Jyotiṣa Fundamentals

2nd edition

My Master's Words

Visti Larsen

Published by RAMA

Dedication

With immense gratitude I offer this book at the feet of my Jyotiṣa Guru, Pandit Sanjay Rath, to whom I owe my entire knowledge and livelihood.

First edition 2004
Second edition: 2012

RAMA: A PART OF SHRI GARUDA

Signalvej 125

2860 Søborg

Tel: +45 22965939

www.rama-edu.com

Printed in Great Britain

By Lightingsource

First published in India in 2004

Proof for first edition by Sarbani Rath

Cover design by Sagittarius Publications. Revamped for second edition by Mladen Lubura (mladenlubura@yahoo.com)

Charts calculated and displayed from Śrī Jyoti Star (http://www.vedicsoftware.com/). Prastara Aṣṭakavarga charts from Jagannātha Horā (http://vedicastrologer.org)

Preface
To 2nd edition

This publication is the second edition of my previous publication; 'My Masters Words', written in 2003. These publications come as a promise to my teacher; Pt. Sanjay Rāth, who wanted the tradition of Jyotiṣa to be known and recognized in India as well as abroad.

As solicited by the readers, the book in its second edition has been expanded to include much more information on Pañcāñga. Herein each limb of the Pañcāñga has been elaborated upon based on the work and teachings of Pt. Sanjay Rāth. Every section of the Pañcāñga chapter has been expanded upon. In sections where this authors own observations come to fore it has been clearly mentioned. However, it must be clearly mentioned that the entire knowledge existing in this book has arisen due to the teachings of my Jyotiṣa Guru Pt. Sanjay Rāth.

Initially an entire book on Pañcāñga had been planned, spanning two hundred pages in its raw form before deciding to add select portions of it to the second edition of this book.

In subsequent chapters care has been taken to correct previous layout and scripting errors and improving language. Some charts have been removed to avoid repetition while some have been added, in select sections, to add more detail and understanding of the principles at hand.

Nine years have passed since the contents of this book first were written, and in this time through learning the deeper tenants and principles of Jyotiṣa through *Maharṣi Parāśara Horā Śastra* and *Maharṣi Jaimini Kṛtam Upadeśa Sutram,* as taught in the tradition, certain sections of the book have been refined to suit and ease the learning of Jyotiṣa. Admittedly this book is like a small creek in the ocean of knowledge that is Jyotiṣa and this author hopes that students earlier as well as in the future will benefit from the knowledge amassed herein.

In agreement with the previous publisher, Sagittarius Publications, the current edition has been published by Shri Garuda and RĀMA Publications.

नमः सवित्रे जगदेकचक्शुषे जगत्प्रसूती स्थिति नाश हेतवे।
त्रयीमयाय त्रिगुणात्म धारिणे विरश्चि नारायण शङ्करात्मन्॥

Introduction

I, Visti Larsen, born to Kaj and Maymuna Larsen on November 21st 1981 at 6 AM in Nairobi, Kenya.

Grandson of Christian and Agathe Larsen as well as Ali Fakih and Fatma Swaleh.

In tribute to my Guru Sanjay Rath and the lineage of Śrī Acyutānanda Dāsa of Orissa, I hereby present this book, in its second edition, as a fruit of my learning.

Chart 1: Author

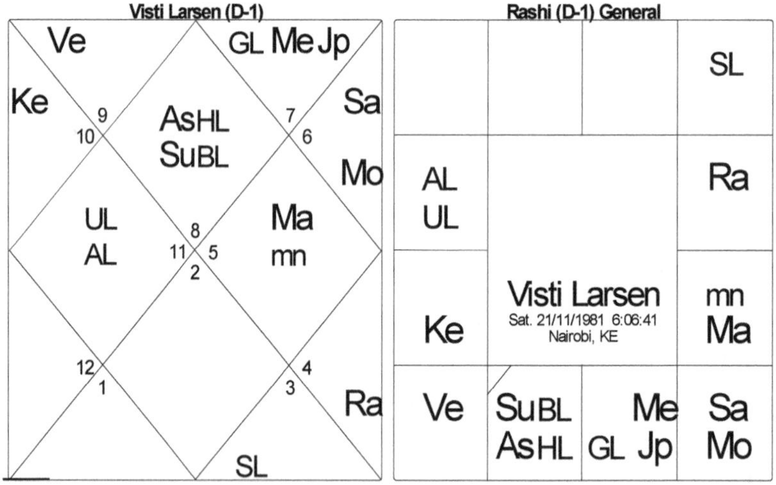

I hope with the publication of this book, the tradition of Jyotiṣa will be recognized by the astrology community, as well as society at large for the traditions depth, understanding and intellectual approach.

Publication

This publication is the result of a promise to my teacher, namely to teach on to others, what I have learned. The book is a contribution to the aspiring astrologers, with knowledge gained both from my personal association with my Guru, and the application of the same knowledge in my own experiences with my clientele.

This book is structured to enable beginners and intermediate level astrologers gravitate to an advanced comprehension and competence, emulating the hightened pace that I was exposed to under the tutelage of my Guru Pt. Sanjay Rath.

To work on the core roots of the subject, the first chapter deals with the 'Pañcaãñga', or the five limbs of the Vedic calendar. This particular area of Jyotiṣa is often overlooked due to lack of knowledge in application on part of the astrologer, and also the idea that it is merely a calendar system, and hence overlooked completely by astrologers following the Western Astrology System. To give a more practical use of the pañcãñga, I have introduced some very useful methods of application to identify flaws in the quality of time, and how it relates to the chart.

Suffice to say, that this is 'only the tip of the iceberg'. This chapter may seem difficult for beginners, and I do recommend students to give themselves adequate time to understand this. This chapter is however given first, as this is the first thing that an astrologer is taught to see before analyzing the chart… the reader will appreciate why, after reading it.

The subsequent chapters deal with more commonly known concepts, such as Graha, Rāśi, Bhāva, Kāraka, etc. however to avoid a repetition of already available literature, I have added a deeper understanding to aspects of the topic which are lesser known, such as Māraṇa Kāraka Sthāna, Bhāva and Graha Tithi, use of day/ night births, planetary castes and the Varṇadā Lagna, Upagraha – just to mention some topics under the Graha chapter. In a similar vein, I have given some deeper understanding and principles on the use of the Rāśi as well as the Bhāva, and a particularly important topic, namely Sambandha or relationships. Two topics which are very close to heart among the members of Sri Jagannātha Centre are Ārūḍha and Kāraka. I have devoted a chapter to each in an attempt to establish a stronger foundation for the use of these techniques, and also an idea of their importance. In fact the entire book deals very strongly with the use of the Ārūḍhas.

Four chapters are devoted to the twelve Bhāvas. Each bhāva has been picked up and with it some extremely practical and repeatable techniques are shown which are not mentioned in the modern Jyotiṣa books.

The last chapter is devoted to the Nārāyaṇa Daśā which is the hall mark of the Jaimini Sutras, and one of my personal favourites. It should however, not be assumed that this Daśā system is the only one used in this tradition. In fact Pt. Jagannāth Rath, the grandfather of Pt. Sanjay Rath, was fond of Vimśottari Daśā, which he used down to a precision of 6 sub-levels in his predictions! Yet, he used to calculate Nārāyaṇa Daśā mentally to confirm the same. These Daśā systems are but a few of the many Daśā systems learnt in the paramparā, but to begin with giving the aspiring astrologers a sidestep from the more commonly used Vimśottari Daśā (or the Aṣṭottari Daśā used in eastern India), I have given some practical use of Nārāyaṇa Daśā.

Acknowledgement

I would like to thank my Guru, Sanjay Rath, for having devoted time and energy to teaching and encouraging the next generation of astrologers, with the knowledge from the paramparā of Śrī Acyutānanda Dāsa. He is further to thank for making the front cover of the book. My thanks go to the members of Śrī Jagannāth Centre, for having established a e-forum for learning, to help the learning process for aspiring jyotiṣas, through intellectual discussions and serious application of scriptural knowledge. For participation the forum can be found through: http://srijagannath.org.

Further, I would like to acknowledge show my gratitude for the tedious and detailed work of Smt. Sarbani Rath in enabling this work to be in its present form. Finally my gratitude goes to the entire staff of Sagittarius Publications which made this book available and worked towards enabling the knowledge of Jyotiṣa to be available to all.

I offer this book for the benefit of all astrologers. Visti Larsen (visti@srigaruda.com)

Table of Contents

List of Charts

LIST OF TABLES

List of Figures

यन्मण्डलं दीप्तिकरं विशालं रत्नप्रभं तीव्रमनादि रूपम्।
दारिद्य दखुक्षयकारणं च पुनातु मां तत्सवितुर्वरेण्यम्॥

1

Pañcāñga
The Five Limbs

Introduction

From a western perspective, the established calendar and the movement of the planets and stars are perceived as completely separate entities, and deemed as mere human instruments attempting to imitate the movements of the equinoxes and its resultant seasons. Specifically, in the established Gregorian calendar, the focus has been to make up for earths movement around the Sun, now approximately 365.25 days, and its resultant effect on the seasons. In this calendar, the year length is 365 days, and one day is added every four years to make up for the ¼ day extra traversed by the earth per year.

Other methods to imitate the planetary movements have been made by the ancients. The Saros metonic cycle appeared to be a calendar system based on the reoccurrence of eclipses. This took into account the movement of the north and south nodes of the Moon, as well as the reoccurrence of the synodic months (from one full moon to the next). Here the calendar consisted of an 18 year cycle, readjusting itself after 18 years, 10 and 1/3rd days.

A most ancient and impressive calendar is found among the Egyptians who had a fixed calendar much like the Gregorian. It had twelve months of thirty days each concluding with five days of worship of the Gods at the end of the year, hence a 365 day year. However, it did not take into account the movement of the seasons which gradually became later and later until they again realigned after 1460 years. Further they checked their calendar not with reference to the seasons and equinoxes, but with the annual heliacal rising of the star Sirius, now situated at the tropical degree of 14° 12′ Cancer.

The Mayans had their hands in the calculation of the Venus-cycle, yet it was used for divination of good/bad times for their land, and it's not apparent that it was used to form their calendar.

Not deeming other ancient calendars as lesser, the Vedic calendar has it all! The movement of each celestial body forms a timescale, where each after a given amount of time would all have traversed the exact same distance individually. In other words, the movement of the Moon around the earth, and the earth around the Sun will after a certain amount of time have traversed equal distances in space, and are therefore exactly in synch. Thus movement in space is actually a movement in time. From this timescale springs forth a variety of time measurements used to divine the auspiciousness or inauspiciousness of the time, the most popular of these timescales being the Vedic Tithi. This is based on the movement of the Sun and Moon, with regards to each other, to form a lunar calendar.

There are five parts of the Vedic calendar named *Tithi, Nakṣatra, Vāra (weekday), Yoga and Karaṇa,* the basis of which form other timescales, and are known wholly as *Pañcāñga* as it consists of five (*pañca)* limbs (*añga*) or parts.

Origin

To understand *Pañcāñga* we must understand the origin of the Vedic calendar. Notably the entire movement of the Vedic calendar consists of sidereal functions of time, i.e. a calendar based on the backdrop of the stars. Here the Vedic philosophy divides the universe in various lokas or abodes. Three of these abodes are physically manifest and are the i) earth or immediate abode known as bhuloka, ii) the sky and planets in this galaxy known as bhuva loka and iii) the stars being svarga loka. The Deva reside in the last mentioned loka, and because the Deva/Gods decide the karma of this world any movement of time must also be decided based on them. Time based on the stars is a sidereal function of time.

The ancient Purāṇa and Siddhānta which describe the functions of the universe always begin their explanation with understanding the smallest measures of time. This initiates with the prāṇa or lifeforce, of which there are for every individual 21600 units in a sidereal day. The following has been culled from the Sūrya siddhānta, chapter 1, verses 11-21.

6 prana = 1 vinadi

60 vinadi = 1 nadi

60 nadi = a sidereal day (the complete rotation of the earth: 23:56 hrs)

30 days make a month.

> 30 sidereal days make a sidereal month.
>
> A lunar month consists of as many lunar days (Tithi).
>
> A civil month consists of as many sunrises.

A solar month happens based on the suns movement in and out of a sign. Twelve such months make a year. This is one day of the Deva. This is the equivalent of a sidereal year.

360 days of the Deva make one year of the Deva.

```
Twelve thousand Deva years is a Chaturyuga (four yugas).

Seventy-one Chaturyuga is a Manvantara or age of the patriarch.

Fourteen such Manvantara is a Kalpa.
```

A Kalpa is a day of Brahma, the end of which brings the dissolution of all that exists. The night is of a similar length. One hundred of such is the maximum age of Brahma. We are now in the 51st Kalpa.

Note that the Kalpa is the maximum time span for the created universe. The universe has been described as an egg or an elliptic circle encompassing the border limit of the universe. The length of its circle being described in the measurement of Yojanas as: 18,712,080,864,000,000. Here the brilliance of the Vedic system shines through, as all planets, nodes and stars would in a period of a Kalpa traverse, in their own orbits, a distance equal to that length described in space, showing the equivalence between time and space.

Example: The Moon will traverse an orbit of 324,000 yojanas, and in a kalpa it will do so 57,753,336,000 times. The two multiplied will reveal the full distance traversed by the Moon in space, namely 18,712,080,864,000,000.

Similarly the Suns orbit being 4,331,500 yojanas and in a Kalpa will do so 4,320,000,000 times, the full distance being equal to that traversed by the Moon and the circle of the Kalpa. Therefore all movement in space is exactly synchronous with the progression of time.

Notably, it is found that the definition of a year is based on a sidereal function of time and not a mere solar return as we know it from the Gregorian calendar. This difference between a solar year and a sidereal year brings the emergence of the Ayanāmśa. At present the difference between the two types of years is only a few hours. Yet, this difference has with time caused that the present solar New Year and the present sidereal New Year are 23 days apart and growing. When the two are 365 days apart the two new years will again be the same. The last time these were aligned was said to be about 1500 years ago and is today known as the Lahiri Ayanāmśa.

Pañcāñga

An important but often ignored and misunderstood tool of jyotiṣa, are the five limbs or 'pañcāñga'. The pañcāñga is the Vedic method of reckoning time and is the backbone of the Vedic Calendar. Most dismiss this as merely a calendar or the cosmology of Jyotiṣa however it is very useful for predictive Jyotiṣa. It comprises of five different date systems called:

- Tithi - lunar day
- Karaṇa - first or second halves of the lunar day
- Vāra – weekday; Monday, Tuesday, etc.
- Nakṣatra - one of the lunar asterisms occupied by the Moon

❖ Yoga – The asterism attained by the progressed lunar day

It is said in the Vedas, with the use of pañcāñga, the person becomes free from all his sins.

- Knowledge of *karaṇa* leads to success in all endeavours.
- Knowledge of *Tithi* brings prosperity.
- Knowledge of *Vāra* prolongs Life.
- Knowledge of *Nakṣatra* removes sins.
- Knowledge of *yoga* gives immunity from diseases.

These five limbs are linked to the five elements (tattva): earth (Pṛthvī), water (Jala), fire (Agni), air (Vāyu) and vacuum (Ākāśa) respectively. These five Tattvas make up the various elements of our creation, and are popularly understood as causing the birth of the material elements. These same elements are the object of the five action oriented senses[1] and the five knowledge acquiring senses[2], with which the mind merges to experience various actions and emotions.

The principle behind the pañcāñga emerges from the knowledge that the mind is experiencing the world through these elements, and these elements makeup the basic world we live in, and hence any incompatibilities or inauspicious combinations of the same can result in a major flaw in the native's quality of time.

Further, just as the planetary placements indicate the karma and will of God, the pañcāñga represents how we as beings interact with the karma that has been created. Therefore the pañcāñga acts as a filter for our experiences of karma.

Hence it becomes important to check the pañcāñga before indicating the strength of a planet, as well as its auspicious or inauspiciousness. The description of the pañcāñga is given in the following section.

1 Known as Karmendriyas; speech, grasping walking, evacuation/cleaning and procreation.
2 Known as Gyānendriyas; smell, taste, sight, hear and touch/feel.

1.1 Nakṣatra: The flow of prāṇa (Vāyu Tattva)

The Nakṣatra form the basis of the Zodiac and among the five limbs of the Pañcāñga the Nakṣatra represent the element of Vāyu or wind/gas.

A great deal has been written on the Nakṣatra already. Yet, until the release of the book Bṛhat Nakṣatra, by Sanjay Rath, most writing on the Nakṣatra has focussed on mythology, story-book like descriptions of the Nakṣatra and personalities, or just simply listed the Nakṣatra without a proper application of the same.

In light of the new release by Sanjay Rath, the following paragraphs only serve to highlight some aspects of the Nakṣatra taught in the tradition. For further detailed reading on the Nakṣatras please refer to the book by Sanjay Rath.

Table 1: Yoga Tara

No.	Constellation	Degrees
1	Aśvinī	00 - 13:20 Aries
2	Bharaṇī	13:20 - 26:40 Aries
3	Kṛttikā	26:40 Aries - 10:00 Taurus
4	Rohiṇī	10:00 - 23:20 Taurus
5	Mṛgaśirā	23:20 Taurus - 6:40 Gemini
6	Ārdrā	6:40 - 20:00 Gemini
7	Punarvasu	20:00 Gemini - 3:20 Cancer
8	Puṣyā	3:20 - 16:40 Cancer
9	Aśleṣā	16:40 - 30:00 Cancer
10	Maghā	00 - 13:20 Leo
11	Pūrva Phalgunī	13:20 - 26:40 Leo
12	Uttara Phalgunī	26:40 Leo - 10:00 Virgo
13	Hasta	10:00 - 23:20 Virgo
14	Chitrā	23:20 Virgo - 6:40 Libra
15	Svāti	6:40 - 20:00 Libra
16	Viśākhā	20:00 Libra - 3:20 Scorpio
17	Anurādhā	3:20 - 16:40 Scorpio
18	Jyeṣṭhā	16:40 - 30:00 Scorpio
19	Mūlā	00 - 13:20 Sagittarius
20	Pūrva Aṣāḍhā	13:20 - 26:40 Sagittarius
21	Uttara Aṣāḍhā	26:40 Sagittarius - 10:00 Capricorn
22	Śravaṇā	10:00 - 23:20 Capricorn
23	Dhaniṣṭhā	23:20 Capricorn - 6:40 Aquarius
24	Śatabhiṣaj	6:40 - 20:00 Aquarius
25	Pūrva Bhadrapadā	20:00 Aquarius - 3:20 Pisces
26	Uttara Bhadrapadā	3:20 - 16:40 Pisces
27	Revatī	16:40 - 30:00 Pisces

The Nakṣatra are the basis of the zodiac. They are based on the stars but do not form star-signs per say, just as the zodiac signs or Rāśi also do not form discernable visible star-constellations of thirty degrees each. Further, whilst the word 'zodiac' is used to depict the stars-signs as animals, when we refer to the Nakṣatra the word Kālapuruṣa is more appropriate as we are now describing the limbs of God. The Nakṣatra and the Rāśi are based on individual stars that signify the beginning of the signs, normally based on the beginning of Aries or Libra. These stars are known as Yogatara, and occupy a degree in space. I.e. the Yogatara of Chitrā Nakṣatra would be Chitrā itself yet occupies only the current tropical degree of 23° 57′2.03″ Libra. Chitrā is in the modern context recognized as the star Spica. One-hundred-eighty degrees opposite Chitrā's Yogatara forms the beginning of sidereal Aries (Aditya 1997), and thus the beginning of the sidereal zodiac. This zodiac of three-hundred-sixty degrees is then divided into twenty-seven or twenty-eight parts to form the Nakṣatra Maṇḍala, or circle of Nakṣatra.

The Nakṣatra and their number are based on the lunar return of the Moon. The Moon takes 27 days and 7¾ hours to make a lunar return, and from this we arrive at two schemes of Nakṣatra. One scheme rounds down the number to 27 and gives us the same number of Nakṣatra, i.e. 27. Another includes the remaining seven hours, which is roughly the equivalent of ¼ day, and adds an intercalary Nakṣatra called Abhijit forming a number of 28 Nakṣatra. Abhijit Muhūrta is also the name of the time of exact midday and is roughly six hours after sunrise, and said to be presided over by Viṣṇu. Thus this time of day is also named Viṣṇu Gāyatri. The natural sign of midday is Capricorn and therefore Abhijit is naturally given its position in this sign.

These two schemes of Nakṣatra are not contradictory but complimentary to each other, where one excluding the use of Abhijit/Viṣṇu carries a more materialistic agenda and the latter includes the spiritual.

The twenty-seven/twenty-eight names of the Nakṣatra are here given:

Each Nakṣatra is given an equal portion of 13°20′ distributed over the zodiac beginning with 0° Aries with the Nakṣatra of Aśvinī. However, this particularly applies to the twenty-seven Nakṣatra scheme which excludes Abhijit.

Abhijit is said to occupy a space of seven and ¾ of a day, or to be exact; 7 hrs, 37 minutes and 35 seconds, which is an equivalent of 4°14′13″ in space. This spans starts from 6°40′ Capricorn, or the second Navāṁśa of Capricorn, and ends at 10° 54′ 13″ Capricorn. This overlaps the end of Uttara Aṣāḍhā and almost the first degree of Śravaṇā Nakṣatra. Adding to our list of names we will get the twenty-eight Nakṣatra scheme, which is used in many methods of prediction, especially the popular Sarvatobhadra chakra.

A day consists of four portions, namely of the times between: i) morning and midday, ii) midday and evening, iii) evening and midnight and iv) midnight and the following morning. So also the Nakṣatra have four portions called Nakṣatra pada. These portions are exactly 1/4th of the Nakṣatra length, i.e. 13°20′ divided into four portions of 3°20′ each. This span is called a Nakṣatra pada. Abhijit is also given four pada or parts.

Etymos logos

Many different meanings of the word Nakṣatra have been given by authors in the past, two of which are given in the tradition are presented here.

- The initiating sound *na* is a specific reference to the Moon. Here the sound *ma*, which represents our self, is suffixed to show our name, viz.: *nāma*. Therefore the first use of the Nakṣatra is to find the suitable name of the person, or that part of the Moon which is ours. The word *kṣatra* then represents the Moons sovereign over its own space, where just as the Sun is the sovereign of the sun signs, so also the Moon is the sovereign of the lunar constellations or

Nakṣatra.

- *Nakṣa* also refers to the approaching darkness which is about to envelope the world due to the lack of sunlight. The sound *tra* added to the end of this comes from the word *trayi* which means to protect or give shelter. Hence the other meaning of the word Nakṣatra refers to that which protects one in darkness. Specifically the word *trayi* has its root in the word *rayi* which means food or sustenance and therefore the nature of the protection is in the form of sustenance and the Nakṣatra also have the function of granting longevity.

Because the Nakṣatra gives us the sound or name and this is said to protect us, the first mantra given to a person is their name itself, of which the first sound of the name is the cause of the soul's bondage, i.e. if the name is *Visti* then the first syllable is *va* and the cause of bondage or the Hamsa bīja is *vaṁ* (S. Rath, A Course on Jaimini Maharishi's Upadesa Sutra 2007). This Hamsa bīja will give knowledge of the self. For more knowledge about Mantra and the name please refer to the Dattātreya Upanishad. The next step for those well versed in Sanskrit and Vedic numerology is to delineate the meaning of the sound to understand the cause of rebirth. This will not be described in this work.

Table 2: Loka and Mantra (S. Rath, A Course on Jaimini Maharishi's Upadesa Sutra 2007)

Loka/Chakra	Syllables	Mantra
Satya/Sahasrara	64	Mana Pada
Samudra	32	Anusthubh
Tapa/Ājñākhya	16	Ṣoḍaṣi
Samudra	8	Mantra pada (Gāyatri)
Jana/Viśuddha	4	Bija, carana
Samudra	2	Bīja/nāma
Mahar/Anāhata	1	Haṁsa

There are other stages of mantra initiation which are meant to help the person cross the samudra or oceans of unrest between the seven lokas/chakras, as well as cross the loka/chakra itself. This begins with the heart chakra moving upwards.

This underscores the need for selecting a suitable name for the child born, so their mantra can lead them towards their life's goal. The Sanskrit syllables are placed in the Nakṣatras and their four parts in the Hoḍa chakra, which will be explained in this chapter.

Ṛkṣa (Moons Nakṣatra)

The Moon rules the time span of a Kṣaṇa which is the instantaneous occurrence of an event as it's interpreted by the mind. The Moon is the mind as the mind was attained when the seed of the father caused the impregnation in the mother's womb, i.e. once the soul coming from the father (Sun) was conceived, it is said that the mind and body immediately followed suit and were instantaneously joined to the soul (Varahamihira). As this happened as a result of conception, the Moon/mother represents the māna/mind and the śarīra or the sheath of the body. Therefore the Moons Nakṣatra and the Nakṣatra which follow it will also represent the limbs of the physical body itself also known as the Nakṣatra puruṣa.

Since the mind controls the senses, i.e. the five karmendriyas or acting senses, and the five jñānendriya or knowledge-acquiring senses, the Nakṣatras have a direct bearing on our actions. Yet they do not create our actions but affect our mind and form the basis of our actions! This inspiration is seen in the Nakṣatras and is called kriyā śakti, i.e. the power to influence action.

Notably the boundaries of each Nakṣatra are defined by the passing of a day or Vāra, and therefore Agni again acts as the vehicle of the Gods and brings the presence of the Deva or Divinity in the Nakṣatra.

The stars are where the Deva reside, and the Moon is the māna or mind of all beings. Hence, we have a luni-zodiacal scheme where we can measure the divine inspiration arising from the Deva in the stars, and how it affects the mind of the individual.

Table 3: Nakṣatra lordships

#	Nakṣatra	Graha
#	Nakṣatra	Graha
1	Aśvinī, Magha, Mūla	Ketu
2	Bharaṇī, P. Phalgunī, P. Aṣāḍha	Venus
3	Kṛttikā, U. Phalgunī, U. Aṣāḍha	Sun
4	Rohiṇī, Hasta, Śravaṇā	Moon
5	Mṛgaśirā, Chitrā, Dhaniṣṭha	Mars
6	Ārdra, Svāti, Śatabhiṣaj	Rāhu
7	Punarvasu, Viśāka, P. Bhadra	Jupiter
8	Puṣya, Anurādha, U. Bhadra	Saturn
9	Aśleṣā, Jyeṣṭha, Revatī	Mercury

As the Nakṣatra will have an impact on the mind which carries us throughout our life, the Moons Nakṣatra will show the theme of our life and the impact that we will have on the world. Here each Nakṣatra is presided over by a devatā whose mythology and symbol will decide the theme of life and natives impact on the world. Further the nine grahas are given three Nakṣatra each to preside over, and when the planet presiding over the moons Nakṣatra is strong the native will leave this impact on the world they live in. Nakṣatra lordships

The order of lordship of the Nakṣatra beginning from the Sun is: Sun, Moon, Mars, Rāhu, Jupiter, Saturn, Mercury, Ketu and Venus. This list begins from the head of the Nakṣatras namely Kṛttikā and continues three times to envelope all the Nakṣatras.

The reason for the scheme is derived as follows:

The nine graha in the order of weekdays or Vāra are the basis of all schemes of planets, viz.: Sun, Moon, Mars, Mercury, Jupiter, Venus, Saturn, Rāhu and Ketu. Then in a process of three steps the nodes eclipse and change the order to suit the Nakṣatra.

Table 4: Nakṣatra lordships

	Sun, Moon, Mars		Mercury, Jupiter, Venus		Saturn, Rahu & Ketu
Vāra order - Unchanged					
1	Sun, Moon, Mars	**Rāhu**	Mercury, Jupiter,	Venus	Saturn & Ketu
The first three steps to establish dharma are taken by Sun, Moon and Mars in their order, after which Rāhu interferes to bring about the first change in the scheme.					
2	Sun, Moon, Mars	Rāhu	**Jupiter, Mercury**	**Saturn, Ketu**	**Venus**
In the second step two reversals happen caused by the two nodes again. Note that the order of the first three cannot be changed as that would reverse dharma itself. Mercury and Jupiter who follow Rāhu reverse their positions. Thereafter Venus exchanges places with Saturn and Ketu.					
3	Sun, Moon, Mars	Rāhu	Jupiter	**Saturn, Mercury**	Ketu & Venus
In the third step another reversal happens where Saturn in his newly found position exchanges places with Mercury. This brings the final order to: Sun, Moon, Mars, Rahu, Jupiter, Saturn, Mercury, Ketu and Venus.					

The Nakṣatra lord is analysed from the perspective of longevity or ayuṣa first and foremost. How the persons longevity is and how this affects one's life is interpreted by ascertaining the placement of the Nakṣatra lord w.r.t. the seventh house and its lord. In this way the Nakṣatra lord is termed Jīva or the living being.

There are many ways to interpret longevity and this method gives an idea as to what causes the longevity to be strong or weak. Notably, the seventh house is also the door to the outside world and if this lord is strong it ensures good karma in the interaction with the world and also good longevity, but if weak then one's interaction with the same would become less and problematic.

Figure 1: Ayuṣa and Nakṣatra

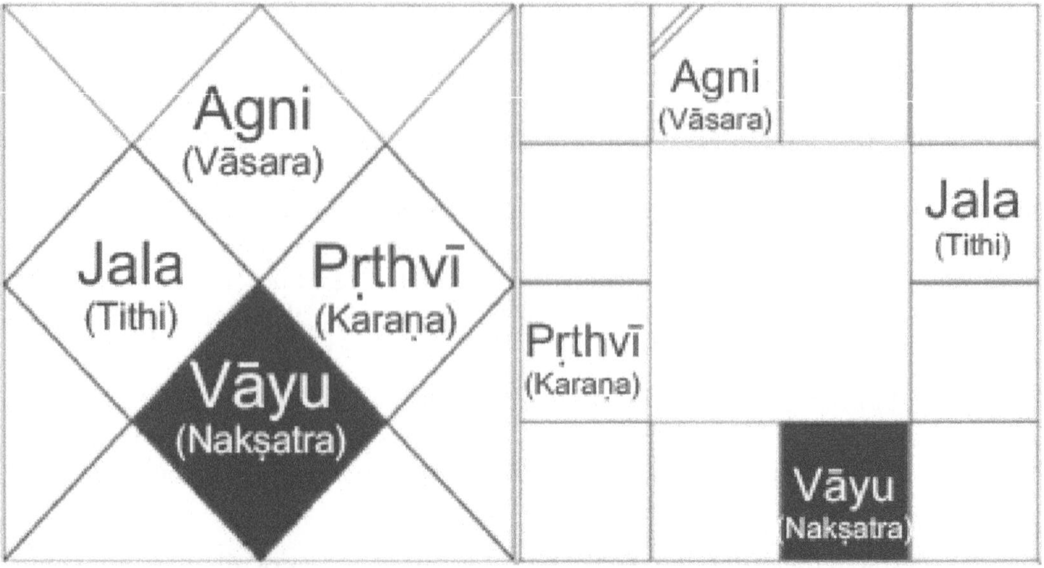

As the Nakṣatra lord is of the nature of Vāyu, the placement of the same in Vāyu signs (Gemini, Libra or Aquarius) or with Vāyu planets (Saturn and Rāhu) promotes good prāṇa and long life. Conversely placement in Pṛthvī Rāśi shows lack of movement in the prāṇa and stagnation. Thus also diminished health and longevity. Agni or fiery signs are good for Prāṇa and if the Nakṣatra lord is connected to the weekday lord, or Vareśa, the person may have great achievements in life. Conversely, placement in watery signs is not auspicious showing Prāṇa failing due to emotions. A similar situation comes to pass when the lord of the Tithi is connected to the Nakṣatra lord.

Should the Nakṣatra lord be in the seventh house or joined the seventh lord it promotes strong prāna or life force and long life. If badly placed from the seventh or obstructed by another graha (argalā) then this is not so. Afflictions to the Jīva can lessen longevity suddenly. Māraṇa Kāraka Sthāna is pivotal to be estimated in this context.

Chart 2: Sanjay Gandhi

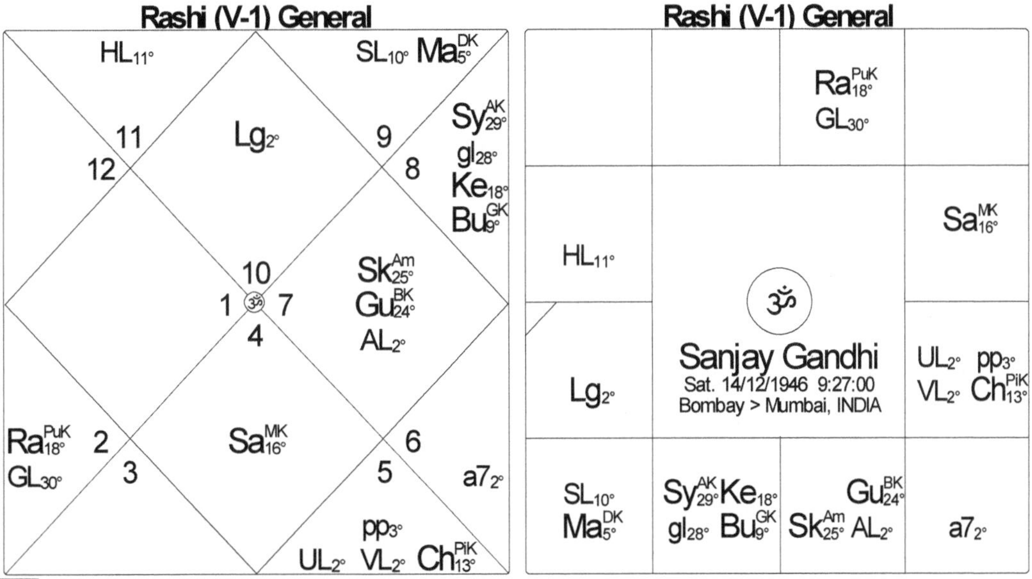

Chart of Sanjay Gandhi, born 14th December 1946, at 9: 27 AM, Mumbai, India.

The Moon occupies the eighth house in Maghā Nakṣatra whose lord is Ketu. Weekday lord is Saturn who also lords the Tithi.

Upon an initial assessment of the seventh house we find a well placed Saturn which promotes good prāṇa and longevity. However, with lord Moon placed in the eighth house in Māraṇa Kāraka Sthāna this seems more difficult. Weak Moon tends to give health problems in childhood but the strong placement of Jupiter and Venus in the tenth house would ward off the same.

The lords of the first, eighth and tenth houses are a good means to ascertain the longevity (Jaimini, 1997). The first lord Saturn is well placed in the seventh house, the eighth lord is somewhat problematically placed with Ketu, as the tenth lord Venus is in its own sign. An initial estimate would be that at least 2 out of 3 indicators point towards middle life span due to the well placed Lagna and tenth lords. However, we note that should Ketu dominate over the planets in the eleventh house that this forms a line of malefic grahas in the two signs following that of Jupiter and Venus which would block these two benefics from giving longevity. Ketu indicates accidents and with the Sun indicates such occurring in the air. Ketu is in the Navāṁśa of Sagittarius which causes fall from a height.

It cannot be ignored that this Ketu is placed in the house of obstruction or Bādhaka (ref 10.3.1 Bādhaka: the source of obstacles). In most cases the planets in the house of Bādhaka shows actions performed against the society one lives in. Ketu shows mistakes or actions which are against the growth of family[3]. As we have also noted, Ketu being the Nakṣatra lord is placed in a watery sign joined earthy Mercury which isn't good for longevity.

In 1976 the Nārāyaṇa Daśā of Libra began. Libra is occupied by Jupiter and Venus and most notably Venus in the tenth house whilst aspected by the Moon causes Mahānta Yoga for entrepreneurship and acumen for business, but the purpose of these activities will be seen from the Moon's placement and being in the most malefic eighth house does not bode well for the outcome of these activities. Venus being Amatyakāraka in the tenth house promises huge rise in career and this will be in politics as Rāhu is in a sign of Venus. During this time the India Emergency occurred and Sanjay rose to take up official work through the support of his mother and Prime Minister at the time, Indira Gandhi.

Libra's Bāhya Rāśi (refer Dvāra and Bāhya) is placed in Cancer and would indicate important events related to his interaction with society and the world. Cancer receives the sign aspect of the combination of planets in Scorpio which can bring activities related to his longevity. At this time during Libra Mahādaśā and Libra Antaradaśā Sanjay Gandhi had officers carrying out family planning vasectomies and sterilizations in the slums of Delhi. Whilst these activities were supposed to be voluntary, cases of force and abuse were noted by many inhabitants. With this followed also forced relocation of 250 thousand people for the purpose of 'clearing the slums'. When the Antaradaśā of Scorpio followed these cases became a means to warrant the arrest of Sanjay Gandhi, and his mother Indira Gandhi, for actions performed during the India emergency. Sanjay Gandhi was able to initiate many of these activities without holding any elected post in parliament.

With the advent of the Antaradaśā of Aquarius, which aspects the powerful Libra by sign aspect, Sanjay took an elected position in parliament. However, when counting from Libra to Aquarius and the same distance there from we arrive at the sixth house of Gemini. This being the sixth house of enemies is terrible for work. The lord Mercury is further joined Ketu whom we deemed as difficult for longevity. Further as Aquarius is the second house in the chart it bodes difficult for health during this time. In June of the same year Sanjay Gandhi died in an airplane crash along with his pilot. He had aged 33.

This principle of counting from the Mahādaśā to the Antaradaśā and the same distance therefrom is like a Daśā Bāhya (refer Dvāra and Bāhya*). Just as the Bāhya Rāśi shows the*

3 ketum kulaśya unnatim.

interaction with the larger society at a whole, this Antaradaśā Bāhya shows the same for just that particular Antaradaśā and is useful to ascertain the exact results of that Daśā.

Chart 3: Alan-Fournier

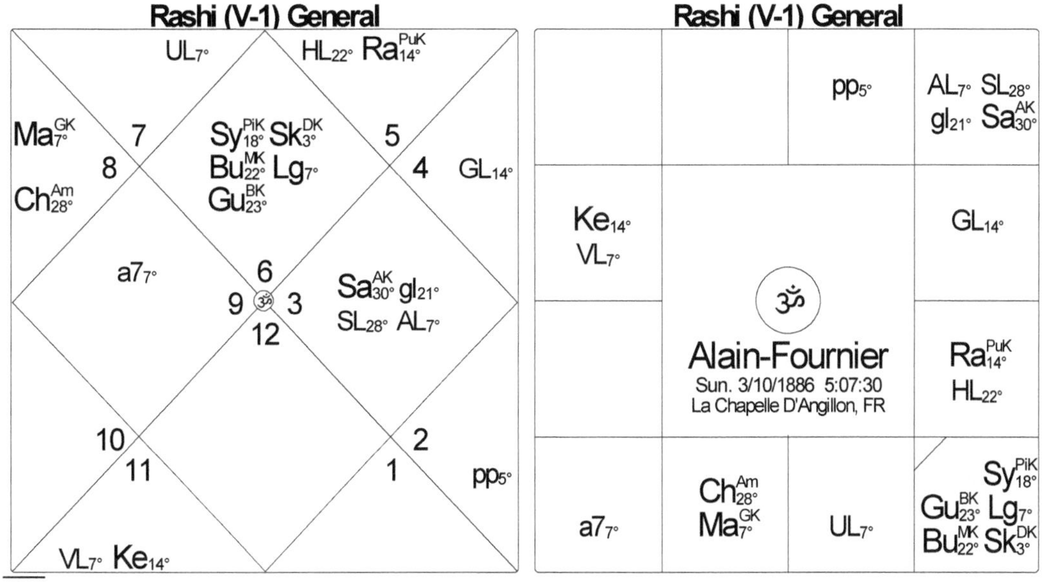

Chart of Alain-Fournier, born Henri Alban Fournier, 3rd October 1886, 5 AM, La Chapele D'Angillon, France.

The Moon is placed in the Nakṣatra of Jyeṣṭhā lorded over by Mercury. Saturn is the weekday lord as Venus lords the Tithi. The fourth Nakṣatra is lorded over by the Sun giving a strict upbringing in a family which may have political connections (Sun). Sun is placed in Virgo joined Mercury, Jupiter and Venus. Being the most malefic therein it gives the results of most benefit Jupiter making the family predominantly academically minded. The Sun is the Pitṛkāraka as Venus is Matṛkāraka joined Virgo indicating that both parents, as both fourth and ninth lords join the sign indicating that both parents may belong to this path. Further as this all occurs in the fourth from the Ārūḍha Lagna the native himself will belong to a school or organisation with its focus on academia.

The native was born to parents who were both schoolteachers in Paris. They further held very good connections to send the young Henri to the most prestigious secondary school at the time namely *Lycée Lakanal* in Sceaux, France.

Notably, the four planet combination in the Lagna is Pravrājya Yoga. With tenth lord involved it in regular practice promises that the house of conjunction suffers greatly and anything joined the house is similar to a bottomless pit! Yet, in concordance with the advice of Parāśara (Parashara, 1999), but one planet combust in this combination will surely grant great abundance in life. Here Mercury and Jupiter are both combust and will surely prove beneficial, yet as Mercury is also the lord of the Moon's Nakṣatra this combustion will not support longevity. This is further diminished by joining an earthy sign with Mercury who is also the Tithi lord!

Jupiter is the seventh lord and its union with the Nakṣatra lord is auspicious for longevity. However, it is also combust by the Sun and further Sun, Jupiter and Mercury are all in Hastā Nakṣatra whose lord Moon is debilitated and joined Mars in Scorpio. This can give serious threats to life, especially as the Moon is in Gaṇḍānta. As the fourth from the combination is Sagittarius this can happen in a battleground-like setting.

At ten years of age his Vimśottari Daśā of Venus began. Venus despite being ninth lord is debilitated and is more likely to act as Māraka or killer for Virgo Lagna due to its second lordship. During Venus Daśā, Mars Antaradaśā he began his secondary schooling. Mars being lord of the Moon sign and thus Śubhapati, as well as being in the third house from the Daśā Rāśi bring good luck, however being in the third house from the fourth, ninth and tenth lord makes him work very hard and much disciplined.

Despite his hard work, he didn't manage to clear his exams to attend the *Ecole Normale Supérieure* to become a teacher himself. Instead he studied at the Merchant Marine School in *Brest*.

When Venus Daśā, Jupiter Antaradaśā arrived he interrupted his studies to undergo two years of military service! Who would have thought that Jupiter would take one to the military? The dilemma arises in that Jupiter being the seventh lord is severely combust by the Sun would put him into dangerous situations due to being an afflicted seventh lord. During this time he produced many poems and short stories which were later collected to be known as *Miracles*.

Exactly as Jupiter ended he ended his two years of military service and began to make his career. He began as a journalist in Saturn Antaradaśā. The writing or journalist profession suggests that his Navāṁśa Lagna is Pisces with Jupiter and Moon in trines to each other making the time 5:7:30 AM. His work herein was as a critic.

Saturn is placed in the tenth house in the Rāśi giving a career focus. Being the Atmakāraka would require extensive soul searching and this would not be easy. Being the fifth lord in the tenth house promises huge fortune and being associated with wealthy and influential people. The Ātmakāraka is the king of the horoscope and being in the house of the king can promise huge achievements, especially with tenth lord on the Lagna in Digbala which crowns one for ones mastery of knowledge. Saturn is further the lord of Varṇada Lagna which will make a significant mark on his profession).

Following this he became employed as private secretary to a businessman and politician (Ātmakāraka in Gemini) whom he had met during his work. During this latter portion of Saturn Antaradaśā he finished his first fiction novel: *'Le Grand Meaulnes'* (The Lost Estate). The Ārūḍha of the third house is placed in Aquarius lorded over by Saturn. In 1913 in Mercury Antaradaśā the book was published.

Despite working on several other novels the negatives of Mercury Antaradaśā were about to set in. He was drafted for World War I which broke out in 1914 and with the fourth from Mercury being Sagittarius he was to enter the battle field. He had at this time already begun work on his second book *'Columbe Blanchet'* (the white dove). Birds are signified by the Sun and Leo, and herein we find that Leo is placed in the third from Ārūḍha Lagna which will bring the demise. Mercury signifies the northern direction and in Venus Daśā, Mercury Antaradaśā, Rāhu Pratyantaradaśā he was sent to the northern most part of France to the area of Saint-Rémy-au-Bois. Rāhu being placed in Leo in the third from Ārūḍha Lagna makes it very dangerous. Further from the Ārūḍha of the eighth house (A8) the months of Virgo and Leo are very deadly as these are occupied by the lord of A8 and are in trines to A8 respectively.

One month later during this same Pratyantaradaśā he was killed in battle on 22nd September 1914 as the Sun was transiting Virgo. The Tithi was that of Tritīyā lorded over by Mars. The Tithi of demise will have its lord influencing the fifth lord from Lagna. The fifth lord Saturn is alone in Gemini and receives only the Graha Dṛṣṭi of Mars suggesting that either the Tithi of Mars or Saturn would cause the demise. Mars is stronger in own sign and thus causes the demise.

With the Ātmakāraka in the tenth house as its lord is in the Lagna fame can come posthumously for ones work. The unfinished works of Henry were published after his demise and brought him fame from the same. Movies were made from his initial published work as well of his draft of *Columbe Blanchet.* His works are recorded as part of the classical literary heritage of France.

The method of applying the Nakṣatra lord for longevity produces startling results when applied to the charts of those who died prematurely especially before their twenties. This somewhat gory subject has not been delivered in this book but readers are suggested to analyze this with respect to such charts. However, making predictions about the demise of a child before it has reached its twenties is not performed in the tradition as it incurs the error of Brahmā Doṣa upon the Jyotiṣa, hence readers are asked to tread gently and recite the Gayatri Mantra to avoid this flaw.

1.2 Yoga: Cooperation (Ākāśa Tattva)

Besides relating to the various means of attaining union with God, the term Yoga has different meanings in the astrological context:

- yoga can relate to Sambandha, i.e. association with others;
- yoga can indicate a specific type of combination of planets giving rise to certain results in one's life;
- it can also relate to which of the Nakṣatra the moon is placed in and thus gives rise to chandra yoga;
- finally it also relates to a specific point found through the addition of longitudes of the Sun and Moon called the yoga sphuta.

Thus there are different aspects of the word yoga. The latter among these meanings is dealt with in Pañcāñga.

From among the pañcāñga, the Tithi and yoga emerge as a result of the movements of the Sun and the Moon. In case of Tithi, we deduct the longitudes of the Sun from the Moon, to arrive at the distance of the Moon from the Sun. In case of yoga, we add the two longitudes.

These two formulas symbolize to the two gurus as depicted in the Vedas, namely Bṛhaspati (Jupiter symbolizing the accumulation of longitudes) and Śukrācārya (Venus symbolizing the differentiation of longitudes). The former (yoga) is the embodiment of the ākāśa tattva or the binding element which keeps all forms together and at peace, whilst the latter is the embodiment of the jala tattva (watery element) which ensures prosperity and sustains the native in this birth, just as the rain feeds the earth and causes the growth of crops.

As Yoga relates to union, it is symbolic of the union of Puruṣa (Holy Spirit or father personified - sun) and Prākṛti (nature or mother personified - moon) for the purpose of all creation. This union gives rise to twenty-seven different combinations of which one is cause of one's own birth.

Yoga is therefore seen as a very auspicious point which indicates one's union with God/the world. The stronger one's yoga the better one's connection with the society, world and God is. It therefore shows the nature of the people whom one will share this space with, and how fortunate this space will be for the person.

Yoga is found by:

1. Adding the longitude (starting from Aries) of the Sun and Moon.
2. This result should be divided by 13°20′ degrees.
3. This quotient plus one, result in a Nakṣatra number.
4. The resultant number will reveal one of the twenty seven yogas, and should be counted from Puṣyā Nakṣatra (3°20′ Cancer or 93°20′).

The reason for the counting starting from Puṣyā is because its deity is Bṛhaspati who is the guru of the Deva. The greatness of Bṛhaspati finds its place in the Gita where Śrī Kṛṣṇa said; "Among guru's I am Bṛhaspati". Bṛhaspati is known as an abbreviation of the name Brahmaṇaspati or "the governor of the followers of the creator" and is eulogized as the greatest teacher of the Veda or spirituality. Those who wish to be good teachers of Jyotiṣa or any limb of the Veda are advised to worship him.

The twenty-seven yoga and their Nakṣatra equivalents are here given beginning with Puṣyā.

Table 5: Yoga and Nakṣatra

#	Yoga	Nakṣatra, Devatā	#	Yoga	Nakṣatra, Devatā
#	Yoga	Nakṣatra, devatā	#	Yoga	Nakṣatra, devatā
1	Viṣkambha	Puṣya, Brihaspati (Jupiter)	15	Vajra	Śravaṇā, Viṣṇu
2	**Prīti**	Aśleṣā, Sarpa/Ahi	16	Siddhi	Dhaniṣṭha, Vasudeva
3	**Ayuṣmān**	Magha, Pitri	17	**Vyātipata**	Śatabhiṣaj, Varuna
4	**Saubhāgya**	Pūrva phalgunī, Bhaga	18	**Variyān**	Pūrva bhadrapada, Ajaikapada
5	**Śobhana**	Uttara phalgunī, Aryaman	19	**Parighā**	Uttara bhadrapada, Ahirbudhanya
6	Atigaṇḍa	Hasta, Savitri/Arka	20	**Śiva**	Revatī, Pūshan
7	**Sukarmā**	Chitrā, Vishvakarma/Tvasta	21	Siddha	Aśvin, Aśvin kumar
8	Dhṛti	Svāti, Vāyu/Marut	22	**Sādhya**	Bharaṇi, Yama
9	**Śula**	Viśāka, Sakrāgni	23	**Śubha**	Kṛttikā, Agni
10	Gaṇḍa	Anurādha, Mitra	24	**Śukla**	Rohiṇī, Prajapati
11	Vṛdhi	Jyeṣṭha, Indra	25	**Brahmā**	Mṛgaśirā, Soma
12	Dhruva	Mūla, Nirriti	26	Indra	Ārdra, Rudra
13	**Vyāghāta**	Pūrva aṣāḍha, Apah	27	Vaidhṛti	Punarvasu, Aditi
14	Harṣana	Uttara aṣāḍha, Vishva Deva			

Yoga refers to the union or sambandha/relationship with the people around you. The twenty seven yogas and their lords as per the Viṁśottarī scheme are here tabulated.

Table 6: Yoga lords

Yoga #	Name	Graha
1,10,19	Viṣkambha, Gaṇḍa, Parighā	Saturn
2,11,20	Prīti, Vṛdhi, Śiva	Mercury
3,12,21	Ayuṣmān, Dhruva, Siddha	Ketu
4,13,22	Saubhāgya, Vyāghāta, Sādhya	Venus
5,14,23	Śobhana, Harṣana, Śubha	Sun
6,15,24	Atigaṇḍa, Vajra, Śukla	Moon
7,16,25	Sukarmā, Siddhi, Brahmā	Mars
8,17,26	Dhṛti, Vyātipata, Indra	Rāhu
9,18,27	Śula, Variyān, Vaidhṛti	Jupiter

The addition of the degrees of Sun and Moon reveals not only a specific Nakṣatra but a specific degree. This degree point is known as the yoga sphuta. Sheshadri Iyer taught the use of this particular sphuta and taught three points of Yogi point, Saha or Duplicate yogi point and Ava yogi point.

Table 7: Yoga point

Term	Meaning	Sanskrit term
Yogi point	Yoga Nakṣatra	Yogabha or yogārkṣa
Saha or Duplicate yogi point	Yoga Rāśi	Yogakṣetra
Ava yogi point	14th Nakṣatra from the yoga Nakṣatra	

The lords of these Nakṣatra or Rāśi are used in prediction to determine the native's extent of fortune. However, this point can be expanded to the use of Navāṁśa positions and other relevant varga positions also termed yogāmśa.

While the Yogi point and Duplicate yogi point are directly linked to the Nakṣatra and Rāśi of the Yoga sphuta, the Ava yogi point is the fourteenth Nakṣatra there from. The fourteenth Nakṣatra in the natural zodiac is Chitra from which we ascertain the starting point of the zodiac as zero degrees Aries is exactly opposite the position of Chitra. This Ava yogi is normally considered inauspicious. The term Ava refers to that which is descending or coming down and thus refers in this case to the Ākāśa descending or being pulled down and is in converse to the Yogi point itself which causes the Ākāśa to rise.

Tārā

Just as the Moon's movement caused the boundaries of the Nakṣatras to be created, the Nakṣatra are said to be the wives of the Moon, a role in which he takes on the name *Soma*.

Nakṣatra or its synonym Tārā represents the wife of Bṛhaspati who was kidnapped by Soma, the Moon. Shortly after the kidnapping had been resolved and Tara returned to her husband after all the tumult, it was noticed that Tārā was pregnant, resulting in another dramatic situation between Bṛhaspati and Soma as to find who was the father of the child to come. After much coercion from Bṛhaspati, Tara admitted that the child to come was the offspring of Soma.

The child born was a son and was named Budha (not to be confused with Buddha – the enlightened one). Budha is symbolic of this human birth itself, which is said to be a bastard birth being that it has separated us from Guru (Bṛhaspati) and the knowledge of the divine. This birth of ours took place as a result of the Moon kidnapping a Nakṣatra/Tārā which also is our birth Nakṣatra. However, with his birth Budha was given the choice to either follow his biological father (Soma/Moon) and his less than lawful ways, or his mother's husband (Bṛhaspati, Jupiter or Lagna) who moves on the path of the seers. This battle of choice is between the Nakṣatra of the Moon vs. that of the Yoga sphuta i.e. follow your emotions, senses and ways of the public (Moon) or follow own reasoning and logic (Jupiter).

Regardless of which of the two paths one may follow, the Moons Nakṣatra will always dominate in a person's childhood and upbringing. This is because the Moon represents the mother and will show the mothers impact on the child's mind and world-view. This is regardless of whether one has been raised by ones biological mother or not. This in turn will affect the person's entire theme of life, hence the amount of scripture available which is devoted to mere analysis of Nakṣatra to determine the native's life events.

The tradition takes this analysis a step further in that the Nakṣatra of the Moon vs. that of the Yoga are analysed to determine whether they wish to continue on their singular path of feeding themselves in this world or on the worldly path of sharing with the world and seeing the world as one family.

In my personal research I have found that in the charts of all prominent spiritually realised souls, the planets in or lording over the Yoga Nakṣatra are always stronger or more prominent than that of the Nakṣatra lord of the Moon sign in the chart. Whilst the spiritually realised are not alone in treating the world as their family, these difference between what one gives and what one takes is more evident in the charts of the sincere preachers of God.

Chart 4: Sri Chaitanya Mahaprabhu

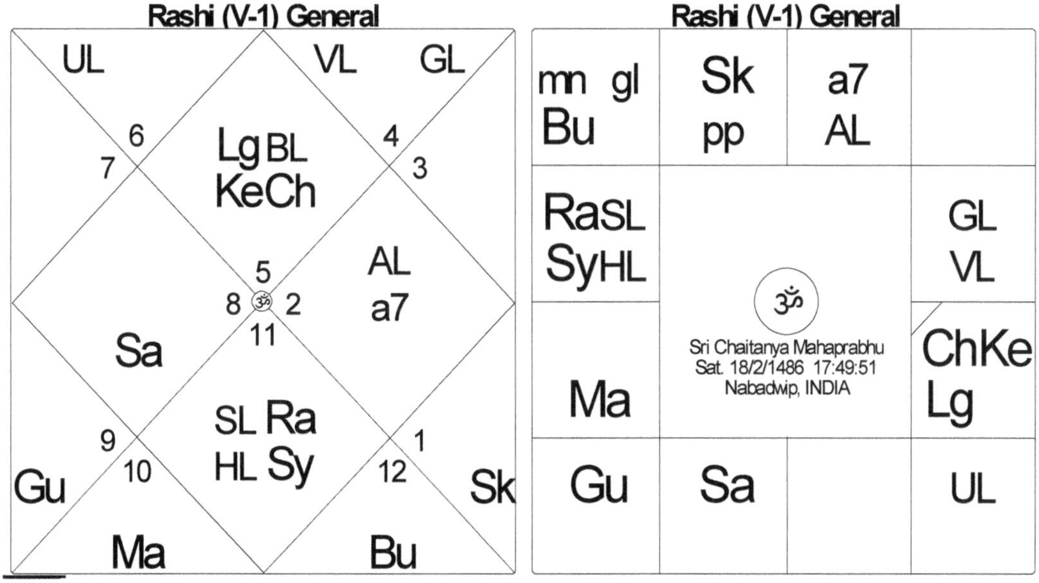

Chart of Śrī Chaitanya Mahaprabhu, born 18th February 1486, at 5:49 PM, Nabadwip, India. Moon is in the Lagna in the same Nakṣatra which is a criteria for the birth of a Viṣṇu Avatara, and being Pūrvaphalguṇī sets the stage for an incarnation of the Moon itself, i.e. an aspect of Śrī Kṛṣṇa. With the ninth lord Mars placed in Capricorn Rāśi and associated with Saturn, Sun and Jupiter in the Navāṁśa Chaitanya fulfills all the necessary criteria for being an incarnation of Śrī Viṣṇu.

He was born during a lunar eclipse, and whenever specifically the junction of Sun and Rāhu arises either a great Guru is born or misfortune due to ignorance arises. The difference is decided based on Jupiter and being that Jupiter is placed in a trine to the Lagna a great teacher is born who will overcome the ignorance of many. Being in the fifth house he will restart the ancient traditions of knowledge. This yoga is known as Dakṣiṇamūrti Yoga by some.

The Yoga is Dhṛti residing in Svatī Nakṣatra, lorded by Rāhu. With Moon's Nakṣatra being lorded over by Venus in the ninth house, the placement of Yoga lord in a Kendra makes it stronger and more prominent. Also we find that the Yoga lord is causing the Dakṣiṇamūrti Yoga in the chart. It therefore becomes evident that the Yoga lord is directly linked to the spiritual agenda of the native.

Chart 5: Śrī Lahiri Mahasaya

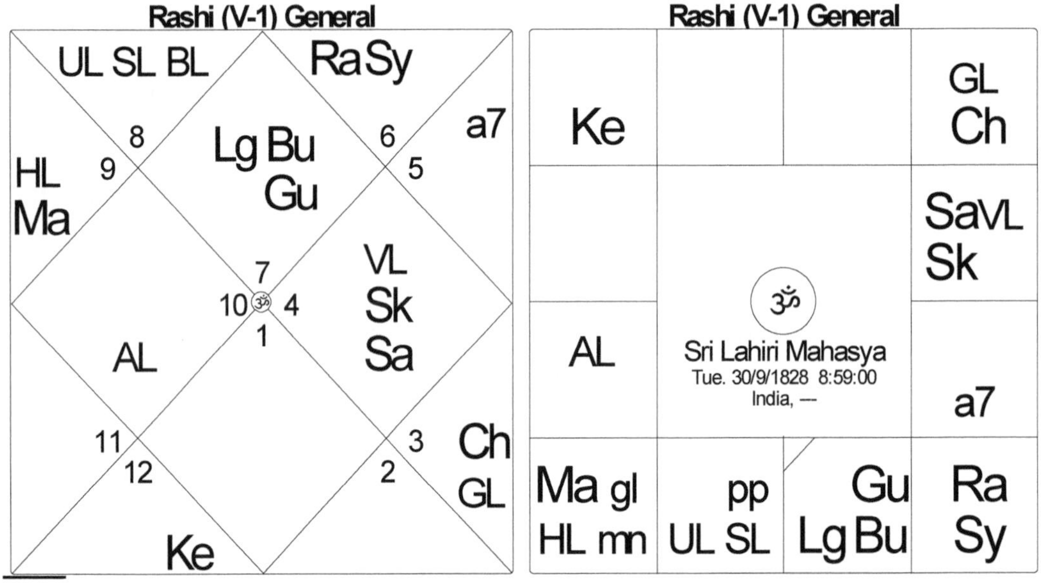

Chart of Śrī Lahiri Mahasaya, born 30th November 1828, 8:59 AM, 87e5, 26n28, India.

Nakṣatra of the Moon is Ārdrā, lorded by Rāhu, as the Yoga is Variyan, in Viśakhā Nakṣatra lorded over by Jupiter. As Lagna and Jupiter occupy Viśakhā Nakṣatra the Yoga dominates significantly over the indications of the Nakṣatra lord and is much stronger placed in the Lagna.

Lahiri embarked on a career of government service proving the initial interest in social service, and since ninth lord Mercury is joined Jupiter in the Lagna the meeting with his Guru made him turn towards spirituality in a major way to become the teacher of modern day Kriya Yoga.

Again most notably the union of Sun and Rāhu exists as Jupiter occupies a trine to the Lagna.

Chart 6: Ramana Mahaṛṣi

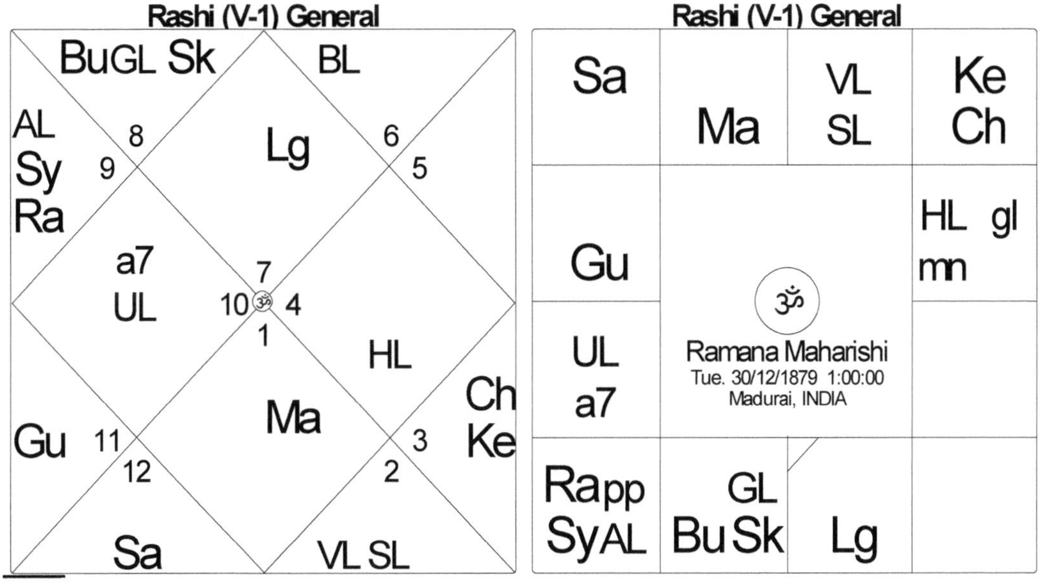

Chart of Ramaṇa Mahāṛṣi, born 30th December 1879, 1 AM, Madurai, India.

Moon occupies the Nakṣatra of Punarvasū, the Yoga is Indra occupying Ādrā Nakṣatra. Where the Nakṣatra lord Jupiter seems stronger placed due to its position in the fifth house, Rāhu being the Yoga lord is in an exchange with Jupiter in the chart. This suggests that the Yoga lord has a profound influence on affairs of the Nakṣatra lord and again we find the union of Sun and Rāhu as Jupiter is placed in a trine.

The eclipse has a profound impact on the chart of great spiritualists and the analysis of the Yoga lord with such views in mind will prove as a sure indicator to the pursuits of the native towards sharing their knowledge with the world.

1.3 Tithi: Fructification of all Desires (Jala Tattva)

The Tithis are based on the movement of the Sun and Moon. Specifically their amount is based on the time between two full moons, namely twenty-nine and a half days. This number is rounded up to thirty Tithis spread equally over a span of 360 degrees. This gives each Tithi a length of twelve degrees.

Unlike the Nakṣatra which are solely based on the Moon, the Tithi are based on the movement of both the Sun and the Moon. Yet, unlike Yoga which is also based on the same, the Tithi are based on the separation and not cumulative sum of their movement. This separation is said to embody the exact desire which caused rebirth of the soul, and for this reason is symbolized by Venus and the watery (Jala) element. Tithi not only symbolizes the desire for rebirth, but also all how these desires are projected upon the souls we share this life with. Thus, we can analyze the Tithi to understand the native's love life, marriage, and the relationship with the souls with which we have to share this world with. For this reason Pārāśara Muni designates the time span of a Pakṣa/fortnight to Venus (Parashara 1999, I-31).

The association of the watery element with Tithi is also associated with food. The Moon due to its separation from the Sun reflects or absorbs the Sun's light and this light is said to be the food for all beings which we presently measure through the control the Moon has over the tides. This food is symbolically said to be absorbed into the Nakṣatra of the Moon where the food quantity is said to indicate the longevity of the living being. Therefore the Tithi indicates the ability to catch or pull the food down to the living beings as the Nakṣatra of the Moon shows how long this food will last and thus give longevity.

These thirty Tithis spread over two pakṣa/fortnights (time between full moon and new moon). The phase of waxing, i.e. increasing motion towards the full moon is called Śukla Pakṣa or bright fortnight. The phase of waning, i.e. decreasing motion from full moon to new moon is called Kṛṣṇa Pakṣa or dark fortnight. These two Pakṣa are also known as Tara and Kali Pakṣa respectively, indicating the two forms of the divine mother. The Tithis are hence divided into two halves; those which occur in Śukla Pakṣa, and those which occur in Kṛṣṇa pakṣa. This gives us fourteen Tithis which repeat twice (14x2=28), whilst the last two, the full moon and the new moon occur only once a month, giving a total of 28+2=30 Tithis in a month.

Here is illustrated the means of calculating the Tithi for a person with the Sun at 5°07′ Scorpio, and Moon at4°37′ Virgo. Moon displaced 299°30′ ahead of the Sun. Dividing this figure by 12° we attain the quotient of 24 and a remainder of 11°30′, indicating that the 25th Tithi is undergoing and 0°30′ is left of it. Since the Tithi value is higher than 15 it implies that the Tithi resides in Kṛṣṇa Pakṣa (Dark fortnight). Deducting 15 from the attained value of 25 we get 10 as the result indicating that the 10th Tithi of the Dark fortnight is undergoing, or Kṛṣṇa Daśamī Tithi.

Table 8: Tithi Lords

Tithi	Tithi name	Graha lord
1 and 9	Pratipada, Navamī	Sun
2 and 10	Dvītiyā, Daśamī	Moon
3 and 11	Tṛtīyā, Ekādaśī	Mars
4 and 12	Caturthī, Dvādaśī	Mercury
5 and 13	Pañcamī, Trayodaśī	Jupiter
6 and 14	Saṣṭī, Caturdaśī	Venus
7 and Full moon	Saptamī, Pūrṇimā	Saturn
8 and New Moon	Aṣṭamī, Amāvasyā	Rāhu

The graha presiding over the Tithis is given by Harihara in his work Prasna Marga. The given table illustrates the same. The tradition teaches that the basis of the order is simply the natural weekday order of planets from Sun to Rāhu completing the Tithi from Pratipada (1st) to Aṣṭamī (8th). This order continues from Navamī (9th) to Caturdaśī (14th) yet the fifteenth Tithi being either Pūrṇimā (full moon) or Amāvasyā (new moon) is presided over by Saturn and Rāhu respectively. Ketu finds no mention in this scheme as it doesn't cause rebirth and instead grants mokṣa or final emancipation to the individual. Therefore, when Harihara explains the Tithi and the graha presiding over the same, he also explains the kāla chakra which is the basis of both Hindu and Buddhist beliefs.

Figure 2: Kāla chakra

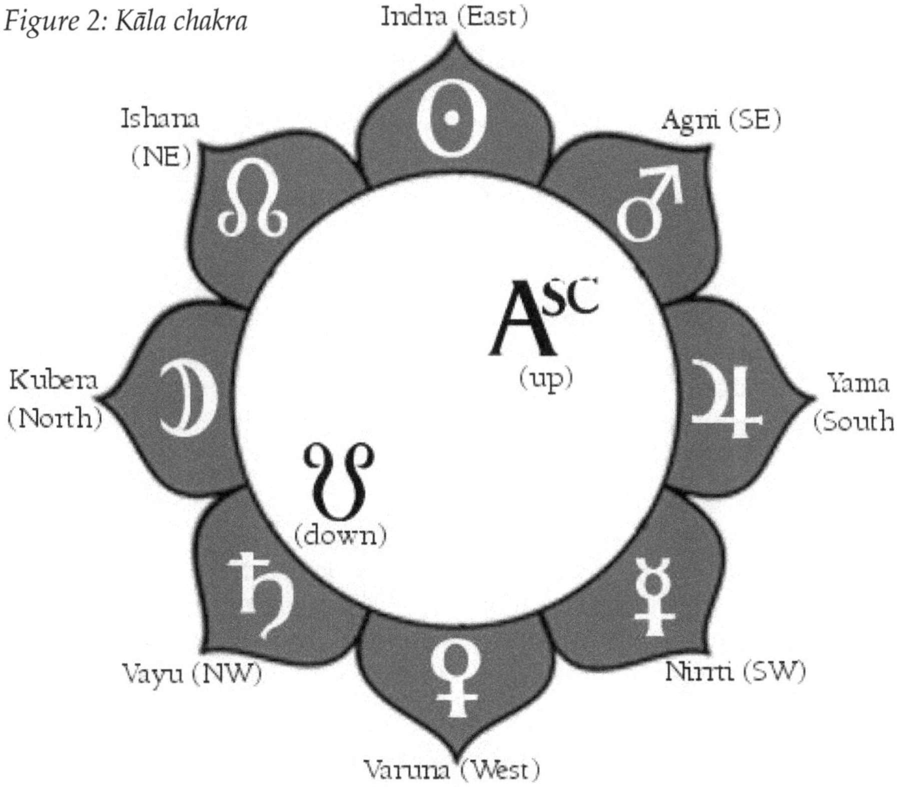

In the kāla chakra, the eight graha from Sun to Rāhu rule the eight directions in the horizontal plane, whereas Ketu rules the vertical downwards plane as the Lagna or Ascendant rules the upwards direction. Notably this is opposite in the Dig chakra. The Kāla chakra also forms the basis of the soul or atma which has eight spokes and also the basis of the chāra kāraka scheme.

Nandādi Tithi

The fifteen Tithi are distributed into five groups symbolising the five elements or Pañca Tattva. The names of these five groups are Nanda, Bhadra, Jaya, Rikta and Pūrṇa in order. The first, sixth and eleventh Tithis belong to the Nanda group. The second, seventh and twelfth Tithis belong to the Bhadrā group and in this order the remaining Tithis are distributed. This is here tabulated.

Table 9: Nadādi Tithi

Group	Nanda	Bhadra	Jaya	Ṛkta	Pūrṇa
Tithi	1st, 6th and 11th	2nd, 7th, and 12th	3rd, 8th and 13th	4th, 9th and 14th	5th, 10th and 15th
Tattva	Agni	Pṛthvī	Akaśa	Jala	Vāyu

Pakṣa Bala (strength of the Moon)

The strength of the Tithi or Pakṣa Bala defines the auspiciousness of the Moon in the chart. If the moon is devoid of light it is considered *krūra* or cruel. Otherwise its considered *saumya* or benevolent.

Two methods exist to define the strength of the Moon based on the Tithi. One method is simply that during the bright fortnight (Śukla Pakṣa) the Moon is strong and during the dark fortnight it is weak. This does not really indicate the strength of the Moon but speaks of the Moon's agenda. When in the bright fortnight the Moon is heading towards the full moon which symbolises prosperity and a materialistic agenda. Instead when in the dark fortnight the Moon is heading towards the new moon and therefore takes on a more spiritual agenda.

A more sound method of defining the Moon's strength is based on the Moon's proximity to the new or full moon. If the Moon is closer to the full moon than to the new moon it is considered strong, otherwise weak. This is loosely defined as the Moon occupying the Tithis between Śukla Aṣṭamī (8th Tithi of the bright fortnight) till Kṛṣṇa Aṣṭamī (8th Tithi of the dark fortnight).

Deva and Tithi

To help these souls God has manifested in different forms on different Tithis to show the way back to God. Knowledge about these Tithis are essential for astrologers, as we not only get to know the means to curtail the bonds which have brought us here, but also which Tithis are more or less difficult for various purposes in this abode.

Table 10: Tithi Devatā

Tithi	Devatā	Tithi	Devatā	Tithi	Devatā
1	Īśa	6	Guha	11	Viśva
2	Vahnika	7	Ravi	12	Hari
3	Gaurī	8	Śiva	13	Agni
4	Gaṇeśa	9	Durgā	14	Śiva
5	Sarasvati	10	Antaka	15	Kali/Narayana

Auspicious and Inauspicious Tithi

Traditionally the inauspicious Tithi are said to be the three Tithi in proximity to the New Moon namely Kṛṣṇa Chaturdaṣī (14th Tithi of the dark fortnight), Amāvāsya (15th Tithi of the dark fortnight) and Śukla Pratipada (1st Tithi of the bright fortnight). Their inauspiciousness stemming from the lack of light attained by the Moon during these Tithi.

Figure 3: Relationships and Tithi

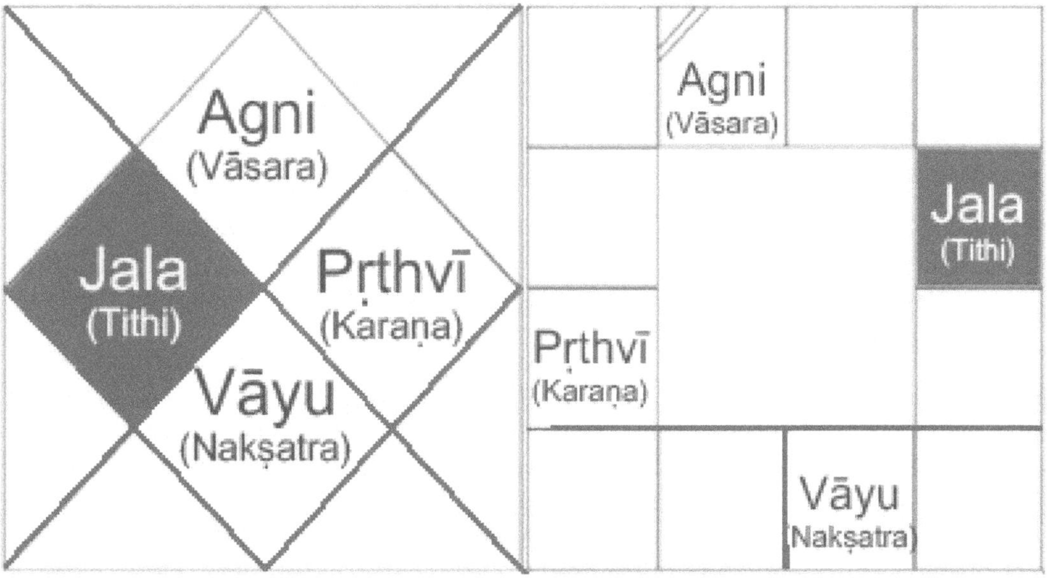

Further the three Rikta Tithi (refer: Nandādi Tithi) are also considered inauspicious, namely Chaturthī (4th Tithi), Navamī (9th Tithi) and Chaturdaśī (14th Tithi).

Figure 3: Tithi and Jala

In the interpretation of the Tithi, the lord of the Tithi should be taken into examination. Herein specifically we are to analyse it for the person's relationships in life. This is done from two perspectives:

- How the person interacts with the partner is seen from the Tithi lord's placement from the fifth house.
- How the emotional aspect of the relationship and its long term potential is seen from the placement from the fourth house and lord (Rath, Vedic Reading Process, 2010).

- Similarly malefic influence on the fourth house or lord is pivotal in ensuring healthy married life if any.
- The Tithi being watery by nature is best placed in watery signs and worst in fiery signs. Earthy signs are good for a relationship with rules and boundaries, whilst airy signs encourage negative movement and separation in the couple. The persons attitude towards relationships must be seen from the Tithi lords placement from Lagna.

Chart 7: Carol Kane

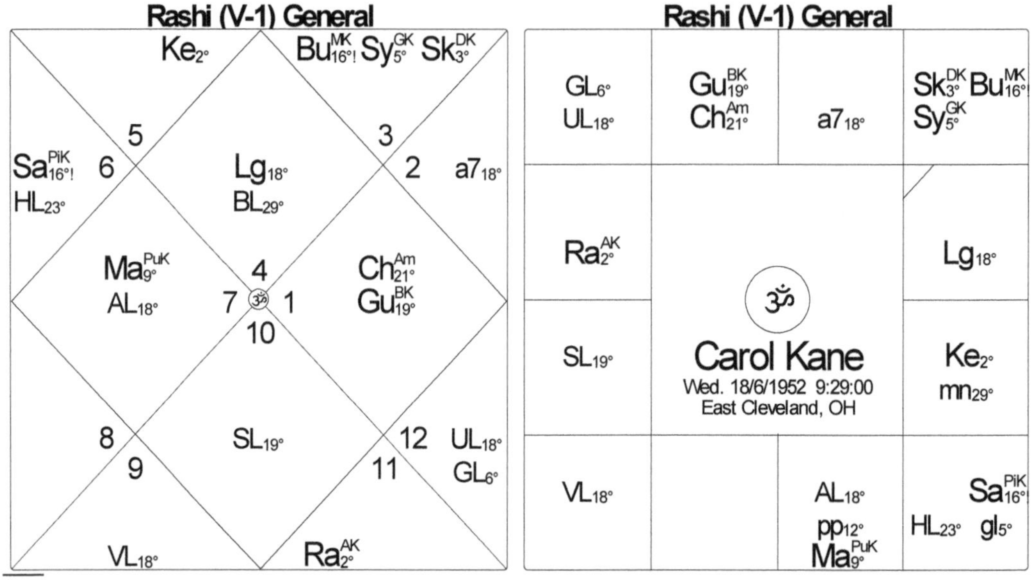

Chart of Carolyn Laurie Kane, better known as Carol Kane, born 18th June 1952, 9:29 AM in East Cleveland, Ohio, USA. Tithi of birth is. Kṛṣṇa Dvadaśī Tithi lorded over by Mercury. Tenth lord Mars is placed in the fourth house which can prove trying for the the relationship between mother and father. As Mars is the lord of the Moon sign the differences between parents would appear from birth. As Mars lords the fourth Nakṣatra from Moon this would further have a significant impact on Carolyn's childhood and upbringing.

The second house represents family and whilst Ketu in there is excellent for the wealth of the family due to being in Leo, the lord Sun is placed in the twelfth house in Māraṇa Kāraka Sthāna which works towards the detriment of the family, and especially family. Among the ninth and fourth lords representing father and mother, the ninth lord is badly placed in the eleventh from the second lord causing the father to break from the family. As the Sun is furthermore occupying the Manasa Nakṣatra (Rath, Brhat Nakshatra, 2008) these experiences would have a negative impact on the young Carolyn's mind and could be carried by her for a long time. Insted the fourth lord Venus is extremely auspicious and supportive as it is also lord over the Ārūḍha of the ninth house (A9) giving lifelong comfort.

Carolyn was born of Russian emigrants with the mother being an artist active with Jazz singing, dancing and playing the Piano whilst the father was an architect who worked for the World Bank. Despite being born in Cleveland, Kane with her parents moved to New York when she was eight years of age. The Mahādaśā was fourth lord Venus in the Antaradaśā of Mercury who is joined the fourth lord to support the move.

When the Mahādaśā of the Sun began at the age of ten the family differences began to manifest. The Sun being second lord in Māraṇa Kāraka Sthāna is difficult for family matters and especially during the Antaradaśā of the planets badly placed from the same. Among the Graha only Moon and Jupiter are badly placed from the Sun but Moon being the lord of Lagna represents the native herself and not one among the family members. When the Antaradaśā of ninth lord Jupiter arose as Kane was twelve years old the parents divorced.

Despite its misgivings for the father and family happiness, the union of Moon and Jupiter as first and ninth lords in the tenth house is a fantastic combination for name and fame lasting beyond one's lifetime. This becomes all the more prominent with their placement in the seventh from Ārūḍha Lagna ensuring financial security in life. With equal number of Graha in the second and fourth houses the potentiality of fortune from a young age is assured. The Daśā of fourth from Ghaṭika Lagna and tenth from Horā Lagna are sure indicators to earning reputation and wealth and so also as both are lorded and conjoined by Mercury the same occurred during Mercury Antaradaśā. At 14 she had her professional theatre debut in the act *The Prime of Miss Jean Brodie.*

Her first film debut came in 1971 in Moon Mahādaśā, Jupiter Antaradaśā. As would be expected from this combination her contribution to the film industry would leave a lasting impression. She has since gone on to act in 50 movies since then as well as played a minor role in 34 TV series. She is still quite active on the acting scene. Her most noteworthy role was acting on the series TAXI. During Mars Mahādaśā she played Simka Dahblitz-Gravas, wife of Latka Gravas played by Andy Kaufman. Mars is placed in Libra whose lord Venus signifies vehicles and transportation. Mars there will signify a place for repairs or mechanics and so also the main theme of the series was set in a taxi-company's garage. Her main fame in the series occurred during Mercury Antaradaśā which previously had made her initial theatre debut. This continued during Ketu Antaradaśā which is well placed in the second house in Leo.

Despite her professional success Kane has never married. The seventh lord Saturn is well placed in the third house and surely gave relationships. Further Tithi lord Mercury and fourth lord Venus are conjoined which is indicative of serious long term relationships. However, the conjunction of the Sun with Venus in the previously mentioned Manasa Nakṣatra leave a less desired outcome of any long term relationship where excessive emotional strain on the mind leaves her vulnerable towards much anxiety. Such hurdles are quite difficult to overcome and Rudrābhiṣeka once a month as well as wearing a 4-faced Rudrākṣa bead would have been advisable to overcome these hurdles. Tithi lord Mercury placed in an airy sign with the fiery Sun shows unfortunate outcomes in relationships, and the placement in the twelfth house leaves much to wish for in ones attitude towards relationships.

Mars being the fifth lord and Putrakāraka plays a pivotal role in bringing children into her life and having Argalā on the Lagna should have paved the way for the same. Yet this Mars' Argalā is fully obstructed by Jupiter and Moon in the tenth house which was meant to assure her professional success and legacy.

Chart 8: David Letterman

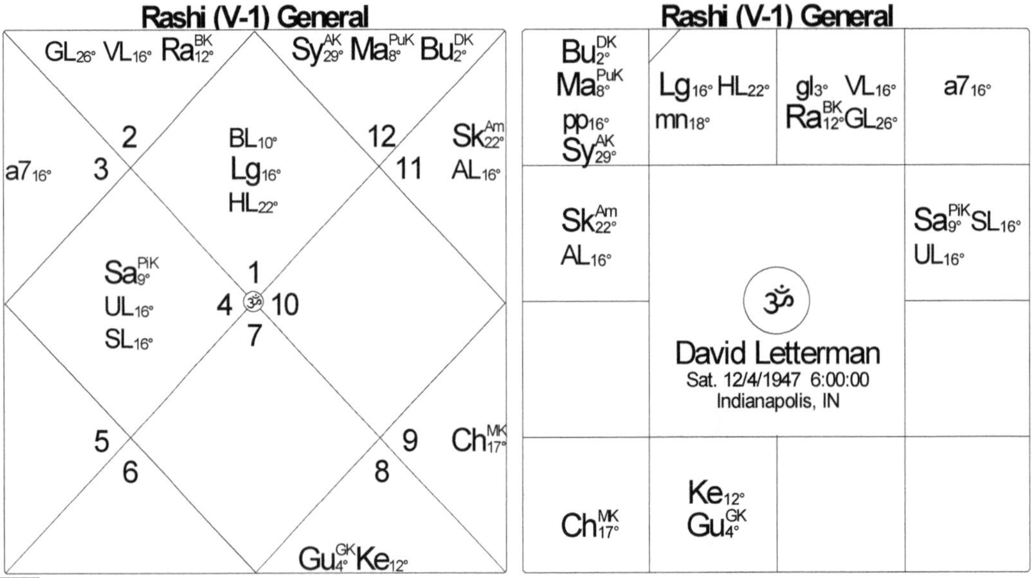

Chart of David Letterman, born 12th April 1947, 6 AM, Indianapolis, Indiana, USA. Tithi is Kṛṣṇa Saptamī which is lorded over by Saturn. Saturn is placed in the fourth house which is supportive towards long term relationships and marriage as it lords over the Tithi and placed in a watery sign. However, being a malefic it as Tithi lord in a Kendra or eighth house proves detrimental towards health and longevity as the Tithi lord is responsible for the water in the body. Jupiter being retrograde in the eighth house and joined a malefic further accentuates a very dangerous time in childhood; however Jupiter being Śubhapati will protect the native and more so as it has sign aspect on the Lagna. It further aspects an afflicted twelfth and second house to completely keep the evils of them at bay. Thus Jupiter becomes a great protector of the chart, yet will be negative for father due to its ninth lordship.

The fourth lord Moon is placed in the ninth house which can prove difficult as it is placed in the sixth house from the fourth, and promotes physical separation from the partner and issues/lack of intimacy. This is further a bigger problem in that seventh lord Venus is placed in the eleventh house where it blocks the Argalā of Moon on the fourth house.

This causes a most peculiar situation in that Venus is not only the significator of relationships and partnerships but also seventh lord who is responsible for bringing the same into his life. Hence, that which is bringing the mate into his life is also pushing out the partner. This creates a problem to sustain a relationship because of 'new' partners entering the relationship. This becomes all the more perplexing when we see that Venus is joined the Ārūḍha Lagna which promises fortune through the limelight, and further in that Venus lords over the Ārūḍha of the ninth house (A9) which gives lifelong comfort.

Born to Harry and Dorothy Letterman in the Utpanna Viṁśottari Daśā of Rāhu and Antaradaśā of Jupiter. Letterman whilst growing up admired his father's high spirit and this brought him into the realm of comedy which became the focus of his career from the advent of his school days.

In 1969 with the advent of Jupiter Daśā, Venus Antaradaśā Letterman graduated from the Ball State University from the department of Radio and Television. Venus being among the largest blessings in his chart would pave the way for his career in the entertainment industry and being the Amatyakāraka would surely do so.

Venus being the seventh lord also brought him to his first marriage during the same year. Venus further joins the seventh lord Rāhu in the Navāṁśa justifying the timing of marriage. A great dilemma arises in that the Upapada in Cancer is placed in the sixth house from Venus and indicates a marriage which may not be born out of right intentions or cannot last long due to lack of affection. This would later come true as the couple would separate.

Letterman got inspired by the then talk show host Paul Dixon in whose footsteps Letterman wished to follow. By then he had already worked on the student-run radio stations.

He began his career as a radio talk show host and further as a weatherman and anchorman in the Indianapolis TV station. Therein he received some recognition for his humorous pieces. He further appeared in different contexts as a reporter for the TV station.

The family was always worried for Letterman's father who suffered a heart attack when Letterman was four during the Daśā of Rāhu and Antaradaśā of Mercury. Mercury is in an exchange with Jupiter and would thus bring about its results.

The Dvādaśāṁśa has Libra Lagna as the ninth house is Gemini. From Gemini the Māraka houses are Cancer and Sagittarius. Their lords, Moon and Jupiter, are in mutual aspect where Jupiter retrograde in own sign is much more evil for fathers health. This makes Jupiter Mahādaśā the problematic and so also in the Mahādaśā of Jupiter and Antaradaśā of Moon Letterman's father passed away due to a heart attack. Letterman was 26 at the time.

Chart 9: Letterman D-12

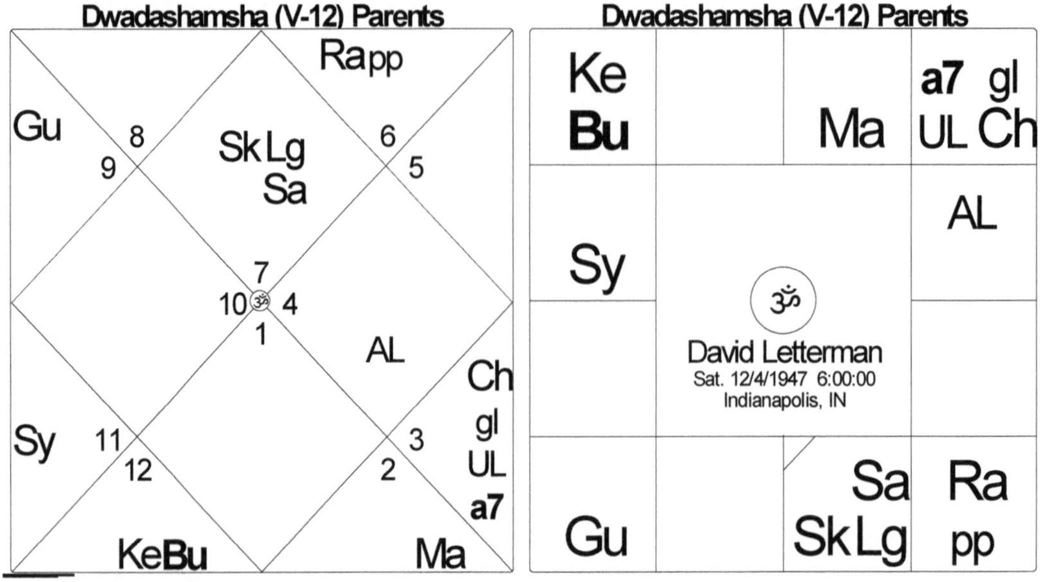

Encouraged by his then wife, Michelle, and friends, Letterman moved to Los Angeles, California to become a comedy writer. He loaded up his truck and drove to California to begin a new life. He began writing material for Jimmy Walker and further appeared at The Comedy Store performing for himself. Rāhu is the lord of the Ārūḍha Lagna and dispositor of the most fortunate Venus and so also when Rāhu Antaradaśā began he embarked on this new career.

Unfortunately, his new found career also brought many tests to his marriage. By 1977 in Saturn Daśā, Saturn Antaradaśā his wife urged Letterman to divorce due to the nature of the relationships he was entertaining in California. Saturn clearly supports Venus due to dispositing the same and being the seventh lord from the Upapada would surely strain marriage due to external parties. Saturn lords the eighth from the Upapada and gives room to the next partner. So also from 1978 during the same Antaradaśā he began a long term relationship with Merrill Markoe, who sharing his career pursuits was instrumental in contributing many of the ideas which Letterman still uses on his show. Venus is joined Aquarius and shows a strong love relationship and Rāhu being the lord of the same has gained eleven Navāṁśa giving at least eleven years of the relationship.

Saturn being the tenth lord would give a new lift in his career. After a year of various jobs he began appearing on the Johnny Carson show several times and was widely liked by the host as well as the audience. He attributed Mr. Carson as having the most profound influence on his career.

With the advent of Mercury Antaradaśā he began his own morning show (Sun is conjoined) amidst game shows and soap operas. Despite being critically acclaimed for his performance the ratings were low and the show was cancelled (Māraṇa Kāraka Sthāna) the same year. Eying his success NBC gave him slots at night which made the show take off in the public eye and gathered a cult following, especially among college students. The show debuted at the end of Mercury Antaradaśā and continued for ten years after which Letterman began his show independently of NBC.

In 1988 the relationship with Markoe ended in Moon Antaradaśā. Moon becoming strong during its Antaradaśā puts up a fight with Venus and pushes it out of Letterman's life and so also due to Markoe moving to pursue her writing career elsewhere, the relationship ended. During the same year Letterman began dating Regina Lasko who would become his future wife.

Moon being the dispositor of the tenth lord also brought a new beginning to his career and so also Letterman signed with CBS to launch the *Late Show with David Letterman.*

With Virgo being the third from the Upapada it signifies his third long term partnership with Regina Lasko. As Mercury lords this Upapada and is debilitated in the twelfth house it indicates a relationship which may not be solemnized into a marriage. Mercury being in a Kendra to the Moon receives cancellation of its debilitation and paves the way for an opportunity to marry once Mercury becomes strong. So also it took until Mercury Mahadaśā, Jupiter Antaradaśā (exchange with Mercury) until the couple wedded in 2009. By then their son Harry was 5 years old and had been born during the previous Moon Antaradaśā. Moon lords the Saptāṁśa (D-7) Lagna and is placed in the ninth house to bring the first child.

Chart 10: Letterman D-7

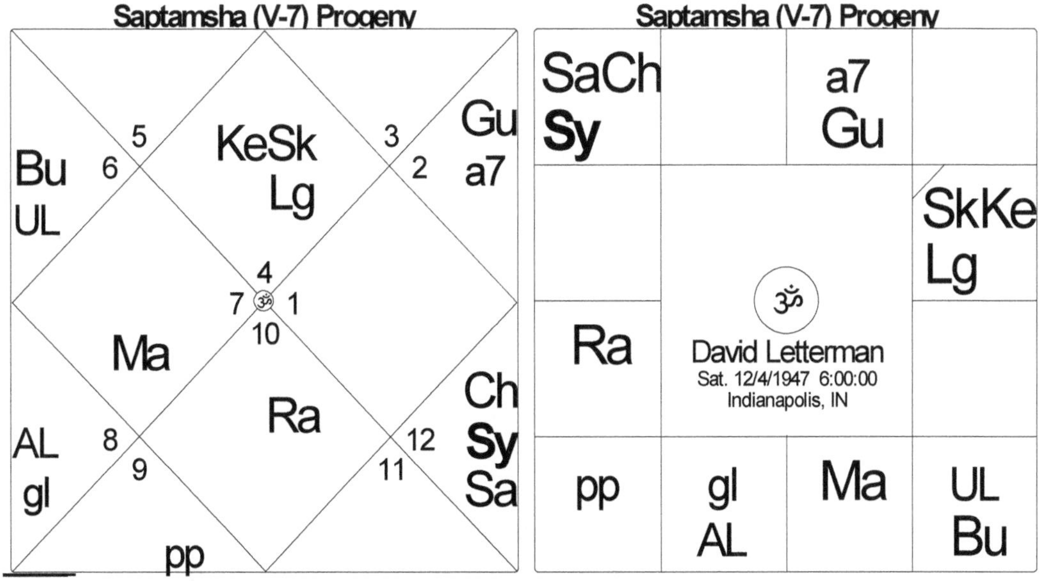

However, Venus lords over the second house from Virgo and being the source of Letterman's limelight strains the marriage due to extramarital affairs. With Rāhu aspecting Libra from Taurus by sign aspect and further lording over the Ārūḍha Lagna risk of scandal due to relationships would arise. Jupiter being the ninth lord in the eighth house brought about this problem during the same Antaradaśā and a few months after their wedding. We must recall that Jupiter is also a great protector in the chart but being the ninth lord would require truthfulness above all. Letterman was forced to reveal that he had been the victim of extortion by a couple who threatened to reveal that Letterman had engaged in relationships with members of his staff. He revealed this on his show to the viewing audience. He claimed that these incidents had occurred prior to his marriage. He continues to be married to his wife and rumors are that he has been forgiven, however the trials to the relationship are evidently on account of the negatives of Venus.

Tithi Bīja

Previously, the Graha presiding over the Tithi have been defined to w.r.t. the Kāla Chakra. The Kāla Chakra (lit. wheel of time) signifies the bondage of the individual soul by the movement of time. Herein time is described as circular (or elliptic) and moving at different timescales at different levels of existence (or consciousness). The age old example of the time of the Gods vs. that of the humans comes to fore in this principle where what may seem as one year for the human beings is but a day for the Gods. Having to succumb to a particular existence and thus a particular timescale is the bondage of time that all living beings are subject to.

The Graha which presides over the Tithi thus indicates that aspect of the Tithi which has caused us to be enslaved by time and this has occurred due to desire as is the nature of all Tithis. The Graha which lords over the Tithi indicates the main flaw of the Tithi and analysis of the Tithi will also reveal how this flaw will manifest. Specifically, it is the desire (seventh house) indicated by the Graha presiding over the Tithi which brings about the problem, and it is thus also through desire that every being is reborn according to the classical literature. The Tithi is responsible for yoking two individuals together and prominently for relationships and progeny. Two individuals who have come together for the purpose of having children must 'match Tithis' to be able to have children together. In essence the couple is yoked together to cause new rebirths of individuals due to that bond which caused themselves to be reborn in the first place. In an individual's chart the affliction of this Tithi Bīja also reveals problems for this yoking to happen and can thereby delay or deny marriage as well as children.

Practically, the seventh house from the Graha lording over the Tithi represents the desire of the Tithi, whilst the manifestation of this desire is brought about by ascertaining the *Tithi Bīja*.

Whilst other traditions may term this principle differently, the *Tithi Bīja* is ascertained in line with the principle of calculating the Ārūḍha pada.

i) Count from the Rāśi of the Moon to the Rāśi in the seventh from the lord of the Tithi and count the same distance from the seventh from the Lord of the Tithi. The Rāśi arrived at is the *Tithi Bīja*.

ii) Should the arrived at Rāśi be placed in the Moon Rāśi or opposite Rāśi then an exception applies. Count to the tenth Rāśi from the mentioned Rāśi to arrive at the Tithi Bīja.

As is the case with the Ārūḍha calculations, some ignore the exception to arrive at the result, however this does not become an Ārūḍha but instead the Bahya. Therefore it may be appropriate to term these special points as *Tithi Ārūḍha* and *Tithi Bahya* respectively.

Calculation example for a person born during Kṛṣṇa Tṛtiyā as the Moon is in Aquarius and Mars (lord of Tṛtiyā Tithi) is placed in Virgo.

i) Mars lords over the Tṛtiyā Tithi and being in Virgo requires us to count from the Moon sign (Aquarius) to Pisces (seventh from Virgo). Pisces is the second Rāśi from Aquarius. Counting the same distance (second) from Pisces we arrive at Aries. This is then the Tithi Bīja Rāśi for the person.

ii) There are no exceptions required therefore the Tithi Bāhya and Tithi Ārūḍha are the same.

In interpreting the chart, should the Rāśi of the Tithi Bīja is one among the Duṣthāna from the Lagna it may pose a problem in marriage or progeny. Specifically the 6th house delays permanent relationships, forcing abstinence and thus children, the 8th can give a premature end to the relationships whilst the 12th can deny one of a lasting lineage. The remaining houses can pose problems if the occupants or lords of these houses are badly placed.

Chart 11: Empress of Japan Michiko Shoda

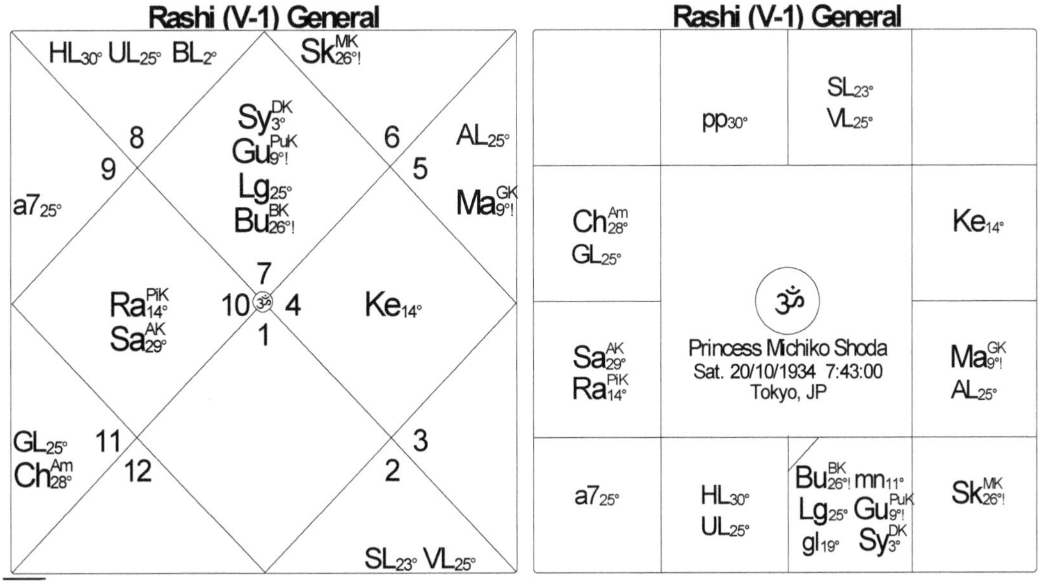

Chart of Empress of Japan Michiko Shoda, born 20th October 1934, 7:43 AM in Tokyo, Japan. She is born during the Tithi of Śukla Trayodaśī whose lord is Jupiter as Saturn is the Ātmakāraka. Empress Michiko was not born into a Royal family, yet was a commoner who married the then Crown Prince Akihito, son of Emperor Hirohito. The Lagna lord is very important for Raja Yoga and here it is Venus debilitated in the twelfth house not boding well. It however attains Nīca Bhañga Raja Yoga, or Raja Yoga due to cancellation of debility, due to lords of its exaltation and debilitation signs, Mercury and Jupiter, being placed on the Lagna. Mercury and Jupiter further are strong in Digbala showing the blessings of knowledge (Iśana) and wealth (Kubera) after rise from a low position (debilitated Lagna lord). Michiko Sodha was the first commoner to marry into the Royal family belonging to the Chrysanthemum Throne.

We find further that Mercury is the Navāṁśa dispositor of the Ātmakāraka Saturn justifying that this rise and wealth of Mercury will come through royal association, and she will thereafter belong to the royal family as Mercury is further joined the Navāṁśa Lagna. Mercury is further the ninth lord and shows the blessings coming from own father. Her father was a wealthy industrialist and being so enabled Michiko to interact with the elite in society.

The Tithi of birth is Śukla Trayodaśī which is among the more auspicious Tithi. Jupiter is placed in Libra and its seventh house is Aries. Counting from Moon in Aquarius to Aries is three signs. The third sign from Aries is Gemini which becomes the Tithi Bīja. Notably the Tithi Bīja being Gemini is lorded by the same Mercury which brings about her main blessings and rise in life, and is further placed in the ninth house which is a blessing.

Despite the promise of marriage and fortune, her marriage into the royal family of Japan was no walk on roses. With the Sun debilitated on the Lagna the then Princess was bothered by strong feelings of inadequacy, low self esteem due to feeling unable to live up to the expectations of her family and some within the public eye. Further with the twelfth house from the Moon being joined by Saturn and Rāhu, pressure will be immense in marriage and marital disharmony was bound to occur. Saturn and Rāhu are in the fourth house suggesting that mother or mother-in-law would be the cause of these difficulties leading to anxiety and nervous breakdowns, events which were known to have affected the Empress.

Chart 12: Emperor of Japan Akihito

Chart of Emperor of Japan Akihito born 23rd December 1933, 6:39 AM, Tokyo Japan. Birth is during Śukla Saptamī Tithi and the Ātmakāraka is Jupiter. The Lagna lord and lord of the Ārūḍha Lagna is the same Ātmakāraka Jupiter showing fame due to his status or position. He is today known as the only reigning monarch in the world. It is notable that Emperors as well as Empresses of Japan have a strong connection between the Ātmakāraka and the sign Virgo.

Birth is during Saptamī Tithi and its lord is Saturn placed in Capricorn. The seventh sign from Capricorn is Cancer and we need to count from Moon in Aquarius to Cancer. The count gives us six as the result and we need to count to the sixth sign from Cancer which is Sagittarius. Sagittarius becomes the Tithi Bīja. At first glance we find that the Tithi Bīja of Emperor Akihito and his spouse Empress Michiko Shoda are in opposite signs from each other, i.e. Gemini and Sagittarius. Being in Kendra Rāśi from each other is positive and shows a positive match between couples enabling them to have children. This is further in the 1st house for the Emperor granting marriage and fortune of progeny. Further comparison finds that their seventh lords are also in signs which are well placed from each other, confirming a very positive match for conjugal life and offspring.

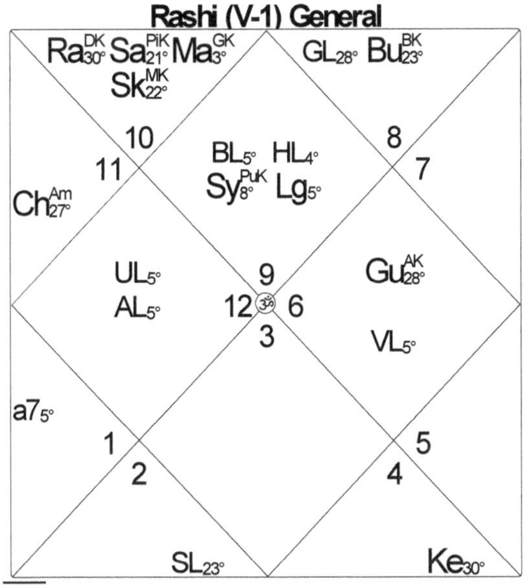

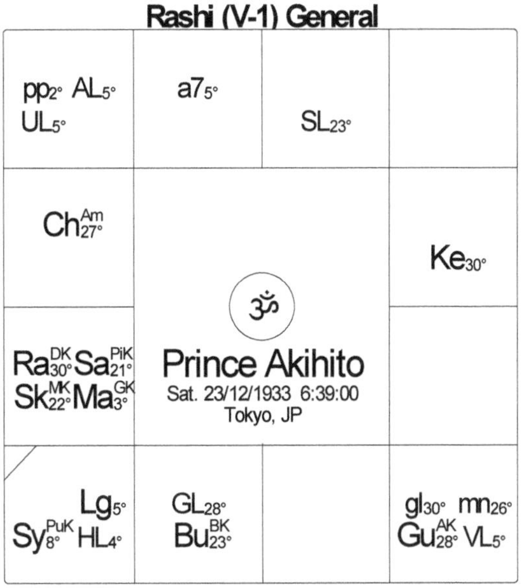

Sagittarius being the Tithi Bīja of the Emperor is lorded over by the previously mentioned Ātmakāraka showing that the off spring will continue in the royal lineage to which he belongs. The fifth lord is Mars and being exalted in Rāśi and Navāṁśa gives the fortune of up to three children (Parashara 1999). The couple has two sons and a daughter.

Chart 13: Nicholas II, Czar of Russia

Chart of Nicholas II, Czar of Russia, born 19th May 1868, 0:15 AM, St. Petersburg, Russia. The Tithi is Kṛṣṇa Dvadaśī and the Ātmakāraka Moon. The Kārakāṁśa is that of Aquarius and its lord Saturn is placed on the Navāṁśa Lagna justifying his royal-aristocratic heritage. However, the same Saturn is badly placed in the twelfth house in the Rāśi chart and will give defamation and risks to destroy the lineage to which he belongs. Saturn being placed in the ninth house from the Ārūḍha Lagna shows that this bad name arises out of following the advice of well-wishes that leads to his infamy. Nicholas II is infamous for being the last Czar of Russia, wherein a series of fatal mistakes and wrong decisions on part of the Czar, led to the Russian Revolution of 1917 ending the reign of the Czars in a bloody execution of the entire royal household. Most notably Saturn is also the second lord and acts as Rudra in the chart due to its placement and affliction. Saturn rules the policies of the peasants and carries the agenda of socialism which would be the cause of his undoing.

Rashi (V-1) General

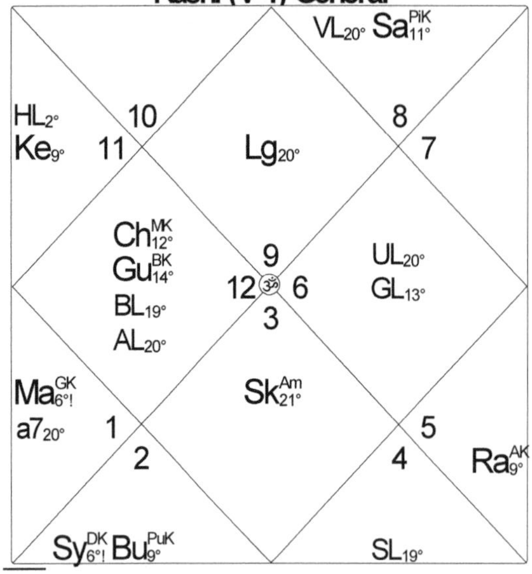

Rashi (V-1) General

Lagna lord Jupiter must be analysed and here Jupiter is well placed in the fourth house in a Gaja Keśari Yoga with the Moon. This further is a MahāntaYoga (Jaimini 1997) making the Czar very socially aware and a very progressive ruler on behalf of the people. His reign saw great improvement in matters of laws and he was the one to instigate the first formal agreement on weapons armament in Europe to encourage peace in the region. His acts and affinity with the Russian Orthodox Church led to the canonization of himself and his family following his demise. This great Raja Yoga is tainted by the Moons eighth lordship showing premature end. Further Venus being the only Graha with Rāśi Dṛṣṭi on the Yoga is further the sixth lord in Bādhaka Sthāna showing enmity arising out of thin air and for reasons which are hard to fathom or justify.

In light of these dreadful omens, the future of the lineage and its continuation has to be analysed in the chart. The birth Tithi being Dvadaśī is lorded over by Mercury which is placed in Taurus. The seventh from Taurus is Scorpio and counting from Moon in Pisces to Scorpio we get the count nine. Counting to the ninth sign from Scorpio we arrive at Cancer which is the Tithi Bīja. This being the eighth house and lorded by the same Moon indicates a risk of end to the lineage, and threatens the aristocracy due to the Moon being Ātmakāraka.

The fortune of any person is directly measurable in the fortune they see as parents. The fifth lord is Mars who is placed in it Mūlatrikoṇa (two) Rāśi and has also progressed two Navāṁśa, both confirming the fortune of having two children. However, as the Czar and his wife Alix did not produce a male heir in their initial attempts to have children, they had three girls after which the male heir Alexei was born. The exceeding of the two promised births is enough to indicate misfortune, but to add the birth of a son after the birth of three daughters is said to cause Tridevi Doṣa which brings about the anger of the divine mother in her three forms as Mahālakṣmī, Mahāsarasvatī and Mahākāḷī. Similarly, the anger of Brahmā, Visṇu and Maheśvara arises out of a daughter being born after the birth of three sons. Such a misfortune was bound to seal the fate of the Russian Royal lineage.

The male heir was not only born amidst anxiousness towards the need for a male heir, but also contracted Haemophilia which presented him with many challenges. Finding no solace in medical science, the Czar and Czarina turned towards the mystics for help, which they found through Siberian priest, Grigori Rasputin. With Rāhu in the ninth house showing risk of being misled by priests and mystics, as its lord is placed in the sixth house showing the priest becoming the enemy, this turn of events would be the sure nail in the coffin for the future of the Czar's family.

Rasputin, who seemingly offered spiritual protection where medical doctors and other mystics could not, was now the Czarina's personal priest to ensure the protection of the male heir. Some saw him as a prophet whilst some took him as a fraud, with horrid rumours from his days in Siberia involving highly promiscuous behaviour and unbefitting conduct under the banner of priesthood. He had an unusual philosophy that to truly be spiritual one had to know sin, a philosophy which made his bedroom an open door to the many ladies who sought his blessing in St. Peterburg.

Dvadaṣottari Daśā is applicable in the Czar's chart as the Navāṁśa Lagna falls in sign associated with Venus. Rāhu Mahādaśā had just begun in 1904 when the male heir Alexei was born. The first Antaradaśā was Mars which is the fifth lord in the fifth house bringing the child. The same year war broke out with Japan during the Russians expansion to the east. Mars in the tenth, first or fifth houses from Lagna will surely cause evil to any position of Jupiter in the chart. Further, the Papakartari Yoga of Mars and Ketu spells unrest to the people as it occurs on the fourth house. With Mars' advent the peaceful policy of the Czar and his good social intentions were thrown out the window as he heedlessly spent the Russian treasury on war. Mars is in the second house from Ārūḍha Lagna showing defeat as its placement in the tenth from the śatrupada (A6) benefitted the enemy. Japan repeatedly struck the Russians culminating in a complete wipe-out of the Russian fleet in the east. Only following this shocking incident did the Czar accept mediation and peace talks with the Japenese, leading to further dismay among the people following the event of Bloody Sunday earlier in the year. During this time he made an attempt to pacify the people by introducing a governing body under the aristocracy called the State of Duma.

This Antaradaśā lasted until 1906 and had already brought Rasputin under the appreciation of the Royal court in 1905.

With the end of Mars Antaradaśā the involvement of the Czar in the state of Duma seemed to pave the way towards less civil unrest, however, many saw this as no more than an extended autocracy of the Czar that in no way represented the interests of the people. Yet, this brought peace until the advent of the First World War in 1914. Ketu Antaradaśā began in May 1914 just days before the war broke out on the Serbian-Austrian border, again bringing unrest due to the Kartari Yoga. The military and people saw harsh times as the war-machine brought huge losses whilst the winter deprived the people of food both in the trenches and at home. To boot, in light of the losses in the war he dismissed the commander in chief and instated himself in the formers place. He was now in direct control of the military and also directly responsible for the ongoing war and its toll on the Russian people. Nicholas had headed to the front and left the Duma in political unrest with the Czar's unavailability.

Mercury's Antaradaśā had arisen following November 1915 and is a dire Māraka and threat to life during its period being the lord of the seventh from the Moon and combust by the Sun whilst afflicted by retrograde Saturn. Being the tenth lord under such affliction would cause the throne itself to be deprived from the Czar. With growing rumours that Rasputin was wielding the hand in the Czar's decisions during the war, Rasputin was murdered quite brutally in the December of 1916 due to a plot among the other aristocrats (Mercury is the dire enemy of Rāhu and Māraka to the ninth house). With the people starving, riots had broken out in the capitol. The military seeing it unable to cope with the way the Czar had handled the war rallied with the Duma and forced him to abdicate in March 1917. He spent the time thereafter with his family under confinement.

Rāhu being in Maraṇa Kāraka Sthāna from the Lagna bodes evil for the health of the Czar, as further the Sun is its dispositor and placed in the third from Ārūḍha Lagna indicating risk of demise due to firearms. Whilst Mars lords the second house from the Moon, it was unlikely to kill in 1904 due to being in own sign. Instead due to being aspected by the Māraṇa Kāraka Sthāna Rāhu made Rāhu Antaradaśā a most dire and deadly Māraka from August 1917-August 1919. We note that it was the same Mars who brought the birth of his fourth child and the first war with Japan in 1904-1905.

The Bolsheviks (Saturn) assumed political control and administered the family under their confinement in Tobolsk and later in Yekaterinburg both situated along the Iset river (Cancer). In the middle of the night, with the excuse of moving the family from their holding place, the entire family along with their staff were executed by gunfire on 17th July 1918. This occurred during the Pratyantara Daśā of Moon being the eighth lord from Lagna and the cause of the end of Raja yoga.

Chart 14: King of Sweden, Charles XII
Chart of King of Sweden, Charless XII, born 27th June 1682, 6:45 AM, Stockholm, Sweden. Birth is during Kṛṣṇa Saptamī Tithi as the Ātmakāraka is Rāhu. Seventh lord is placed in Lagna indicating that the Dvisaptati Sama Daśā is applicable.

The Navāṁśa Lagna is Aquarius which is lorded by Rāhu justifying his birth in the aristocracy. Birth is during a Saturday and being the eighth lord show Raja yoga through an inheritance, and this is through father as ninth lord Jupiter is joined Saturn. With an exchange between first and ninth houses great fortune is promised through father. Sun is placed in the twelfth house from the ninth lord and can show loss of father. Due to many reforms and expansions during the time of his father

Charles XI, the young Charles XII stood to inherit a Swedish Empire at its highest glory and a very able and trained army. The sudden demise of his father occurred when he was but fourteen and he was immediately instated as king.

Rashi (V-1) General

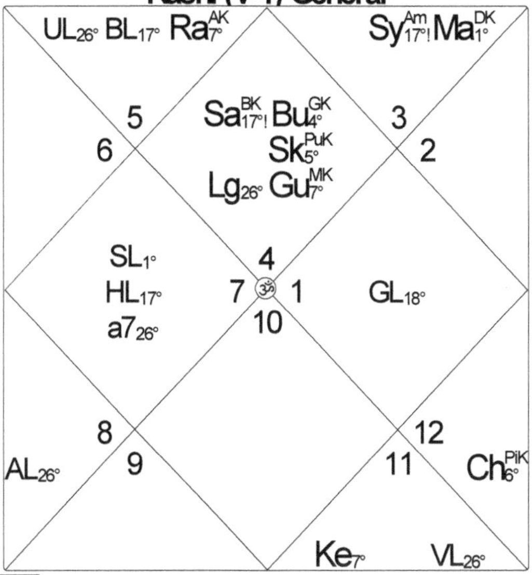

Rashi (V-1) General

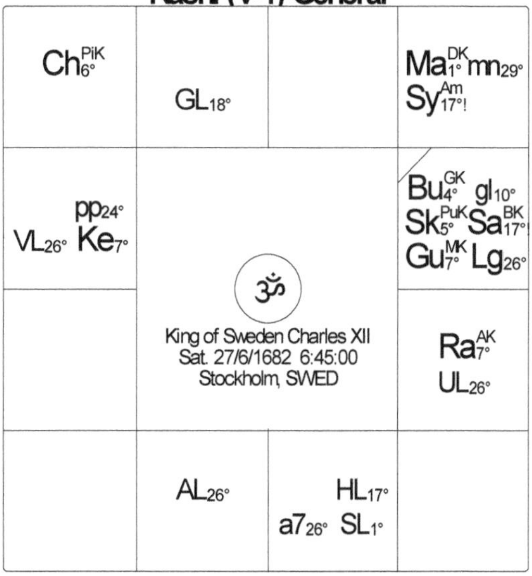

With the most auspicious conjunction of Jupiter and Mercury on the Lagna, the young king was born with a very gifted mind for mathematics, architechture, poetry, art and other intellectual pursuits. Coupled with the exchange between Jupiter and the Moon endowed him with great writing skills as well and great reputation. However, Saturn on the Lagna as Mars is in the twelfth is horrible for reputation and Mars will bring such reputation through battles and fighting.

As the fourth lord Venus as well as being Bādhakeśa is defeated in planetary war with Mercury, it threatens loss of land and the lessening of the empire with the coming of the new king. Three years after the news of the young king's coronation, the previously conquered Danish-Norwegian alliance declared war on Sweden, thinking the young king to be unprepared for the battle. Russia and Poland also joined in to declare war on the Swedes and began advancing towards Swedish occupied territory in the Empire.

With such difficulties arising with his ascendance to the throne, the tenth house has to be analysed for afflictions. The tenth house is Mars as its lord is causing a Kuja Doṣa from Moon and Lagna. This brings restlessness, ill health, short life and torment through secret enemies as soon as his ascension occurs. With the Papakartari on the Lagna by Rāhu, Mars and the Sun the situation is absolutely terrible for the young king and Sweden.

He was the only heir to the Swedish throne and it therefore becomes necessary to analyse the Tithi Bīja for further heirs. The lord of the Tithi is Saturn placed in Cancer. We need to count from Moon in Pisces to Capricorn which gives us the count of eleven. The eleventh Rāśī from Capricorn is Scorpio which is the Tithi Bīja. This being the fifth house is auspicious at first glance; however the lord of the same is the noted Mars and risks denying marriage and progeny. Being the fifth lord as well the risk of having no heirs is strong. To add Mars is highly weak due to being in the first degree of Gemini increasing its malificence. Yet, this Mars is the lord of Ārūḍha Lagna and Ghaṭika Lagna indicating quick and sudden victories through battle.

In May 1697, the Dvisaptati Sama Daśā of Sun-Saturn occurred during his coronation. Sun is joined the Navāṁśa Lagna and is further causing Raja Sambandha Yoga for association with power, due to being the Amātyakāraka and joined the tenth lord Mars. Saturn is the eighth lord and joined ninth lord Jupiter and justifies his inheritance and coronation.

With the declaration of war against Sweden in 1700, the Mahā-Antara Daśā was Moon-Mars. Moon is a Māraka to the Sun, as is Mars to the Moon. Further the advent of Mars Antaradaśā instigates the terrible Kuja Doṣa which would push the king into military campaigns. Charles XII immediately attacked Denmark with 43 ships and forced a peace treaty with Denmark-Norway in August of the same year, putting a quick end to one foe in the war. Three months later the king attacked King August II of Poland and Peter the Great of Russia in the battle of Narva, and despite being outnumbered four-to-one managed to split the enemy armies in half and send them fleeing into the winter. The Swedes lost but 667 men compared to the 17,000 of the enemy army. In just a year the king had attacked and won over four great nations and had expanded their influence as a result. Two years later the king did so again in Moon-Jupiter Daśā as he ignored previous treaties signed in Parliament and captured many cities of the Polish-Lithuanian Commonwealth. Jupiter gives the effects of Saturn and makes him ignore Jupiter and ignore peace. However, this Saturn is in Māraṇa Kāraka Sthāna and this decision to go against Parliament would later have severe consequences.

It was not until Moon Mahādaśā ended that the luck of Charles XII would turn. Mars Mahādaśā began in November 1707 and the Kuja Doṣa was to take its effect. Being largely undefeatable due to the lordship of Mars, the Antaradaśā of Mercury defeating the fourth lord Venus in planetary war, would be of great detriment to the Empire as the Antaradaśā began in 1709. Charles XII had yet ended the war with Russia, and with repeated skirmishes and Russia regaining strength, the king decided to attack Moscow. This proved to be a huge mistake as the Russian winter, insufficient supplies and more skirmishes reduced the Swedish armies fighting capacity to bare minimum before the battle of Poltava even began. The king himself had been incapacitated by a coma (Papakartari Yoga) due to his injuries and the fight was a complete humiliation to the Swedish war machine. The king escaped south to Bender in the Ottoman Empire where he set up camp. This turn of events is said to mark the fall of the Swedish Empire and rise of the Russian Empire.

He stayed in Bender until 1713 whereafter he was put under house arrest (twelfth house) in Constantinople for his constant scheming between the Turks and Russians, which at one point even had led to war between the two powers. Finally fleeing his arrest he returned to Sweden, his Empire significantly smaller than what it had been before he left it in 1709. He attempted once more to regain the Swedish Empire by attacking Norway in 1718. Mercury Mahādaśā is running which is a Māraka to the Sun and also causing the defeat of Venus in planetary war. Jupiter Antaradaśā is giving the effects of Māraṇa Kāraka Sthāna Saturn, and in November the Pratyantaradaśā of malefic Mars was running. At this time the Swedes themselves had grown angry and tired at his war-mongering and during the battle the king was shot in the head on the battlefield in November. Uncertainty as to who delivered the final bullet still remains. The third house from Ārūḍha Lagna is Capricorn and is aspected only by Rāhu (duṣtha māraṇa yoga) in Leo (politics) showing political machinations and scheming as the cause of death.

The placement of Mars lived up to its fullest prediction in this chart where not only was marriage and progeny denied, but also complete ruin of the reputation apparent and sealed by the inauspicious yogas on the Tithi Bīja Rāśi.

Chart 15: B. Annapūrṇa

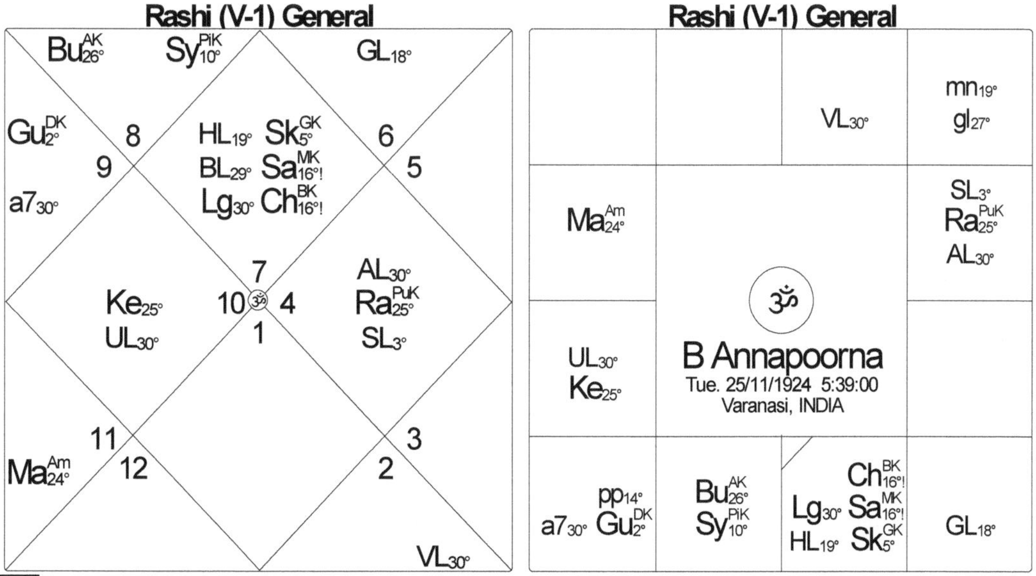

Chart of a mother born 25th January 1924, 5:40 AM, Varanasi, India. Born on the border between Kṛṣṇa Trayodaśī Tithi and Kṛṣṇa Chaturdaśī Tithi, we shall examine the effects of both and ascertain the correct one. For Kṛṣṇa Chaturdaśī Tithi, as its lord Venus occupies Libra and the Moon occupies the same. Counting from Moon to the seventh from Venus we get the number seven. Counting to the seventh from the same we get Libra again. As the Ārūḍha cannot fall in the first or seventh from Libra itself, we need to count to the tenth therefrom which comes to Cancer wherein the Tithi Bīja will be.

For the Tithi being Kṛṣṇa Trayodaśī, the lord Jupiter is placed in Sagittarius and its seventh house is Gemini. Counting from Moon in Libra to Gemini we get nine. Counting to the ninth therefrom we arrive at Aquarius which is the Tithi Bīja for Trayodaśī Tithi.

As her husband has his Tithi Bīja in Sagittarius and joined lord of Aquarius, Rāhu we find stronger indications suggesting Tithi Bīja to be Aquarius and her Tithi being Trayodaśī and not Chaturdaśī. This places the birth time at 5:39 AM.

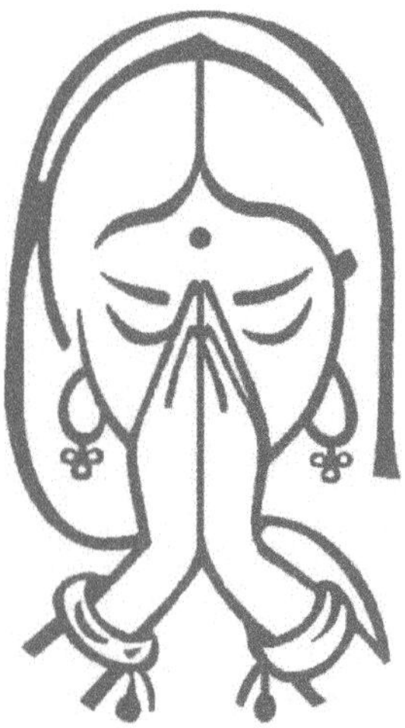

Ātmakāraka is Mercury and lords over the Navāṁśa Lagna confirming birth in a well disposed aristocratic family. In the Rāśi chart Mercury lords over the ninth house bringing this blessing through father and is joined Chara Pitṛkāraka Sun to confirm this blessing from an early age. Her father was among the close legal advisors (Mercury) to the royal court in Varanasi. Mercury is however afflicted by Saturn and Rāhu in the Navāṁśa indicating that the fortune will be short lasted due to pitṛdoṣa. Notably, the remedy in this case is to worship the original progenitors, namely the Ṛṣi and specifically that of Marīcī in this ladies case.

This doṣa repeats in the Rāśi chart due to Saturn aspecting Rāhu, and Ketu is further in Capricorn lorded by Saturn. In such cases it becomes pertinent to examine the ninth house from Sun and fourth house from Moon for father and mother respectively.

The fourth house from Moon is Capricorn and is occupied by Ketu. This is a most unpleasant placement for Ketu which some consider the Māraṇa Kāraka Sthāna placement for Ketu and can cause issues with longevity for the people indicated by Ketu. Saturn is the lord and despite being exalted is defeated in planetary war by the Moon. The close conjunction and war also causes a Chara Kāraka replacement which leave Mars to fend for mothers life and further afflicts the Moon. Mars receives the Rāśi Dṛṣṭi of Saturn, Rāhu, Venus and Moon, among which all but Moon end up afflicting Mars. This suggests serious consequences to her mothers health from very early on, and as confirmed in the Dvādaśāṁśa (D-12) divisional chart, due to Moon and Chara Matṛkāraka's position in the eighth house, her mother had an early demise. Rāhu is joined Moon and Matṛkāraka in the Dvādaśāṁśa and confirms the pitṛdoṣa and this event happening in her Rāhu Daśā lasting for her first 5 years of life. Antaradaśā was of Venus which lords malefic houses for mother in the same divisional chart.

As Rāhu is placed in the ninth from the Sun another Māraṇa Kāraka placement becomes apparent. This is further aspected by Saturn confirming that Pitṛdoṣa affects both mother's and father's longevity. The lord of the same is the Moon which we have seen also suffers from the Chara Kāraka replacement.

To confirm the incident we again resort to the Dvādaśāṁśa chart. As the Pitṛdoṣa affects both parents, we would expect the Daśā to be associated with the same as was the case with the mother. First Mahādaśā of Rāhu is not inauspicious for father as Rāhu lords over a Kendra house from the ninth. Jupiter follows this and aspects the Pitṛdoṣa by Graha Dṛṣṭi and can give the effects of the same. Jupiter lords the eighth and eleventh houses from the ninth making it very inauspicious and can cause problems. During Jupiter Mahādaśā, Jupiter Antaradaśā father passed away. Jupiter in own Rāśi indicates that father may have been well aware of his demise, and so also he had prepared for the same prior to the destined event.

The new mother is to be seen from the Grahas in the fourth house from Moon in the Rāśi, and herein we find Ketu indicating that a very spiritual lady may adopt the child. Ketu is second lord and suggests a family relation. The ladies aunt who had previously renounced to live as a Sanyasī, came out of her renunciation to raise the child. The Ātmakāraka Mercury has Rāśi Dṛṣṭi on Ketu and shows that an important desire of the soul became fulfilled with the coming of this aunt, and that the purpose of all these dire events was to ensure that her soul became thoroughly acquainted with spiritual knowledge. It is therefore not appropriate in this case to judge any event as good or bad, as it is obvious that this soul required her aunt to come out of her renunciation to guide this soul. Only a very spiritual soul can be able to truly endure such events for this purpose.

With Jupiter placed in the third house, whilst aspecting the seventh, as well as lording the seventh house in Navāṁśa marriage was likely to arrive during Jupiter Mahādaśā. Upapada (UL) resides in the Rāśi of Capricorn and indicates that the spouses Lagna could be an earthy Rāśi (Capricorn, Virgo or Taurus) or Cancer or Libra. Her husband's Lagna is Cancer.

Saturn Mahādaśā began from 21 years of age and lasts until 40, during which the couple attempted to have children as Saturn is the fifth lord and lord over the Tithi Bīja in Aquarius. However, Saturn is again causing Pitṛdoṣa and is likely to bring about much suffering related to children as well. As Putrakāraka Rāhu is also part of this Doṣa this is guaranteed. As Mars is in the fifth house and aspected by Saturn especially male children would suffer.

The couple endured a significant delay in having children, and the lady went to lament her situation to Satya Sai Baba. Venus lords the ninth house from Ātmakāraka in the Navāṁśa. Hence it is either during its Antaradaśā or those associated with Libra when she approached her Guru. Learning of her situation, the Guru advised her to eat a Khajur date and throw the seed of the same into a specific well. Let us examine this remedy: Dates are fruits usually consumed whilst dry hence belonging to either the category or the Sun or Mars. She was asked to consume the same as Mars is second lord. Seeds correspond to the Sun, and we find that the specific ṛṣi of Marīcī which is the remedy is also signified by the Sun. This seed (sun) has to be thrown into a specific well which is signified by Scorpio. Therefore the remedy was to strengthen the placement of second lord Mars in the fifth house. This is a most peculiar method of giving a remedy which only great souls like the Sai Baba can imitate.

Following the advice of the Guru, the lady consumed the date but didn't throw the seed in the appropriate well. Following this the couple gave birth to a son. Yet, after the child was but three months he died due to an epileptic fit (afflicted Mars-nervous system disorders). Following this the couple conceived twice more however both children died at birth due to being born prematurely.

Years passed and Saturn's toll on them made them detached from the idea of having children and they had grown increasingly spiritual. Mars Antaradaśā arrived in summer of 1959, and the couple partook on a long pilgrimage. At this stage the husband was aged 43 and the mother 35. Mars is again the second lord and is responsible for expanding the family. Further it aspects and disposits the ninth lord from atmakāraka in the Navāṁśa, confirming that the blessings of the Guru at to arrive during this Daśā. They visited Jagannātha Puri (Pisces), Dvāraka (Capricorn) and finally Badrinātha (Aquarius - 5th house and Tithi Bīja). There she prayed hard to have a child and if a boy she would name him Narāyaṇa and if a girl then Lakṣmī. Following this they visited Satya Sai Baba where she again narrated her difficulties and prayer. He inquired about the date seed and understanding the error of hers and its resultant consequences, Sai Baba manifested a Rakṣa (thread for protection), giving it to her and proclaimed that she would have a daughter who would live long!

The number of pregnancies can be gleaned from the Navāṁśas progressed by Saturn. Being in Libra Rāśi it should have given three children, but being in Aquarius in Navāṁśa four signs would have passed and instead indicates four pregnancies. First is signified by Libra, which is male and suffers pitṛdoṣa which didn't survive. Second is seen from Scorpio again indicating male due to the Sun's placement which didn't survive. Third is seen from Jupiter in Sagittarius which caused another son which didn't survive. Last is Capricorn housing Ketu being a girl who can survive! Beyond this there would be misfortune if more children were born.

Later the same year the lady had a vision whilst reciting the Bhagavad Gīta (Sun). She saw that a young girl of 9-10 years of age (Tripurasūndarī Devi - Mercury) carrying two infants and running. Considering the young girls predicament the lady asked how the girl at such a young age could care for two children. The young girl then placed one of the infants in the ladies arms and that infant happened to be a girl, after which her vision ended. Following this the lady immediately conceived and gave birth to a girl in Saturn Mahādaśā, Rāhu Antaradaśā and Rāhu Pratyantaradaśā all lording over the fifth house in the Rāśi. The ārūḍha of the fifth house is placed in Gemini, and the seventh is stronger indicating the childs Lagna being that of a fiery Rāśi. Her Lagna is Sagittarius. Jupiter's position in Sagittarius suggests a great blessing to the family's life once a child is born with that Lagna. The daughter grew up healthy, despite some initial worries during her birth, and holds an important position in furthering knowledge on spirituality and dharma for the Balaji temple in Tirupati (Aquarius).

This story proves that no matter the hurdles, diligence and remedies do indeed work and can help overcome problems in having children when the Tithi Bīja is afflicted.

Tithi doṣa: Naraka Chaturdaśi, Amāvāsya and Tithi kṣaya

Naraka Chaturdaśi

Naraka Chaturdaśi or 'hellish' chaturdaśi is the fourteenth Tithi in the dark fortnight of the month, i.e. Kṛṣṇa Chaturdaśi. During this Tithi, the anger of Śiva is said to be the strongest, as it is said that the Moon/Soma, kidnapped the wife of Bṛhaspati on this particular day. Based on the amount of the Tithi progressed, six sins or ripus will be present, and as a result Śiva will cast his anger on one of the six odd houses from Lagna, ruining their sustenance ability. In this form, Śiva's anger causes Rudra, the holder of the life force or prāṇa, to leave the native and cause a fall in the longevity.

Table 11: Chaturdaśi effects (Parashara 1999)

1/6th part	Bhāva affected	Effects
First	First bhāva	Auspicious effects
Second	Third bhāva	Evils/danger to father
Third	Fifth bhāva	Evils/danger to mother
Fourth	Seventh bhāva	Evils/danger to maternal uncle
Fifth	Ninth bhāva	Danger to brothers
Sixth	Eleventh bhāva	Danger to children

The effects can be understood more in detail by analyzing the house which has been affected. The third bhāva is a māraka bhāva from the ninth house, and hence when malefic, causes the ill health or demise of father, guru, etc. Similarly the first bhāva is said to give auspicious effects, being that it is a Māraka to the twelfth house of secret enemies in the horoscope. However the first house is also Māraka to the seventh house and can cause the ill health of the spouse as well.

This comes under the group of Gaṇḍa Tithis. The remedy to mitigate the inauspicious effects of this Tithi is to worship Lord Śiva in his form depicted with a crescent Moon on his forehead and seated on Nandi, i.e. as Śrī Somanātha.

Amāvāsya birth (darśa jātāna)

Amāvāsya is the time of the New Moon, where the Moon is no longer visible due to being eclipsed by the Sun's rays. This follows exactly after 'Naraka' Caturdaśī and so also follows in the story of Soma's venture to kidnap the wife of Bṛhaspati. It was during Amāvāsya that Soma consummated his desire with Tara, and impregnated her.

Hence for this reason those born on this particular day will not enjoy the glance of Bṛhaspati/Jupiter upon them. The effects given are; poverty, lack of children and fortune. Also for women this is said to cause distress and ill-health to the husband.

The reason is here given: Bṛhaspati is the name of the graha Jupiter, and when Jupiter decides not to bless a person with his glance then also such a person will suffer in the matters related to Jupiter's kārakatva or signification. Jupiter is the kāraka of the wealth controlling Bhāvas; second and eleventh Bhāvas. He is the kāraka of the fifth and ninth houses additionally which control the children and fortune of an individual. Finally Jupiter is the kāraka for husband in a women's chart.

In addition to the effects mentioned above, the position and yoga's of Jupiter in ones natal chart are observed to be quite fruitless, in case of births on Amāvāsya Tithi.

The remedy lies in worshipping the Sun and Moon on every Amāvāsya, in the south-eastern[4] corner of one's house (Parashara 1999).

Just as in the case of Caturdaśī doṣa, Amāvāsya is also divided into portions. The first 1/8th of Amāvāsya has no malignant effect on ladies (Dikshita 1992). Further, the malignant effect of Amāvāsya will affect mother and sisters if in the first half, and in the second it will affect father and brothers (Narada n.d.).

Traditional teaching

The planets joining the Sun and Moon when the Amāvāsya doṣa occurs bring negative results to the houses lorded by the planets, i.e. if the lord of the first house is joined, then the first house significations of health, name, reputation, etc. suffer. Which of these is most afflicted will then depend on the analysis of the significators of health, reputation, etc.

Further, based on the principle of calculating the Tithi Bīja, count from the Moon to Rāhu, and then count the same distance there from. The resultant distance will reveal a house and a sign. This house treated from the ascendant will reveal the main problem faced by the native as a result of the Amāvāsya doṣa. Based on this the remedy for the native can also be given.

Chart 16: Graf, Steffi

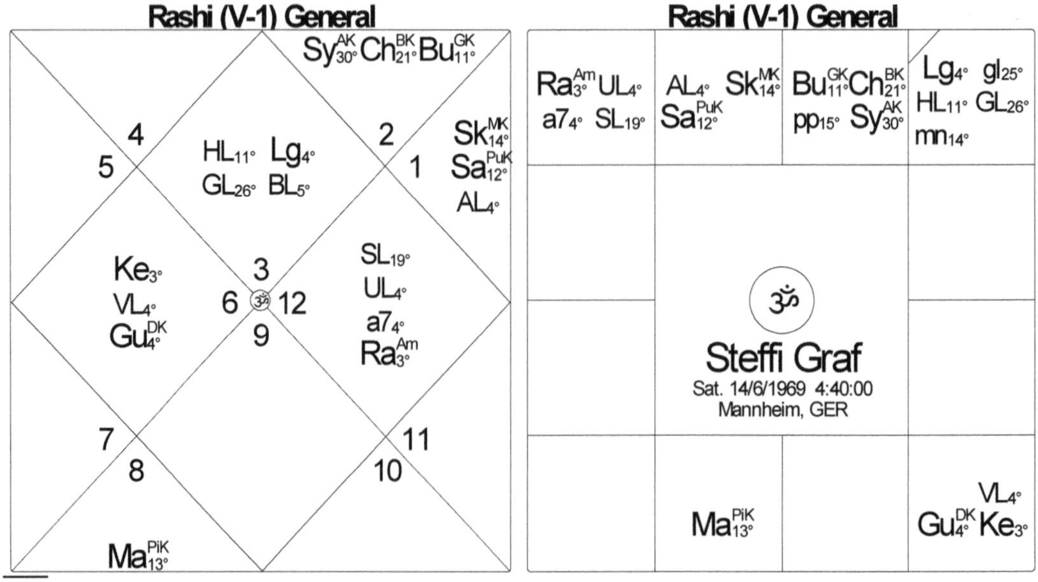

4 The translation of Bṛhat Parāśara Horā Śāstra by Santhanam and Sharma both translate the word 'vahni kona' as the south-western direction. However, 'vahni' refers to the direction of 'agni' which is the commonly known as the south-eastern direction.

Chart of Stefanie Maria Graf, born June 14th, 1969 at 4:40 AM, in Mannheim, Germany. She is born during the Amāvāsya Tithi where 25% of the Tithi has been covered. As less than half of the Tithi has been covered the effects should be detrimental towards mother and sister(s).

Ascertaining the Tithi Bīja we find it falling in Capricorn, the eighth house of debt, demise and sudden transformations/changes. This happens to be the ninth house from the Sun indicating that father will bring about these unpleasant experiences, yet the lord Saturn is also the weekday lord and its Mūlatrikoṇa being the ninth house promises Rājayoga, but Duryoga as well.

In the year 1990 during the Adhana-Vimśottari Daśā of Mars Mahādaśā, Rāhu Antaradaśā a story ran in the German tabloids about a 22 year model claiming Steffi's father, Peter Graf, to be the father of the models new born child. A four month court case ensued which was followed very closely by Germans and struck deeply with Steffi and her family. The course ended with a settlement and later arrest of the model and a boxing promoter for blackmailing Mr.Graf.

Again in the following Antaradaśā of Rāhu in the Mahādaśā of Rāhu, Steffi's father was sentenced to four years in jail for tax evasion of 7.4 million $. In the same Antaradaśā Steffi ended her tennis career and began a long term relationship with another tennis star, Andre Agassi.

It is evident that the coming of Rāhu played havoc in the life of Steffi, proving that Rāhu truly brings the effects of Amāvāsya to fore in life.

Chart 17: Loretta Young

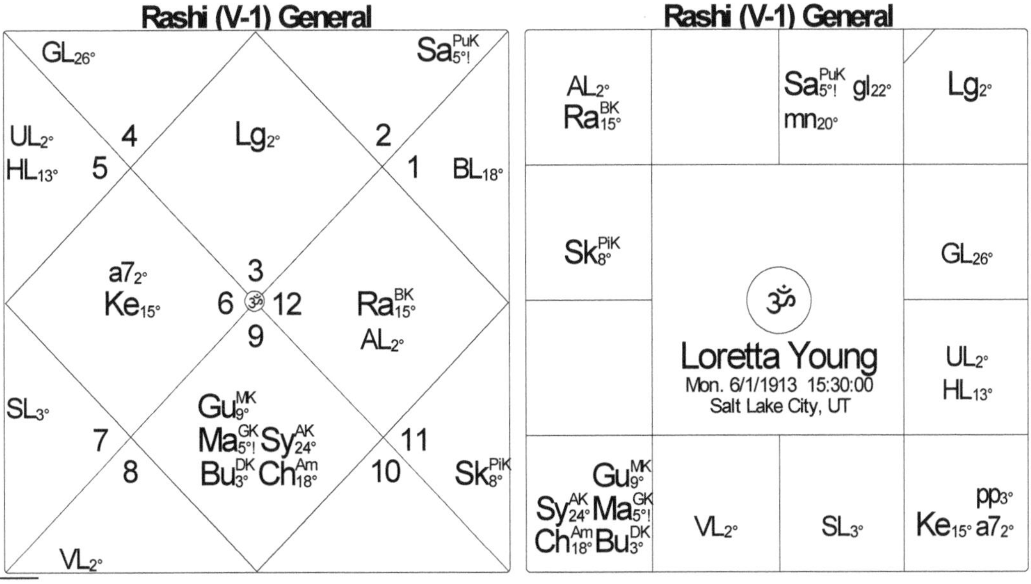

Chart of Gretchen Michaela Young, later known as Loretta Young, born June 1st, 1913 at 3.30 PM, in Salt Lake City, Utah, USA. She is born during Amāvāsya as 53 % has passed. This is the second half of Amāvāsya which affects father and brothers.

The Tithi Bīja is placed in Pisces which is the tenth house. The tenth house is a very negative house for both parents as it causes separation between the two, and as this is placed in the fourth house from the Moon the mother is likely to carry this into her life.

At the early age of three in the Vimśottari Daśā of Venus-Rāhu Gretchens parents divorced and her mother moved with Gretchen and Gretchen's two elder sisters to Hollywood. There the mother opened a boarding house to make a living. With the following Guru Antaradaśā Gretchen was already starring in movies with her two elder sisters from the age of four and was well on her way to become a movie starlet.

The joining of the Sun and Moon in the seventh house is bound to make its mark on relationships. Herein Mercury the Darakāraka can give shocks in relationships due to the influence of the Amāvāsya Doṣa. In Sun Daśā, Mercury Antaradaśā she eloped with co-actor Grant Withers. Ketu aspects Mercury by Raśī Dṛṣṭi and will give realization of mistakes and wrong doings. Therefore with the advent of subsequent Ketu Antaradaśā the couple annulled the marriage. Subsequently Young had affairs with Spencer Tracy and in 1935 at the age of 22 in Moon Daśā, Rāhu Antaradaśā she entered an affair with Clark Gable.

Rāhu itself being in Pisces can augment terrible suffering during the periods of Rāhu and Jupiter, and as this is joined the Ārūḍha Lagna it will give a bad reputation. The subject of infamy will be related to Jupiter and indicates husband, children, teachers, gurus, money or similar indications of Jupiter. As Rāhu is the ninth lord in this chart the subject may specifically have to do with a pregnancy or child.

The then married Gable was at the height of his career, and so when Young became pregnant she entered a difficult dilemma. Being a devout catholic she would not end the pregnancy and decided to conceal it to avoid scandal. She did so successfully and once born she gave the child up for adoption. The child was born during the subsequent Jupiter Antaradaśā in November 1935.

Five years later she marries producer Tom Lewis during the auspicious Moon Daśā, Venus Antaradaśā. Venus is placed in the ninth house promising great fortune after marriage and further twenty years of good and blissful marriage.

When Jupiter Mahādaśā arrived in 1967 the stage was set to bring out the negatives of the Amāvāsya Doṣa. Rāhu is alone in Pisces and with Jupiter aspecting it Jupiter is about to pick up a good fight against all the negatives of the Amāvāsya.

With the advent of Jupiter Young, seeing the entertainment industry changing with the popularity of Television, decided to travel and begin seeing the world from a different perspective. Seemingly giving up her career and abandoning her fans, she visited Taiwan, China, India, Iran and parts of the orient at length to broaden her world view. Arriving home after a good years travels she had lost interest in her career and began to tend to the family and her movie and television rights. In 1969 in Jupiter Antaradaśā she ended her marriage with Tom Lewis in a bitter divorce.

Subsequently in Jupiter Daśā and Mercury Antaradaśā Young was awarded $ 550,000 in her 6 year long suit against NBC for not living up to terms of agreement in allowing foreign television outlets rerun her old TV-series. However, one year later a scandal emerged reg. her son Christopher Lewis. Mercury being a dire enemy of the nodes and being Lagna lord will attempt to protect Young but can cause damage to children as Rāhu is the ninth lord. In 1973 Christopher whilst working with Lyric Productions was charged with child molestation and filming and distributing child pornography along with 13 other men. The scandal was huge with victims from 6-17 being suspected to have performed lewd acts form the men in the movies. Despite the heavy charges Christopher was merely fined USD 500 $.

With the end of Jupiter Mahādaśā Young entered a new era of her life. After the demise of her ex-husband Tom Lewis in 1988, she in 1991 in Saturn Daśā, Venus Antaradaśā remarried. She married fashion designer Jean Louis. Unfortunately the marriage only lasted a few years where in Saturn Daśā, Rāhu Antaradaśā Jean died. In the subsequent Antaradaśā of Guru in the year 2000 worries of Young's health began to emerge. Saturn is the eighth lord and being retrograde in the twelfth makes it extremely evil for health. Rāhu is notably in the Nakṣatra of Saturn as Saturn aspects the second house and sixth house which bode negative for health. This Mahādaśā could not be a walk on roses due to being in the sixth house from the Sun and Lagna lord. Being in the third from Ārūḍha Lagna cemented the possibility of severe disease, and being in a Venusian sign could bring this in the ovaries. When she downplayed all worries and entered the hospital under an alias it became known that she was battling with a vastly progressed ovarian and colon cancer. The doctors removed a very large cyst from her colon and she was permitted to go home. A month later on 12th August 2000 she left her body as a result of the cancer.

It is evident that the periods of Rāhu as well as Jupiter proved pivotal in the career and personal life of Mrs. Young, and justifies the importance of these grahas when analyzing the presence of Amāvāsya in the chart.

1.4 Karaṇa: The Road to Accomplishment (Pṛthvī Tattva)

Karaṇa is a half Tithi, and thus if there are 30 Tithi in a month, there will be 60 Karaṇa in the same lunar month. Where a Tithi spans over 12 degrees, the Karaṇa will span over half that namely 6 degrees. There are eleven different Karaṇa, four fixed and seven un-fixed or movable.

The four fixed are: Śakuni, Catuṣpada, Nāga and Kintughna. In this order they always occupy the last half of the 14th Kṛṣṇa Caturdaśī Tithi until the first half of the 1st Śukla Pratipada Tithi.

The seven movable are: Bava, Balava, Kaulava, Taitula, Garija, Vanija and Viṣṭi. Viṣṭi Karaṇa is also known as Bhadrā Karaṇa. These remaining seven, in the given order, occupy continuously the Tithis spanning from the second half of Śukla Pratipada until the first half of Kṛṣṇa Caturdaśī.

Essentially the four fixed Tithis span over the darkest part of the new Moon when the Moon is weakest in strength. This has been tabulated below.

Table 12: Karana

Pakṣa →	Śukla Pakṣa		Kṛṣṇa Pakṣa	
Tithi ↓	1st half	2nd half	1st half	2nd half
Pratipada (1)	Kintughna	Bava	Balava	Kaulava
Dvītiyā (2)	Balava	Kaulava	Taitula	Garija
Tṛtīyā (3)	Taitula	Garija	Vaṇija	Viṣṭi
Caturthī (4)	Vaṇija	Viṣṭi	Bava	Balava
Paìcamī (5)	Bava	Balava	Kaulava	Taitula
Ṣaṣṭī (6)	Kaulava	Taitula	Garija	Vaṇija
Saptamī (7)	Garija	Vaṇija	Viṣṭi	Bava
Aṣṭamī (8)	Viṣṭi	Bava	Balava	Kaulava
Navamī (9)	Balava	Kaulava	Taitula	Garija
Daśamī (10)	Taitula	Garija	Vaṇija	Viṣṭi
Ekādaśī (11)	Vaṇija	Viṣṭi	Bava	Balava
Dvādaśī (12)	Bava	Balava	Kaulava	Taitula
Trayodaśī (13)	Kaulava	Taitula	Garija	Vaṇija
Caturdaśī (14)	Garija	Vaṇija	Viṣṭi	Śakuni
Pūrṇimā/Amāvasyā	Viṣṭi	Bava	Catuṣpada	Nāga

Karaṇa means *doing, making, effecting, causing* and refers to the karma done in life. From the planet presiding over the Karaṇa we can determine the karma yoga available for us to do, and also whether we will be successful in doing so.

The Karaṇa are to be interepreted w.r.t. to the Lagna for the availability of the work, fourth house for the ease of learning it and tenth house to see how easily the work is practiced or performed.

The Karaṇa being of Pṛthvī Tattva, or earthy nature, is most auspicious when placed

Table 29: Karaṇa Lords

No.	Karaṇa	Graha
1	Bava	Sun
2	Balava	Moon
3	Kaulava	Mars
4	Taitula	Mercury
5	Garija	Jupiter
6	Vaṇija	Venus
7	Viṣṭi	Saturn
8	Śakuni (Brahmā)	Rāhu
9	Catuṣpada (Viṣṇu)	Ketu
10	Nāga (Maheśa)	Rāhu
11	Kinstughna (Sūrya)	Ketu

in earthy signs. The best placement is Virgo which ensures great business acumen and fortune. Worst is the airy signs which cause fleeting fortune and requires one to be extremely flexible in monetary matters. A career which requires much travel and movement is recommended. Fiery signs will require one to be a leader be it for mundane affairs or in spiritual matters, yet not appear to ask for money from ones followers. Watery signs are also auspicious and encourage earnings from healing people. A lot of socialising is indicated by the Karaṇa lord associated with watery planets and signs.

Examining the Karaṇa lord in the Daśāṁśa (D-10) will reveal the focus or intentions of the person in matters of work.

Essentially choosing the work of the Karaṇa graha ensures success, but this may be delayed based on planets associating with the Karaṇa lord.

The planets presiding over the Karaṇa determine the type of karma. The following is taught in the tradition in the table below.

The dreaded Viṣṭi Karaṇa which is said to cause poverty has naturally been presided over by Saturn. Yet, this dreaded aspect of Viṣṭi Karaṇa should not be taken for granted and depending on Saturn's placement in the chart the birth during this Karaṇa can be quite auspicious and grant Raja yoga.

Four Karaṇa are lorded over by the nodes, namely those which arise from the sec-

Figure 5: Wealth and Karaṇa

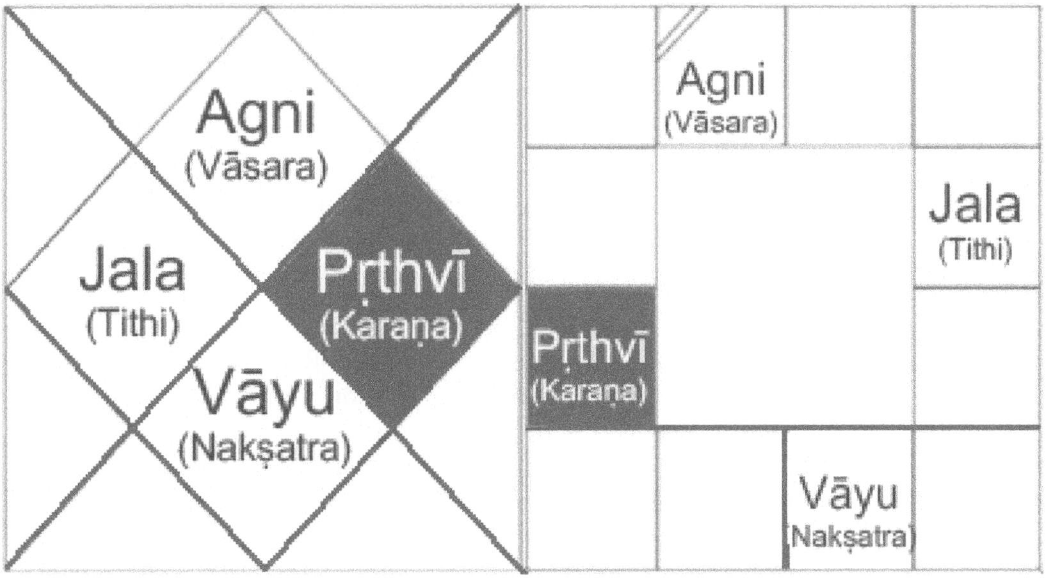

ond half of Kṛṣṇa Chaturdaśī until the first half of Śukla Pratipada. These Karaṇa are the darkest among all the Karaṇa and are said to be cursed. It was during these four Karaṇa that Soma, the Moon God, kidnapped Tārā and therefore also the nodes enact their negatives over the Moon during this time.

Birth during these last four Karaṇa risk causing financial problems. These will arise due to the reasons indicated by the Rāśi of Rāhu and the Nakṣatra of Ketu. Grahas joining them in their Rāśi or Nakṣatra will further colour the sources of these problems. Especially Rāhu will bring about infamy and scandals whereas Ketu will deprive of resources due to mistakes. Their placement from the Ārūḍha Lagna becomes pivotal as this can make or break a person's life and career, or cause huge changes. As the nodes tend to act in halves one can infer that one half of the career is extremely fortunate as the other half is the exact opposite. The event which marks this change is then based on the position of the nodes.

Chart 18: Tiger Woods

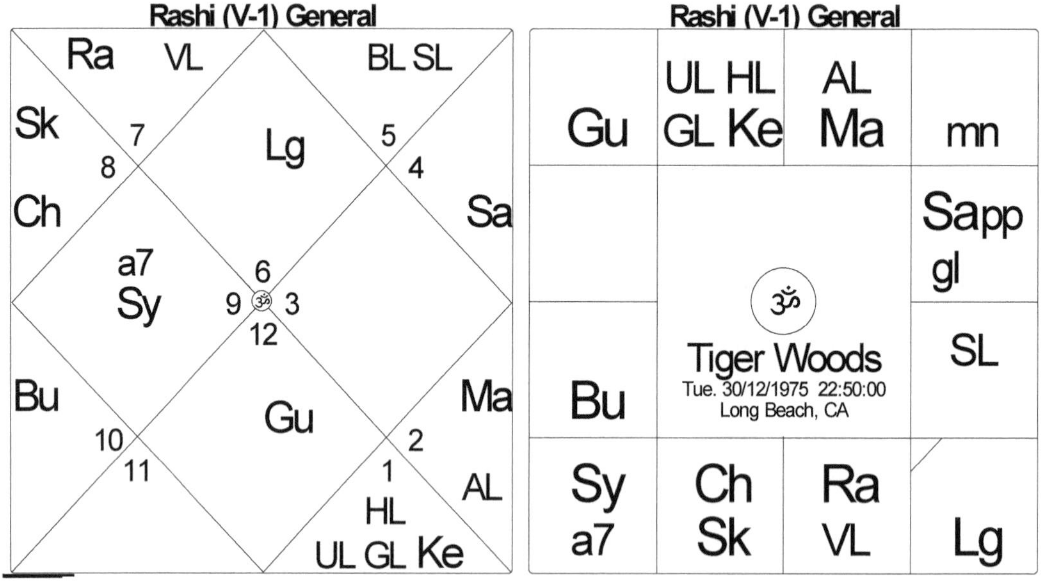

Chart of Tiger Woods, born Eldrick Tont Woods, December 30th 1975, 10:50 PM Long Beach, California, USA.

The fourth house is important for childhood and here the fourth Nakṣatra is lorded by the Sun as Sun is placed in the fourth house itself suggesting a strict childhood upbringing with a strong religious influence. Woods was brought up as a Buddhist and practices the same throughout his life.

Birth is during Shakuni Brahmā Karaṇa, lorded by Rāhu. Rāhu is placed in an airy sign requiring lots of travelling and movement. He is an international golf champion. Being in the second house it is well placed from Lagna, 4th and 10th houses showing early career and good education. Its sixth lordship makes him a master at strategy. Moon is in Jyeṣṭhā Nakṣatra as is the Yoga sphuta indicating that the lord Mercury holds an important sway over the life of the native. Mercury is Vargottama and joined the Lagna in the Navāṁśa suggesting a career either in writing or sports and this would be an extremely successful career as it lords over the Yoga. Being in a Saturnian sign Mercury is not likely to support academia and thus supports sports instead. With Mercury being the tenth lord in the fifth house it will crown Woods with a prestigious title within his profession.

The Karaṇa lord is Rāhu, a dire enemy of the Sun and will oppose his religious tenants, and is placed in the second house in Libra. Being placed in a trine to the tenth house is very auspicious and suggests a successful career. This being placed in the sixth house from the Ārūḍha Lagna suggests wealth and progress in career as well.

Woods was introduced to golf by his athletic father before the age of two. When the Utpanna Vimśottari Daśā of Rāhu began at age seven he began a winning streak over the next nine years. During this time he won the Junior World Golf Championship six times, of which four of these times were consecutive. He further went on to win the Junior Amateur Championship three times following this. The years from 1991-1994 during Rāhu Daśā, Mercury Antaradaśā were highly influential and brought him into golf stardom among his peers. When he left college in 1996 he left his amateur status and began his professional career in Venus Antardaśā. His career did not calm down following this and with Venus forming Bhagya Yoga in the third house he went on to sign advertising contracts worth USD 60 Million $ in the year 1996 alone and was named Sportsman of the year.

The Sun Antaradaśā was not auspicious for him with his form dwindling, presumably due to new training on his swing. Sun is not a friend of Rāhu and being in the fourth house brings closer focus on family than on work. He broke the temporary slump in the Antaradaśā of the Moon where he began his victory streak again. This continued into Mars Antaradaśā.

Jupiter is in the seventh house in own sign suggesting that his future wife would be his lady-luck in life and would contribute greatly to the life of Woods. One year into Jupiter Daśā, Jupiter Antaradaśā he met his Swedish girlfriend Elin Nordegren, a model and at the time nanny. Two years later they tied the knot on October 5th, 2004 at 5:40PM in Holetown, Barbados.

With Saturn largely bringing good with him, being the Chara Pitṛkāraka does give suffering to father. At the end of Saturn Antaradaśā in May 2006, father and mentor Earl Woods passed away due to prostate cancer. Saturn joined the Praṇapada can cause a loved one to pass away from one's life and this would require some strength to overcome. This is a notable event as the ninth lord exchange between Mars and Venus does become very sensitive. With the advent of Mercury Antaradaśā in the fifth house the couple saw the birth of their first daughter and with Ketu Antaradaśā their son was born.

Rāhu saw the greatest rise of Woods through the beginning of his career and with the advent of Jupiter he is seen settling down into his family life. Therefore notably, as Rāhu is also sharing Rāśi Dṛṣṭi with the Ārūḍha Lagna a scandal of ill repute will arise in the native's life. The nature of such a scandal is seen from the Rāśi occupied by Rāhu and being in a sign of Venus will bring this in matters of relationships. As Rāhu is also the sixth lord from Lagna placed in the second house this matter will bring enmity within the family.

In light of the above the native's relationships have to be studied carefully. The exchange between Mars and Venus along the third and ninth houses is a difficult predicament as Venus in any association with the ninth house gives an ideal that in matters of relationships 'the grass is always greener on the other side' and can make the person be ever on the lookout for new relationships. With Mars getting involved with Venus the sex drive will last until the native is 100 years old (Jaimini, 1997) and when this occurs in the third, seventh or eleventh houses the native will surely be presented with or embark on extra marital affairs. With the Moon associated with Venus a stamp of approval is given that this will surely happen. The amount of relations expands to abnormal limits as Rāhu's second aspect is on Venus. Venus occupying the sign of Scorpio will give open promiscuity in this regard. As the Upapada is in the eighth house the ninth house and the previously mentioned yogas become responsible for making or breaking the marriage.

To stop such a Venus requires the influence of Ketu. Ketu is placed in the eighth house of marital separation and shares a sign aspect with Venus curtailing this situation after some separation from spouse. However, when Jupiter is in the seventh house in own sign the person marries their lady luck and a break in such a relationship would be devastating for the person's life in all aspects of life. With Mars and Ketu following in a line after Jupiter without any beneficial influence is terrible for such a relationship and as the tenth house follows after this line the career will be the target of such a fall.

Despite an ongoing successful golfing career with a great many endorsements, in November 2009 after a small car accident involving Woods in the vicinity of his home, Woods admitted to having family problems. This was a day after a tabloid claimed that Woods had an extra-marital affair with a New York City night-club manager. Within days pressure increased in the Woods household as more women brought forth claims of his affairs with them. In December he released a statement admitting his infidelity which brought about a huge scandal. Within the months which followed Woods finally mentioned that during his five year marriage he had been unfaithful with a staggering number of one-hundred-twenty different ladies. Notably the union of Mars and Venus occurs in the eighth house in the Navāṁśa showing the massive number of affairs causing a break in marriage. By October 2010 during the same Venus Antaradaśā Woods and Nordegren divorced whilst sharing custody of their two children. Nordegren appears to have moved to Sweden following this. In the months up to this event most of his sponsors withdrew their deals with Woods. His losses in these deals were estimated between USD 5 and 12 billion $.

As is evident, the scandal's vastness and career implications were all linked to Rāhu being the Karaṇa lord. Clients with such indications should be warned about the problems associated with the nodes associated with the Karaṇa and remedies be advised to lessen the damages. Woods still plays golf professionally, however his reputation as a Golfing star and idol for children to look up to has been hampered for life.

Bhadrā (Viṣṭi) Karaṇa

Bhadrā refers to the Devi born from the body of Śiva for the purpose of fighting the Daityas (among the Asuras or ungodly ones). She is depicted with the face of a donkey, having three legs, seven arms and a long tail. She is black in colour. After doing the bidding of Śiva she resides in his ear as an ornament and calendar-wise she is similarly placed in the seventh Karaṇa also known as Viṣṭi Karaṇa.
According to Ratna Kośa her eight occurrences during a month depict her with eight different names namely: Hansī, Nandinī, Triśirā, Sumukhī, Karalikā, Vaikṛtī, Raudramukhī and Chaturmukhī.

Kālachakra and Bhadrā

Her first occurrence begins from the second half of Śukla Chaturthī Tithi and her movement through the various other Karaṇa can be depicted in the Kāla Chakra. Herein being born from the body of Śiva she resides in the western direction wherein the bull and snake reside which are notably also the vehicles of Śiva. Being opposite the eastern direction which is presided over by the Sun she is also said by some to be born of the Sun God.

Being that the western direction is presided over by the Devatā Varuṇa some modern authors tend to confuse Śiva with Varuṇa claiming the former to be a modern depiction of the latter, however this is incorrect and a misunderstanding of the Kāla Chakra. Instead Śiva actually resides in the north-eastern direction in the form of Iśana.

Table 13: Bhadrā Karaṇa

Tithi	Tithi Half	Name
Śukla Aṣṭamī	1st	Hansī
Pūrṇimā	1st	Nandinī
Śukla Chaturthī	2nd	Triśirā
Śukla Ekadaśī	2nd	Sumukhī
Kṛṣṇa Saptamī	1st	Karalikā
Kṛṣṇa Chaturdaśī	1st	Vaikṛtī
Kṛṣṇa Tṛtiyā	2nd	Raudramukhī
Kṛṣṇa Daśamī	2nd	Chaturmukhī

From this western direction which is the fifth direction from the east, Bhadrā moves to the sixth direction from herself in clockwise direction, i.e. her second step will come to the south-east and her third will come to the north, etc. Notably, if one were to count the number of the direction resided by her from the eastern direction, the number will reveal whether her Karaṇa occurs in the first or second half of the Tithi based on whether the resultant number is less or more than four respectively, i.e. she begins in the west which is the fifth direction from the east hence being more than four she starts in the second part of the Tithi, and then moves to the south-east which is the second direction from the east which is less than four and is thus the first half of the Tithi.

Figure 6: Bhadrachakra

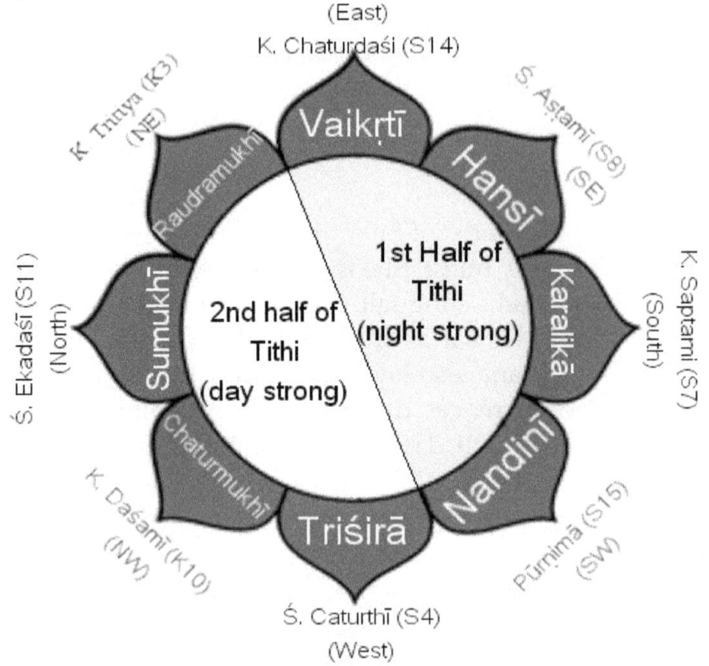

Her fourth step will come to the south-west after which she has completed her four occurrences during the Śukla pakṣa or bright half of the month. To begin her movement during the Kṛṣṇa Pakṣa she begins her step from the opposite direction of that of her last occurrence, i.e. she last resided in the south-west which initiates her next step from the north-east. Only in this case her steps are in reverse and therefore means that the sixth direction has to be counted in anti-clockwise order. Therefore starting from the north-east which would be the first occurrence in the Kṛṣṇa Pakṣa, her second occurrence will occur in the south which is the sixth direction reckoned in the reverse from north-east. In this way she covers all eight directions and their presiding Devatā starting from the west with Varuṇa and ending with the east with Indra.

Mouth and tail of Bhadrā and Prahāra

The Bhadrā Karaṇa is divided into four parts or Prahara, during which the Devī's body is depicted as spread out through the span of the Karaṇa with its head/mouth initiating and tail ending the same.

It is said that her mouth is most inauspicious as the tail is auspicious and these reside in the beginning and ending fractions of the Karaṇa. Further, her position is not fixed but moving. I.e. if the mouth is in the first $1/4^{th}$ of the Karaṇa, the tail will be in the last $1/4^{th}$ of the Karaṇa. Similarly should the mouth move to the second $1/4^{th}$ of the Karaṇa the tail will be in the first $1/4^{th}$ of the Karaṇa. In this way the body is actually moving through the different quarters of the Karaṇa throughout the various Tithi.

The derivations of the movements are actually based on Tithi and eight portions of the same and can be understood from the movement of Bhadrā through the Kālachakra as depicted under the previous heading. For ease these have been calculated in a simplified manner dividing the Karaṇa into four for the reader hereunder.

Throughout these portions the mouth of Bhadrā occupies a span of time of five Ghaṭika or two hours. This corresponds loosely to the time of one Rāśi Lagna or one-twelfth portion of a day or one-sixth portion of a half day. Herein it should be understood that these spans are relative to the length of the Tithi or Karaṇa. As the orbiting bodies sometimes move slower and sometimes faster it is not appropriate to base our estimations of these portions based on time. The number of Ghaṭika for the mouth to occupy in a day will vary based on the speed of the Sun and Moon. Therefore an appropriate method is to estimate this based on degrees.

Table 14: Mouth and Tail of Bhadrā

Tithi	Tithi Half	1/4th part occupied by the mouth	Direction of the mouth	1/4th part occupied by the tail	Direction of the tail
Śukla Chaturthī	2nd	1st	West	4th	North-east
Śukla Aṣṭamī	1st	2nd	South-east	1st	West
Śukla Ekadaśī	2nd	3rd	North	2nd	South-east
Pūrṇimā	1st	4th	South-west	3rd	North
Kṛṣṇa Tṛtiyā	2nd	4th	North-east	3rd	South
Kṛṣṇa Saptamī	1st	3rd	South	2nd	North-west
Kṛṣṇa Daśamī	2nd	2nd	North-west	1st	East
Kṛṣṇa Chaturdaśī	1st	1st	East	4th	South-west

A Karaṇa changes every 6° of separation between the Sun and Moon; therefore ¼ of a Karaṇa is 1°30′. A one-sixth portion of the Karaṇa (one-twelfth portion of a Tithi) is therefore 1°, and therefore we can conclude that fraction-wise the mouth of Bhadrā exists for two-thirds ($^2/_3$) of every quarter portion of a Karaṇa. Similarly the tail occupying the last 3 Ghaṭika or seventy-two minutes of the one-fourth portion will occupy a degree span of 0°36′ at the conclusion of the ¼ portion in question.

Example: Sun: 5°7′ Scorpio. Moon: 4°37′ Virgo. With the given values the Tithi is that of Kṛṣṇa Daśamī which spans over the twelve degrees from 23°7′ Leo to 5°7′ Virgo. The Tithi occupies the second half spanning from 29°7′ Leo to 5°7′ Virgo and is therefore Viṣṭi or Bhadrā Karaṇa. Based on this we have tabulated the degree spans of the four parts of the Karaṇa:

Table 15: Bhadrā calculation example

¼ part	Span (1°30′ each)	Portion
1	29°7 Leo - 0°37′ Virgo	Tail
2	0°37′-2°7′ Virgo	Mouth
3	2°7′-3°37′ Virgo	Arms
4	3°37′-5°7′ Virgo	Legs

During these four spans our previous table shows that the mouth during this particular Tithi and Karaṇa should reside in the second part and the tail in the first part. Notably the Moon (4°37′ Virgo) is not placed in this span. Further, the mouth in the second portion will occupy a whole degree spanning from 0°37′ Virgo until 1°37′ Virgo. Similarly the tail will occupy the last 0°36′ of the first ¼ which spans from 0°1′ to 0°37′.

The interpretation of Bhadrā or any Karaṇa must be held with the concept of Karaṇa. The Karaṇa deals first and foremost with ones work and karma yoga and the planet lording over the Karaṇa carries the responsibility of giving the effects of the Karaṇa. This graha should be interpreted w.r.t. the tenth house in the chart where its placement from it reveals the natives experience of their career (Rath, Vedic Reading Process, 2010).

Should the Bhadrā Karaṇa be in the first half of the Tithi as birth is in the night, the results of the Karaṇa are said to be auspicious, similarly for the second half of the Tithi during the daytime (Acharya, 2003, p. 34). However, in this authors own practice it is apparent that the negatives do manifest despite this principle but the outcome tends to be in favour of the native.

Chart 19: Male accident – Viṣṭi Karaṇa

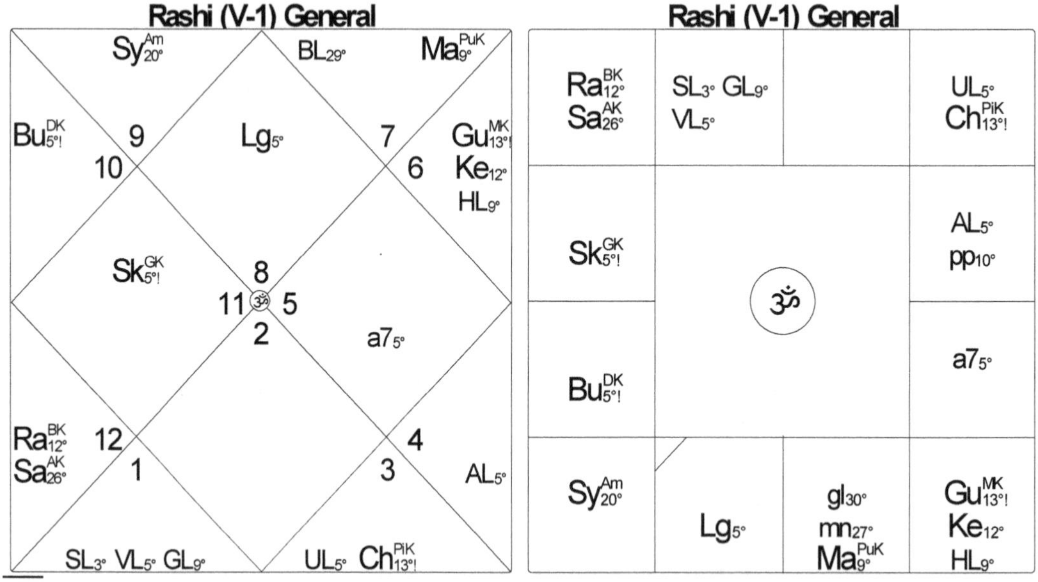

Male born 3rd January 1969, 4 AM, Novi Sad, Yugoslavia. Birth is in the first half of Pūrṇimā Tithi which is Viṣṭi Karaṇa. Further this is in the last part of the same which is occupied by the mouth of Bhadrā at the given time and makes it quite negative.

The effects of the Karaṇa are to be interpreted from the lord Saturn. Saturn is placed in the ninth house with Rāhu which is a Śraddha Doṣa wherein the native suffers due to not performing the last rites of one of the parents. This in turn being the fourth lord will surely give difficulties with mother as a result. Two malefic in the fifth house and further being the Ātmakāraka further risks jail sentence or some type of confinement, besides a fatal threat to life as this is also aspecting the third from the Ārūḍha Lagna. Being in the fifth house also presents a risk to a child but Jupiter aspects the fifth house to protect the same.

This man had throughout life prolonged friction with his mother for a variety of reasons arising from mothers lack of support in his marriage and a sibling rivalry with his sister, all arising due to the Śraddha Doṣa. When he reached the age of thirty-three (33) in Adhana Vimśottari of Jupiter Daśā, Saturn Antaradaśā whilst driving (fourth lord) in an October month with his mother and his sisters mother in-law, the car was involved in a terrible accident due to being hit by a truck! The sister's mother in-law died in this accident as the mother and the man received serious injuries. His wife was supposed to join him in the car but decided not to in the last minute... it became known weeks later that she was carrying their second child at the time of the incident!

The incident struck an already strained cord between the native and his mother and further estranged them with the mother blaming him for the accident. This further led to some estrangement from his brother in-law and his sister who had become favoured by the mother. He himself was indicted in a 2 year long criminal case risking imprisonment for the incident.

We further see that Saturn is placed in the eighth house from the tenth showing a change of jobs or profession. The native is a mechanic and the injuries he sustained caused him to be unable to work for a few months following the incident. Yet, he didn't lose his job as these are placed in the fourth house from the Sun.

The legal case put a serious dent on the couple's finances. Saturn and the nodes aspect the twelfth house from the Ārūḍha Lagna shows huge losses, especially as the Moon is involved. The two year long court case with risk of jail time further caused worry and pressure on the family. With the advent of Mercury Antaradaśā the table was set for the problem to be cleared. Mercury is placed in the third house and its aspect on the ninth by Graha Dṛṣṭi causes great fortune. Mercury further despises court cases and will end them as soon as possible. Mercury is the Chara Dārakāraka and supports help through wife. His wife was able to get her bosses company lawyer (Mercury) to take the case and this proved fruitful yet expensive. With the advent of Mercury the lawyer was able to prove that the native was not at fault and further that he was to be compensated for the incident. The court ruled in his favour and further freed him of any doubts in the case. With the financial perturbations being over the native regained some respite. The maternal issues have yet to subside however.

1.5 Vāra: Strength to perform (Agni Tattva)

The word *Vāra* is short for the word *Vāsara*. *Vāsa* means *to stay, abide, dwell in*, whilst *Ra* is a reference to Agni the God of fire much like the name given to the Egyptian Sun God. Hence the word *Vāsara* implies an abode for the God of fire. Similarly, a weekday/Vāra is a resting place for the Agni, and all the functions of the weekdays arise from this principle.

Agni is a reference to the fire-element, as well as the Devatā who carries the same. Symbolizing one of the five base elements, some scholars have equated the worship of Agni to a more pre-hindu period where the worship mainly consisted of the visible elements of the universe such as water, earth, trees, air, etc. With that, some scholars have divided the various facets of God, such as Śiva, Gaṇeśa, Agni etc. into two groups of *Vedic deities* and *Hindu deities* thinking that with time the deities have changed their form or identity, or simply new names/Gods have come into existence in the minds of the population.

However this is not the case, as the traditions of India would agree that deities of the Ṛg Vedic period are the same as that of today, only their names may have changed slightly. I.e. in the Rig Veda the name Iṣa is used for Iśvara/ Śiva, and the name Gaṇapati is an obvious name for Gaṇeśa. Garutman has become Garuda today, and similar different names exist i.e. Kṛṣto and Kṛṣṇa.

Agni has always been worshipped as Agni, and the worship of Agni has been constantly maintained by the Agni hotris, who specifically are Agni-worshippers, and more recently the Brahma and Arya Samaja's of India. Here the latter two go as far as rejecting any other physical form of God, and only worship Agni and offer the various mantras of the Ṛg Veda to the fire.

This practice is not wrong per say, as Agni is said to be the vehicle between the worshipper and the Devatā. For this reason he carries another name *Vahni* which stems from the word *vhni* meaning the conveyor, carrier or bearer (also refer *vahana*). This is said to be symbolic of the third eye (ajñakhya chakra) where Agni rests, and from which the prayers are transmitted to the Devatā of worship. Hence also, the worship of Agni is essential for the grace of the Devatā of worship and as its ultimate purpose gives the worshipper enlightenment through the blessing of Śiva (S. Rath, A Course on Jaimini Maharishi›s Upadesa Sutra 2007). For this reason the first śloka of the Ṛg Veda is dedicated to Agni:

अग्निमीळे पुरोहितं यज्ञस्य देवंऋत्विजं। होतारं रत्नधातमम्॥

agnimīḷe purohitaṁ yajñasya devamṛtvijaṁ| hotarāṁ ratnadhātamam||

In fact the entire first sukta of the Ṛg Veda is dedicated purely to Agni, and shows the importance of Agni worship.

In the cosmology Agni is born from Maharishi Kaśyapa. Astrologically Kaśyapa Gotra is associated with Sun and Saturn. Sun because Kaśyapa is the father of the twelve Adityas or sunsigns and Agni. Saturn because is is also the father of all the asuras, daityas and danavas. Daitya is from the word *diti* meaning disjoined or unconnected which can refer to being disjoined from ones family or lineage, therefore the latter may also partly be the reason why those who do not know their Gotra are asked to take the name of Kaśyapa during certain rituals and rites.

[1]Agni has two wives/śaktis, namely *Svāhā* and *Svadhā* who represent the oblations for the deva/Gods and pitri/ancestors respectively. Thus mantras ending in either of these two words specifically refer to the object of the offering being either God or ancestors, i.e. *om agnaye svāhā* or *om pitṛbhyo svadhā* are common uses.

Agnikoṇa is a reference to one among the ten directions and here Agni is a *Dikpāla*. Dikpāla litteraly means *protector of direction* and here specifically refers to Agni as a devatā who rules the south-eastern direction. The Dikpāla are devatā who rule the directions of karma and their wives are the givers of fruits of these paths or directions. No fruit arises without the blessings of one of these Dikpāla, or rather their śaktis namely the Dikvadhu. Therefore Agni has a very central position in ensuring the fruits of karma, being one among the Dikpāla.

In this regard Agni is also a Lokapāla presiding specifically over this earth namely Bhūloka. Therefore Agni helps us cross this world and the existance in this world and those with strong Agni in their lives will surely suceed in their lifes objective in this world.

This role of Agni is closely associated with *Ignis,* a greek deity carrying similar functions as Agni. From this word came the word *ingineer,* thus reffering to the function of Agni. The south-eastern direction is ruled by Venus and therefore gives rise to people who are great designers or can make great scetches or plans in their mind, and are masters of inventions such as those seen by the Sri Paraśurāma Avatara.

Among the planets and luminaries Sun and Mars are associated with fire, where Sun is more closely associated with the light emanating from fire, whilst Mars is specifically referred to as being of the fiery element. For this reason Mars' placement in the *arthatrikona* in the dasamsa chart can show engineering as a profession.

Among sounds Agni is associated with the consonant *ra* and carries significance akin to the Egyptian Sun-God. This is known as a sound of the seers/rishis as the seers are said to be channels/pathways towards God, and here the two paths of moving upwards towards God (ra-fire) or bringing God down to oneself (la-earth) are governed by the rishis. The sound *ra* is commonly added to the mystic seed/bija mantras, i.e. hrīm, śrīm and krīm (viz. ka+ra+ī+m) are common uses of the same and represent this upwards movement.

Agni is depicted with seven tongues or *jihva* with which he accepts the offerings people make and transmits them to the Gods. In this form he is known by the name *Vahni* and is eulogized as he acts as a vehicle between the worshipper and Deva. The seven tongues (jihva) symbolize the seven weekdays during which the offering are accepted.

Table 16: Saptajihva bīja

Jihva	Bija
hiranyā	srūm
gaganā	hrūm
raktā	śrūm
Kṛṣṇa	vrūm
suprabhā	lrūm
bahurūpā	rūm
atiraktā	yrūm

The seven jihva are named hiranyā, gaganā, raktā, Kṛṣṇa, suprabhā, bahurūpā and atiraktā. They each have a bija or monosyllable mantra consisting of the bija *rūm*, and prefixed by one of the seven semi-vowels.

These seven tongues have seven sounds associated with them, and are also associated with the five planets and two luminaries.

Agni in life

To understand the role of fire or Agni in interpreting a chart, we need to understand the role of Agni in daily life. In the body Agni is the digestive fire which resides in the stomach and is signified by the sign Leo. The importance of good digestion cannot be emphasized enough as this alone can make or break even the healthiest of lifestyles, hence the Sun signifying ones health and vitality also lords Leo. From the lord of the weekday itself we will understand how the digestive fire is working in the body and to what extent the person is healthy or not and how the body is heated, by seeing it's placement from Leo. Any weakness to this digestive fire is therefore also a great weakness to health which has to be analysed from Vāra Ghātaka. Here we are concerned with the strength of the body as well which is signified by Mars and its natural lordship over the first Rāśi Aries.

From fire or heat is produced energy. This energy gives direction and the ability to pursue any particular direction in life. It gives the availability of resources and therefore also plays an important role in financial assessment in the chart. From here we enter the concept of Agni and Rājayoga, wherein which we need to assess the lord of the weekday in the chart with respect to lordship and position from other Graha to know where the Agni of the native is being directed.

From fire comes light. This light is the light of self realisation, be it realisation of one's present state and the world, or the higher realisations of God. Here we enter the concept of Agni as the vehicle between God and us; hence the presence of God in one's life is also ascertained by analysing Agni in a chart. Agni is therefore appropriately depicted as sitting in the third eye or Ājñakhya Chakra which affects ones perception, sight and divine sight as well. It is from here that the fruition of all our prayers arises. Here we have to determine the appropriate weekday for worship, the importance of God in the weekday we are born in, how God manifests in the various yoga of the Graha, how the weekday connects to God on each of the seven weekdays, etc.

Tattva-Devatā

The five elements or Tattva correspond to the Pañca Devatā or five main Devatā of worship which devout seekers worship every day. They are Gaṇeśa, Āditya, Viṣṇu, Śakti and Śiva for the elements of Pṛthvī, Agni, Akaśa, Jala and Vāyu respectively. Some give different lists for the same for different purposes. In this case the purpose of the Devatā is to correct the negatives of the element in question. Being that they are associated with the Tattva or elements, the Devatā are said to be formless (nirankara) as the elements have yet to mix to make discernable forms. These forms of worship are said to be very old as a result.

The order of this list also corresponds to the Devatā residing in the seven chakras in the body. Here Gaṇeśa sits in the Mulādhara, Kāma in Svādhisthāna, Āditya in Maṇipura, Viṣṇu in Anahata, Śakti in Viśuddha, Śiva in the Ajñakha, and finally Sadaśiva in the Sahasrara. Herein the worship of Kāma and Sadaśiva is left out to furnish the order of the Pañcadevatā in daily worship.

Table 17: Dvadaśāditya (S. Rath, A Course on Jaimini Maharishi's Upadesa Sutra 2007)

Rāśi	Āditya	Vāra
Aries	Dhātā/Savitur	Sunday
Taurus	Aryaman	Thursday
Gemini	Mitra	Wednesday
Cancer	Varuṇa/Aruṇa	Monday
Leo	Indra	-
Virgo	Vivasvan	-
Libra	Puṣan	-
Scorpio	Parjanya/Dakṣa	Saturday
Sagittarius	Aṁśuman/Aṁśa	Tuesday
Capricorn	Bhāga	Friday
Aquarius	Tvaṣṭā	-
Pisces	Viṣṇu	-

Whilst Agni is the divinity which presides over the fire element, the Devatā which corrects and purifies the same is Āditya. The name Āditya corresponds to the first created as the beginning syllable (A) is the first among the Sanskrit syllables. Āditya is a common name for the children of Aditi, and just like Agni the parents of Āditya are Brahmaṛṣi Kaśyapa and his wife Aditi. The Āditya were initially seven in number corresponding to the seven weekdays, and are extolled in the Ṛg Veda. In these seven forms they began creating the entire universe which initially manifested as an egg called Mārtaṇḍa. This egg then broke into two halves where the upper represented the sky, the lower the earth and the middle the air between (S. Rath, A Course on Jaimini Maharishi's Upadesa Sutra 2007), and possibly these three symbolise the creation of the three manifested Loka (Bhur, Bhuva and Svarga). This breaking of the egg brought about five more Āditya giving a final number of twelve Āditya corresponding to the twelve sun signs.

The Agni element holding this energy to create one's life is thus purified by the original creators themselves namely the Āditya.

Vāra and worship

Based on the weekday, the deities who help us overcome the various karma associated with each planet's significance are worshipped. The megalomaniacs (Sun-ego) ever eager for power, fame and position worship Śiva (Sun) on Mondays to keep their egos in check and maintain their power. Those wishing to become good mothers, or good providers (Moon) worship Durgā (Moon-Monday) on Tuesdays to live up to that ideal. In this manner the deity is worshiped on the weekday following that which the deity's planet/luminary presides over.

Table 18: Vāra and Devatā

Day	Monday	Tuesday	Wednesday	Thursday	Friday	Saturday	Sunday
Deva	Śiva	Devī	Gaṇeśa and Skanda	Viṣṇu	Guru	Lakṣmī	Nārāyaṇa

On these days, Agni is prepared to bring the offering to the Gods, to the benefit of the worshiper.

Auspicious and Inauspicious Vāra

Traditionally the weekday presided over by a malefic Graha are to be avoided for embarking on auspicious activities. This omits the weekdays of Tuesday and Saturday for auspicious activities, where the Sun in some cases is also omitted. Depending on the nature of the activity specific weekdays are avoided based on the Kāla

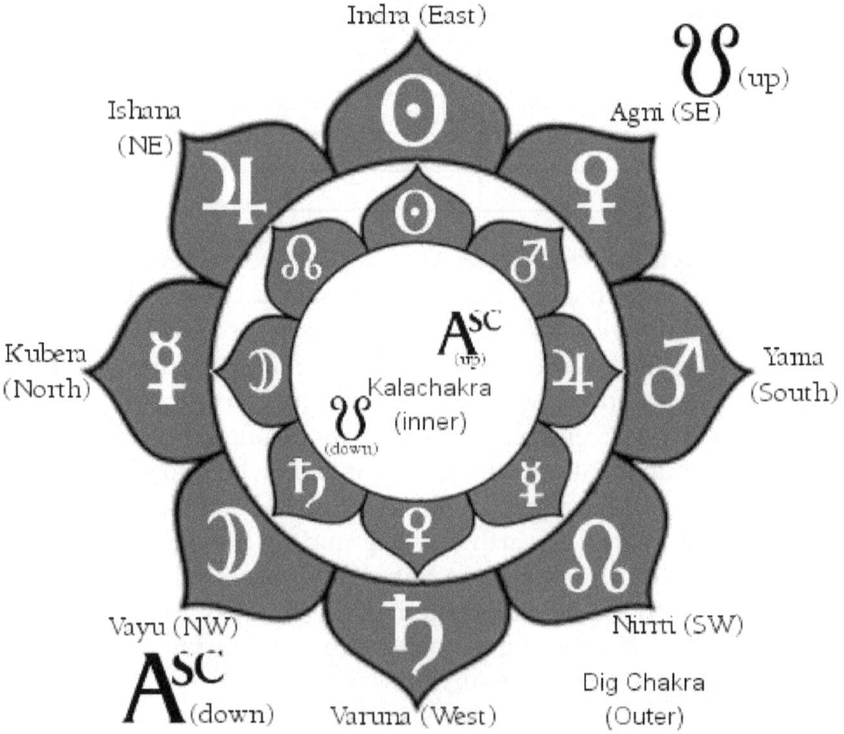

Chakra and its relation to the Dig chakra.

Herein Venus presiding over the south-eastern direction in the Dig Chakra is said to represent all events such as marriage, travel, new partnerships, etc. and the same direction in the Kāla Chakra is presided over by Mars which blocks the auspicious activities of Venus. Hence for this reason marriage, travel and other activities presided over by Venus are to be avoided on the days of Mars, i.e. Tuesdays. Similarly, important objectives dealing with work and enterprise (Mercury) are to be avoided on Mondays, activities related to governance and political purposes (Sun) are avoided on Sundays, certain foods and drinks (Moon) are not to be consumed or offered on Saturdays, and embarking on detoxification of the body (Saturn) and other cleansing practices are to be avoided on a Friday.

Whilst this advice is given generally to all, the individual chart of the native will reveal the most auspicious activity to embark on some specific activities. Example: if one's tenth house is lorded by Jupiter, then embarking on important career moves is recommended on Thursdays for the native, regardless of the actual position of Jupiter in the person's natal chart. Should this conflict with the general advise given earlier, then the general advice is always followed for the overall good of the activity in focus.

Origin of Vāra

The origin of the seven weekdays and their presiding energies arises from the movement and speed of the five planets and two luminaries, as far as earth is concerned. The Vāra lasts from one sunrise to the next comprising of one day and one night. This is known as *ahorātra* meaning day and night, or a division of a day (Vāra) into two parts. This division into two is done with reference to the twelve signs, where the twelve signs give their results in the day and the same twelve in the night. From the word *ahorātra* is derived the word *horā* of which there are twenty-four in a day (twelve times two), just as there are twenty-four hours.

Table 19: Vāra and Horā

Sunday												
1	2	3	4	5	6	7	8	9	10	11	12	
Sun	Ven	Merc	Mo	Sat	Jup	Mars	Sun	Ven	Merc	Mo	Sat	
13	14	15	16	17	18	19	20	21	22	23	24	25
Jup	Mars	Sun	Ven	Merc	Mo	Sat	Jup	Mars	Sun	Ven	Merc	Mo
												Monday

These twenty-four *horā* move according to the speed of the planets' beginning with the slowest and ending with the fastest. This is of course from an earth-centric perspective as it is with reference to those living on earth that we wish to measure the quality of time. The order of the speeds is thus: (1) Saturn, (2) Jupiter, (3) Mars, (4) Sun, (5) Venus, (6) Mercury and (7) Moon. This sequence traverses throughout the day beginning with the planet lording the day. Example: If we were to define the week as starting from the Sun, the order would be: (1) Sun, (2) Venus, (3) Mercury, (4) Moon, (5) Saturn, (6) Jupiter and (7) Mars. This then repeats until all twenty-four

horā are covered. The planet initiating the twenty-fifth Horā is then the lord of the next day.
Thus, based on the movement of the seven grahas through the twenty-four horā of a day, the lords and presiding planets of the seven weekdays are formed.

The Horā of the day begins with the advent of the day. This advent of the day is defined in three ways in the tradition which also have three distinct usages.

Table 20: Dinapraveśa

Starting time	Term	Usage
Sunrise	Kālahorā	Natal charts
6 AM LMT (Local Mean Time)	Mahākālahorā (1)	Muhūrta
6 AM LST (Local Standard Time)	Mahākālahorā (2)	Praśna

The Horā is to be applied using the same principles as those given for the Vāra for day-to-day planning of activities.

Having embarked on the timescales, it is necessary to define their usage within the spectrum of Jyotiṣa. Maharṣi Pārāśara[5] describes the Grahas presiding over each timescale. In this scheme the Moon rules a Kṣaṇa, or the smallest timescale which is an instantaneous moment. The tradition teaches that this moment can last up to an hour and is best equated to the Horā at birth.

Table 21: Timescales

Timescale	Significator
Kṣaṇa (moment)	Moon
Vāra (day)	Mars
Pakṣa (fortnight)	Venus
Māsa (month)	Jupiter
Ṛtu (season)	Mercury
Āyana (six months)	Sun
Varṣa (year)	Saturn

Knowing this, we can equate the quality of the Horā at birth with that of the Moon. The tradition teaches that from the Horā of birth we can get to know the areas of life where the native focuses their minds attention. It shows the area where the māna will reside for the individual and its strength. Essentially the energy indicated by the Vāra has to be focussed somewhere and this 'somewhere' is the placement of the Horā lord.

Similarly, Since Mars rules a weekday and Mars rules the strength of the body, we can see the strength of the body we are born with from our weekday of birth. Similarly the Tithi can be used for relationships and conjugal life, etc. The Māsa (month) is based on the Suns transit, and so the dispositor of the Suns sign will show the extent of wealth (Jupiter), rājayoga and blessings from the Devas that the native enjoys. In this manner each of the timescales can be understood.

However, the Vāra and Horā holds special significance in this regard. Since the first Horā of a day is the overlord of the day, the first Vāra of the month or year is the lord of the entire month/year. Here the definition of the month or year must be defined with regards to the Nakṣatra and signs as they show the impact of the Devas on our world. Hence, the solar entry into Aries is the beginning of the year, and the solar entry into a sign is the beginning of the month. The days during which this

5 Bṛhat Parāśara Horā Śāstra, Grahaguṇasvarūpādhyāya, śloka 33.

occurs will indicate the lord of the entire year/month.

Since a year is presided over by Saturn, the Vāra ruling the year will show the sorrow or sins that we must experience in this life and also how we overcome the same. That Graha in the natives chart will show the source of this sorrow. Further, as per Maharṣi Pārāśara the Devatā of Saturn is Brahmā and therefore the lord of the year can help one attain Brahma Jñana provided the native is able to overcome ones weaknesses. When analysing the lord of the year, Jupiter and its aspects must be carefully scrutinised as the movement of Jupiter takes one year per sign and defines the quality of the year.

Similarly, since a month is presided over by Jupiter, the blessings and happiness given by God is found from the Vāra ruling that month. Here the relationship to the Sun must also be carefully scrutinised as the Sun's transit through the signs corresponds to one month per sign. From here the wealth/resources that are given to the native can be ascertained.

Interpreting Vareśa

The placement of the Vareśa is vital for health as it shows the energy of the body. Here the placement from the Lagna will speak of the persons overall health which is decided from the persons liver, stomach and other parts of the digestion. Its placement from the Moon will have an impact on longevity as well. To understand the strength of the person's digestion the placement of the Vareśa from Leo is to be ascertained. I.e. if Vareśa is placed in Pisces or Capricorn bad digestion is seen due to excess water or slow digestion respectively. Similarly the strength or energy of the brain is seen from the Vareśa's placement from Aries.

Figure 4: Health and Vāra

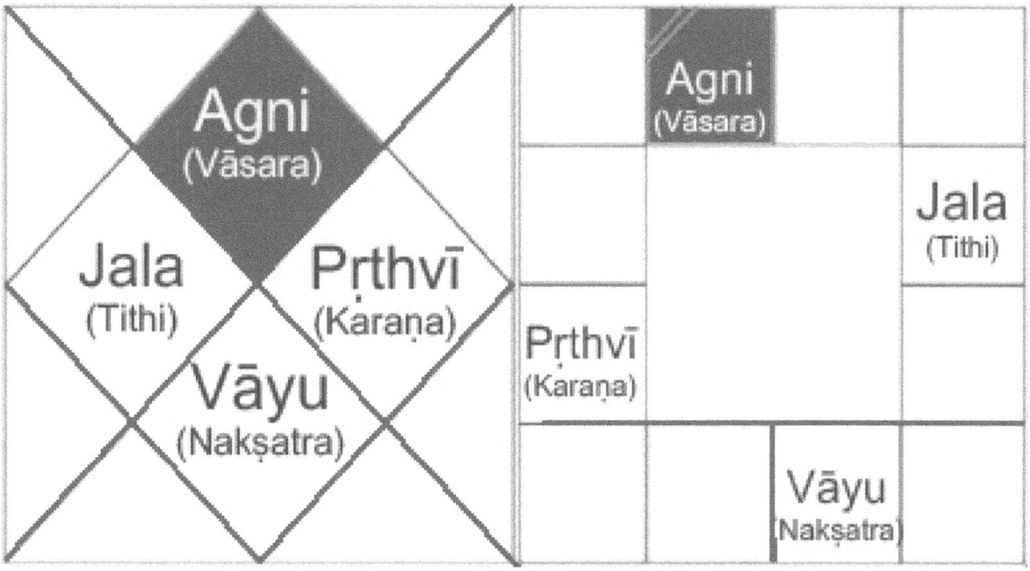

The sign of the Vareśa decides the energy level in the body. Vareśa is best placed in fiery signs as it's nature is fire or Agni itself. So also its worst placed in watery signs where energy is very low. Airy signs will feed the fire whilst the earthy will put it out. If Vareśa is afflicted then the limbs of the body may suffer. This can risk reducing mobility or worse. Care should be taken to not give gems or items to wear which can reduce or obstruct the influence of Vareśa in the chart, i.e. should the Vareśa be giving Argalā to the Lagna then it gemstones of Graha obstructing this Argalā should never be strengthened.

The nature of the Vareśa will decide its auspiciousness with respect to Rājayoga, i.e. malefics (weak Moon, ill associated Mercury, Sun, Mars and Saturn) lording over the weekday will bring negative results, whilst benefics (Jupiter, Venus, strong Moon and well associated Mercury) will give auspicious results. The source of the auspicious/inauspicious results is indicated by the significations of the Graha in question, i.e. birth during a Sunday, being presided over by the Sun will give disfavour from the king or government, troubles through heat or fire, financial problems, etc. The tradition adds that specifically the Mūlatrikoṇa Rāśi of the Vareśa will indicate the extent of the Rājayoga. Herein the Mūlatrikoṇa being in the duṣthāna (3rd, 6th, 8th & 12th) for malefics as Vareśa is considered auspicious since the suffering at the hands of the king, etc. occurs to the enemies and the native benefits. Koṇa (5th & 9th) are considered auspicious for all Graha, whilst Kendra is auspicious for benefics.

Vāra chakra

Beginning from the origin of this galaxy, namely the Sun, the remaining grahas follow starting from Sun and ending with Ketu. This forms the natural weekday order including the two nodes which form the borders between the beginning (Sun) and end (Saturn).

Table 22: Vāra chakra

#	Vāra lords
1	Sun
2	Moon
3	Mars
4	Mercury
5	Jupiter
6	Venus
7	Saturn
8	Rāhu
9	Ketu

This order serves various purposes. Not only is it the natural order referred to in the ancient astrological texts, but it also serves as a means to understand planetary yogas. Here the principle is: add the number of the planets presiding weekdays together. If it's larger than nine, then deduct nine from this. The resultant number is the planet and deity blessing/cursing the yoga.

Example: The yoga between Jupiter and Mars is said to give the blessings of the mother (Rāhu or Moon). Add the number of Mars (3) and Jupiter (5). The result is 8, and equals to the number of Rāhu. Hence the auspicious conjunction between Mars and Jupiter gives the blessings of the divine mother Durgā.

Example 2: the yoga between Saturn and Mars is very inauspicious and gives madness and other such problems to the native. Let us try to understand the deity causing this blemish: Adding the numbers of Mars (3) and Saturn (7) we get 10. This is larger than 9 and thus we will remove 9 from this result and get 1. The number 1 is the equivalent of Sun in the Vāra chakra, and shows that the anger of Śiva arises when the yoga of these two planets occur. The anger of Śiva became ever more prominent in his encounters with Kāmadeva. One such encounter brought about the birth of Kārtikeya, and as a result if the Mars-Saturn yoga occurs in the signs of Saturn where both planets are well placed, can give the blessing of being nursed by six mothers (the Kṛttikā mothers of Kārtikeya) or having six sisters.

Vedic numerology and the Vāra chakra

Table 23: Guṇa chakra

#	Numerology lords
1	Sun
2	Moon
3	Jupiter
4	Rāhu
5	Mercury
6	Venus
7	Ketu
8	Saturn
9	Mars

The Vāra chakra also helps us understand the relationships between the grahas, and how they affect each other in various yogas. But to understand this we have to divide the grahas in groups depending on their qualities or guṇa.

There are three main guṇa known as satva, rajas and tamas, which divide the planets in three moods of sustenance, creation and destruction respectively. The three in the satva group are Sun, Moon and Jupiter respectively. The two in the rajas group are Mercury and Venus respectively. The last group being tamas belongs to Saturn and Mars respectively. Rāhu and Ketu split the i) satva and rajas group & ii) rajas and tamas group respectively. This chakra is therefore appropriately known as the guṇa chakra.

Based on this new scheme of grahas, we can learn more about the interrelationship of planets with each other. The ninth planet is Mars – the protector and strength of the native. So also count to the ninth from any planet in the Vāra chakra to ascertain the protector/*kavacha* of any planet. Example: In the Vāra chakra, the ninth Graha from the Sun is Ketu, hence spirituality, meditation, recluses, etc. become the source of protection for the soul/ātma. If this protection of Ketu becomes weak, then people signified by the Sun will loose their ability to protect themselves from disease, enemy action, etc.

The fourth planet in the numerology chart is Rāhu who is the natural cause of obstacles of this birth. So also if the fourth from any planet in the Vāra chakra is badly placed, it can show obstacles in the attainment of one's hopes and desires. Understanding this, each and every Graha holds some importance in supporting or protecting each other. Among the most important grahas, the fourth, sixth and eighth grahas are of primary concern as they indicate the obstacles, sins and punishment respectively that each planet carries.

Chart 20: H.C. Andersen

Chart of author Hans Christian Andersen, born April 2nd 1805, 1 AM in (10°23′ East, 55°24′ North).

The lord of the weekday is Moon. Despite a most difficult placement of the Moon in the sixth house promising ill health, its Mūlatrikoṇa sign is the seventh house which grants Rājayoga. The lord Venus is in the fifth house and exalted and can grant this through poetry. With Karaṇa lord placed in the fifth, this is assured and enormous success is granted through this.

Further we find Jupiter in the ascendant breaking a Śakata Yoga as fifth lord which

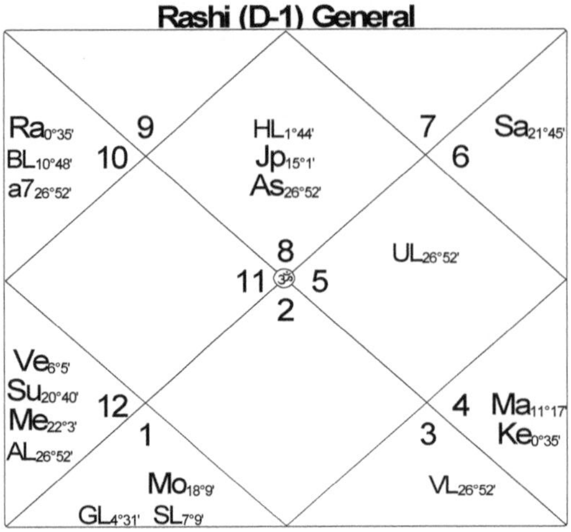

normally promises marriage, children and good education/learning. Jupiter aspects the Moon in the sixth house and links the Horā Lagna, Ghaṭika Lagna and Lagna creating a Mahāyogada for name and long lasting fame through. This can happen through writing as Jupiter and Moon give authorship. However, the fifth house itself is under a severe affliction having the junction of Sun and Venus there. The reason being that from the Sun in the Vāra Chakra Venus is the sixth Graha therefrom causing their union to be quite destructive towards the lives of the being indicated by the house in question. As Venus is the seventh lord this combination will also have a bearing on the marriage and relationships of the native.

In such cases the placement of 1) the lord of the fifth house and 2) kāraka Jupiter is necessary to ensure the continuation of progeny. Here Jupiter is both the lord and Kāraka of the fifth house and despite being in the Lagna is not likely to support the fifth house as it's retrograde. This can give deep learning and literacy however will require one to strive very hard towards having children and also relationships as seventh lord Venus is placed in the house of Jupiter (fifth house).

Should a scenario arise that neither lord nor kāraka of the house in question can support the activity, the tradition teaches the next step to be to analyse the *number graha*. The *number graha* is ascertained by:

1. Adding the values of all the grahas joined the house in question. The value of the Graha is based on the Vārachakra.
2. From the number attained divide by nine, ignore the quotient and keep the remainder.
3. Deduct the number attained from nine. This is the result and the number will reveal which of the Grahas in the Guṇachakra has become the *number graha.*

In this case Sun, Mercury and Venus are joined the fifth house. Their values in the Vārachakra are one, five and six respectively. Their addition becomes twelve and after division by nine the remainder becomes three. Removing three from nine we get six and in the Guṇachakra the sixth Graha is Venus. Venus is not better placed as it is joined the destructive yoga in the fifth house.

As the fifth house from Jupiter also has this particular yoga it is clear that it will be difficult for the native to have children and bring children into this world. We see the same scenario with his relationships as the seventh lord from Venus is the same Mercury placed in the fifth house.

Due to this problem the world renowned author neither married nor had kids of his own, despite a very strong desire to do the same due to Jupiter being retrograde in the Lagna whilst aspecting the fifth and seventh houses.

Chart 21: Queen Marie Antoinette

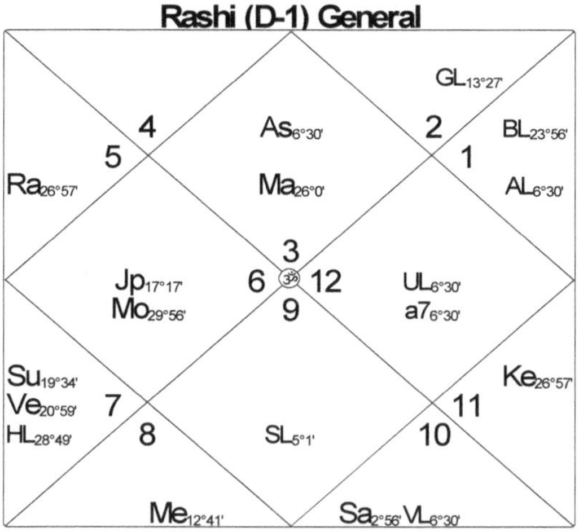

Chart of Queen Marie Antoinette, born November 11th 1755, 7:30 PM in Vienna, Austria. With Lagna joined the Ātmakāraka Mars and lording the Ārūḍha Lagna birth and life in the royal family is guaranteed. Ātmakāraka Mars and Pitṛkāraka Mercury are in Parivartana Yoga bringing about support from a lineage or dynasty, and being in the sixth can bring the greatest enemies together to establish dynasties. Here the rivals of Austria through Marie-Antoinette married the royal prince of France as a means to end the enmity between Austria and France.

This same Mars is however placed in the third from the Ārūḍha and will also show demise on account of this same royal lineage and all due to own mistakes and specifically due to frivolousness or befriending the 'wrong people' due to being placed in Gemini whilst Mercury is in the sixth house of Scorpio. Further, she is born during the Chaturdaśi Tithi which surely gives problems with terrorists, gangs or rebels due to the negatives of Ketu (S. Rath, Brhat Nakshatra 2008). Here Ketu is in the ninth house and being the sixth from the fourth will bring all this in a country foreign from her birth place (France). The fifth house is the house of power, and here the second lord and Marakeśa Moon is placed and is weak due to its pakṣa bala. Further the Sun is weak and is the kārakaof one's dynasty showing that her entrance into the royal family can prove to destroy the lineage. Her end came with the advent of the French revolution where after the reign of the monarchy also came to an end in France.

Sun and Venus are again joined the fifth house, just as the case with the author H.C. Andersen. The lord of the fifth is also Venus confirming this problem. However, instead Jupiter is well placed in the fourth house and will grant children into the life of the Queen namely, Marie-Thérèse Charlotte, Louis Joseph Xavier Francois, Louis Charles and Sophie Hélène Béatrice. Queen Marie Antoinette had four children clearly showing the break of the destructive yoga. Notably Jupiter is afflicted by the fourth dṛṣṭi of Mars and the second dṛṣṭi of Rāhu indicating some suffering in this respect.

The destructive yoga involves the fifth lord and will hurt the health of the children despite the kāraka Jupiter granting the same children. The second aged seven, the third aged ten and the fourth lived for barely a year. Only the first born Marie-Thérèse lived through adulthood until the age of seventy-two.

Nārāyaṇa Daśā works quite well in the cases of royalty. The children were all born in her Nārāyaṇa Daśa of Virgo (1773-1783) housing Jupiter and breaking the destructive yoga, and the following of Taurus (1783-1788) whose lord Venus is placed in the fifth house. Being that Taurus also receives the Rāśi Dṛṣṭi of the destructive yoga in Libra, the latter part of the Daśā also brought about the demise of the youngest child Sophie (1786-1787. One year after Taurus Daśā started the eldest son Louis Joseph fell seriously ill and with the advent of the Daśā of Capricorn joined Saturn and aspected by Rāhu (yoga for dead spirits) he met with his demise due to serious fever ailments.

The younger son also met with his untimely demise yet only two years after Queen Marie had met with the guillotine of the French revolutionaries.

A careful note is that whilst children are seen in the fifth house for both men and women, ladies ability to conceive and procreate arises from the ninth house. For ladies this is reversed in case of even signs ascending in the Lagna and instead of the ninth house the fifth house will come under focus.

Chart 22: Queen Victoria Ena

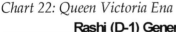

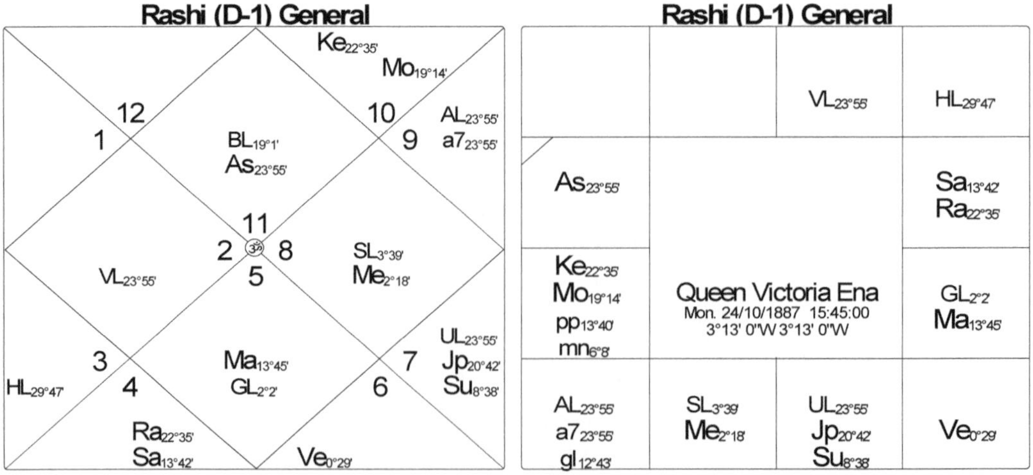

Chart of Queen Victoria Ena, born October 24th 1887, 3:45 PM in Balmoral Castle,

Scotland. Herein Jupiter and Sun are joined which form a destructive yoga as the Sun is the sixth Graha from Jupiter in the Vāra Chakra. The lord of the same is Venus which is debilitated, as the Kāraka Jupiter is further involved in the same yoga causing the destruction of the ninth house to be severe. The *number graha* needs to be analysed. The values of Sun and Jupiter are 1 and 5 respectively. Adding them gives the value 6 and deducting the same from 9 gives the number 3 which is the value of the *number graha*. In the Guṇa Chakra the 3rd Graha is Jupiter which becomes the *number graha*. Jupiter is placed in the same yoga sealing the fate of the indications of the ninth house.

Being in the ninth house this will affect the father. Her father was Prince Henry of Battenberg. The ninth house from the Sun will represent the father's longevity, and here Gemini is that sign and the most undesirable Shraddha Yoga of Saturn and Rāhu is formed in the second from Gemini and causes the airy signs to be very malefic. During the Pitṛ Śula Daśā of Libra in her initial nine years of age, her father had his demise due to malaria (watery disease) contracted during a military campaign in Africa. This specifically occurred during 20th of January 1896.

As the Lagna is an odd sign the ninth house will also represent children in this ladies chart. As the destructive yoga involves male planets the male children are likely to suffer on account of this, however as the Jupiter is in the ninth children will be born but may yet suffer. Queen Ena had seven children of which five were male and two were female. All but one of the male children contracted haemophilia excepting one who was stillborn. The daughters did not contract the same. Of these three remaining sons, two died prematurely due to car accidents and the last suffered serious physical infirmities.

Chart 23: Martha Argerich

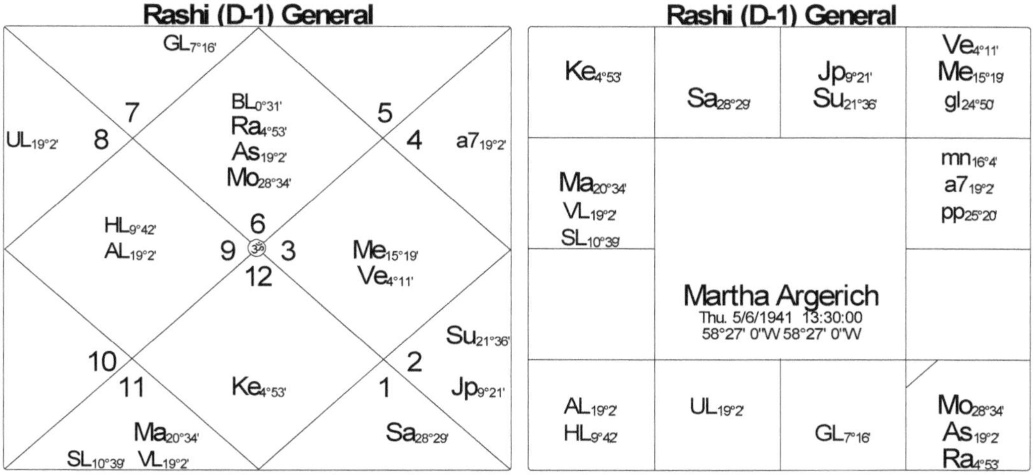

Chart of Pianist Martha Argerich, born June 5th 1941, 13:30 PM in Buenos Aires, Argentina. With Lagneśa in the tenth house forming Siddha Yoga for excellence and perfection in one particular field of expertise. Ninth lord Venus is joined the same bringing about a Raja Yoga, and as this also occurs in the tenth house form the

Moon it gives great reputation and career.

Jupiter and Sun are joined bringing about a destructive yoga, however both Sun and Jupiter are of a Sattvic nature and therefore their placement in the ninth house is considered auspicious for dharma. Venus is the lord of the tenth and is well placed promoting the house as well.

The ninth house is an important house for marriage as well as children in ladies charts, and the lady has three children with three different husbands! Notably children did not suffer as the Lagna is an even sign and the children will be seen from the fifth house instead. The main point being that she married each of the men she fell in love with which from a Dharmic perspective is considered praiseworthy. Further with each of them she had a child.

A clue to the broken marriages can be seen from the seventh house and tithi lord. The tithi lord is Mars which in itself does not bode well for relationships. Being in an airy sign in the sixth house one will feel deprived in relationship matters and surely seek comfort elsewhere. Any node in the seventh house risks infidelity (Sharma 1986) and here Ketu is placed. Ketu is placed there and the sixth Graha in the Vārachakra from Ketu is Jupiter which is placed in the ninth. This implies that each time the native falls in love with another man Jupiter being in the ninth house of Dharma breaks her marriage in favour of the new, and this brings about children. Here the destructive yoga broke the persons Dharma or promise of marriage only to bring about a recreation of the same.

Chaitra Pratipada chakra (Mundane charts)

Tradition tells us that the chart drawn for Chaitra Pratipada or the new moon of the month of Chaitra is combined with the charts of the various solar ingresses to make predictions (S. Rath, Focus on Nepal 2006). The Chaitra Pratipada chart is said to show the karma of the ruler and the country. The ruler of the day will specifically represent this ruler in the chart and his/her fortunes; hence special care was always drawn to making this chart.

The solar ingress charts show those whom are carrying out the will of the ruler and act like ministers of a monarch/ruler. Specifically the day lord of the solar ingress into Aries will indicate the military chief, whilst the day lord solar ingress into Libra can show the minister of trade or finances, thus the function depends on the nature of the sign wherein the ingress is made. Among the signs special care is taken to the solar ingress to the four movable signs as they attend to the most important issues for a country.

The rulers of the day of all these solar ingress are examined in the chart drawn for the Chaitra new moon to see how the various ministers are acting in respect to the ruler. The Rajjyotiṣa or Jyotiṣa for the rulers are taught specific types of spiritual penance to prepare an analysis of such a chakra and thus be able to predict the events for the country or region in the year ahead.

Chart 24: Kingdom of Denmark Chaitra Śukla Pratipada (1849)

Rashi (D-1) General

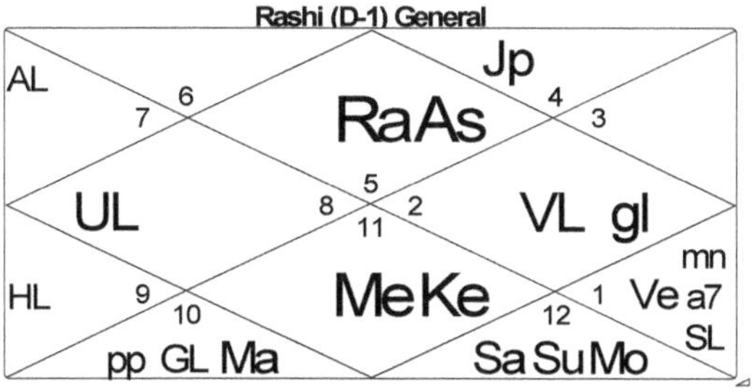

Rashi (D-1) General

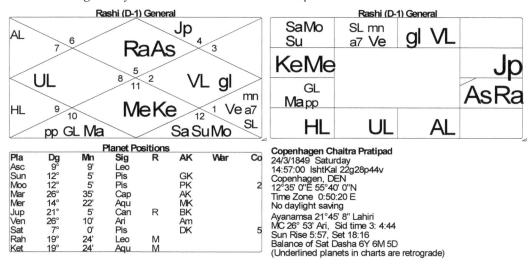

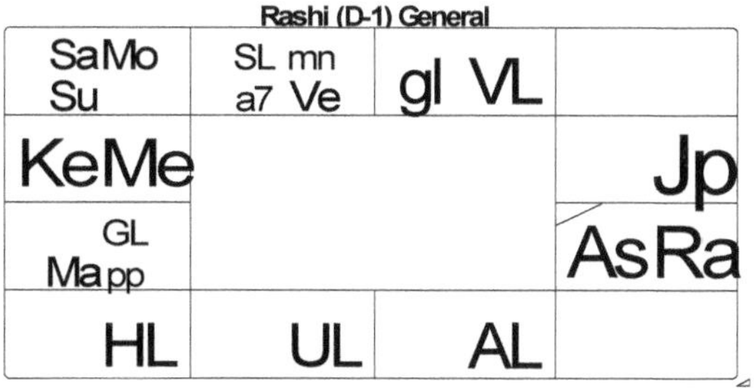

Planet Positions

Pla	Dg	Mn	Sig	R	AK	War	Co
Asc	9°	9'	Leo				
Sun	12°	5'	Pis		GK		
Moo	12°	5'	Pis		PK		2
Mar	26°	35'	Cap		AK		
Mer	14°	22'	Aqu		MK		
Jup	21°	5'	Can	R	BK		
Ven	26°	10'	Ari		Am		
Sat	7°	0'	Pis		DK		5
Rah	19°	24'	Leo	M			
Ket	19°	24'	Aqu	M			

Copenhagen Chaitra Pratipad
24/3/1849 Saturday
14:57:00 IshtKal 22g28p44v
Copenhagen, DEN
12°35' 0"E 55°40' 0"N
Time Zone 0:50:20 E
No daylight saving
Ayanamsa 21°45' 8" Lahiri
MC 26° 53' Ari, Sid time 3: 4:44
Sun Rise 5:57, Set 18:16
Balance of Sat Dasha 6Y 6M 5D
(Underlined planets in charts are retrograde)

1849 was a big turning point in Danish history where the monarchy was substituted for constitutional monarchy out of fear of the earlier revolutions in France affecting the Danish rule, as nationalism had been growing in the country which consisted of 1/3rd ethnic Germans. The solar ingress in to Aries occurred on Wednesday the 11th of April 1849 and we must analyse the position of Mercury in the Chaitra Pratipada chart for the prime-minister or chief of the army, whilst Saturn represents the king or monarch in the chart itself as the event occurred on a Saturday.

At first glance the nodes along the 1/7 axis do not bode well for the monarch and the neighbours where tense ties can erupt as a result.

Saturn representing the monarch is in the eighth house showing long life and lasting presence, but is joined the Lagna lord Sun indicating that this will have to occur after a change in the monarchy which can lessen or deprive the regent of his/her importance. Mercury bring the prime-minister shows the entry of a young man in an old man's (Saturn) world, and a risk of the newcomer falling and hurting the kingdom badly due to a mistake (Mercury joined Ketu causes breakage of bones). Mercury aspects the Lagna and is Vargottama and shows the prime-minister taking on the roles of the regent, and being in the seventh house (Māraṇa Kāraka Sthāna) it shows that he will make terrible mistakes in the diplomacy and foreign policy which will affect the taxes (eleventh lordship) and treasury (second lordship) of the country. Since Mercury is Mātṛkāraka this will affect the state of the people living in the country and this will be based on the differences in language and writing (Mercury).

Saturn lords the seventh house of diplomacy and sixth house of enemies, showing that the change in the monarchy will give a completely new stance towards the neighbours of the country showing how neighbours can become foes and the old foes becoming defeated. The borders will be carved out by the ninth house and lord and with ninth lord Mars in the sixth house and exalted it shows a very strong enemy which will shake the borders of the country, but the kingdoms borders will not change as the ninth lord is exalted and this enemy will come from the south (Mars) and being Bādhakeśa he will note show his real motive. Rāhu and Saturn which afflict the Lagna and Lagna lord respectively rule the west and south-western directions.

As it was, Denmark was involved in a civil war with the region of Prussia. This consisted of the northern part of Germany and the south/south-western part of Denmark (Saturn & Rāhu). Prussia at the time made up 1/3rd of the population of Denmark and ½ of its earnings (Mercury's lordship). The reason for the occurrence was the lack of male heirs to the throne of Denmark (Surya doṣa) after the demise of the then monarch the previous year. The real trigger was the then instalment of the king's sister (Moon joined Saturn), which being a lady was considered an illegal action as it went against the then laws of the region. A truce had failed during February earlier the same year, and on 3rd April just nine days after the New Moon, during the compressed Vimśottari Daśā of sixth lord Saturn fighting renewed.

Mercury Mahādaśā followed from 13th April to 5th of June and the new regents or prime-minister was set to reform the monarchy. Constitutional monarchy was installed on June 5th 1849. Mercury will give the results of Ketu due to the conjunction and throughout this time the war with Prussia raged on and the Danish treasury dwindled.

After continuous months of fighting with Prussia on 10th June 1849 peace talks were held. The Mahādaśā running was Ketu which will give the results of Mercury and thus a temporary peace was to come. Yet, Mercury is in Māraṇa Kāraka Sthāna and any agreement signed is not likely to be lasting. Help came from Germany (south – Mars the secret enemy) which suggested the instalment of a sovereign who was neutral to both Denmark and Prussia and ensured peace for one year (Mercury guarantees peace) for the exhausted Prussian region.

Vimshottari (1yr)

Start Date			Age	Dashas
15/	2/	1849	-0.1	Sa
13/	4/	1849	0.1	Me
5/	6/	1849	0.2	Ke
27/	6/	1849	0.3	Ve
28/	8/	1849	0.4	Su
16/	9/	1849	0.5	Mo
16/	10/	1849	0.6	Ma
6/	11/	1849	0.6	Ra
30/	12/	1849	0.8	Jp
15/	2/	1850	0.9	Sa
13/	4/	1850	1.1	Me
5/	6/	1850	1.2	Ke

Mars is also the Bādhakeśa in the sixth house showing a very secret or hidden enemy coming to ensure the borders are kept (Mars is exalted). Fate would have it that later Prussia became annexed by Germany in the second war between Prussia and Denmark, and finally completely during the First World War. Thus under the guise of being a supporter, Germany later went on to redefine the borders of Prussia and Denmark.

Chart 25: Tehran Chaitra Śukla Pratipad (1978)

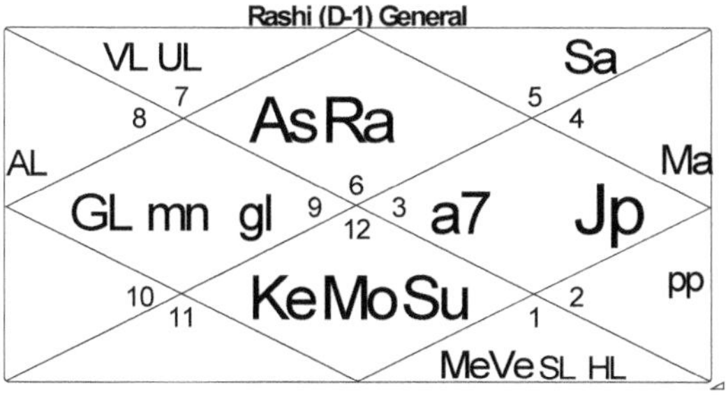

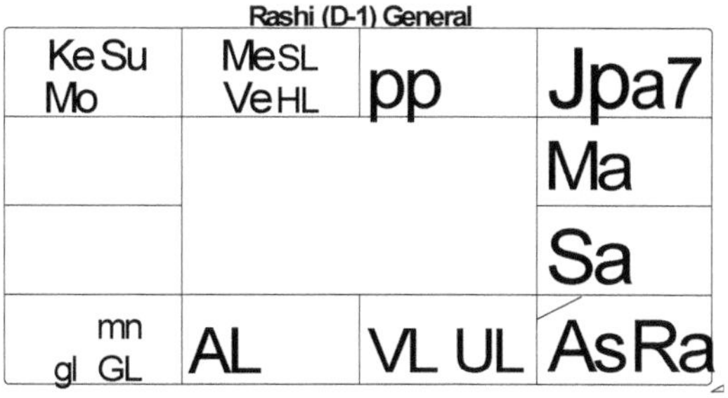

Planet Positions

Pla	Dg	Mn	Sig	R	AK	War	Co
Asc	27°	34'	Virg				
Sun	23°	53'	Pis		AK		
Moo	23°	53'	Pis		Am		1
Mar	5°	23'	Can		PK		
Mer	0°	41'	Ari	R	GK		
Jup	5°	50'	Gem		MK		
Ven	12°	18'	Ari		BK		
Sat	0°	23'	Leo	R	DK		
Rah	11°	53'	Virg	M			
Ket	11°	53'	Pis	M			

Tehran 1978 Chaitra Pratipad
7/4/1978 Friday
20:14:00 IshtKal 32g24p25v
Teheran, IR
51°26' 0"E 35°40' 0"N
Time Zone 4: 0: 0 E
Daylight Saving of 1 hour
Ayanamsa 23°32'47" Lahiri
MC 0° 3' Can, Sid time 7:41:53
Sun Rise 7:16, Set 19:57
Balance of Mer Dasha 7Y 9M 16D
(Underlined planets in charts are retrograde)

Aries Solar ingress: Thursday (Jupiter)

Chaitra Krishna Pratipada (Full Moon): Sunday (Sun)

The Islamic revolution in Iran 1978 culminated in the removal of the previous constitutional monarchy wherein the Shah's of Iran reigned, and the instalment of an Islamic republic. The events that led to this began more prominently from the early 1970's, but it was the year of 1978 unto early 1979 which brought about the main steps towards the creation of the republic.

The monarch or Shah of Iran is seen from the day lord Venus which is placed in the eighth house. This is further joined first and tenth lord Mercury showing that the role of monarch and governance of the country are held by the same person namely the Shah Muhammad Reza Pahlavi and his rule is coming to an end or he will be forced to flee his country. With Rāhu in the Lagna the Shah is highly unpopular and danger is there to his life.

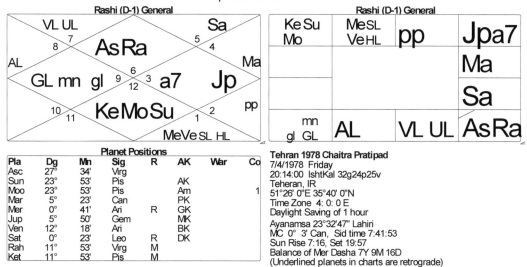

Jupiter lords the day of the Aries solar ingress and will represent Dr. Shapour Bakhtiar the then prime-minister. Jupiter indicates intellectual and idealistic rule and is placed in the tenth house of governance, and rules the Ghātaka Lagna showing the ability to wield power, and is further Bādhakeśa due to its lordship of the seventh house indicating support from foreign countries. The then Shah was branded as a human rights violator by the US Government (Gemini), under Jimmy Carter, and gave the prime-minister the needed edge to exercise a strong opposition towards the Shah. Jupiter is further in the Navāṁśa of Scorpio which is the third house of battle and war in the chart.

Jupiter and Venus though both being Gurus are enemies, where Venus runs the camp of materialists, as Jupiter runs the camp of divine seekers. The Sun is the day lord of the Chaitra Krishna Pratipada (Full Moon) and will represent the spiritual leader or *marja's* in Iran who are a select few proficient in the Quran and authorised by their teachers to declare the laws of Islam based on the same. They are also known as *Grand Ayatollah*. The Sun (Grand Ayatollah) has a naturally friendly relationship with Jupiter (prime minister) but is a dire enemy of Venus (Shah). The Sun is in the Navāṁśa of Capricorn which is the fifth house of power in the Rāśi chart and shows great popularity and support for the rule of priests. Ayatollah Khomeini had grown increasingly popular and despite being exiled from Iran, had continued a political campaign against the Shah.

Using compressed Viṁśottari Daśā for one year; Mercury Daśā (Shah's downfall begins) began the year and saw several demonstrations and destruction of hotels, cinemas, banks, government offices and other symbols of the Shah's regime. One such major occurrence which also took the lives of many due to clashes with security forces occurred during Ketu Daśā, Rāhu Antaradaśā.

Ketu lords the third house of battles and clashes and is joined the Sun ruling the clerics of the country. Religious leaders and students (Sun disposits fifth lord Saturn) took to the streets in riots against the then Shah's rule.

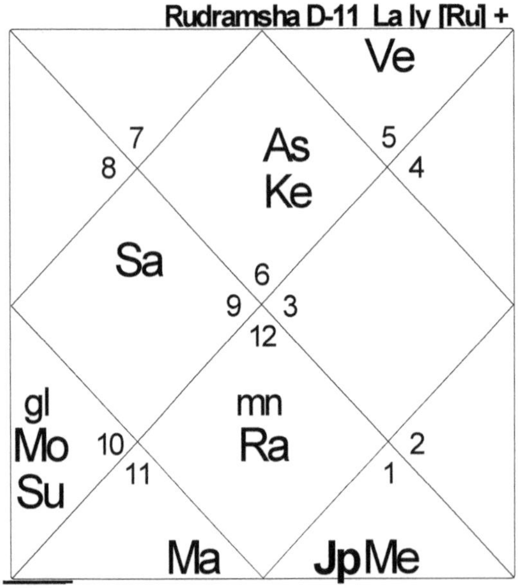

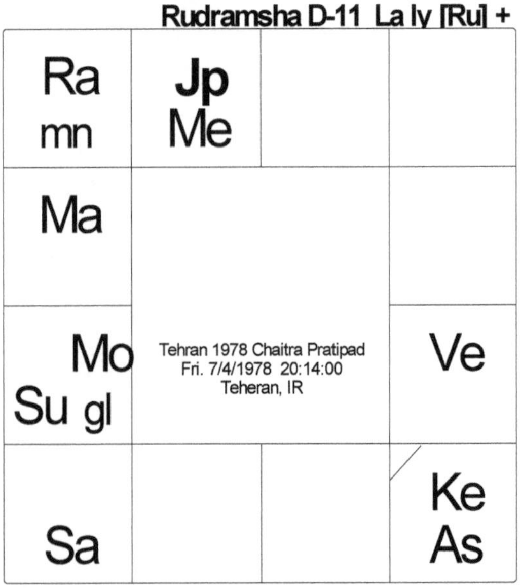

The Rudrāṁśa (D-11) chart is the most appropriate to analyse the battles of the country. Herein Ketu is joined the Lagna and guarantees trouble for the leader and country. The third, sixth and eleventh house shows those who will attack the country, whilst the first, tenth and eighth house show the country and its longevity itself. Rāhu is the sixth lord in Bādhaka Sthāna showing that the enemies are within the country and that the government will be in disarray as to whom they can trust or not in the country. Notably Venus (Shah) is placed in the twelfth house of loss and the lord of that house is the Sun (Ayatollah) ruling his fate. This same Sun is placed in the fifth house of power. During this time Ayatollah Kazem Shariatmadari joined Khomeini's cause, when one of Kazem's followers was shot dead by security forces in front of him.

In an attempt to appease the people, the Shah attempted to create a stable economy by dampening inflation and cutting costs. He also sacked his head of security and promised free elections the following June. Venus (Shah) lording the second house shows the power to affect finances and security (ninth lordship), but being placed in the eighth house shows that he will cause his own undoing. Mercury being the tenth lord shows that the countries efficiency will fall and many young workers (Mercury) were sacked to create the cutbacks and these same workers living in the city slums then joined the demonstrations in massive numbers. This grew even stronger in the Mahādaśā of the Sun (Ayatollah) which lasted over the summer and shows the massive support for the Ayatollah.

Vimshottari (1yr)

Start Date			Age	Dashas
10/	3/	1978	-0.1	Me
1/	5/	1978	0.1	Ke
23/	5/	1978	0.1	Ve
25/	7/	1978	0.3	Su
13/	8/	1978	0.3	Mo
13/	9/	1978	0.4	Ma
4/	10/	1978	0.5	Ra
27/	11/	1978	0.6	Jp
13/	1/	1979	0.8	Sa
11/	3/	1979	0.9	Me
2/	5/	1979	1.1	Ke
23/	5/	1979	1.1	Ve

Over the late summer of 1978 the Shah sought help from the USA to quell an impending revolution. The Daśā's of Sun and Moon are running and are both joined the Sun in the seventh house representing the Ayatollah and showing that the neighbours and partners (seventh house) will not support the Shah. This was particularly because of the bad reputation the Shah's rule had gotten by the government of President Carter. Despite complete disarray Iran, the CIA brought forth and analysis in August starting that Iran wasn't at risk of revolution in the near future! Surely this is the result of Bādhaka at work where the allies do not help because they either misunderstood or deliberately do not want to interfere.

The confusion caused by the Bādhaka was so intense that despite demonstrators repeatedly targeting and burning movie theatres and killing 400 people, the Shah was blamed by the family and relatives of the demised for all the incidents. Even claims that the Shah's security force had done so to frame the opposition were raised.

The situation became even more intense as the Shah declared martial law in Moon Daśā, Venus Antaradaśā resulting in a massive protest killing 84 demonstrators by security forces, the particular day being known as Black Friday.

Mars Mahādaśā had come and being the third lord as well as dispositor of the Lagneśa and Venus (Shah) the Shah was to flex his muscles. Yet, Mars is debilitated in the eleventh and could bring a largely opposite result. Mars is placed in the sixth house in the Rudrāṁśa showing that the enemy will be suffering and being in Aquarius this can cause displacement (lorded by Rāhu). Ayatollah Khomeini ran his campaign from the neighbouring Iraq, and the Shah drawing on his influence sought to get the Ayatollah deported. The Ayatollah was forced to travel to Paris after being rejected entry into Kuwait (Mars shows difficulty at borders). He then finally travelled to Paris, but this ended up becoming a great source of support for him (Shah failed: third lord is debilitated) as he became the news of the world then, appearing in magazines and interviews all over the world. Further the Ayatollah's exile had been heard in Iran where his support had become even stronger as Rāhu Daśā passed and gave the Shah a further bashing to his reputation (Rāhu in Lagna and in Bādhaka sign in Rudrāṁśa).

With the advent of Jupiter Daśā the end was near. In Rāśi Jupiter represents the prime-minister who is clearly supporting the Ayatollah and clerics of the country (Sun). Jupiter is placed in the eighth house of the Rudrāṁśa (D-11) and shows religious disturbances in the country as well as many demonstrators (Mercury) who are lacking work filling the street squares of the capitol (Aries) and asking the Shah to leave the country (eighth house is the end of longevity of the ruler). Two million demonstrators filled the streets at this time asking for the removal of the Shah at this time. The Daśā-Antaradaśā was Jupiter-Mercury which are the exact two Grahas in the eighth house in the Rudrāṁśa. Again we see the Rudrāṁśa giving very accurate results.

Loss of power/position can only come once the fifth house has had its say. Fifth lord is Saturn placed in the twelfth house (loss of power) and is placed in the sign Leo (Grand Ayatollah – Sun). During Saturn Daśā, Mercury Antaradaśā the prime-minister asked the Shah to leave his post and the country. During Saturn Daśā, Venus Antaradaśā Ayatollah Khomeini arrived back in Tehran after his long exile. Venus representing the loss of power of the Shah sealed the arrival of new leaders, and so began the *Decade of Fajr* from February 1st until February 11th. The prime-minister invited Khomeini to form a Vatican state in the city of Qom. Jupiter always works on the behalf of the Sun as it is the natural kāraka or *doer* on behalf of the Sun. On arrival Khomeini clearly rejected the proposal of then prime-minister Bakhtiar's to form a government. Whilst Jupiter works for the Sun, Sun is the Vedhaka or piercer/knower of weaknesses of Jupiter, and a New Moon Sun will never accept the ideals of Jupiter, as Sun is himself the king! On February 4th in the same Daśā-Antaradaśā Khomeini appointed his own competing interim prime-minister for elections! He further claimed that 'since I have appointed him he must be obeyed'. It was 'Gods government' he warned, and disobedience against which was 'a revolt against God'. On February 9th during Saturn Daśā, Venus Antaradaśā fighting broke out between the imperial guard loyal to the Shah (Venus), and pro-Khomeini rebels with Khomeini declaring Jihad on the soldiers! The fighting ended on February 11th just a day before the advent of the Sun Antaradaśā.

The fighting was over and later that year in June Iran presented its first constitution and declared them as an Islamic republic.

Chart 26: Washington Chaitra Śukla Pratipada (2008)

Rashi (D-1) General

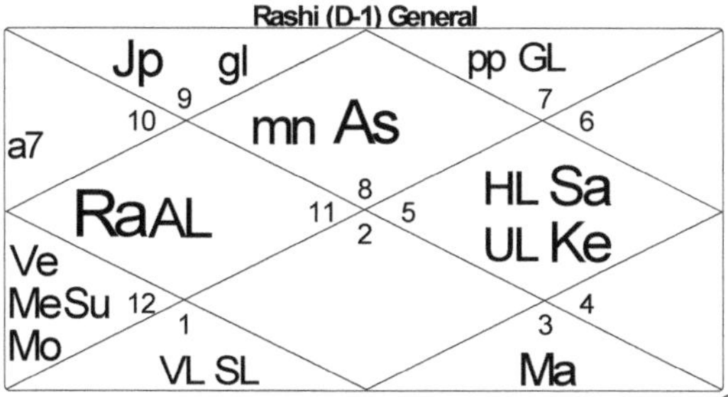

Rashi (D-1) General

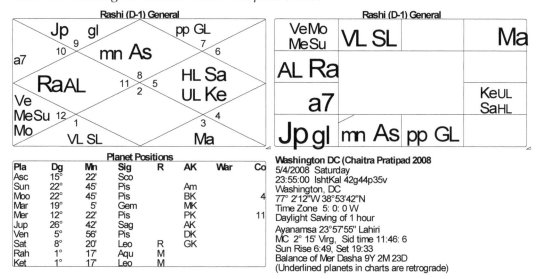

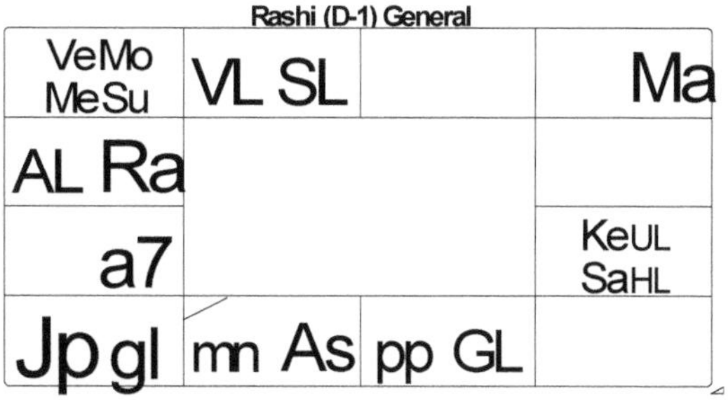

Planet Positions

Pla	Dg	Mn	Sig	R	AK	War	Co
Asc	15°	22'	Sco				
Sun	22°	45'	Pis		Am		
Moo	22°	45'	Pis		BK		4
Mar	19°	5'	Gem		MK		
Mer	12°	22'	Pis		PK		11
Jup	26°	42'	Sag		AK		
Ven	5°	56'	Pis		DK		
Sat	8°	20'	Leo	R	GK		
Rah	1°	17'	Aqu	M			
Ket	1°	17'	Leo	M			

Washington DC (Chaitra Pratipad 2008
5/4/2008 Saturday
23:55:00 IshtKal 42g44p35v
Washington, DC
77° 2'12"W 38°53'42"N
Time Zone 5: 0: 0 W
Daylight Saving of 1 hour
Ayanamsa 23°57'55" Lahiri
MC 2° 15' Virg, Sid time 11:46: 6
Sun Rise 6:49, Set 19:33
Balance of Mer Dasha 9Y 2M 23D
(Underlined planets in charts are retrograde)

Solar ingress	Vāra (Vedic weekday)
Aries	Sunday (Sun)
Libra	Thursday (Jupiter)

In every annual new year chart for Washington DC since 2003, the weekday lord or vareśa is joined or lording the third or sixth house in the chart showing the tides for war in the country. In the 2008 chart Mars is the weekday lord and lords the sixth house confirming that the nation is still at war. Mars further aspects the eleventh house and shows that all the taxes of the country are being used for this purpose, and its Rāśi dṛṣṭi on the fifth house of voters where twelfth and eighth lords Mercury and Venus are placed is causing Viparīta Raja Yoga for the country at the cost of the voters or people. In addition the fifth house of the voters are suffering from Pravrājya yoga due to four planets being joined the same. On account of the Pravrājya yoga the Raja yoga of the ninth lord joined the two Kendra lords cannot function until the Daśā of a combust Graha. Herein Moon and Mercury are combust but Mercury being the eighth and eleventh lord is not benefitting the voters at all and instead making it harder for them on account of bad contracts. This no doubt must indicate the inappropriate amount of loans given by the banks to consumers. Moon on the other hand is more auspicious but due to being weak is quite malefic in the chart and can show support but not without anxiety affecting the public.

The particular cause of the Pravrājya yoga is seen from the strongest Graha, here Venus. Venus is the eighth and third lord from the fifth house and indicates that the voters have borrowed too much and are suffering for this, in this case at the hand of the banks who are also doing the same (Mercury).

The Keśari Yoga of Jupiter in Kendra to the Moon is auspicious and as Jupiter is the lord of the fifth house of voters and placed in the second house of treasury it guarantees great support coming from the countries own coffers. Jupiter is the vareśa for the solar ingress into Libra and shows that the ministers of finance will come to the rescue and ensure the continuity of the finances of the public.

The government voted over a bank bailout plan twice. Once during Mars Daśā Ketu Antaradaśā yet unsuccessfully and later in Mars Daśā, Venus Antaradaśā with success. The Bhrātṛkāraka is the Moon and its activation causes laws and policies to be changed. Venus joins the Moon and brought about the policy change. The actual use of the money will occur during Jupiter Mahādaśā.

The next Chaitra Śukla Pratipada chart has Jupiter as the lord of the weekday and unlike the last six years of charts, there is no association with the third or sixth houses showing an end to the battles faced by the US in the coming year.

Chart 27: Washington Chaitra Śukla Pratipada (2009)

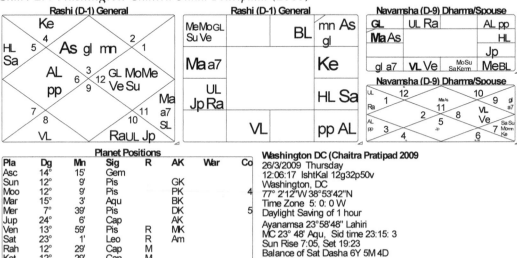

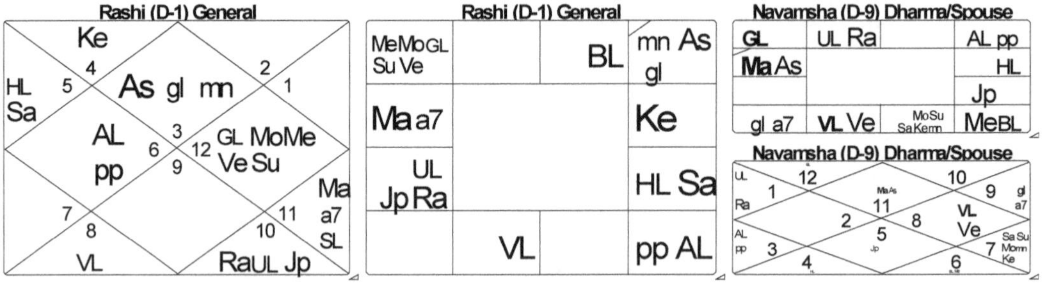

Planet Positions

Pla	Dg	Mn	Sig	R	AK	War	Co
Asc	14°	15'	Gem				
Sun	12°	9'	Pis		GK		
Moo	12°	9'	Pis		PK		4
Mar	15°	3'	Aqu		BK		
Mer	7°	39'	Pis		DK		5
Jup	24°	6'	Cap		AK		
Ven	13°	59'	Pis	R	MK		
Sat	23°	1'	Leo	R	Am		
Rah	12°	29'	Cap	M			
Ket	12°	29'	Can	M			

Washington DC (Chaitra Pratipad 2009
26/3/2009 Thursday
12:06:17 IshtKal 12g32p50v
Washington, DC
77° 2'12"W 38°53'42"N
Time Zone 5: 0: 0 W
Daylight Saving of 1 hour
Ayanamsa 23°58'48" Lahiri
MC 23° 48' Aqu, Sid time 23:15: 3
Sun Rise 7:05, Set 19:23
Balance of Sat Dasha 6Y 5M 4D
(Underlined planets in charts are retrograde)

The chart for the following year in Washington DC has Vareśa Jupiter placed in the eighth house in debilitation with Rāhu which does not bode well for the leader or causes some great unrest for the leader. Being the tenth lord it clearly affects the incumbent party and being the seventh lord it also affects the neighbours and allies. Yet, Jupiter is not associated with the third or sixth houses in anyway and shows that the previous years[6] of armed conflict are coming to an end. To see exactly what this entails for the nation it's essential to analyse the Navāṁśa. If Jupiter is associated with Rāhu herein then great shock may hit the country due to the demise of someone. If this associates with the twelfth and eighth houses then the leader(s) of the country will be killed, whilst if associated with the second or sixth houses then a major enemy or opponent suffers the same fate.

In the given Navāṁśa, with Aquarius Lagna, Jupiter and Rāhu mutually aspect confirming the previous mentioned risk. Neither are associated with the eighth or twelfth houses showing that the leader is not at risk. Instead Jupiter lords the second house and presents this risk to a major enemy. Jupiter is in Leo showing that it is surely a politician and could have their Lagna associated with Leo or a strong Sun.

Ātmakāraka is Jupiter and shows that the leader is taking on this karma personally

---

6 April 5th 2008, 23:56; March 18th 2007, 22:44:06; March 29th 2006, 6:15:57; April 8th 2005, 16:32:39; March 20th 2004, 18:38: 43; April 1st 2003, 15:17:59; April 12th 2002, 15:23:13.

and the reputation of the nation and the leader will be negatively affected by this. However, this will end up benefitting the nation as the vareśa is the lord of the Kendra in the Rāśi chart and is a sure promise of prosperity for the nation following this, and specifically in the growth of foreign ties due to the lordship of the seventh house.

Rāhu and Jupiter Daśā will arrive at the end of the year beginning from around November. It is during this time that we can expect to see its results.

The fifth house of voters is not out of the rut yet. The fifth lord Venus despite being exalted is joined debilitated Mercury in a Pravrājya yoga in the tenth house. The incumbent party is amassing a great deal of resources and with the twelfth lord Venus placed there the expenses are huge. This Pravrājya will break in the second quarter of this year with the coming of Mercury Mahādaśā and again in September with the coming of Moon Mahādaśā. This will bring new ways out of the financial issues and is sure to benefit the population and government. However, the financial issues of the population will not begin to be overcome until the year of 2010 with the advent of the next Chaitra Śukla Pratipada Chakra.

1.6 Five Areas of Life

The five limbs can be roughly divided into the following areas:

Table 24: Five areas of life

Limb	Area
Vāra	life, energy
Karaṇa	activity, work in society, achievements
Tithi	marital relationships, passions, love life
Nakṣatra	disease, death, bodily ailments
Yoga	general relationships, the company one keeps, friendship circle, spirituality

If there is an affliction to one of these limbs, it will affect the planet which is linked to that limb. For example, Sankrānti (sun's entry into a sign) is considered a Vāra (weekday) affliction, and the Vāra in which one is born will indicate the area of suffering. There are some divergent views on what to consider the birth Tithi, i.e. should it be the Tithi at the time of birth or the Tithi running at sunrise. The paramparā teaches that the Tithi at the time of birth should be used, no matter what the Tithi at sunrise was.The sunrise tithi can be used to time the day occurence of an event.

1.7 More application of the Pañcāñga

Tattva conflicts

Each of the Tithi, yoga, etc. has an element or tattva associated with it. Tattva conflicts occur, when there is a graha linking the conflicting tattva with each other. The main conflicting tattvas are:

Table 25: Pañcāñga Sambandha

Limb	Afflicted by	Supports
Agni (Vāra)	Jala (Tithi)	Vāyu (Nakṣatra)
Jala (Tithi)	Vāyu (Nakṣatra)	Pṛthvī (Karaṇa)
Vāyu (Nakṣatra)	Pṛthvī (Karaṇa)	Agni (Vāra)
Pṛthvī (Karaṇa)	Agni (Vāra)	Jala (Tithi)

Ākāśa/Yoga has no conflicts and will remove any conflicts presiding in the other tattvas. Hence; if birth happens on a Tithi whose lord is also lord of the Vāra, predict that there is a tattva conflict. For example, should birth be on Saptamī Tithi on a Saturday, the houses lorded by Saturn will be weak in the horoscope.

Table 26: Quick Pañcāñga Table

Graha	Vāra	Tithi	Karaṇa	Nakṣatra	Yoga
Sun	Sunday	1st and 9th	Bava	3rd, 12th, 21st	5th, 14th, 23rd
Moon	Monday	2nd and 10th	Balava	4th, 13th, 22nd	6th, 15th, 24th
Mars	Tuesday	3rd and 11th	Kaulava	5th, 14th, 23rd	7th, 16th, 25th
Mercury	Wednesday	4th and 12th	Taitula	9th, 18th, 27th	2nd, 11th, 20th
Jupiter	Thursday	5th and 13th	Garija	7th, 16th, 25th	9th, 18th, 27th
Venus	Friday	6th and 14th	Vaṇija	2nd, 11th, 20th	4th, 13th, 22nd
Saturn	Saturday	7th and Pūrṇimā	Viṣṭi	8th, 17th, 26th	1st, 10th, 19th
Rāhu	-	8th and Amāvasyā	Śakuni Brahmā, Nāga Maheśa	6th, 15th, 24th	8th, 17th, 26th
Ketu	-	-	Catuṣpada Viṣṇu, Kintughna Sūrya	1st, 10th, 19th	3rd, 12th, 21st

Sankrānti

Sankrānti is the time when the Sun has entered the sign and resides in the first degree of the sign (0 °-1°). Find the day on which the Sun enters zero degrees of a sign. That entire day will have Sankrānti doṣa. The day in which this happens is relevant, causing seven types of Sankrānti.

Table 27: Sankrānti and weekday

Day	Type of Sankrānti
Sunday	Ghorā
Monday	Dhvamsī
Tuesday	Mahodarī
Wednesday	Mandā
Thursday	Mandākini
Friday	Miśra
Saturday	Rākṣasā

Ghorā means awful, frightful…it refers to a malefic Sun, whilst the goal of the Sun is to become Aghorā, which is a name for Śiva (a deity indicated by the Sun). Śamkara also is a name for Śiva, and hence Sankrānti refers to the ire of Shiva, in his various forms. We may hence infer that Sankrānti makes the graha which lords the day of birth inauspicious, and the native suffers the anger of Śiva. For this reason we must study the lordships of that graha in the horoscope and decide the negative circumstances arising out of this.

Ghātaka

Birth during specific Nakṣatra, Tithi, Vāra or janma Rāśi, can cause pain/suffering from the grahas in the horoscope. This can also indicate the times of accidents/ physical suffering as well as emotional suffering on account of relationships. This principle is called ghāta and means to hurt, maim, kill, slay, bruise, injure, etc. Ghātaka refers to the one who performs this act of killing, i.e. the killer.

Table 28: Ghātaka Cakra[7]

Rāśī	Moon	Tithi	Day	Nakṣatra	Lagna	
1	2	3	4	5	Lagna-1 Same Sex	Lagna-2 Opposite Sex
Aries	Aries	Nandā	Sunday	Maghā	Aries	Libra
Taurus	Virgo	Pūrṇa	Saturday	Hastā	Taurus	Scorpio
Gemini	Aquarius	Bhadrā	Monday	Swāti	Cancer	Capricorn
Cancer	Leo	Bhadrā	Wednesday	Anurādhā	Libra	Aries
Leo	Capricorn	Jayā	Saturday	Mūlā	Capricorn	cancer
Virgo	Gemini	Pūrṇa	Saturday	Śravaṇa	Pisces	Virgo
Libra	Sagittarius	Ṛktā	Thursday	Śatabhiśāj	Virgo	Pisces
Scorpio	Taurus	Nandā	Friday	Revatī	Scorpio	Taurus
Sagittarius	Pisces	Jayā	Friday	Dvīja	Sagittarius	Gemini
Capricorn	Leo	Ṛkta	Tuesday	Rohiṇī	Aquarius	Leo
Aquarius	Sagittarius	Jayā	Thursday	Ārdrā	Gemini	Sagittari-us
Pisces	Aquarius	Pūrṇa	Friday	Aśleṣa	Leo	Aquarius

Based on the Rāśi occupied by the Moon, derive the following from the table:

❖ *Ghāta Candra*

When the moon is transiting this Rāśi it indicates *ghāta* coming in the form of disappointment, emotional suffering, etc.

❖ *Ghāta Tithi*

Partners born on one's Ghātaka Tithi will be the source of *ghāta* in relationships. This should be used in marriage matching.

❖ *Ghāta Nakṣatra*

During Moon's transit through the *ghāta Nakṣatra* physical *ghāta* will come.

❖ *Ghāta Vāra*

During the Vāra causing *ghāta* on the janma Rāśi health wise predict inauspicious tides.

7 This Chakra is from Sanjay Rath's lecture on Ghātak – 2003.

❖ *Ghāta Lagna*

People's Lagna in *ghāta* to your janma Rāśi will come to cause you *ghāta*. Also if the transit Lagna is one of the *ghāta Lagna* it can cause evil results during its period.

Similarly one can also reckon one's birth Vāra, Tithi, Nakṣatra and derive results.

❖ *Ghāta Tithi*

Signs which are *ghāta* to one's janma Tithi will indicate the source of *ghāta* in relationships. This can also show the suffering of the native's parents in the horoscope. If the Sun falls in one of these signs, it's called Dagdha Tithi and causes considerable sorrow to father prior to the time of one's birth. Incase of Moon placed in either of these signs, it is said that the mother sees sorrow prior to the natives birth. This is called Śunya Tithi

❖ *Ghāta Nakṣatra*

If one's Moon Nakṣatra at birth happen to be *ghāta* to a sign, then those ārūḍas and grahas in that sign will suffer physical injury.

❖ *Ghāta Vāra*

The signs which receive *ghāta* from one's Vāra of birth will indicate diseases/ailments suffered by the native.

Eka Nakṣatra Doṣa

When two immediate family members are born in the same Nakṣatra, the younger of those born suffers. If this is merely same Nakṣatra, the wealth/happiness of the younger suffers. If this is the same Nakṣatra pada, then the health of the younger suffers severely. This suffering begins when the two natives are detached from each other, i.e. when one decides to leave home, or live independently of the other.

1.8 Case Studies

Tattva Conflict

Chart 28: Śuklā Navamī on a Sunday

Chart of male native, born 25th August 1974, 2.32 PM, Patratu, India.

In the given chart, Tithi is Śukla Navamī (S 9) and Vāra is Sunday. As per Table 26, both are lorded by the Sun, and we may expect the sign Leo to be inauspicious for the native. The native is born with Sagittarius Lagna, and the 9th house is Leo occupied by the Sun, Mercury and Mars. Without consulting the pañcāñga it would be difficult to say why the premature demise of father happened for the native, but the 9th house being Leo and suffering from the Tattva conflict ruins the 9th house and causes the premature demise of the father.

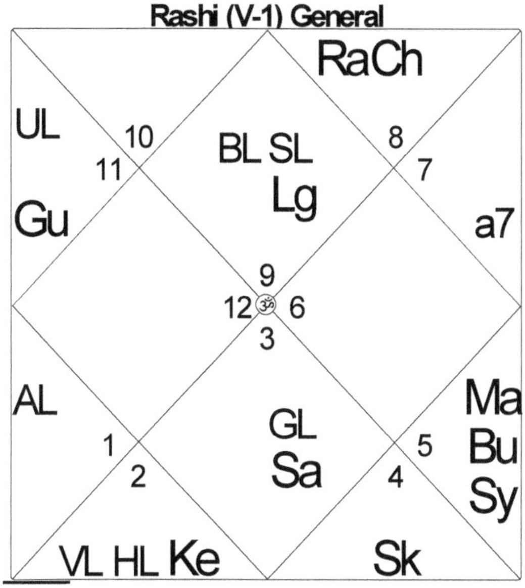

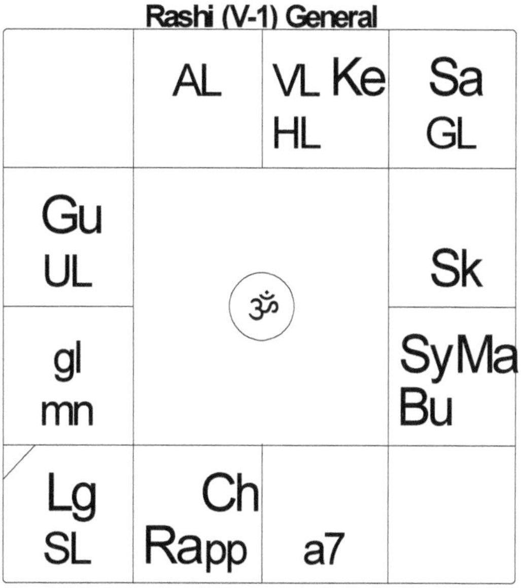

Chart 29: Śukla Tṛtīyā on a Tuesday

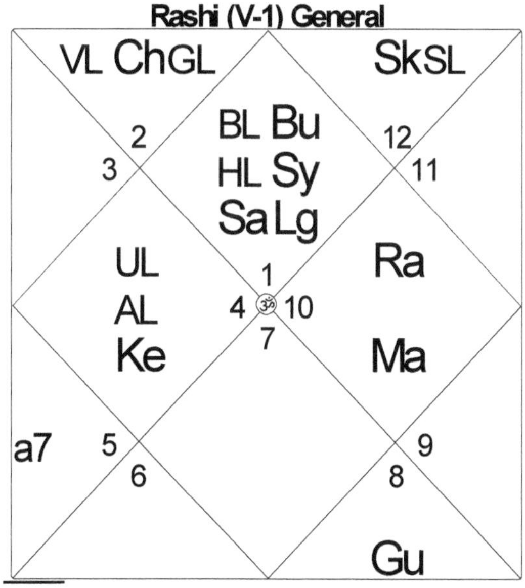

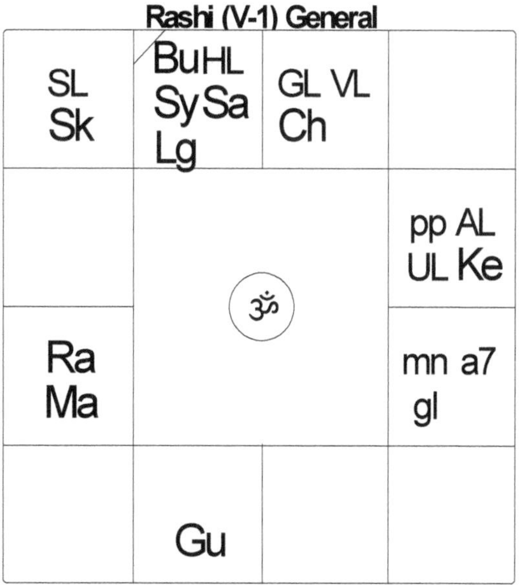

Chart of male native, born 27th April 1971, 6.33 AM, Andheri, India.

In the given chart, birth is during Śukla Tṛtīyā on a Tuesday, causing Mars and its signs to act inauspiciously. Lagna is Aries in the chart, and hence Mars lords the Lagna and 8th houses. The native could not find happiness in his birth country (Lagna) and has hence moved abroad. As A10 occupies Aries, Mars also promises to cause a loss of job and insecurity in profession, and this will be due to battles or war as Aries is involved. After the incident of September 11th, the native found himself without a job for a long period of time, due to insecurity on the job-market.

Sankrānti

Chart 30: Sankrānti on a Monday

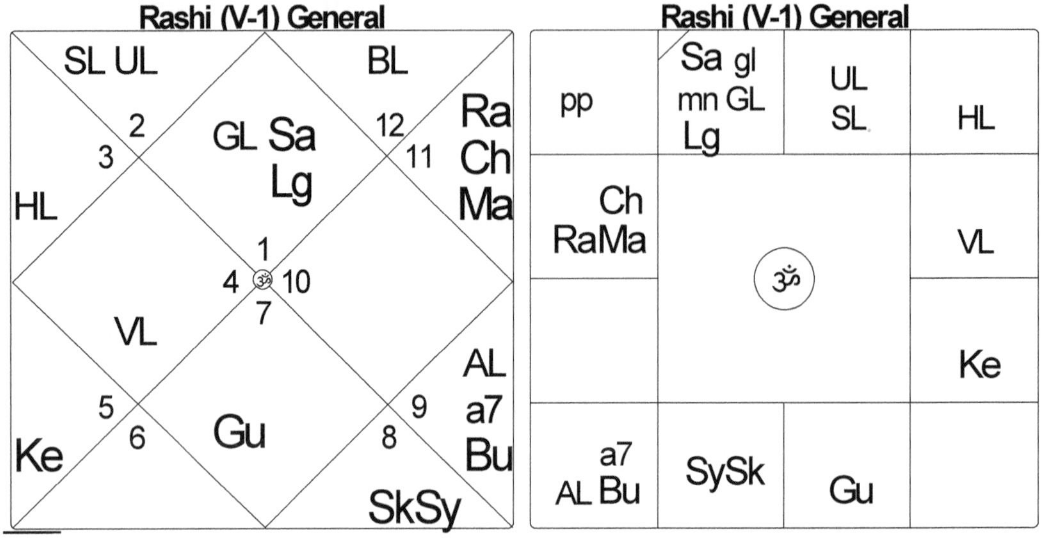

Chart of female native, born 15th December 1969, 2.06 PM, 75w17, 43n6, 5 hrs West of GMT.

In the given chart, the person is born on Dhvanksī Sankrānti (Sankrānti on a Monday) causing the Moon to turn extremely malefic for the person. Moon happens to be Ātmakāraka and lords the 4th house, indicating that a lingering desire of the soul to have a home, be established, create a family. This has been delayed for the person and the native was advised to perform a Sankrānti doṣa ritual and recite the Mṛtyuñjaya Mantra for Śiva.

Chart 31: Sankrānti on a Thursday

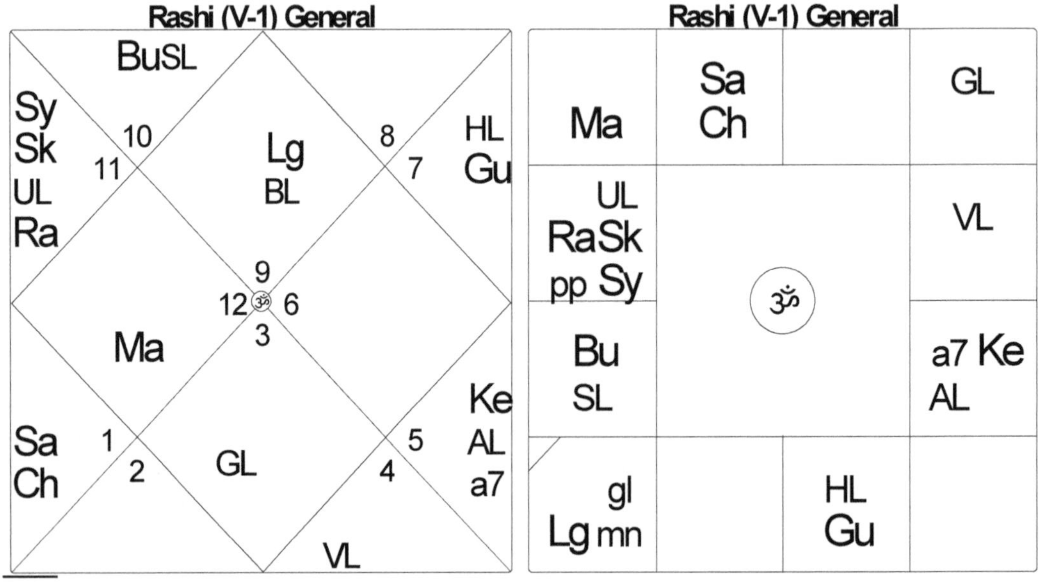

Native born 13th February 1970, 3:53 AM, New Delhi, India.

The given chart suffers from Mandākini Sankrānti, due to birth during a Sankrānti occurring on a Thursday. Jupiter is the lord of Thursday and in the chart is lording over the Lagna and the 4th house. Due to the lordship of Lagna, the native could not establish himself in his own country, and decided to move abroad. As Mars is placed in kendra it supports the native and being 12th lord it makes the native go abroad. Mars will require the native to have property abroad. The native is doing very well in a foreign country, but has never been able to establish himself in his birth-country. If any such attempt should be made by the individual to settle in their birth place, the native should perform the Sankrānti doṣa ritual.

Ghātaka

Chart 32: Śūnya Tithi, Ghātak Vāra.

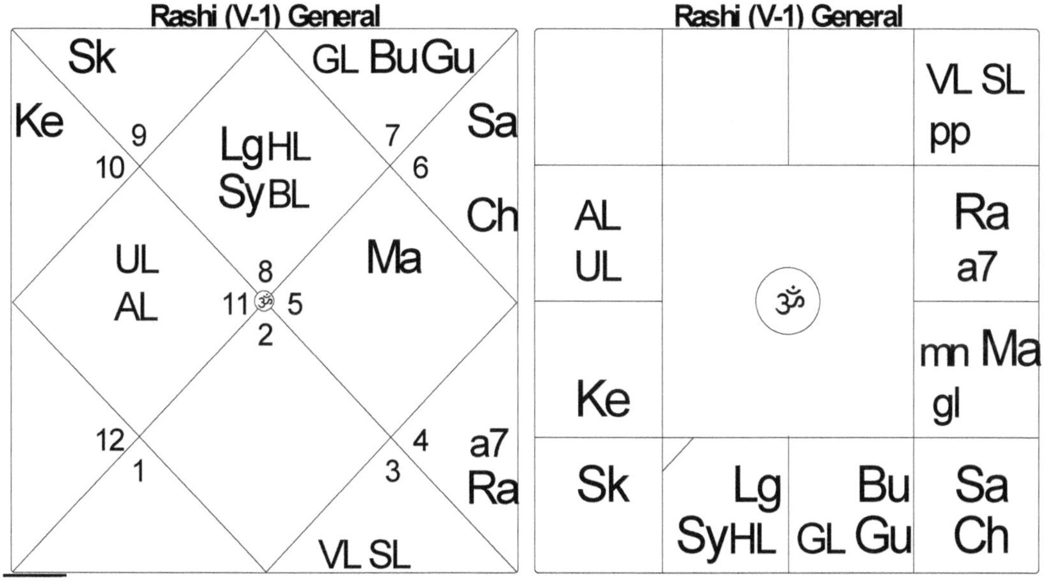

Male native born 21st November 1981, 6:06:41, Nairobi, Kenya.

The native is born on Kṛṣṇa Daśamī Tithi. This is a Pūrṇa Tithi and the signs Taurus, Virgo and Pisces suffer Ghāta from this Tithi. The natives moon is in Virgo, hence causing Śūnya Tithi, this caused the native's mother to suffer some anxiety at the time of the native's birth. This was due to the demise of the native's maternal grandfather, who in tradition, the native was to be named after. The native was born on a Friday, and this day causes Ghātak to the signs Scorpio, Sagittarius and Pisces. In the native's chart, Sun is in Scorpio in the Lagna ruling the head. The native has suffered twice injuries to the head in his childhood whilst swimming. The 2nd house is Sagittarius ruling the face, and is occupied by Venus. The native has had excess toxins in his blood resulting in acne and boils on the face. These manifested on the left side of the face as Venus is in the 2nd horā of Sagittarius. The issues calmed down significantly following his marriage (seventh lord Venus).

Chart 33: Śūnya Tithi, Ghātak Vāra

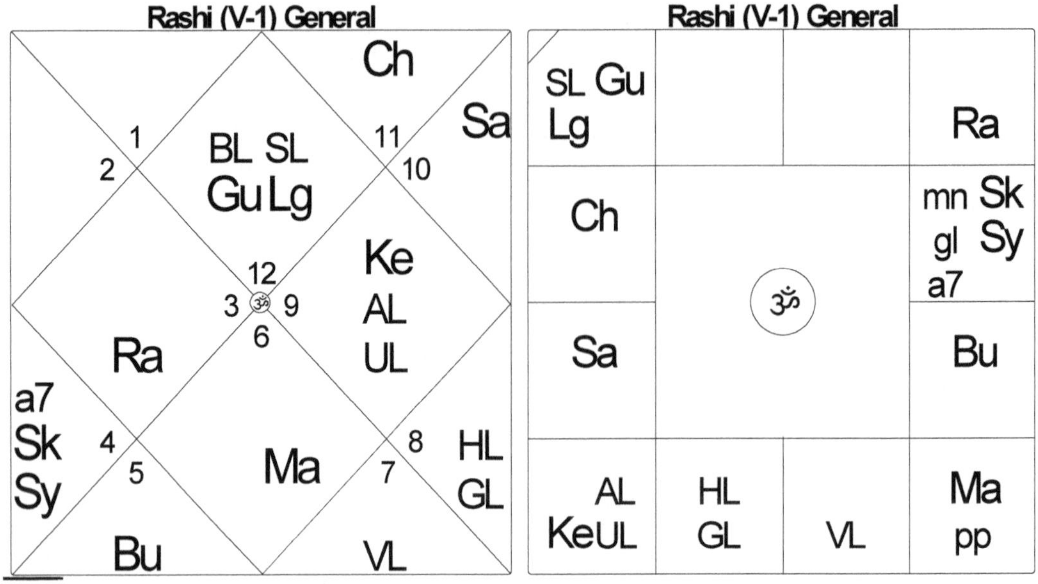

Male native born 7th August 1963, 9:15 PM, Sambalpur, India.

The native is born on Kṛṣṇa Tṛtīyā Tithi. This is a Jayā Tithi and the signs suffering Ghātak from this Tithi are Leo, Sagittarius and Aquarius. The native has Moon in Aquarius hence causing Śūnya Tithi. The native's mother was very depressed around the birth of the native, due to the recent demise of a grandmother. Furthermore, the birth also was quite complex and required the use of forceps to deliver the child. The native was born on a Wednesday, which happens to be Ghātak to the sign Cancer. Sun and Venus occupy Cancer, which has resulted in severe heart problems to the native due to Sun's position, as well as blood pressure due to Venus' association with the Moon.

As Bādhakeśa Mercury is placed in the 6th house, it promises trouble from servants, pets, enmity, etc. Since Mercury is in the Navāṁśa of Leo, this will arise in the form of large canines such as dogs, tigers, and such. As Ghātaka is formed on the basis of the Lagna, to time the Vāra when it will strike should again be seen from Lagna. From Table 10 we see that Friday is Ghātak to Pisces Lagna. However for injury to come to the body the Moon must transit the Ghātak Rāśi of the natal Moon. Natal Moon is in Aquarius and its Ghātak Rāśi is Sagittarius. It was a Friday on February 14th, 1969, whilst Moon was transiting Sagittarius, the inevitable was to occur and the native suffered a severe dog bite, resulting in hospitalization.

This proves that the knowledge of Ghātak becomes very useful in predicting the time of ghāta.

Eka Nakṣatra doṣa

Chart 34: Sister: Rohīṇi Nakṣatra

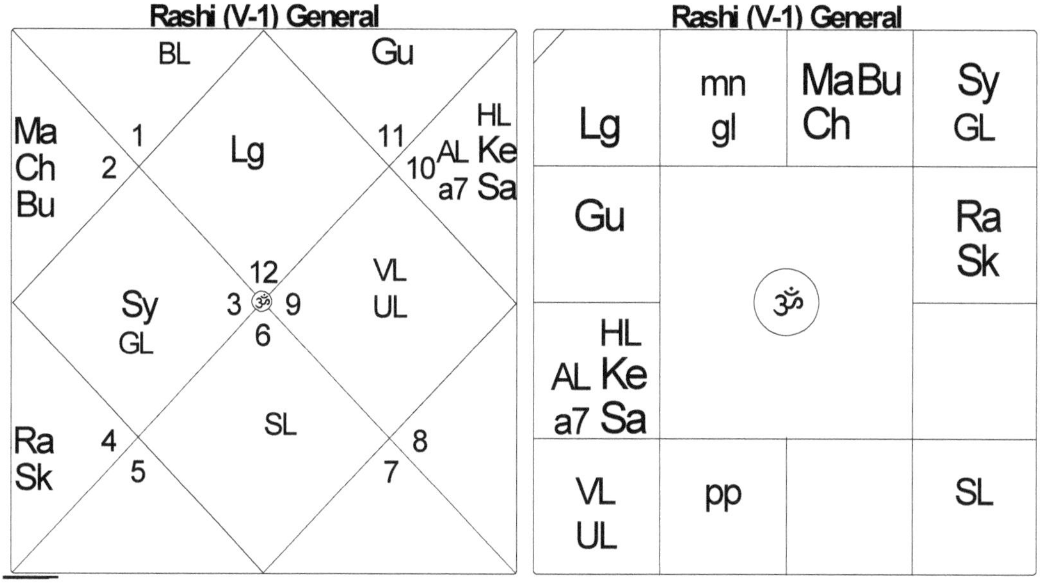

Female native born 30th June 1962, 0:13 AM, Calcutta, India.

Chart 35: Eldest brother: Rohīṇi Nakṣatra

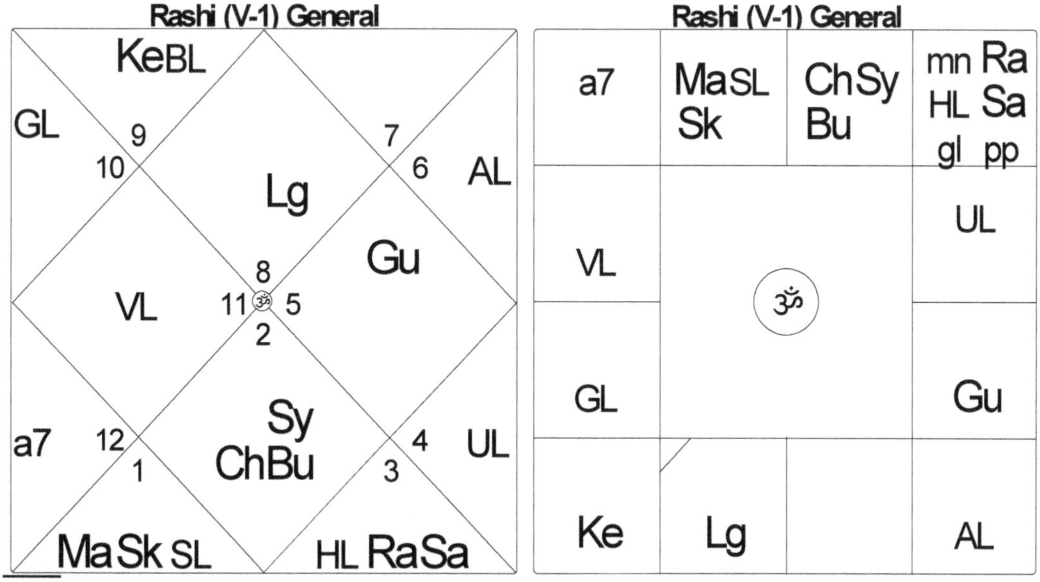

Male native born 9th June 1945, 5:20 PM, Calcutta, India.

The two natives are siblings. They both share the same Nakṣatra but not the same Nakṣatra pada. The fortunes of the younger sibling has been vastly different compared to her other siblings who are earning from well-paying jobs in the family business. The younger sibling also had some misfortune and delay in marriage, likely because the moon is in the 3rd Nakṣatra of Rohīṇi, which indicates marriage, relationships, conjugal life, etc. These misfortunes started at the time when she left home for studies. The remedy lies in worshipping the deity of the Nakṣatra. The deity of Rohīṇi is Brahmā or Prajāpati. The native performed a pujā for Prajāpati and has seen much improvement in her life, especially in her relationships. It should be noted that the suffering did not start until the two siblings lived separately. This proves that the time of separation becomes the instigator for the problems, as moon is the kāraka for the 4th house of home.

यन्मण्डलं देवगणैः सुपूजितं विप्रैः स्तुतं भावनमुक्तिकोविदम्।
तं देवदेवं प्रणमामि सूर्यं पुनातु मां तत्सवितुर्वरेण्यम्॥

2

Rāśis & Grahas

Grahas

There is already plenty of information available concerning the usage of the various planetary indications with regard to Jyotiṣa. However not much of this information originates from classical texts such as Bṛhat Parāśara Horā Śastra, nor is much of that information properly understood, such as the concept of planetary seasons, planetary times, the status of the planets, etc. In this chapter I have touched upon the philosophy and use of some of these concepts and added some very practical information on the usage of various principles, as I have learned from the tradition.

Planetary Castes

Table 30: Graha & Rāśi Varṇa

Varṇa	Graha	Rāśi
Brahmin	Jupiter and Venus	Watery
Kṣatriya	Sun and Mars	Fiery
Vaiśya	Moon and Mercury	Earthy
Śudra	Saturn	Airy
Caṇḍāla	Rāhu	-
Jātyāntara	Ketu	-

Caste is a concept that is understood in southern Asia to be hereditary and decided upon birth, however, upon reading the old texts it is apparent that caste is decided solely upon ones profession. This is quite evident in eastern India where the caste was selected by the Gaṇapati or local regent of the area, and the work decided based on ones skillset. The nature of the work was always connected to the divinity of the area where the worker had some task to fulfil for the temple and society. By performing this work the native fulfilled their role towards God and society and thus also fulfilled the role of their caste to its fullest. Similarly the signs also have castes[1].

1 The given list is as per the parampara, but it should be noted that in Jaimini's Upadeśa the airy signs have become Vaiśya and the earthy signs have become Śudra. The list given by Jaimini is given for a different purpose than seeing a person's profession.

Table 31: Overview of Varṇa

Varṇa	Occupation
Brāhmiṇ	Teachers, writers, entertainers, consultants, priests, scientists
Kṣatriya	Politicians, guards, warriors, protectors
Vaiśya	Businessmen, dealers, traders, accountants, salesmen
Śudra	Workers, servants, maintenance workers
Caṇḍāla	Those who work with the dead, border officials or other professions which require onet to be at the border of two worlds or places. Some mystics are attributed to this.
Jātyāntara	Sub-divisions of other castes

The application of the above is done by using the Varṇadā Lagna. The calculation of the same is now explaied.

Varṇadā Lagna

Some authors assume that the calculation of the Varṇadā Lagna must be performed with reference to the actual degrees of the Lagna and Horā Lagna; however no scriptures mentioning the calculation have this mentioned. While such discussions may seem cumbersome, the position of the Varṇadā Lagna in some charts may vary with or without the usage of degrees. Regardless of opinions, the following are the calculations for the Varṇadā Lagna:

1. Count the position of the Lagna or Horā Lagna. This is to be counted forward from Aries if they occupy an odd sign and backwards from Pisces if they occupy an even sign. In both cases the result should be an odd number.

2. If the Lagna and Horā Lagna both occupy odd signs or both occupy even signs add their values. If they occupy signs of different oddity then deduct their values from each other and find their difference. In either case the result should be a positive even value.

3. With the resultant value count the same number forward from Aries if the Lagna is in an odd sign, or backwards from Pisces if the Lagna is in an even sign. The result is the Varṇadā Lagna.

After having performed this exercise, if you have omitted the degrees of the Lagna and Horā Lagna, then the result should be in an even house from the Lagna.

An example is given with the following chart:
Figure 7: Paramparā Guru Śrī Acyuta Dasa

1. The Lagna is in Virgo, an even sign, hence counting from Pisces in reverse to Virgo we get the 7th sign.

   The Horā Lagna is in Taurus another even sign, hence counting from Pisces in reverse to Taurus we get the 11th sign.

2. Both Lagna and Horā Lagna are in even signs hence their results are to be

added: 7+11 is 18.

3. As Lagna is an even sign (Virgo), we must reckon this result in reverse from Pisces. The 18th sign is equal to the 6th sign (18-12=6) hence the 6th sign in reverse from Pisces must be found. This is Libra, which is the position of the Varṇadā Lagna.

Libra is a śūdra sign hence we may infer that Śrī Acyuta Dasa was given śūdra type work, i.e. service. The lord of varṇadā Lagna is Venus and is placed in a watery sign indicating that he would change to Brāhmiṇ work, and would enjoy a lot of happiness from the exaltation of the same. Venus is unconjoined hence it alone will indicate the type of Brāhmiṇ work. Among Brāhmiṇs Venus indicates consultants and advisors, i.e. like astrologers, therapists, doctors, etc., whilst Jupiter indicates teachers, singers, actors, etc.

Hence Śrī Acyuta Dasa would have been involved in a consultant related profession. He was a very renowned Jyotiṣa for the heads of Orissa.

Planetary Status

Maharṣi Parāśara and many other ancient astrologers have specified the status or role of the planets, but practitioners have implemented its usage to the application in natal charts, and that too loosely mentioned among the various kārakatva of the grahas.

Table 32: Graha and Status

Graha	Status
Sun and Moon	King and Queen
Mercury	Prince
Jupiter and Venus	Advisors and Ministers
Mars	Army General
Rāhu	Spies, Attacking force
Ketu	Defense
Saturn	Workers/Servants

The paramparā teaches, that this finds its most literal usage in mundane horoscopy for a nation or governing body, whilst its relevance in individual horoscopy, is restricted to those who deal with people in such circumstances. This can easily be applied in swearing-in charts of nations, to see whether the ruling party (Sun) will last its tenure, and what will be the experience of the tenure as well as the opposition from other parties (Mercury), and whether the other parties will take over when the tenure is over. The use of military (Mars, Rāhu and Ketu) during the tenure, the governments decisions and advise (Jupiter and Venus) will also be indicated, as well as the state and treatment of the social workers (Saturn) can hence be seen from the chart.

Similarly the cara kārakas also are important in this context.

Table 33: Chara Kāraka description

Abbr	Name and Description
AK	The King is the Ātmakāraka.
AmK	The opposition of the government is the Amātyakāraka.
BK	The policy of the nation will be seen from Bhrātṛkāraka.
MK	The home/mental peace will be seen from Mātṛkāraka.
PiK	The values of the nation, and the promises made by the government will be indicated by Pitṛkāraka.
GK	The close neighbours of the nation (family) are indicated by Jñātikāraka.
DK	The relationships/partners of the nation in business or war (ex. NATO) are indicated by Dārakāraka.

The Putrakāraka is excluded from this list, as a seven cara Kāraka scheme is required for entities which cannot produce children.

Examples

Chart 36: Swearing in of Vajpayee 1999

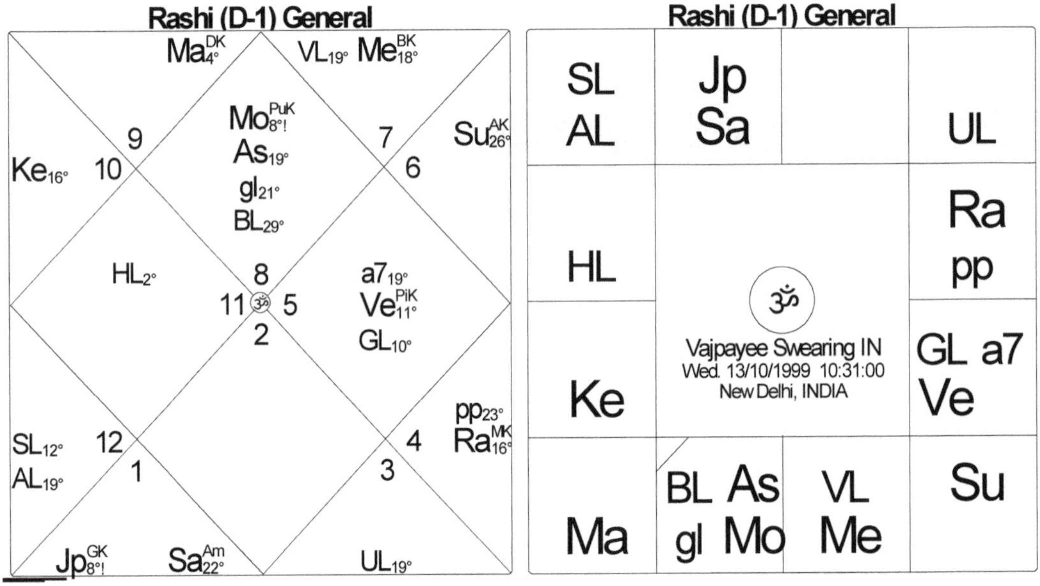

The swearing in chart of the Vajpayee Government, New Delhi, India 1999. Swearing in occurred 13th October 1999, 10:31 AM, New Delhi, India.

The Sun is in the focus being the indicator of the king in the chart, and is well placed in the 11th house. Furthermore, it is the temporary king (AK) and will surely confer long lasting power. Since the 10th lord (opposition) is also the Sun the champion of the opposition will be favoring the Sun and hence Vajpayee. *The PiK shows the promises made by the government.*

In this case, AmK Moon is 9th lord. Hence a promise regarding the establishment of dharma or building of a temple is indicated. This was the very heavily disputed Śrī Rāma temple. However Jupiter replaces this PiK hence the focus went on 2nd and 5th houses matters instead, i.e. economy and education.

Chart 37: Swearing in of George Bush 2001

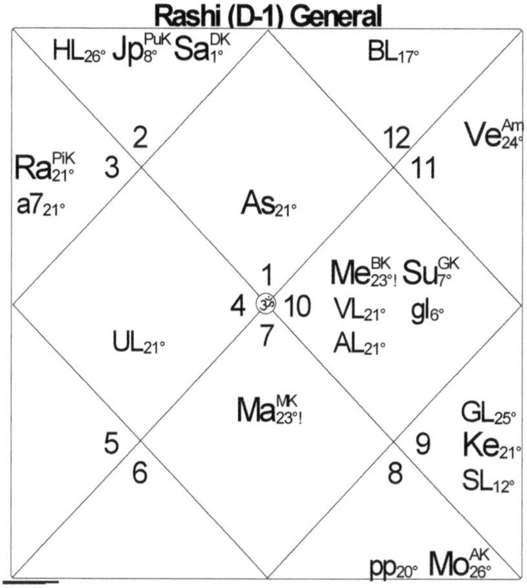

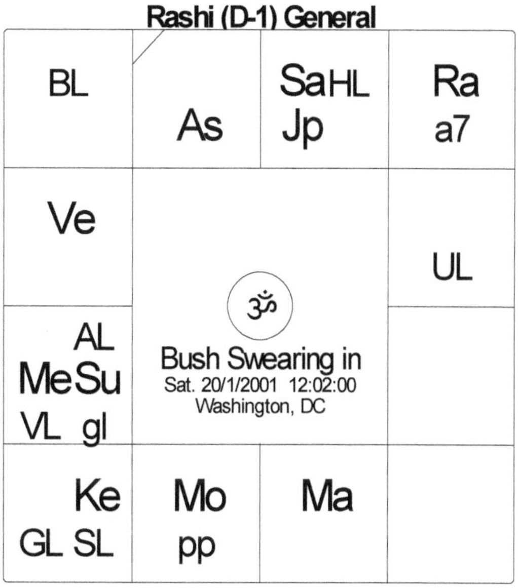

Swearing in chart of the government of George William Bush, 20th January 2001, 12:02, Washington DC.

The strong Sun ensures that the naturally expected tenure of four years will last. The Lagna lord is in maraṇa Kāraka sthāna showing that the reputation of the person under consideration will not be auspicious. Similarly see the AK Moon in maraṇa Kāraka sthāna.

Sun's position in its own Aṣṭākavarga receives bindus from all grahas except Mercury. Hence only Mercury will be able to pull down the Sun. Mercury is the competition and is the Kāraka for 10th house. *Among the cara kārakas AmK is the Kāraka for the 10th house as well and should be seen along with naisargika Amk Jupiter.* Mercury is in 10th and 10th lord Saturn is joined Jupiter in a trine. These two facts are very powerful indicators for the opposition's power, and will fight against the current government indicated by Lagna lord Mars, AK Moon and naisargika AK Sun.

The strength of these same planets can be viewed in the election time chart to see how the opposition will be able to sway/win the elections. This is especially so in Tithi Praveśa or Chaitra Pratipada charts.

Chart 38: NATO Attack on Serbia

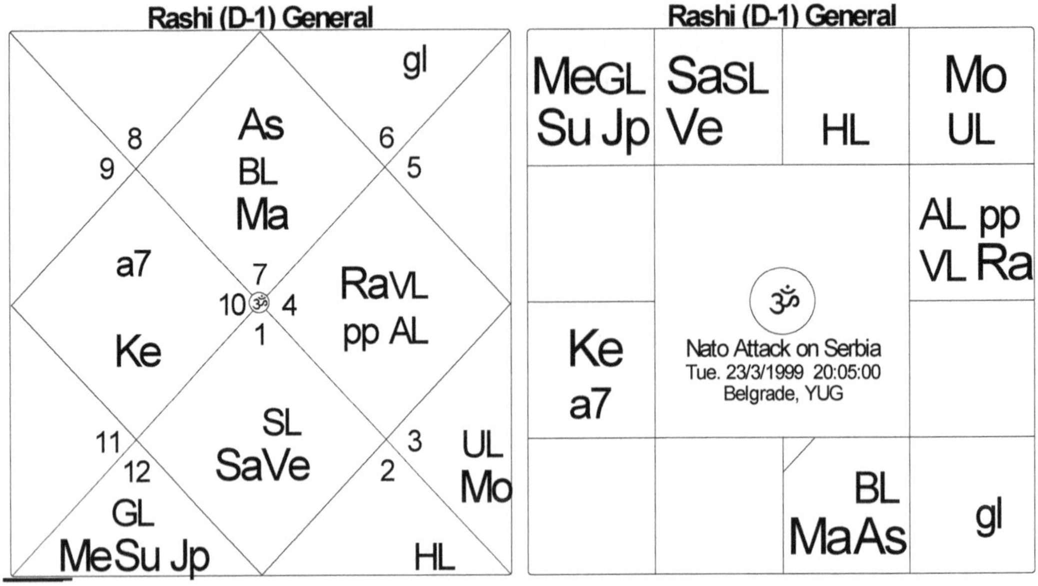

Chart of the NATO attack of the republic of Serbia and Montenegro, 23rd March 1999, 8:05 PM, Belgrade, Serbia and Montenegro. Note the two indicators of the army, Rāhu and Ketu. Lagna is the attacker and the 6th is the victim of the attack. The 7th house shows those who will defend the victim. Rāhu is in 10th and will be favouring the Lagna because it has dṛṣṭi on the 6th (victim) and the (11th) indicating the intention of Rāhu to destroy and punish the victim, which in this case is Serbia. The support of the nodes of the attacker promotes the winner to be the attacker namely NATO itself. It was an uneven battle as Serbia was being attacked by NATO and was without much support to defend them. Despite a very advanced Serbian military and support from Russia, the battle was in favour of the attacking forces with a countries inhabitants forced to expect regular bombings and raids which as in all cases rarely is without civilian casualties.

Day/Night strong planets

According to Parāśara[2] the planets which are strong in the day are the Sun and the benefics, whilst Moon and the malefics are strong during night. Parāśara indicates that Mercury is strong at both times. This can also be interpreted as Mercury is strong during the junctions between day and night.

Day Strong:	Sun, Venus and Jupiter
Night Strong:	Moon, Mars, Saturn, Rāhu, Ketu
Twilight:	Mercury

Whenever there is talk of day or Vāra, it is naturally linked with the Agni Tattva (refer Chapter 1). When the Agni of a graha is strong, that graha will not cause

2 Grahaguṇasvarūpādhyāyaḥ (chapter on grahas), śloka 36.

physical suffering.

The use of this is practical when ascertaining the actual auspiciousness of a planet/lordship. Planets who normally are able to kill or cause suffering may relent causing physical suffering if they are strong due to day/night birth. Planets can attain the ability to kill in various positions/lordship. One such position is Māraṇa Kāraka Sthāna.

Māraṇa Kāraka sthāna

Jātaka Pārijāta, by Vaidyanātha Dikṣita, mentions in the chapter on Kāla Chakra Daśā, the various inauspicious bhāvas for the eight planets, excluding Ketu. These are known as Māraṇa Kāraka Sthāna. The tradition adds that for Mercury and Ketu the fourth house placement gives effects akin to Māraṇa Kāraka Sthāna and thus is added. Some further add the second house for Ketu.

Table 34: Māraṇa Kāraka Sthāna

Graha	MKS	Remedy
Sun	12th	Nārāyaṇa
Moon	8th	Nārāyaṇa
Mars	7th	Lakṣmī
Mercury	7th	Lakṣmī
Jupiter	3rd	Rudra
Venus	6th	Nārāyaṇa
Saturn	1st	Śiva
Rāhu	9th	Guru
Ketu	4th	Gouri

A planet in Māraṇa Kāraka Sthāna can give death like suffering; however this inauspiciousness is removed if the graha is strong due to day/night birth.

Should the graha be placed in own or exalted sign then the native despite being exposed to the Māraṇa Kāraka effects will work hard to overcome them, yet the negative effects will be visible and the person will lack good judgement in the matters pertaining to the house whose lord is placed in Māraṇa Kāraka Sthāna.

The suffering of the Māraṇa Kāraka Sthāna is enhanced by malefic affliction to the sign lorded by the Graha in Māraṇa Kāraka Sthāna. I.e. should tenth lord by placed in such a position then afflictions to the tenth house itself will be the cause of suffering. If two or more malefics afflict such a sign a curse has arisen which can give terrible suffering.

The remedy in either case is to worship the Pratyadhi Devatā of the house Kāraka. I.e. for Mars in the seventh house the Kāraka Venus will give the remedy. The Pratyadhi Devatā of the same is Śrī Lakṣmī and is the remedy for the problem.

Examples

Chart 39: Ninth lord in Māraṇa Kāraka Sthāna

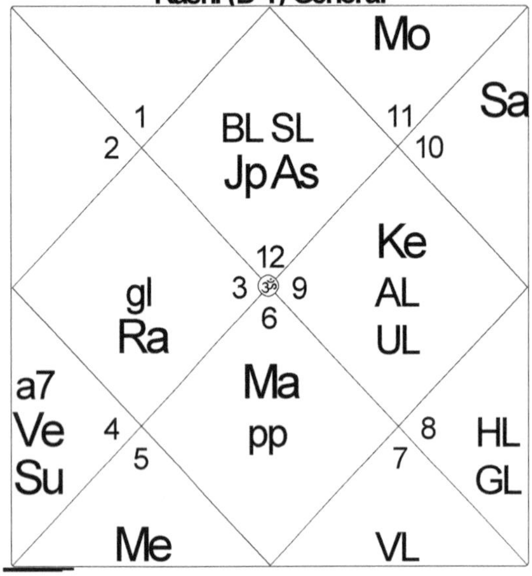

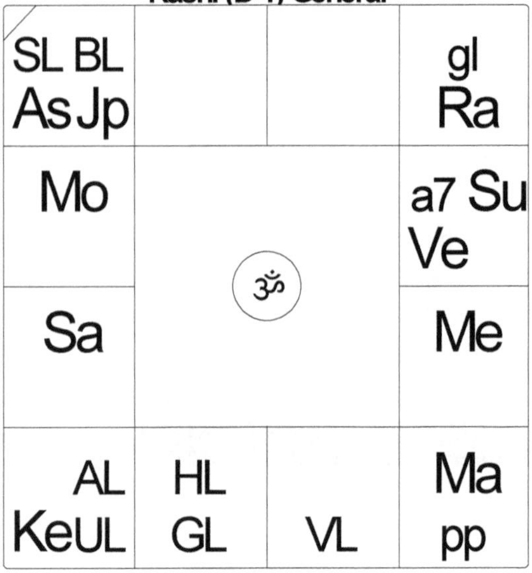

Male native born 7th August 1963, 9:15 PM, Sambalpur, India.

The native has 9th and 2nd lord Mars, in the 7th house making it Māraṇa Kāraka Sthāna. Neither Aries nor Scorpio receive the full Graha Dṛṣṭi of any malefic mitigating the suffering somewhat. This position would cause death-like suffering on account of family/finances and father/guru/elders. However the native is born during the night making Mars' life-force or Agni Tattva strong. When the time came the father implicated the native into a financial mess, which nearly brought the native into troubles with the law. The native has however averted these due to Mars' night strength.

Chart 40: William Soutar

Chart of William Soutar, born 28th April 1898, 5:15 AM, Perth, Scotland, United Kingdom.

Venus joins the Lagna in strength providing good health and upbringing. Venus lords the fourth Nakṣatra from the Moon confirming the good upbringing and schooling. He was born to a well-established joiner and thrived in his school as a sportsman and later in poetry. With Venus in Lagna and Moon in the third he was known as a leader among his peers and very popular due to Yanavanta Yoga.

Sagittarius Nārāyaṇa Daśā was undergoing when he attended Perth Academy, and with the Bāhya Rāśi in the third house with Moon his popularity in school was peaking. Sagittarius being the eight house and joined a debilitated Rāhu would present him to the battlefield and in 1917 during Scorpio Antaradaśā he would join the Navy during World War I (Saturn in seventh brings the blessings of Varuṇa).

His two year stint in the Navy was uneventful and peaceful as the Nārāyaṇa Daśā of

Cancer had begun, however Cancer is the third house occupied by the Moon which gives rise to health problems due to bad food. Mercury being the Ātmakāraka, retrograde and afflicted in the twelfth house presents a worse problem in that the body becomes unable to fully absorb all nutrients, and with its conjunction with the Sun this will affect the bones.

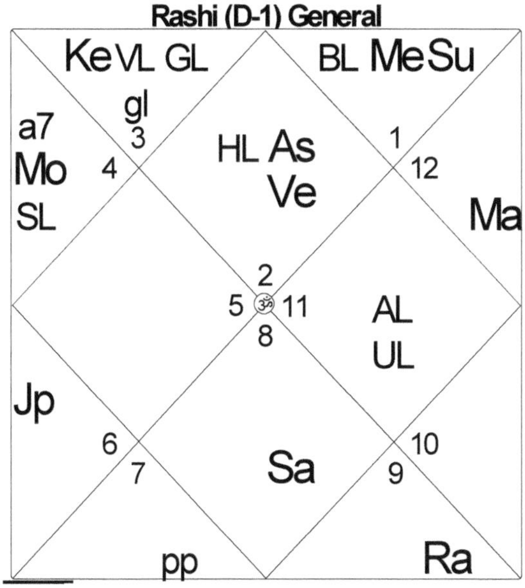

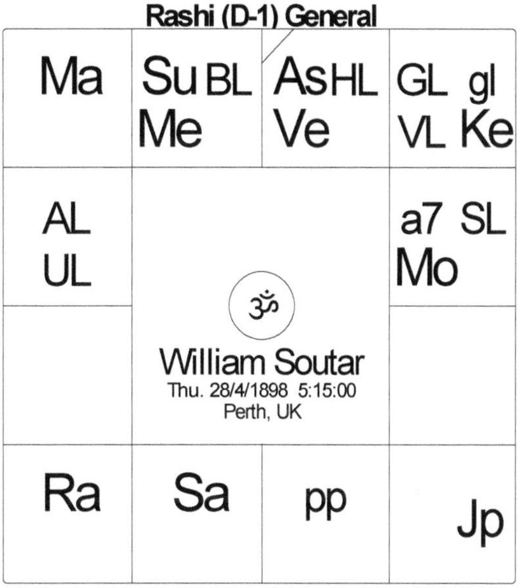

With the Sun being placed in Māraṇa Kāraka Sthāna as Leo is afflicted by Rāhu and Saturn this was to prove highly dangerous for Soutar's health. Soutar began feeling pains in his legs and feet proving painful to walk. Despite this he attended university to study English and just months prior to his graduation in he published his first volume of poetry *Gleanings of an Undergraduate* in February 1923. The Bāhya Rāśi is placed in Virgo with the well placed Jupiter as the Antaradaśā is Pisces aspecting the same.

To Soutar's disappointment the advent of Aquarius Antaradaśā brought bad news. As his pains now extended to his lower back and began to immobilise him he could not attend teacher training college. Consoling himself that he was now free to become a poet he and his parents moved into a new home with an extension built for Soutar.

1925-1934 was the Śūla Daśā of Leo with lord Sun in Māraṇa Kāraka Sthāna, and in 1930 Soutar found himself permanently confined to his bed due to the diagnosis of Ankylosing Spondylitis. The Nārāyaṇa Daśā was of Aquarius whose lord Saturn is also the ninth lord which controls movement of the legs.

During the 1930's in the Mahādaśā of Virgo he managed to produce his most well known works and a number of bairn-rhymes for children. Virgo is joined the well placed Jupiter giving fame and name for his work,

The next Aries Mahādaśā also published three of his works. Aries houses the Ātmakāraka Mercury bringing forth some of his more personal works. However,

Aries housing the cause of his disease would be the most detrimental towards his health.

Śūla Daśā of Libra was to arrive in at the age of 45 in 1943. Lord Venus despite being in own sign is in mutual aspect with the Moon causing Rudra Yoga. Three months after the advent of the Daśā he was diagnosed with Tuberculosis and five months later he left his body due to the same.

More than often the graha in Māraṇa Kāraka Sthāna has some influence on the persons cause of demise.

Chart 41: Traits

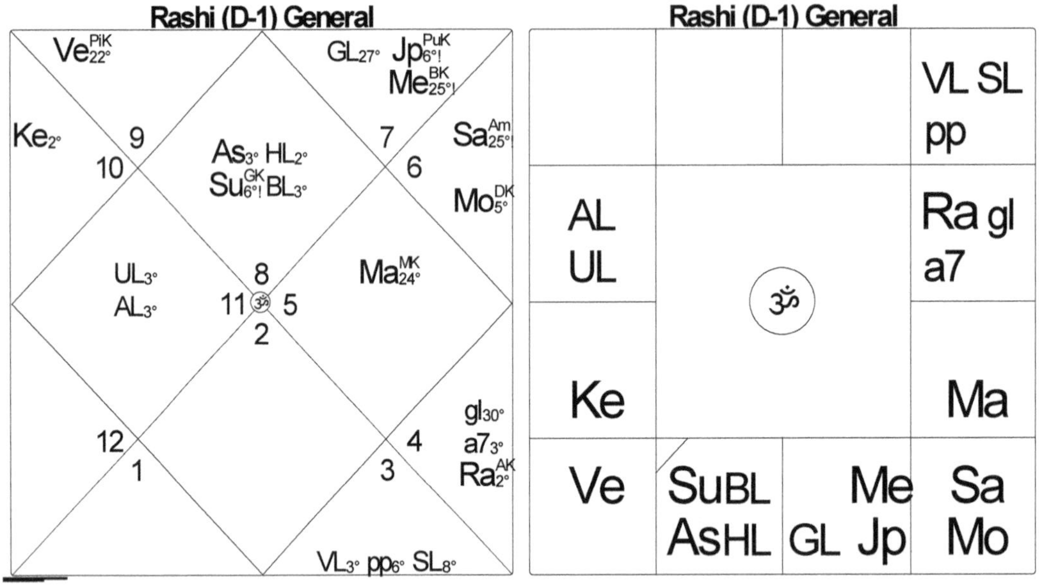

Chart of male native born 21st November 1981, 6:06:41 AM, Nairobi, Kenya.

Another method of using the day/night birth is to see the prominent traits of a person. It is often stated that Mars' position will make the native aggressive and cruel; however this will not be as prominent for those born during the night. In the given chart Mars is the Lagna lord and placed in the 10th house, however the native rarely exhibits anger and cruelty towards others.

The native is born during the twilight however the night-half of the twilight making Mars very strong. However, the Sun's placement in the Lagna is not strong due to the night birth and will bring out the negative effects of the Sun namely arrogance. This can also be used to see the stronger lordships and the 10th and 11th houses must be seen specifically in reference to career. The natives 10th house is lorded by the weak Sun who is weak; hence the native's work-output will become a problem. However the 11th lord Mercury is very strong due to the twilight birth, ensuring more gains from the work-output than expected from the natives work. In this manner the day/night birth indications can be used.

2.1.7 Periods of Planets

The sages have stated the following to be the time-periods of the planets:

While astrologers have committed the use of these time periods to praśna, its use in natal charts has not been left out by Maharṣi Parāśara[3]. Maharṣi explains that the year, month, day and Horā are stronger than each other in ascending order. The paramparā teaches that the lords of each of these should be delineated in the chart. The method of application has been given in by Kalyan Verma, who explains that the graha lording the day during the start of a year, month, etc. should be considered as the lord of that entire period, i.e. year, month etc.

Table 35: Graha timescales

Graha	Period
Moon	Muhūrta or Horā
Mars	Vāra
Venus	Pakṣa
Jupiter	Māsa
Mercury	Ṛtu
Sun	Ayana
Saturn	Samvatsara

The definition of a year and month is now required. In the study of Jyotiṣa, the definition of a year is the revolution of the Sun, as per Mantresvara's[4] advice to use solar years for Udu and other daśās. The beginning of this year hence depends on the Suns entry into any of the twelve signs, depending on the purpose of the year. The financial New Year begins from the entry of Sun into Libra, this is because Libra symbolizes the market place and business. The New Year for farming, agriculture and the workers of the society starts from the entry of Sun into Capricorn, which is known as Makara Sankrānti. Whilst many such definitions of the New Year exists, the beginning of the Zodiac is the beginning of Aries, and the day of Sun's entry into this sign should be considered as the general New Year for all mankind.

Similarly the month in which one is born, starts from the day the Sun entered the sign in which one was born. The day should be understood as starting from sunrise and ending on sunrise the next day. The lord of the year, month or day, depends on the planet which governs the day in which these incidents happened. If the Sun moved into Aries on a Monday, the Moon will govern the entire year, and the month of Aries. Those who are born during such a year/month or day should see the lords of these year/month or day in their charts to decide the results. These results are of the nature of the natural lords of the year/month/day or Horā.

- The *year* is naturally governed by Saturn, hence the lord of the year, will decide what sins and punishment one must experience in this life.
- The *month* is naturally governed by Jupiter; hence the lord of the month will indicate which blessings and fortunes one has come to experience in this life.
- The *day* is naturally governed by Mars, hence the lord of the day will indicate our strength, power, skills and vitality and how this manifests in our lives.
- The *Horā* is naturally lorded by the Moon; hence the lord of the Horā will indicate our primary focus in life, namely what our mind is constantly contemplating.

3 Grahaguṇasvarūpādhyāyaḥ (chapter on grahas) śloka 38.

4 Phala Deepika, Ekonavimsho'adhyāyaḥ (chapter 19) śloka 4.

Examples

Chart 42: Rajiv Gandhi

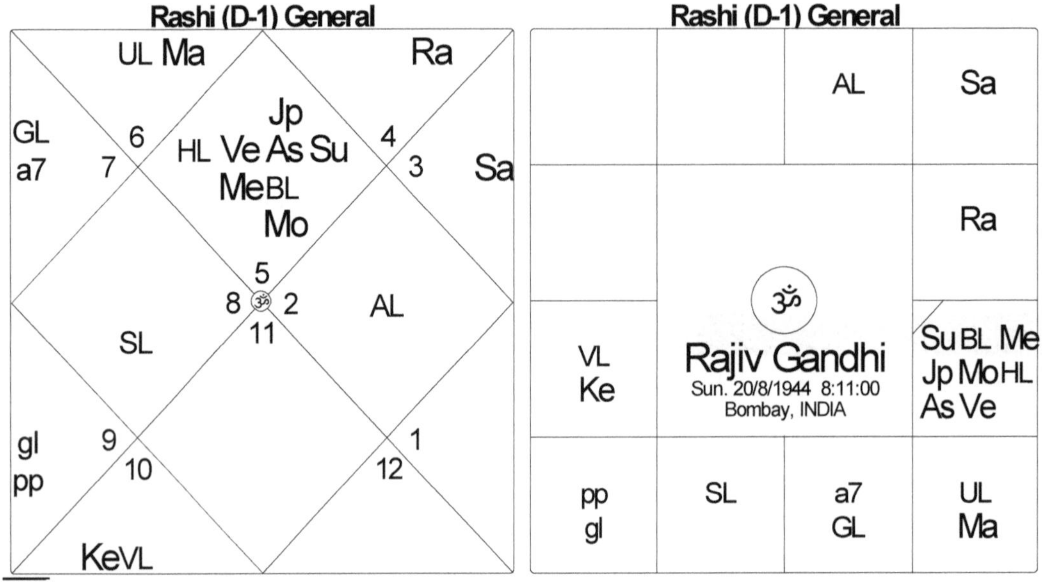

In the chart of Rajiv Gandhi, the lord of the year is Jupiter who is placed in Mahārāja yoga with Sun the Lagna lord. Rajiv Gandhi never wanted to come into power nor become the prime minister of India, hence indicating that his position as prime minister came as punishment to him through the loss of a mother, and later on as a source of his own demise. Jupiter is 8th lord indicating that the power was inherited.

Year Lord	Jupiter
Month Lord	Mercury
Day Lord	Sun
Horā Lord	Sun

The month lord is Mercury, involved in a very strong Dhana yoga with 5th lord Jupiter and Mercury itself being 11th lord. This paved the way for enormous wealth for Rajiv Gandhi, which came as a blessing to him. As Mercury is AK and 2nd lord it supports a very strong if not royal family. The day lord is the Sun well placed in the Lagna indicating good solid health and character. The Horā lord is again the Sun giving Mr. Gandhi an enormous focus on his name/fame and how people perceived him. He would be very particular about his behavior in public, and always be very respectful and righteous towards others due to this.

2.1.9 Bhāva/Graha Tithi

A method used to judge the outcome of a house or graha is through the calculation of Tithi. This Tithi calculation tells one about the amount of light shed on that bhāva/graha, and hence how great the blessing is on the bhāva/graha. A popular method is given in Phaladīpikā to find the bhāva Tithi.

1. Find the distance in longitude of the Moon from the suns position.
2. Multiply this by the number of the bhāva in question, i.e. for Lagna 1, for 5th house 5, etc.
3. Find the resultant Tithi after this calculation, and judge accordingly.

Tithi

A general way of distinguishing the Tithis is that Tithis falling in śukla pakṣa are auspicious, whilst those in kṛṣṇa pakṣa are otherwise. Of those Tithis which fall in kṛṣṇa pakṣa,

- Pratipada (1) to Śaśti (6) are delay causing
- Saptamī (7) to Daśamī (10) are compulsory for remedial measures
- Ekādaśi (11) to Amāvasyā (15) can deny results altogether.

Some Tithis are particularly inauspicious independent of pakṣa as here tabulated.

Table 36: Tithi Doṣa

Tithi	Remedy
Caturthī (4)	Śrī Gaṇeśa – Any bhāva falling under such a Tithi has its results blocked, and it becomes utmost necessary to worship Gaṇeśa to remove the blocks. Preferably one with the glaum bīja in it, i.e. om glaum gaṇeśāya namaḥ।
Caturdaśī (14)	Śrī Śiva – Any bhāva falling under a caturdaśī suffers from the anger of Śiva and remedial measures are utmost necessary.
Navamī (9)	Śrī Durgā has been angered and requires propitiation.

Incase of the three above Tithis reading of the pūrana devoted to them helps. Incase of Gaṇeśa any purānas will do as he wrote them all. The remedies for the other Tithis are as follows:

Table 37: Tithi Devata and Remedy

Tithi	Devatā	Remedy
Kṛṣṇa Pratipada	Santāna (baby) Gopāl	Mantra Japa
Kṛṣṇa Tṛtīyā	Durga/Caṇḍī	Mantra Japa
Kṛṣṇa Panchamī	Kula Devatā	Mantra Japa
Ṣaṣṭī	Śrī Subramanyā	Mantra Japa
Saptamī	Śaṇkara Nārāyaṇa	Rath Yātra
Aṣṭamī	Śrī Kṛṣṇa	Worship Bal Gopal or Janmāṣṭamī pujā
Kṛṣṇa Daśamī	Devi	Feed 1000 Brahmins
Kṛṣṇa Ekādaśī	Viṣṇu	Do pujā at pilgrimage center
Kṛṣṇa Trayodaśi	Viṣṇu and Indra	Jaya bali, Indra puja, victory pujas
Dvādaśī	Śurya	Feed Brahmins in Śrāvaṇa Month
Amāvasyā	Pitṛs/ancestors	The Pitṛ's have been angered and need propitiation. This can be through performing their last rites, i.e. srāddha.

If the pakṣa is not specified, the remedy applies to both pakṣa.

Viṣṭi Karaṇa

If the calculated Tithi falls on Viṣṭi Karaṇa, the native suffers from Viṣa or poison. It indicates Sarpa doṣa and the native will be tormented by the snakes. If this occurs in Śukla pakṣa the problem is recent and the anger would have come in this birth or a recent birth. In case of Kṛṣṇa pakṣa- this has been an error for a long time. The occurrences of Viṣṭi Karaṇa can be seen from "Table 12: Karana" on page 60.

Graha Tithi

The Tithi for the grahas hold special significance as they show the relationship and problems in the relationship with that specific person/graha/deity, i.e. the Tithi for Jupiter shows the expectations one's guru has for one. The Tithi for Mercury indicates one's approach towards knowledge and also which deity wishes to bless you with knowledge or vidyā, hence its called vidyā Tithi.

The graha Tithi is calculated by finding the distance progressed by the Moon from the graha, i.e. in case of Mangal Tithi, we would be interested in the distance traversed by the Moon from Mars' position. The Tithi calculated from Sun is the Tithi normally calculated in the horoscope and most relevant as it deals with the self.

Example of guru Tithi: Assume we want to know what expectations the guru holds for a native with Moon at 4°38′ Virgo, i.e. 5s 4° 38′ and Jupiter at 5°13′ Libra, i.e. 6s 5°13′.

Moon is 11 signs ahead of Jupiter (12th from Jupiter), hence we can form our calculation as;

Moon 11s 4° 38′
Jupiter 0 s 5° 13′

The Moon is 30° 35′ behind Jupiter. Removing multiples of 12° we get approximately 2½ Tithis remaining before the New Moon, i.e. the Tithi is the 3rd before the New Moon, or the 13th after the Full Moon – Kṛṣṇa Trayodaśi.

Chart 43: Authors Promise to his guru

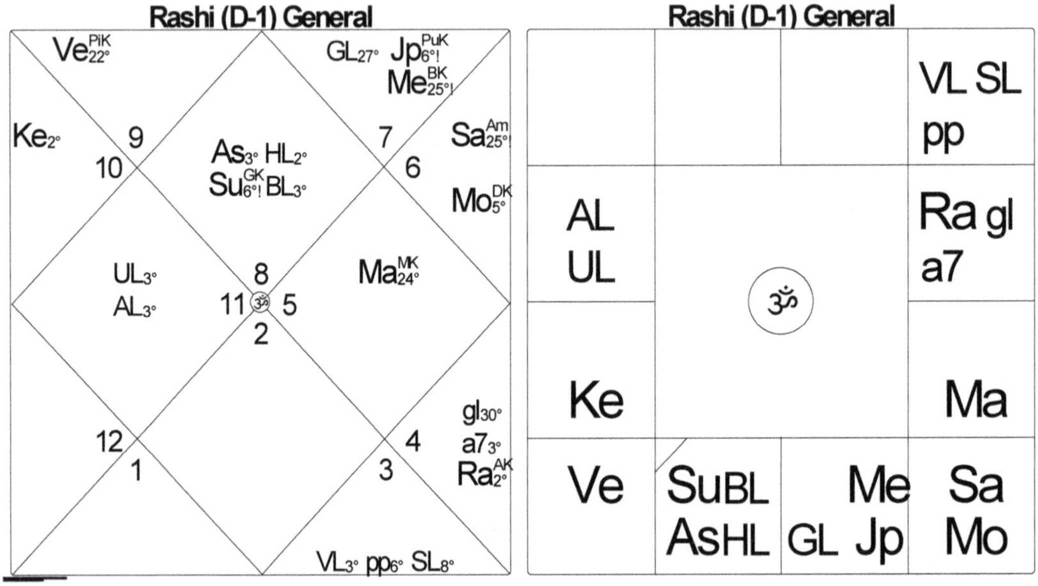

The chart of the author. Born 21st November 1981, 6:06:41 AM, Nairobi, Kenya.

The lord of Trayodaśi as per Table 2: Tithi Lords, is Jupiter. Jupiter is 5th lord, hence an important expectation from the guru is to give knowledge, or produce knowledge. Jupiter is joined Mercury who is Kāraka for students and writing. Hence the native is required to teach students and give knowledge through writing. As Mercury is 11th lord, this knowledge must comprise the nature of Jyotiṣa.

As this Tithi occurs in Kṛṣṇa pakṣa, a great deal of Pūja is required to finish such an attempt. This should be in the form of deities which give victory, i.e. Jaya Bali. Before commencing the writing of this book, the author spent time with his guru and performed austerities to ensure that he could commence and finish this book.

Upagraha

The basic understanding about the Upagraha is that they are only inauspicious. This understanding and the fact that there are 10 Upagraha tends to scare away most astrologers from the application of the Upagraha, as their calculation can become time consuming (and at times disputed) and their usage is often misunderstood by many.

Aprakāśa grahas

First it is necessary to clarify that among the upagrahas, five are known as aprakāśa grahas, and are calculated differently from the upagrahas like Gulika, etc.

The word aprakāśa means 'without effulgence' or 'without glow'. These are: Dhūma, Vyatīpāta, Pariveṣa, Indra Chāpa and Upāketu.

Their calculation is solely based on the Sun and depicts actual earth phenomena, which however is not visible but measurable. A small example arises from the calculation of Dhūma – Dhūma is exactly 133:20 degrees ahead of the Sun. If one were to draw a chart where Sun would be in the 9th house, then Dhūma would fall in the Lagna. It is this time of day which is the hottest, and when the suns rays are the most deadly. This is solely caused by Dhūma being on the Lagna.

First find the longitude of the Sun.

1. Add 4 signs (120°) and 13°20′, i.e. 133°20′ to get the position of Dhūma.
2. Deduct 360° from the longitude of Dhūma, and add the result from Aries to get the position of Vyatīpāta.
3. Add 6 signs (180°) to the position of Vyatīpāta to get the position of Pariveṣa.
4. Deduct 360° from the longitude of Pariveṣa, and add the result from Aries to get the position of Indra Chapa (also known as Indra Dhanus).
5. Add 16°40′ to Indra Chāpa to get the position of Upāketu.

Add 1 sign (30°) to the longitude of Upāketu and one should reach the longitude of the Sun again – to confirm that one has calculated correctly.

- Notably the 5 steps given above begin and end with the suns longitude.
- The calculation of Pariveṣa (step 3) is always exactly opposite Vyatīpāta.

- Calculations of Vyatīpāta (step 2) and Indra Chāpa (step 4) are interesting as their result is a mirror or image of Dhūma and Pariveṣa.

The usage of the Aprakāśa grahas has been given as follows by Pārāśara:

- □ If an Aprakāśa graha joins the lord of the Sun sign, one's lineage, i.e. children and followers, suffers.
- □ If an Aprakāśa graha joins the lord of Moon sign, one's longevity suffers.
- □ If an Aprakāśa graha joins the lord of Lagna, one's intelligence suffers, and insanity can be experienced.

Yama grahas

Table 38: Yama Graha

Graha	Upagraha
Sun	Kāla
Mars	Mṛtyu
Mercury	Ardha Prahāra
Jupiter	Yama Ghaṇṭaka
Saturn	Gulika

The five Upagraha are mentioned in standard literature. The tradition mentions seven to be the appropriate number for the seven graha and are based on time periods in a day, and are hence known as Yama grahas because they follow the sunrise and sunset of the Sun. Yama is the name of the God of death who happened to be the son of the Sungod himself. Because the portions they occupy are called Vela they are also known as Vela graha.

Eight Yama will progress between the sunrise and sunset, and Eight more will progress between the sunset and the following sunrise.

If the native is born in the daytime, then one must only calculate the Yamas progressing between sunrise and sunset. Otherwise, in case of night birth, this is done from sunset to the subsequent sunrise.

The eight Yama are lorded by the seven Grahas and Śūnya (void). These will progress in the order of weekdays, ended by Gulika. The beginning of the Yama will depend on the day of the week, i.e. on Tuesday the first Yama will be of Mars.

Table 39: Yama example

Timespan	Yama
6:40-8:10	Sun
8:10-9:40	Moon
9:40-11:10	Mars
11:10-12:40	Mercury
12:40-14:10	Jupiter
14:10-15:40	Venus
15:40-17:10	Saturn
17:10-18:40	Śūnya

Each Yama is of an equal length. The length depends on the length of day/night.

Example of Daytime birth on a Sunday, with a day-length of 12 hrs (1 Yama = 12 hrs/8=1½ hrs).

Sunrise at 6:40 and sunset at 18:40.

In the night time the Yama will commence from the fifth weekday from the one lording the day, i.e. for the above example the 5th weekday from Sunday is Thursday lorded by Jupiter, which will start the night-time Yama. This will progress in the same order of weekdays.

The Upagraha will depend on the degree of Lagna at the time it rises. The Upagraha rise at the middle of the Yama portions.

In the given example of Sunday, the Upagraha will rise at the following tabulated times:

The Parampara teaches that the names of the Upagraha, deal with their ability to overcome others, i.e. Yama Ghaṇṭaka shows the ability of Jupiter to obstruct or stop Yama from doing his work, namely causing death. Here Jupiter has taken the role as jīva or life to avoid the evil of the death and demise. Gulika indicates the ability to take on the sins and evils of other beings, i.e. drink the poison created by others. This is symbolized by Shiva as Viṣa-hara drinking the poison created from the churning of the ocean, whilst Māndi does the exact opposite and gives others the poisons we have created. In this manner the other Upagraha are to be understood.

Table 40: Upagraha example

Upagraha	Rising time
Kāla	7:25
	8:55
Mṛtyu	10:25
Ardha Prahāra	11:55
Yama Ghaṇṭaka	13:25
	14:55
Gulika	16:25
	17:55

Since Yama Ghaṇṭaka has the power to obstruct death of any bhāva, it becomes pertinent to understand when remedies for the various bhāvas should be performed, using this same Upagraha.

1. Add the degrees of Lagna and Yama Ghaṇṭaka.
2. The result should be multiplied by 1 if you want a remedy for the Lagna. 2 for the 2nd house, and so on, depending on the bhāva.
3. The result will reveal a Rāśi. When transit Jupiter has Rāśi dṛṣṭi on this bhāva, it is the best time to perform remedies for the bhāva in question.

This method reveals when the guru will bless the bhāva in question, and when the remedy will work.

There are other simpler methods, but this is quite reliable.

Examples

Chart 44: Beverly Sills

Female native born 25th May 1929, 1 AM, Brooklyn, Kings, NY, USA. The Sun is at 10°38′ Taurus.

1. Adding 4 whole signs, we reach Virgo and adding 13°20′ we reach 23°58′ Virgo for the position of Dhūma.
2. We are now asked to deduct 12 signs (360°) from Dhūma. 6°2′ is remaining of Virgo, added to the 6 signs remaining from the end of Virgo to the beginning of Aries. Hence the result is 6s6°2′. Adding this to Aries we get 6°2′ Libra revealing the position of Vyatīpāta.
3. Adding 6 signs to the position of Vyatīpāta we reach the exact opposite position of Vyatīpāta namely 6°2′ Aries which will be the position of Pariveṣa.
4. We now have to deduct the position of Pariveṣa from 12 signs (360°). 23°58′ is remaining of Aries from the position of Pariveṣa. The signs remaining from end of Aries to beginning of Aries are 11. Hence the result becomes, 11s

23°58′ which must be added to the beginning of Aries. The result is 23°58′ Pisces revealing the position of Indra Chapa.

5. Adding 16°40′ to the position of Indra Chapa, we get 10°38′ Aries. This is the position of Upāketu. To confirm our calculations add 1 sign to the position of Upāketu, i.e. 10°38′ Taurus. This is same as the Suns degree, hence we have calculated correctly.

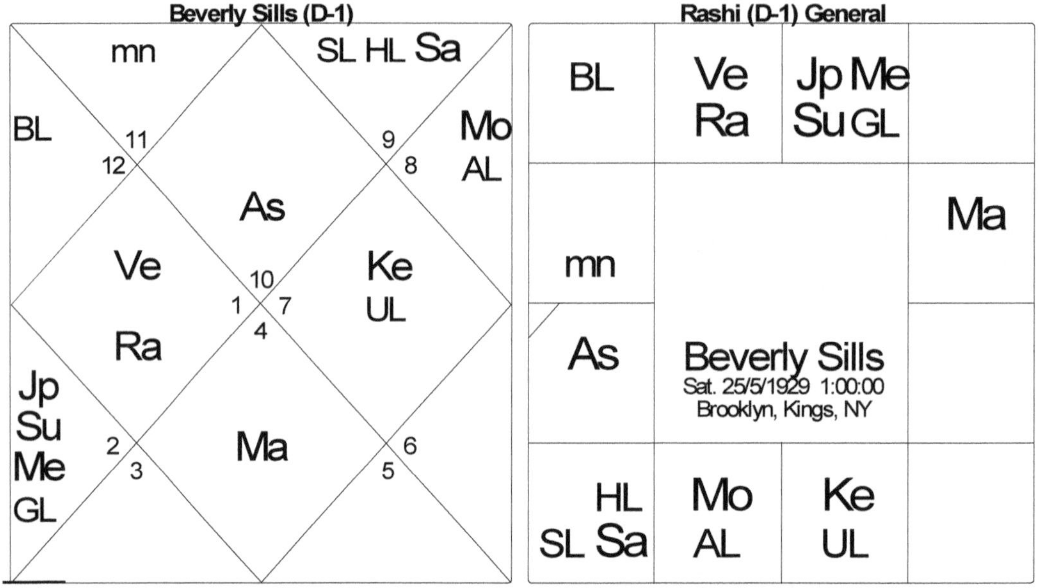

In the native's chart the Sun is in Taurus with lord Venus joined Pariveṣa and Upaketu. This in itself is enough to hurt the lineage and children. Venus is well placed in Digbala in the fourth house and gave brilliance in music and acting. Sills was a musical prodigy and through her career met her husband Peter Greenough. Upapada is lorded by Venus and houses Ketu suggesting marriage to a divorcee.

After the birth of two children, the Mahadaśā of Sun and Antaradaśā of Rāhu arose in the advent of 1962. Rāhu is joined Venus and would give the results of Venus'conjunction, herewith the effects of the Upagraha. The couples two children were diagnosed with the eldest being deaf and the youngest mentally challenged and autistic! This terrible news arose in a matter of weeks with the advent of Rāhu Antaradaśā. The couple took leave from work to dedicate to their ailing kids, yet Sills still managed to run the City-Opera as a co-director due to the blessing of yogakāraka Venus.

Chart 45: Brain Tumour
Male native born 5th October 1976, 9:27 PM, New York City, NY, USA.

Moon's dispositor is afflicted by Mṛtyu ensuring a threat to the longevity of the native. The native was met with the unfortunate news that he had a brain tumour.

Using the principles of Kalpadruma yoga, let us analyze the health of the native. Venus is Lagna lord and the dispositor of the same will indicate the health of the native. Venus is again the dispositor of Lagna lord and is placed in the 6th house with

Rāhu and Mars. Whilst the own sign-placement is beneficial towards the native giving a strong fighting ability, this same position has caused his ill health due to the placement of Rāhu and Mars with it. Mars is 2nd lord from Lagna lord – Venus, indicating that this is a chronic problem which endangers him and a change in attitude/mentality is needed to remove the problem.

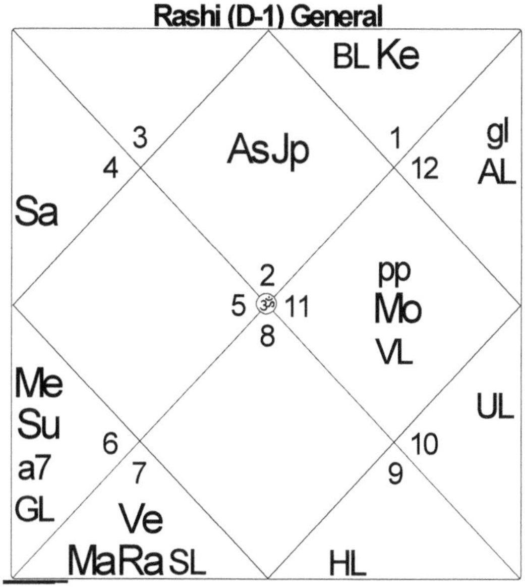

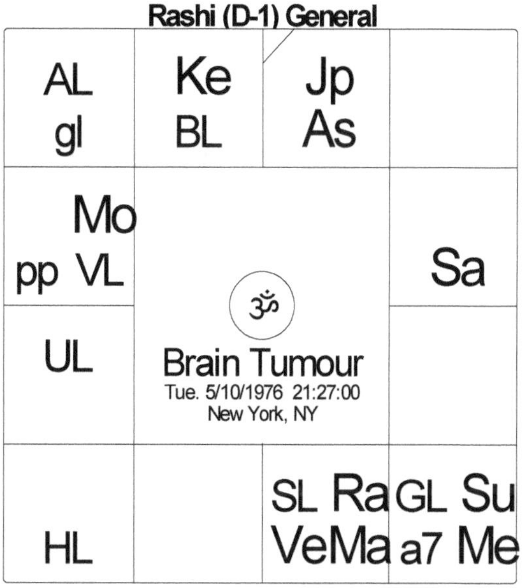

Jupiter is fortunately in Lagna, and will benefit the native, however with some delay due to Jupiter's retrogression.

Chart 46: Epilepsy

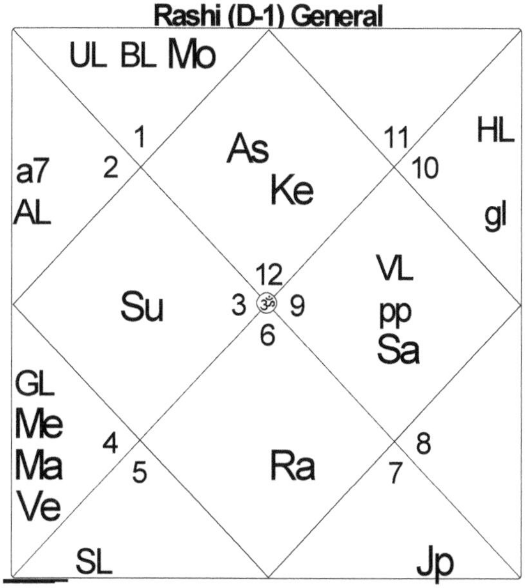

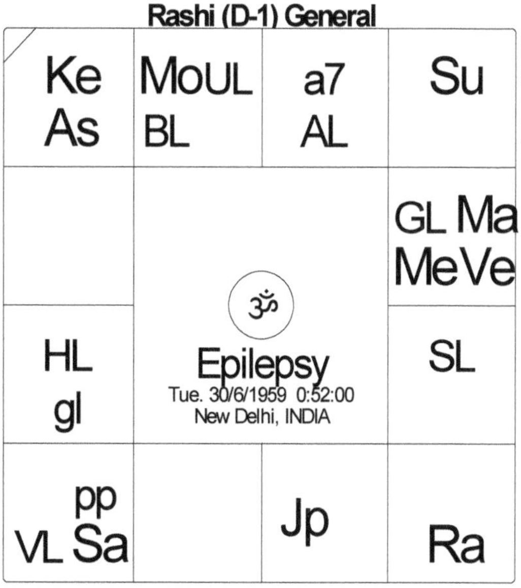

Female native born 30th June 1959, 0:52 AM, New Delhi, India. The given chart is of a native who suffered a severe case of epilepsy, to the extent that it caused mental abnormality and physical problems due to the strong medication.

The Lagna lord is joined Dhūma hence intellectual difficulty is promised.

The Moon's dispositor is unconjoined any Upagraha, but being debilitated affects the longevity of the native.

Applying the rules of Kalpadruma yoga, the dispositor of the Lagna lord is Venus, which will decide the health of the individual. Venus is joined 2nd lord Mars, indicating disease and suffering, as well as Mercury. These 3 planets associated with the 2nd from Lagna, ārūḍha Lagna and Lagna lord, leaving no room for a curing the problem. As these are in the 3rd from Ārūḍha Lagna, her ailment was the cause of her premature death.

Chart 47: Autistic child

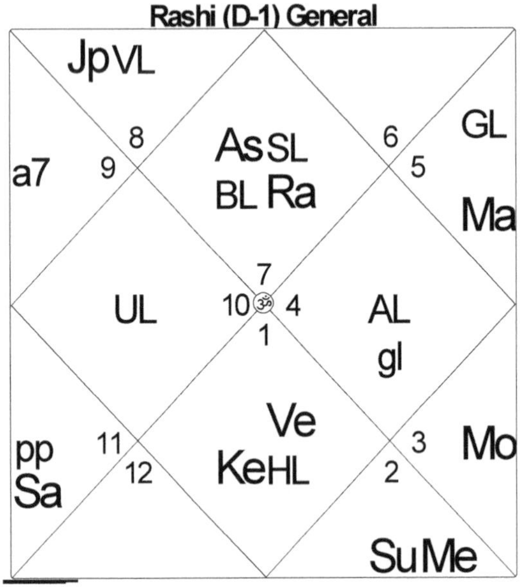

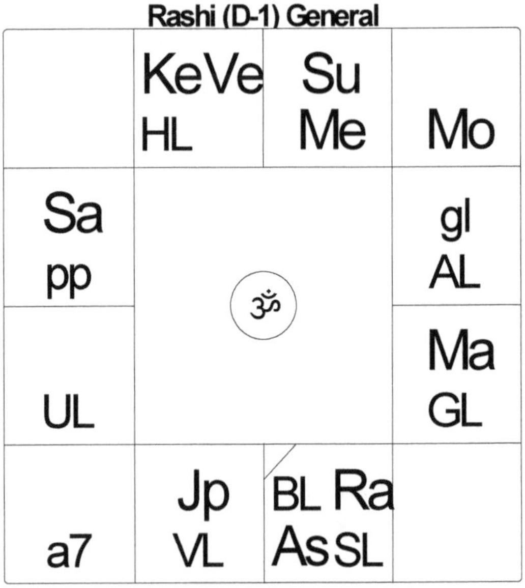

Dhūma is in Lagna creating excess heat on the head. However the real problem is Venus joined Upaketu in the seventh house indicating the ailment. 9th lord joined Bādhakeśa will certainly obstruct the remedies from working easily, hence a time should be selected for the native's family to perform remedies effectively.

The child is born during the daytime on a Thursday. Sunrise was at: 5:24:40 and sunset occurred at; 19:13:55 giving a day length of 13hrs 49 min 15 sec. The result divided by 8 gives; 01 hr 43 min 39 sec, per Yama.

As the birth is on a Thursday and we are seeking the position of Yama Ghaṇṭaka, we merely need to add ½ Yama to the sunrise time to reach the rising time of Yama Ghaṇṭaka.

5:24:40 +51:50 = 6:16:30 as the result.

At 6:16:30 AM the Lagna was at 28° 21′ Taurus, which is the position of Yama Ghaṇṭaka.

Now to find the time to perform the remedy;

1. Lagna degree is 9° 59′ Libra, i.e. 6s 9° 59′, added to the position of Yama Ghaṇṭaka which is 1s 28° 21′. The result is 8s 7° 59′ i.e. 7° 59′ Sagittarius.
2. If this is multiplied by 1 for the Lagna, we get the same result.

Hence when Jupiter is in dual signs, remedies must be performed to help the native's health and intelligence.

The Rāśis

Pārāśara Muni, whilst discussing with Maitreya, listed out the indications of all the 12 signs and how to understand them. This is an example of Pārāśara teaching Maitreya about the sign Aries;

raktavarṇo bṛhadgātraścatuṣpādrātrivikramī || 6||

pūrvavāsī nṛpajñātiḥ śailacārī rajoguṇī |

pṛṣṭhodayī pāvakī ca meṣaRāśiḥ kujādhipaḥ || 7||

"The sign Aries has a blood-red complexion, has a large and bulky body, is a quadruped sign (4-legged), and excerts its strength in the night. Aries resides in the east, is acquanted with royalty and wanders in hills. It has a predominance of Raja guṇa. It rises with its back, is the son of agni and is lorded by the planet Mars."

Pārāśara Muni has given the description of Aries very freely, listing out all the various indications of the sign Aries in the following order; complexion, body-type, number of feet, time of activity, direction of residence, acquaintance, place of pastimes, guṇa, rising, lineage, planetary lordship. At times the symbol, length, distance and other traits are listed when we read subsequent ślokas. These effects which apply for all the signs have been tabulated in the following paragraphs.

Masculine and feminine signs

The sign is either positive "masculine", or negative "feminine". The odd numbered signs (as reckoned from Aries) are the Male or Odd signs while the even numbered signs are Female or Even signs.

- The Odd signs, viz. Aries, Gemini, Leo, Libra, Sagittarius, and Aquarius are masculine signs.
- The Even signs, viz. Taurus, Cancer, Virgo, Scorpio, Capricorn, and Pisces are feminine signs.

Day/Night signs

Among the 12 signs, half are strong during the day time and the other half are strong in the night time. This knowledge is used for various purposes especially in Prasna[5]. In a natal chart, this can also be used to see the strength of the persons daily cycle.

5 Question chart, also known as Horary Chart.

Planets[6] which are strong during day time and placed in the day-strong signs become strong for activities done during the day. In Lost Horoscopy, where the birth time is lost, this knowledge can be used in Praśna to help determine when the person was born. In this manor there are several uses of the Day/Night principle of the signs.

Rising of signs

Figure 8: Day/Night Chakra

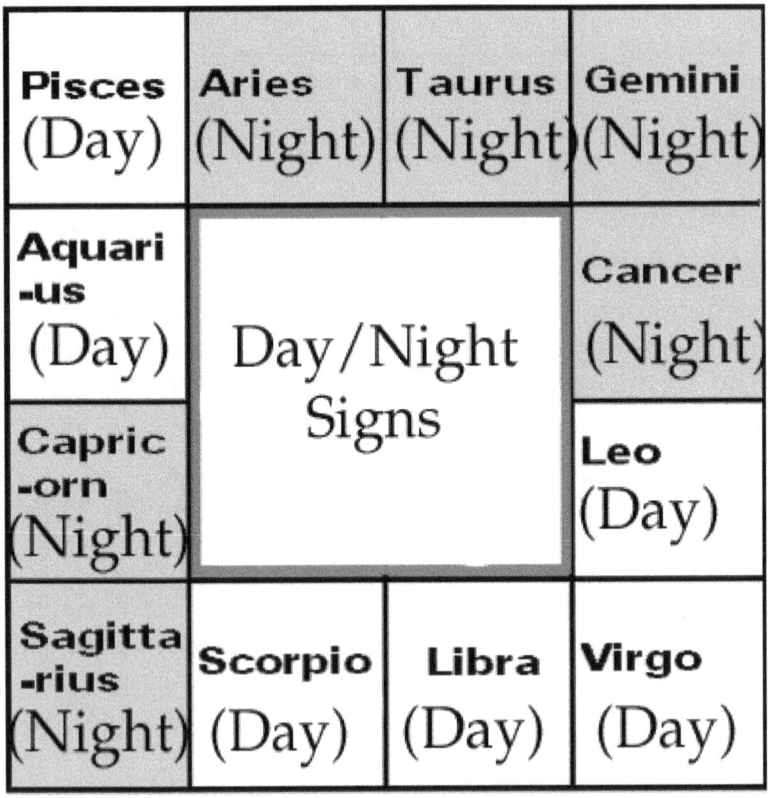

All signs rise with a specific portion of their body. Rising can occur with the (i) head first, (ii) back first or (iii) both head and back. This is useful in many instances. An example would be to determine whether the birth of a child happened with their feet first or their head first. This is also used to see the effects of planetary periods in life, i.e. when will the sign/planet give the various effects of its nature, placement, etc.

Table 41: Udaya

Head rising (śīrṣodaya)	Leo, Virgo, Libra, Scorpio and Gemini
Back rising (pṛṣṭhodaya)	Aries, Taurus, Cancer, Sagittarius and Capricorn, Aquarius
Both Rising (ubhayodaya)	Pisces

6 Refer to the Lesson on Planets/Grahas.

Figure 9: Udāya Chakra

Pisces (both)	**Aries** (back)	**Taurus** (back)	**Gemini** (head)
Aquari-us (back)	Udaya (Rising)		**Cancer** (back)
Capric-orn (back)			**Leo** (head)
Sagitta-rius (back)	**Scorpio** (head)	**Libra** (head)	**Virgo** (head)

The quadrants and the three guṇa's

Mobility: Each sign is movable (**chara**), fixed (**sthira**) or dual (**dvisvabhāva**). Thus every fourth sign reckoned from Aries is movable, every fourth reckoned from Taurus is fixed and every fourth reckoned from Gemini is dual in nature.

This similarity of every fourth counting is called the quadruplicity of the sign. The movable signs have excessive energy and are capable of easy movement showing the predominance of **rajas guṇa**.

The fixed signs have low energy and have an inability to move thereby showing a predominance of **tamas guṇa**.

The dual signs are a balance between the excessive mobility of the movable signs and the immobility of the fixed signs thereby showing a predominance of **sattva guṇa**. *Guṇa is the inner attribute of the sign and this inner nature of the sign manifests externally in different ways, mobility being one of them.*

Table 42: Guṇa and signs

Rāśi	Mobility	Guṇa
Aries, Cancer, Libra and Capricorn	Movable	Rajas
Taurus, Leo, Scorpio and Aquarius	Fixed	Tamas
Gemini, Virgo, Sagittarius and Pisces	Dual	Sattva

Directions and distances of the signs

In Jyotiṣa it's important to know in which direction events will happen, and how far away they will occur.

The signs are divided into the 4 main directions indicated by the trines to each of the movable signs.

Table 43: Direction of signs

Rāśi	Direction
Aries, Leo and Sagittarius	East
Taurus, Virgo and Capricorn	South
Gemini, Libra and Aquarius	West
Cancer, Scorpio and Pisces	North

The distances are of 3 types – Far/overseas, between travel and close to one's residence. These are based on the sign being movable, dual or fixed respectively.

Table 44: Distance and signs

Rāśi	Distance
Movable signs (Aries, Cancer, Libra and Capricorn)	Far/overseas
Dual signs (Pisces, Gemini, Virgo and Sagittarius)	Between travel
Fixed signs (Aquarius, Taurus, Leo and Scorpio)	Close to one's residence

One use of this information arises when we look at the sign containing the 10th lord to see whether one will travel far to get their job or whether it will be near the home. Similarly; we can also predict how far away one will meet their marriage partner, reunion with family, friends, etc.

The trines and the five elements (Tattva)

Each sign belongs to one of the triplicity of fire, air, earth and water (Refer Tattva below). *Triplicity* means triplicate or *three of a kind* and there are three signs of each of the four types of elemental forms. The ancients called these the fire triplicity (Aries, Leo and Sagittarius), because there are three zodiac signs for each element. We will stick to this terminology instead of using the more refined term 'energy'. Since these signs are similar, this triplicity, trine or **trikoṇa** represents harmony or similarity of nature/ interest. These signs are 120^0apart.

Table 45: Tattva and signs

Tattva	Rāśi
Fire (Agni)	Aries, Leo and Sagittarius
Water (Jala)	Pisces, Cancer and Scorpio
Air (Vāyu)	Aquarius, Gemini and Libra
Earth (Pṛthvī)	Capricorn, Taurus and Virgo
Ether (Ākāśa)	all signs

Notably the Ākāśa Tattva is in all signs, binding the other signs together. Also note that all Fiery and airy signs are odd, whilst all watery and earthy are even signs. This adds to our understanding of the Tattva of the signs.

Essentially the main cause of suffering on the account of others is caused by the bad relationship between the Tattva or lack of Ākāśa Tattva in the relationships. Hence the problems most people suffer from when it comes to relationships is due to the mismatch of the 4 Tattva, be it in marriage, between friends, students and teacher, etc.

Its use is of a very spiritual level, what some call the 'third level' of Jyotiṣa, where the independent use of the Kārakāmśa to time events in a native's life, finds its place.

These 4 trines are also linked to the 4 Yugas of time as follows;

Table 46: Yuga and signs

Tattva	Yuga
Fire (Aries, Leo and Sagittarius)	Kṛta (Satya)
Water (Pisces, Cancer and Scorpio)	Tṛta
Air (Aquarius, Gemini and Libra)	Dwapara
Earth (Capricorn, Taurus and Virgo)	Kali

The knowledge of the Yuga's helps one to decide the overall auspicious/inauspicious results of a sign placement. A planet in a Kali Yuga sign (especially Capricorn) will give results with difficulty. Planets in Satya Yuga signs will give results with ease.

Physical embodiment of the signs

The physical embodiment of a sign helps us tell how the native looks/appearances are. It also helps us determine the size of objects which are a part of our everyday life.

Following are the facial and bodily characteristics of the signs. It should be kept in mind that the planets position in a sign moderates the appearance of the sign. For example, if Saturn is in Leo in the Lagna, then the person will have primary saturnian traits. This will be modified through the sign of Leo, as a person with Saturn in Cancer will have a different appearance than one with Saturn in Leo.

Table 47: Bodily features and signs

Rāśi	Body	Features
Aries	Prominent limbs	Triangular face, dark and thick eyebrows and long neck
Taurus	Full limbs	Full face, small eyes, short thick neck, wide nostrils and mouth
Gemini	Even body	Dark hair, hazel and bright eyes
Cancer	Round/Bulky body	Round face, delicate features, small or flat nose and eyes
Leo	Large	Full body, broad, well set shoulders and an oval face
Virgo	Medium	Slender, neat and prim and a long nose
Libra	Medium	Large eyes, large hips, smooth hair, round and sweet face
Scorpio	Slender/lean and hair	Broad face, dark and curly hair with small dark eyes
Sagittarius	Even body	Oval face, high forehead, prominent nose and clear eyes
Capricorn	Large	Thin face, long chin, thin neck, dark hair and weak knees
Aquarius	Medium	Long face and hazel eyes
Pisces	Medium	Round shoulders, large face, sleepy or fish like eyes

Each sign also has a complexion and colour[7], as well as an average length. The complexions are based on the planets lording the sign, whilst the colours are based on the signs themselves.

The length of a sign is used to determine the size of objects and the length of a native's limbs (proportionate to their body). Some believe that the length of signs are used to determine the height of a person.

Table 48: Sign colour, complextion and lengths

Rāśi	Colours	Complexion	Length
Aries	Blood red	Reddish	Short
Taurus	White	Dark	Short
Gemini	Parrot Green	Dark	Medium
Cancer	Reddish white	Fair	Medium
Leo	Yellow white	Reddish	Long
Virgo	Grey	Dark	Long
Libra	Black	Dark	Long
Scorpio	Yellow	Reddish	Long
Sagittarius	Golden	Fair	Medium
Capricorn	Variegated	Bluish	Medium
Aquarius	Blue/Violet	Bluish	Short
Pisces	Fish Color	Fair	Short

7 The colors are used to see the colour of objects (horary queries Prasna), however the complexion of a sign is determined by the complexion of the planet lording it, or placed in it. In the table the complexion is given as per the Graha lording it.

यन्मण्डलं ज्ञानघनं त्वगम्यं त्रैलोक्यपूज्यं त्रिगुणात्मरूपम्।
समस्ततेजोमयदिव्यरूपं पुनातु मां तत्सवितुर्वरेण्यम्॥ ३॥

3

Bhāva
The houses

3.1 Bhāva Indications

The Bhāvas hold the key to the divination of the chart. The 12 signs being the embodiment of God with his various limbs, find a similar disposition for the particular individual. In a sense we become droplets of the Supreme Being. The 12 Bhāvas begin from the Lagna or ascendant, which is the sign and degree in which the sunlight intercepts with the ecliptic at that particular time. Each sign following the Lagna is allotted to a house. For those familiar with Western Astrology, this is known as a 'whole-sign' house system. However there are other methods to calculate the houses, as popularized by Western Astrologers and sanctioned by Pārāśara Muni.

There are three main approaches to distribute the Bhāvas: the first treats the entire sign as a bhāva and is known as Rāśi Chakra. Another method depends on the exact degree of Lagna, from which the distribution of houses is 15 degrees before and after the Lagna degree (known as Bhāva chakra). The third method(s) depends on the exact point of midday (known as the midheaven) after which the space/time between the sunrise and midday is equally distributed between the houses to ascertain the Bhāva spans – this is seen in the distribution methods of Śripati, Placidus, Porphyry, Koch and others. The latter is known as Bhāva Chalit Chakra. The latter two techniques are not wrong, but require a different application of principles to understand the chart, as they find their basis within boundaries which are breaking that of the physically created universe, namely the signs.

These various distribution techniques are beyond the purview of this book, yet some refined principles to understand the Bhāvas are here bye given.

3.2 Bhāvat Bhavam

Bhāvat Bhavam is a principle through which one can see the manifestation of houses results. For Example, death is seen from the eighth house and the circumstances of death are seen from the eighth from the eighth house, i.e. the third house. This is why the third house from the Ārūḍha Lagna is seen for death, as per Jaimini. This similarly works with other Bhāvas i.e. the sixth from the sixth is the eleventh house and Jaimini calls these the Daṇḍa and Hara Bhāvas, i.e. where the punishment and the cause of death himself (Rudra) sits respectively. The tenth from the tenth is the seventh house, and hence one's relationships with others tell a lot about the success of one's karma yoga. In this manner, the principle of Bhāvat Bhavam should be understood.

3.3 Reckoning relatives from the Bhāva

The twelve Bhāvas show different areas of life, each comprising various issues as for example the exclusive use for determining family related affairs. In this scheme the concept of studying 'Bhāvas from the bhāva' or treating a house as the focal point and reckoning the houses from this house, is understood and interpreted.

This is best understood through an example. The Lagna is the self and hence the father of the self is seen from the ninth from the Lagna. The father of the father is therefore seen from the fifth house, which is the ninth from the ninth i.e. in this way we can also see the fathers' mother in the twelve house, which is the fourth from the ninth house. For the mother this reckoning starts from the fourth house. The mother's father is seen from the twelve house, which is ninth from the fourth house. The mothers' mother is seen from the seventh house, which is the fourth from the fourth house. Maternal Uncle is seen from the third from the fourth house, namely the sixth house from the Lagna. In this manner, one can reckon one's relations in the horoscope.

Some may wonder why the houses of mother (fourth) and father (ninth) are not opposite to each other, making them each other's spouses. The reason arises from the role the parent has towards the self/native. The mother is responsible for carrying the child and nurturing the child, whilst the father is responsible for guiding and protecting the child. It is only during the act of intercourse (leading to the conception of the native) between the father and mother that the houses change.

3.4 Bhāva Classification

The following steps will explain how to use the Bhāvas, by dividing them into various groups, and what the purpose of those groups are i.e. kendras, trikoṇas, dusthānas, etc.

3.2.1 The Four Trines

Having covered the principle of opposites, it now becomes necessary to understand the trines. The trikoṇa or trines are the houses placed in fifth and ninth houses from any particular house/sign. These houses share the same ideals as that of the particular sign they are in trines to. With reference to the Lagna, the fifth and ninth houses from it become the dharma trikoṇa. Similarly, the trines to each of the four houses viz. 1st, 10th, 7^{th,} and 4th are known as the dharma, artha, kāma and mokṣa trikoṇa.

Table 49: Trikoṇa bhāva

Houses	Trikoṇa/Trine Name
1st, 5th and 9th	dharma (goal, duty, nature)
10th, 2nd and 6th	artha (wealth, sustenance, profession)
7th, 11th and 3rd	kāma (desires)
4th, 8th and 12th	mokṣa (liberation)

Planets or signs in the dharma trikoṇa will show grahas who share the same ideals as the native, i.e. the ninth house shows the father, teachers, guides and elders, which all have the purpose or ideal of protecting and guiding the native's interest. Similarly, the fifth house shows one's followers and children whom one protects. Whether these people will also protect one's ideals, needs to be understood from the concept of sambandha, which means relationships.

Additionally both the fifth and ninth houses also have to do with the worship the native does, hence planets in the fifth or ninth houses will indicate worships or prayers that the native performs consciously or unconsciously for the realization of his aspirations.

3.2.2 The Three Quadrants

Just as the signs in quadrant to each other have a similar dignity as being movable, fixed and dual, the houses in quadrants to each other also have a similar dignity depending on the Lagna rising in the chart.

Table 50: Kendra bhāva

Houses	Quadrant Name
1st, 4th, 7th and 10th	Kendra
5th, 8th, 11th and 2nd	Paṇaphara
9th, 12th, 3rd and 6th	Apoklimā

Example: **Cancer Lagna**

Kendra: Cancer, Libra, Capricorn and Aries

Paṇaphara: Scorpio, Aquarius, Taurus and Leo

Apoklimā: Pisces, Gemini, Virgo and Sagittarius

The basis of these three quadrants arises from the understanding of the trines. From the Lagna, find the first, fifth and ninth houses. The quadrants to these houses become the Kendra (first), Paṇaphara (fifth), and Apoklimā (ninth) respectively.

These quadrants are the four pillars to the three trines and become necessary in judging the indications of a chart i.e. the 4th house from the ninth is the twelfth house and shows the happiness one achieves from fulfilling our dharma (ninth), namely good sleep and liberation from the world. Similarly the fourth house from the first shows how fulfilling our personal ideals, gives us happiness and stable mind.

Specifically the quadrants to the Lagna will indicate which type of personality we take on. The tenth house indicates the personality we take on due to our work and karma yoga. This house has the strongest influence on our personality. The seventh house indicating the influence of our spouse on our nature, then the fourth house, showing how our childhood experiences mould our nature, and lastly the Lagna itself showing our own innate nature, follow this. The strongest planets in quadrants to the Lagna will indicate our personality and nature, as well as our aspirations in life.

3.2.3 Dusthāna: Houses of Suffering

Among the twelve houses, there are three, which cause suffering to the native, due to the effects of past births. Maharṣi Parāśara calls these houses Duḥ houses; the present nomenclature knows them as Duḥ – sthāna or dusthāna.

These houses are:

- Sixth (sins/weaknesses, strife, punishment, enmity, fights, arguments, battles)
- Eighth (evil karma, past life mistakes/wrong doings, death, shock, sorrow)
- Twelfth (loss, theft, secret enemies, expenses)

The sixth and eighth houses both become important when diseases are concerned, among which the sixth shows diseases arising from own weaknesses, while the eighth shows the long term diseases and trials arising from the wrong doings in the past births.

The twelfth house indicates losses needed to release one from one's past debts, which could be forced away from the native, provided the native is not prepared to give. The people who cause this loss act as secret enemies or thieves. From the positive angle, the twelfth house can give good expenses to charitable organizations and similar causes.

3.2.4. Upachaya: Houses of Growth

Among the twelve houses, four houses are called upachaya. Upachaya means accumulation, quantity, elevation, increase, growth, etc. These houses have the special ability to help one's growth, and make one fulfill one's objectives in life.

The upachaya houses are:

- Third (action/initiative, weapons, enemies action, copulation, actions needed for growth)
- Sixth (sins, strife, punishment and hard work)
- Tenth (profession, social activity, karma yoga)
- Eleventh (fulfillment of desires and gains, fruits)

The houses, which are not upachaya, are called anupachaya.

The basis of the upachaya houses becomes clear if we treat Aries as Lagna, and depict the natural zodiac. The third and sixth houses from Aries become Gemini and Virgo respectively, which are both lorded by Mercury. Mercury signifies communication, learning, relations with one's friends and kin, and one's ability to smile/joke/laugh, it is the student among the grahas and is eager to learn. These traits of Mercury become very important for one's growth. If Mercury becomes negative, one will not be able to adapt to social groups, new knowledge, work, etc which cause a negative impact in one's growth. Having expressed such negative traits in one's previous lives, we experience the results in this life through enmity, strife, punishment, diseases and such negative 3rd/6th house indications.

Similarly, the tenth and eleventh become Capricorn and Aquarius respectively, which are both lorded by Saturn. Here Saturn decides our karma yoga and from whom we shall reap the fruits of the same. This is decided based on how much good karma (tenth) we did in the past as well as how much we took/reaped (eleventh) from the world in the past lives.

The negative aspect arising from the upachaya houses, is that with one's own growth and success, another's growth will be hampered/destroyed. This is especially so with the 3rd, 6th and 11th houses known as the triṣaḍāya houses, as in the natural zodiac, these are the exaltation, mūlatrikoṇa and own signs of Rāhu (Gemini, Virgo and Aquarius respectively).

3.2.5 Māraka: Killers

Two houses attain the special ability to take us away from this abode, i.e. kill us. These are:

Second (food, sustenance, or lack of the same)

Seventh (the time for rebirth)

The second house causes one's sustenance to disappear in the body, thereby bringing closer the time of demise. Similarly, the second from any house rules the sustenance of that house, and can make or break the house depending on whether it is auspicious or not, i.e. the eighth house is the second from the seventh house, and hence can indicate the end of marriage if malefics are there, while benefics will protect the marriage.

The seventh house is the house of rebirth, and desires, and when its time comes, death is possible as for rebirth to happen, one must leave one's body. Hence, the seventh house can also cause death.

3.2.6 Caturāśraya: Houses of Protection

The fifth house from any house is its shelter or āśraya i.e. the fifth house from Lagna shows the shelter of the native, and indicates the children or followers who will take on and continue the native's goals and ideals in life.

As the fourth house shows one's home, the shelter of the same becomes very important. The shelter of the fourth house is the eighth, being the fifth from the fourth. Hence, the fourth and eighth houses become caturāśraya in the chart.

Table 51: Chaturāśraya bhāva

Houses	Name
Fourth and eighth	caturāśraya

This is why Jātaka Bharaṇam states that the Sun's placement in the eighth house in Sagittarius can give landed property. This will make Taurus the Lagna and Sun the fourth lord in a Jupitarian sign. However, this is so, if Jupiter is well placed from the Lagna lord Venus, otherwise it will not act as a caturāśraya, and instead act as a dusthāna.

An important principle is derived from this statement. The sixth house is both a dusthāna and an upachaya. It will work as an upachaya if the sixth lord is friendly towards the Lagna lord, otherwise it will prove to be a dusthāna lord. Similarly, the eighth lord will act as a dusthāna lord unless it is friendly towards the Lagna lord.

3.2.7 The Second and Twelfth Houses: Parāśraya

The second and twelfth houses have a special role to play, as they are the adjacent houses to the Lagna. These adjacent houses are the cushions of the native's life, and placement of malefics there can cause tension, strain, misery, and similar evil tides. Benefics there will act as a great blessing and can protect the native throughout their life. They give a happy and tension-free life. The ancient astrologers have explained these results in the yogas named aśubha and śubha yoga's respectively. Equal number of planets in these adjacent houses can cause bandhana, or incarceration/imprisonment/isolation/solitude. If the planets are benefic, this is usually for one's own protection, or for the sake of solitude, i.e. in an effort to complete a task. Malefics will however not be auspicious in such houses and can cause severe tension, torture, incarceration, etc. They are similar to a curse when they are two or more in number.

3.3 Lordship

The Lagna lord is called Lagna-īśa or lagneśa. Its other names are lagneśvara, Lagnapati or Lagnapa for short. The sign in which the lagneśa is posited is called pāka Lagna. In various compilations different names maybe used for the lagneśa, which are usually given in the initial chapters of that particular compilation. Whilst the Lagna is the native as an entity moving in this world, the lagneśa is that entity with intelligence applied in its interaction with the world. This can be described as follows:

- The Lagna can be compared to a body moving down a street. Whilst it can see groceries, animals, people and other entities, it is separate from them and without interaction.
- The lagneśa is the Lagna when it has started to interact, i.e. talk to the people on the street, and hence the time when the intellect has been applied.

Because the intellect is being applied, Jupiter becomes the karaka for the lagneśa.

Similarly, for other individuals, the lord of their house shows the application of their intellect. Malefics who are inimical towards Jupiter will damage the intelligence if joined Lagna lord and can cause psychotic disorders, whilst planets who are friendly towards Jupiter will benefit the intelligence when joined Lagna lord.

Dhīmanta Yoga, which is a combination for a person who is very eager to explore and study the universe, occurs when the Lagna or its lord is associated with the 3rd, 5th or 6th Bhāvas from Lagna. Similarly, because the karaka for the Lagna is the Sun, the Lagna lord will carry the qualities of the Sun to whichever bhāva it is posited in. The placement of the Lagna lord from the Sun can contribute to the health of the individual; similarly, the Sun's placement from Lagna itself should also be seen for health and vitality in particular.

Placement of the Lagneśa

A bhāva prospers if its lord is placed in the kendra or trikoṇa. The reasons for the same are given as follows:

- If the lord of a bhāva is placed in a kendra, the native will identify himself with that graha, and hence always protect its lordship. This can be either positive or negative. If a person has sixth lord in a kendra, they will tend to obstruct their marriage, as the sixth lord causes celibacy, be it voluntary or involuntary.
- If the lord of a bhāva is placed in a trikoṇa the native will consciously or unconsciously worship that ideal indicated by the graha, and hence always support its lordship i.e. if the seventh lord is in the ninth house, the native will constantly be praying for a spouse, especially if that wish has not been fulfilled yet.

A bhāva tends to suffer when its lord is placed in a dusthāna house (6th, $8^{th,}$ or 12th). However, the different houses in the dusthāna will give different results.

- If the lord of the bhāva is in the sixth house, very inauspicious effects are to be experienced as the graha will consider the native as an enemy and will not protect the Bhāvas that graha lords for the natives benefit.
- If the lord of the bhāva is in the eighth house, it indicates a karmic debt to that graha and the native will have to face many hardships from that bhāva the graha lords.
- If the lord of the bhāva is in the twelfth house the native is forced to feed that graha as long as one exists, otherwise the bhāva lorded by that graha will cause expenses and loss to survive because of the bhāva it lords.

In all cases of dusthāna placements of bhāva lords, the results are inauspicious unless the bhāva lords are themselves lords of a dusthāna. In the latter case, this will prove to be beneficial to the native as the inauspicious Bhāvas will be suppressed and will not be able to cause inauspicious effects, i.e. if sixth lord is in the eighth or twelfth houses, the natives enemies will suffer. This rule also applies to the third house and its lord, as the third house is the karma yoga (tenth house) of the enemy (sixth house), and is hence the reason why some consider the third house as a dusthāna.

All life must come from somewhere, and similarly the lagneśa's placement in any bhāva will deprive that bhāva of the life force and give it to the Lagna. This is akin to a tree that with time and growth starts to deprive the plants around it from their life force. For this reason Parāśara states that lagneśa in the fifth house is inauspicious for children. Similarly, lagneśa in the ninth house is inauspicious for father. The extent to which this is inauspicious must be analyzed in further detail and these yogas cannot be taken in isolation. Just as the bhāva the planet is placed in, is deprived of its life force, another bhāva becomes more auspicious. Count from Lagna lord back to the Lagna. The resultant amount of signs will indicate the bhāva who prospers.

Example: If lagneśa is in the fifth house, the Lagna is in the ninth from the lagneśa. This increases the prosperity of the ninth house, hence Parāśara states that not only will there be misfortune to children if lagneśa is in fifth house, but blessings from elders will also be there. Personal experience tells that if a person with lagneśa in fifth house has children, they tend to develop some issue towards their children, and begins to perceive the children as a burden.

Because the Lagna lord carries the kārakatva of the Sun to the bhāva it is placed in, lagneśa in the seventh house causes the spouse to be dominating, just as Sun placed in seventh house will do. Such a person will let themselves be dominated by people other than the spouse as well. If such a lagneśa is in seventh or twelfth and afflicted, it can cause serious disturbances in the intelligence of the person and they may consume aphrodisiacs or psychotropic substances. This can lead to addictions as well if Rāhu is strongly influencing.

The placement of the D-1 lagneśa in the vargas is very relevant. Since the lagneśa deals with intelligence, the placement of the d-1 lagneśa in Navāṁśa will indicate how easily the person can grasp and understand various concepts. This lagneśa should be well placed from Navāṁśa Lagna and preferably not in an inimical sign.

Since the Sun's natural year of maturity is the 22nd year (21/22), the results of the bhāva in which the lagneśa is placed may arise in the 22nd year.

- **Example 1:** if lagneśa is in the tenth house, Siddha Yoga and a boost in career will begin in the native's 22nd year.
- **Example 2:** if lagneśa is in the ninth house, whilst Rāhu influences Pitṛ pada (A9), it can cause premature demise of the father in the 22nd year.

Similarly, since the Lagna lord itself has the kārakatva of Jupiter, the lagneśa's auspicious placement may be bestowed on the native in the 16th year.

- Example: This author has lagneśa as Ketu involved in a Kāla Amrita Yoga. This author's interest in astrology and spirituality began in his 16th year.

The subsequent ages of maturity for the planets are as follows: Sun, 21, 22, 48 and 70 and Jupiter, 16, 31, 32 and 56 are equally relevant for judging the results.

Chart 48: Nash, John Forbes Jr.

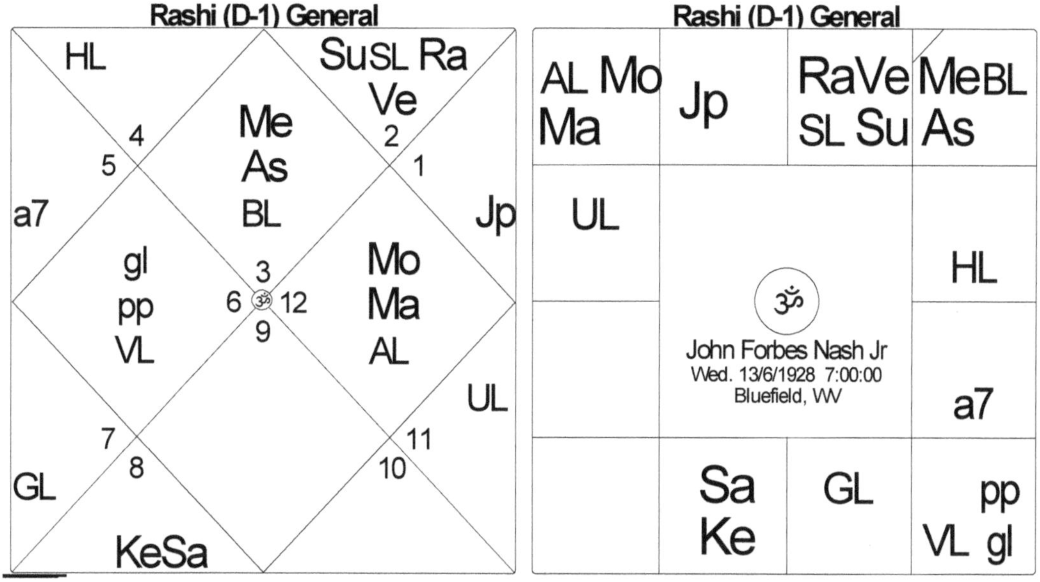

Chart of John Forbes Nash Jr., born 13th June 1928, 7 AM, Bluefield, WV, USA.

In the given chart, of the Nobel Prize winner of 1994, the Lagna lord is well placed in the Lagna, promising excellent thinking capacity and ability intellectually. This is forming Bhadrā Mahāpuruṣa yoga however, this is ruined by Mercury's debilitation in Navāṁśa, which would curtail the effects of this yoga and his health. Whilst Nash was an excellent mathematician, he was very shy and introvert, and had problems in socializing. Fifth house is unoccupied whilst its lord is in the twelfth house with Rāhu and Sun, and aspected by Saturn. Nash developed schizophrenia, which became abundantly clear after the birth of his second child (from his second affair). This occurred at the juncture of the Nārāyaṇa Daśās of Virgo and Taurus. Virgo has the mṛtyupada, showing that disease will be prevalent during this time. Taurus being the next Daśā has the afflicted fifth lord, indicating the ruined intelligence. To see the native's sense of awareness and direction during a Nārāyaṇa Daśā, treat the lord of the Daśā sign as Lagna, and see the placement of Jupiter there from. Here Jupiter is in the twelfth from Daśā lord, so the onset of a disease in the intellect is more prominent during such a time.

Chart 49: Taylor, Elizabeth

Chart of Elizabeth Taylor, born Elizabeth Rosemond Taylor, 27th February 1932, Hampstead, UK.

In the given chart of the famous actress Elizabeth Taylor, the Lagna lord(s) is not in the seventh house or the twelfth house, however Mars is in Aquarius with the Sun which is co-lorded by Rāhu and hence the yoga for consuming poisons is complete. Rāhu itself is joined Venus the seventh lord, indicating that this dependency may

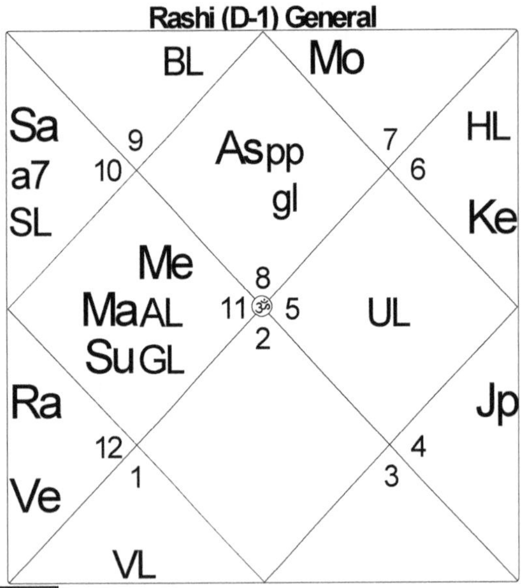

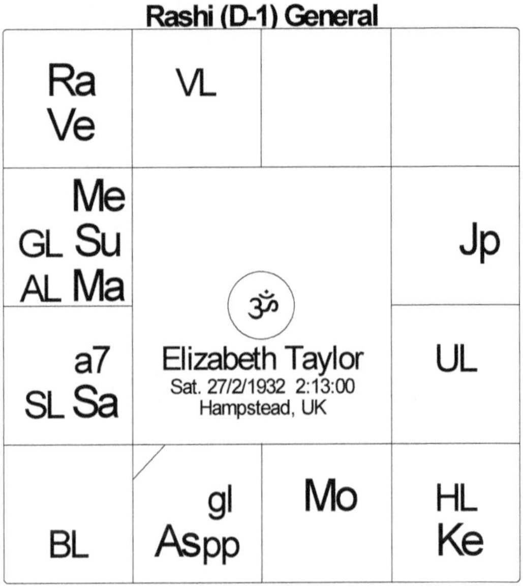

come as a result of shocks in relationships/marriages. Due to the break up with Richard Burton, Taylor had to be admitted to the Betty Ford clinic due to a dependency of alcohol (Saturnine sign) in 1983. This was during Taurus Daśā whose lord itself is joined Rāhu, hence causing the problem. She went into greater doldrums when her former husband died in 1984. This instigated an addiction to pain-killers which though being legal, sent her back to the Betty Ford clinic in 1988 during Sagittarius Daśā, which receives the sign aspect of Rāhu and Venus.

3.4 Planets associated with the bhāva lord

Whilst the placement of a bhāva lord maybe auspicious, planets joining the same lord can change the picture completely.

- Should the bhāva lord be joined a benefic such as Jupiter, Venus or Moon, the lord will prosper in abundance. Even in cases of debility, the conjunction of a strong natural benefic can make things very auspicious.
- Should the bhāva lord be joined with either Rāhu, Saturn, Mars or Ketu, the bhāva will undoubtedly suffer. Even if a planet is placed in its exaltation sign, the junction of the nodes will disrupt that graha from giving results easily.

The results of these placements can be understood from the lajjitādi avasthās.

3.4.1 Kalpadruma yoga

Parāśara states that if the Lagna lord, its dispositor, its dispositor and the formers Navāṁśa dispositor are placed in exaltation, own sign, kendra or trikoṇa, the Kalpadruma yoga is formed. The native born with Kalpadruma yoga is like a mighty lord or sovereign power. His supremacy and sway hold good. He is pious and merciful, yet strong and fond of battles. The celestial tree (pārijāta) grants his wishes.

Here it becomes important to understand the nature of these dispositors.

- The lagneśa itself represents the native's intelligence, and all general matters of the Lagna.
- The dispositor of the lagneśa (also known as pākeśa) is like the Sun and will represent the health of the individual.
- The dispositor of the pāka lagneśa (also known as pāka pākeśa) is like the Moon and will represent the native's ability to provide sustenance or wealth for himself.
- The Navāṁśa dispositor of the above pāka pākeśa (also known as pāka-pākeśa-amśeśa) will represent the luck of fortune of the individual in achieving the wealth.

If all four planets mentioned are in kendra/trikoṇa or exalted/mūlatrikoṇa or own sign, in the rāśī, then the native will be granted anything he asks and will have strong ideals. Such a person is a mighty sovereign, according to Parāśara. It maybe inferred that if Lagna lord is in the Lagna, then three out of the four dispositors will be well placed, but the fortune of the native is solely dependent on the Navāṁśa dispositor.

By distinguishing one dispositor from the other, we can get a good understanding of various parts of the native's life, just by understanding the particular dispositor. The dispositor of the lagneśa will help in determining health problems. This is an addition to looking at the placement of the Sun from the lagneśa. If the pākeśa (dispositor of lagneśa) is badly placed, then during its Daśā, surely problems with the native's health will occur.

The dispositor of pākeśa in the chart becomes very relevant to see whether the native can provide for himself or not. If badly placed from the Lagna, a wrong investment of energy may occur, leading the native into financial insecurity. If all three i.e. lagneśa, pākeśa, and dispositor of pākeśa are well placed, but the Navāṁśa dispositor of the latter is not, then though the native may apply themselves well in all fields, luck will not shine upon them. This luck is the blessing of God and will ensure bhāgya/fortune on the native.

The Navāṁśa dispositor can also be used on each of the three above, independently.

Example 1: the Navāṁśa dispositor of the lagneśa will reveal the luck the native has through their interaction with the world.

Example 2: the Navāṁśa dispositor of the pākeśa will reveal the luck the native has in improving their health.

This knowledge can also be applied to any other Bhāvas, but must be done intelligently. In usual practice, dispositor of the particular bhāva lord is most important as it can reveal very important facts about that particular Bhāvas health i.e. dispositor of fourth lord, will show the mothers health.

Chart 50: Gandhi, Mahatma

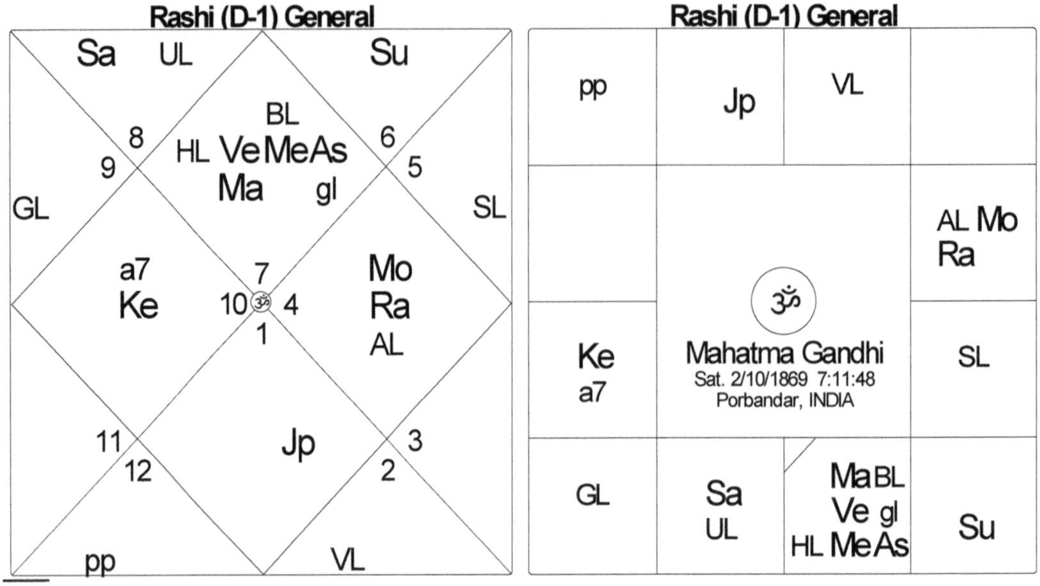

Chart of Mahatma Gandhi, born Mohandas Gandhi, 2nd October 1869, 7: 11, Porbandar, India.

A superficial look at the given chart will reveal Mālavya Mahāpūruṣa Yoga. However, such a yoga cannot be fully functional unless the Navāṁśa dispositor is also well placed. Venus is in Taurus Navāṁśa hence confirming the unbreakable mahāpūruṣa for Gandhi, which promises success in his endeavors.

This knowledge can also be applied to any other Bhāvas, but must be done intelligently. In usual practice dispositor of the particular bhāva lord is most important as it can reveal very important facts about that particular Bhāvas health. I.e. dispositor of 4th lord will show the mothers health.

3.4.2 Auspicious Placements: Yoga Kārakas

Yoga Kāraka literally means bringer of union. The type of yoga is that union between one's character, work, ideals and traits (kendra) and the prayers we make (trikoṇa). A graha becoming yoga Kāraka is considered very auspicious because of this union, and will confer great blessings upon the native. The combinations that make a graha a yoga Kāraka are given as follows.

If a lord of a kendra and a lord of a trikoṇa associate with each other, those grahas become yoga kārakas. This association can happen in four ways.

1. The two lords are the same graha.
2. The lords are in conjunction.
3. The lords are in each other's houses.
4. If the lords have mutual aspect on each other.

3.4.3 More Placements of the Lagna Lord

The placement of the bhāva lord in the various houses, colors the effects of the house it lords and the house it is placed in. For grahas lording more than one bhāva, the graha will protect both the Bhāvas it lords, but the house it is placed in will experience more dominant effects than the Bhāvas it lords, depending on the strength of the graha.

For Pisces Lagna, the eleventh and twelfth houses are lorded by the same planet, namely Saturn. Hence, Saturn becomes responsible for bringing both the gains and the losses/expenses to the native. These two adjacent/conflicting indications will be settled through Saturn's placement, i.e. whether Saturn is supporting Aquarius or Capricorn. This aspect of the lordship will be dealt with in the higher levels. If assumingly Saturn was giving its lordship of Aquarius and was placed in the seventh house Virgo, it would act as twelfth lord in seventh house and could give marriage to a foreigner, foreign travel at the time of marriage, or some hidden/secrecy associated with the marriage. If instead it were supporting Capricorn, Saturn would act as eleventh lord in the seventh house. This would give a lot of gains/wealth at the time of marriage, as well as social support and friendships. A source of income for the native would be business and such involvements. However, in both cases of Saturn's placement, Saturn would be responsible for protecting the physical aspects of both Capricorn and Aquarius, the difference lies in whose results would Virgo experience.

Knowing this, it become pertinent to understand the results of the Lagna lord in each bhāva.

3.3.5.1 Various Bhāva Placement of the Lagna Lord

The Lagna lord is the most important graha in the chart. It shows where the fruits and ideals of the Lagna are going to manifest, i.e. whilst every individual may have some ideals in life, whether we are able to achieve the same, depends on the placement of the Lagna lord.

Based on this principle we may infer the following:

- If the Lagna lord is placed in a kendra, the native will work diligently for their ideals.
- If the Lagna lord is placed in a trine, the native will seek and gain favors from others to attain their goals.
- If the Lagna lord is placed in the third or eleventh, the native will always balance their ideals with their efforts, but could be scrupulous.
- If the Lagna lord is placed in the sixth or eighth houses the native has a lot of bad luck in attaining their ideals, this is either because they are constantly fighting (6th house) or are trying to clear their karmic debts to society, be it monetary or through physical effort.
- If the Lagna lord is placed in the second or twelfth houses, there is a general wrong timing in when to work for one's ideals and when to fulfill others ide-

als. The second house will generally show a great focus on immediate family, whilst the twelfth shows the focus on one's spouse and such supporters.

It is evident that the placement in the second, sixth, eighth and twelfth houses are not conducive towards supporting the ideals of the Lagna. Similar principles arise when judging the placements of planets placed from each other (refer Tatkālika Sambandha).

3.5 Judging Dual Lordship

In cases of dual lordship, it becomes necessary to differentiate between the signs lorded by the graha in order to judge which of that lord's results will dominate. For this, Maharṣi Parāśara has given us some practical clues.

1. If the bhāva lord is in one of the signs it lords, that lordship will dominate.
2. If the bhāva lord is having seventh house graha dṛṣṭi on either of the signs it lords, then that bhāva will dominate.
3. If the bhāva lord is in an odd sign, the even sign it lords will dominate, and vice versa.

Chart 51: Malcolm X

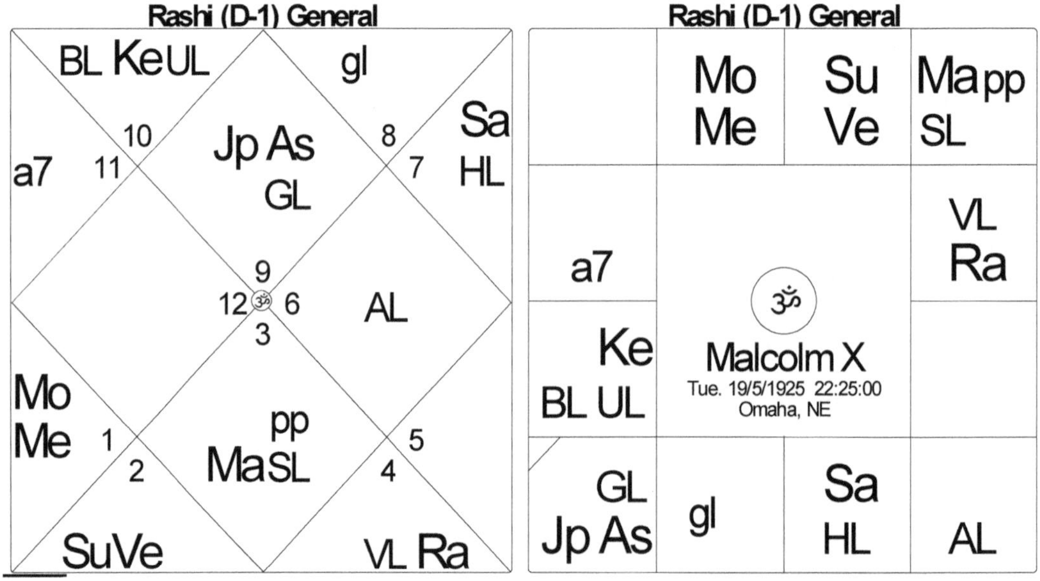

Chart of Malcolm X, born Malcolm Little, 19th May 1925, 10:25 PM, Omaha, Nebraska, USA.

The Moon occupies Aśvinī Nakṣatra and the fourth Nakṣatra from it is lorded over by the Moon itself. Moon in fifth house is not considered the worst position, but with solely malefics and a Venus in Māraṇa Kāraka Sthāna occupying the *graha māla yoga* following the Moon sign it bodes a negative outcome for the mother (fourth house precedes the yoga) and especially father (ninth house succeeds the yoga).

The negatives to father are further accentuated by the affliction of Jupiter by Saturn and Mars. Because Jupiter is the ruler over the natural ninth (Sagittarius) and twelfth (Pisces) father and teachers tend to bring about some suffering in the person's life. As the ninth lord Sun is placed in the sixth house with the badly placed Venus it accentuates the troubles to father's health. Finally the bad mutual placement between the cursed Jupiter and ninth lord Sun seals a difficult fate for father.

The Sun being the ninth lord can bring such difficulties after the age of six as its length in the Vimśottari Daśā is six years. At the age of six in September 1931 Malcolm's father was killed in a vehicular accident.

Chart 52: Malcolm X Dvādaśāṁśa

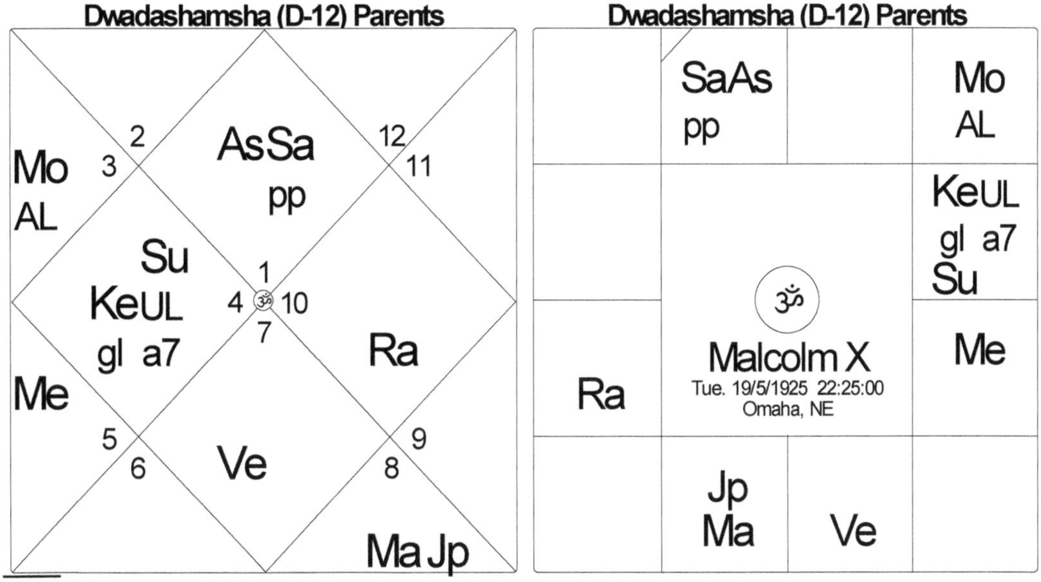

Accidents are caused by Ketu or Sagittarius and for parents the Dvādaśāṁśa chart must be analysed for the same. Herein we find that the Ārūḍha of the ninth house falls in Libra where the third there from is Sagittarius itself confirming the accident. Moon's aspect on Sagittarius by Rāśi Dṛṣṭi confirms the incident. Suspicion of foul play was involved because an attempt had been made previously on the father and his family. When Malcolm was four the family's home in Michigan was burnt to the ground by a white supremacist group due to the father's work as a Baptist preacher. In the Rāśi the fourth house precedes the *graha māla yoga* suggesting the troubles to property. Further the fourth houses from Moon and Lagna are afflicted suggesting the troubles in the fourth year.

Attempts on his life is confirmed by the aspect of Rāhu on the eighth house from Ārūḍha of the ninth house, but Rāhu's lack of involvement with the third from the same does not suggest this at his demise.

Due to the father's demise the family was soon in dire straits due to the added pressure on the mother to earn for the family. Previously the trials to the fourth house have been mentioned, and specifically as the Moon is in the fifth house from fourth lord Jupiter the mother risks suffering from diseases of the mind. As Malcolm completes his seventh grade at the age of thirteen his mother is declared legally insane and institutionalised. This causes Malcolm's family to be split up as they are sent to live in foster care.

At this stage Malcolm had showed excellence among his peers in school, traits which are promised by Jupiter in own sign. However, the Mars placed in Māraṇa Kāraka Sthāna in the seventh house is a difficult position and its lordship of the fifth house and twelfth house would surely trouble children and his own personal freedom. As Mars joins or aspects neither of the signs it lords over, its placement in an odd sign suggests that its lordship of the twelfth house Scorpio will be the most trying.

In 1940 Aries Nārāyaṇa Daśā began and he left his eighth grade of schooling due to a remark about his future by his teacher. Ninth or fifth lords in the seventh house tend to bring knowledge/education which will not be applied by the native, however in this case the education itself became disliked by the native as Mars is badly placed. He was placed in a series of foster homes to white foster parents and a year later he left these in favour of his older half-sister Ella Little Collins in Boston. He held a few short jobs during this time and with the advent of the next Daśā of Pisces he moved to Harlem, New York. The first time Jupiter was associated with the Nārāyaṇa Daśā Rāśi Malcolm lost a home and his father. This second time would also activate the curse but to a lesser extent. Saturn is the most malefic graha in the curse and lords the tenth house from the Moon indicating its effects in his profession. During Malcolm's stay in New York he took to dealing drugs, gambling, robbery and racketeering as his means of livelihood.

When Scorpio Nārāyaṇa Daśā arrived in the beginning of 1945 he returned to Boston, MA, just as he had during the prior Daśā of Aries. Only this time his intentions were more sinister, as he brought with him a group of associates, who with him carried out elaborate robberies of white homes. With his freedom being threatened due to the badly placed twelfth lord, in January 1946 during Scorpio Daśā, Aries Antaradaśā he was arrested whilst trying to pick up a stolen watch from a jeweller. He was sentenced to jail for ten years for robbery and carrying firearms.

Venus is the significator for the seventh house where Mars is badly placed and if well placed will help overcome the negative placement of Mars. Venus despite being in the sixth house is joined the Sun which suggests a means to overcome the negative placement. Sun is the ninth lord and brings higher education and religion. During his time in jail he under the influence of elders began self-educating himself. Further some two years into his sentence his brothers (Mars) began suggesting that he turn to religion to diminish his jail sentence. He reconsidered his initial dismissal of religion, which had arisen due to his childhood animosity towards his father, and turned to Islam. Thus also with the end of Scorpio Daśā, three years prior to his end of sentence, he was released on parole in 1952 during Cancer Daśā at the age of twenty-seven.

Cancer Daśā is occupied by Rāhu and ends the negative *graha māla yoga* on the Moon being the lord of Cancer. When the Moon is in such a state and Rāhu is involved, anti social behavior bordering bigotry is possible. This had already marred Malcolm's experiences in his childhood as Moon lords over the fourth Nakṣatra from the Moon and would come to fore in his life from the advent of Cancer Daśā. As Cancer houses the Varṇadā Lagna it will do so through career.

Malcolm joined the Nation of Islam, an African-American religious group with the purpose of improving the spiritual, mental, social and economic conditions of the African-American community. He renounced his last name (Moon is joined Mercury), replacing it with X as an act of renouncing the name that had been imposed on his ancestors by their slave masters. The group, led by Elijah Muhammad, preached racial segregation from white influence and a final goal of immigrating to Africa, where they believed to hold their roots. They further preached black supremacy. In 1953 Malcolm was appointed as minister in their Detroit temple, and soon advanced by opening new temples and attracting new members all over the USA. He was commended on his eloquence and great sense of presence which was impressive and commanded respect.

Gemini Daśā began in 1955 with its Bāhya Rāśi being Sagittarius. Jupiter in the Lagna in Sagittarius catapulted Malcolm to fame. He was invited to talk shows and interviewed regularly as the face of the organization. Jupiter is further Vargottama in Sagittarius as Ātmakāraka suggesting a grand purpose for his birth associated with his fame.

Further, with Gemini being the seventh house and its lord in exchange with the fifth lord, marriage and children will come to pass during this time. In 1958 during Gemini-Pisces he and Betty X married. In the years that followed the couple produced six daughters of which twins were born posthumously.

The fourth from Ārūḍha Lagna shows the organization and here Jupiter is placed in the Lagna confirming the fame he made through the organization. However, Jupiter is retrograde herein and suggests leaving the organization. As this is the Bāhya Rāśi and associated with Jupiter the excuse will be regarding children. By 1964 the organization had grown from 500 at the time of Malcolm's entry to 25,000. Malcolm had grown to a position that overshadowed that of the leader Elijah and this caused great jealousy within the organization. Further the leader Elijah had been accused of adultery and fathering children with several of his previous secretaries, which was a direct break from the ideals of the organisation and had disgusted Malcolm. Malcolm left the organisation in March 1964 during the Daśā of Gemini-Scorpio.

Scorpio Antaradaśā is lorded over by Mars which afflicts Jupiter in the Lagna. If a curse exists in a chart the Antaradaśā of the malefics involved will surely bring about the negatives of the affliction.

This would thus put an end to the Hamsa Mahāpuruṣa Yoga caused by the placement of Jupiter as it implied leaving the organisation that brought him his stardom. Shortly after he met with Martin Luther King Jr. and further travelled to Mecca to attend the Hajj. Malcolm came back transformed with a new belief that people of all races could live together as he had witnessed in Mecca. He formed two new organisations, namely Muslim Mosque Inc., and the Organisation of Afro-American unity. He began preaching ideals of non-segregation and of unity beyond race and religion and wished that African-Americans seek out help and support if persecuted.

He was met with strong support and was well treated by the media, as his former organisation began suffering from the loss of Malcolm. Throughout 1964 leaders of the Nation of Islam railed against Malcolm and openly threatened him in their conversations and publications. Aquarius Nārāyaṇa Daśā began in the beginning of 1965 housing the Ārūḍha of the sixth house bringing about serious problems from enemies. This being in the sixth from the Ārūḍha Lagna further brings about enmity and aspecting Saturn in the second from the Ārūḍha Lagna which further threatens life. Śūla Daśā had arrived at Aries whose lord is placed in Māraṇa Kāraka Sthāna further threatening life. Aries is also the Bāhya Rāśi of the Nārāyaṇa Daśā. In such cases the third from the Ārūḍha Lagna needs to be observed which here is aspected by the nodes promoting Duṣṭha Māraṇa Yoga. Moon's aspect bring about a crowd or many people who will witness or be involved in the demise.

In February 1965 after the Nation of Islam had reclaimed Malcolm's house in a suit, the house was burned to the ground. One week later on the 21st of February 1965, during a meeting in the Organisation of Afro-American unity, Malcolm was shot by gunmen. They fired upon him sixteen times before fleeing. The gunmen, belonging to Nation of Islam, were later arrested and convicted of their crimes.

यन्मण्डलं गुढमति प्रबोधं धर्मस्य वृद्धिं कुरुते जनानाम्।
यत्सर्व पाप क्षयकारणश्च पुनातु मां तत्सवितुर्वरेण्यम्॥ ४॥

4

Sambandha

Relationships

4.1 Naisargika (natural) Sambandha

Naisargika Sambandha helps to understand what the natural disposition of the graha are towards each other. While the word Naisargika means "natural," there is more than one type of natural relationship between the graha. These natural relationships depend on the focus of the relationship.

The concept of natural relationships or "Naisargika Sambandha," which is commonly used among astrologers, is based on the Mūlatrikoṇa sign of the each graha. This method of seeing relationships is focused on the purpose or job of the graha. The graha will distribute the work to those signs, which are friendly towards its Mūlatrikoṇa sign. The lords of those friendly signs will benefit by attaining a job or a qualification of sorts, whilst those left out will have no purpose to fulfil.

Maharṣi Parāśara gives the Naisargika Sambandha as follows:

- FROM the graha's Mūlatrikoṇa sign, see the signs in upachaya (3rd, 6th, 10th and 11th) and seventh (7th) from it. The graha is inimical to those signs, and their lords.
- It is friendly towards the remaining signs (1st, 2nd, 4th, 5th, 8th, 9th, and 12th), and its exaltation sign.
- If a planet happens to lord both lord of an inimical sign and friendly sign, then that planet is considered neutral.

Some scholars disagree about the friendship status of the fifth house.

Example:

Consider the Sun and its Naisargika Sambandha. The Sun's Mūlatrikoṇa sign is Leo. Libra (3rd), Capricorn (6th), Aquarius (7th), Taurus (10th) and Gemini (11th) are the inimical signs of Leo, the rest are friendly.

Among the lordships of the inimical signs, Mercury rules both an inimical sign (Gemini) and friendly sign (Virgo); hence, the Sun is neutral towards Mercury. Sun has become highly inimical towards Saturn, Rāhu and Venus, neutral towards Mercury and friendly towards the rest of the grahas.

Table 52: Ravi Sambandha

Sun	
Inimical Sign and Lord	Friendly Sign and Lord
Libra (Venus)	Aries (Mars)
Capricorn (Saturn)	Cancer (Moon)
Aquarius (Saturn and Rāhu)	Virgo (Mercury)
Taurus (Venus)	Scorpio (Mars and Ketu)
Gemini (Mercury)	Sagittarius (Jupiter)
	Pisces (Jupiter)

The Parampara teaches that a neutral graha can take either a friendly or an inimical stand, depending on which of its two lordships it supports more. If the neutral graha supports the inimical sign, it acts as inimical, whilst if it supports a friendly sign, then it will act friendly. To see which it will prefer, one must decide which lordship is predominating. The rules are as follows:

1. If the planet is placed in the sign, then that sign dominates.
2. If the planet is in the seventh from the sign, that sign dominates.
3. If the planet is in an odd sign, the even sign lordship will dominate and vice-versa.

To continue with the example of Sun's Naisargika Sambandha, Mercury lords the impure and promiscuous sign Gemini and the pure, celibate sign Virgo, among which the Sun is inimical towards Gemini, and friendly towards Virgo. Should Mercury be placed in Gemini or Sagittarius, and if neither, then in an even sign (except Virgo), then the Sun will be inimical towards Mercury.

The most important planet in the chart is the Ātmakāraka. The job of the Ātmakāraka is to guide the soul through this life. The Ātmakāraka will distribute its work to other planets, to help it reach its goal. The signs, which the Ātmakāraka remains friendly towards, will prosper and have growth, but those it is inimical towards will suffer, and not give auspicious results, especially the sign in the seventh from the Mūlatrikoṇa sign of the Ātmakāraka.

4.1.1 Examples

Chart 53: Broken relationships

Male native born 4th September 1969, 1:50 AM, Delhi, India.

The native of the given chart has Mars as AK. Mars' Mūlatrikoṇa is Aries, and hence the inimical signs become Gemini, Virgo, Libra, Capricorn and Aquarius. Among these signs, Mars will hate Libra the most, as it is the seventh from Aries. Venus is

Rashi (D-1) General

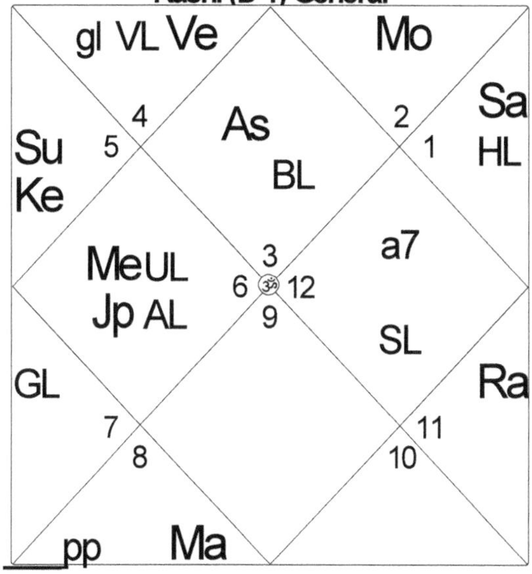

Rashi (D-1) General

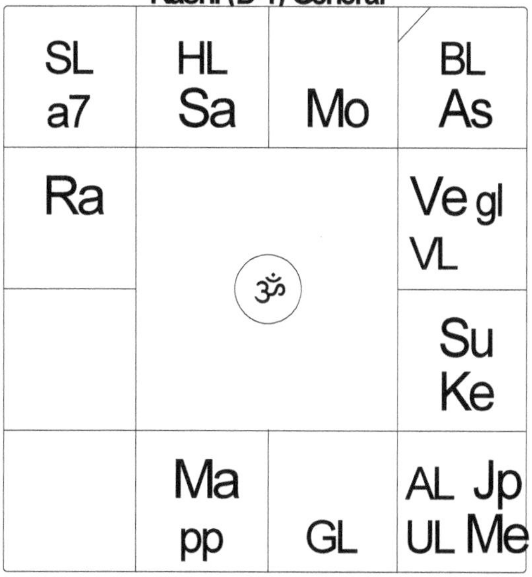

in Cancer, hence supporting Libra, where it has the disfavour of Mars, promising troubles in relationships.

In the chart, Libra happens to be the second from the Upapada and Ārūḍha Lagna, whilst Upapada and Ārūḍha Lagna both fall in Virgo, which Mars also is inimical towards. The native had a relationship in which his marriage proposal was turned down and the partner decided to marry someone else and left the country. The final blow was caused by the lord of Upapada, which is defeated in planetary war, hence, similarly the native felt defeated.

The eighth from Upapada is lorded by the Ātmakāraka, hence marriage is promised and will be hard to break, at least until Mars has finished his tenure. Mars is furthermore in the sixth house, so a requirement for this marriage is celibacy, which is quite uncommon in marriages. The native married an equally spiritual person but they have no conjugal relations. However, Saturn is in Aries, and as Mars does not like Saturn, there is a possibility of separation in the marriage. The native married an elderly woman as signified by Saturn but due to differences and the forced celibacy, both natives live apart from each other.

Chart 54: Marriage and Children

In the given chart, Moon is Ātmakāraka. The Moon's Mūlatrikoṇa is Taurus, which is inimical towards Cancer, Libra, Scorpio, Aquarius and Pisces. Libra is the second from Upapada and its lord Venus is in Aquarius, another sign which the Moon finds little room for. The native was married but due to financial strain she left her husband (second lord is joined Venus, hence a requirement for the marriage is money, and sixth lord in the seventh will cause separation from spouse) and kept the children.

Saturn lords both the seventh and eighth houses in the chart, and being in an even sign it will support Aquarius over Capricorn, making Saturn act as eighth lord in the chart. Saturn is in Bādhaka Sthāna, and had it acted as the seventh lord major

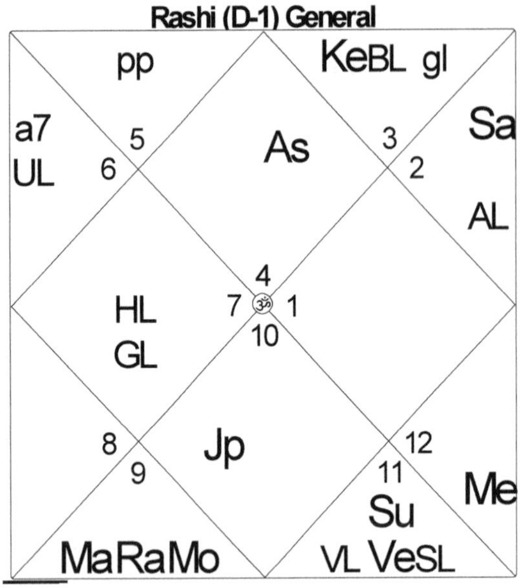

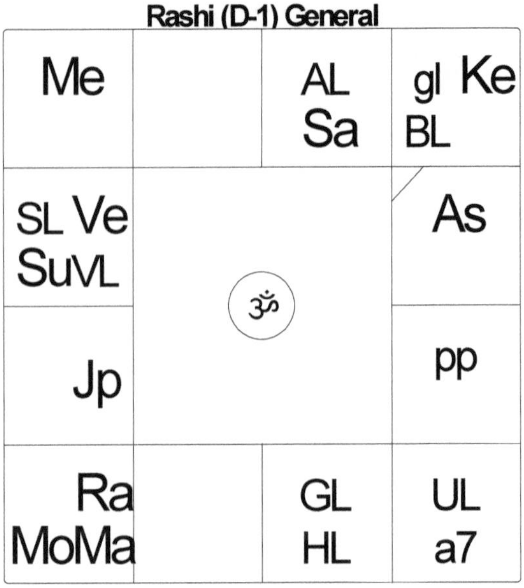

obstacles in getting married would arise, however instead Tattva doṣa exists and health problems will arise as a result. Saturn supporting the eighth house would also be more potent in breaking the marriage, as Moon has become greatly inimical towards Saturn.

The story is however not over yet. Moon as Ātmakāraka is in the sixth house joined fifth lord and eighth lord. This indicates the loss of children, health problems and all this will be initiated with the separation in marriage, as Moon is Lagna lord, and sixth lord is in the seventh house, indicating the separation from husband. After leaving the husband, the native lost the ability to have children due to health problems, followed by the premature demise of her already existing children, leaving her alone without children and a partner.

Readers will note a very intense curse of mother existing in the chart (refer **5.1.2.2 Curses or Śāpa**), and this too on the Ātmakāraka which will dominate the chart. This proves that the Ātmakāraka is truly the king of the chart and yogas involving the AK will surely happen. Lagna lord Moon joined fifth lord Mars, is going to promise power and position as well, however not until the native has recovered from her shocking experience (Rāhu).

4.2 Tatkālika (temporary) Sambandha

Tatkālika Sambandha means temporary relationships. This term cannot be used loosely as the temporal relationship also depends on the purpose of the relationship. Largely there are two types of Tatkālika Sambandha.

i. Sambandha based on support and Rāja yoga, taught by Maharṣi Parāśara.

ii. Sambandha based on physical disposition or bhāva Sambandha.

4.2.1 Bhāva Sambandha

The mutual placement between grahas forms the bhāva Sambandha, i.e. planets placed in quadrants, trines, 2/12, 6/8, or 3/11 to each other. The result of this placement is given partly in the bhāva chapters, but is reproduced here in short form:

- Mutual quadrant placement of planets is conducive towards excellent relationships, as the two grahas will always support each other.
- Mutual trine placement of planets is very auspicious and indicates a mutual goal of the two grahas.
- Mutual 3/11 placement is fruitful, but requires some struggle to get the good results.
- Mutual 2/12 placement causes a lack of or wrong timing in the grahas attempt to help each other and this causes delay or denial of results.
- Mutual 6/8 placement indicates a complete mismatch in ideals and physiology. When one graha wants to start the work, the other graha does not and vice-versa.

This Sambandha is especially useful in judging how two or more grahas work together. This will not indicate whether the two grahas support each other, nor will it indicate their friendship towards each other. Examples of these are reproduced in the four chapters on the topic of Bhāva.

4.2.2 Rājya Yoga Sambandha

Figure 10: Tatkālika Sambandha Chakra

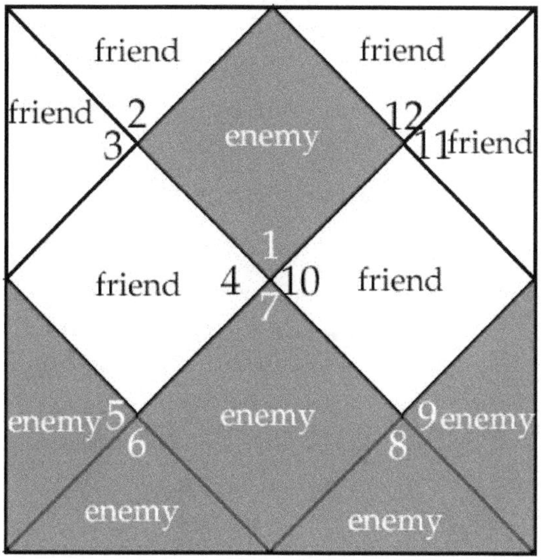

Sambandha based on getting Rājya yoga depends on the support one has. This support can come from both friends and foes, and does not include those one has to share one's power with. Maharṣi Parāśara explains this form of tatkālika Sambandha as follows:

❖ The grahas in the 10th, 11th, 12th, 2nd, 3rd and 4th houses from the graha are friendly, while the rest are not.

The depiction of this Sambandha resembles an upside down umbrella, with the pole going through the first and seventh houses, whilst the shade spreads along the 5th, 6th, 7th, 8th and 9th houses. Those signs, which fall under the shade of the umbrella, are those in which one can seek shelter.

Whilst all the planets in the friendly houses, act auspiciously towards one, special care is taken for the fourth house. The fourth house shows support from those who wish to replace you one day, i.e. they will one day become the fifth house, and inherit your merits and fruits of labour, and question is only that of time. If benefics are in the fourth house, then they will take your wealth when you have given it up, i.e. when you are ready to be replaced. This is otherwise in case of malefics, and indicates cheating and deceit, resulting in the loss of one's wealth and is known as Kapaṭa Yoga.

This principle can be applied from any graha or position, but most importantly it should be applied from Lagna and the lord of Lagna, to see the support the native gets in society.

Examples are given in the chapter on sixth house.

4.3 Graha Sambandha

There are four types of Sambandha formed by the grahas.

i. Parivartana

ii. Conjunction

iii. Mutual aspect by graha dṛṣṭi

iv. Rāśi dṛṣṭi on each other's signs

These graha Sambandha give the graha the power to give each other's results, i.e. if the fourth lord is joined the fifth lord, then the fifth lord can give the results of the fourth lord and vice versa. This is especially helpful in deciding the results of Daśā.

Chart 55: Lyndon B. Johnson

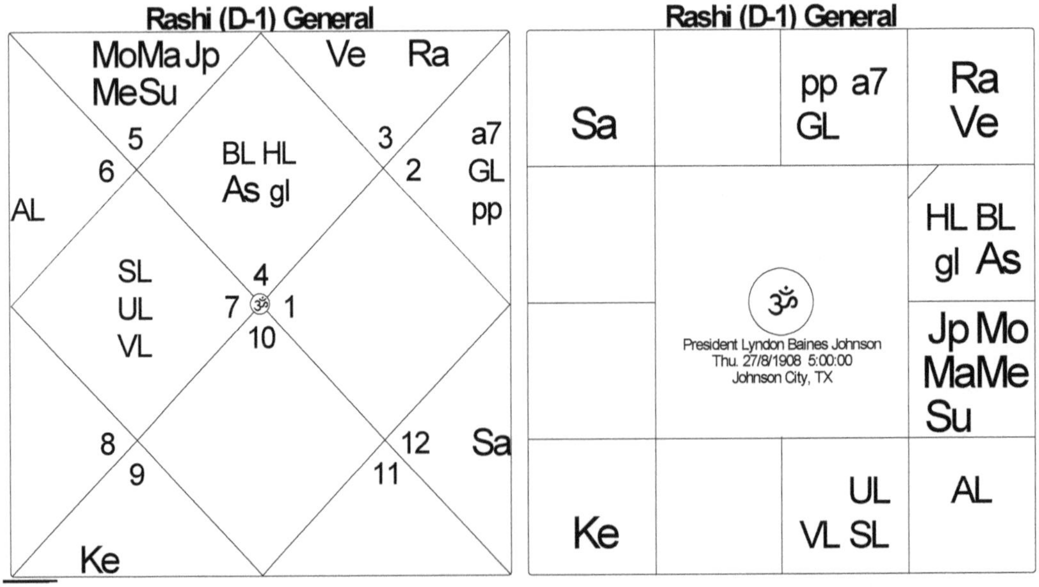

Chart of President Lyndon Baines Johnson, born 27th August 1908, 5 AM, Johnson City, Texas, USA.

In this chart we find five graha joined in the second house. These graha will give the results of each other and therefore the task of the Jyotiṣa is to ascertain the exact effects of each of them. The graha that are conjoined are Sun, Moon, Mars, Mercury and Jupiter. To understand how the conjunction works we need to pair the graha with each other based on the natural benefic and malefic nature of them. First we shall place them in a hierarchy based on their beneficence:

1	Jupiter
2	Mercury
3	Moon
4	Sun
5	Mars

Here Moon is considered less benign than Mercury as Moon is closer to the new Moon and thus harbouring less light.

The next step is to pair the most malefic graha with the most benefic. These pairs will indicate which results the graha are giving rise to in their Daśā.

1	Jupiter & Mars
2	Mercury & Sun
3	Moon - alone

Having allotted the most benefic with the most malefic the same step is taken with the remaining graha. Should an odd number of graha be joined then one graha will remain without a pairing and will give its own results in the Daśā. This is primarily to be attributed to the Mahādaśā effects of the graha but does find its usage in other principles of Jyotiṣa.

When four or more planets join they form Pravrājya Yoga for renunciation and penury, however this is the opposite for those graha which are combust in such a yoga which all of them are!

In the chart the Moon occupies Pūrva Phalguṇi Nakṣatra lorded over by Venus, and the fourth Nakṣatra from it is lorded by Mars. Mars will bring the effects of Jupiter and so also Johnson was brought up in a good, peaceful and strict household. Jupiter is placed in the twelfth from the Ārūḍha Lagna ensuring that he is the eldest among his siblings as the third lord therefrom is Mars who is joined four graha to give four younger siblings. Jupiter supports religious upbringing and being the fourth lord from the Ārūḍha Lagna ensures joining a spiritual organization as well. Johnson like his grandfather was a member of the Christian Church.

The Kṣema Vimśottari Daśā is applicable for Johnson and so also the first Daśā was Mars, Jupiter Antaradaśā and his grandfather declared that this child would be a United States Senator. Jupiter signifies paternal grandparents and this shows a pronounced influence of them in Johnson's life. As Jupiter is placed in the fourth house from Ghaṭika Lagna it promises popularity and fame as well as power. Mars Daśā was until the age of 5.

Rāhu Daśā began for the next 18 years until 23 and is joined the fourth lord Venus. Venus will give the effects of Rāhu and vice versa, so also the main focus of Rāhu Daśā was education due to the fourth lordship of Venus. Venus further lords over the eleventh house from Lagna and tenth house from Moon, which would bring a focus on work and income. During Rāhu Daśā, Venus Antaradaśā Johnson enrolled to become a teacher. As Venus is joined Rāhu this choice of study would not be smooth and he had to break with his education for one year in 1927 during the same Venus Antaradaśā. During this time he taught at the Wellhausen School in Cotulla. He continued his education the following year with the advent of Sun Antaradaśā and graduated in 1930 during Rāhu Daśā, Moon Antaradaśā. He began teaching speaking and debate to high school students during the same Antaradaśā, but as Moon is further lord over the Lagna and Horā Lagna name and fame would become the focus of his life. Further as Rāhu is the Amatyakāraka political career is guaranteed and with great success as it is joined Venus the Ātmakāraka.

His father, being politically well acquainted, ensured that in 1930 Johnson campaigned for the Texas Senator Welly Hopkins. This happened just before the advent of Jupiter Mahādaśā, the graha which caused his grandfather to predict the child's success. Being in the first house from the Sun, Jupiter Daśā would prove to be one that brings great fame. Jupiter will give the effects of Mars who is a yogakāraka due to its lordship of the fifth and tenth houses and causes Simhasana Yoga by being placed in the second house. So also when Jupiter Daśā started in November 1931 he continued to follow the political ladder and was elected to the House of Representatives. This led to a recommendation to congressmen Richard M. Kleberg who appointed Johnson as his legislative secretary. This enabled him to interact with many of the political aides in the capitol and a view of how the Congress worked.

Before the end of Jupiter Antaradaśā Johnson was elected speaker of Little Congress, an organisation of congressional workers.

Saturn Antaradaśā arrived in the beginning of 1934. Saturn is the seventh lord from Lagna, lords the Navāṁśa Lagna and is well placed from the seventh lord in Navāṁśa Lagna, all indications that point to entering an important relationship. The Upapada is in the fourth house in a Venusian sign suggesting a meeting through a vehicle or the likes or in connection with his home. On a trip home to Texas he met Claudia Alta Taylor. He decided almost instantly that they should marry and so also at the end of the year on 17th November 1934 the two tied the knot. Saturn is placed in the ninth house suggesting some education or furtherance of knowledge and so also during the year Johnson briefly attended a Law school in Washington DC.

Saturn Antaradaśā does not support his work in Washington during Jupiter Mahādaśā being in the eighth from it. Further Saturn in the ninth causes one to work for social causes of deprived individuals. In 1935 he resigned his post in the capitol to take a post as the Texas Director of the National Youth Administration.

The program was designed to enable young people to get jobs.

Two years later in 1937 he ran for election to Congress. Mercury Antaradaśā was running which is the lord of the Ārūḍha Lagna giving fame and name, but being the third and twelfth lord saw him leave his responsibilities in the youth program. Mercury is further the eighth lord in the Daśāṁśa (D-10) chart causing resignation from post, but being in trines to Jupiter in the same divisional chart ensures continued success.

Johnson would successfully hold this position in Congress until 1948! In 1947 Saturn Mahādaśā began, which was the same graha that ensured Johnson's marriage. Saturn is not considered auspicious in the ninth house as the native may use scrupulous means to get what they want and money will be the motivating factor, yet at the same time they will be very concerned about the poor and downtrodden. Saturn is placed in the eighth from the Sun which is an auspicious position for Saturn, but would bring him in a situation where others reaped the fruits of his work. Saturn associates strongly with Lagna lord, Horā Lagna and the Ghaṭika Lagna in the Drekkaṇa chart ensuring powerful influence during this time, and with Saturn being the seventh lord from Lagna and Horā Lagna Johnson's wife would be that blessing that would take him to power. Finally, as Saturn is the seventh lord placed in the ninth, the ninth lord Jupiter shares Raśī Dṛṣṭi with the seventh house forming a temporary Rāja Yoga that Jupiter instigated in its Daśā.

In 1948 Johnson ran for Senator in a highly disputed election. Johnson won by a small margin and became Senator. It later became evident from ballot lists that a lot of the registered voters for Johnson arrived at the end of the voting, in alphabetical order and had already passed away before the election took place! Despite this he became a Senator in Saturn Daśā, Saturn Antaradaśā. He held his position very well in the senate and was notorious for his persuasion skills.

Johnson was considered the favourite of the southern democrats due to his influence in the Senate and earlier position in the House of Representatives, and therefore was encouraged to run for president in 1960. The Democratic National Convention was held in July 1960 during Saturn Daśā, Mars Antaradaśā. Mars is the Yogakāraka that we had mentioned earlier and was sure to be a boon for Johnson. Being a malefic in the sixth from the Mahādaśā, Mars was sure to bring battles and the possibility of winning. Mars rules the southern direction and so it was that his main support came from the southern states of the USA.

Yet, the Rāja yoga granted by Mars is strong but the many grahas joined Mars and it being deeply combust implies that this Rāja yoga must be shared and a much stronger leader signified by the Sun will precede him. Johnson was second to John F. Kennedy in the democratic nomination and despite not winning was asked to join Kennedy as his Vice Presidential candidate. Later that year the pair would win the Presidential election.

Despite the pairs success Kennedy despised Johnson and made him virtually powerless in the White House. The two had feuded vigorously in the Democratic nominations and this had continued into the White House. However, Rāhu Antaradaśā was about to start and besides being the Amatyakāraka is joined the Ātmakāraka in a Rāja Sambandha Yoga promising enormous power. However, Rāhu is the eighth lord and will have to do so through the demise of another. This is in tune with the philosophy of Mahādaśā lord Saturn who when giving Rāja yoga will cause the fall of another. So also in Saturn Daśā, Rāhu Antaradaśā Kennedy was assassinated and in November 1963 Johnson was instated as acting president.

Continuing in the footsteps of Kennedy, Johnson broke the delaying debate of the southern democrats to sign the Civil Rights Act of 1964, having a focus on overcoming racial segregation. Following this he met with several civil rights activists among which included Martin Luther King Jr. Jupiter Antaradaśā had started bringing the tides of peace following the horror of the assassination. The grand blessing carried by Jupiter brought Johnson into the presidential election of 1964 where in November 1964 he attained a landslide victory against opponent Barry Goldwater. The next two years of Jupiter Antaradaśā were largely successful for Johnson, instigating the Great Society program with the purpose of enabling aide to education, attack on disease, Medicare, Medicaid, urban renewal, beautification, conservation, enabling everyone to vote, and many other society conscious issues. With this program he was able to tackle many problems experienced by the poorer regions of the USA and further was influential in creating a larger middle class.

In November 1966 Mercury Mahādaśā began. Mercury will give the results of the Sun which is a dire Māraka for Cancer Lagna afflicting health. Being in the fourth house from the Ghaṭika Lagna this will affect his popularity as well. Johnson had joined an administration which was deep into the Vietnam War which caused his popularity to plummet in the newspapers (Mercury). Further he began receiving resistance from his own party which had now become divided into four fractions.

A resignation of post is expected due to Mercury's lordship in the Daśāṁśa (D-10) chart. Mercury is the fifth lord from Ghaṭika Lagna affecting power and position and so also during the same Antaradaśā he indicated that he would not run for a second term as president. The Democrats lost their seat to Nixon in the 1968 elections.

Johnson retired to his Texas ranch to complete his memoirs. He had indicated earlier that he felt he wouldn't survive a second term as president due to heart issues. Ketu Antaradaśā arose from 1969 to 1970 following his presidency and being exalted in the fifth from the Mahādaśā graha it indicates happiness, rest and expansion of family. His daughters Luci and Lynda both delivered their second child and their families were set to grow even bigger over the next few years.

Venus Antaradaśā arose from 1970 to 1973 and is placed in the unfortunate eleventh from the Mahādaśā indicating punishment and troubles. This is further accentuated by its junction with eighth lord Rāhu showing health problems. Just before the end of Venus Antaradaśā Johnson passed away in his bed. He passed away due to his third heart attack. He died a month before a ceasefire was signed in Vietnam.

यन्मण्डलं व्याधि विनाश दःुखं यद्दग्यजुः सामसु संप्रगीतम्।
प्रकाशितं येन च भूर्भुवः स्वः पुनातु मां तत्सवितुर्वरेण्यम्॥ ५॥

5

Tools

5.1 Dṛṣṭi: Sight of Signs and Planets

The Sanskrit equivalent to aspects is dṛṣṭi, which means sight and is derived from the word *dṛś*, which means 'to watch' or 'to see'. Keeping this in mind, the concept of dṛṣṭi as a line of sight becomes apparently clear. All sight and visibility depends on light, and this light is the bringer of knowledge. This is why the Sun is the source of all knowledge in the universe.

There are two types of knowledge in the universe.

1. Knowledge, which is readily available, and comes naturally.
2. Knowledge, which one desires, and hence pursues.

These two categories can be understood in the following terms: rāśī dṛṣṭi, and graha dṛṣṭi respectively which are the sight of signs and planets respectively. We can infer from the above, that though a body may have a desire to 'see' or attain knowledge, it may not have the ability to do so, or the knowledge is not available. In a similar way, a wall blocks us from seeing an object placed behind it. This is the vital difference between these two types of dṛṣṭi.

In popular western astrology, aspects are determined through the mutual placement of planets. This mutual placement results in a relationship between two or more bodies allowing the reader to assess the relationship. Two bodies having a tense relationship with each other may give bad results in the specific area of life. Some translate the concept of dṛṣṭi as the equivalent of the western aspect, but they are evidently different in application.

5.1.1 Rāśi Dṛṣṭi (sight of signs)

Just as a home has windows, through which it shares sight with other buildings and their occupants, the signs have a view or sight, which it shares with other signs and the planets occupying them. Rāśi dṛṣṭi can be compared to a neighbourhood of signs. The signs, which share vision, belong to the same neighbourhood.

Table 53: Rāśi Dṛṣṭi

Sign	Aspects
Aries	Leo, Scorpio, Aquarius
Taurus	Cancer, Libra, Capricorn
Gemini	Virgo, Sagittarius, Pisces
Cancer	Scorpio, Aquarius, Taurus
Leo	Libra, Capricorn, Aries
Virgo	Sagittarius, Pisces, Gemini
Libra	Aquarius, Taurus, Leo
Scorpio	Capricorn, Aries, Cancer
Sagittarius	Pisces, Gemini, Libra
Capricorn	Taurus, Leo, Scorpio
Aquarius	Aries, Cancer, Libra
Pisces	Gemini, Virgo, Sagittarius

This sight, or aspect does not change based on the planet, but is fixed based on the sign. This type of sight is circumstantial in nature, and shows the ability of various signs to influence other signs through their presence.

This sight can drastically alter the nature of a sign. If an evil element (malefic body) moves into one's neighbourhood, it will make one agitated, scared, depressed, etc while a good element (benefic body) will cause happiness, and well being to those present in the neighbourhood.

Rāśi dṛṣṭi depends on the sign in question.

- If the sign is a movable one, it will see the fixed signs, except the fixed sign adjacent to it.
- Similarly, a fixed sign will see the movable signs, except the movable sign adjacent to it.
- All dual signs see each other.

The planets in these signs, will share the same vision as the sign it is placed in.

Example of Rāśi Dṛṣṭi:

In the example chart, Scorpio (marked in dark dray) has mutual 'sight' with the signs: Aries, Cancer and Capricorn (marked in light grey). Among these, Cancer has Rāhu, whilst Capricorn has Ketu, which will shape the results of Scorpio.

Figure 11: Rāśi Dṛṣṭi Example

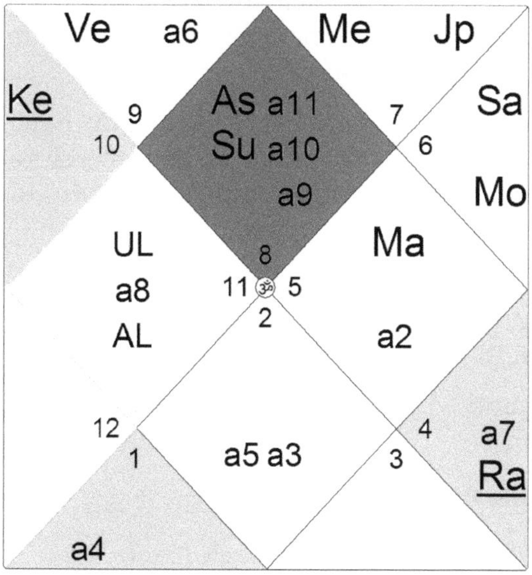

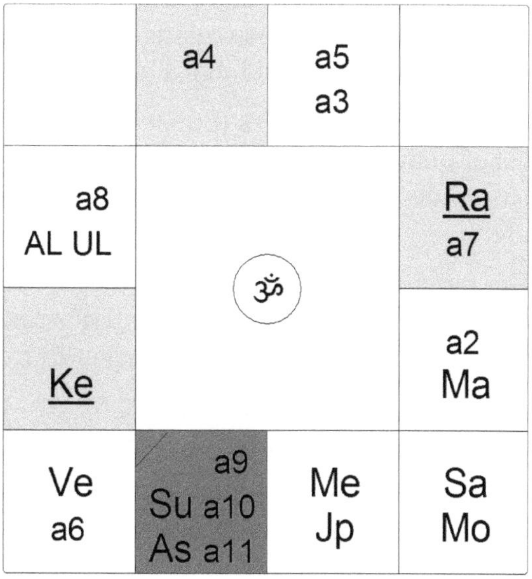

Rāśi dṛṣṭi is a very practical tool to understand the chart. A small practical example is given. Whilst describing the grahas, Maharṣi Parāśara has stated that the Sun, Jupiter, and the nodes give knowledge, while the Moon enables the person to repeat what has been told.

The use of this dictum is as follows. See which of these grahas have Rāśi dṛṣṭi on the Lagna and you will know how much intellectual capacity the native possesses. In the example chart, Sun is in the Lagna, receiving the Rāśi dṛṣṭi of Rāhu and Ketu. Hence, one may infer that the native presides over a good amount of intellectual capacity.

5.1.1.3 Abhimukha

Of the three signs having sight on the relevant sign, the sign having an oddity (odd/even) different from the two other signs will have a stronger strength of vision and influence. This is the concept of 'Abhimukha'. Abhimukha means 'front-facing' literally, and indicates the signs, which face each other, and will have direct sight.

Table 54: Abhimukha

Abhimukha Sign Pair	
Aries	Scorpio
Taurus	Libra
Gemini	Sagittarius
Cancer	Aquarius
Leo	Capricorn
Virgo	Pisces

The Abhimukha principle is used to emphasize the most influential bodies involved in an event. When comparing this to our scheme in the neighbourhood, the Abhimukha sign will be your closest neighbour, and who will have a stronger influence on you than the other neighbours. Hence in the earlier example, among the signs: Leo, Scorpio and Aquarius, Scorpio will have the strongest impact on the affairs of Aries, as will Scorpio's occupant – the Sun.

5.1.2 Graha Dṛṣṭi (sight of planets)

Just as Rāśi dṛṣṭi is based on the sign, graha dṛṣṭi is based on the planet. Graha dṛṣṭi can be understood as the bodies' individual nature or desire, which is irrespective of circumstances. Hence using graha dṛṣṭi, we can see the native's desires and it is these desires that will have a bearing on their actions in society.

Among the nine bodies (Sun to Ketu) in Vedic Astrology, Ketu is excluded from the list of planets having graha dṛṣṭi, as Ketu has no head and cannot see, and therefore has no desires. It is for this reason that Ketu has the power to curb one's desires in life.

The remaining eight bodies, all desire to see the seventh house from it. The seventh house is the house from which all desires spring; therefore, it is natural that all bodies with desires would see the seventh from it.

The bodies also see the 3rd, 10th, 5th, 9th, 4th and 8th houses from them, with partial desire/intensity[1]. The grahas see the

- seventh house with full (100%) intensity;

1 Commonly astrologers discard these 'partial sights', and use the full aspects only, however such practice is not recommended, as fact remains that a Grahas partial aspect may turn out to hold a stronger influence than its full aspect.

- fourth and eighth houses with ¾ (75%) intensity;
- fifth and ninth houses with ½ (50%) intensity;
- third and tenth houses with ¼ (25%) intensity.

Figure 12: Graha Dṛṣṭi Chakra: dṛṣṭi strength

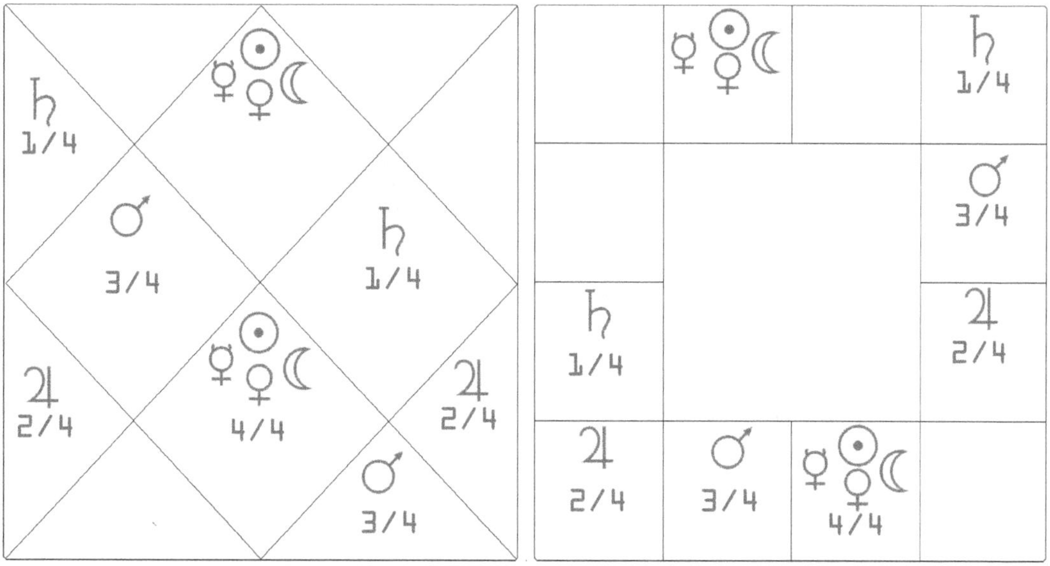

The outer planets Saturn, Jupiter and Mars, as well as Rāhu additionally have full dṛṣṭi as follows:

Saturn: 3rd and 10th houses from it.

Jupiter: 9th and 5th from it.

Rāhu: 9th, 5th and 12th (2nd in regular motion, as Rāhu is always retrograde)from it.

Mars: 4th and 8th houses from it.

The outer bodies have this special strength of dṛṣṭi, due to their position relative to the earth, which enables a "better view." The root reason for their 'special sight' and hence 'special desire or focus' can be understood from the nature of the planets, as given below.

Saturn desires to see the third and tenth houses from it, as these are two among the four houses of growth (Upachaya[2]). The third house specifically shows our habits and the arsenal we carry, be these rosaries or weapons. The tenth shows the actions or karma performed in society. If these actions are without purity, we may leave this earth too early. Hence Saturn is interested in keeping us pure and strong to ensure longer life through which we experience our karmas.

Mars desires to see the fourth and eighth houses from it. The fourth house shows our home and protection, and Mars being the natural soldier, desires to ensure that the home is well guarded. The eighth house shows death and new beginnings, and

2 3rd, 6th, 10th and 11th houses are upachaya sthānas or houses of growth.

as a soldier, Mars will ensure protection of the home, even if deadly force is required.

Jupiter desires to see the fifth and ninth houses from it, as these show the past and future. Jupiter looks at all the good deeds we did in the past life, and ensures that they come into fructification in the future (pūrva puṇya[3]).

Rāhu sees all the bad deeds we did in our past (ninth) and this results in little fortune in the future (fifth). This is the exact opposite of Jupiter, who wishes to bless the native for their good deeds. Rāhu also sees the twelfth from his position as he is always looking to see what is transpiring behind his back. Astrologers may note that since Rāhu is retrograde, his twelfth house is actually the second house from himself, when counted in zodiacal order.

Chart 56: Example of Graha Dṛṣṭi

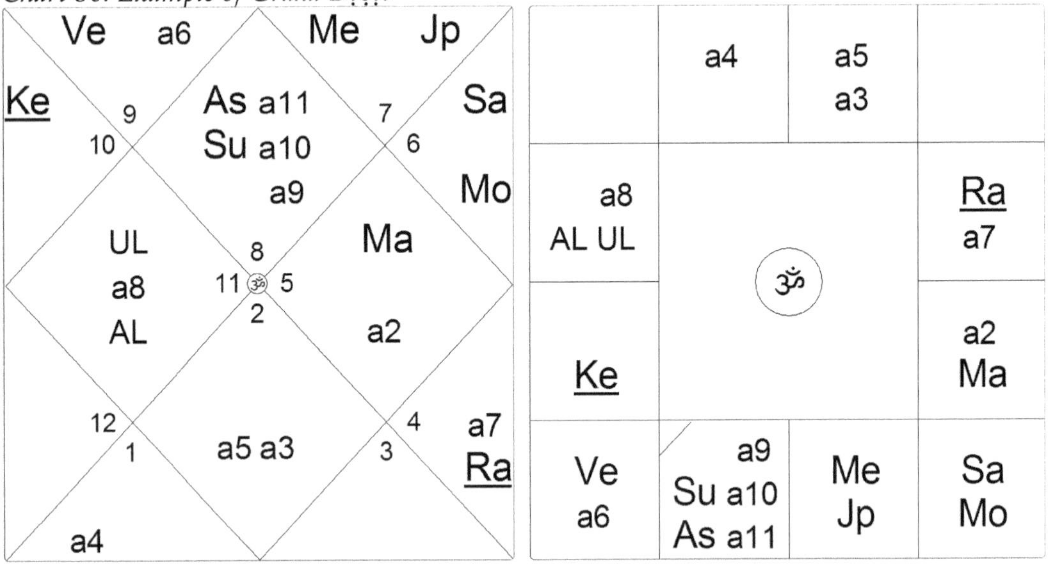

An example is given above. Jupiter in Libra desires to see Aquarius (5th from it), Aries (7th), and Gemini (9th). Rāhu in Cancer desires to see Leo (2nd from it), Scorpio (5th), Capricorn (7th) and Pisces (9th). Mars in Leo desires to see Scorpio (4th), Aquarius (7th) and Pisces (8th). Saturn in Virgo desires to see Scorpio (3rd), Pisces (7th) and Gemini (10th).

It may be inferred that the bodies can only see the 3rd, 4th, 5th, 7th, 8th, 9th, 10th (and 2nd/12th) houses from their position. The houses excluded from this scheme are the 6th and 11th houses, which are the houses of punishment (Daṇḍa[4]) and end (Hara[5]) in this world, respectively. Hence, none of the grahas has the desire to see such positions in the chart, and only God has the final say on these two areas of life.

---

3 Pūrva (past/previous) Puṇya (fruits/results), hence fruits of past life.

4 Daṇḍa means punishment and the sixth house shows the six sins (ṣaòripu) we have committed and must suffer for. The sixth house is also used to see the punishment we receive after death.

5 Hara is the form of Śiva as the destroyer of the universe, also known as Rudra. This is the basis for the Rudrākśa (D-11 Varga chart).

5.1.2.1 Magnitude of Dṛṣṭi: Sphuṭa Dṛṣṭi

Having ascertained the dṛṣṭi of the various grahas it becomes important to ascertain the strength of this dṛṣṭi. The strength of dṛṣṭi will indicate the power of the graha to influence the decisions, or actions of another graha/bhāva, and show the focus of the specific graha i.e. if there are no grahas in the Lagna, the graha having the strongest graha dṛṣṭi on the Lagna will have the strongest sway on the native's personality.

Calculation of Sphuṭa Dṛṣṭi

i. First, choose the appropriate chakra resembling the grahas dṛṣṭi, i.e. if it is either of Sun, Moon, Venus or Mercury, choose the one in Figure 12.

ii. Choose the relevant graha/bhāva/point, to focus the dṛṣṭi on.

iii. Expunging signs, decide whether the degree of the graha is higher or lower than the bhāva of focus.

- If the graha has a higher degree, check the difference in the 'dṛṣṭi strength' (Refer: Figure 12) between the bhāva of focus and the bhāva in the twelfth from it.
- If the graha has a lower degree, check the difference in 'dṛṣṭi strength' between the bhāva of focus and the bhāva in second from it.

iv. Divide the difference by 30 degrees to ascertain the dṛṣṭi strength per 1 degree.

v. Expunging signs again, determine the exact difference in degrees between the graha and the point of focus

vi. Multiply the difference with the result of #4.

vii. Add or deduct the result of #6 from the percentage of the point of focus, depending on whether the point of focus has a lower or higher degree respectively.

Some do not ascribe to this view of applying degrees to aspects.

Chart 57: Example Chart

In the given chart, we are interested in the strength of Sun's dṛṣṭi on Mars.

1. Treating Sun as Lagna, it has 25% (1/4) dṛṣṭi on the third house from it (Refer: Figure 12).
2. The degree of Sun is 21° Cancer whilst Mars occupies 13° Virgo.
3. Expunging signs, Mars occupies a lower degree w.r.t. Sun.
4. Since Mars occupies a lower degree, we must consider the dṛṣṭi strength of Sun on the second from it, compared to the third from it. The second from Sun has 0% intensity, compared to the 25% intensity in the third from Sun, making the difference 25%.

5. The difference is 25% and this is divided by 30 degrees to get = 25/30 = 5/6 % per 1 degree.
6. The difference between 21° and 13° is eight°.
7. Eight degrees is multiplied by 5/6 = 40/6 or 6+1/6%.
8. As the degree of Mars is less than that of Sun, the 6+1/6 % is deducted from 25% = 18+1/3%. Hence the result of Sun's dṛṣṭi sphuṭa on Mars is 18+1/3%

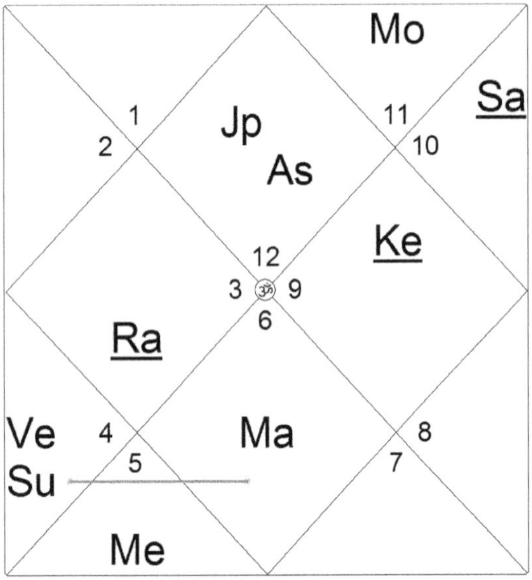

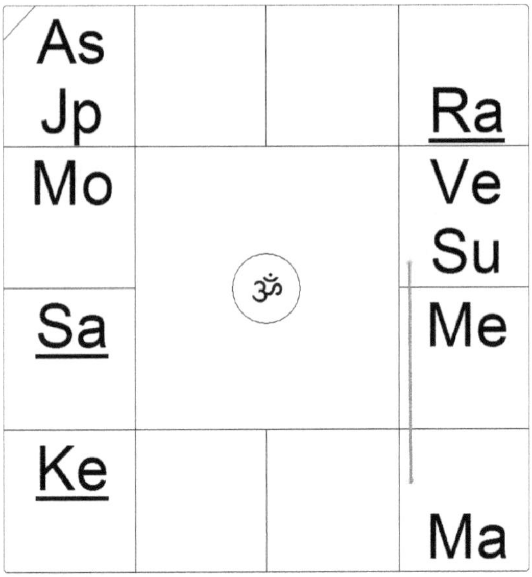

A quick formula to work out the calculation is:

$D^{\circ} * (P\%/30) + p\% = X$

D = is the degree difference between the graha and the point of focus, after expunging signs.

P = is the number ascertained in #3.

d = is the percentage full percentage value, from the point of focus which must be added or deducted.

X= is the result of the calculation.

5.1.2.2 Curses or Śāpa

A curse or an evil eye is caused due to a malign/evil intent towards another individual.

Due to such cruel attitudes towards another person in past lives, we are inclined to suffer in future lives to come. To see what evil we caused to another individual, we have to see the graha dṛṣṭi or conjunction of malefics on other planets. Each of the malefics represents a state of emotional suffering, of which two or more such malefics constitutes a curse.

- If this dṛṣṭi/conjunction of malefics is on a bhāva, it gives a wrong attitude towards the area of life indicated by the bhāva.

- ☐ If the dṛṣṭi is on a graha then it indicates suffering arising out of a person who suffered at your hands in the past birth.

The latter constitutes a curse. The planet(s) joined/aspected by malefics indicate the type of curse.

- Jupiter – Curse of Brahmins, priests, spiritual people, guru's or deva
- Ketu – Curse of nāgas or sādhus/renunciate
- Moon – Curse of mother
- Venus – Curse of spouse or sister
- Mercury – Curse of uncle
- Sun – Curse of father
- Mars – Curse of brother
- Saturn – Curse of elders, forefathers, deceased.
- Rāhu – Curse of sarpas/snakes

If more than one curse exists in a chart, then the most benefic planet involved in the curse will dominate the effects of the curse. The reason being that a more benefic planet is a more pious planet, and its prayers will always fructify... be the prayer a curse or a blessing.

The malefics, who are causing the curse, indicate the type of suffering and from which areas of life the suffering will be experienced.

- ☐ If Rāhu is involved in the curse, then the houses occupied by Aquarius will indicate the negative impact of the shock/deceit suffered.
- ☐ If Saturn is involved in the curse, the houses occupied by Capricorn and Aquarius, will indicate the result of the sorrow/shock suffered.
- ☐ If Mars is involved in the curse, then the houses occupied by Aries and Scorpio will indicate the result of the anger/violence suffered.
- ☐ Sun and Ketu are not considered malefics for this purpose.

Different connotations arise from other bodies joining this curse, of which two are most important.

- If the Lagna lord joins this curse, then the suffering of the curse is very intense and can cause terrible emotional states bordering insanity.
- If the Ātmakāraka is involved in the curse, then the suffering is very deep and hard for the native to express/understand.
- In cases where both Ātmakāraka and Lagna lord are involved in the curse, the suffering experienced will cause emotional blockages, and can hinder the natives' emotional progress in life.

5.1.2.3 Examples

Chart 58: Śrī Rāma: Brahmin Śāpa

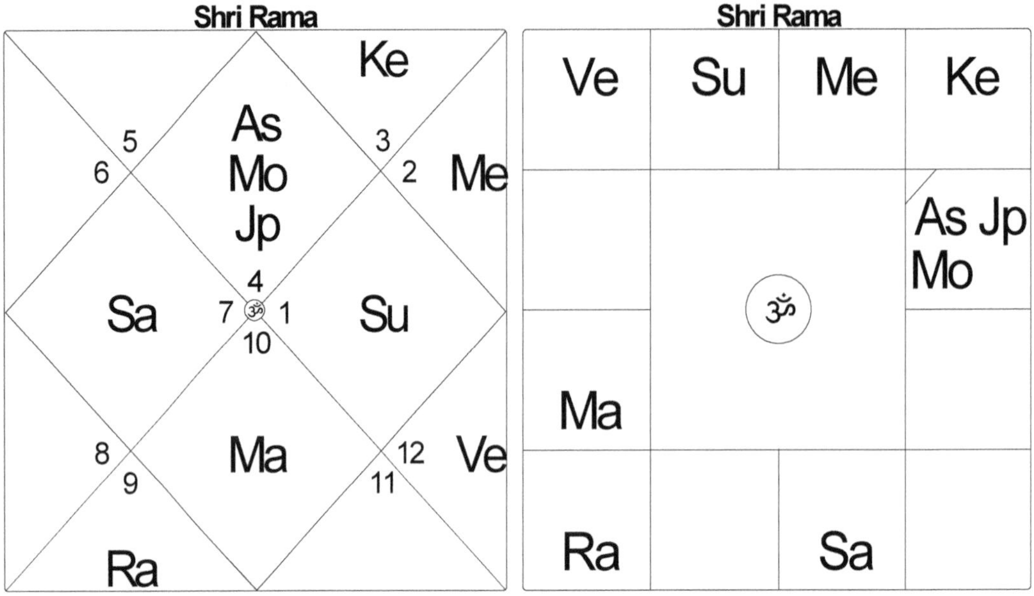

Śrī Rāma born Treta Yuga, Chaitra Śukla Navamī, Abhijīt Muhūrta, Karkaṭaka Lagna.

In the chart of Lord Rāma, Saturn, Mars and Rāhu all have graha dṛṣṭi on the Sun in his tenth house. However, Jupiter and Moon also receive the dṛṣṭi of Mars and Saturn. Since Jupiter is the most benefic planet, it indicates a curse of Brahmin or Deva. Jātaka Pārijāta states that if sixth lord is involved in the curse, there is talk of a Brahmin and not a Deva. The Parampara teaches that this applies to eighth and twelfth lords as well, to fulfil the requirements for the yoga of a perfect Brahmin[6].

Due to Jupiter and Saturn being sixth and eighth lords respectively there is a curse of Brahmin. Saturn's lordship will indicate the sorrow/suffering experienced due to this curse. Saturn lords the seventh house indicating that the suffering will be because of spouse, and that too separation from the spouse as Saturn lords the eighth house as well.

Mars indicates where the anger will come from. Mars lords the fifth house and tenth house. It so happens that the Brahmin which cursed Śrī Rāma in previous births was none other than Devarṣi Nārada, a devotee (5th house) of Śrī Vishnu. Devarṣi Nārada cursed Śrī Viṣṇu, when Viṣṇu prevented him from getting married. Just as Nārada lost his wife, so did Śrī Rāma.

As Lagna lord is Jupiter, the separation from spouse would have caused a lot of suffering and torment, but as the same Jupiter is forming a Hamsa Mahāpuruṣa yoga, whilst there was suffering, Śrī Rāma showed mercy on his enemy, Ravaṇa, when he gave him a chance to hand over his wife and stay on peaceful terms.

---

6 Should moon be in a Duṣthāna and Saturn be in Lagna, the birth is that of a perfect Brahmin.

The remedy lies in worshipping the planet causing the curse. In case of Jupiter, the worship of Sadāśiva is advised. Śrī Rāma installed the Rāmeśvaram Śiva Linga, which ended the curse, and later took on the worship of Śrī Cāmuṇḍi Devi (Mars) to end the war with Rāvaṇa. He did this with the Cāmuṇḍā Hṛdaya Mantra, also known as the Ram Caṇḍī mantra because Śrī Rāma added the Praṇava AUM to the mantra: om aim hrīm klīm camuṇḍāyai viccai.

Chart 59: Kalatra Śāpa

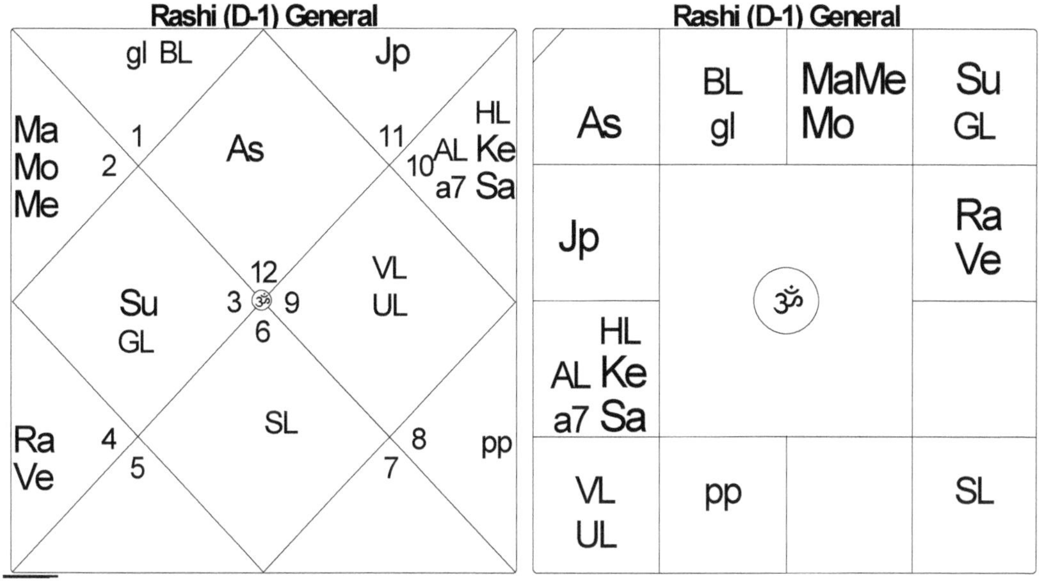

Female native born 30th June 1962, 0:13 AM, Kolkata, India.

The native's Venus is joined Rāhu and receives the graha dṛṣṭi of Saturn. This forms Kalatra Śāpa or the curse of spouse. Saturn is in and lords the 11th house where the Ārūḍha Lagna is placed, hence this curse would have caused her a bad name or reputation, as well as the loss of income/work. Rāhu is lord of Aquarius where Jupiter the Lagna lord is posited. The shocks (Rāhu) arising out of this experience would have left a deep scar on her intelligence. This can give insecurity and a severe lack of self-esteem. As Venus is eighth lord, it was triggered through the separation between her and the partner.

Whenever analyzing the fortune of marriage, the ninth lord should also be analyzed and whenever the yoga exists between the eighth and ninth lords, premature death of spouse can occur. Here Venus the eighth lord has Rāśi dṛṣṭi on the ninth house, whilst the ninth lord has Rāśi dṛṣṭi on the eighth house; hence the danger of premature death of a partner is there. The presence of Kāla Sarpa Yoga has intensified the curse, and made it hard to break, however with the strengthening and purification of Venus, the native's curses will end. This could be done through intense worship of Śrī Lakṣmī, or Śrī Kamalātmikā Devi.

Chart 60: Curse of Sādhu

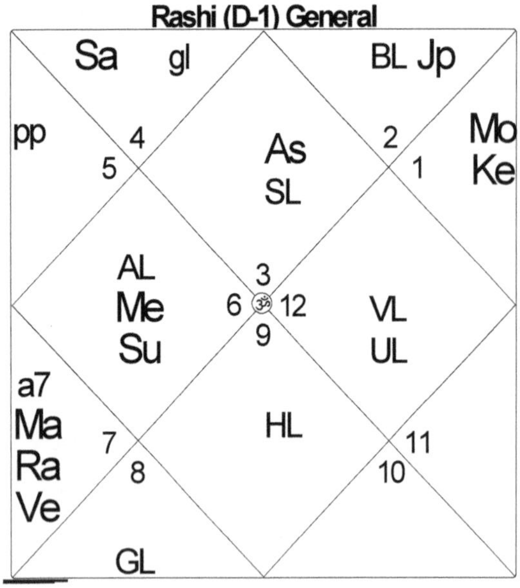

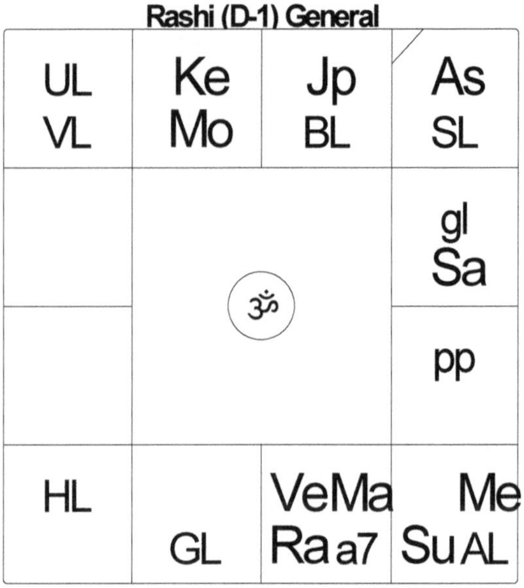

Male native born 9th October 1976, 10:06 PM, Vineland, New Jersey.

The native had visited a Śuka Nāḍi reader and learned that he had incurred the curse of a Sādhu in previous births. Let us confirm this from his chart.

Ketu indicates curses from Nāgas and Sādhus, which must be analyzed. Ketu is in Aries, receiving the graha dṛṣṭi of Saturn and Mars. The aspect of Rāhu on Ketu is always ignored. We can hence confirm that curse of a sādhu definitely exists. However, this is not the primary curse, which is curse of a spouse (Venus).½

Rāhu lords the ninth house in the chart, hence the native may have a shocking experience related to teachers/gurus. Rāhu in the fifth house indicates places of learning or related to knowledge, students, etc, and its conjunction with Venus will definitely indicate issues of an intimate nature. Saturn lords the eighth house and can indicate sorrow due to the demise of their loved ones. The native has experienced separation between him and his gurus/guides due to the guru's premature demise, illicit affairs with other students, or their reproduction of wrong knowledge to the native. It should be noted that all the gurus the native has had problems with, had taken vows of celibacy or renunciation (Ketu).

As there is Kāla Sarpa Yoga in the chart, again formed along the curse axis, the remedy advised must be in the form of the benefics joined the nodes. These are Moon and Venus, whom the native should strengthen/purify. This could be through Devi worship due to Moon, or the worship of Śrī Lakṣmī. The intelligent astrologer would advise Śrī Kamalātmikā, however Venus being Ātmakāraka would make such worship very painful and difficult, hence instead the worship of Śrī Bhuvaneśvarī should be advised, accompanied with the worship of Śrī Lakṣmī or the Iṣṭa Devatā.

5.2 Avasthā (states of planets)

Avasthā refers to the state of a planet. There are many avasthās, which are used for various purposes, and their use is solely for understanding the state of the person through which one experiences. For example, if a planet is in a depressed state, then only when the native is in a depressed state will they get the results of the planet, similarly planets in a delighted state will only give results only when the native is in a delighted state. Whether the graha puts the native in that state or the native himself move towards that state, is left open for debate.

5.2.1 Dīptādi Avasthā: 'exalted' and other states

Table 55: Dīptādi Avasthā

Term	Emotion	Placement
Dīpta	Excited	Exaltation
Svastha	Confident	Own sign
Pramudita	Glad	Friendliest sign
Śānta	At peace	Friendly sign
Dīna	Timid	Neutral
Duḥkhita	Distressed	Enemy
Vikala	Agitated	Joined an inimical graha
Khala	Shaking	Debilitation
Kopa	Enraged	Combustion

The Dīptādi avasthā refers to mental states experienced through the fructification of yogas given by the grahas. A simple way to use this knowledge is to take a chart and look for exalted and debilitated planets. The bhāva in which an exalted planet is placed is a source of great enjoyment, i.e. exalted planets in fourth house will make the person enjoy all activities dealing with the home. This is opposite for debilitated planets.

5.2.2 Bālādi Avasthā: 'infant' and other states

Table 56: Bālādi Avasthā

Name	Meaning	Degree span
Bāla	Infant	0° - 5:59°
Kumāra	Young	6° - 11:59°
Yuvā	Adult	12°- 17:59°
Vṛddha	Old	18° - 23:59°
Mṛta	Dead	24° - 29:59°

The tabulated designation of degrees is opposite in even signs, i.e. the first six degrees of an even sign is Mṛta, the next is Vṛddha, and so on. The Parampara teaches, that it is again opposite if the planet is retrograde, as the age of a planet depends on when its entering and exiting a sign, just as one enters and exists life.

The Bālādi avasthā is used to see when one gets the results of a specific planet, i.e. which state one is in when one gets the fruits of the planet. If a Daśā of a planet in an infant state is running, one gets the results prematurely or earlier than expected from the Daśā.

A planet in yoga will give results depending on which state it is in. A planet in Mṛta avasthā will give one results after death.

Chart 61: Padre Pio: Postmortem Fame

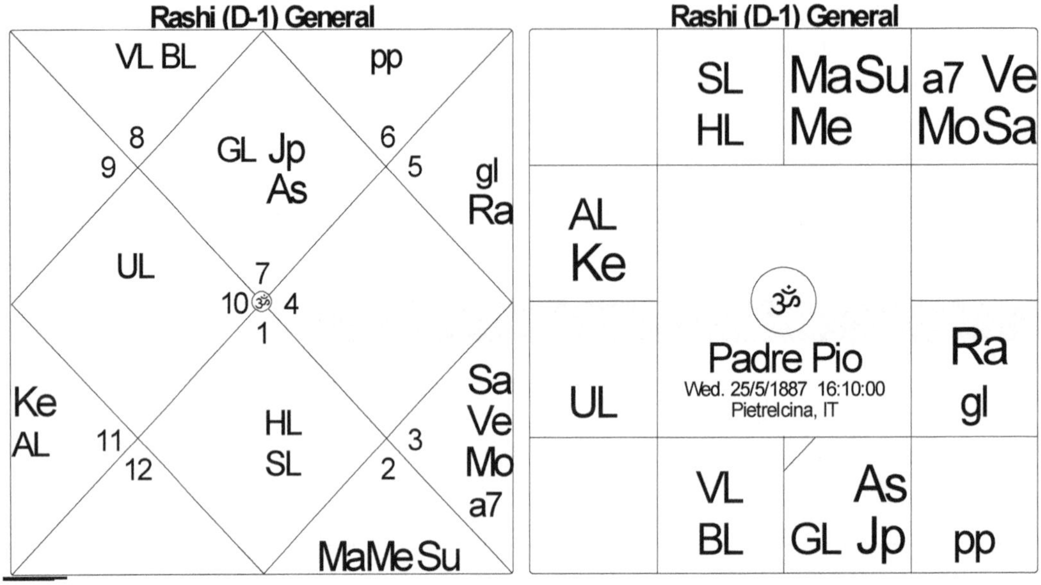

Chart of Padre Pio, born Francesco Forgione, 25th May 1887, 4:10 PM, Pietrelcina, Italy.

The given chart is of an intriguing and well known priest, Padre Pio. He was held in esteem for his very intense experiences of Christ, in which he would begin bleeding profusely from his wrists thus exhibiting signs of Stigmata. The church being weary of such incidents conducted a thorough investigation and isolated the Padre from the public. In public, however he showed enormous powers through the touch of his hands, and is renowned for some fantastic miracles. Many years after leaving his body, the church decided to commend his achievements. The fame given to him is indicated by Jupiter in Lagna. Jupiter is at 4° 53′ in Libra and retrogrades, putting it in Mṛta avasthā. Hence, the fame arose post-mortem fulfilling this dictum.

5.2.3 Lajjitādi Avasthā: 'shameful' and other states

Table 57: Lajjitādi Avasthāt

Term	Emotion	Placement
Lajjita	Ashamed	Joined Nodes, Sun, Saturn or Mars
Garvita	Proud	Exalted or Mūlatrikoṇa sign
Kṣudhita	Agitated	Association with an enemy planet/sign, and a malefic
Tṛṣita	Desirous	In a watery sign, aspected by an enemy and without bnefic aspect
Mudita	Delighted	Friendly association and associated with a benefic

Term	Emotion	Placement
Kṣobhita	Disturbed	Combust, malefic aspect and enemy aspect

The Lajjitādi Avasthā is similar to the Dīptādi Avasthā, and is very useful in evaluating the native's mental state during the fructification of Yogas. A planet joined a malefic is bound to give the emotion connected to the Lajjita state. People suffering from depression would be in Kṣudhita Avasthā. People in a state of dissatisfaction and frustration might be in a state of Kṣobhita Avasthā. Similarly, the Jyotiṣa must judge from the chart.

Chart 62: Broken relationship

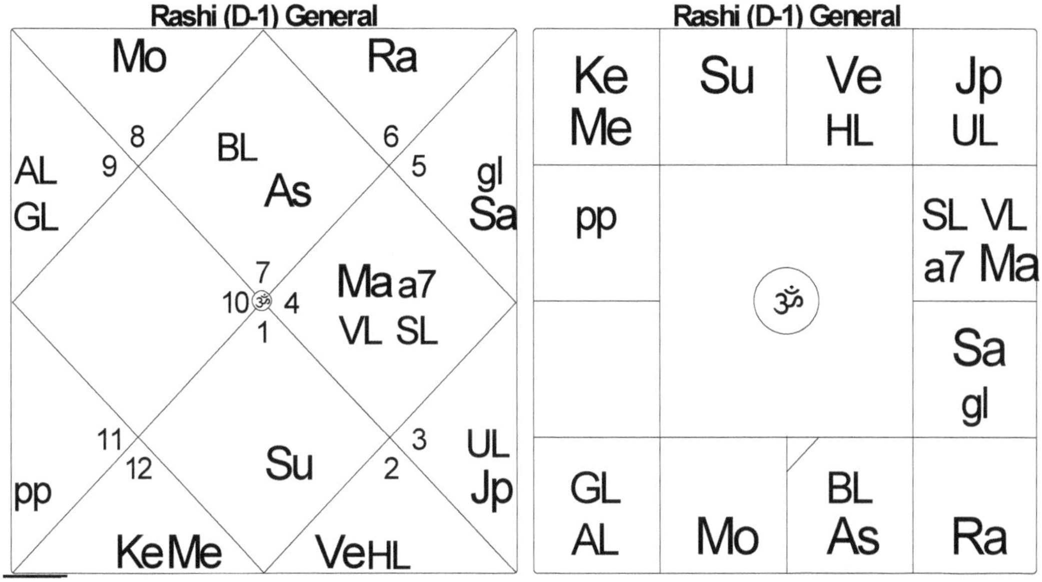

Male native born 25th April 1978, 6:50 PM, New Delhi, India.

The native of the given chart has debilitated AK Mercury joined Ketu in the sixth house. This is a highly undesirable situation where the Ātmakāraka has gone to Kṣudhita avasthā. When such incidents occur in chart, the native undergoes an intense transformation due to deep and important lessons being learnt by the Ātmā, and tendencies towards self-torture/punishment arise (Sixth house). Mercury lords the Upapada in the ninth house, which could be the source of the suffering, i.e. heartbreak.

However due to birth at sunset, Mercury has become extraordinarily strong, and will help ward of the evil. The best remedy in such a case is to worship the Iṣṭa Devatā, which is Jupiter in the native's chart. Hence, the worship of guru is vital for the native to overcome such experiences. The native was advised to worship Maharṣi Vyāsa, which gave excellent results for the native.

5.3 Aṣṭākavarga

Aṣṭākavarga is one of the popular, yet highly misunderstood tools among many Jyotiṣa. Aṣṭākavarga is extolled by Parāśara[7] as being one of the necessary tools for this Kali Yuga due to the degraded intellects of human beings, acquired through sinful deeds. Given below is an introduction to the Aṣṭākavarga system.

5.3.1.1 Aṣṭākavarga

Aṣṭākavarga consists of the words; Aṣṭa-ka-varga.

- Aṣṭa means eight
- Ka is the Brahma bīja, which causes the entire creation, from which the word kṣetra is derived which signifies the Rāśi chart itself. This interpretation is disputed by author's interpreting words such as 'Lagna-amśa-ka', or 'Kāraka-amśa-ka'.
- Varga means division, or part.

Hence, in Jyotiṣa terminology, the word Aṣṭākavarga means eight divisions in the Rāśi chart. In these eight divisions, the astrologers list out the contribution of 'rekha' from the seven grahas and the Lagna.

5.3.1.2 Rekha

Rekha means line, and is akin to the tilak put on the forehead/3rd eye during religious rites. This Rekha symbolizes a blessing and a potentiality and is masculine in nature. Once this potentiality has caused creation, the unused energy is depicted as a bindu or dot. The line shows how the potentiality has been used and the dot is that which is unused or inaccessible.

Table 58: Total Rekhā

Graha	Rekha
Sun	48
Moon	49
Mars	39
Mercury	54
Jupiter	56
Venus	52
Saturn	39
Lagna	49
Total	386

Jyotiṣa uses the rekha to see the potential that a chart has. The reksha will show the actual strength of a graha/bhāva, whilst the bindu will show the lack of the same.

5.3.2 Aṣṭākavarga Rekha at a Glance

A total of 386 Rekha needs to be distributed, among the twelve Bhāva in the eight vargas. This constitutes an average of 28 Rekha per bhāva, most of which is conducive towards auspicious results, otherwise inauspicious results follow. Sun, Moon, Mars, Mercury, Jupiter, Venus, Saturn and Lagna rule the eight Vargas. The nodes being the cause of rebirth are excluded in favour of their creation, the Lagna. Some newer scriptures include the Aṣṭākavarga schemes of the nodes; however, this does not adhere to the views of the ancient astrologers. A simple fact being, that more graha schemes, means more than the eight Vargas, which is implied by the word Aṣṭākavarga. Each of the eight Vargas has a specific amount of contribution.

7 Bṛhat Parāśara Horā Śāstra, Aṣṭakavargādhyāya.

Each varga has a specific distribution of rekha and bindu for each of the eight grahas. Given below is an example of the Sun's Aṣṭākavarga:

Table 59: Distribution of Sun's Rekhā

Graha	1st	2nd	3rd	4th	5th	6th	7th	8th	9th	10th	11th	12th
SUN	I	I		I			I	I	I	I	I	
MOON			I			I				I	I	
MARS	I	I		I			I	I	I	I	I	
MERCURY			I		I	I			I	I	I	I
JUPITER					I	I			I		I	
VENUS						I	I					I
SATURN	I	I		I			I	I	I	I	I	
LAGNA			I	I		I				I	I	I

The distribution of the Rekha in other vargas can be learnt from any textbook on Jyotiṣa.

5.3.3 Quick Conclusions using Aṣṭākavarga

5.3.3.1 Samudaya Aṣṭākavarga (SAV)

'Samudaya' means collective or accumulated, and shows the entire amount of accumulated rekhas for each bhāva. Samudaya Aṣṭākavarga or SAV will show the amount of potential energy one can spend in one area of life. The average being 386/12 = 32 rekha. Hence anything more than 32 rekha is auspicious whilst anything less than 32 is inauspicious. Those who use Varāhamihira's variation for SAV, exclude the use of the Lagna varga and hence the rekha average would be 337/12=28 rekha. Astrologers should keep this difference in mind before deducing the results of the SAV scheme.

A more than average SAV rekha in a bhāva will give a lot of focus on that specific bhāva i.e. higher rekha in the tenth house will indicate a karma yogi, whilst more rekha in the eleventh house will indicate a Bhogi or someone who strives to enjoy life's fruits. In this manner we see where there is more rekha to distinguish where all the energy of the native is spent. The Jyotiṣa will find this useful in overall assessments of a bhāva, but this is not conducive towards improving predictive accuracy.

5.3.3.3 Bhinna Aṣṭākavarga (BAV)

Each of the eight vargas deals with a specific part of one's life. Find the Kāraka of the house of focus. Open the specific varga of the chosen Kāraka and see its contribution to the house of focus. The maximum amount of rekha a bhāva can attain is eight rekha; hence, average is four rekha per bhāva.

Example of Sun's BAV

Figure 13: BAV of Sun

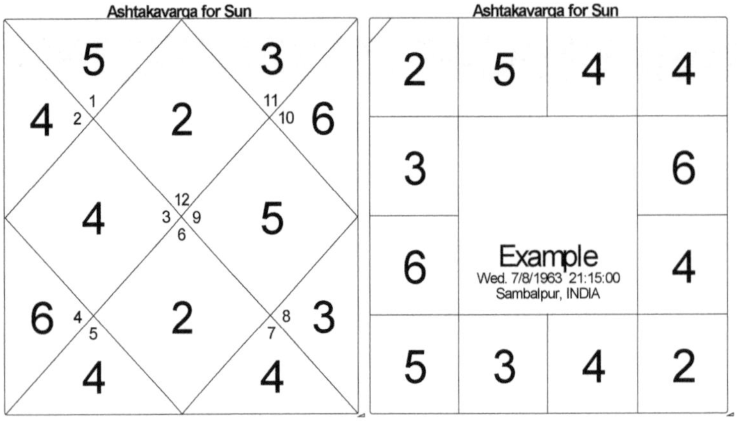

Sun is the primary Kāraka for the Lagna, having the role of protecting the native's health. The native's Lagna is Pisces and the Sun contributes two Rekha to Pisces, which is much below average. The native's health is quite unstable. By using the Sun's Aṣṭākavarga in a similar manner, the health of other family members can be quickly evaluated from the chart. The fourth house Gemini has four rekha indicating a mother with average/good health, whilst the ninth house has three rekha showing that the father has below average health.

Example of Lagna's BAV

The Lagna's contribution will show the intelligence of the person in the chart and the amount of attention the native puts in various areas of their life. The native's Lagna is Scorpio, which has a contribution of four rekha in the Lagna Aṣṭākavarga, indicating a native with average intelligence.

Figure 14: BAV of Lagna

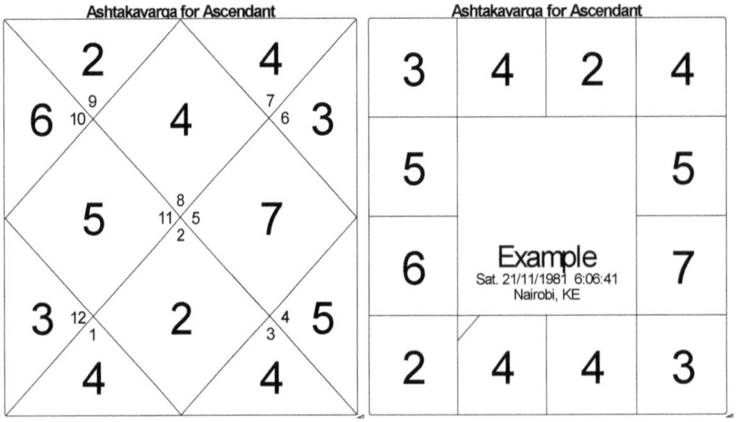

Example of Mars' BAV

Figure 15: BAV of Mars

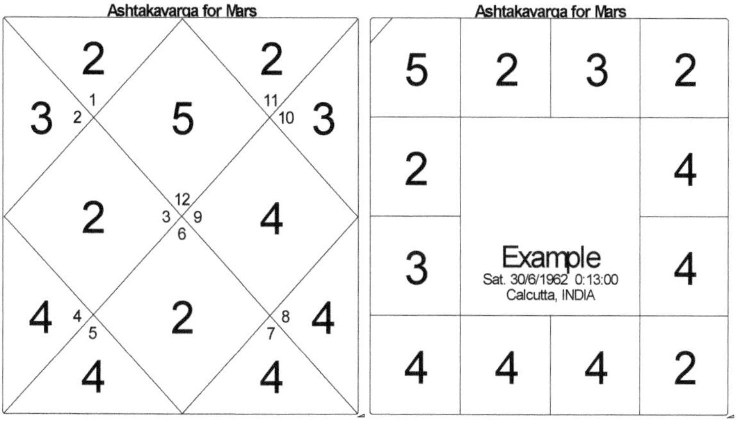

Another useful technique is treating the Kāraka as Lagna and judging the results there from. Mars is the Kāraka for co-born and the third house there from shows the maximum amount of co-born the native may have in their life. In the given chart, Mars is placed in Taurus and the third there from is Cancer, which has a contribution of four rekhas. The native has four brothers. Again, this method gives the Jyotiṣa an overall assessment, and is not conducive towards enhancing predictive accuracy.

Prastara Aṣṭākavarga (PAV)

Figure 16: PAV of Sun

Su Ma	Su Mo Ma Me Sa	As Su Ma Me	As Ma Me Ve
As Su Sa	PAV		Su Mo Ma Me Ju Sa
As Su Me Ju Ve Sa	Sun		As Su Ju Sa
As Mo Ma Me Ve	Mo Ju Sa	Su Ma Me Sa	Ma Sa

'Prastara' or 'spread-out' Aṣṭākavarga is a detailed exposition of the Bhinna Aṣṭākavarga. Each contribution of a rekha by a graha shows which grahas (people) are contributing to which bhāva (areas of life) in the Bhinna Aṣṭākavarga. This is useful in determining the effects of Antaradaśā on a person. This use of Aṣṭākavarga is conducive towards predictive accuracy!

See the Daśā running. Find the specific PAV, i.e. Sun's PAV for health and Lagna's PAV for intelligence. See whether the Antaradaśā graha contributes to the house in focus. If so, predict that the house will be activated during the Antaradaśā of that graha.

Example of health

The native of Pisces Lagna, has notably only two grahas contributing to the Lagna in Sun's BAV. Upon opening the PAV we learn that these two grahas are Sun and Mars. One can infer that during the Antaradaśās of Sun and Mars the native will have very good health. Whilst the native was running Jupiter mahā Daśā, Sun and Mars Antaradaśās, the native had exceedingly good health and took up physical exercises and sports.

Examples

Chart 63: Male: Marriage & Children

Rashi (D-1) General

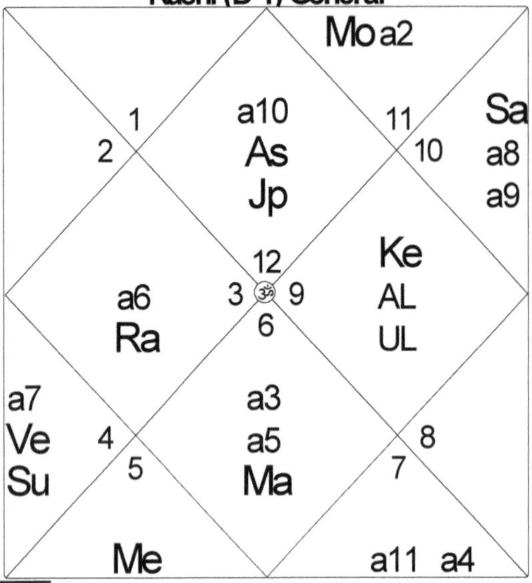

North Indian chart — placements:

- Mo a2 (top)
- a10 As Jp (house 1/2); Sa, a8, a9 (houses 10/11); Mo a2
- a6 Ra (house 3); Ke AL UL (house 9)
- a7 Ve Su (houses 4/5); a3 a5 Ma (houses 7/8)
- Me; a11 a4 (bottom)

Rashi (D-1) General

a10 Jp As			a6 Ra
Mo a2	ॐ		a7 Su Ve
a8 Saa9			Me
AL KeUL	a4 a11	a5 a3 Ma	

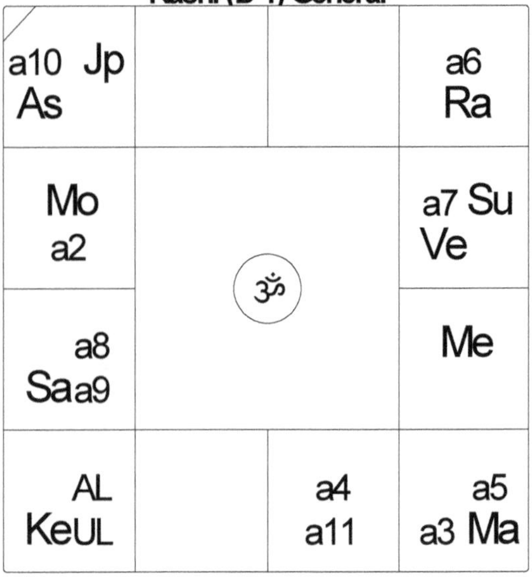

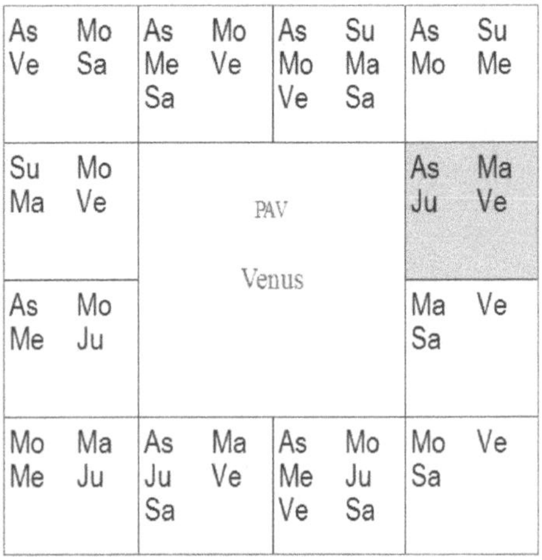

Male born 7th August 1963, 21:15, Sambalpur, India.

In the PAV of Venus, the seventh house Virgo has the contribution from Venus, Moon and Saturn. Further Mars is in the seventh house. The native was married in the Daśā Saturn-Moon. Eighth lord Venus is afflicted by Sun, Saturn and Rāhu showing physical separation in the relationship, while the Upapada in Libra has Mars as its lord placed in Māraṇa Kāraka Sthāna showing that the separation is due to divorce. Separation happened in Mercury-Venus as Venus contributes to the eighth house. Mercury-Moon brought the divorce where Moon also contributes to the eighth house. As Moon also contributes to the seventh house as well as aspecting he second house and A2 family expansion was to happen in the same Daśā. The native enjoyed his second marriage during the same Mercury-Moon Daśā.

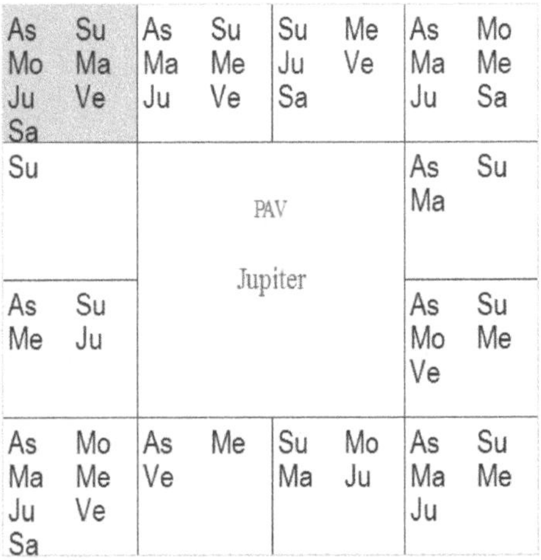

In the PAV of Jupiter, the fifth house from Lagna has the contribution of Mars, Sun and the Lagna. In case of the Lagna's contribution the daśās of Rāhu or Ketu can give results.

The native had children in the daśās Saturn-

PAV Venus

As Ve / Mo Sa	As Me Sa / Mo Ve	As Mo Ve / Su Ma Sa	As Mo / Su Me
Su Ma / Mo Ve	PAV Venus		As Ma / Ju Ve
As Me / Mo Ju			Ma Sa / Ve
Mo Me / Ma Ju	As Ju Sa / Ma Ve	As Me Ve / Mo Ju Sa	Mo Sa / Ve

PAV Jupiter

As Mo Ju Sa / Su Ma Ve	As Ma Ju / Su Me Ve	Su Ju Sa / Me Ve	As Ma Ju / Mo Me Sa
Su	PAV Jupiter		As Ma / Su
As Me / Su Ju			As Mo Ve / Su Me
As Ma Ju / Mo Me Ve	As Ve / Me	Su Ma / Mo Ju	As Ma Ju / Su Me

Mars and Saturn-Rāhu, and these were a girl and boy respectively.

This technique of timing events using Aṣṭākavarga, though quite simple requires refining in finding which graha will bring the event. For this the relevant varga is required and the use of graha Sambandha as given in the Sambandha chapter.

Chart 64: Male: Marriage example

Male born: 12th December 1945, 12:01:56 PM, Sindal, Denmark. In the PAV of Venus,

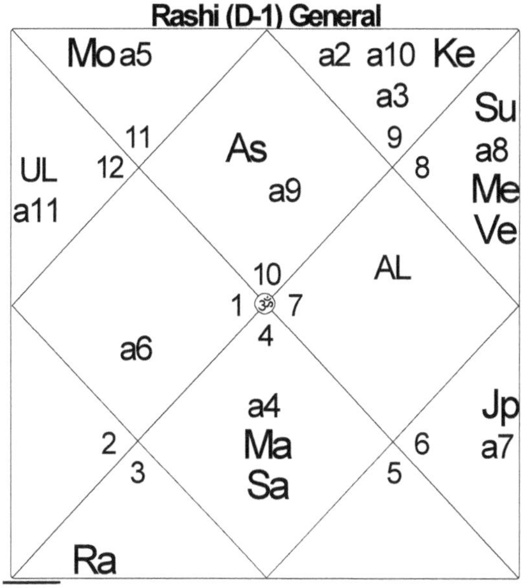

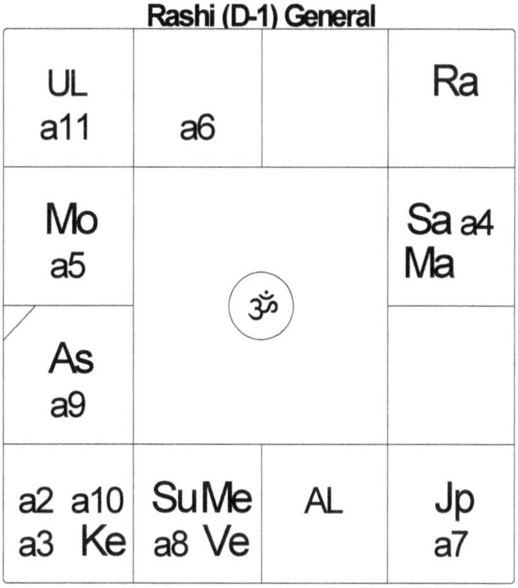

the seventh house Cancer has the contribution from Mercury, Venus and Jupiter.

Having ascertained the three possible Daśā, the Navāṁśa can be used to fine tune the specific Daśā.

In the Navāṁśa the Mahādaśā must have a strong yoga with the lagna or its lord to justify any events pertaining to marriage. (Rath, Crux of Vedic Astrology - Timing of events, 1998) If not then the person is not personally invested in such activities. Here a strong link is found through conjunction, aspect (graha dṛṣṭi) having unobstructed Argalā or obstructing negative Argalā.

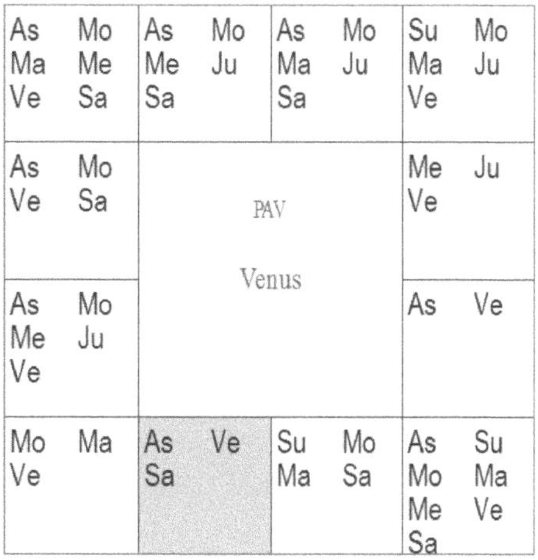

In the given chart the Navāṁśa Lagna is Leo and unoccupied. The lord is Sun placed in the eighth house. Mars and Jupiter aspect the Sun but their Mahādaśā are not likely being that he was born during Jupiter Daśā and Mars is his last Daśā. Sun is also a contender being the Lagneśa but would solicit a significant delay as it arises when he is seventy years of age. Truly the likely Mahādaśā are either of Saturn or Mercury which covers the ages from 7 to 43 where most people get married. Among these Saturn gives Argalā to the Sun but is completely obstructed by Venus and Mercury. Therefore the likely Mahādaśā is that of Mercury who is also a contender as per Aṣṭakavarga.

Chart 65: Male: Marriage example Navāṁśa (D-9)

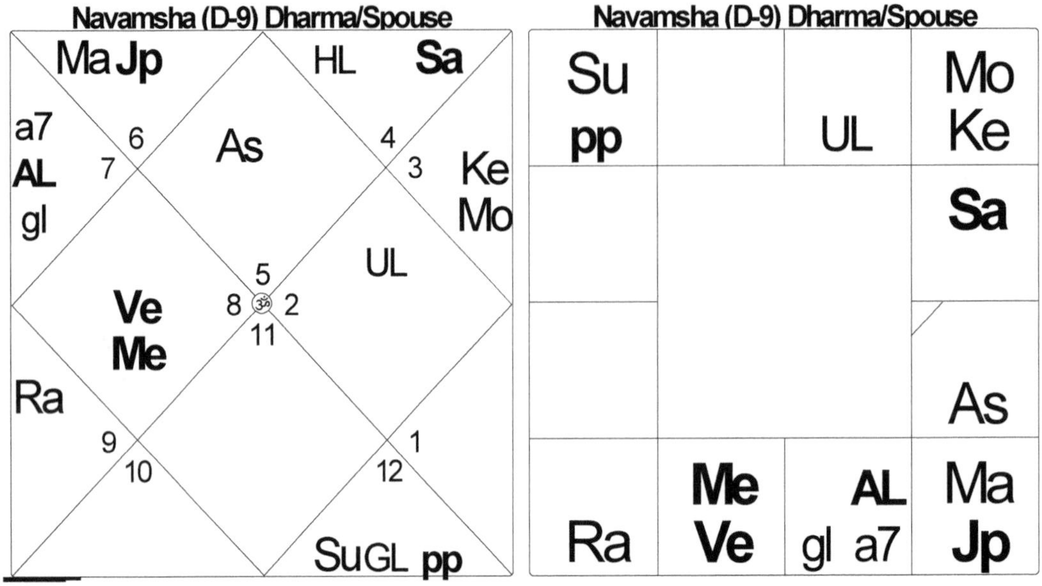

In the Navāṁśā the Antaradaśā should be linked to the house signifying the particular spouse in question, i.e. for first spouse we see the seventh house and lord. Herein the Antaradaśā should be strongly associated with the lord of the sign. Herein in addition to the principles for the Mahādaśā planets placed in the 5th, 9th or 12th from the lord can give the event. It is worthwhile to examine Argalā very thoroughly in this case as well. This works very well when used with the Aṣṭākavarga calculations given earlier.

In the given chart we have ascertained Mercury, Jupiter and Venus as possible Daśā / Antaradaśā for the event. The seventh lord in the Navāṁśa is Aquarius which is lorded by two planets, i.e. Saturn and Rāhu showing two potential spouses. Among these Rāhu is weaker due to its debility. Also Ātmakāraka is Jupiter who will not prefer Rāhu and instead supports Saturn in Cancer. This being the twelfth house suggests a wife in a foreign country. Jupiter being a contender for the Daśā is placed in the third from Saturn and does not suggest that Jupiter Antaradaśā can bring the marriage. Venus and Mercury are both strong in trines to Saturn and will bring the marriage. At this stage there is very little separating Mercury and Venus in their ability to give the marriage. Among the two, Mercury has higher degrees in its sign as well as stronger Ṣaḍbala making it stronger to give the event. The wedding happened in Mercury-Mercury-Saturn Maha-Antara-Pratyantara Daśā.

यन्मण्डलं वेदविदो वदन्ति गायन्ति यच्चारण सिद्ध सङ्घाः।
यद्योगिनो योगजुषां च सङ्घाः पुनातु मां तत्सवितुर्वरेण्यम्॥ ६॥

6

Ārūḍha

The image

Ārūḍha Padas tend to be dismissed by some authors, their reasoning being either lack of understanding or lack of appreciation. Often this stems from confusing the application of Lagna with that of Ārūḍha Lagna. It is important to understand that the Bhāvas from the Lagna show all the karma, which is coming our way, i.e. the 11th house shows where the wealth is coming from, the second house shows where the food is coming from and the sixth house shows where the enemies are coming from. How we react to this depends on the Ārūḍha Lagna! This forms a 3-dimensional sphere of understanding the Lagna vis-a-vis the Ārūḍha Lagna.

For example, the native's gains are seen from the eleventh from Lagna. If malefics are there, the wealth comes through some inauspiciousness, i.e. Saturn indicates sorrow or loss, whilst Mars indicates that some fights or anger has transpired. The eleventh from Ārūḍha Lagna will indicate how the native goes about in taking this wealth from others. If malefics are there the native will adopt a cruel disposition in taking the wealth. Saturn in eleventh from Ārūḍha Lagna will never give poverty, because such natives will take the wealth without considering other people's feelings.

Hence, the application of Lagna and Ārūḍha Lagna simultaneously can give very deep insight into the nature of the native and their life events. Based on reactions, which benefit the native, he or she attains fortune in life, because the event will put them in a state of happiness and satisfaction.

6.1 Placements from Ārūḍha Lagna

The placement of planets from the Ārūḍha Lagna will indicate the actual influences of events on the native whether the events are auspicious or not. A person may loose their job, but as a result, they get a new and a better job in a field of work, which turned out to be more lucrative than the previous one. Similarly, a gain in one area may prove inauspicious in the end. This method of judging the chart is done by reckoning the positions of planets from Lagna initially followed by the Ārūḍha Lagna in order to determine the result.

Consequently, it becomes important to understand the auspicious and inauspicious placements from the Ārūḍha Lagna. These positions are static and easy to remember:

- Strong benefics are auspicious for material wealth in the 1st, 2nd, 4th, 5th, 8th and 10th houses from the Ārūḍha Lagna.
- Strong malefics are auspicious in the third and sixth from Ārūḍha Lagna. Weak benefics here are also auspicious for material wealth. Instead, weak malefics and strong benefics can cause defeat or loss but they are good for spiritual direction.

The strength of the graha should be understood from its dīptādi avasthā, i.e. whether it is exalted, debilitated, etc, and should be judged from both Rāśi and Navāṁśa.

Additionally some results are as follows:

- All grahas (even upagrahas) are auspicious in the ninth and eleventh houses from Ārūḍha Lagna.
- Any graha in the seventh or twelfth from Ārūḍha Lagna tends to cause inauspicious results, more so if it is a malefic. If a benefic, it will indicate expenses though on good deeds and occasions.

6.1.1 Examples

Chart 66: Dean, Howard

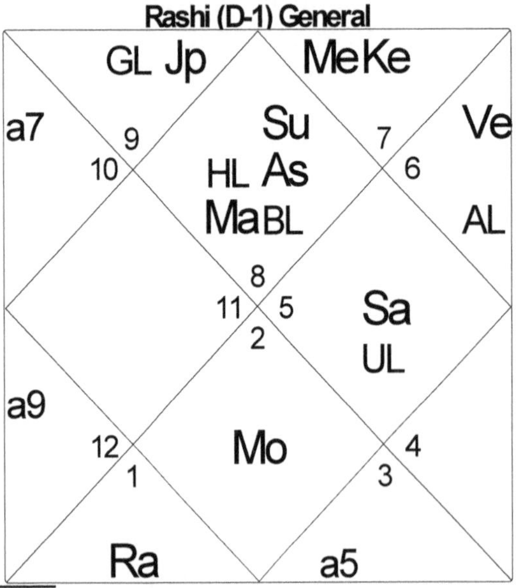

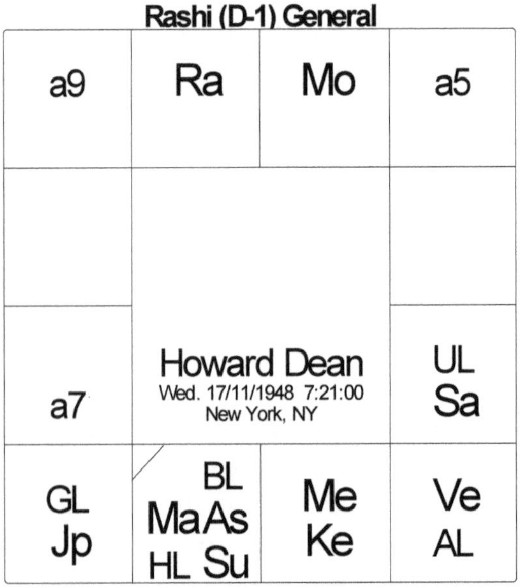

Howard Dean, born 17th November 1948, 7:21 AM, New York, NY, USA.

Howard Dean was one of the Democratic Candidates running for the elections of US President 2005. Having a strong Ātmakāraka in Lagna in mutual aspect with the Putrakāraka Moon exalted in the seventh, Howard Dean grew popular very quickly and looked like a very strong threat to President George Bush Jr. Analyzing the planetary positions from Ārūḍha Lagna for Dean, we see that Ārūḍha Lagna is in Virgo and occupied by Venus while Mercury and Ketu occupy the second from it. Two malefics are in the third from it, Jupiter is in the fourth, Rāhu in the eighth, Moon in the ninth, and Saturn is in the twelfth house. Among these, Saturn, Rāhu and debilitated Venus are inauspicious.

Mercury would seem extremely strong and fortunate in the second however, it is debilitated in Navāṁśa. This position of Mercury requires more clarification. Mercury in the second house from Ārūḍha Lagna in Rāśi promises lots of wealth and leadership of many communities. Seeing this promise unfolding, Dean was optimistic from his campaign. However, Mercury's debilitation in Navāṁśa indicates that the fortune indicated by the promise will be denied. Hence, during Saturn-Mercury Daśā Dean led a very strong democratic campaign, only to realize that he had spent too much, too early and ran out of funds to continue his campaign. Mercury is joined Ketu putting it in Lajjita Avasthā, hence this incident would give Dean a feeling of being ashamed when this incident happened. Dean started his campaign in Saturn-Saturn. A careful look at Saturn in the twelfth from Ārūḍha Lagna reveals an excessive amount of expenditure on poor people, and workers/servants. Dean led a campaign with the focus on attracting more people from the middle and lower classes into the ellections.

Chart 67: Naveen Patnaik

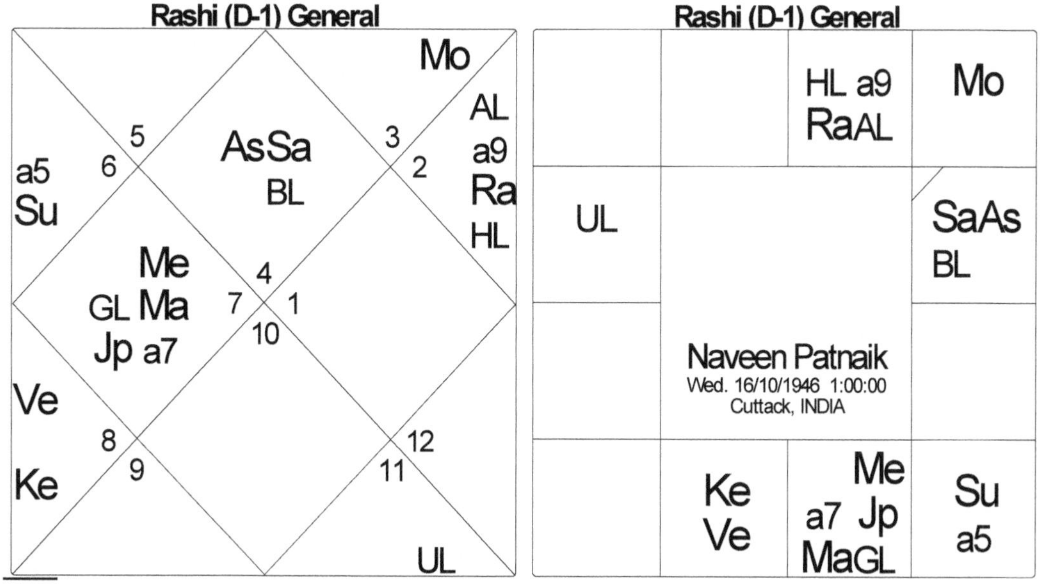

Naveen Patnaik, born: 16th October 1946, 1:00 AM, Cuttack, India.

Ārūḍha Lagna is in Taurus in the given chart. Saturn is placed in strength in the third house from Ārūḍha Lagna, while Mars is strong in the sixth there from. However, both Jupiter and Mercury are conjoined Mars, which can give loss and misfortunes in battles. If one were to ignore the Navāṁśa, one would miss that Mercury and Jupiter are both debilitated, hence enforcing a very strong Rājya yoga in the Rāśi for Patnaik. During Saturn-Jupiter, he became a cabinet minister in the Indian Government. Later with the advent of Mercury Daśā, he became the Chief Minister of Orissa.

Notably in the two charts of government officials, Mercury has played a major role. Mercury and Venus are both very important in the study of the Ārūḍha Lagna, as they are both rājasik in nature
and are responsible for binding us to society. Mercury does so through career and work, while Venus does so through relationships and bonds in marriage. These two facets of life are however renounced by illumined sages and ascetics; hence, the analysis of Venus and Mercury is quite important in the charts of those who have renounced the world.

Chart 68: HH. Śrila Prabhupāda

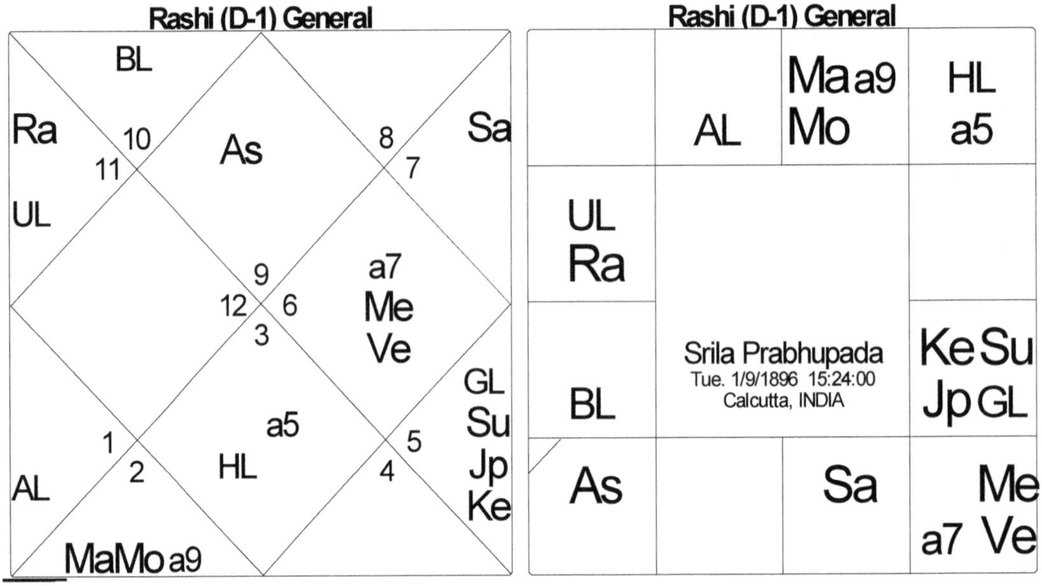

Srila Prabhupāda, born 1st September 1896, 3:24 PM, Tollygunge Suburb, Calcutta, India.

In the chart of H.H. Śrila Prabhupāda, Mercury and Venus are together in Virgo in the sixth from Ārūḍha Lagna. Whilst the position of Mercury is strong and indicates the potential of renouncing career and aspirations, Venus is weak indicating an inability to renounce marriage and relationships. For a long time he did not renounce, though his guru requested him to do so, and whilst he worked and had a career, he failed miserably due to repeated theft of his money and belongings.

Venus is however receiving nīcabhañga by Mercury as it is lord of Venus' debilitation sign, and Mercury is in a Kendra from Lagna. Hence it may be inferred that when Mercury Daśā begins the native will experience Pravrājya Yoga, i.e. the loss of everything, whether or not the person chooses to. In Mercury Daśā-Venus Antaradaśā, he renounced his wife and family and became more active in teaching and spreading spirituality to the world.

Chart 69: Swami Vivekananda

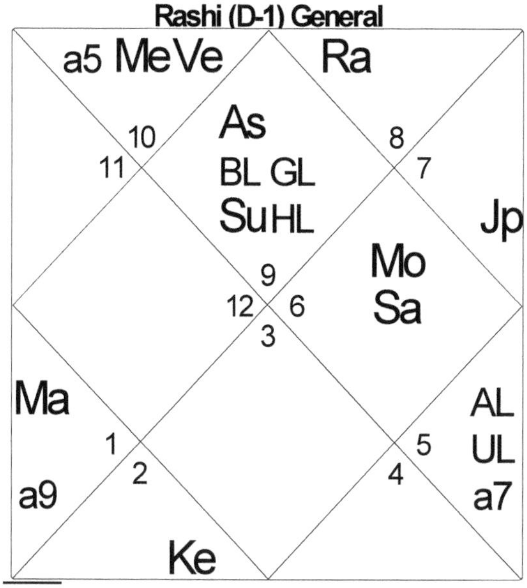

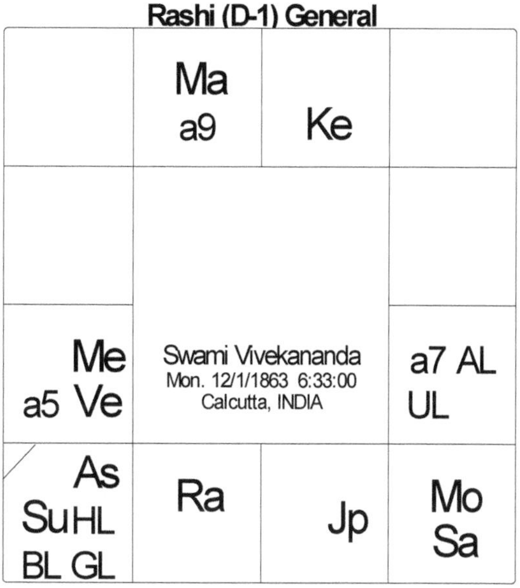

Swami Vivekananda, born 1st February 1863, 6:33 AM, Calcutta, India.

Ārūḍha Lagna is in Leo and Mercury and Venus are joined in Capricorn. Furthermore, Venus is exalted in Navāṁśa. This shows a chart with a very strong potential for Parivrājya Yoga. After Swāmīji lost his father and his marriage was called off, he spent about a year trying to get a job and establish his career. Simultaneously, his guru Śrī Rāmakṛṣṇa Paramahamsa, was trying to get Swāmīji to join him and renounce worldly bonds. Having failed to establish himself in life and coping with the loss of his father, Swāmīji finally took to the life of a sanyāsī and renounced the world.

Chart 70: Śrī Ramaṇa Mahāṛṣi

Ramaṇa Mahaṛṣi, born 30th December 1879, 1 AM, Madurai, India.

In the chart of Śrī Ramaṇa Mahāṛṣi, Venus and Mercury are again joined, however unlike the former charts, these are together in the twelfth from Ārūḍha Lagna. The placement of Venus and Mercury in the twelfth from Ārūḍha Lagna shows a complete and utter rejection of the qualities of both Venus and Mercury. Mahāṛṣi renounced the worldly life at a very young age during his early teens, living as a beggar and spending most of his time in meditation of the Supreme. As Venus is Dārakāraka and Mercury is Amātyakāraka, the renunciation is complete, and confirms a chart of a true monk.

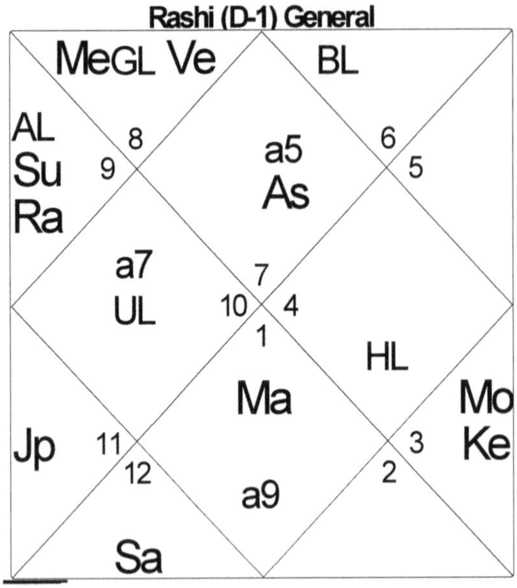

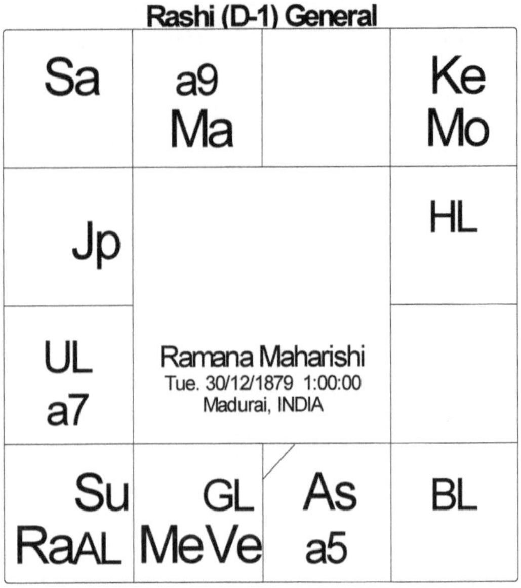

6.2 Ārūḍha and Sambandha

Whilst Sambandha between the Lagna and its lord has its own application, Sambandha from the Ārūḍha Lagna is the most important, as one's own perception of good and bad is solely dependant on the Ārūḍha Lagna. For this, one must apply two methods; Chara Kāraka and lordship from Ārūḍha Lagna. This Sambandha shows how people in one's social circle have an impact on one's life. For example, for father, one must see the ninth lord from Ārūḍha Lagna and the Chara Pitṛkāraka and their placement from the Ārūḍha Lagna.

- If this placement is inauspicious then the native suffers because of the specific relative.
- If the two mentioned indicators are demonstrating conflicting results, one will dominate depending on how these planets are placed in the varga i.e. for seventh lord and DK, the one that lords or is in trines to the seventh house in Navāṁśa will give effects of the first spouse's behaviour. Similarly judge from the other spouses (second, ninth, etc).

The auspicious and inauspicious positions are reckoned using the standard rules from Ārūḍha Lagna.

6.3 Examples

Chart 71: Relationship with Father
Female native born 30th June 1962, 0:13 AM, Calcutta, India.

In the native's chart, the Ārūḍha Lagna is in Capricorn. The father's impact on the native is seen from the placement of the Chara Pitṛkāraka Moon and ninth lord

Mercury (ninth lord from Capricorn). The Moon is exalted in the fifth from Ārūḍha Lagna, indicating a father who will have a very positive impact on the native. The fifth house involves knowledge, interests, and followers/students. The native was always gifted with the best among teachers and always studied in the best schools.

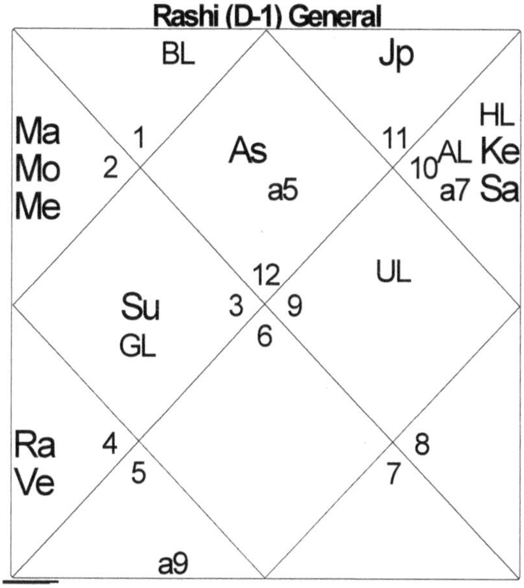

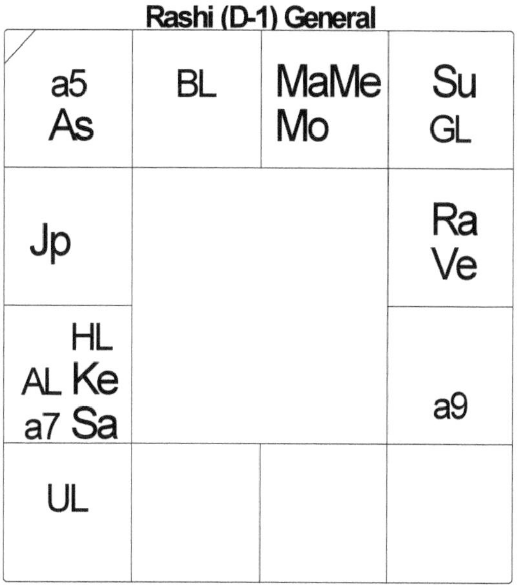

The native also met many influential people through her fathers associations. Mercury is also joined the combination of an exalted Moon, indicating Śāradā yoga, which gives deep knowledge of many fields of study.

Chart 72: Relationship with Husband

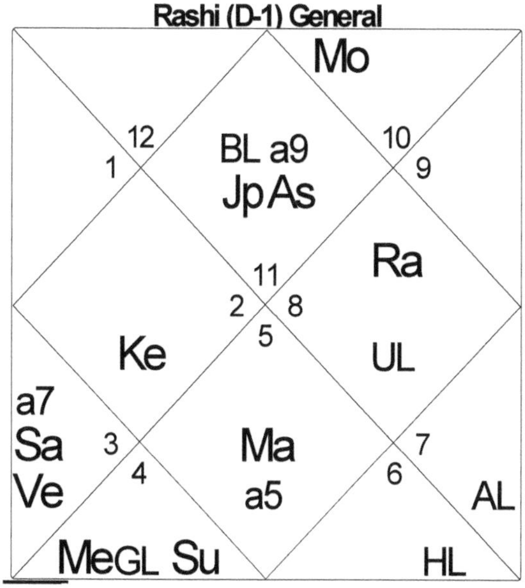

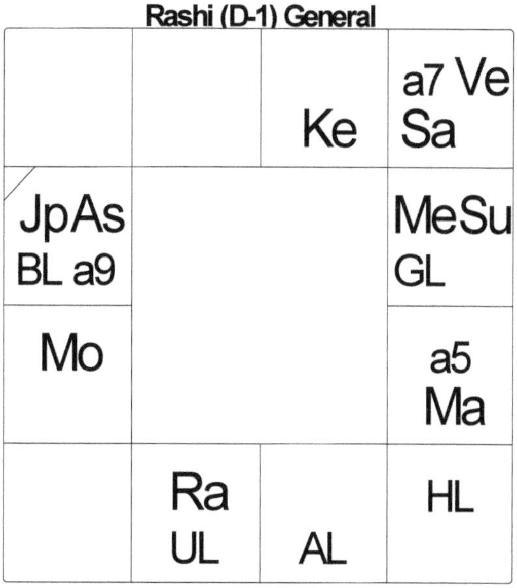

Female native born 3rd August 1974, 7:58 PM, Delhi, India.

In the native's chart, the Lagna is Aquarius, having two lords, Saturn and Rāhu. In these cases, two Ārūḍhas for the Lagna will prevail. The stronger Ārūḍha will also decide which lord of Lagna is dominating; hence, a careful judgment of the chart should be made. The native has Saturn in the fifth house. Lagna lord in fifth house will give problems with children and childbirths, however such incidents will manifest after the person has become a mother. Since Saturn is in the second from Ārūḍha Lagna, this indicates poverty, or financial distress because of rejecting money as Saturn is Lagna lord. Hence, Saturn will dominate the choice of Ārūḍha when the native decides to earn independently.

Let us look at Rāhu now. Rāhu is in the tenth house in Upapada. It is forming a Sarpa Yoga broken only by Jupiter in the Lagna. This Jupiter also lords the second from Upapada, indicating separation or divorce in the marriage, due to the bad relationship between Jupiter and Rāhu. Consequently, Rāhu as Lagna lord will only be prominent during marriage, after which Saturn will dominate. Thus to analyze the influence of the spouse on the native, one must consider Rāhu as Lagna lord and hence the Ārūḍha Lagna will fall in Taurus.

The seventh lords from Taurus, the Ārūḍha Lagna, are Mars and Ketu. The Chara Dārakāraka is Mercury. Among these three grahas, Mars will be the most prominent because it lords the seventh house in the Navāṁśa, indicating that the nature of the first spouse will be that of Mars in her chart. Mars is in the fourth from Ārūḍha Lagna in the Rāśi, which is a very inauspicious placement from the Ārūḍha Lagna. It causes anger, arguments and fights, as well as over-protectiveness, loss of possessions and a distressed situation. No malefics are auspicious in the fourth from Ārūḍha Lagna. The native's marriage ended due to intense fights between the couple and the native's dissatisfaction due to her husband's criminal activities.

6.3 Graha Ārūḍha

The Grahārūḍha is an Ārūḍha for the grahas. Since grahas are people, the Grahārūḍha will reveal the self's perception of others and the others perception of the self. This perception can lead to favouring a specific graha over another. As people come into our lives to manifest specific events, the placement of the Grahārūḍha will reveal how we experience the behaviour of a specific graha.

- The Grahārūḍha is calculated by counting from the graha to its sign and the same distance there from, like bhāva Ārūḍha, except the counting starts from the graha. Same exceptions apply to the Grahārūḍha, as is the case with the bhāva Ārūḍha, only difference is with reference to the grahas position.

- In case of a graha lording two signs, calculate Grahārūḍha for both signs.

The perception that people have of one'self is seen from the Grahārūḍha of the Lagna. Find the lord of Lagna (excluding nodes) and calculate the Grahārūḍha keeping the Lagna as the lordship of the graha. The resultant placement will indicate how others perceive the native, irrespective of what the native believes.

A Grahārūḍha in quadrants or trines to the Lagna is a graha favoured by the native. Otherwise, the native will not favour the graha, or may feel uncomfortable with the graha.

6.3.1 Examples

Chart 73: George W Bush Jr.

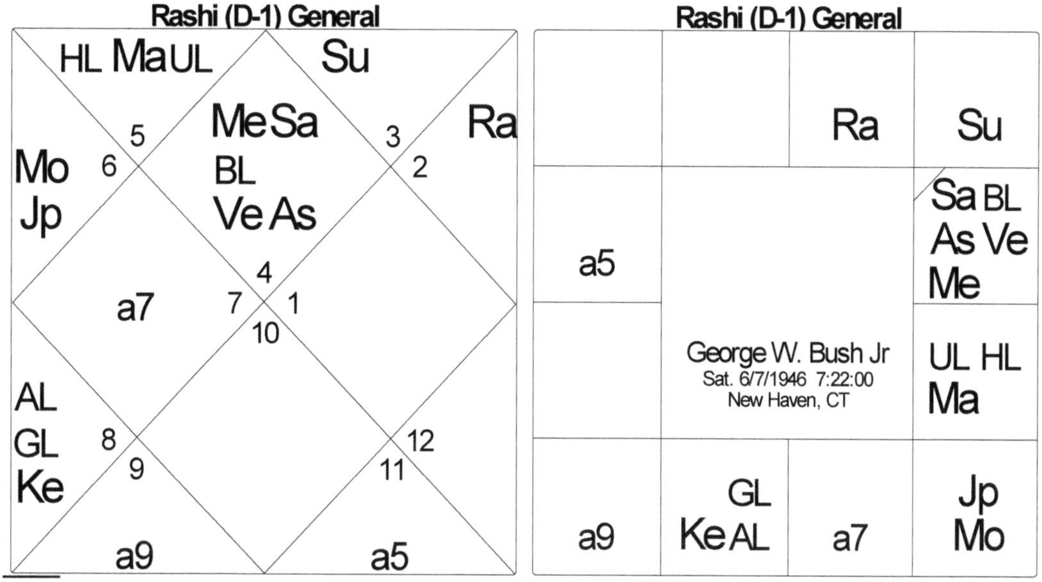

George W. Bush born 6th July 1946, 7:22 AM, New Haven, CT, USA.

In the chart of President Bush, the calculation of the Grahārūḍha of Lagna lord will tell us how others perceive Bush, and how Bush tends to present himself to the world. The Moon is in Virgo, and its sign Cancer is in the eleventh from it. We are required to count to the eleventh sign from Cancer, which is Taurus. Taurus is occupied by Rāhu indicating that Bush is perceived as a good planner, a person eager to fight/vengeful, and a very powerful person due to Rāhu's strength. As the Ārūḍha Lagna is in Scorpio, this indicates that Bush tries to adopt the exact opposite approach from how the society perceives him.

Bush won the elections in 2000/2001 defeating Al Gore, another Cancer Lagna. The impact of another Cancer Lagna is seen from the Grahārūḍha of Moon in Bush's chart, which by mere placement in the eleventh house indicates fortune, however at the cost of another person as it is a triṣaḍāya bhāva.

Chart 74: Al Gore

Albert Arnold Gore, born 31st March 1948, 12:53 PM, Washington, DC, USA.

If we analyze Al Gore's chart and ascertain the Grahārūḍha of Moon, we find it in the eighth house, indicating that Gore would incur severe losses and depression in the advent of a fight with another Cancer Lagna. This is why Gore stood in the shadow of Bill Clinton another Cancer Lagna. However, Gore's presence gave great strength to the work of Clinton due to the Grahārūḍha of Moon in Lagna in Clinton's chart, promising name, fame, and reputation.

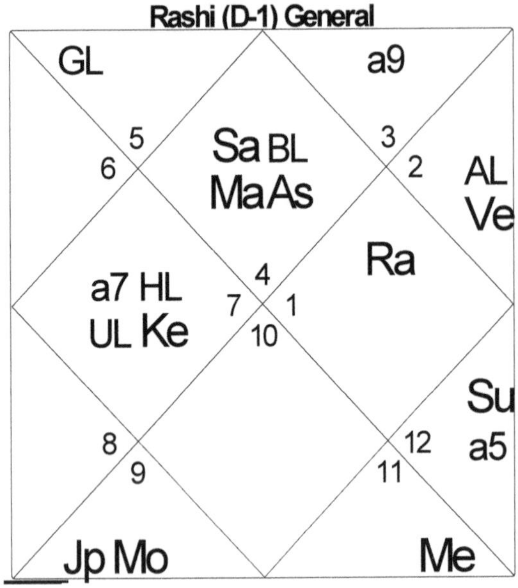

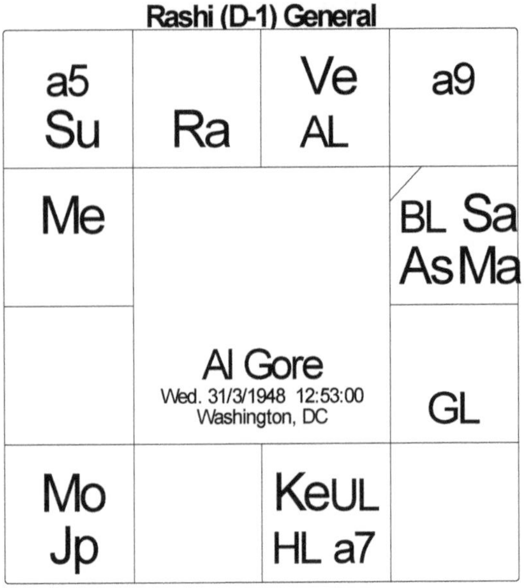

Vimshottari

Start Date	Age	Dashas	
18/ 5/ 1987	**40.9**	**Sa**	**Sa**
21/ 5/ 1990	43.9	Sa	Me
29/ 1/ 1993	46.6	Sa	Ke
8/ 3/ 1994	47.7	Sa	Ve
8/ 5/ 1997	50.8	Sa	Su
20/ 4/ 1998	51.8	Sa	Mo
22/11/ 1999	53.4	Sa	Ma
30/12/ 2000	54.5	Sa	Ra
8/11/ 2003	57.3	Sa	Jp
18/ 5/ 2006	**59.9**	**Me**	**Me**
17/10/ 2008	62.3	Me	Ke
14/10/ 2009	63.3	Me	Ve
13/ 8/ 2012	66.1	Me	Su
18/ 6/ 2013	67.0	Me	Mo
19/11/ 2014	68.4	Me	Ma
17/11/ 2015	69.4	Me	Ra
3/ 6/ 2018	71.9	Me	Jp

Figure 17: George W. Bush Vimśottari Daśā

Returning to Bush's chart, the Daśā in which he came to power was Saturn-Rāhu. As the Antaradaśā indicates those people/souls which enter into our lives, their impact should be seen from the Grahārūḍha. Rāhu is in Taurus and Aquarius is the tenth from it. The tenth from Aquarius becomes Scorpio, however the Grahārūḍha of Rāhu cannot fall in either Taurus or Scorpio, hence we must count to the tenth sign from Scorpio, which is Leo. Leo is the second from Lagna, indicating a lot of worry, near-death incidents, and financial tension. This accompanied the events of the September 11th incident which followed in the year of Mr. Bush' presidency.

The next Antaradaśā is that of Jupiter and Jupiter is in Virgo. Jupiter has two Grahārūḍhas as it lords two signs. The Grahārūḍha of Jupiter as lord of Sagittarius and Pisces fall in Sagittarius and Gemini respectively. Both these placements are inauspicious indicating experiences of fighting/revolt and backstabbing respectively from his peers. Bush became quite unpopular at this time. As Jupiter is in the third house it was due to weapons, wars, fighting, etc. Gajakeśarī yoga in the third house is highly conducive towards war. This started during Rāhu's Antaradaśā as Rāhu has graha dṛṣṭi on the third house, and the insecurity following the placement of its Grahārūḍha in the second house. Bush also became unpopular due to the incidents following his invasion of Afghanistan and Iraq in his fight against terrorism. This was especially from his close allies in Europe who were unhappy about his policies in the Middle East.

In this manner, the Grahārūḍha can be used to decide the outcome of events, and associations.

यन्मण्डलं सर्वजनेषु पूजितं ज्योतिश्चकुर्यादिह मर्त्यलोके।
यत् कालकालादिमनादिरूपं पुनातु मां तत्सवितुर्वरेण्यम्॥ ७॥

7

Kāraka
Significators

7.1 Naisargika (natural) Kārakas

Whilst the texts give many significations of the grahas, the proper use of the grahas comes first into light when applied with reference to the Bhāvas. Each bhāva has a primary Kāraka for it.

These primary kārakas have multiple uses, which arte discussed in other chapters, however it is important to note, that while these are primary kārakas, secondary kārakas also exist.

Table 60: Bhāva Kārakas

Bhāva	Graha
1st	Sun
2nd	Jupiter
3rd	Mars
4th	Moon
5th	Jupiter
6th	Saturn
7th	Venus
8th	Saturn
9th	Jupiter
10th	Mercury
11th	Jupiter
12th	Saturn

Example: Moon is the Kāraka for the fourth house with reference to mind, mother and home, which is most important among the fourth house indications. Secondarily, Venus is the Kāraka for vehicles, Mars for lands and property, Mercury for education, Ketu for buildings, Jupiter for happiness, Saturn for unhappiness, etc. In this manner, each house should be examined for its significations and the relevant graha should be ascertained.

These various kārakas help to determine the different facets of a house, i.e. the fourth house shows many aspects of life, as can be seen from the above example. These various aspects shape differently dependant on the kārakas.

It is common among astrologers to mix the qualities of a graha and the Bhāvas it signifies. However, this is not the correct approach. Let us give an illustration. It is said that Jupiter is sātvik in nature and he is the Kāraka for wealth. The first quality that is Jupiter's sātvik nature is used when understanding the influence Jupiter has on a particular area of life. The second aspect, that is Jupiter's kārakatva of wealth, is used when judging the strength of the second house and its wealth giving aspect. The two indications need to be differentiated to make a proper assessment of the karakas.

Table 61: Graha Kāraka

Sun First house: soul, health, spirituality, head Second house: resources Fifth house: parā vidyā (spiritual knowledge) Ninth house: faith, father, dharma, prospectus of marriage Tenth house: eyesight, kingship/Rāja yoga	**Moon** First house: disposition, body Second house: family, lineage, face Fourth house: home, birthplace, mother, emotions, doctors Fifth house: strength of mantra Seventh house: desires of the heart Twelfth house: recovery from diseases
Mars First house: strength Third house: sense of timing, fighting skills, reflexes, siblings Fourth house: land Fifth house: authority Sixth house: enmity, battles, accidents/bruises, ulcers, cuts	**Mercury** Second house: speech Third house: communication skills Fourth house: education Fifth house: students Seventh house: business partners, sense of discrimination Tenth house: career Eleventh house: friends and social circle
Jupiter First house: sense of awareness, wisdom Second house: wealth and sustenance Fourth house: happiness (sukha) and satisfaction Fifth house: children and memory Ninth house: teachers, especially the spiritual guide/priest, luck Eleventh house: gains	**Venus** First house: physical beauty Second house: eyeballs Fourth house: cars, chairs, sofas and other comforts Fifth house: love affairs and romance Seventh house: spouse or partner Twelfth house: sleep comfort
Saturn Fourth house: sorrow or dukha Sixth house: weaknesses, ailments, strife Eighth house: diseases, financial debts/poverty, longevity, death, renunciation Tenth house: workload Twelfth house: expenses or that, which causes loss	**Rāhu** First house: ego Seventh house: rebirth Ninth house: misfortune/adharma Twelfth house: foreign residence or travel, bondage and imprisonment **Ketu** Fourth house: buildings, flats Twelfth house: samādhi, nirvāṇa, mokṣa, liberation

The above list is not final; in fact, some subtle indications of each bhāva can be linked to the various grahas. The above list is recommended for general purposes. The list will not explain how a graha acts in the various Bhāvas, but which indications it seeks to protect in them.

7.1.1 Judging the Kāraka

The three viz.: house, lord and Kāraka form the most important aspects of the chart. If all three are weak or afflicted, only then can we say that a particular area of life is ruined in the native's life. The method of judging is given in subsequent chapters, but an introduction is given below.

The relationship between the lord and the Kāraka will show the native's interaction with others.

- Count from the lord to the significator to know what the native has to do.
- Count from the significator to the lord to know what the native can expect.

Example: If when judging a relationship, the seventh lord and Venus are in trines to each other, then the interaction is a give (fifth) and take (ninth) relationship, which is very healthy, as the roles are defined. Instead, if the seventh lord and Venus are in sixth/eighth from each other, then a lot of misunderstanding can occur between the native and their partner.

The relationship between the Kāraka the house will show the native's luck.

- Count from the significator to the house to know the native's attitude.
- Count from the house to the significator to know the fortune.

Example: If the Sun is in the eighth house from the Lagna, the native will have a very wrong attitude towards keeping themselves healthy and fit, and could neglect himself. The result of this attitude is bad health.

7.1.2 Strength of the Kāraka

When judging the placement of the Kāraka, the various houses and relationships need defining. To judge the happiness one gains from one's interaction with the world, one should judge the bhāva lord with reference to the Kāraka of the house. For example, the primary fifth house Kāraka is Jupiter, which is the Kāraka for children. Other external manifestations of the fifth house are students (Mercury), lovers (Venus), subordinates (Saturn) etc. Similarly, other planets signify other indications of the fifth bhāva. To judge the native's fortune with respect to his relationship with his children, see the position relationship between Jupiter and the fifth lord.

- The Kendra placements are auspicious and show that children will be naturally drawn towards the native, and there is a good relationship between the native and the children.
- The trikoṇa placement is auspicious and shows a healthy mutually reciprocal relationship between the native and his children. This also indicates an active interest in relating with his children.
- The 3 - 11 relationship is conducive towards a growing friendship with children.
- The 2 - 12 relationship shows a mismatch in timing and the relationship will be very unbalanced and requires either a lot of giving (12th) or expenses (2nd).

- The 6 - 8 relationship is the worst, and indicates complications and complete mismatch in ideals and character. A lot of misfortune with children is experienced due to this.

7.2 Chara (temporal/changing) Kārakas

There are eight Chara kārakas given in case of humans and living beings, each depending on the degrees of the eight grahas from Sun to Rāhu. In case of non-living beings or beings that do not have the faculty to reproduce, the Chara Putrakāraka is omitted making it a scheme of seven Chara kārakas, with the exclusion of Rāhu.

Expunging signs, the planet with the highest degree in its sign becomes the Ātmakāraka. The one's following will become the Amātya, Bhrātṛ etc. kārakas. One must keep in mind that Rāhu's degree should be reckoned in reverse, i.e. subtracted from 30.

Following are the eight Chara kārakas:

Table 62: Chara Kārakas

#	Kāraka	Description
1	Ātmakāraka (AK)	The soul, self, the king
2	Amātyakāraka (AmK)	Advisors, ministers and employers.
3	Bhrātṛkāraka (BK)	Friendly address of someone close, i.e. brother, guru, etc
4	Mātṛkāraka (MK)	Mother/Maternal relatives
5	Pitṛkāraka (PiK)	Father/Paternal relatives
6	Putrakāraka (PK)	Children and followers
7	Jñātikāraka (GK)	Kinsmen, relatives
8	Dārakāraka (DK)	Spouse, lover. This is also seen for wealth and business.

These eight Kāraka show how we as souls are interacting with different parts of our lives. These are pivitoal in chart analysis to examine to what extent we are truly experiencing or enjoying certain fruits of the society. E.g. the placement of the Dārakāraka can singlehandedly decide our marital and financial happiness, as it alone represents our soul in its interaction with these aspects of life. Similarly the Amātyakāraka has the same significance w.r.t. our work and profession.

These Chara Kāraka must be well placed from the houses they are kāraka of, or at least otherwise well placed in the chart to provide the native with the fruits of that aspect of life. Herein the bhāva kāraka have to be derived:

Table 63: Chārakāraka Bhāva

#	Kāraka	Bhāva
1	Ātmakāraka (AK)	First and eighth houses
2	Amātyakāraka (AmK)	Tenth house
3	Bhrātṛkāraka (BK)	Third, ninth and eleventh houses
4	Mātṛkāraka (MK)	Fourth and twelfth houses
5	Pitṛkāraka (PiK)	Ninth house
6	Putrakāraka (PK)	Fifth house
7	Jñātikāraka (GK)	Sixth house
8	Dārakāraka (DK)	Second and seventh houses

These eight Chara kārakas can be divided into three groups as follows:

Table 64: Chara Kāraka Grouping

#	Kāraka	Description
1	Ātmakāraka	Those who play a role in realizing one's souls purpose.
2	Amātyakāraka	
3	Bhrātṛkāraka	
4	Mātṛkāraka	Those who play a role in realizing one's desires.
5	Pitṛkāraka	
6	Putrakāraka	
7	Jñātikāraka	Those who are the object of one's desires.
8	Dārakāraka	

7.2.1 Ātmakāraka: the king

The most important among the Chara kārakas, is the Ātmakāraka. This shows one's soul's purpose and that which is important in one's life; as well as those one considers highly, almost as a king.

- The placement of the Chara Ātmakāraka in Rāśi is known as the Kāraka Lagna, which shows how the important soul lessons manifest in this birth.
- In Navāṁśa, it is known as the Kārakāmśa and indicates the soul's purpose in this birth, as well as the deity who has favored one to realize this purpose and will eventually cause liberation to the native.

The Chara kārakas (specifically the Ātmakāraka) change depending on the purpose of the native's birth, as he is guided through various existences, finally aiming at achieving mokṣa/liberation, which is signified by the planet Ketu. Hence Ketu is excluded from the above scheme of Chara kārakas, as it causes liberation from the repeated births, and is the true goal of all souls. However, before one can attain this goal, one has to undergo a series of events to unlearn some of the negative traits that cause repeated bondage in this world. The bondage of the soul is indicated by the planet becoming the Chara Ātmakāraka. How one faces these lessons is indicated by the house placement of the Chara Ātmakāraka.

Table 65: Ātmakāraka Grahas (Rath, Charakaraka and Spirituality, 2002)

Ātmakāraka	Indications
Sun	Ego, self-importance, ideals, name, reputation become the pivotal issues in the native's life, and he should learn to subdue his own ego.
Moon	Emotions and compassion towards others becomes a big issue. Due to excessive emotional dependence, the native may always be looking for relationships, or relationships will be looking for them.
Mars	Short temper, or excessive anger/violence may be expressed or experienced by the native, and the native should make a conscious step to throw away any weapons and grudges and learn the path of non-violence or ahimsa.
Mercury	When to speak and when not to speak becomes a major issue either for the native or his/her social circle. Such people should be particularly careful of what they say, and to whom they say it.
Jupiter	The most important issue for such people is whom they consider as a teacher/guide and whom they do not consider. Such people should learn to respect their teachers and elders. There is a risk of the person neglecting their spouse, or suffering separation from their spouse. They should care well for their children.
Venus	Relationships and sex becomes a major issue for such people. The person should always try to maintain purity in relations, and not to overindulge.
Saturn	Either the native sees a lot of sorrow in life, or gives a lot of sorrow to others. The native should learn to take away the sorrow of others, but not give sorrow to others.
Rāhu	The person trusts others too easily, and as a result often finds himself cheated or deceived, and a risk is there that the same person may cheat others in return in a never-ending cycle of cheating. The person should learn to accept deceit and move on. Foreign people/places also have a vital role to say with this graha.

The above indications ALSO apply to the lord of Kārakāmśa.

The Ātmakāraka is literally the king of the chart. If the Ātmakāraka is auspicious, the whole chart is auspicious, if otherwise the entire life will seem meaningless. As mentioned in the chapter on "dṛṣṭi," if a curse involves the Chara Ātmakāraka, then the effects of the curse are experienced very intensely by the native. Any relationship with a person strongly indicated by the Ātmakāraka will be a very important soul-level relationship, be it a harsh lesson or a spiritually fulfilling and long-lasting relationship.

7.2.2 Kāraka Lagna: Ātmakāraka in the Rāśi

The Kāraka Lagna is the sign occupied by the Ātmakāraka in the Rāśi chart. This Lagna can be analyzed independently to understand the inclinations of the native at a more subtle and unconscious level and in conjunction with the yogas from the Lagna, to see the important soul-level events, which may manifest in life. Independently, the yoga of the karaka Lagna with other grahas shows the strong inclinations of the native. Jaimini has given some of these indications for our benefit:

- If the lord of Kāraka Lagna (Kāraka Lagneśa), aspects or joins the Kāraka Lagna, the native will always maintain a good physique.
- Should the Kāraka Lagna be associated with the 2nd or 7th houses/lords from Kāraka Lagna, the native will be driven by an inclination to earn money and wealth in this world.
- Instead, if the 3rd, 6th or 5th houses/lords are involved, then the inclination is towards knowledge.
- The association with the fourth house/lord makes the person happy and contented.
- Association with the tenth house/lord gives name and fame.
- The association with the twelfth house/lord causes the person to be spendthrift, whilst the association with the eighth house/lord can give poverty or lack of wealth.

These lordships should be analyzed from the Kāraka Lagna and can be analyzed from the Lagna and Ārūḍha Lagna as well. Whilst the above list can help to understand a persons own personal and sometimes unconscious inclinations, a more noteworthy use of the Kāraka Lagna is to analyze its presence in the natal chart, with respect to Lagna, Ārūḍha Lagna, etc. Since the Kāraka Lagna will show how the soul is realizing some important lessons in life, its position is very important and a few examples are given to illustrate this.

Chart 75: Franklin Delano Roosevelt

The Ātmakāraka is Jupiter and is joined a debilitated (fall, destruction) seventh lord Saturn (marriage). In such a scenario one may expect the dictum of 'neglect of spouse' to function as the marriage suffers. Jupiter is the fifth lord and indicates romances causing the problems in the marriage, and Roosevelt had an extramarital affair with a colleague. Due to Jupiter being Ātmakāraka, truth dominated and Roosevelt publicly admitted to having an affair. However, the Rogapada (a6) joins this combination; disease is likely to strike the native following the adharma[1] of this affair. This is in the ninth house of legs/thighs and Saturn is sixth lord, so the legs are likely to be affected. Saturn is in a sign of Mars which is a yoga for loss of legs and polio afflicted Roosevelt's legs making him unable to walk or use his legs.

---

1 Malefics in the 9th house cause one to perform acts which are against dharma, and proves to be very unlucky for the person.

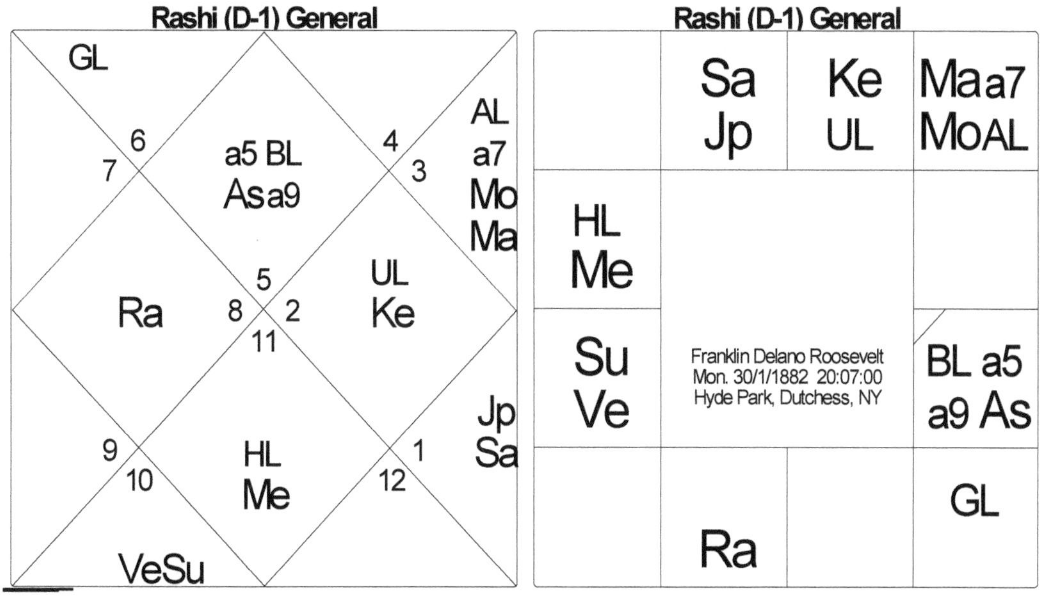

Chart 76: Princess Diana

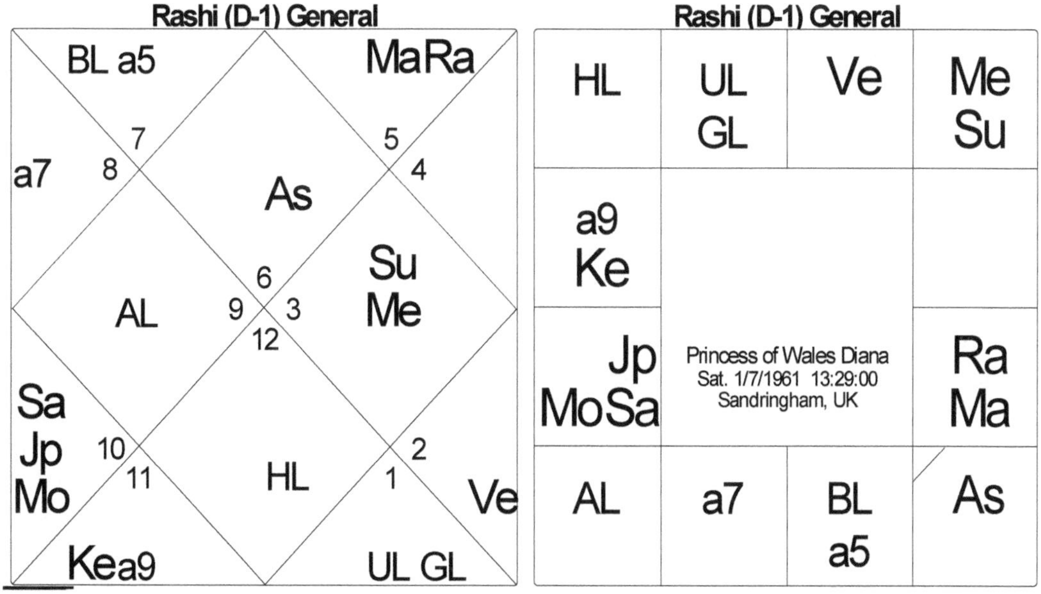

The Moon is the Ātmakāraka and is in Capricorn with the seventh lord Jupiter and the fifth lord Saturn. Just as in the case of Roosevelt, the seventh lord is debilitated and joined the fifth lord. This will give extra-marital romances causing the fall of marriage. The presence of Ātmakāraka Moon confirms this, causing the native to seek other 'attachments'. However, in the present case, the three planets have Rāśi dṛṣṭi on the second house from Upapada, causing the breakage of marriage. Venus is there confirming the excuse being extramarital affairs. Saturn is also the sixth lord and karaka for servants, hence causing the problem w.r.t. servants specifically..

Chart 77: Bill Clinton

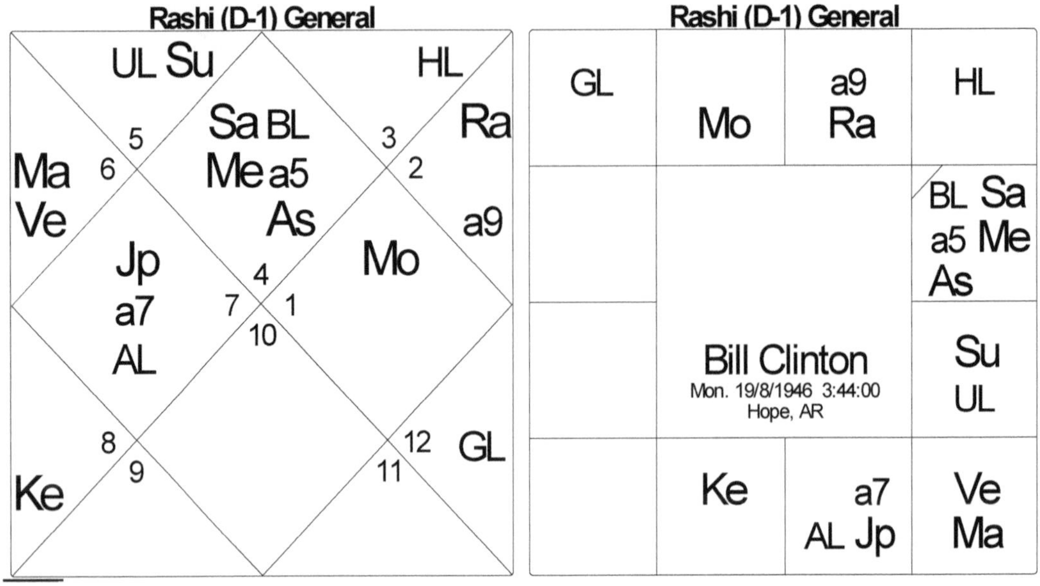

Moon is the Ātmakāraka just as in the case of Princess Diana and is well placed in the tenth house conferring long lasting name, fame and reputation. Additionally Saturn is in Cancer. When Saturn is in Cancer in either the first or the tenth houses, aspirations for great power will be present. Some powerful yogas for fame and power are also there.

α) The ninth lord Jupiter is in the seventh from Kāraka Lagna giving Rāja yoga of a great order.

β) The tenth lord and Amātya Kāraka are joined giving Rāja-Sambandha yoga or the association with people in power.

The latter is also a dispositor of the Kāraka Lagna, but is unfortunately placed in the second from Upapada causing disturbances in the marriage. Observe that seventh lord Saturn has gone to the Lagna, which is akin to debility for Saturn (maraṇa Kāraka sthāna). Saturn is in turn joined Mercury who happens to be the dispositor of the fifth lord Mars, again bringing the connection between fifth lord and a weak/ fallen seventh lord, as in the previous cases. Venus in the second from Upapada caused the disturbances due to 'extramarital affairs'. In case of both Princess Diana and Bill Clinton, the Ātmakāraka Moon is either joined Mercury, or strongly associated with Mercury in the Navāṁśa. This is a specific yoga for the native indulging in promiscuity and extra marital relations. This brings us to the importance of Kārakāṁśa when judging the placement of Ātmakāraka.

7.2.3 Kārakāṁśa: Ātmakāraka in Navāṁśa

The sign of the Ātmakāraka in the Navāṁśa is called Kārakāṁśa. Whilst the Ātmakāraka planet indicates the important issues we need to learn and overcome in this life, the planet owning the Kārakāṁśa shows wthich new issues we may be creating for the next life. It is not hard to understand why mahāṛṣis Parāśara and

Jaimini were only concerned about the Kārakāmśa and not the Ātmakāraka.

Parāśara, Jaimini and Mahādeva[2], have given a list of evils associated with the sign becoming the Kārakāmśa. One must be careful that these evils apply to the placement of any planet in Navāṁśa and not just the Kārakāmśa. Since the Navāṁśa is said to show our luck as given to us by God, the evils pertaining to each amśa are the omens that God gives us to protect us.

Table 66: Navāṁśa Signs

Amśa	Affliction (Jaimini)
Aries	trouble from rats, cats, etc.
Taurus	troubles from quadrupeds (cows, bulls, etc)
Gemini	troubles like itches, skin infections and overweight (stomach disorders)
Cancer	trouble from watery diseases, hydrophobia and leprosy
Leo	danger from dogs, tiger and such canines
Virgo	gives the same as Gemini Navāṁśa
Libra	trouble from trade and business
Scorpio	trouble from watery diseases, reptiles and snakes besides shortage of mothers milk (debilitation of Moon)
Sagittarius	danger from accidents and fall from height
Capricorn	danger from aquatic creatures, birds and spirits besides skin problems and/or psychic disorders
Aquarius	construction of lakes, tanks, garden, roads, temples, etc or troubles from the same
Pisces	law abiding religious person (danger from swimming/drowning should be added)

2 Author of Jātaka Tattva.

Chart 78: Lady having stomach disorders

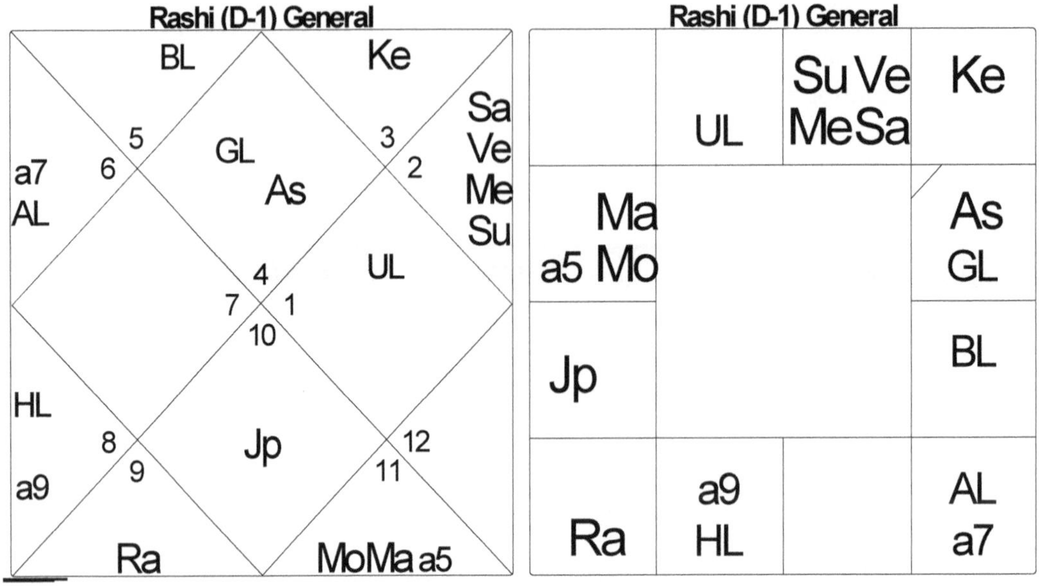

Lady born 25th May 1973, 11:18 AM, Smithtown, NY, USA.

In the given chart this lady was suffering from chronic stomach disorders during the event of house move. As one can see in the Navāṁśa, Ātmakāraka Saturn is in Virgo Navāṁśa, giving overweight and stomach disorders as well as skin problems. Saturn is in the seventh house in Navāṁśa, and this may occur during important events related to the opposite sex. Later, as she came closer to the point in time where she was shifting from her house she was involved in a small car accident, which resulted in a very painful spinal injury.

Chart 79: Lady having stomach disorders Navāṁśa (D-9)

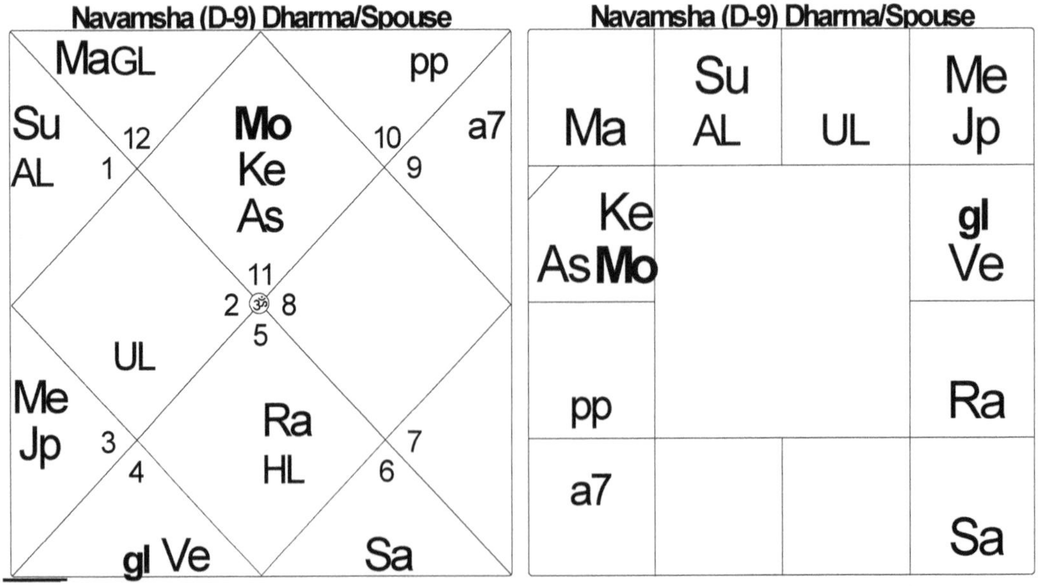

In the Rāśi, Saturn is lord of the seventh and eighth, being responsible for killing (Māraka) and causing diseases (8th lord). This shows that Saturn will bring results pertaining to death and diseases/chronic injury. The placement of and planets joining Saturn will show through which activities this will manifest. Saturn is in the Bādhaka Sthāna (eleventh from movable signs) from Lagna, with Bādhakeśa Venus, who is also fourth lord (vehicles). This is joined with Mercury who is third and twelfth lord (short distance travel and staying far from home), and second lord Sun (Māraka and lord of finances). Sun is also Karaka for the bone/spine. Further, Mṛtyupada (Ārūḍha of the 8th house), is there, confirming the chronic injury. The results manifested in Saturn Mahādaśā – Mercury Antaradaśā.

Since Saturn is the Ātmakāraka and seventh and eighth lord, and Mercury is the Navāṁśa dispositor of Saturn, as well as the third and twelfth lord, it brought about the a move.

Mercury is in Rohiṇī Nakṣatra, which is lorded by Lagna lord Moon, signifying that health and personality will be her focal point during this Daśā. When she complained about her painful ailments from the accident, the author enquired whether currently she had skin or stomach problems. She answered in the affirmative to the stomach disorders, after which, the mantra for the Iṣṭa Devatā Durgā (Rāhu in twelfth from Kārakāmśa) was given, and later an aṣṭākṣarī Āditya mantra for her Lagna was given. It was later revealed that the intention of the house shift was to live closer to a man she had recently met, yet had not formalized a relationship with.

Chart 80: Example from VRA

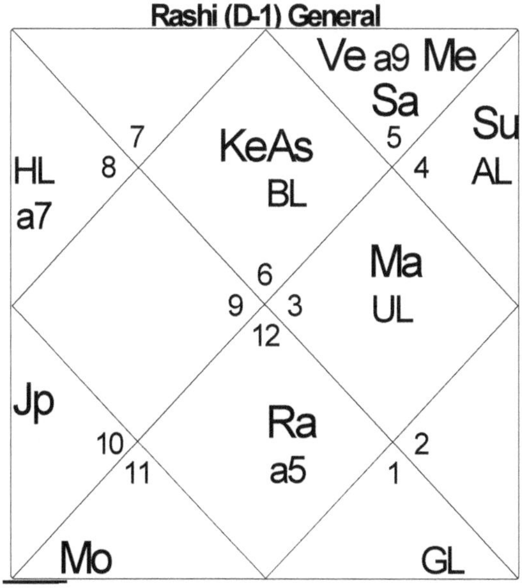

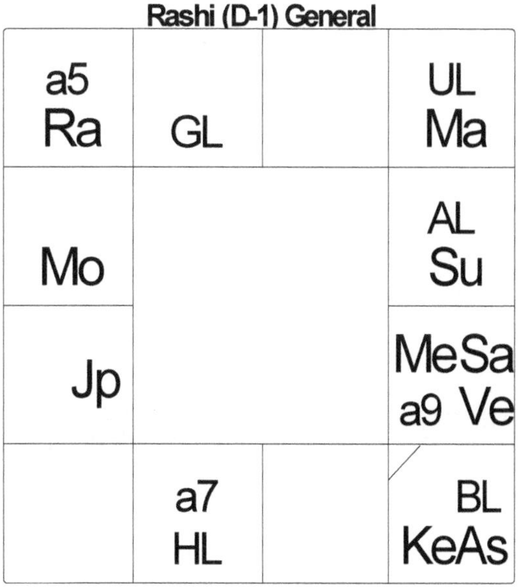

The following example is from the book *Vedic Remedies in Astrology* by Sanjay Rath.

In the chart, Ketu is in Lagna aspected by Mars, causing Piśāca Bādhā. This indicates troubles from spirits and possession. Since there are no benefics in the Kendras to Lagna, this yoga will surely manifest as the native dabbles in activities such as black magic, etc. Further, there is Sarpa Yoga, due to the occupation of three malefics in the Kendra from Lagna, confirming the immoral activities of the native. The Lagna lord is important as it shows how the native manifests his activities. In this case, it is Mercury, conjoined Saturn and Venus in the twelfth house. This is dangerous as the Lagna lord represents the sense of awareness (Dhī śakti), the significator of which is Jupiter. As a result, any grahas inimical towards Jupiter will cause obstructions to the brain/intelligence. Saturn performs this function in the present case. Venus in the twelfth house, afflicted by the fifth lord, also causes devotion to dark spirits or black magic.

When judging obstructions, it is necessary to analyze the Bādhakeśa. Jupiter is the Bādhakeśa, and is in the fifth house. This shows that he neglected to worship his deity in his last life and consequently the deity was angry with him. As Jupiter is debilitated and retrograde in a trine, it shows a curse from the past life, from the deity. The retrogression of the Bādhakeśa shows that the deity will not listen to any prayers/mantras, and is very angry! This happens in Capricorn Navāṁśa and we can expect mental disorders to result from this. This is an example of using planets other than the kārakāmśa. During Jupiter Daśā Venus Antaradaśā, the native started tampering with the dark arts, and during the subsequent Sun Antaradaśā, there was a terrible fire, after which the native became schizophrenic. The ailment has remained incurable.

Venus is placed in the twelfth indicating the devotion to dark forces. Sun is dispositor of the planets in the twelfth house and khāreśa[1], thus punishing the native for continuing his ill deeds in this life. However due to Jupiter's retrogression in a debilitation sign the native, though being mentally unstable, was married to a very caring wife, who helped take care of him and bore him two children. Hence, Jupiter did not act completely unfavorable to the native.

7.2.4 Navāṁśa Lagna and Kārakāmśa

The placement of the Navāṁśa Lagna from the Kārakāmśa will indicate the purpose of he native's current birth. Here the reference from the Kārakāmśa becomes important as this will show the intentions that the ātmā has for this birth. To make this easier for the reader, the placements are given from Navāṁśa Lagna.

Table 67: Kārakāmśa Bhāvas

Karakāṁśa	Results
First	Birth in a powerful/political family if the dispositor is strong. The native is required to lead others. Much depends on the strength of the Sun. If the Ātmakāraka has Rāśi dṛṣṭi on the Navāṁśa Lagna, then the association is there from birth, whilst if merely the Navāṁśa Lagna lord is connected to Ātmakāraka, then the native rises to reap a position of power/authority after birth.
Second	Highly spiritual, may renounce life if Saturn is strong, otherwise if Venus is strong the native will perform severe penance.

Karakāṁśa	Results
Third	Wealthy, succeeds in almost anything, has friends in very high places and is very sociable.
Fourth	Birth of a karma yogi. The person's career becomes important and the native may attain fame if Moon or Jupiter is strong, whilst if Saturn is strong, the work itself becomes the focus. If Sun is strong the native will enjoy Rāja yoga.
Fifth	The native follows dharma diligently, is blessed by his/her father, and enjoys fortune if the Sun is strong.
Sixth	Birth is for purging past sins. The person may suffer from chronic diseases. Worship of Saturn as the embodiment of truth or Lord Satyanārāyaṇa, and fasting on full Moon days is advised.
Seventh	The native enjoys life and has a good heart. The strength of Venus promises a very fruitful marriage.
Eighth	The native is troubled by enemies and enemy action. Is defeated in battle, and has many weaknesses. Worship of Saturn as the embodiment of truth or Lord Satyanārāyaṇa, and fasting on full Moon days is advised.
Ninth	The native is pious, wealthy and fortunate.
Tenth	The native has a clean heart, and puts much importance in a good home and family. This also depends on the strength of the Moon.
Eleventh	Success in battle, bravery and excellent executive ability is granted, and if Mars is strong Rāja yoga is granted.
Twelfth	The native has the blessings of Lakṣmī and attains great wealth.

The results as given above are based on the position of the Kārakāmśa from the Navāṁśa Lagna i.e. if the Kārakāmśa is in the ninth from Navāṁśa Lagna, then the results of the ninth house will be seen.

Chart 81: Princess Diana - Navāṁśa (D-9)

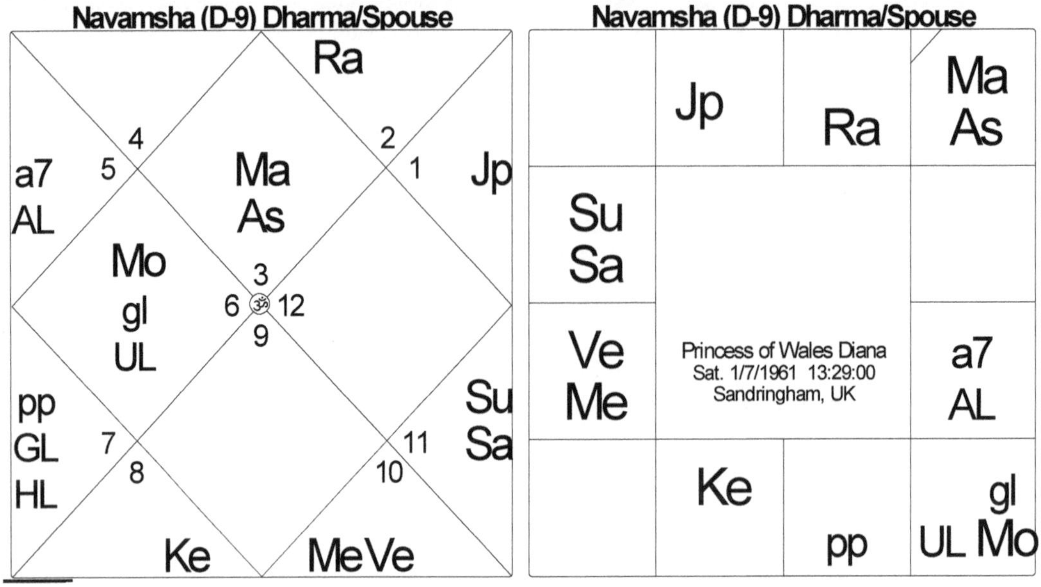

Diana, Princess of Wales, born 1st July 1961, 1:29 PM, Sandringham, United Kingdom.

The Ātmakāraka Moon is in Virgo Navāṁśa, which becomes the Kārakāmśa. Princess Diana has Navāṁśa Lagna and Kārakāmśa in Virgo. This indicates the birth in a royal family. The princess's father is the Earl of Spencer, and it was due to this family connection that the young Diana met with the Prince of Wales and later became the Princess of Wales.

Parāśara and Jaimini explain that the association with royalty is due to the placement of Venus in the first or fifth from 'svāmśa', whilst associated with the Moon or Jupiter. Here svāmśa refers to the Ārūḍha Lagna, Navāṁśa or Kārakāmśa Lagna. The latter two are seen in the Navāṁśa and indicates a more intimate connection, i.e. through marriage or such a relationship. In the Navāṁśa of Diana, Venus is in the fifth from Navāṁśa Lagna as well as the Kārakāmśa and Moon is itself in the Kārakāmśa, indicating the Rāja-Sambandha yoga. These yogas came together to cause the royal association for Princess Diana.

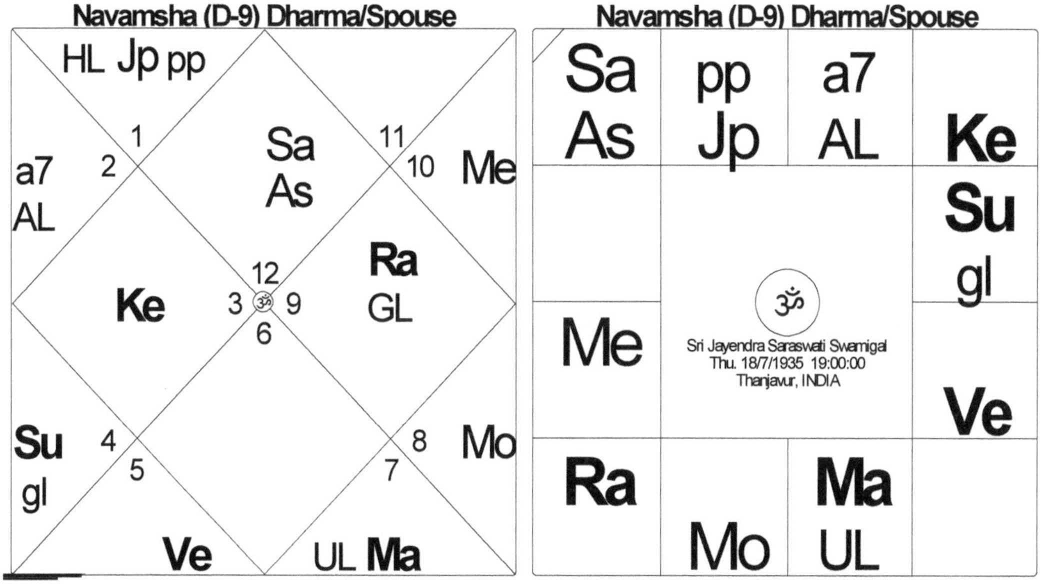

Chart 82: Clinton, Bill - Navāṁśa (D-9)

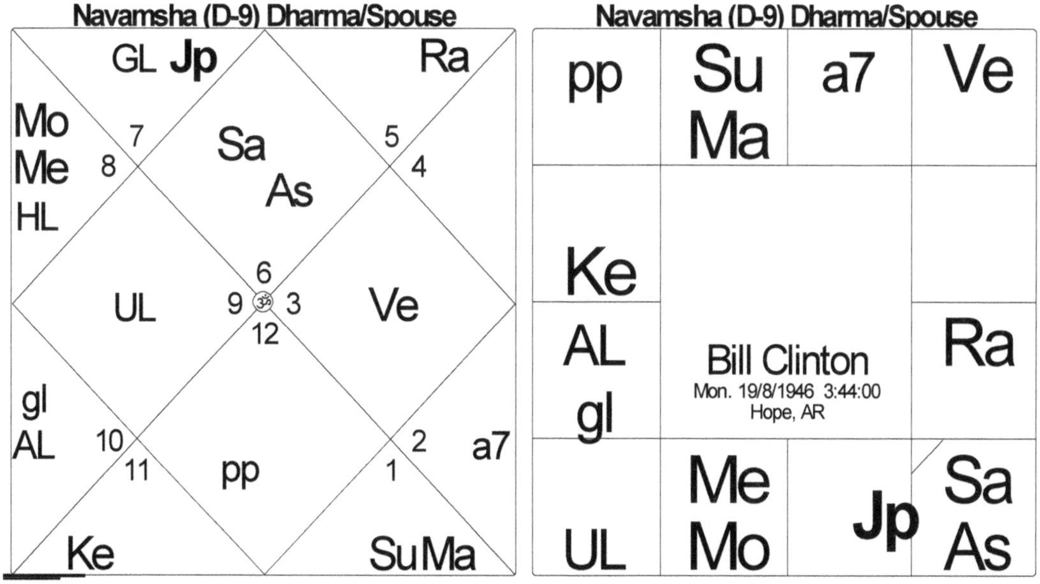

Clinton was not born in a powerful or influential family, but rose to such a high position later in life. In the Navāṁśa of Clinton the Lagna is Virgo and Kārakāṁśa is Scorpio. Scorpio neither aspects nor joins Virgo, hence the association with power since birth is not indicated.

Instead, the lord of Navāṁśa Lagna, Mercury is in the Kārakāṁśa confirming a rise later in life. This yoga of Navāṁśa Lagna lord and the Kārakāṁśa is also a Moon-Mercury yoga. This combination is said to give extramarital relations and other such activity. Hence the coming to power would also have ignited this aspect of his life. In fact most of Clinton's extra-marital relations have been with his secretaries whilst he was in power.

Chart 83: H.H. Śamkarācārya Jayendra Sarasvatī - Navāṁśa (D-9)

Śrī Jayendra Sarasvati Swamigal, born 18th July 1935, 7 PM, Thanjavur, India.

In the chart of His Holiness Jayendra Sarasvatī Swāmīgal, the Śamkarācārya of Kānci, the Ātmakāraka is Jupiter, and is placed in Aries in Navāṁśa which becomes the Kārakāmśa. The Kārakāmśa is in the second house from Navāṁśa Lagna, indicating a high level of spirituality and the possibility of renunciation. Between Saturn and Venus, Saturn is retrograde and is placed in the Navāṁśa Lagna and is much stronger than Venus in the sixth. Hence, Saturn will dominate fully and lead the native towards renunciation. The Ātmakāraka is also lord of Navāṁśa Lagna promising a great rise in life. Unlike the previous Śamkarācārya, Jayendra Sarasvatī has traveled extensively and holds a great sway in the leading political parties of India.

Chart 84: Swami Vivekananda

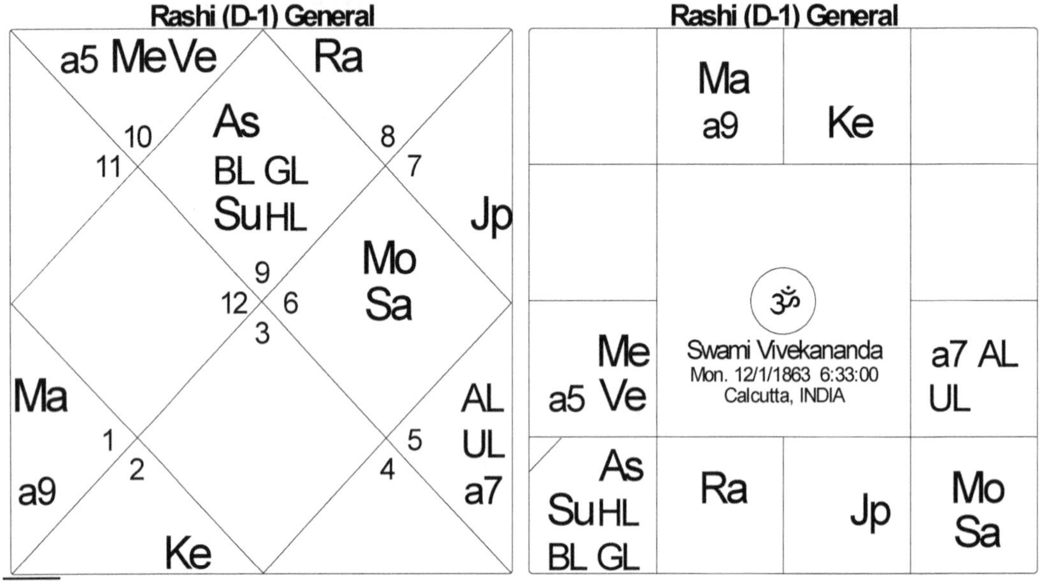

Ātmakāraka is the Sun, and is in Sagittarius in Navāṁśa, which becomes the Kārakāmśa. The Kārakāmśa is in the second from Navāṁśa Lagna, just as in the previous case, hence indicating a soul born for a very spiritual purpose. Between Saturn and Venus, Venus is exalted in the trines to Navāṁśa Lagna, but Saturn is also strongly aspecting the Navāṁśa Lagna from the seventh house. Hence, both planets are indicating renunciation (Saturn) and penance (Venus). In fact, Swāmīji is known for his penance in various parts of India such as Almora just to name a few.

Chart 85: The Author

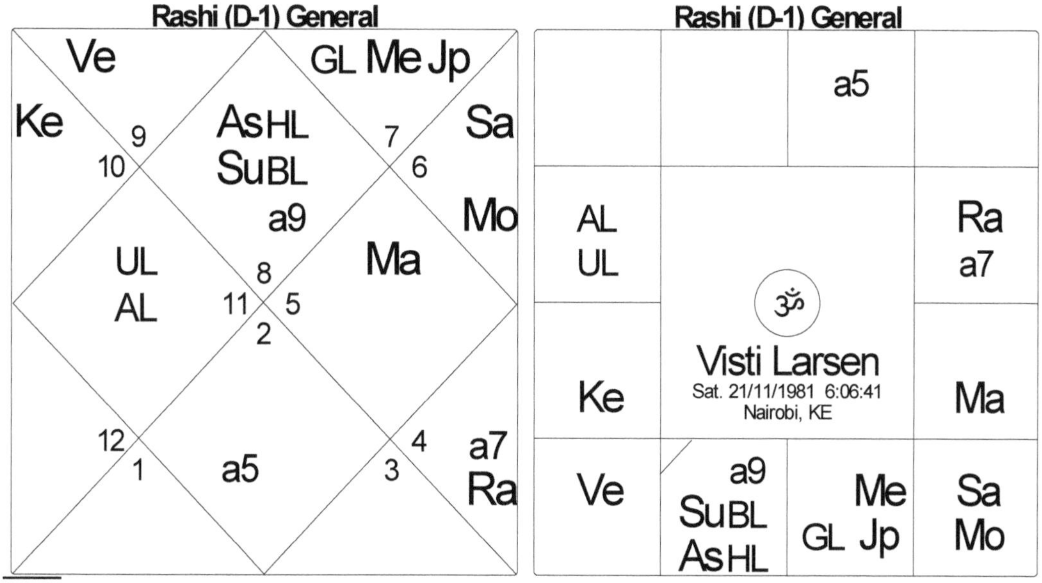

The author has Kārakāṁśa and Navāṁśa Lagna in Cancer. However, the dispositor of the Kārakāṁśa, Moon, is in the eighth house in Navāṁśa and in a parivartana with Ātmakāraka Rāhu. Hence, the prospect of birth in a political family or an influential family is ruled out. In fact, the opposite may be expected. The native's parents lived a very simple life prior to the native's birth, but following the native's birth his father had a significant rise in profession through a transfer. Since the Rāja yoga has not occurred at birth itself, it will instead rise later in life. The parivartana occurring in the Navāṁśa shows that the significant change will occur after marriage.

7.2.5 Ātmakāraka and Rājya Yoga

Since the Ātmakāraka acts like the king of the horoscope, its yoga with the various planets will show important soul-level associations, which can bring one fame, name, reputation, power and authority. Parāśara and Jaimini give a lot of importance to the following yogas:

- If the Ātmakāraka and Putrakāraka have yoga, then there is Mahārāja Yoga and great power is bestowed upon the native. The same applies to the yoga between Lagna lord and fifth lord.
- If the Ātmakāraka and Pitṛkāraka have yoga, then the native is blessed by elders and has Rāja yoga. The same applies to the yoga between Lagna lord and ninth lords, which is known as Lakṣmī Yoga.
- If the ninth lord from Lagna joins the Kāraka Lagna, the fifth from it or the seventh from it, then Rāja yoga occurs and the native attains heights well beyond his peers.

Chart 86: Siddhartha a.k.a. Śrī Gautama Buddha[3]

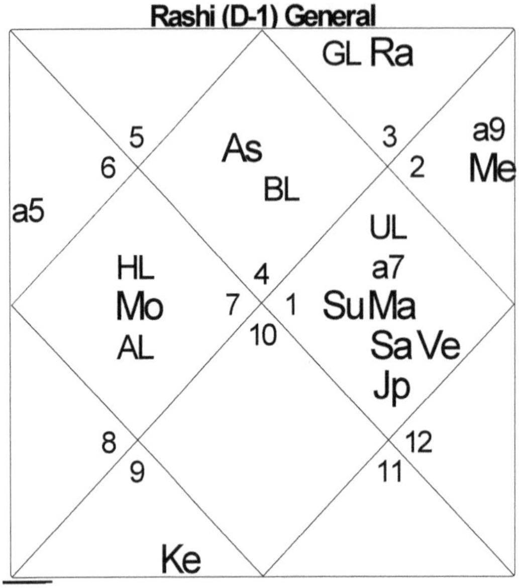

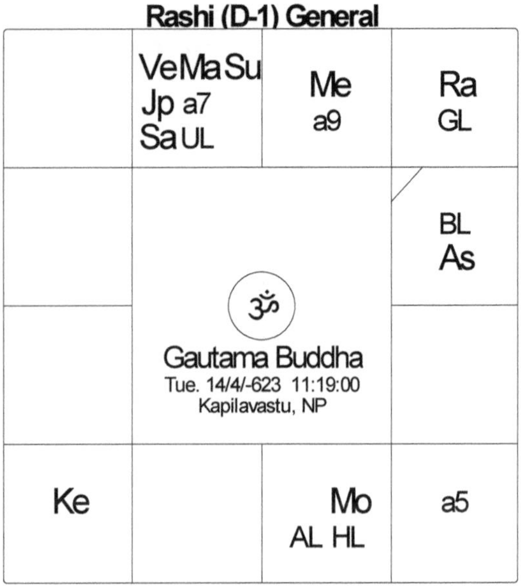

The chart of Siddhartha, later known as Śrī Gautama Buddha, ought to indicate some powerful Mahārāja yogas for the young Siddhartha to have been born in a royal family of great esteem and power. The Sun is the Chara Ātmakāraka and is placed in Aries. Jupiter the Putrakāraka also occupies this position causing the Mahārāja Yoga. The fifth lord Mars is in a mutual graha dṛṣṭi with the Lagna lord Moon, again conferring Mahārāja Yoga and proving his birth in a royal family. Finally, the lord of Ārūḍha Lagna and lord of fifth from Ārūḍha Lagna are conjoined in this Yoga, conferring a complete Mahārāja Yoga of great esteem and power.

Since the second lord is in the tenth house with the tenth lord, it gives Simhāsana[4] Yoga, which confers one a seat on the throne, i.e. kingship. This is accompanied by the combination of the ninth lord Jupiter with the Kāraka Lagna. These same combinations give Parivrājya Yoga, caused by the combination of four or more planets in a sign, in a Kendra to the Lagna, with the involvement of the tenth lord. Siddhartha, therefore, may reject the monumental yoga for power. This corroborates with the prediction given by Sage Asita to the father of Siddhartha, shortly after the latter's birth. The Simhāsana yoga still functioned and Siddhartha introduced Buddhism to the world, now regarded by many almost as a separate religion and enjoying a massive following in different parts of the globe.

3 The chart has been used with reference to the book "Notable horoscopes", by BV Raman.

4 Literally the seat of the lion, or the throne room symbolizing kingship. This is formed by the 10th lords placement in the 1st or 2nd houses, or associated with their lords.

Chart 87: Rajiv Gandhi

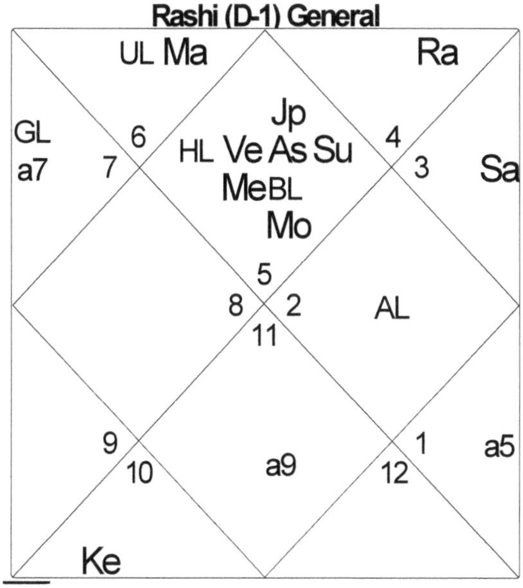

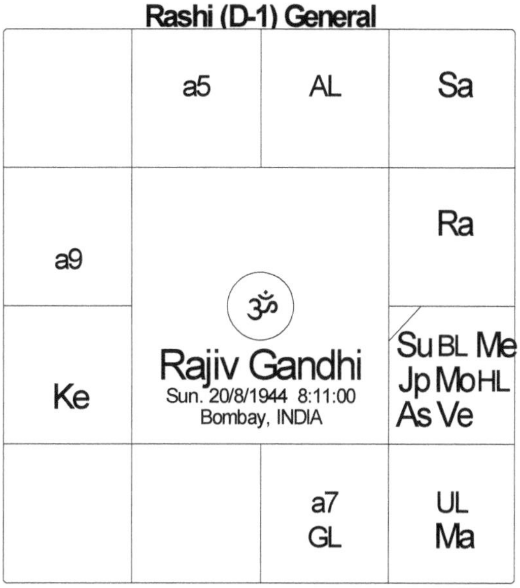

In the chart of Rajiv Gandhi, there is once again a five-planet conjunction. Mercury being the Ātmakāraka is in Lagna with the Lagna lord Sun and is joined the fifth lord and Putrakāraka Jupiter, forming a Mahārāja yoga, which will work from the time of birth, just as in the case of Siddhartha. Further, the lord of Ārūḍha Lagna and the lord of fifth from Ārūḍha Lagna are joined, just as in the case of Siddhartha promising a very powerful Mahārāja Yoga. The tenth lord is forming Simhāsana Yoga by being placed in the Lagna.

The difference is in a pāpakartāri yoga on the Lagna, showing the difficult circumstances under which he may be pushed to the throne. Gandhi was asked to step into politics after the assassination of his mother Indira Gandhi, the then prime minister of India. This was preceded by the death of his brother Sanjay Gandhi who was active in politics. In fact, the Parivrājya Yoga in the chart does hint at an initial disinterest in politics which is true since he was employed as an airlines pilot with Air India for a considerable period of time and led a completely non-political life. Rajiv Gandhi went on to become the Prime Minister of India and enjoyed considerable power and was lauded for ushering economic reforms.

Chart 88: Adolph Hitler

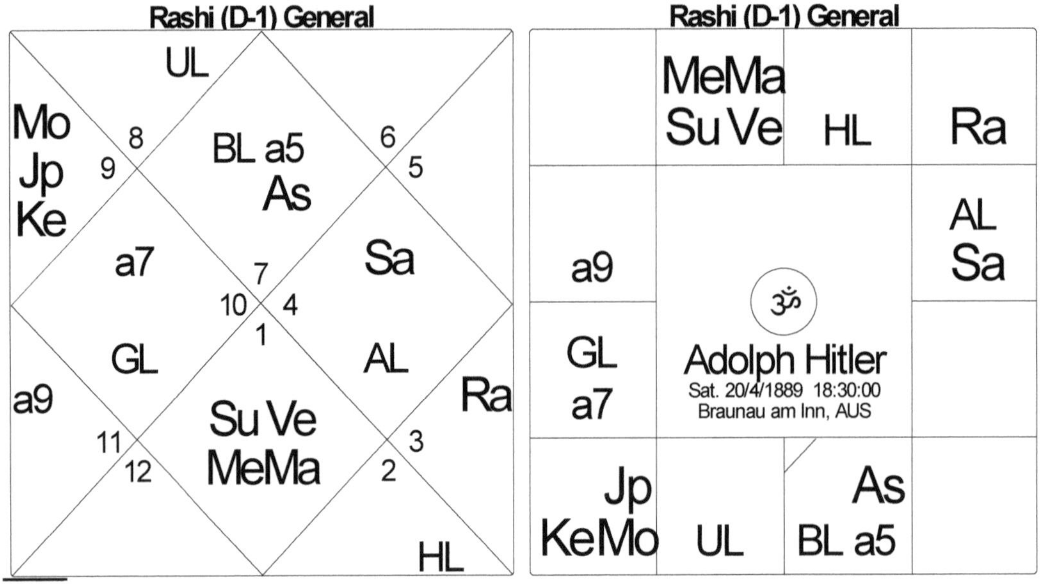

Adolph Hitler, born Adolph Schicklgruber, 20th April 1889, 6:30 PM, Branau, Austria.

The Chara Ātmakāraka Venus is joined the Putrakāraka Sun in the seventh house, conferring Mahārāja Yoga or great power/support from followers. Lord of Ārūḍha Lagna Moon is joined Ketu who is lord of the fifth from Ārūḍha Lagna, indicating that he will enjoy power and authority. The conjunction of the ninth lord with the karaka Lagna and Lagna lord confers the blessings of elders and great fortune in his actions. However two disturbing aspects of the chart come to light with these yogas:

α) Rucaka mahāpuruṣa yoga is formed in conjunction with the Kāraka Lagna, indicating that the world (9th lord) must see war if such a man comes into power.

β) An inauspicious Śakti Yoga for destruction is formed along the 3/9 axis involving the planet of peace and life Jupiter, causing the destruction of peace in the world and great devastation of life.

These two aspects of the chart shows the birth of a tyrant, and that the world would see dark days in his coming to power.

Chart 89: Queen Victoria

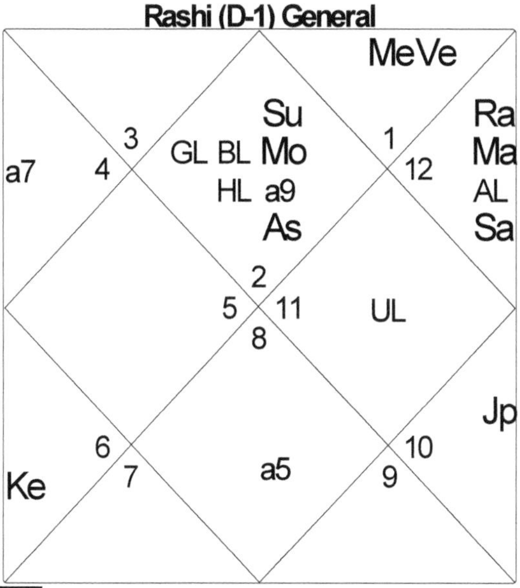

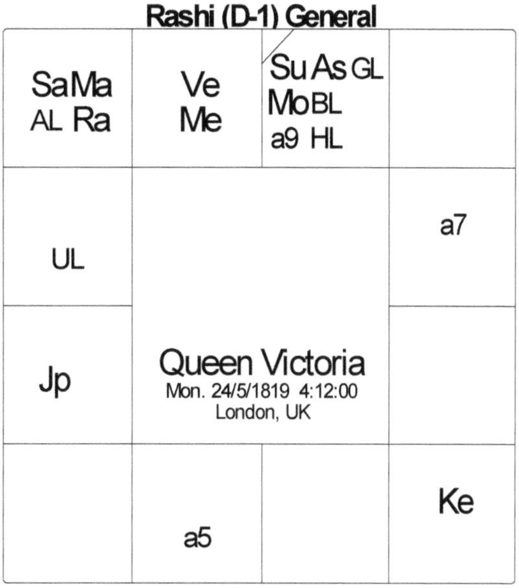

Queen Victoria, born 24th May 1819, 4:12 AM, London, United Kingdom.

Lagna lord Venus and fifth lord Mercury are joined, whilst Ātmakāraka Mars and Putrakāraka Saturn are simultaneously combined together forming a strong Mahārāja Yoga for Queen Victoria. As the Lagna lord and fifth lords are in the twelfth house, the primary focus of this yoga would be in foreign nations and communities, and rightly the great extent to which her Rāja yoga worked, was in foreign trade and the occupation of foreign soil, which lifted England to a very high status in the world. The ninth lord is joined the Kāraka Lagna again, just as in the previous chart, promising great achievements in the world.

Chart 90: Bill Gates

William Gates, born 28th October 1955, 8:49 PM, Seattle, WA, USA.

In the chart of multi billionaire Bill Gates, the Ātmakāraka and Putrakāraka are joined in the fifth house. However the Lagna lord and fifth lords are not joined, nor is the yoga from Ārūḍha Lagna working. This proves that Gates was not born with a silver spoon in his mouth and as a layman had to work his way up. The ninth lord Saturn is joined the Kāraka Lagna confirming two of the conditions for Mahārāja Yoga. Rightly this occurs in the second house from Ārūḍha Lagna showing that the main focus will not be power but wealth. Venus is joined the karaka Lagna and ninth lord and among the three planets it is the most benefic and will give the effects of the ninth lord. During Venus Mahādaśā (1982-2002) Gates became the richest man in the world and commanded a lot of respect and power in the computer industry. This was followed by Sun Daśā (2002-2008) which has continued to keep him among the topmost men in the world.

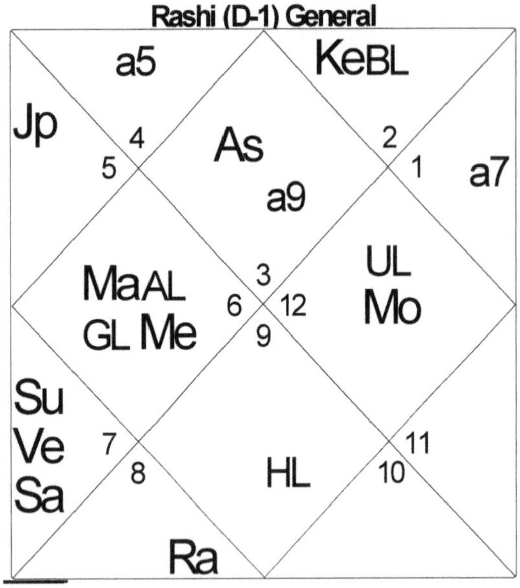

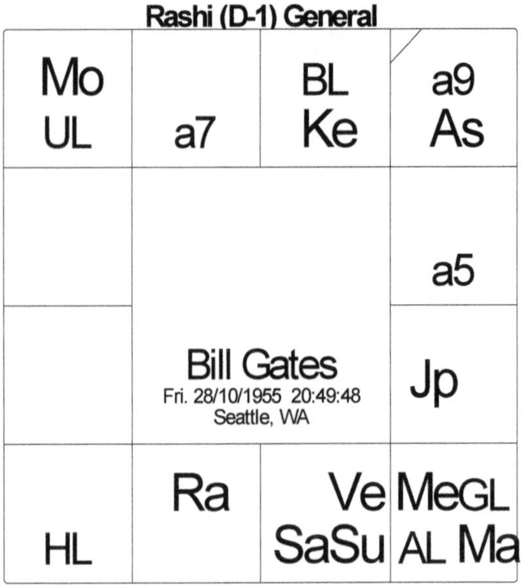

To conclude, the readers may find some of these Rāja yogas formed in the charts of those less privileged than the examples above. To answer such doubts, an in depth study of the vaiśeṣikāmśa as defined by Mahāṛṣi Parāśara is required to understand the extent of the natives rise in life. This is however beyond the purview of this publication, but the above yogas will give a very good indication of where the native's life is heading.

यन्मण्डलं विष्णुचतुर्मखाख्यं यदक्षरं पापहरं जनानां
यत्कालकल्प क्शयकारणं च पुनातु मां तत्सवितुर्वरेण्यम्॥ ८॥

8

First, Fifth & Ninth

The Dharma trikoṇa

8.1 Lagna (First House)

The Lagna is the most important bhāva among the twelve Bhāvas in the horoscope. Based on the Lagna, one should make the final decision regarding the auspiciousness of a planet, the native's basic and changeable nature, the predominant influences on his life, his health, strength, appearance, focus, spirituality and his intelligence. Some practical tools for analysis and chart rectification are hereby described.

8.1.1 Complexion

Each sign has a complexion and colour, as well as an average length. The complexions are based on the planets lording the sign, whilst the colours are based on the signs themselves. The length of a sign determines the size of objects and the length of a native's limbs (proportionate to their body). Some believe that the length of signs determines the height of a person however this is a misconception. The height is derived from the planets placed in quadrants to the Lagna, and this size is measured in añgula, which is relative to the average width of one's fingers.

The scriptures give a method to find the complexion of a person based on the Chandrāṁśa, which is the Navāṁśa of the Moon. The Parampara teaches the following:

1. Take the Lagna degrees and minutes and divide the number into two.

2. Count the quotient from the Lagna.

3. The resultant sign will indicate the complexion.

Example: The Lagna is 14° 20′ Pisces. When divided by 2, the result is 7° 10′. This is equal to the 8th degree. The eighth sign from Pisces is Libra, and its lord Venus will indicate a dark complexion. The colours are from the grahas lording the signs, and not the signs themselves. The complexions are given in the table. It should be kept in mind that the colour arrived at is relative to that of one's family, i.e. darker, lighter or otherwise compared to one's family relations. This technique is valuable for rectification purposes.

Table 68: Colours and Complexions

Rāśi	Colours	Complexion	Length
Aries	Blood Red	Reddish	Short
Taurus	White	Dark	Short
Gemini	Parrot Green	Dark	Medium
Cancer	Reddish White	Fair	Medium
Leo	Yellowish White	Reddish	Long
Virgo	Grey	Dark	Long
Libra	Black	Dark	Long
Scorpio	Yellow	Reddish	Long
Sagittarius	Golden	Fair	Medium
Capricorn	Variegated	Bluish	Medium
Aquarius	Blue/Violet	Bluish	Short
Pisces	Fish Colour	Fair	Short

8.1.2 Nature and Character

The character of a person is broadly defined in two ways; being happy and pleasant (saumya) or cruel and cold (krūra). This is based on the natural characteristics of the grahas as given by Parāśara:

- Sun, Saturn, Mars, the darker Moon, Rāhu and Ketu are krūra.
- Mercury becomes krūra if associated with krūra grahas.
- Jupiter, Venus and the brighter Moon are saumya.

Parāśara defines the Moon's strength from the perspective of light. This light depends on the amount of solar rays received by the Moon during its orbit. A standard definition of this strength is seen from the Tithis i.e. from śuklā aṣṭamī to Kṛṣṇa aṣṭamī, the Moon is strong due to the light received by the Sun.

The uses of saumya and krūra grahas are given below:

- If the Lagna lord is krūra, the native is krūra and saumya if the Lagna lord is saumya.
- If this lord is krūra and joined a saumya graha then the native is sometimes saumya, and vice versa.
- If the Lagna has krūra grahas, the native will become krūra after the age of maturity of that graha in Lagna.
- Grahas having graha dṛṣṭi on the Lagna will cause temporary changes in

nature due to the influence of that graha; however, this is not the internal nature of the native and is caused by the native's involvement with the society.

A person's nature may change because of other associations or circumstances, depending on the planets occupying the Kendras.

- Lagna shows the inner nature as described above.
- Fourth house shows the experiences in childhood, which may change one's nature.
- Seventh house shows the experiences because of partnerships and marriage, which change one's personality.
- Tenth house shows how work modifies one's nature.

The influence of these Kendras is strong in ascending order, making the tenth house the strongest. Similarly, the lordship of those planets placed in quadrants gain considerable strength and influences the native's life.

8.1.3 Planets and Knowledge

Of the nine grahas, Maharṣi Parāśara has specifically stated that the Sun, Jupiter, Rāhu and Ketu are dhīmān. This means that these four grahas make one knowledgeable. Hence, when deciding how much intellectual capability a person has, one has to study the influence of these four grahas in the chart.

Specifically, intelligence is seen from the Lagna or Pāka Lagna (the Lagna lord's sign placement). This requires differentiation. If the influences are on the Lagna, the native has an inborn intellectual capability, which enables him to be a good thinker. If the influences are on the Pāka Lagna, then the native will get the intellectual ability through guidance of a guru/teacher. This is because the natural guru, Jupiter is Kāraka for the pāka Lagna. Finally, to see whether it becomes a part of the native's work to spread or work with knowledge, see the influence of these grahas on the Varṇadā Lagna, or its lord.

Additionally Parāśara states that the Moon is vākya, meaning that the Moon enables one to speak/narrate/re-tell knowledge. Hence, the blessing of the Moon enables one to carry on the knowledge of the seers.

8.1.4 Spirituality

To understand how to see spirituality in a chart, refer to Sāravalī:

आत्मा रविः शीतकरस्तु वेतः सत्त्वं धराजः शशिजोऽथ वाणी।
गुरुःसितो ज्ञानशुखे मदश्च राहुः शानी कालनरस्य दुःखम्॥१॥

ātmā raviḥ śītakarastu vetaḥ sattvam dharājaḥ śaśijo'tha vāṇī|
guruḥsito jñānaśukhe madaśca rāhuḥ śāniḥ kālanarasya duḥkham||1||

The Sun is the Ātmā, Moon is the mana, Mars indicates the strength, Jupiter and Venus show knowledge and happiness respectively, one's ego is indicated by Rāhu and Saturn is the cause of grief.

ātmādayo gaganagairbamlibhirbalavattarāḥ|▫

The Ātmā and other significations will be strong if their placement in the heavens (Bhāvas) is auspicious.

In the first śloka of Sāravalī, we find a clear outline of the significations of the grahas. He continues stating that these indications will be strong, if the placements of the grahas are auspicious. Kalyāṇ Vermā specifically uses the word *gagana*, meaning sky and implies using the Bhāvas as the sky is based on the movement of the Lagna (rising) with reference to the Sun's position. Hence, Kalyāṇ Vermā is asking us to look at the bhāva position in the chart to judge the strength of the significator.

For deciding the source and spiritual strength, our focus is on the Sun. The Sun is the Ātmā, and its strength bestows more ātma*jñā*na (knowledge of the soul) to the native. Whether the native is moving towards this knowledge or away from this knowledge will determine whether the person is spiritual or not. This is seen from the relationship between the Lagna lord and the Sun.

- Placement of the Sun in trines or quadrants from the Lagna lord is highly conducive towards spirituality or moving on the spiritual path. Other combinations suffer from some flaw, and require correction.
- In case of other combinations, determine if a single planet links the Lagna lord and the Sun, through aspect, lordship, conjunction, etc. If so, then that planet will bring spirituality if it is propitiated.

Even if the native's spiritual path is lacking, the mutual relationship between Jupiter and the Lagna lord is conducive for spiritual life, indicating that the native will be guided towards spirituality by a competent guru or guide. The Ātmakāraka is analyzed to judge the inner spirituality of the person. This may or may not manifest outwardly depending on the previous rules given for the Lagna lord. If neither of the above-mentioned links exists, there is no reason to study the native's Vimśāmśa Chart (D-20) for their spiritual practices.

8.1.5 Case Studies

8.1.5.1 Nature and Character

Chart 91: Author

Visti Larsen, born 21st November 1981, 6:06:41 AM, Nairobi, Kenya.

Lagna is Scorpio having two lords, Mars and Ketu. Both planets are krūra indicating krūra behaviour. The Sun being in Lagna will dominate the behaviour and make the person very giving like the Sun but very arrogant.

The Lagna degree is 2°42′. Dividing this by 2 we get 1°21′. Rounding this number up to the next integer we get 2 or the 2nd house. Thus the complexion will be defined from the second house from Lagna. The second house is Sagittarius lorded by Jupiter suggesting a very fair appearance. However, the exchange with Venus gives a brown appearance. The native's mother is from Africa having a brown complexion as father is European and is fair showing how the parivartana gives this mixed complexion.

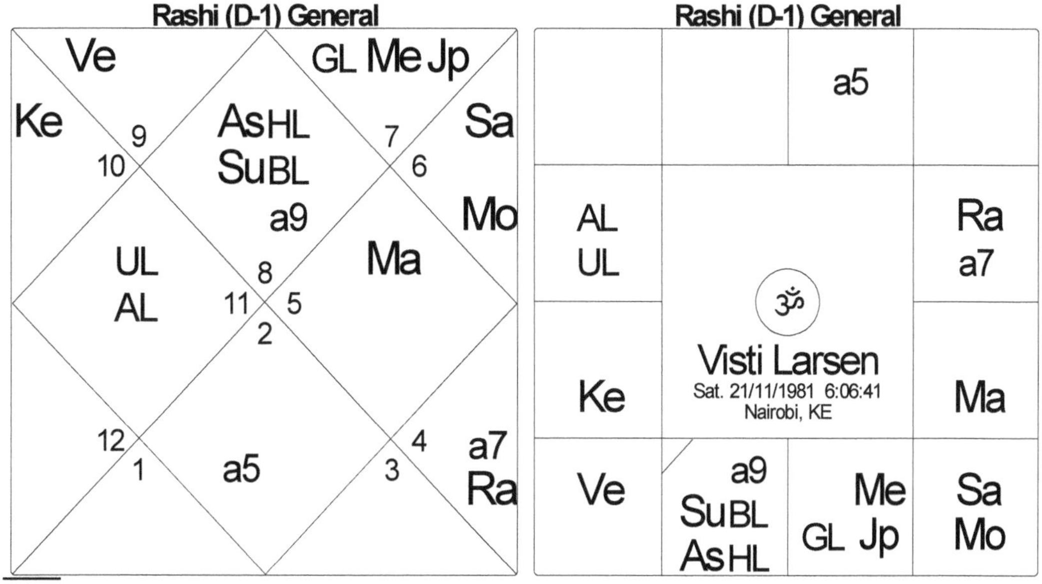

Chart 92: Male Native

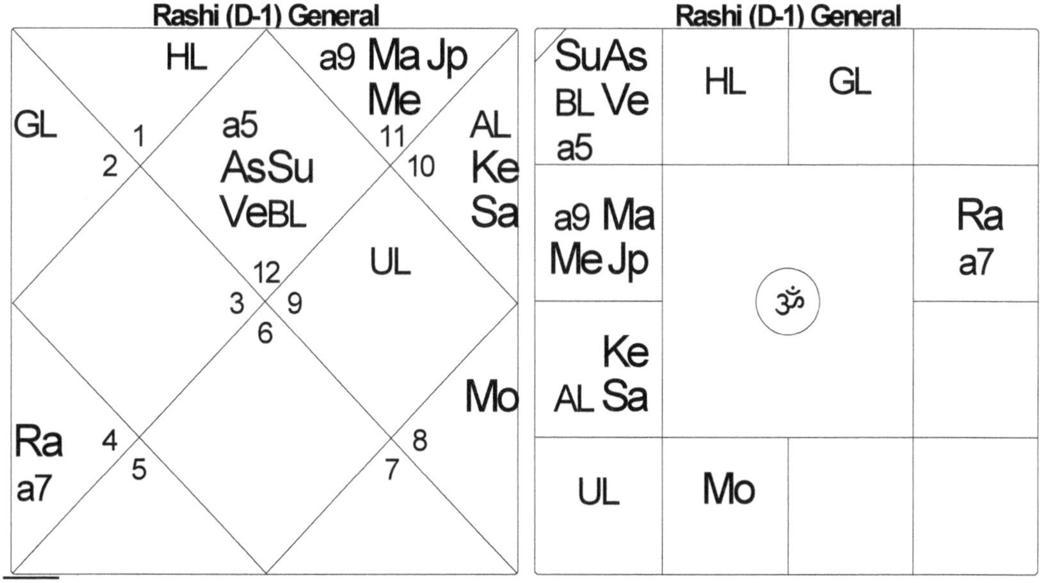

Male born 28th March 1962, 6:29 AM, Kiri Buru, India.

The native has Pisces Lagna with Sun and Venus in the Lagna, whilst Lagneśa Jupiter is joined Mars and Mercury in the twelfth house. Focusing on the grahas in Lagna, the native will act like the Sun after the age of 21/22, and after 25/26, the native will be extremely saumya due to Venus. However both traits will remain, making the native extremely arrogant in matters related to knowledge and authority due to the Sun, whilst towards women the native will be extremely saumya due to Venus. After the age of 30 (Jupiter) the native became extremely krūra, due to the close conjunction of Mars with Lagna lord Jupiter. Mars causes relationships to break, and hence the krūra attitude arose from the bitterness of a broken relationship.

Chart 93: Female Native

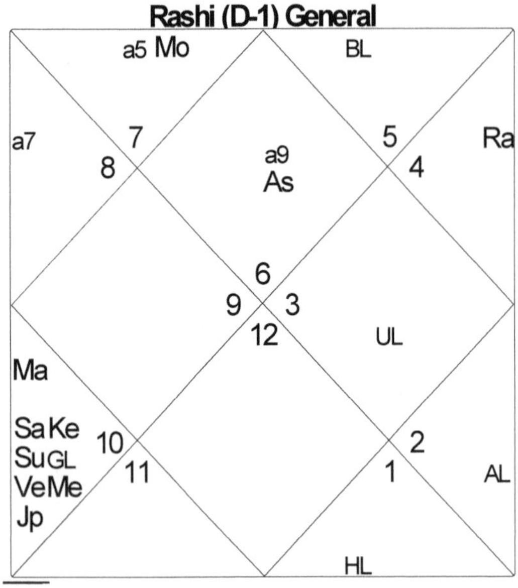

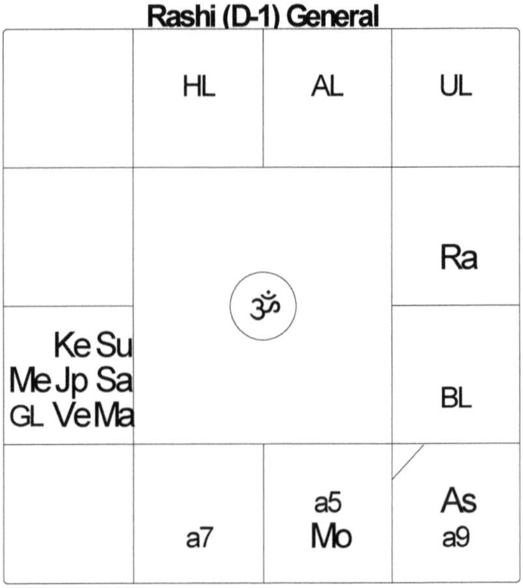

Female born 27th January 1962, 10:15 PM, Huntington, WV, USA.

The native has Virgo rising with no grahas in Lagna. The Lagna lord Mercury is joined six planets, Mars, Sun, Jupiter, Venus, Saturn and Ketu. Depending on the native's associations, she will change her nature. Due to association with gurus (Venus is BK) the native is very saumya, while the same applies for association with astrologers (Jupiter). However, in relationships, the native could take on a very defensive Martian nature, which can be negative.

Chart 94: Male Native

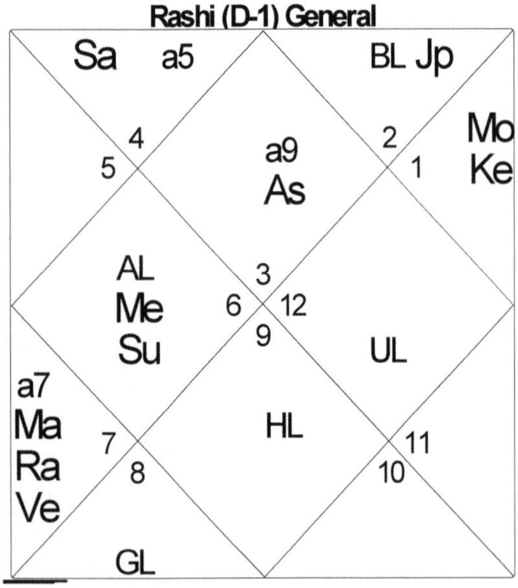

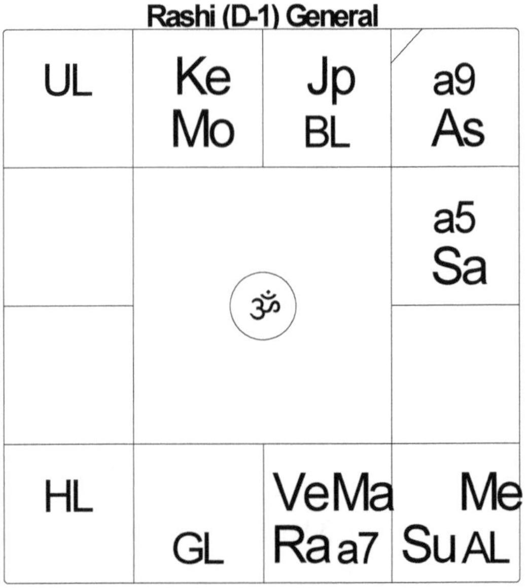

Male born: 9th October 1976, 10:06 PM, Vineland, NJ, USA.

Gemini Lagna with Mercury conjoined Sun in the fourth in Virgo. The native tends to be very arrogant when he takes a leadership role, and when it concerns knowledge. As Mercury lords ṛtu, during the summer months (gṛṣma ṛtu), when the Sun/Mars is the strongest, the native will be overly influenced by the Sun. However, this nature tends to become very saumya due to his association with his guru as Jupiter has graha dṛṣṭi on Mercury and the Sun.

8.1.5.2 Spirituality

Chart 95: Standard Nativity

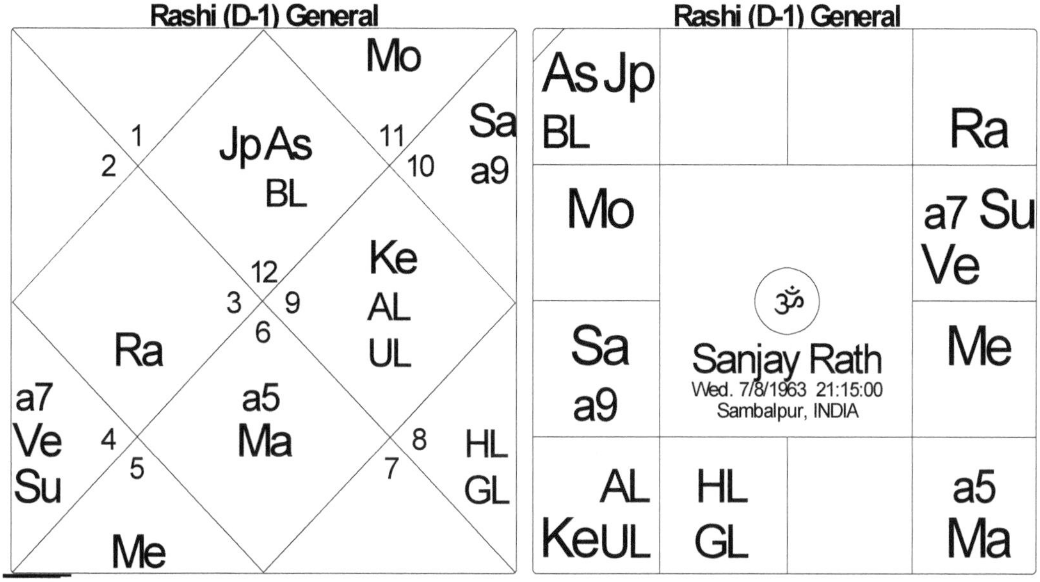

Pt. Sanjay Rath, born 7th August 1963, 9:15 PM, Sambalpur, India.

In the given chart, the Lagna lord is Jupiter placed in Lagna, ensuring the guidance of the guru upon him. Sun is in trines to this and is aspected by Jupiter ensuring a strong sense of spirituality, with its source coming from the guru. The native was born in a family of pious spiritualists, who taught him about God and the intricate details of the universe in the form of astrology and spiritual tools such as mantras and yantras.

Chart 96: Spiritual Aspirant (1)

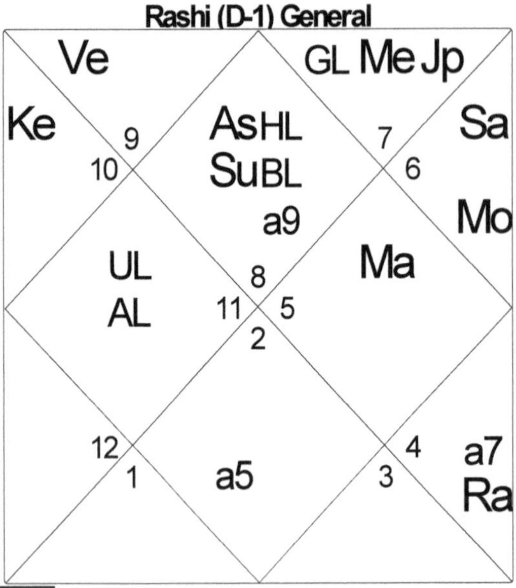

The native has Scorpio Lagna with two Lagna lords. As Kāla Amṛta yoga exists in the chart, Ketu will dominate until 45. The Sun is in the eleventh from Ketu, indicating some struggle spiritually, however Jupiter is in quadrants ensuring that the guidance of the guru will strengthen his spirituality and lead him towards God. The native was not born in a spiritual family, but was surrounded by various facets of spirituality practiced in his community, yet did not approach it, as the requirement was a that of a guru to teach. When the native began studying Jyotiṣa (eleventh lord Mercury), he attained the guidance of an experienced guru to teach him about spirituality (Jupiter is joined Mercury indicating a guru-śiśya Parampara).

Chart 97: Śankarācārya Candraśekharendra Sarasvatī

H.H. Chandraśekhara Sarasvati Swamigal, born 20th May 1894, 1:22 PM, Villupuram, India.

In the case of H.H. Chandraśekhar Sarasvatī, Sun is Lagna lord in a Kendra, ensuring strong and deep spirituality. This Sun is furthermore conjoined Jupiter in the tenth giving proper guidance and teaching, as well as an occupation with a large number of followers (Jupiter is fifth lord forming Mahārāja Yoga).

As Venus is placed in the eighth house it curtails sexual desire and activity, a must for true spiriritual aspirants. *Whenever Venus is placed in the second or eighth house whilst also being the dispositor of the Chara Ātmakāraka and Lagna lord, the native renounces to join the worship of the Divine Mother.* Herein we find that Lagna lord Sun is in Taurus whose dispositor is Venus. Saturn is the Ātmakāraka and is not in a sign of Venus, but its dispositor is also in Taurus thus giving a link to Venus. He renounced to be the Śankaracharya of the Kamakoti Pītha whose worship is of the Divine Mother form Kāmakṣī.

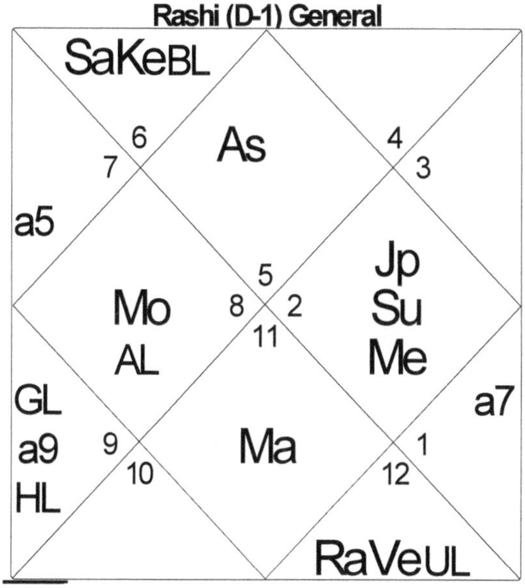

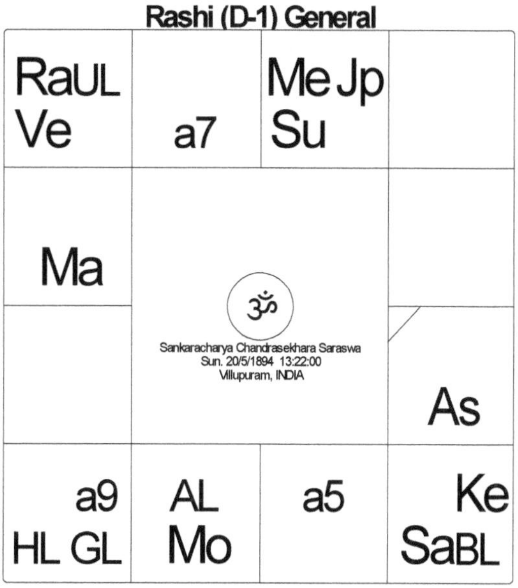

8.2 The Ninth House

The ninth house deals with a variety of issues, of which the father, the guru and the employer are prominent. The higher-education prospects of an individual are seen from the ninth house, as well as the issue of foreign residence. For a fixed sign Lagna, the ninth house becomes a source of bādhā, thereby transforming the bhāgya of the ninth house into obstacles. While everyone has a father, not all remain constantly in their children's life, and hence it is very important to ascertain the father's presence and its duration in the native's life. The employers presence is solely dependant on whether the native is employed or not, yet it can colour the job situation quite thoroughly.

8.2.1 Father

At the time of birth, the child has no choice but to be in the company of their mother, who is giving birth to them, but their father may not be present. After the time of birth, the father may be absent and finally if the father's longevity is weak the quality of time spent with the father can be disappointing, or if longevity is long, troubles may arise due to arguments, misunderstandings or conflicts of a similar nature. A few useful tools are below to determine these factors.

8.2.1.1 The Father at Birth

The scriptures agree unanimously that if the Moon does not see the Lagna, then the father will not be present during the native's birth. The Sun indicates the father in cases of day birth and by Saturn in cases of night birth.

Day Birth

If simultaneously the Sun is in the visible[1] signs (excluding the tenth), the father may not be close to the birth chamber or have no knowledge of the birth. If this same Sun is in a movable sign in the eighth or ninth, then the father is in a foreign country or overseas, while in a fixed sign the father is in the vicinity, but not close to the birthplace location. Dual signs will indicate a father in transit.

Night Birth

If the Moon does not see the Lagna and Saturn is in Lagna or Mars in the seventh, the father will not be present during the native's birth.

8.2.1.2 Premature Demise of Father

The premature demise of the father is caused by the evil influence of Rāhu or Saturn. The paramparā teaches that if Rāhu and/or Saturn associate with the A9, then premature demise of the father can happen. If the Sun also associates with the A9, the premature demise can be averted. Similarly, the health of the father must be seen from the ninth lord's dispositor, as per Kalpadruma Yoga (refer chapter 3: Bhāvas). Having found reasons to believe that the father may not live long, treat the ninth house as Lagna and see the 1st, 10th and 8th lords[2] there from; this is the method of three lords and will reveal evils such as premature death etc.

8.2.2 Guru and Spirituality

Before looking for the traits of a spiritual guru it is important to ascertain whether the person is spiritual or not. This is done as per the steps in the section on the first house.

> *bhāgyaprabhāvagurudharmatapaḥśubhāni sañcintayennavamadevapurohitābhyām*
> Luck/fortune, might/inherit strength/supernatural powers, teachers, dharma, penance, all round good, should all be considered from the ninth house and the priest of the gods (Jupiter and bhrātṛkāraka).
>
> *Jātaka Pārijāta*, Saptāṣṭamanavamabhāvādhyāyaḥ, śloka 65

Vaidyanāth Dīkṣita lists out the significations of the ninth house. Among these, our focus is on the supernatural powers, teachers and penance of the native. The spiritual guide comes in various forms, be it through physical contact or through revelations. The Naisargika Kāraka for guru is Jupiter, whilst the Chara Kāraka for the same is the Bhrātṛkāraka. The Chara Bhrātṛkāraka indicates the knowledge the guru wants to teach. This is the essence and soul of the guru. This knowledge relates to spirituality in one way or the other, and links to various other sciences. For example, a person may learn spirituality through astrology, martial arts, meditation, etc. but the fact remains that they are learning spirituality and the Bhrātṛkāraka or the planets conjoined it indicates the tool used.

1 *Sāravalī*, Grahaguṇādhyāyaḥ , Śloka 1 and 2

The highest ambition and goal for spiritual aspirants is to learn the parā vidyā knowledge from the guru. This knowledge is indicated by Jupiter's presence in the chart. Planets that are joined Jupiter will indicate which fields of knowledge will accompany the parā vidyā knowledge.

Finally, whilst the level of knowledge presided over by the guru maybe very high, the native will meet that guru unless the ninth lord has a strong association with either the Bhrātṛkāraka or Jupiter. This association is seen in both Rāśi and Navāṁśa, just as in the case of the Lagna lord and the Sun/Jupiter. If the above combinations do not exist in the Rāśi, then there is no reason to examine Vimśāmśa (D-20) chart for the spiritual guru.

8.2.3 Case studies

8.2.3.1 Father

Chart 98: Night Birth, Father in Delhi

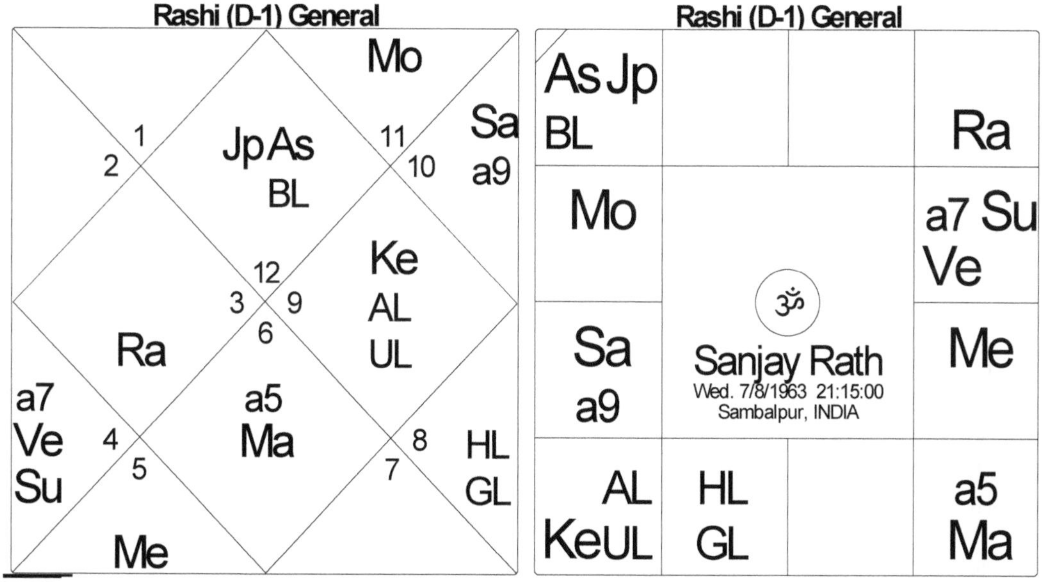

In this case, the native was born during the night. The Moon does not have Rāśi dṛṣṭi on the Lagna; hence, we may infer that the father was not present when the native was born. Mars is in the seventh house, indicating that the father will be in a foreign place during the native's birth, or will have no knowledge of the native's birth. Mars is in a dual sign, Virgo indicating that the father was travelling in a neighbouring state or was in transit (Delhi).

Chart 99: Premature Day Birth, Father in USA

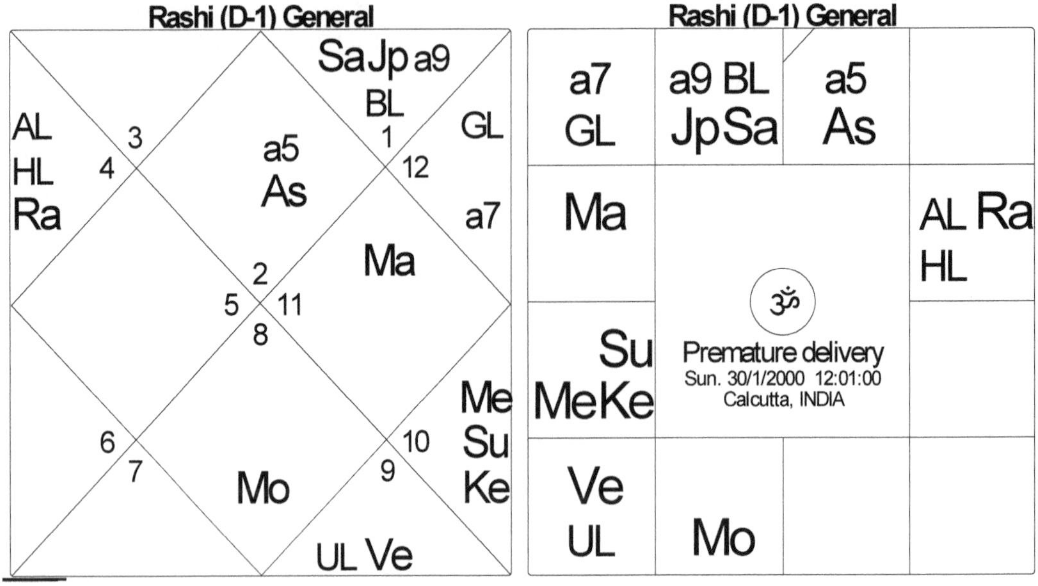

Female child born 20th January 12:01 PM, Calcutta, India.

In the given chart, the father had enquired from the author about the prospects of his newborn daughter. The author noticed the Lagna degree being close to the border and hence sought to rectify the chart. The author told him, "If Taurus is the Lagna the child was born prematurely, while you (the father) were in a foreign country." The father answered in affirmative, and the chart was confirmed accurate with Taurus Lagna.

The Lagna lord in the eighth house, while the Moon is debilitated, indicated the possibility of bālariṣṭa or premature death, but Venus in the eighth house averts this. Venus is Śukrācārya, the recipient of the Mṛtyunjaya mantra, and it saved the child from premature death by lording or being in the eighth house. This saving factor however also causes premature birth of the child in the seventh month.

The next step is to see the Moon. Moon is in Scorpio and whilst it does have graha dṛṣṭi on the Lagna, it does not have Rāśi dṛṣṭi on the same, confirming that Rāśi dṛṣṭi should be used for this purpose. As the person is born during the daytime, the Sun's position needs to be analyzed. The Sun is in the ninth house, in a movable sign, indicating that the father was not present during the birth and that too in a foreign country.

Chart 100: Case 1: Four Months before birth

In the given chart, the Pitṛpada (A9) is in Sagittarius occupied by Rāhu and Mars. The Sun has no association with the A9, and is in the Ārūḍha Lagna in Libra joined the 12th lord from it, i.e. Mercury suggesting some loss related to father.

The 2nd and 8th houses from the 9th are occupied by Venus and Moon. Venus is debilitated and does not bode well for father as it hates the 12th from its position whilst

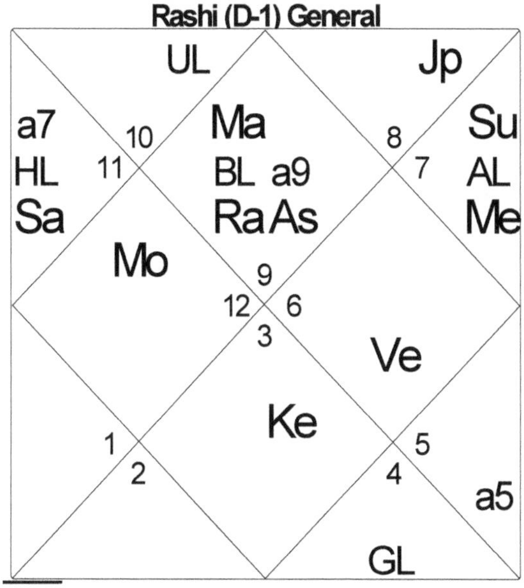

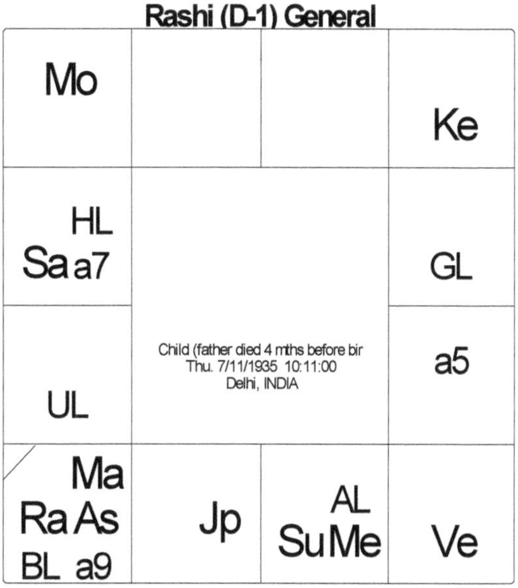

Moon will seek to protect being a benefic. However due to Moon occupying the 8th Navāṁśa from its Rāśi position it becomes very negative and does not protect father.

The ninth lord from Sun is occupied by debilitated Ketu as Mars, Rāhu and debilitated Venus are in Kendra from the same which is not auspicious for father. Moon is the only auspicious graha in this context and as analysed previously cannot protect father. The native's father died four months prior to the native's birth, and hence has never seen the child's face. We may infer that the Dvādaśāṁśa Lagna is Pisces in this case to justify the lack of father's presence in life.

Chart 101: Case 2: Premature Death of father

The Ārūḍha Lagna in the tenth house or Virgo is always a problem for the fathers health. Herein Ārūḍha Lagna in the tenth house has the ninth house in twelfth therefrom showing risk of loss of father. This has to be substantiated with further analysis.

Rāhu lords and has Rāśi dṛṣṭi on the A9 in Aquarius. The ninth lord Jupiter is in the eighth from the ninth house as Saturn afflicts the Sun in Māraṇa Kāraka Sthāna. Finally the ninth lord from the Sun is Mars placed in Māraṇa Kāraka Sthāna. These factors are enough to decide a premature affliction to the father. It is apparent that the Pitṛkāraka, Moon replaces the Mātṛkāraka Sun in a Chara karaka replacement. This makes Saturn the new Pitṛkāraka, which is in the 12th house from Lagna, and AK, confirming the premature demise. Moon indicates the 1st year of birth. The native's father passed away within the 1st year of birth.

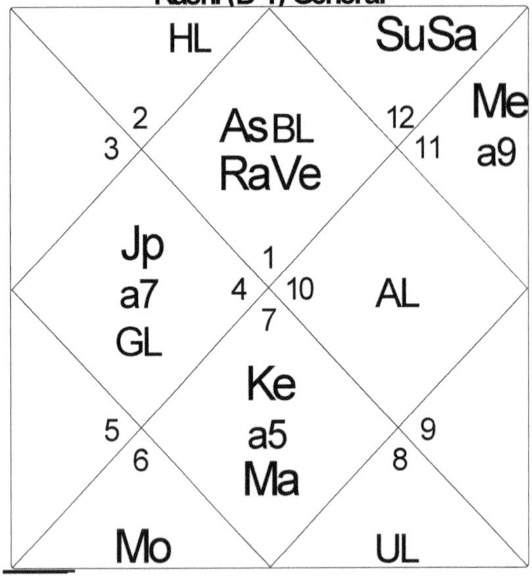

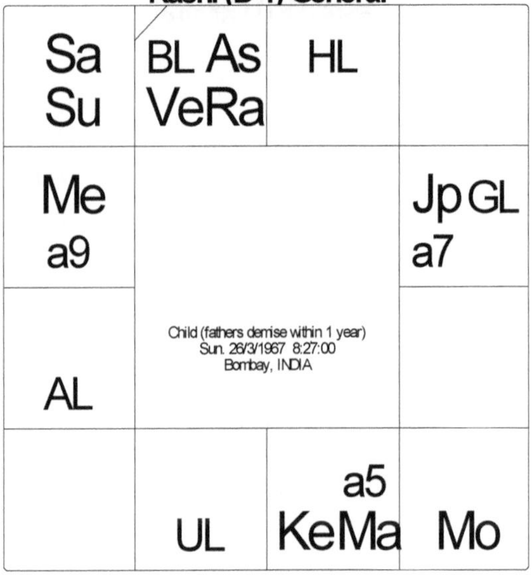

8.2.3.2 Guru and Spirituality

Chart 102: Parampara Guru Śrī Acyutānanda Dasa

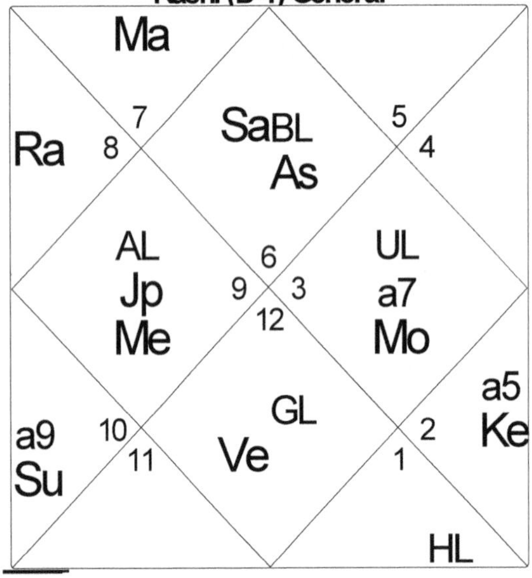

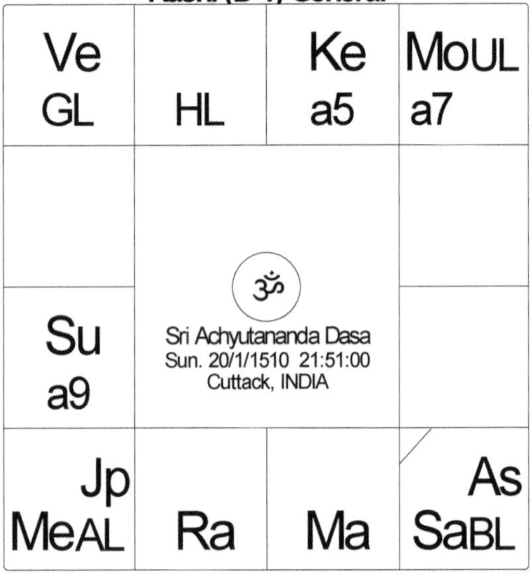

The guru of Śrī Acyuta Dāśā was none other than Śrī Caitanya Mahāprabhu, said to be a partial incarnation of Śrī Kṛṣṇa. This should be visible from the chart. The ninth lord is Venus, exalted in the seventh house. This Venus has mutual Rāśi dṛṣṭi with Jupiter and Mercury, among which Jupiter is Chara Bhrātṛkāraka. Hence ninth lord Venus, Jupiter and the Bhrātṛkāraka are associated with each other, fulfilling this dictum. As Jupiter and Mercury are joined, the appearance of the guru indicated the beginning of the guru-śiśya paramparā.

The timing of the Guru's arrival is best done with the Navāṁśa (D9) and Viṁśāṁśa

(D20). Herein the ninth from the Kārakāṁśa in the D9 chart shows the arrival of the Dikṣa Guru and a very important and lasting Dikṣa arises from this.

Chart 103: Parampara Guru Śrī Acyutānanda Dasa

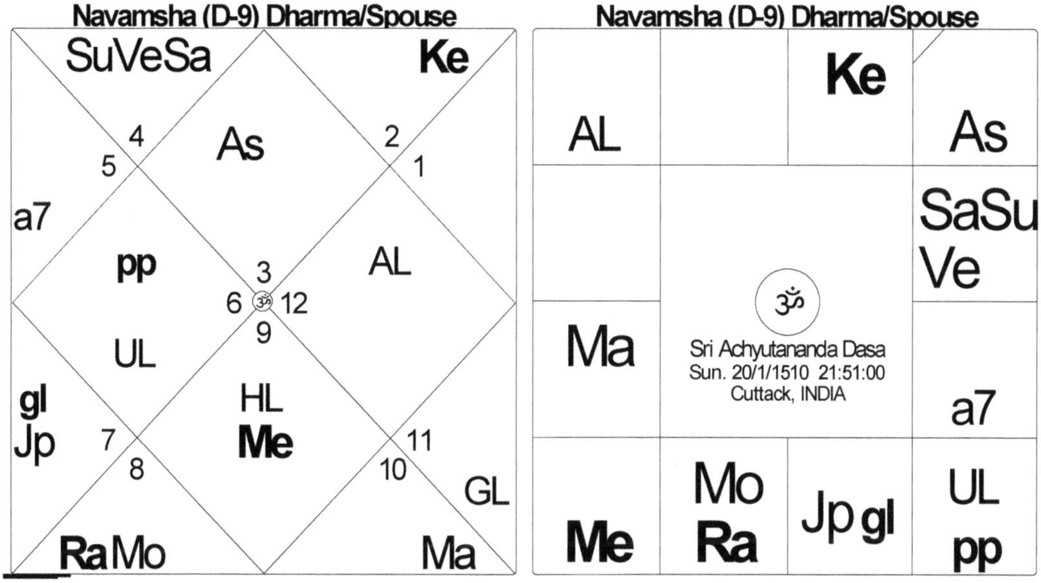

In the Navāṁśa the Ātmakāraka Mercury is placed in Sagittarius. The ninth house therefrom is Leo whose lord Sun is joined Venus and Saturn in Cancer. During the Vimśottari Mahādaśā of Moon and Antaradaśā of Saturn Śrī Achyutānanda met his Guru and received his first mantra. Notably the Daśā has been calculated from the Ātmakāraka Mercury in this case.

Chart 104: Śrī Lahiri Mahāśaya

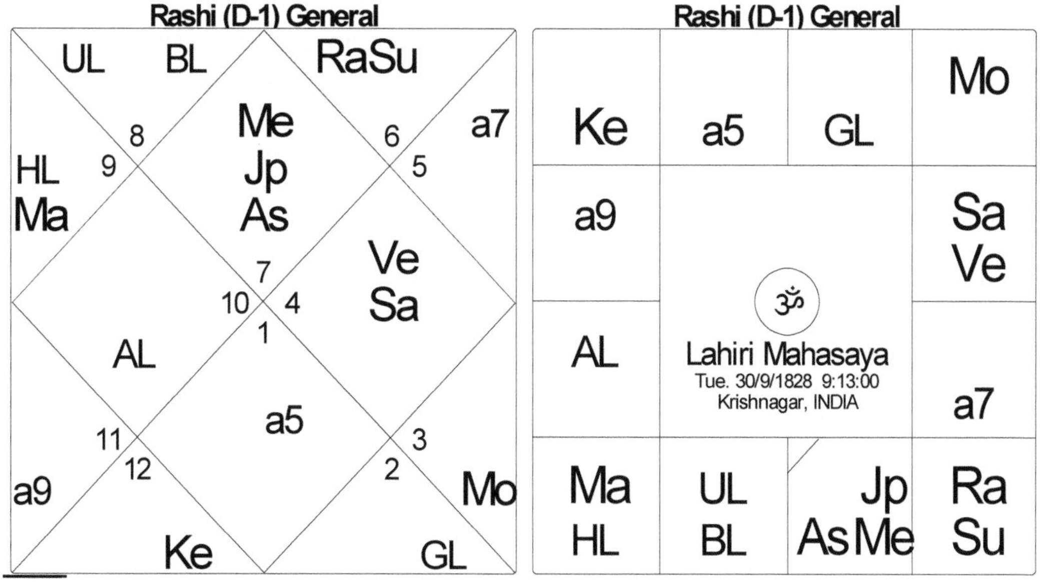

The guru of Śrī Lahiri Mahāśaya was Gorakhnath Babaji. It is said, that Babaji appeared in front of him out of no-where while he was trekking in the mountains. After this meeting, he learnt Kriyā yoga and spread the knowledge to his students. The ninth lord is Moon and in the eighth house it is in Kendra to Naisargika and Chara Bhrātṛkāraka Jupiter, confirming the presence of a great guru. As Jupiter is fifth lord and joined Mercury this became the start of the guru-śiśya paramparā.

8.3 The Fifth House

The fifth house deals with progeny, knowledge, students/followers and spiritual practices. It is a house associated with "pūrva puṇya" as it shows the future and how it is modified by the fortunes we carry over from the past. It shows the aspects of life we wish to study and find interesting, and gives us good knowledge about the subjects the native occupies his mind with as well as the songs and mantra he will like.

8.3.1 Children

8.3.1.1 Conception

Before venturing into the sex of children and their impact in one's life, it is necessary to analyze whether one can conceive at all. The third house has to do with mating and the Ārūḍha of the third house indicates the result of the same, i.e. whether one can actually conceive. The ninth house being the seventh from the third house deals with the same w.r.t. the partner, and hence the Ārūḍha of the ninth house is to be examined. If these Ārūḍhas are in the $2^{nd}/12^{th}$ or $6^{th}/8^{th}$ from the Sun, then the native has physical problems connected with conception and needs medical help.

The Sun as the giver of light does not shine on the $2^{nd}/12^{th}$ or 6th /8th from its position, resulting in darkness and hence lack of life. As Ārūḍhas reside in the abode of the mind, they resemble the Moon and hence the Kāraka for Ārūḍha Lagna is the Moon. Just as the Moonlight is a reflection of the Sun, the life of the Ārūḍha is dependant on the light of the Sun. As the Sun is the giver of light and life, one can determine whether a soul is willing to be born into the world through the native is seen from the Ārūḍha of the third and ninth houses from the Sun known as As3 and As9. If so, then remedies will be very effective in bringing about the pregnancy and childbirth.

To summarize, the A3 and A9 are used to see the physical ability to conceive or cause conception, while the As3 and As9 are used to see whether a soul is willing to be born from the native. Both these strengths are reckoned from the Sun's position. In case of a conflict between the Ārūḍhas, the stronger will dominate the results, but the weaker may come into play later on, indicating an ability to conceive. If the inability to conceive is not one's own but instead that of the spouse, the Upapada and the second there from should be perused.

8.3.1.2 Children from various relationships/marriages

The fifth house in the Rāśi is used for a general understanding of the native's fortune concerning children. Here the state of Jupiter and that of the fifth lord is crucial. Even if the fifth lord and Jupiter are in a good relationship, the state of Jupiter is important in sustaining pregnancies. The placement of planets in the fifth house may at times seem harmless; however, Lagna lord in the fifth house tends to give multiple miscarriages. The reason for this is that wherever the Lagna lord is placed, the life of that bhāva will be depleted. Even after having children, these natives tend to have problems with their children and feel drained by their presence.

To differentiate the children from various relationships/marriages, it becomes necessary to use the Upapada. Here some knowledge of marriage and relationships is necessary as well, and should be understood from the chapter on the seventh house. The ninth from Upapada indicates the children of the specific marriage/serious partnership. Here the ninth is analysed as the Ārūḍha deals with manifestation and the manifestation of any bhāva occurs based on the bhāvat-bhāvam principle. I.e. death is seen in the eighth house but manifests in the eighth from the eighth house, namely the third house and specifically from the Ārūḍha Lagna. Similarly children manifest in the ninth house from the Upapada.

- Should eunuch planets such as Saturn and Mercury be placed there or associate, they will deny children, especially if they are strongly associated with the Upapada or the second there from, indicating an inability to conceive.
- Venus will give excessive sexuality, depleting the ability to procreate, especially if debilitated or joined Mercury.
- Saturn and Mars' association with the ninth house will bring children through adoption.
- Moon will bring one child only.
- Rāhu, Jupiter and Sun will bring many children. If Venus is well placed/strong then Rāhu can bless with twins, triplets, etc.
- Children's birth will be delayed if planets giving children and those denying them are involved.

8.3.2 Knowledge

Knowledge is the result of interest and eagerness to study. This eagerness to study makes one a dhīmanta. Hence, to identify whether a person is interested in studying and learning from the universe it becomes necessary to look for Dhīmanta Yogas in the chart. Whilst Dhīmanta Yoga is not the only knowledge giving yoga, it is also necessary to analyze other related yogas and understand them from the perspective of knowledge and education.

Students come as a result of one's knowledge, hence to see the blessings of students in one's life, it is necessary to analyze the fifth lord's relationship with Mercury.

8.3.2.1 Dhīmanta Yoga

If the first house lord is in the third or sixth house, or associated with the third or sixth lord, then Dhīmanta Yoga is formed. The native born will be a researcher and intellectual with great interest in studying and will raise questions. This yoga is also formed through the association with the fifth house/lord.

A dhīmanta is a person whose focus (Lagna/lord) is on understanding and acquiring knowledge. The manifestation of the yoga leads the native to become a researcher, scientist or people of similar disposition. The third and sixth houses of the natural zodiac are Gemini and Virgo respectively. Mercury rules both these signs, and hence the first lord associated with these houses will make the person a researcher or one seeking to answer questions. Since the fifth house is the seat of knowledge in the natal chart, it has associated with the Lagna can produce a person that is interested in acquiring knowledge.

If the lord of Lagna is merely in the third, sixth or fifth houses, then whilst the native may strive for knowledge, the knowledge will not be available unless the lord of the specific house is connected to the Lagna lord or the Lagna.

Chart 105: Dhīmanta Yoga

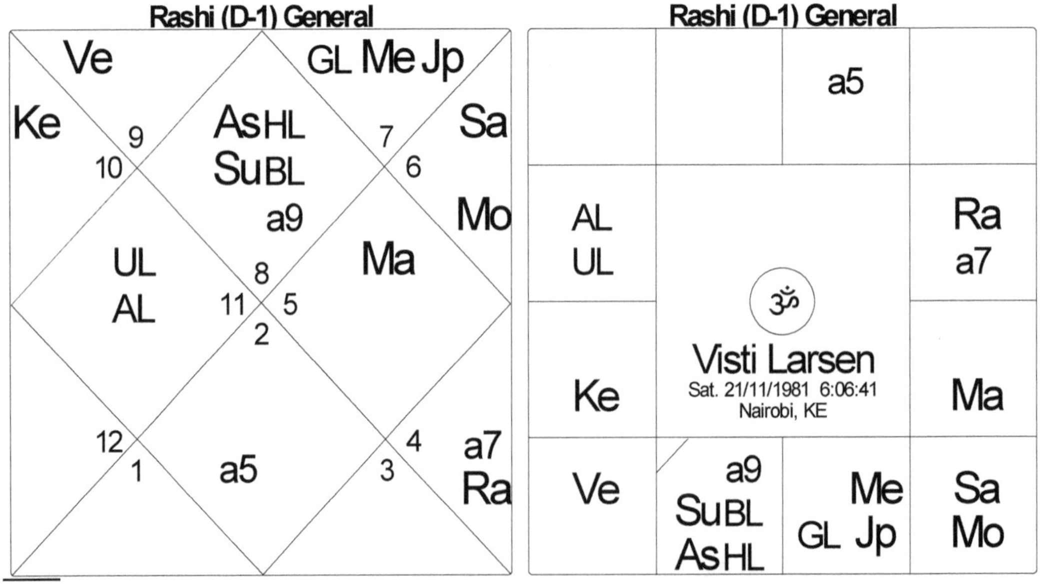

In the given chart, the native has dhīmanta yoga formed by Lagna lord Ketu placed in the third house. However third lord Saturn aspects neither Lagna nor its lord by Rāśi dṛṣṭi, showing that the knowledge is not readily available. The graha dṛṣṭi of Saturn on the Lagna merely indicates the desire of the native to seek the source of the knowledge, yet the knowledge must come through other sources. Saturn's placement in the eleventh house can show that this must come through a Jyotiṣa

Parampara (lineage).

One must note that this yoga need not be formed from Lagna alone, but also Ārūḍha Lagna and Kāraka Lagna can be taken into account, to see a mind and/or a soul born with the purpose of study and research.

8.3.3 Mantra and Spiritual Practice

The fifth house reveals what type of spiritual practices interests the native. These can be very dark if an afflicted Venus is associated as Venus is the guru of the asura (those who do not follow the direction of the Sun), but the mere association of Jupiter will put the native on the right path and correct their mistakes. Moon is the protector of the mind and thus also the Kāraka of prayer and mantra. Mercury signifies words and its association with the fourth house or in Kendra to Moon gives various abilities of using words to influence the mind. How these words are used is seen from the placement of Mercury, i.e. if in third or sixth house the words are used for battle and overcoming enmity whereas in 9th or 12th these are used for higher spiritual objectives.

Kāla Sarpa/Amrita Yogas along the fifth house axis can block one's prayers and mantra's, and tends to cause a lot of dissatisfaction in the native and lead them into wrong practices or generally make them confused or frustrated in life. The nature of the planets in the fifth house or if none, then those joined the lord, will indicate the root cause for the native's interest in worshipping.

- If the Sun is associated with the fifth house the native worships radiant, father-like, knowledge-giving figures, like Lord Śiva, or the Sun itself.
- Moon indicates deities who are motherly, nurturing caring, soothing and give peace and calmness, like Śrī Umā/Pārvatī.
- Mars indicates celibate deities, who are endowed with power and weapons, which they use to protect and fight.
- Jupiter indicates deities immersed in knowledge, teachers and forms, which are non-physical.
- Venus' association with the fifth house indicates a desire to worship deities who give blessings in relationships, gives long life, healing and all the luxuries of life, like Śrī Lakṣmī.
- Saturn indicates forms, which are immersed in darkness, are lazy or claim ignorance. In such cases, the native is advised to worship forms like Niramkāra or Nārāyaṇa, to protect their own intelligence from falling.
- Rāhu indicates forms, which are mysterious in nature, which are highly aggressive and volatile (like snakes); due to their eagerness to battle and which bestow results easily, no matter the cost. In such cases, the native is advised to worship Durgatināśinī or Durgā, to ensure they do not follow a wrong

path in their worship.

- Ketu indicates forms, which lack direction or a body of their own, like spirits, deceased individuals, etc. If Ketu is associated with the Sun the graha attains a body and that too from Śiva, hence this is supposed to be the son of Śiva that is Gaṇeśa. Hence, where there is Ketu's influence people are generally advised to worship Gaṇeśa to ensure that Ketu does not destroy their intelligence and direction in life.

Should these grahas be afflicted, the darker side of the deity emerges, whilst sātvik influences enhance the purer sides of the deities and leads the native towards spirituality and emancipation.

Having ascertained the native's preference of worship, the next step is to analyze the success in doing so, i.e. whether they will be steady in their worship or obstructions will come.

The regular prayer or engagement in worship is seen from the Ārūḍha of the fifth house. Saturn or Rāhu influencing the same causes irregularity in one's worship. Jupiter and Sun will make the native steady and immovable in one's worship. The place of worship is indicated by the ninth house; the tāmasik planets influencing the ninth house will cause problems.

Saturn:	dirt accumulates in the place of worship, due to negligence
Mars:	idols and artifacts brake in the place of worship, or fires start
Nodes:	insects tend to accumulate in the place of worship

One's faith is seen from the Ārūḍha of the ninth house. The tāmasik planets can disturb, shake or change one's faith. Rāhu will make one question, Saturn will make the native loose faith completely and leave their religion, whilst Mars will cause fanaticism and distract the native from the essence of the spirituality they practice. Sātvik prayers or worship will remove the obstacles caused by the tāmasik grahas.

8.3.4 Case studies

Chart 106: Queen Consort Alexandra – 6 children
Queen Consort Alexandra, christened Alexandra Caroline Marie Charlotte Louise Julia; born 1st December 1844, 6:30 AM, Copenhagen, Denmark.

Ātmakāraka is Mercury and is associated with the Lagna in Rāśi and Navāṁśa confirming birth in the aristocracy. Mercury lords the ninth house showing the linkage coming through father and its twelfth lord continues this through marriage. Mars is the dispositor of Mercury as well as seventh lord confirming the continuance of the aristocratic life through spouse.

The Upapada (UL) is placed in the fourth house in Capricorn and despite joined a Saturn in own sign shows unhappiness following marriage, despite long married life as second lord from Upapada is Saturn and well placed in Rāśi and Navāṁśa

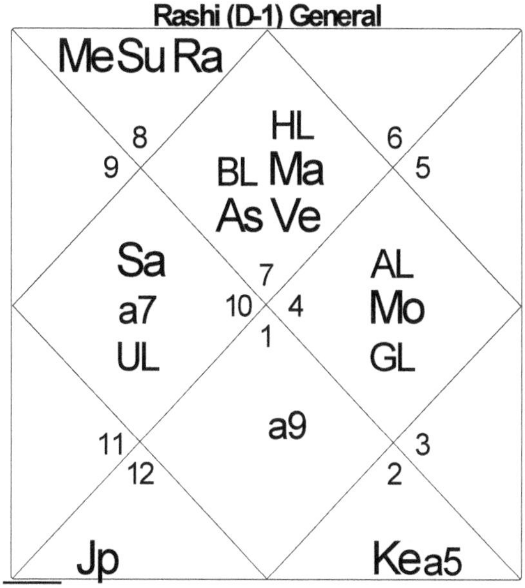

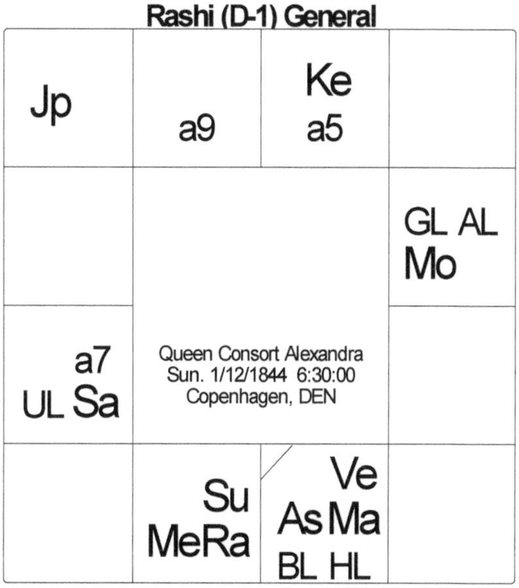

(11th house), yet it's debility in Navāṁśā and joined Ketu shows terrible sexual desires (Sarpa Śāpa) and disease (debility) falling on the spouse. As second from Upapada in Rāśi receives the Rāśi Dṛṣṭi of Mars and Venus jointly extra-marital affairs will surely be there. With Mars and Venus joined in the Kāmatrikoṇa (3rd, 7th or 11th) from the seventh house these will be the philandering of the spouse and not her! Instead had the yoga occurred in the Kāmatrikoṇa from the Lagna then the native herself would be at fault.

With Upapada in the fourth house early marriage is indicated. Prince Edward, heir to King Albert and Queen Victoria, was introduced to Alexandra on 24th September 1861 when Alexandra was 16 years of age. Upapada in the fourth house does not bode well for father in-law as the twelfth therefrom is the third house which represents father-inlaw (9th from 7th). Therefore either the father will travel away or he may pass away before or during the wedding. So also only one year later, after the passing of King Albert, did Prince Edward and Alexandra get engaged 9th September 1862 in Belgium. In this one year Prince Albert had caused a small scandal by having an affair with an Irish actress and the repercussions of the same were said to have strained the then King Albert's health.

The couple were wedded 10th March 1863 when Alexandra was 18 years of age during Venus Daśā, Mars Antaradaśā.

True to the indications of the chart the now King Edward VII kept an entourage of relationships aside from his marriage, a number of liaisons estimated to be up to fifty-five during their forty-seven years of marriage.

Despite Edward VII's philandering, the marriage produced children. The Upapada in Capricorn has Virgo in the ninth from it. Jupiter aspects the same as lord Mercury is joined Sun and Rāhu proving very good for children. Rāhu is placed in Ayuṣ debility proving some of the children to have illness, but the Sun and Jupiter still augments many children.

One method of counting the number is based on the progressed Navāṁśa of the fifth lord(Sharma, 1986). Two fifth lords are evident from Saturn and Rāhu's common lordship of Aquarius. Saturn is placed in Capricorn Rāśi and Aries Navāṁśa suggesting up to three children. Rāhu is placed in Scorpio Rāśi and Libra Navāṁśa which gives a count of up to eleven children (12th sign – 1 = 11 issues). A more detailed examination is now required to see the exact number of children based on the signs progressed as examined in the Navāṁśa.

Table 69: Queen Consort Alexandra childbirths

Rāśi	Issue	Comment
Scorpio	No issue due to Ayuṣ debility	-
Sagittarius	No issue due to debility	-
Capricorn	No issue due to malefic Saturn	-
Aquarius	First issue: Prince Albert Victor	Lord Rāhu is debilitated giving short life
Pisces	Second issue: King George V	Jupiter grants him the kingdom
Aries	Third issue: Princess Louise	Mars in Rājayoga made her Princess Royal
Taurus	No issue due to malefic Ketu	
Gemini	Fourth issue: Princess Victoria	Mercury is the lord and Ātmakāraka making her the closest to the Queen
Cancer	No issue due to enmity between Moon and Rāhu	
Leo	Fifth issue: Princess Maud	Lord Sun gives good life and royalty as Queen of Norway
Virgo	Sixth issue: Prince Alexander John	Mercury supported the earlier born and not the next. Short life of but 24 hours.

The progression of the Navāṁśa of the fifth lord does not replace other methods of estimating the number of children, yet is nevertheless an important technique. Should the number of children exceed that of the progressed Navāṁśa misfortune hits the native. How this manifests depends on the chart in particular and remedies need to be resorted to. Being a delicate subject, Jyotiṣa should be wise in advising the appropriate number of children to the client for good fortune in life.

Rashi (D-1) General

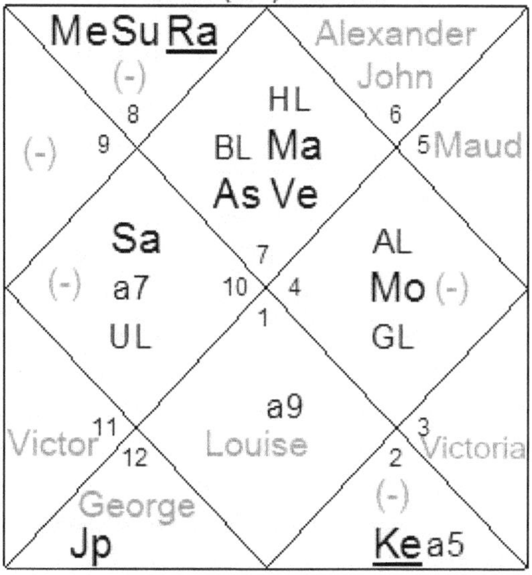

Rashi (D-1) General

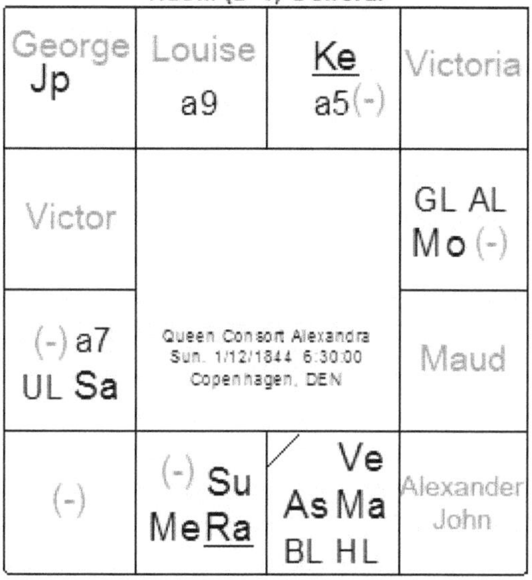

Chart 107: Cher

Rashi (D-1) General

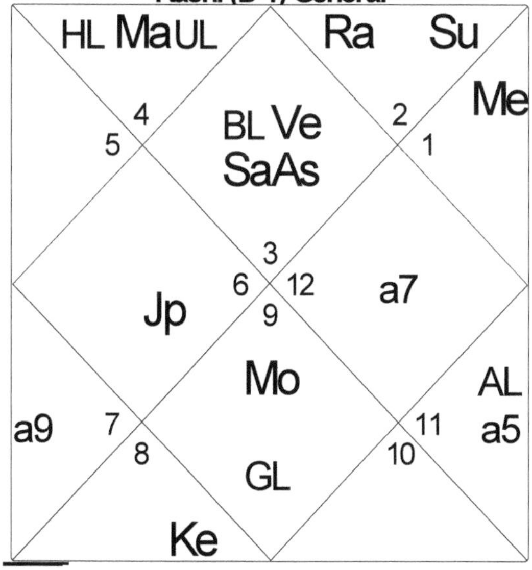

Rashi (D-1) General

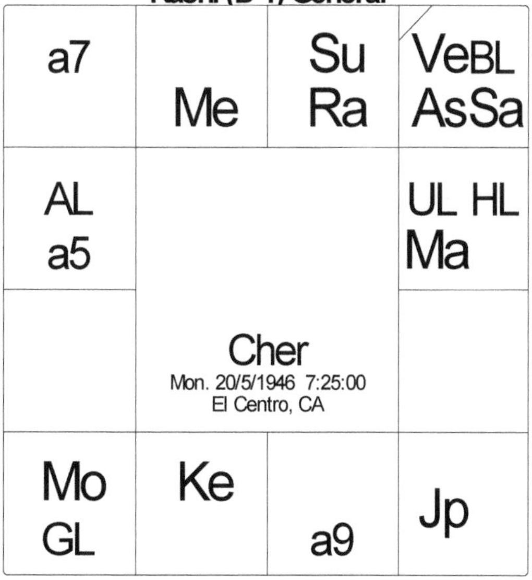

Cher, born Cherilyn Sarkisian, 20th May 1946, 7:25 AM, El Centro, CA, USA.

Birth is during Purvāṣaḍha Nakṣatra and the lord of the fourth therefrom is Mars in debility. The debility of Mars gives a poor upbringing however Mars receives cancellation of debilitation by the placement of Jupiter, Saturn and Moon in Kendra from the Lagna showing a rags-to-riches story in matters of home and comfort. Moon is furthermore in the seventh house granting fame and name through mother. Cher's father was an Armenian American who drove trucks for a living as her mother, being of mixed European descent, sought a living as an actress. The parents divorced and the mother subsequently married the banker Gilbert LaPiere who later adopted Cher. This helped Cher's desire to be educated as an actress and singer herself.

Upapada is in second house and seventh lord in fourth suggests early marriage. Upapada joined the debilitated Mars shows that spouse also hails from humble beginnings, and as the lord Moon is granting fame in the seventh house the spouse is the catalyst to long lasting fame. She met Sonny Bono, 11 years senior to her, in 1962. Sonny worked for a record producer through which Cher started as session singer in 1963 at the age of 17. Moon Daśā, Venus Antaradaśā was running at the time. Venus is placed in the tenth from the tenth lord Jupiter suggesting career and new beginnings due to being in Lagna. Venus' lordship over the ninth from the seventh lord Jupiter also suggests intimate relationships beginning.

The couple was married in 1963 but held an official wedding in October 1964 in Mexico. The ninth from Upapada is Pisces, a fruitful sign, which is unoccupied as Moon, Jupiter, Venus and Saturn aspect by Rāśi Dṛṣṭi. Among these Moons aspect from the Abhimukha of Pisces is strongest and suggests one child from this relationship. Conversely Venus and Saturn in Gemini does not promise children as Jupiter's aspects could give up to three but is placed in the Bādhaka sign from Pisces.

The sustenance of the marriage is seen in the second from Upapada which is Leo. The lord Sun is placed in the twelfth house in Māraṇa Kāraka Sthāna indicating divorce. Sun is in Aquarius in Navāṁśa gaining nine Navāṁśa suggesting that at least nine years of marriage will be strong after which the relationship will dwindle. Sun is in Taurus suggesting extramarital affairs as being the cause. In 1972 Cher had fallen in love with the bands guitarist and the couple maintained a professional relationship for three years before divorcing in 1975.

The cause of the break is the Sun who is joined Rāhu, the lord of the next Upapada in Aquarius indicating marriage following the divorce. So also as the divorce was final in June 1975 three days later Cher married Gregg Allman in Las Vegas. However, as lord of Upapada is in the undesirable Sun-Rāhu yoga this brings marriage to a person who will experiment with psycho-pharmacy. So also Cher sought to dissolve the marriage to Allman 9 days later. Allman convinced Cher to continue the marriage and one year later in July 1976 their son was born. The ninth from Aquarius is Libra, which is a fruitful sign by nature, aspected by Rāhu and Sun promising children, especially sons. The couple had one son.

Upapada in Aquarius is rarely a lasting relationship due to the second house being lorded by Jupiter who doesn't wish to support Rāhu's lordship of Aquarius. Unless other planets are joined Aquarius, these relationships either bring early separation or divorce. Normally the partners find themselves completely opposite in their ideals and lifestyles and quickly end their relationship. The couple divorced after two years of marriage.

Examining the progressed Navāṁśa of the fifth lord Venus we find it placed in Gemini Rāśi and Libra Navāṁśa showing the progression of four Navāṁśa or four potential children. The first child is indicated by Venus joined Saturn in Gemini. The specific combination of Gemini and Saturn suggests a child who will be homosexual. The first born is a daughter named Chastity and claims to be a lesbian. The daughter has further sought to change her sex to a man due to not identifying herself with her female body.

Cancer is the second option but being joined weak Mars will not manifest. The third option is Leo which will manifest. The lord Sun is placed in the twelfth house indicating a child who will be happier in a foreign country. This is further promoted by the junction with Rāhu indicating foreigners supporting him. It is evident that this combination could become very negative in his home country.

Virgo is the next option where Venus suffers debilitation and does not manifest.

Chart 108: Adopted Children

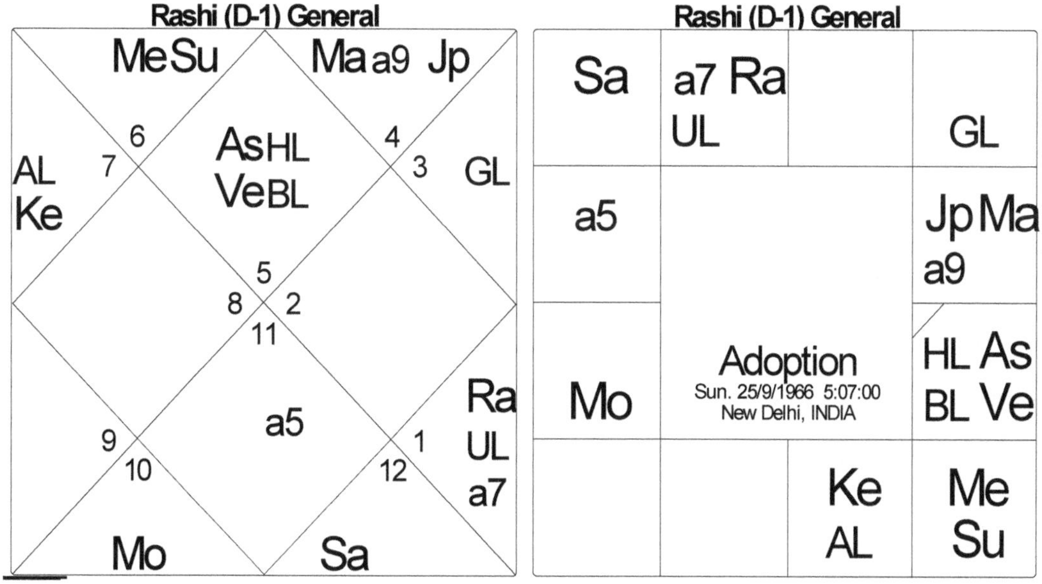

In the given chart, the Lagna lord and second lord are in the second house, which is very unfortunate for children, as they give virodhārgala on the fifth house. The second lord in such a placement can be detrimental for the children. This and the placement of the fifth lord and Jupiter in the twelfth house, which is eighth from the fifth, make it pertinent to analyze the prospects of having children.

The A3 and A9 are well placed from the Sun but the As9 is in the twelfth from the Sun indicating the lack of ability to bring a soul into this world. Finally, to see the outcome the ninth from Upapada needs to be analyzed. The Upapada is in Aries; hence, the ninth there from becomes the fifth house itself. Saturn has Rāśi and graha dṛṣṭi on Sagittarius, while Sun and Mercury also has Rāśi dṛṣṭi on the same. Mercury and Saturn will delay and deny children, whilst the Sun will try to give a child, though weak due to the conjunction with Mercury. Jupiter the lord of the same is joined Mars, hence the way out is adoption, as both Saturn and Mars associate with the ninth from UL or its lord. The native adopted a child, and gave up attempts to procreate.

Knowledge

Chart 109: Albert Einstein, a dhīmanta

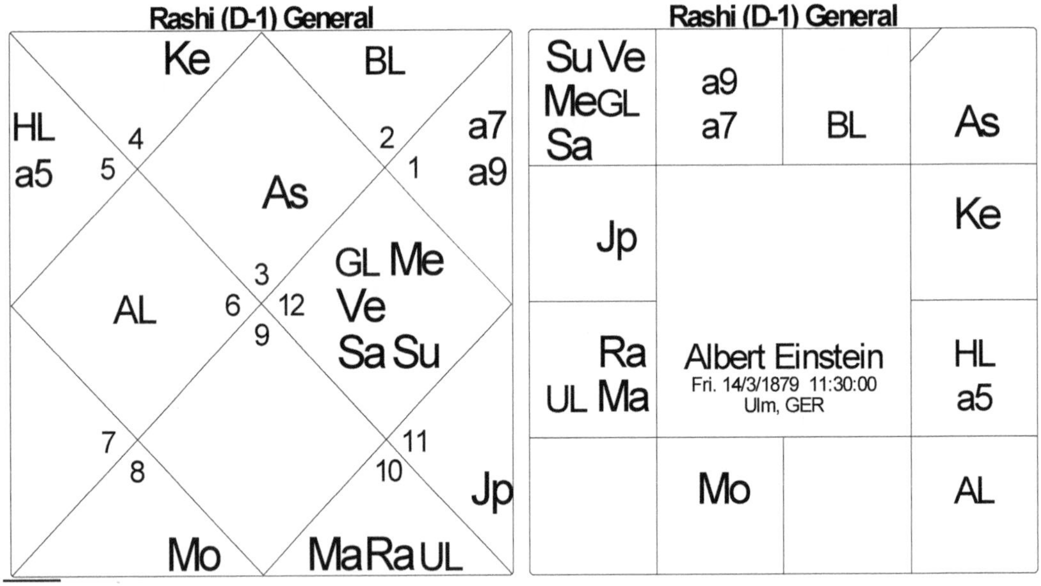

Albert Einstein, born 14th March 1879, 11:30 AM, Ulm, Germany.

Nature of the dhī

In the chart of Albert Einstein, the Lagna is Gemini, and the Nakṣatra is the fourth pada of Ārdrā. Being in the fourth pada, it shows that the inner nature of Einstein is that of attaining inner happiness/satisfaction or even liberation.

Tool(s) of the dhī

Lagna is unoccupied, while its lord Mercury is with the Sun, Saturn and Venus, hence most malefics are joined. Lagna lord being benefic and joined largely malefic planets indicates that Einstein had a strong desire to establish truth in the world.

Dhīmanta yoga from Lagna

As Mercury is in the tenth house (success/career) with third lord Sun, forming Dhīmanta Yoga it ensures that the focus of Einstein's intellect will be study and research. Adding to this the fifth lord Venus is joined Lagna lord Mercury and has Rāśi dṛṣṭi on the Lagna ensuring that the inclination to apply the intellect will be there.

Dhīmanta yoga from Ārūḍha Lagna

Mercury is the lord of Ārūḍha Lagna (AL), and Saturn is the lord of fifth and sixth from Ārūḍha Lagna, again forming dhīmanta yoga, ensuring that research and study will not only be an interest in his life, but will also form his image in society.

Dhīmanta yoga from ātmakāraka

The Chara Ātmakāraka Venus is in the tenth house. The lord of third from Pisces is Venus, while the lord of the sixth is Sun, both of which are in Pisces, forming Dhīmanta Yoga and setting the scene for a soul who's inner most desire is to study and research the depths of the universe.

His success began with the recognition and acceptance of his papers such as *The motion of small particles suspended in a stationary liquid according to the molecular kinetic theory of induction, A heuristic viewpoint concerning the production and transformation of light, The electrodynamics of moving bodies* etc. This happened in Venus Daśā – Rāhu Antaradaśā (Rāhu is ninth lord and is in the Nakṣatra Uttara Āṣāḍa ruled by the Viśvadevas[3]). Later in 1907 his invention of the immortal $E=mc^2$, in Venus Daśā – Jupiter Antaradaśā (Jupiter placed in ninth house).

Chart 110: Swami Vivekananda, a Jñāna Yogi

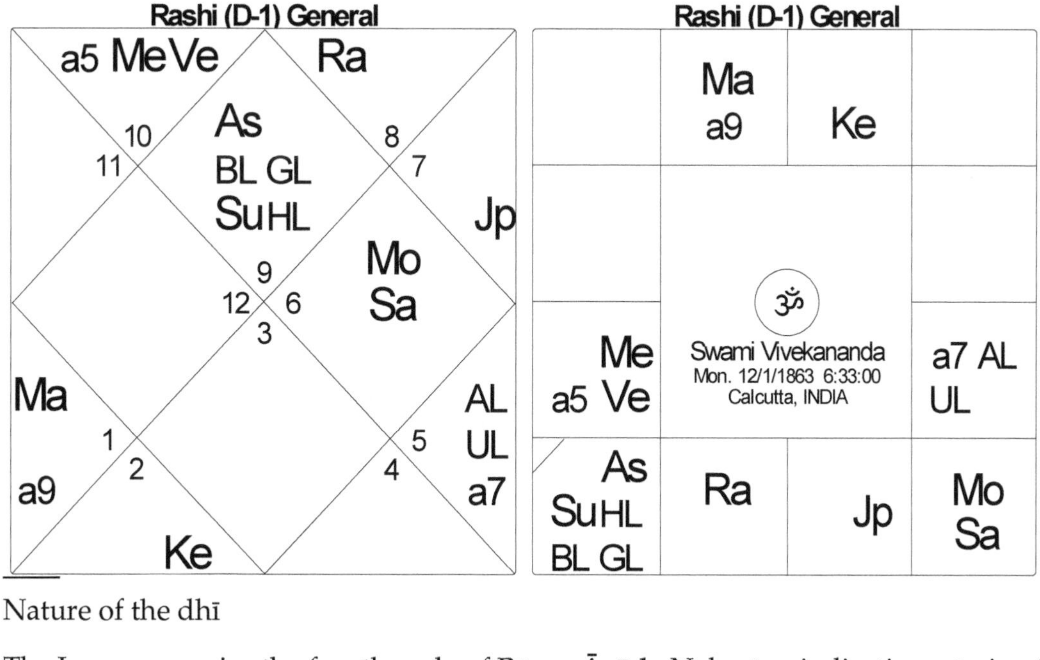

Nature of the dhī

The Lagna occupies the fourth pada of Pūrva **Āṣāḍa** Nakṣatra, indicating a train of thoughts leading towards liberation and inner satisfaction. This is different from the Moon's pada being the third, showing an attitude of spreading happiness among people.

Tool(s) of the dhī

3 Vishwa-Deva, means 'all-gods', where deva is also symbolic of the various lights of God, hence planets here will give events related to understanding or exploiting the universal truths.

The Lagna is Sagittarius occupied by the Sun. By nature, this indicates a person who is strict in his decisions, yet by default a very open and happy person. Sun receives Rāśi dṛṣṭi from Saturn and Moon, one being malefic and the other benefic, hence the native would have an inclination towards both; taking the poison of others (benefic) and causing pain/poison to others. As Moon occupies a higher degree than Saturn does, beneficial results will dominate.

Dhīmanta yoga from Lagna and ātmakāraka

The Lagna and Ātmakāraka are in the same sign Sagittarius, indicating a person reaching for inner self-realization. The lord of Sagittarius is Jupiter, who is in the eleventh house. The eleventh house is the fourth from the eighth house; hence, it gives education in the occult sciences. Jupiter has mutual graha dṛṣṭi with Mars, forming a very powerful Guru-Mangala Yoga, making him righteous and aggressive in the establishment of truth in the world. The placement of Mars in strength in the fifth is important for the native to establish truth and ensures the removal of ignorance. As Mars is also the fifth lord, and placed in the fifth house, it forms a powerful dhīmanta yoga, indicating a soul whose prime focus is to establish truth in this world. His guru (Rāmakṛṣṇa Paramhamsa) gave a more apt description: "He is a burning, roaring fire consuming all impurities to ashes."

Dhīmanta yoga from Ārūḍha Lagna

The Ārūḍha Lagna is in Leo, and its lord Sun is in the fifth there from, in Sagittarius. This forms dhīmanta yoga from Ārūḍha Lagna, and hence the classification of Swami Vivekananda as a dhīmanta is confirmed from the chart. Swāmīji had a large number of students. Fifth lord Mars being well placed from Mercury in the chart confirms this.

Chart 111: Paramhamsa Yogānanda, a Jñāna Yogi

Rashi (D-1) General

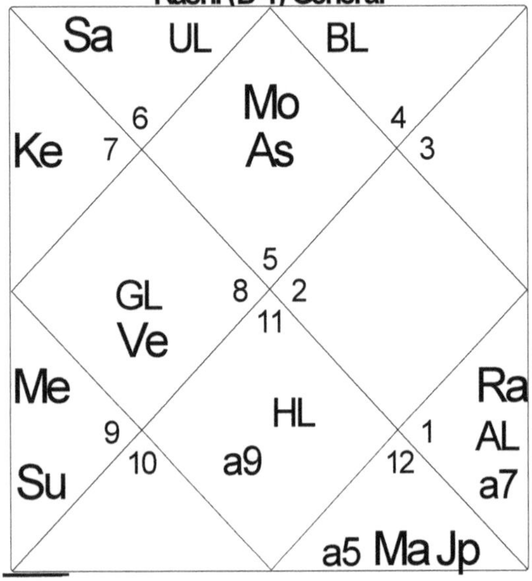

Rashi (D-1) General

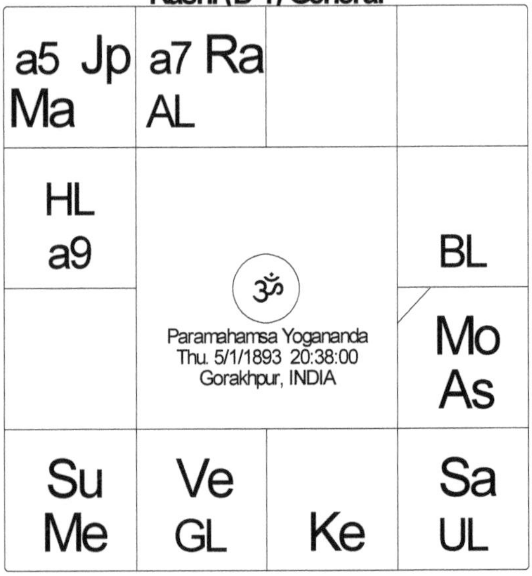

Nature of the dhī

The Lagna falls in the second pada of Maghā Nakṣatra, indicating a train of thought, which is focussed on sustenance i.e. to nurture and ensure fruitful outcomes.

Tool(s) of the dhī

The Lagna being Leo, occupied by the Moon, indicates a person who by nature acts out of goodness. The Moon receives Rāśi dṛṣṭi by Ketu and Rāhu, both malefics hence the native drives towards the establishment of truth in the world.

Dhīmanta yoga from Lagna

The Lagna lord Sun is in the fifth house in Sagittarius, causing dhīmanta yoga. The conjunction between Sun and Mercury in the fifth forms Nipūṇa[4] Yoga, making the native an expert in matters relating to Sagittarius, i.e. dharma, guru, rituals of worship and temples. As Sun is Bhrātṛkāraka, the guru of Paramhamsa Yogānanda had a very important influence in these matters.

Dhīmanta yoga from ātmakāraka

The Ātmakāraka is in Scorpio, and its dispositor Mars is in the fifth from it with Jupiter, forming dhīmanta yoga! This causes the esteemed Guru-Mangala yoga, like in the case of Swami Vivekananda, ensuring a deep yearning to understand the universe.

Dhīmanta yoga from Ārūḍha Lagna

There is no dhīmanta yoga from the Ārūḍha Lagna, though Ārūḍha lagneśa Mars, shares Rāśi dṛṣṭi with the Sun who is the fifth lord from AL. This does not cause a desire to learn and hence there is no dhīmanta yoga from Ārūḍha Lagna. The name of Paramhamsa Yogānanda is therefore not much associated as a searcher for knowledge, but more as a deep mystic crossing the borders of religions due to the position of Rāhu in Ārūḍha Lagna. Notably the fifth lord is Jupiter and is in Kendras to Mercury the Kāraka for students. Yogānanda had a large following and still has many students spread throughout the world.

Paramhamsa Yogānanda was a student of Śrī Yukteśwar, and traveled a lot in the United States, as well as Europe, spreading the knowledge of the Vedas and yoga, and helped found the 'Self Realization Fellowship' foundation.

4 Nipūṇa means 'clever, skillful or expert'; hence, the Nipūṇa Yoga will make the native an expert in a field of study.

Spiritual Practices

Chart 112: Swami Chidananda Saraswati

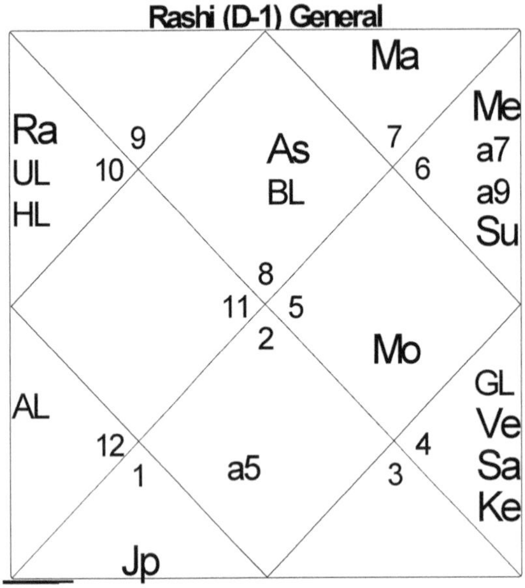

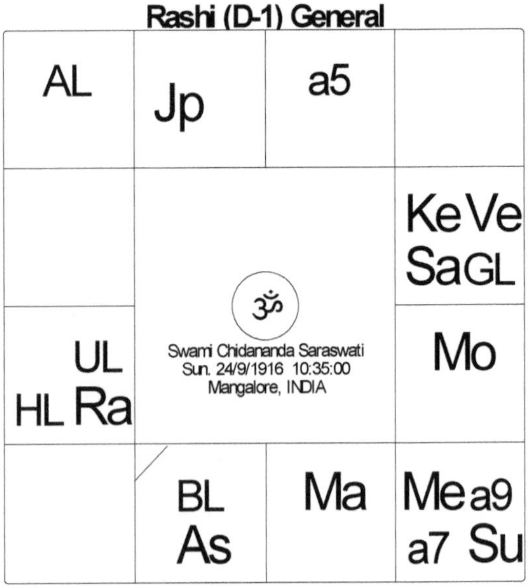

Chart of Swami Chidananda Saraswati, born Sridhara Rao, 24th September 1916, 10:35 AM, Mangalore, India.

He is born during the Kālahorā of Saturn whose placement in the ninth house in Tapasvī yoga caused the family astrologer to immediately pronounce that this was the birth of an enlightened saint! With a life solely focussed on penance this was surely to take a spiritual direction. Further this combination involves 12th from Moon, 7th lord from Lagna and 7th lord from Venus showing a person who will not have any relationships and pursue a life of completely celibacy. However, whenever malefic occupy the 6th and 12th from Moon it bodes difficult for the health of the mother. More so as fourth lord from Moon is Mars placed in the twelfth house. The fourth lord Saturn being joined Ketu shows Shraddha Doṣa coming to mother yet Moon who disposits the fourth lord will protect for at least ten years. So also at the age of ten his mother passed away.

The Tapasvī Yoga exists in the fifth from the Ārūḍha Lagna showing complete dedication to this path. Mercury is the Ātmakāraka and its strength in exaltation and Vargottama shows the presence of a deep understanding of the soul. Being eighth lord this entire knowledge is given to him to overcome the debts of many past lives.

The Karaṇa lord is Jupiter placed in the sixth house. Few placements of benefics in Dusthāna are appreciated, namely Jupiter in sixth where the native overcomes all sins; Mercury in eighth makes one debt free; Venus in twelfth ensures comforts and good marriage. Herein Jupiter in the sixth house shows that his work will be to overcome all weaknesses and as fifth lord his personal mantra will be exactly that. Fifth lord in the sixth house is generally considered inauspicious as it breaks the mantra, but Jupiter in this placement will not be able to do so and it thus protects the mantra and the prayer. Jupiter is alone and suggests that he will like to worship the Guru or Śiva. His mantra was: om namo bhagavate śivānandāya|.

With Jupiters mutual aspect with Lagneśa Mars it forms Rājayoga for many qualified students and disciples, and the focus is meditation as Mars is in the twelfth house. The strength of Mars becomes even more evident as it succeeds a Graha Malika Yoga beginning in the ninth house of religion.

Mars' age would become pivotal for the beginning of his spiritual pursuit and in his 27th year he asked for the permission of his family to renounce and live a monastic life. The Vimśottari Daśā of Sun brought this as Sun lords the twelfth from the Sun. It was Moon Antaradaśā as Moon lords the twelfth from himself, and finally Venus Pratyantaradaśā as Venus lords the twelfth from Lagna, all three ensuring the path towards spirituality and renunciation.

The birth home is seen from the Lagna and the tenth from it can cause one to leave. Herein the lord of the tenth is Sun and is joined Mercury and aspected by Saturn and Rāhu by Graha Dṛṣṭi indicating one among the Tithi lorded by these grahas as the day of the event. Rāhu lords Amāvāsya and rightly so he left his home on 6th March 1943 during Amāvāsya.

Two months later on the 19th of May he found his Guru Swami Śivānanda Sarasvati in Ṛṣikeśa on the full Moon of Buddha Pūrnima. The Sun was placed in Taurus, in trines to the Mṛtyupada, an important position for renunciation. The Antaradaśā had shifted to Mars who lords the ninth house from Moon thus bringing the Guru. The Pratyantaradaśā was Saturn who is placed in the ninth house from Lagna confirming the event of meeting the Guru.

Śivānanda had mentioned to one of his students that the young Rao would become his successor of his ashram. The ashram was the Divine Life Society established by Śivānanda in 1936.

The organisation and its symbols are seen from the tenth house in the chart. Chidananda has the tenth house as Leo suggesting the symbol of a rising body or the Sun or bird. Moon is there suggesting some water or wave in the symbol whilst Jupiter's aspects brings a flower or lotus into the picture. The symbol of the Divine Life Society is an eleven-petaled lotus wherein which the symbol of OM is depicted as rising above a river or sea-body.

Chidananda quickly became popular showing his abilities as a writer and spokesperson. The Dhīmanta Yoga caused by Lagneśa and fifth lord's mutual dṛṣṭi goes far to ensure great intellectual potential. When the Yoga-Vedanta Forrest Academy was in 1948 he was appointed as Vice-Chancellor and professor of Rājayoga by Śivānanda. Moon Mahādaśā had just begun whose lordship of the 11th from Sun gives title and acclaim. Being joined the Varṇadā Lagna and lording the Ghaṭika Lagna it gives work and responsibility in its own Antaradaśā. During the same Antaradaśā Śivānanda nominated him as General Secretary of the Divine Life Society, thus paving the way for his eventual succession to be Śivānanda's successor.

His first year in the Academy further brought about his magnum opus, namely his work Light Fountain. Mars Antaradaśā succeeds that of Moon and is joined the Ārūḍha of the third house granting the manifestation of his written work. Being further in the 3rd from the Moon further justifies this, but a more profound event was to happen due to Mars' lordship of the ninth house from Moon. During Guru Pūrṇima on 10th July 1949 he received his Sanyasa Dikṣa for complete renunciation by Śivānanda. The Daśā was Moon-Mars-Saturn. Saturn's lordship of the third house whilst placed in the ninth brought the exact Pratyantaradaśā of the event. It was at this event that his name was changed to Chidananda.

Chidananda served as General Secretary throughout Moon Mahādaśā and well into Mars Mahādaśā. However, Mars' lordship of the 3rd and 8th from the Sun would bring about an unfortunate event and require many changes, yet being the Lagneśa would give new and positive beginnings to himself. Rāhu is the seventh lord from Moon and placed in the sixth house showing travelling and service. In November 1959 Chidananda was sent to the USA on an extensive tour for which he only returned in 1962 during Mercury Antaradaśā.

Venus is the 3rd lord from the Moon and can bring difficult events related to the Guru. Venus is further joined the third lord from Lagna, Saturn. During Mars Daśā, Venus Antaradaśā and Venus Pratyantaradaśā Swami Śivānanda left his mortal coils. Venus is also the tenth lord from the Moon and so also in the following Pratyantaradaśā of the tenth lord Sun Chidananda was elected president of the Divine Life Society.

The Ārūḍha of the fifth house shows the knowledge that one shares with ones students, and is placed in Taurus. The lord Venus is placed in the Tapasvī Yoga showing that this will be the main teaching. Being in the ninth house this knowledge will reach the entire world and many people will benefit from this knowledge. With Rāhu placed in the fifth house from Sun the Rāhu Mahādaśā will bring this teaching to the many foreign students all over the world. So also in Rāhu Mahādaśā, Jupiter Antaradaśā (5th lord from Moon) he began his world tour for three years managing to teach in many counties all over the world.

Chidananda travelled and taught tirelessly since then and managed to write and publish thirty-four books in his life time.

He left his mortal coils in 28th August 2008 at the age of 91. The Mahādaśā was Saturn who is joined Marakeśā Venus. The Antaradaśā was Venus itself as the Pratyantaradaśā was Saturn. Mars was the Sukṣmāntaradaśā who is placed in the second house from Ātmakāraka. Notably Saturn is also his Iṣṭadevatā, being placed in the twelfth house from Ātmakāraka in the Navāṁśa chart.

Chart 113: Aleister Crowley

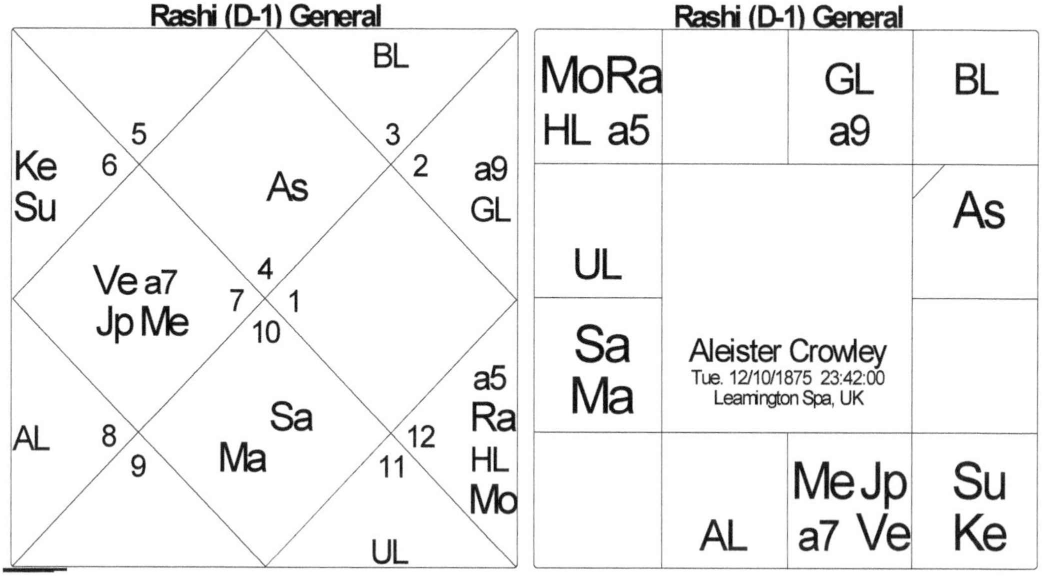

Aleister Crowley, born Edward Alexander Crowley, 12th October 1875, 11:41 PM, Leamington Spa, UK.

Most planets occupy the movable signs showing travel and plenty of foreign exposure. With three benefics in Libra this forms a smaller Māla yoga showing the opportunity for blessings and growth through his travels. With ninth and twelfth lords involved this will surely bring about spiritual growth and the focus is religion. Jupiter is the dispositor of the Moon forming a type of Mahānta Yoga for great contributions towards society. As birth occurs during the Kālahorā of Mercury this is the entire focus of his life, and his work as well due to the Karaṇa lord also being Mercury!

The fourth house will surely rise in childhood and so also his first spiritual influence was from his father, a retired engineer wealthy from shares in a brewery, whom was a preacher for the conservative Christian group Plymouth Brethren. His father would read him and his mother a chapter from the Bible every morning after breakfast and took the Christian ideals very seriously. However, ninth lord in the fourth house is not auspicious for father, especially as it is placed in Naidhanāṁśa due to being in Aquarius Navāṁśa. Venus is the dispositor of Jupiter and will indicate the health of the father. Venus is combust by the Sun suggesting difficult health. As Venus lords the ninth house from Sun, this combustion of Venus implies separation from father due to fathers health. This entire combination occurs in the twelfth from ārūḍha lagna suggesting premature demise of father.

In his childhood the Mahādaśā of Jupiter, Saturn and Mercury occur. Of these the most difficult for father is Saturn being joined the third lord from Sun. The third lord from Moon is Venus joined Jupiter and Mercury which can cause the unfortunate event. During Saturn Daśā, Venus Antaradaśā at the age of eleven Crowley's father died from tongue cancer on 5th March 1887. Crowley inherited his father's fortune making him wealthy.

Venus is in the fourth house and he was subsequently sent to a Plymouth Brethren School, in tune with the family's biblical roots. However, Mercury in Maraṇa Kāraka Sthāna in the fourth house is not going to make school a happy experience, regardless of the two great blessings of Jupiter and Venus. So also Crowley was expelled from one school and left the two subsequent. In 1890 during Moon's Antaradaśā he also began an interest for mountain climbing and climbed his first major mount in Scotland. Moon is the fifth lord from Moon as Saturn is the fifth lord from Sun, and their junction with malefics brings dangerous quests to test their skill.

Besides a dislike for education, Mercury in the fourth also suffers from the flaw of lacking discrimination in sexual matters due to ruining the natural sign of copulation, Gemini. In 1892 Crowley begins at Malvern College. This is during Mars Antaradaśā which is joined 8th lord Saturn in the 7th house showing sexual experiences but being devoid of female counterparts. So he had a homosexual experience. He left this college and began embarking on the same with the opposite sex during Rāhu Antaradaśā which began in July 1892, during which he threw away the puritan beliefs of his parents and interacted with both lady colleagues and prostitutes alike. Rāhu is the 8th lord and he contracted gonorrhoea in the process.

When Jupiter Antaradaśā began he joined Eastborne college. Jupiter in fourth is also the dispositor of the Moon promoting excellent academical achievements. During this time he excelled in the chess club of Eastborne and won titles for the club. However, as the Darapada (A7) is placed in the twelfth from the Lagnapada (AL) the dynamics of the team didn't last and they split during the same Antaradaśā.

He began a three year course at Trinity College in 1895, during the same Antaradaśā, showing excellent results in the first and second classes. As Jupiter disposits the Lagneśa Moon a change in identity was to arise and he changed his name to Aleister during this time. During his studies continued a vigorous sexual life and further partook in a homosexual relationship with the president of the drama club as is evident from Jupiter's conjunction with the Darapada (A7). Jupiter is the ninth lord and Crowley decided that his life was meant for religion and broke with his partner on account of the formers lack of esoteric interests.

Mercury Mahādaśā was looming and in 1897 when it began he left his studies all together without taking any degree! Mercury brought the results of its Māraṇa Kāraka Sthāna and brought complete disinterest in his education. He had maintained his mountaineering activities throughout the previous Daśā, climbing mountains all over Europe. His writing began to take hold of his life and throughout his life from this point he would commit great length of time to his writing and poetry.

Mercury is the Bhrātṛkāraka and brings the Guru or spiritual advisor. Being the ninth lord from the Sun in Rāśi and Ātmakāraka in Navāṁśa it will surely bring the spiritual master. In Mercury Daśā, Mercury Antaradaśā he joined the Hermetic order of the Golden Dawn during the Pratyantaradaśā of Sun.

Mercury is the third lord placed in the fourth house with fourth lord suggesting practice of prayers for the purpose of fighting. As Mercury is in Māraṇa Sthāna this will be for the sake of protection from death or causing the same to others. The fifth lord shows the mood of one's prayer and being in Māraṇa Kāraka Sthana in the seventh house with Saturn forming Yama Yoga, this person is not afraid to use black magic against his enemies. With Mercury in the fourth house the battle will be over property.

Shortly after being initiated, Crowley purchased a new luxury apartment and prepared two rooms, one for white magic and one for black magic. He had one of the clergy members, Allan Bennett, initiate him and teach him the practices of ritual magic as well as the use of psychotropic substances in the same. A year later Bennett travelled to Ceylon (Śrī Lanka) to learn Buddhism, and Crowley found himself searching for more guidance. He acquired a new property in Scotland and began learning from Samuel Liddell MacGregor Mathers, the then ousted leader of the Golden Dawn. Together they formed a pact to repel the rebellion which had ousted Mathers, and reclaim a London temple space, known as the Vault of Rosenkreutz, which had been lost in the struggle. Crowley claimed that then member and author, W.B. Yeats had attempted black magic on him, which Crowley had repelled but had caused his then mistress, Althea Gyles, to leave him.

In the summer of 1900 he left for Mexico. He had begun Ketu Antaradaśā placed in seventh from the Moon, opening the doors to travel. Ketu lords the ninth from Moon and in Mexico he earned a distinction in Freemasonry. During this time he derived the word *Abrahadabra* a derivation of the ancient Aramaic healing-incantation *Abracadabra*. He was encouraged to further control his mind using the Indian practice of Rājayoga. He met Bennett in Hawaii during this time, learned the practice of *Dharaṇa* and the mantra *aum mane padme huṁ*. Upon leaving Mexico City Crowley left for Ceylon to learn more. Together with Bennett they learned Hatha Yoga and embraced Buddhism. Bennett would later travel to Burma to become a Buddhist monk and found World Buddhist Society.

With the advent of 1902 Crowley arrives in Calcutta, India. This is during Venus

Antaradaśā, Moon Pratyantaradaśā. Moon is joined Māraṇa Kāraka Sthāna Rāhu, who is also eighth lord. He falls ill and spends the next three months between being ill with fever and shooting birds and sport in his voyage through India.

During Venus Antaradaśā, Mars Pratyantaradaśā he is almost mugged in Oakley. He defends himself by shooting one mugger as the second gets away. Later that day he lectures for four hours on Buddhism. He met up with Oscar Eckstein where they proceeded to climb the K2 mountain in the Himalayas in Rāhu Pratyantaradaśā. The climb had been unsuccessfully attempted by Europeans before them, and yet also failed by themselves. Venus lords the third from the Moon and is placed in the eighth from it showing a time of disease and danger to health. Rāhu being in Māraṇa Kāraka Sthāna also does not bode well for climbing in cold places. During this expedition Crowley suffered influenza, malaria and snow blindness, but recovered.

The eighth lordship of Venus suggests spiritual or occult exercises as well. Saturn and Rāhu are the eighth lords from Lagna, and in Saturn's Pratyantaradaśā he travelled back to London (Saturn lords the seventh house as well) and began the Abramelin operation. Crowley describes the exercise as follows:

> *The aspirant must have a house secure from observation and interference. In this house there must be an oratory with a window to the East, and a door to the North opening upon a terrace, at the end of which must be a lodge. He must have a Robe, Crown, Wand, Altar, Incense, Anointing Oil, and a Silver Lamen. The terrace and lodge must be strewn with fine sand. He withdraws himself gradually from human intercourse to devote himself more and more to prayer for the space of four months. He must then occupy two months in almost continuous prayer, speaking as little as possible to anybody. At the end of this period he invokes a being described as the Holy Guardian Angel, who appears to him (or to a child employed by him), and who will write in dew upon the Lamen, which is placed upon the Altar. The Oratory is filled with Divine Perfume not of the aspirant's kindling.*
>
> *After a period of communion with the Angel, he summons the Four Great Princes of the Daemonic World, and forces them to swear obedience.*
>
> *On the following day he calls forward and subdues the Eight Sub-Princes; and the day after that, the many Spirits serving these. These inferior Daemons, of whom four act as familiar spirits, then operate a collection of talismans for various purposes. Such is a brief account of the Operation described in the book.*

It is evident that the Holy Guardian Angel bears some resemblance to the Vedic concept of Iṣṭa Devatā. Crowley is said to have believed in the Greek Mythological term *Daemon* as spirits, souls or supernatural beings which are benevolent and can bless. As astrologers we need to be able to judge whether ones actions or even worship can lead to further bad karma, and in this regard we need to be able to judge whether a person is practicing black magic in their worship. This is analysed from the Navāṁśa (D-9) wherein the person's relationship with God is seen, as well as the Viṁśāṁśa (D-20) where the persons relationship with their Guru and spirituality is seen.

Chart 114: Aleister Crowley - Navāṁśa (D-9)

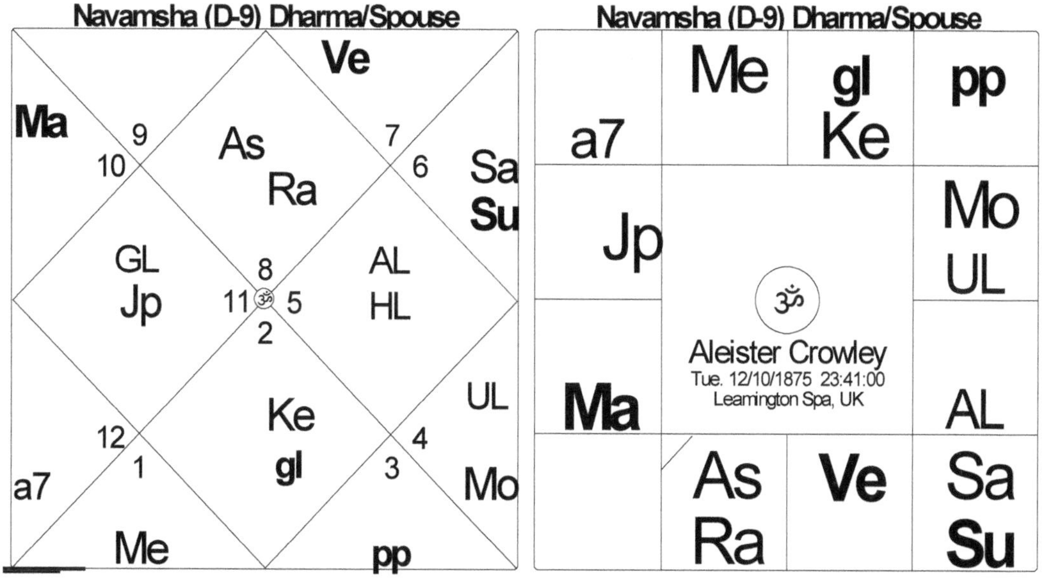

Notably, his Iṣṭa Devatā is seen from Leo, being the twelfth house from the Ātmakāraka Saturn in Navāṁśa, and the lord Sun is joined Saturn thus bringing the Iṣṭa to Saturn. *If such an Iṣṭa Devatā graha is associated with malefics, especially Saturn, is not aspected by Jupiter, nor placed in* 12th *or* 9th *from Kārakāṁśa, nor placed in the signs of Jupiter, nor placed in* 2nd, 5th, *or* 11th *from Kārakāṁśa, thus having no influence of Jupiter at all, then the native may tend towards black magic.* This is the case in the Navāṁśa chart of Crowley where Sun is joined the first house from Kārakāṁśa and has no influence of Jupiter's signs or Jupiter itself. Further with four malefics placed in the trines to Kārakāṁśa Virgo, he is a very powerful practitioner of prayers and can call spirits from the dead (earthy signs)! It is most unusual to find herein that the Ātmakāraka Saturn is not associated with any benefics at all.

However, Crowley being tormented by nightmares (malefic in ninth house) caused him to cease the exercise and he began practicing his knowledge from India. He began practicing the Buddhist practice of *Mahāsatipatthana* during the Sūkṣmāntaradaśā of Mars. This is a meditation practice rooted in the practice of Pratyahara and involves overcoming the minds bodily obstructions in yogic practices. Mars is joined the Ātmakāraka showing focus on body during this period. When Rāhu's Sūkṣmāntaradaśā began he started reciting the mantra *om tat sat om,* and performing daily yogic exercises. Rāhu is placed in the third from Ātmakāraka showing practice of a personal advise or Upadeśa.

Venus Antaradaśā could not help but bring relationships into his life, and being joined the seventh lord from Moon would present an opportunity for marriage. The Upapada (UL) is in the twelfth house from the Lagna lord showing rejecting or indifference towards the spouse. Lord Rāhu is joined the Moon suggesting that the relationship would grow stronger with time, and with Venus in trines to the Upapada this will become a strong love. Seventh lord Saturn's Pratyantaradaśā continues in early August and on 12th August 1903 he marries Rose Edith Kelly. The marriage is one of convenience, but Crowley found himself falling in-love with Rose and successfully winning her affections.

The couple travelled to Egypt in 1904 in Ketu Pratyantaradaśā. Ketu is the fifth lord in the third house and Rose was now pregnant. Third house is the fourth from the twelfth house showing foreign residence and so also the couple began occupying an apartment in Egypt together in Sun Antaradaśā, Sun Pratyantaradaśā. Sun is the Iṣṭa Devatā in the chart and being joined the fifth lord Ketu will bring him to worship his Iṣṭa.

Crowley began another invocation which led to his wife entering a trance and began speaking in the words of a spirit. This continued for a few days as he tried invoking the God Horus with great success. The Iṣṭa Devatā is indicated by the Sun in his chart, and can indicate images of the divine associated with the Sun or birds. Horus is depicted with a human body and birds head.

Horus, by Jeff Dahl

This culminated in him hearing a disembodied voice, said to be a messenger from Horus, who spoke to him what would later be the *Book of Law*. The event happened from 8th to 10th April 1904, during Mercury Daśā, Sun Antaradaśā, Moon Pratyantaradaśā and Mercury Sūkṣmāntaradaśā. Notably all the mentioned grahas are associated with the ninth house from Sun, Moon, Lagna and Ātmakāraka respectively.

This event would later be the cornerstone of his future, but as the voice asked him to steal an artefact from the museum of Cairo and fortifying his own island, Crowley felt somewhat confused with the entire ordeal. He later sent copies of the transcript to his colleagues and put the book aside in relief.

The couple arrived back in Scotland to see their daughter born in Jupiter Pratyantaradaśā on 28th July 1904.

The ninth house indicates the first child in the Saptāṁśa and the lord Jupiter is placed in Capricorn with Saturn suggesting a daughter. The Mahādaśā of Mercury gives argala to the lagna, the Antaradaśā of Sun is in trines to the ninth lord Jupiter, as the Pratyantaradaśā of Jupiter is Jupiter itself. The placement of Saturn with Jupiter does not bode well for the child's health during childhood (1st house) and special care would have to be taken in this. Being the first child the Sun is the significator of the child, but its placement in the sixth house is very inauspicious for the child's health. The Māraka Sthāna from the ninth lord are occupied by Mercury and debilitated Mars, as the lords are Saturn and Moon. During Mercury Daśā, Moon Antaradaśā the child fell sick with typhoid in Burma. Prior to this time Crowley had spent up to five months trying to revive his invocations from Egypt with awkward yet good success with fellow occultist Elaine Simpson. Finishing the same he arrives in June 1906 only to learn that his daughter has died from typhoid in Rangoon,

Burma. The Pratyantaradaśā of the event was the Sun who is joined Moon in the Saptāṁśa. Crowley fell in depression after this, as Rose now began to suffer from alcoholism. The same year his second daughter was born, Lola Zaza. The second child is seen from Aquarius in the Saptāṁśa and its lord Saturn being joined a debilitated Jupiter shows the daughter. Mars Antaradaśā is running which aspects Saturn showing the birth of the child.

Chart 115: Aleister Crowley - Saptaṁśa (D-7)

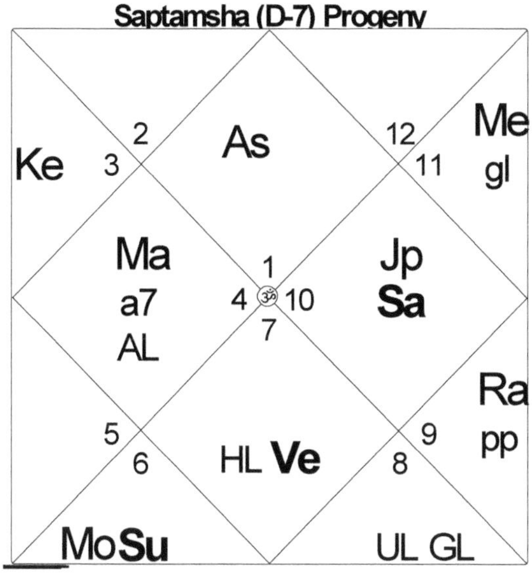

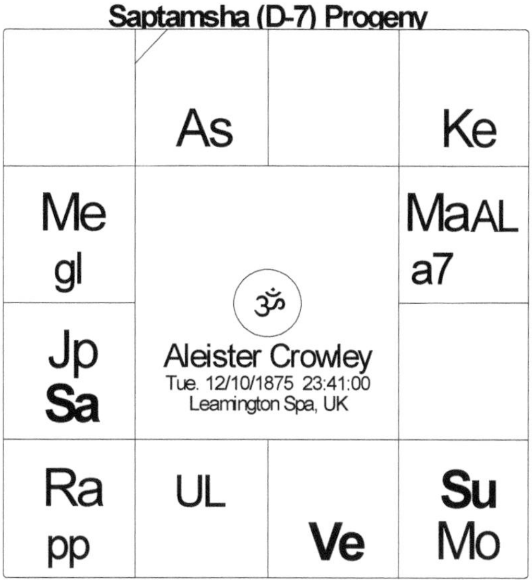

The fifth lord in Rāśi is Mars placed in Vargottama position. This suggests that his luck allows him to have but one daughter and more children following this would signify a change of luck in his life. So also Rose drew more and more into alcoholism as Crowley began having affairs. Rāhu is placed in the second from the Upapada in Māraṇa Kāraka Sthāna showing difficulty sustaining the marriage and addictions being the reason. Rāhu is lording over the twelfth house from Moon and so also marriage troubles became more evident in Mercury Daśā, Rāhu Antaradaśā.

Rāhu lords the fourth house from Ārūḍha Lagna thus signifying the organisation he belongs to, and during this same period he established the successor to the Golden Dawn, namely the Silver Star (Argenteum Astrum). At the end of 1907, during Jupiter Pratyantaradaśā, he and fellow occultist George Cecil Jones began to practice and refine the spiritual rite that Crowley had carried out in Egypt, attempting to unite to his Holy Guardian Angel. He succeeded and through his conversations with Aiwass proceeded to write two follow up books to the initial *Book of Law*. These form what is later called as the *Holy Books of Thelema*.

Rose suffers continuously and Crowley is astounded to find enormous orders of liquor bottles every month. 1908 was spent between Roses' recovery from her addiction and the affairs that Crowley comforted himself with. In July 1909 doctors stated that Rose required institutionalisation for her addiction and Crowley found it appropriate to divorce. Further, Rose had left the house on the complaint that he had beaten her. They agreed to file divorce on the grounds of his affairs to avoid any repercussions on her character. This was uncontested and Rose gained custody of their daughter. The daughter, Lola, would grow up with Roses' brother and wife as Rose fought her addiction. During this time Crowley had found a means to use hashish for his experiments, conceiving that it helped him reach the state of Samādhi. In 1910 he found the ability to do so without the use of the substance but through the ritual he had conceived.

Chart 116: Aleister Crowley - Viṁśāṁśa (D-20)

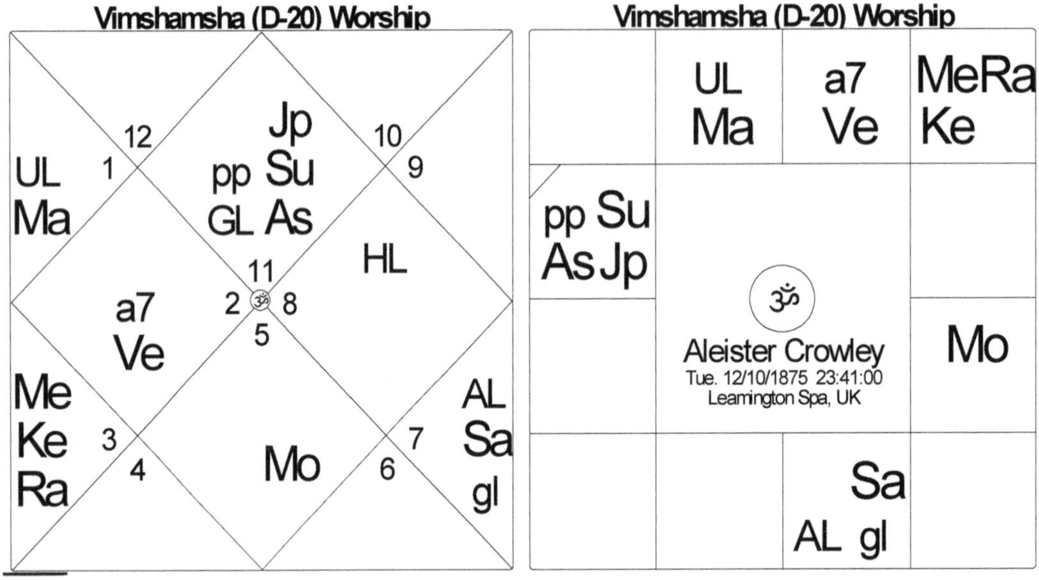

Samādhi and such spiritual practices are ascertained from the Viṁśāṁśa (D-20) chart. Herein the twelfth house causes one to participate in these activities. No planet is in the twelfth house as the lord Saturn is the Ātmakāraka placed in exaltation in the ninth house of Guru or guide. Crowley learned of this practice from Allan Bennett, his first mentor. The exaltation causes a lot of pride related to this topic and the planets, Mars, Rāhu and Jupiter have Graha Dṛṣṭi on it showing the time when he will participate in these activities.

He wrote that he had attained *Nirvikalpa Samādhi* in October 1906. This was during Mercury Daśa, Mars Antaradaśā and Saturn Pratyantaradaśā. The Mahādaśā needs to associate with the Lagna of the chart to justify spiritual activity during this time, and being joined the lord Rāhu justifies his vigorous approach to the subject. The Antaradaśā is Mars and aspects the twelfth lord Saturn justifying the Antaradaśā. The Pratyantaradaśā was of the twelfth lord Saturn itself. Whether or not it was actual Nirvikalpa Samādhi, it is evident that he experienced very deep stages of meditation during this event, however the opposition of Mars and Saturn does not bode well for the mental state during this and Saturn is also the lord of Lagna and the Saturn-Mars opposition causes mental aberration. On March 12th 1907 he tries again with the use of Mescal Buttons, in which the drug mescaline exists. The Daśā was Mercury-Mars-Venus. Venus is the lord of the sign where Saturn is placed to justify the Pratyantaradaśā.

Rāhu Antaradaśā begins and in Jupiter Pratyantaradaśā he with Jones succeeding in attaining Samādhi and uniting with his Holy Guardian Angel. Jupiter is in the sign of Saturn and being in Lagna will bring out the written works which will give him fame. In this process he receives Liber VII and later Liber Cordis Cincti Serpente both in the same Pratyantaradaśā and Sūkṣmāntaradaśā of Jupiter.

All the occurrences with Jones were drug-induced and therefore also in October of the following year he, in Paris, manages to do so without the drug. The Antaradaśā is still Rāhu but the Pratyantaradaśā is now Mercury.

Having founded his new order he travelled to the USA in November 1914. Saturn Antaradaśā is running and lords the twelfth house from Moon in the Rāśi (D-1) chart. During this time he takes the title of Magus (mage or magician) believing himself to have reached an elevated stage of spirituality. Notably, Saturn lords the Lagna in the Viṁśāṁśa (D-20) indicating names and titles. Ketu Mahādaśā is about to start and would bring an end to his the most prolific and important time of his life. Ketu joins the Sun showing a new beginning and being the lord of third from the Sun brings foreign settlement. He stayed in the USA for most of the period of Ketu Mahādaśā. He later claimed to be a spy (Ketu) employed for the British government, which the government confirmed later.

The third house also deals with sexuality, and so also he spent this entire Daśā experimenting with what he called *sex magick*, considering sexual interaction as a means to bring about powerful spiritual realisations. In 1918 he returns to Britain during Rāhu Antaradaśā. Rāhu despite being twelfth lord from the Moon suggesting foreign voyage, brings him home as it is joined the first house from the Moon.

He soon after travels to Italy, arriving in Palermo, Sicily on 1st of April 1920. The Daśā is of Ketu-Saturn. Saturn's 12th lordship from the Moon again brought him to a foreign country. Here he established The Abbey of Thelema, as a means to study the practices that he had undergone with his students. Saturn is the fourth lord from the Ārūḍha Lagna and can make one set up organisations or group-gatherings. He travelled with his then partner, Leah Hirsig and their two month old daughter. The daughter didn't survive beyond October of the same year. During his three year stay, he initiated students and some became his lovers. Venus Daśā began in 1922 which is combust by the Sun. Being the ninth lord from the Sun this indicates difficulties with authorities. Learning of the activities in the Abbey, especially the sexual orgies which took place, the then government of Mussolini expelled Crowley from Italy in 1923. This occurred during Venus Daśā, Venus Antaradaśā and Rāhu Pratyantaradaśā. Venus being the third lord from the Moon and combust does not bode well for living in foreign countries during its Antaradaśā. Rāhu's Pratyantaradaśā is in Māraṇa Kāraka Sthāna in the ninth house showing the problems from rulers.

Following his expulsion from Italy, Crowley was quite inactive. In 1930 he published The Legend of Aleister Crowley, in an attempt to dismiss the ill reputation he earned from the newspapers, following his expulsion from Italy. Rāhu Antaradaśā was at hand, and its placement in the fifth from Ārūḍha Lagna gives a bad reputation. The same placement gives wide suspicion about ones demise. In September of the same year he, whilst attending a funeral in Portugal, fakes his own suicide. For three weeks he remained behind the scenes, until appearing three weeks later in Berlin.

Jupiter is the lord of Rāhu's sign and in Jupiter Antaradaśā he sues Nina Hamnett for labelling him as a practitioner of black magic. Jupiter is placed in the eighth house from Moon which is not auspicious for finance causing Śakata Yoga. He loses the suit, declares bankruptcy and is reprimanded by the judge in the process:

I have been over forty years engaged in the administration of the law in one capacity or another. I thought that I knew of every conceivable form of wickedness. I thought that everything which was vicious and bad had been produced at one time or another before me. I have learnt in this case that we can always learn something more if we live long enough. I have never heard such dreadful, horrible, blasphemous and abominable stuff as that which has been produced by the man (Crowley) who describes himself to you as the greatest living poet.

—Mr. Justice Swift

Ten years later in 1944, Crowley produced *The Book of Thoth*. This occurred in Sun Daśā, Jupiter Antaradaśā. Unlike the previous Antaradaśā of Jupiter, Sun is a friend of Jupiter and brought fortune to him. He sold £ 1,500 worth of his book and then moved to a new house as Jupiter joins Mercury, the fourth lord from Moon.

He would move once more during Saturn Antaradaśā in 1945, as Saturn aspects Mercury, and being in third from the Ārūḍha Lagna, this would prove difficult for his health. Two years later on 1st December 1947 Crowley would leave his mortal coils. The Daśā of the Sun is a Māraka due to its second lordship and further, lording the twelfth from it makes it difficult for health. Venus Antaradaśā is the third and eighth lord from Moon which again is inauspicious for health, and its position in second from the Mahādaśā is again very problematic.

Saturn in the third from Ārūḍha Lagna causes demise due to disease and with Mars could give haemorrhages. Crowley had become addicted to heroin, due to having been administered morphine for his asthma and bronchitis many years earlier. Some say his doctor denying him of his prescription caused the demise, which confirms the doubts and suspicions of his demise, caused by Rāhu's placement. Remarkably, his doctor died within 24 hrs of his own, an event which occurs when either the eighth lord or twelfth lord is in Māraṇa Kāraka Sthāna as in this case.

Chart 117: Dark Worship II

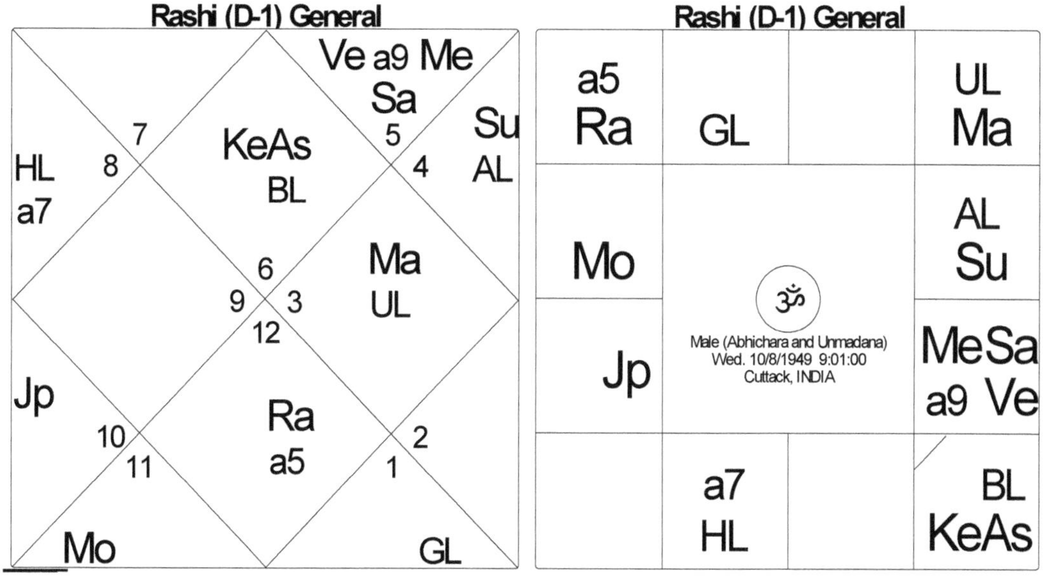

Male native born 10th August 1949, 9:01 AM, Cuttack, Orissa, India. The chart is

Birth is during Wednesday as Mercury is well placed in a fiery sign showing strength, health and good digestion. Being Lagna lord Mercury also strengthens the person and will look very handsome and strong. The person is tall and good looking and interesting in plays and acting. However, being in the twelfth house, it as Lagna lord will make the person cause their own undoing which can end up hurting their health and life. Venus is joined Mercury and will still give comforts in life and not afflict the body. Instead comfort in the form of home and affection from loved ones is indicated, despite some difficulty to health.

Mercury is placed in the third house in Navāṁśā showing struggles with health, and this is confirmed by the placement of Ātmakāraka Venus in the sixth house confirming chronic and long term health issues.

With Ketu on the Lagna aspected by Mars the persons decisions are influenced by Piśācha or evil spirits and Piśācha Bādhaka is formed. With no benefics in Kendra to Lagna to offset this yoga, the person them self may encourage such acts. Usually the person will exhibit very different behaviour after nightfall and be very physically weak during sunrise. Worship during the hours prior to sunrise or Brahma Muhūrta is advised to overcome these difficulties.

The Horā lord will reveal where the focus is. Horā lord is Jupiter placed in the fifth house of Mantra. However, Jupiter is Bādhakeśa and being placed in the house of Mantra indicates either forgetting the mantra or not being aware of the repercussions of one's mantra practice! Jupiter being a benefic is in debility and retrograde. Had this been in a Duṣthāna from Lagna this is a blessing from past life, but in a Kendra or Koṇa this is a very difficult curse. As this is the Bādhakeśa as well it im-

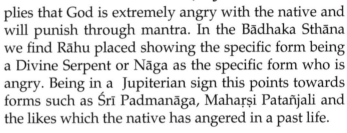

plies that God is extremely angry with the native and will punish through mantra. In the Bādhaka Sthāna we find Rāhu placed showing the specific form being a Divine Serpent or Nāga as the specific form who is angry. Being in a Jupiterian sign this points towards forms such as Śrī Padmanāga, Maharṣi Patañjali and the likes which the native has angered in a past life.

The exact effect of such an angry Bādhakeśa is seen from its Navāṁśa position. Jupiter is placed in Capricorn Navāṁśa showing troubles from spirits, mental aberration, invisible bodies and the likes. Still by Jupiter being Vargottama it will give the blessings of children, despite the bad mantra.

To confirm mental problems the 25th Nakṣatra (Rath, Brhat Nakshatra, 2008) from the Lagna must be occupied by a malefic or afflicted, and more so a fiery malefic such as Ketu, Sun or Mars. In this case the Lagna Nakṣatra is Hastā and the 25th Nakṣatra (including Abhijit) is Aśleṣā. Aśleṣā is occupied by the Sun which can cause serious mental difficulties.

To curtail these issues Abhiśeka of the Śiva liñga is advised or preferably Rudrābhiśeka performed in a temple regularly.

The health problems are brought about by Venus and as Venus lords the second house the second Daśā of Jupiter brought him to practice certain types of dark worship. During Jupiter Daśā, Venus Antaradaśā he dabbled in black magic. Jupiter and Venus are rarely a good combination for a Daśā and being in $6^{th}/8^{th}$ from each other is also very difficult. From the Sun, Jupiter lords the ninth house of spiritual rites, the sixth house of disease, and is placed in the Māraka from the same. From the Moon, the Antaradaśā of Venus is placed in the Māraka house, and lords the ninth house of spiritual rites. When the following Antaradaśā of Sun came his health problems arose. Sun is lords the Māraka house from the Moon and is placed in the sixth house from the Moon showing disease or enmity. Sun is also the lord of the eighth house in the Dṛkāṇa which is very inauspicious for health.

At one of his drama plays a fire broke out. Fires are caused by the fiery planets, or a very angry Jupiter, as is the case. Following the incident he lost his mental balance and developed Schizophrenia. No remedy has been able to reverse his condition due to the retrograde Jupiter blocking all remedies from working. Despite this he has married and blessed with children and a decent salaried job.

Chart 118: Sibly, Ebenezer

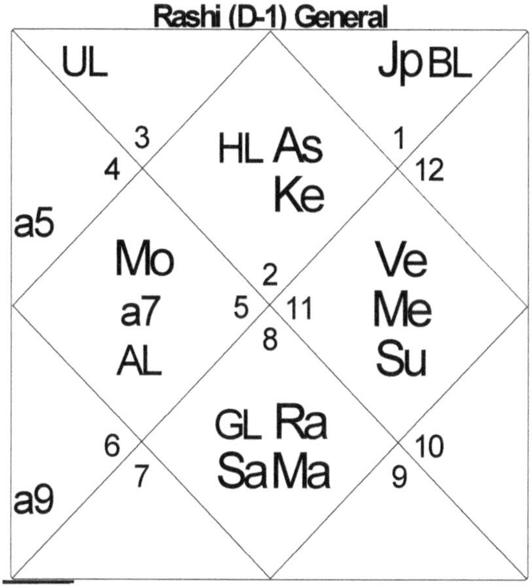

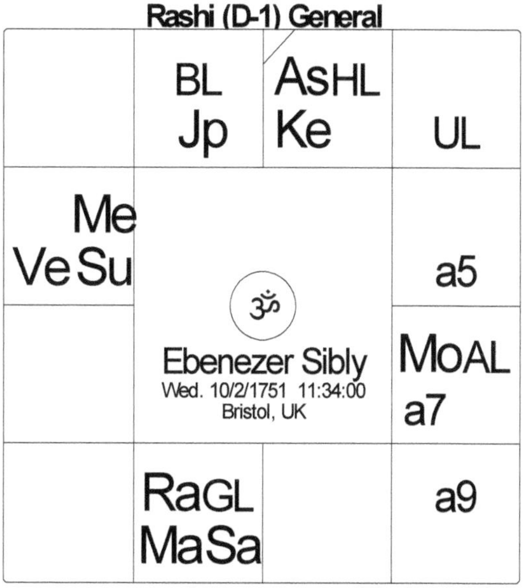

Ebenezer Sibly, born 10th February 1751, 11:23 AM, Bristol, UK. His birth date is recorded as 30th January 1751 using the Julian calendar, which corresponds to 10th February 1751 in the Gregorian calendar. Sibly publishes the time according to his own book as 11:23 AM, but the calculated chart he displays corresponds better to 11:34 AM which we have used.

His Nakṣatra is Magha and the fourth Nakṣatra is lorded over by the Moon. Moon is placed in Leo in Digbala showing a protected and good upbringing. Jupiter's aspects on Moon brought religion and spirituality in it showing his upbringing in a Calvanist Baptist Church.

Lagna lord is joined the Sun giving spiritual leanings, and Sun lording the Ārūḍha Lagna further justifies that he would either lead a profession of politics or that of a preacher/spiritualist.

The weekday is Wednesday lorded by Mercury and is placed in the tenth house in Aquarius giving great strength and energy. Its lordship of Virgo supports prosperity through knowledge (fifth house), mantra, students and children. The Horā lord is Mars placed in the seventh house forming Ruchaka Mahāpurūṣa yoga showing his focus on the topics of Jyotiṣa, Mantra, Tantra, Yantra and black magic as well.

Mars being the Ātmakāraka suggests that his birth purpose is to engage in these activities, however, unlike the case of Crowley, the Iṣṭa Devatā in the Navāṁśa is associated with the signs and houses of Jupiter showing that Sibly does not have a warped view of God and will not engage in black magic, but may instead write or inform others about it.

Ātmakāraka has to associate with the eleventh house from Lagna to give an interest in Jyotiṣa and so also Mars is placed in the Navāṁśa of Pisces which is the eleventh house in the Rāśi chart. Further, with Ketu placed in Digbala from Ārūḍha Lagna he may be an astrologer by profession. Moon is joined the Ārūḍha Lagna and he did receive an education as a doctor. Further the lord of Ārūḍha Lagna is the Sun joined Mercury showing books and written work, as Venus shows working with beauty and design.

Ārūḍha Lagna is placed in the fourth house and his career begins with establishing a home or office. Mercury aspects the third house and in the third Daśā of Sun Sibly opens a book shop with his younger brother Manoah. Both were very adept linguistically and Manoah also had a strong mystical bent of mind. Together they corrected the errors of Worsdale's translation of Tetrabiblos, an error-correction so profound that the work was later referred by many as the 'Sibly edition'. The third lord from the Ārūḍha Lagna is Venus who is joined Mercury indicating the younger brother's involvement in the book shop.

Sibly studied orthodox medicine and was highly interested in Mesmerism and Animal Magnetism, philosophies and practices very much alike that of the eastern traditions of Reiki, as is evident from the strong placement of Mars.

Mars aspects the third house as well, and during this third Daśā he took serious interest in these practices next to his medicine studies.

Ārūḍha Lagna is in the fourth house and so also in the fourth Daśā of Moon he joins the spiritual organisation of Freemasons in 1784 during Moon Mahādaśā, Mars Antaradaśā. Mars lords the ninth from Moon to bring the Guru, as well as the fourth from Moon to bring a new organisation or home. Being that Mars is the Ātmakāraka and lords over the ninth from Kārakāṁśa it brings the spiritual initiation and Guru. Prior to this he had already written extensively on the topic of Astrology. However, it was the influence of the Freemasons and his Grand Master which pushed him to publish his magnum opus: *A new and complete illustration of the celestial science of astrology* in 1784 in two volumes. This occurred in Rāhu Antaradaśā as Rāhu is the dispositor of Venus, the third lord from the Moon.

The contribution of his work in an initial four editions would become the source of his income for the remainder of his life, and became instrumental in reviving the astrological traditions during the 18th century. In 1787 he would finish the third volume and in 1788 the fourth volume was finished. Later the work was renamed to *A New and Complete illustration of the Occult Sciences* as the fourth volume included a serious examination of occult practices, including black magic, which he sought to distinguish the practice of astrology from.

It is evident from his writings that he considered Astrology, the science behind it and its spiritual aspects all an integral part of God. He saw Astrology as a means to understand God and the events that would unfold... a true Vedāñga Jyotiṣa. Spirituality in all its facets is viewed in the Viṁśāṁśa chart. As his written work is still highly regarded today Jupiter is expected to be placed in the first or seventh houses from the Lagna in this chart. He published this during Moon Daśā, Rāhu Antaradaśā as Rāhu aspects Jupiter.

Chart 119: Sibly, Ebenezer - Viṁśāṁśa (D-20)

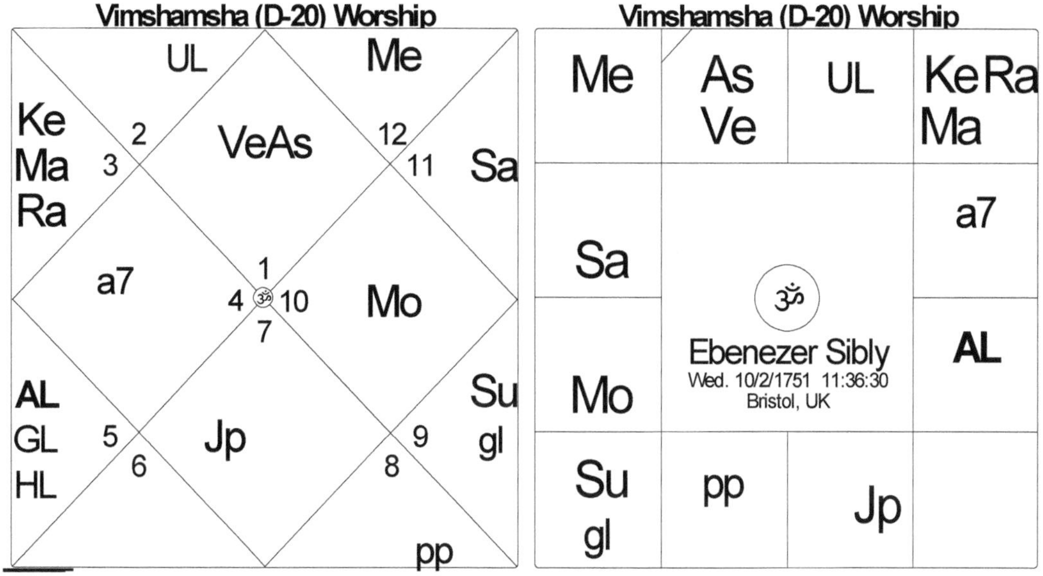

In the Viṁśāṁśa chart the given Lagna is Pisces. A minor change in the birth time places the Lagna in Aries with Jupiter in the seventh house which will justify his fame both then and until now, which is more acceptable. The Ātmakāraka is Mars and lagna lord showing strong spiritual interest and being in the third house of teacher or Guru, his Grand Master's advise would be instrumental towards securing his spiritual life. The placement of this in Gemini with Mars shows Jyotiṣa as the main blessing/advise from his Grand Master.

The Sun is the fifth lord in the Viṁśāṁśa and is placed alone in the ninth house. The ninth house is a trine to the first house showing a form of the Sun God or Savitor as the form of worship. The ninth is adjacent to the tenth house where the mother is worshipped and as a result the specific form can be that of the divine mother in the form of the Sun, i.e. Matāṅgī, Vaiṣṇavī or such forms.

With the fifth lord in the Rāśi placed in the tenth house with the Sun and Venus it is evident that the form is one again of i) a lady, ii) the Sun. The invocation (mañgalacharaṇam) of his work on Astrology includes a two page invocation to the Goddess Urania, the Greek Goddess who is able to foretell the future by the arrangement of the heavens. A small excerpt is here given:

Descend, Urania, with prolific flame, and spread the growing Trophies of thy Name; Disclose to Man a Knowledge of the Skies, whose spangling Beauties draw our wond'ring Eyes.

Instruct young Students in their Care to know, The starry Influence on all Things below; (Sibly, 1784)

Little is known of Sibly beyond his academic and career achievements. In 1791 he began an astrology magazine called *The Conjurer*. The same year the then parliament had tried to suppress Sibly's Astrological and Occult publications. To see the exterior circumstances in society we need to ascertain the Bhāya Rāśi of the Mahādaśā. This is ascertained by counting from the Lagna to the Mahādaśā sign and the same distance there from. Counting from the Lagna to the Moon we get the fourth house. Counting to the fourth from the fourth house we land in the seventh house from Lagna, i.e. Scorpio which becomes the Bhāya or exterior Rāśi. Three malefics are joined this sign showing opposition in life, but as the Mahādaśā sign itself is auspicious the difficulties are solely career-wise. The problem arises herein from the conjunction of Saturn and Rāhu forming Śraddha Doṣa or curse of the demised souls. The graha which can defeat this is Venus which is well placed in Kendra to the Lagna. So also in Moon Daśā, Venus Antaradaśā the Sibly brothers could continue to publish their works by repealing the parliament.

In 1792 during, at the end of Moon Daśā, he received his medical degree. Moon being joined the Ārūḍha Lagna shows his achievement of becoming a doctor and so also he began his work in Sun Antaradaśā which lords over the Moon's sign. His work on astrology is most comprehensive including a very detailed account on the methods of predicting weather, mundane events, personal horoscopy, horary charts, etc. He is most known for his predictions on the American Revolution and is credited for offering the chart of the establishment of the USA.

Prior to earning his medical degree, he had already published *Culpepers English physician: and complete herbal* in 1789 during Moon Daśā, Mercury Antaradaśā. Mercury joins the third lord from Moon justifying the timing. The following Antaradaśā of Ketu would lead to becoming a Fellow of the Harmonic Philosophical Society in Paris. Ketu lording over the fourth house from the Moon would again bring organisations into his life.

His books would continue to be revised and printed by the brothers and in 1794 he would publish *A key to physic and the occult sciences* during the Antaradaśā of Rāhu.

Because of the Ruchaka Mahāpurūṣa Yoga, a life expectancy of at most seventy years is indicated, or in other words a middle lifespan between 36-72 years of age. In this age the Mahādaśā of Moon, Mars, Rāhu and Jupiter occur. Among these Mars and Rāhu are most malefic by placement in the seventh house. Mars is also the third lord from the Sun and is therefore more malefic than Rāhu. The Antaradaśā during this must be placed in Māraka Sthāna from the Moon or associate with these whilst associated with a Dusthāna from the Moon. Mercury is the second lord from the Moon and is joined the Sun and Venus whilst sharing Graha Dṛṣṭi with the Moon. Among these Moon lords a Dusthāna from the Moon and is more malefic. He passed away during Mars Daśā, Moon Antaradaśā. The Pratyantaradaśā was either Saturn or Mercury who are both Māraka for the Lagna.

At present there is no clear record as to why he passed away at such a tender age. Sun, Venus, Mercury, Moon and Ketu all associate with the third from his Ārūḍha Lagna all attempting to contribute to his demise. Among these Ketu is most malefic suggesting some mistake or accident, but being in Taurus this could not be out of any wrong intention. Further being in the Lagna in Taurus can indicate being in the presence of a close lover or person at the time. The sign in the third from AL is the sixth house suggesting a disease was the root cause.

यन्मण्डलं विश्वसृजं प्रसीद्धमुत्पत्तिरक्शा प्रलय ग्रहल्भम्।
यस्मिञ्जगत्संहरतेऽखिलं च पुनातु मां तत्सवितुर्वरेण्यम्॥ ९॥

9

Second, Sixth & Tenth

The Artha trikoṇa

9.1 The Second House

The second house indicates the wealth of the native and hence is an important house indicating the native's sustenance in this world. A select few get enormous wealth, which is far higher than the required amount for their sustenance, whilst others barely earn enough to feed themselves. Fortunately, the wealthy may distribute their money to others through charity or creating jobs whilst the poor may earn through jobs or donations. In some cases, the poor become rich whilst the rich fall into debts and poverty. For these reasons, the analysis of wealth in the horoscope becomes pertinent.

9.1.1 Available Wealth

The second house is the most desired and least applicable house for large parts of society. It is the most desired as it gives wealth in various forms such as property, vehicles, jewellery or even books, all depending on what is considered valuable. It is however the least applicable because the second house also implies savings and most people do not save money but live of their income as indicated by the eleventh house and through this pay of loans or debts (eighth house) on those objects they consider as valuable (second house).

The second house sustains the Lagna, just as food sustains the body, while the twelfth house tends to obstruct the Lagna by causing necessary expenses. Whilst obstruction may seem to be inauspicious, the question is whether a good party causes the obstruction or a bad party i.e. is it caused by a malefic planet or a benefic planet. Benefics in twelfth house are auspicious and indicate wealth spent on good deeds. Benefics in the second and twelfth houses, will protect the native, and give a cushioned life. Malefics will do otherwise and can cause torture or even imprisonment if there is an equal amount of malefics in the second and twelfth houses. The placement of an equal amount of benefics in these houses will not cause imprisonment but may restrain or confine the native to auspicious surroundings, i.e. to write a book or engage in a similar activity. If malefics and benefics occupy the 2nd/12th houses, then scrutiny is required. The nature of the graha in the second house affects ones savings. If one has benefics in second one saves for expenses, whilst malefic cause one to do otherwise. Benefics in twelfth house cause one to spend ones money on the necessary expenses one has, whilst a malefic here will cause one to not pay ones debts or loans. The Lagna has the most important say herein as it can sway ones actions due to the nature of one's character. I.e. malefic in second and twelfth house causing a problematic financial attitude, can be swayed by one benefic in the Lagna which causes one to control ones finances. Malefics in Lagna will do otherwise.

As wealth does not solely imply money but also all resources available to one, these three houses will indicate whether the person is contributing towards the good of society or otherwise. E.g. If a person suffers from Kālasarpa or Sarpa Yoga then by implication the person is said to be a criminal. However, this is only assured if the second, first and twelfth houses show a person who wishes to further eat of society, or instead is fighting the evil yoga by giving good things to society. Conversely Kālāmṛta Yoga will make one a saint or one who gives nectar or amṛta to the world. This again has to be confirmed from the second, first and twelfth houses.

The first, second and eighth houses have a very important role to play in matters of wealth. The planets in the second house shows the way the native is sustained and attains wealth, while the eighth house shows the financial tension one may experience, through debts, loans, etc. Benefics in the second and/or eighth houses gives wealth from good sources, easily payable loans, etc., whereas malefics indicate a need to adopt cruel means to get wealth and serious pressure in taking loans. However, the focal point in this regard is the Lagna. If the Lagna or the grahas occupying it, are not friendly towards the second or eighth houses or its occupants, then the native will dislike the options put before them, and would rather not indulge in such activities. While such a situation causes poverty, the person may be rejecting wrong means of earning a living. This tripod of houses should be examined from Lagna for wealth whilst growing up, from Ārūḍha Lagna for wealth whilst pursuing a career, from Navāṁśa Lagna to see wrong thoughts in wealth matters and finally from the Kārakāṁśa to examine what the souls relationship to wealth is and whether the soul considers wealth an obstruction to its spiritual pursuits.

The eleventh house should be analyzed for wealth, however it will indicate the state of those who have come to give one wealth – i.e. if malefics are in the eleventh the wealth available comes from people who have suffered in some manner, while benefics in the eleventh indicate people who are happy and wish to donate wealth to the native. For moveable signs the eleventh house is also bādhaka sthāna, hence with the wealth acquired, many restrictions and/or burdens will follow, or the native might travel abroad for gaining wealth. The eleventh house acts like Hara, the destroyer, and hence the wealth acquired is merely bringing one closer to one's end, just as a ball of string cannot be pulled forever. The eleventh house then becomes a problem for movable Lagnas as the rajas guṇa[1] is very high in them.

1 Power/desire to create; in this case create new methods of gaining/earning in this world.

Whom or what the native acquires wealth from is seen from the eleventh from Ārūḍha Lagna. The mood of taking the wealth is also seen from here. Malefics there indicate lack of morals/thought before taking the money. Generally, the analysis of the third, sixth and eleventh from Ārūḍha Lagna, is vital in any horoscope.

9.1.2 Sources of Wealth

Whilst the second and eleventh houses indicate the available wealth, the sources of wealth and income are seen in the eleventh house from Ārūḍha Lagna. Any graha joining or having Rāśi dṛṣṭi on the sign or joining its lord will give wealth. However, the willingness of the graha or person to give wealth to the native must be seen from the financial Sambandha. A planet, which is not willing to give wealth will severely, decrease the person's finances during its Daśā period.

Table 70: Sambandha for Finances[2]

Planet	Exaltation/ Debilitation	Own Sign	Friends	Friendly Sign
Sun	Aries/ Libra	Leo	Jupiter	Sagittarius, Pisces
Moon	Taurus/ Scorpio	Cancer	Mercury and Jupiter	Virgo, Gemini Sagittarius, Pisces
Mars	Capricorn/ Cancer	Aries, Scorpio	Mercury and Venus	Virgo, Gemini Taurus, Libra
Mercury	Virgo/ Pisces	Gemini, Virgo	All planets excluding Sun	All signs except Leo
Jupiter	Cancer/ Capricorn	Sagittarius, Pisces	All planets excluding Mars	All signs except Aries and Scorpio
Venus	Pisces/ Virgo	Taurus, Libra	All planets excluding Sun and Moon	All signs except Leo and Cancer
Saturn	Libra/ Aries	Capricorn, Aquarius	Mercury Jupiter Venus	Taurus, Libra, Gemini, Virgo, Pisces, Sagittarius
Rāhu	Gemini/ Sagittarius	Aquarius	Venus, Saturn Jupiter, Mercury	Libra, Capricorn Virgo, Gemini, Pisces, Sagittarius
Ketu	Sagittarius	Scorpio	Sun, Moon	Leo, Cancer, Aries,

2 This table is from Jaimini Upadeśa Sutras by Sanjay Rath. This Sambandha is supposed to be hidden in the last four chapters of the eight chapter long Jaimini Upadeśa.

The amount of wealth will depend on the state of the planets in the sign, i.e. exalted and debilitated planets will give enormous amounts of wealth, followed by own sign and friendly sign. An inimical sign will give least or no wealth at all. These friendly and inimical signs must be ascertained from the Financial Sambandha table.

If the Sambandha is not friendly, the graha will give very little or no wealth. Otherwise, the graha will give its full auspiciousness, which depends on its position. The nature of the graha will indicate whom the wealth is coming from, i.e. Sun indicates father or a father figure, government, etc. When associating with such individuals specific character traits are required from the native to get the wealth i.e. if wealth is coming from the Moon, one has to be willing to soothe and please others in order to get the wealth.

Two specific principles emerge from the above principles.

- The Sambandha of the planet and the sign it is placed in will indicate how much wealth the planet can give.
- The Sambandha of the planet and the lord of eleventh house from Ārūḍha Lagna will indicate whether the planet wants to give the money to the native.

Just as there is a source of wealth, there is also a source of loss or expenses. This is seen from the twelfth from Ārūḍha Lagna by applying the same rules as above. Grahas friendly towards the twelfth lord from Ārūḍha Lagna will give many expenses, through their association with the same.

9.1.3 The Flow of Wealth

The mind of people takes many shapes depending on their focal point. When focusing on wealth, the Horā Lagna shows the state of the native's mind in matters of sustenance and wealth. Planets associating with the Horā Lagna indicate increasing wealth coming to the native. If the planets associating with the Horā Lagna are also associated with the Lagna, the wealth goes solely to the native, otherwise this wealth maybe distributed to others. The seventh from Lagna and Horā Lagna can also give wealth through partnerships/business.

As the Horā Lagna shows resources its nature is like Agni or fire. Therefore also fiery planets or strong planets in the second or tenth house from Horā Lagna can show a lot of wealth. The nature of the planets associated indicate the act through which the money came i.e. Saturn will give money through causing sorrow or need in others and Jupiter will give money after having blessed or helped another person.

9.1.4 Sustenance through Work

The work through which we get wealth is seen from the varṇadā Lagna. Varṇa[3]-dā[4] Lagna shows the type of work you do on a regular basis. The eleventh from the varṇadā Lagna shows the work, which gives an income each time that work is done,

3 Varṇa means occupation, though some have interpreted this as birth-caste.

4 Dā refers to the answer given by Brahmā when the Manuṣya, Rākṣasa and Deva's enquired what their purpose of life was. The Manuṣyas (humans) interpreted this as Dāna (to give, and avoid greed), the Rākṣasa as Dayā (to be merciful and avoid cruelty) whilst the Deva's understood it to be Damaya (self-control). These became the purpose of their creations.

and will ensure one's sustenance in this world. The varṇas can be understood from Chapter 2.

9.1.5 Case studies

Chart 120: Bill Gates

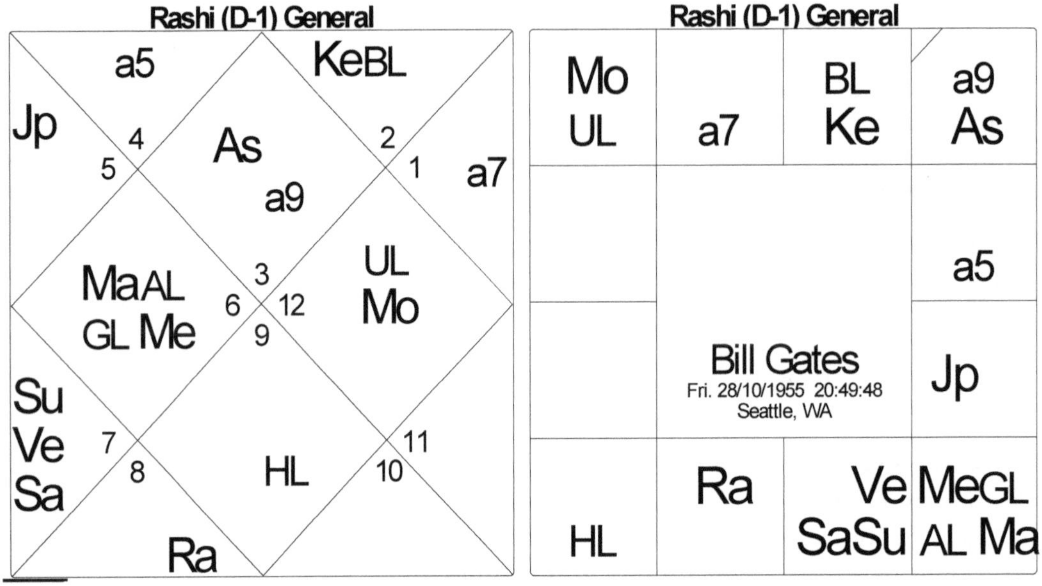

In the chart of Bill Gates, the Horā Lagna is in Sagittarius. The tenth from Sagittarius houses Mars and exalted Mercury which is very auspicious for wealth accumulation. Notably Mercury is also the Karaṇa lord and being in Virgo is excellent for wealth.

With Horā Lagna in Sagittarius whilst the Lagna itself is in Gemini the Varṇadā Lagna is in Pisces. The eleventh from Pisces is Capricorn, which is unoccupied. The lord of the same is exalted in Libra, joined Venus and a debilitated Sun. Here the nature of the planets and the sign will indicate the type of work done and the obstructions to the work. The exaltation of Saturn indicates serving and helping other people. This could be through the automation or simplicity of products and will be the main source of his earnings due to the exaltation of Saturn. The conjunction of Venus will indicate assistance oriented work in the service sector i.e. customer support or hotlines, with the view of troubleshooting. The conjunction of debilitated Sun indicates that the work will involve the networking of people, or uniting people under one common platform, as Sun is debilitated, he will suffer from this. Gates has been accused of monopolizing the IT-industry with his products by acquiring other companies or stealing the inventions of other software developers, the main accusers being Sun Microsystems and the United States Government. Having ascertained the nature of his work, we can now analyze where the money comes from.

The Ārūḍha Lagna is in Virgo, and the eleventh from it is Cancer, which is unoccupied. Ketu and Rāhu have Rāśi dṛṣṭi on Cancer, but among the two, only Ketu has a good relationship with the Moon (refer: Table 70) hence the wealth arising from

Rāhu will be little or none. Ketu indicates gains from foreign cultures and imports. Although Microsoft is an American company, it is dominated by the labor of Indian nationals. Moon itself being the lord indicates gains from the public sector, i.e. government offices, airports, supermarkets, etc. Moon receives the graha and Rāśi dṛṣṭi from an exalted Mercury and Mars indicating a large amount of his wealth will come from the IT and communications sector, whilst Mars indicates the security sector. Mercury's relationship with Moon is friendly promising the large amount of wealth, whilst Mars does not have a good relationship with Moon.

Horā Lagna is in the seventh house receiving the Rāśi dṛṣṭi of the previously mentioned Moon, Mercury and Mars. Moon indicates the act of reaching the public through commercials, whilst Mercury indicates contracts, business deals, writings, etc. Mars' association with Mercury has proved inauspicious, as many have criticized the aggressive tactics that Microsoft adopts to gain business deals in the industry.

The twelfth from Ārūḍha Lagna will indicate the sources of loss for Gates. Jupiter is there, aspected by Saturn, Venus and the lord Sun. Among these only Sun and Jupiter are friendly towards Leo, indicating major expenditure on charity (Jupiter) whilst Sun's debilitation is a major loss coming from the breaking of laws; notice that Sun is again involved in the loss for Gates.

Chart 121: Financial Vicissitudes

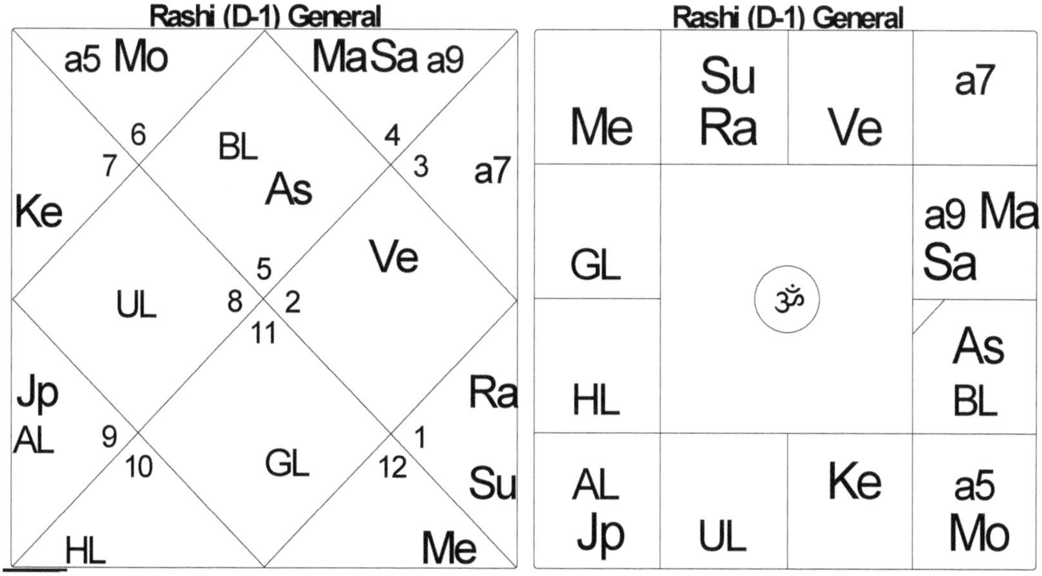

The native has Leo Lagna with Ārūḍha Lagna in the fifth house in Sagittarius. Saturn is lord of seventh house and is in the seventh from Horā Lagna; hence, we can expect Saturn to give wealth to the native although through the dethronements of others. The native travelled abroad (twelfth house) to take up a management position in the telecom company L.M. Ericsson (Israel, Spain and Finland) during the entire Saturn - Saturn Daśā period of 35 months. Saturn aspects the eleventh lord from Ārūḍha Lagna, Venus, and is very friendly to the same, ensuring a lot of wealth and gains from this work. Mercury Antaradaśā followed and both the position and gains came to an abrupt end, as Mercury is debilitated in both Rāśi and Navāṁśa, and placed in the fourth house from Ārūḍha Lagna causing the loss of power and position. Ghāṭikā Lagna is joined Mercury but Mercury is not associated with the Lagna, hence the power/position was given to someone else; eighth house indicates those who take over your work. As Mercury is Ātmakāraka it played a tough role in his life and this was a hard lesson.

Ketu's antara followed Mercury, in the eleventh from Ārūḍha Lagna. At this time, the native started his own consulting company (Ketu in Venus' sign will give consultations with private companies, as Ketu will give the results of Venus and vice-versa). However Ketu is not friendly towards Venus and Libra, hence the native earned very little if not nothing from this work. Venus antara will replace Ketu and is the lord of the eleventh from Ārūḍha Lagna, which promises a substantial amount of gains. However Venus is a strong benefic in the sixth from Ārūḍha Lagna and will cause physical separation from his spouse in the attempt to obtain an income for living. This happened in Saturn's Antaradaśā where the native was commuting between several countries for his job.

Chart 122: Dhirubhai Hirachand Ambani

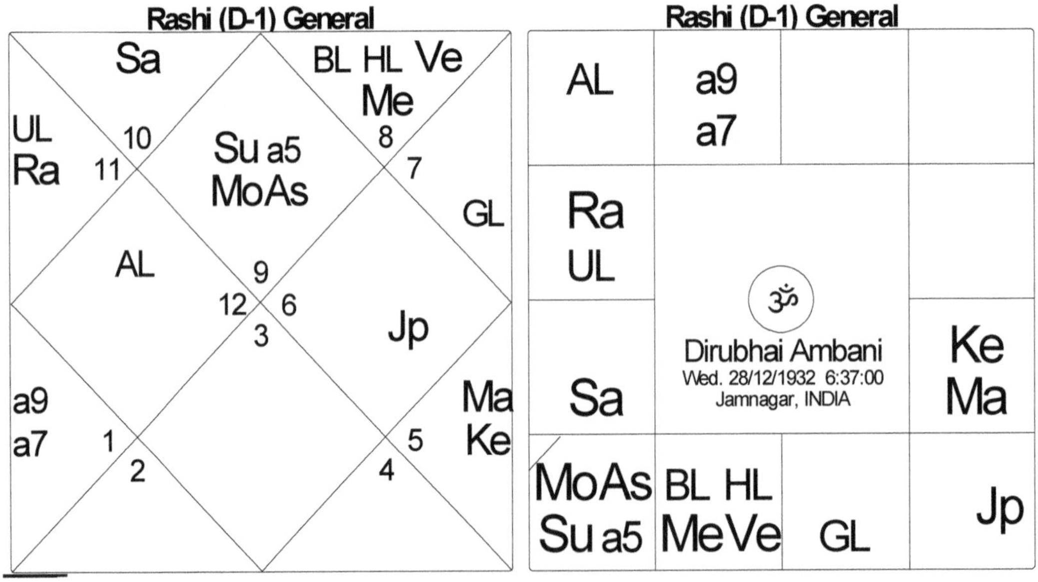

Chart of Dirubhai Hirachand Ambani, born 28th December 1932, 6:37 AM, Jamnagar, India.

Horā Lagna is placed in Scorpio with the second from it occupied by the Sun in a fiery sign, as the tenth from it is occupied by Mars and Ketu conferring very powerful wealth accumulation skills. Karaṇa lord should be seen for wealth and its lorded by the Sun. This is normally not auspicious when in a fiery sign, but as the Tithi lord is also that of the Sun it is an enormous blessing for wealth where water and earth come together.

The native of the given chart, has Sagittarius Lagna, with Saturn in the second house in own sign. Normally Saturn's strength in the second house would confer wealth and sustenance, but this same Saturn is debilitated in Navāṁśa. The native was born in a village, to a schoolteacher. He made his initial living selling snacks and had not seen a hundred rupee (INR) note until he arrived in the big city of Mumbai. This same Saturn in the second house is in the eleventh from Ārūḍha Lagna. The severe poverty suffered in childhood turned into a strong force later in life in an attempt to avoid the same circumstances, i.e. turning a disadvantage into an advantage.

Saturn indicates servants, the poor, the lower class, and workers and the necessities of society[5], hence the native will gain money from the necessities of society. The native's main profit is from the exploration and refining of oil and petrochemical products. Venus, Mercury, Mars and Ketu have Rāśi dṛṣṭi on Capricorn, however among them only Venus and Mercury are friendly towards Saturn and will be eager to give wealth, while Ketu itself is able to give great amounts of wealth, but this may not come to the native himself and will require some parākrama. Venus indicates people in fashion, movies, showbiz, and would give the native money from people involved in the same. The native had a well-known company in the manufacturing of suits, shirts, saris, etc. Mercury indicates people involved in IT, communications, phone's, broadcasting, news and similar areas. The native had another company involved in the mobile and telecommunications markets. Ketu indicates foreign cultures; a great source of income for these companies is through the export of their products. During Saturn Mahādaśā (from 1998), the native was among the wealthiest men in the world, owning a company with a current revenue of US $ 22.6 Billion. It is clear how the Ārūḍha Lagna can change the scenario of the planets placement in the Bhāvas.

9.2 The Sixth House

The sixth house deals with sins acquired by the native in previous births due to lack of purity in mind and body. Should this impurity be physical it results in diseases and ailments during this birth. If this impurity were in the mind and/or actions, it results in enmity in the present birth. The planets in the sixth house or joining the sixth lord indicate the type of injury or ailment that we are prone to, while the Ārūḍha of the sixth house indicate both the nature and actions of the enemy. More important is the outcome of such battles with the enemy, which is seen from the Ārūḍha Lagna itself.

9.2.1 Injury and Ailments

Injuries generally arise from a Martian influence on the sixth house or lord. The Lagnas of Gemini and Scorpio are naturally prone towards accidents and bruises because Mars lords the sixth house. Saturn on the other hand rules pains and ailments. Saturn's signs, Capricorn and Aquarius, would be attributed to the same. The placement of the sixth lord will indicate the body part of the ailment. Grahas joining this planet can moderate the influences. Here the body part is reckoned by dividing the chart into thirty-six body parts, dividing each house into three parts of

5 This is why Saturn in association with the eleventh from Ārūḍha Lagna will never grant poverty to the native.

the body above the neck, the torso and the body below the waist. Grahas joining the sixth lord can moderate this. In the case of some Lagnas the Lagna lord and 6th/8th, lords are the same graha. In such cases the sixth from the sixth, i.e. the eleventh house takes on the results of the sixth house. Similarly, the third lord acts as the eighth lord.

Should the eighth house be involved this ailment becomes chronic. However, the sign of the eighth lord will indicate the disease instead, as per the natural Kālapuruṣa, i.e. Aries is the head, Pisces is the feet, etc. The lords of any other houses involved indicates ailments suffered by that relative lorded by the graha as well. The latter also applies to Ārūḍha Padas falling in the sixth house.

While the sixth and eighth houses indicate bodily pains and ailments of the native, which arise out of accidents or lack of immunity, the second house indicates bodily defects of the native. The planets associated with the second houses from Lagna, Pāka Lagna and Ārūḍha Lagna will indicate bodily defects, which can cause death, i.e. blood disorders, liver problems, etc. Each of the three Lagnas mentioned have different connotations. The second house from the Lagna indicates disorders arising from birth/conditioning. The second house from the Pāka Lagna gives disorders arising from misdirected intelligence, while the second house from the Ārūḍha Lagna shows disorders arising from a wrong lifestyle. The problem area arises from the sapta dhātu, ruled by the sapta grahas.

Table 71: Sapta Dhātu

Graha	Dhātu	Translation
Sun	Asthi	Bone
Moon	Rakta	Blood
Mars	Majjā	Nerves
Mercury	Tvag/Rasa	Skin/Cause of immunity
Jupiter	Vāsa	Fat
Venus	Vīrya	Virility, Semen
Saturn	Snāyu	Muscles

The presence of the planet in the second house or aspecting the same by Rāśi dṛṣṭi will cause problems in that part of body ruled by the dhātu. While Mercury rules skin, planets joining it can give a different connotation. Mercury has the power to not only protect the body through the skin but it can also do so through the immune system. An affliction to Mercury shows an affliction to the immune system of the body, i.e. the red/white blood cells. This tends to cause hormonal problems and overweight, among other things.

A planet joining Mercury in the second house can use the immune system to cause problems in other areas of the body based on the debilitation sign. For example, if Mars joins Mercury, then Mars will use Mercury to debilitate the Moon, causing Rakta doṣa. Mercury itself has the power to debilitate Venus, but needs the help of the Sun who is a great enemy of Venus. In this manner, the astrologer can quickly identify the type of disorders and its effect on the native.

9.2.2 Enmity and War

Those who invite conflicts, usually suffer from the same. Natives with Lagna lord or Ātmakāraka in the sixth house tend to get into conflicts easily, and spend all their time in competition or court battles. The same applies to Lagna lord in twelfth house as it sees the sixth house by graha dṛṣṭi. The sixth lord itself should be in a Kendra from Lagna for the native to be drawn into conflict easily. This will occur in their workplace (10th), married life (7th), childhood and/or home (4th house) or due to their own nature (Lagna). In all cases, this will cause a separation between the spouses, as sixth house is the house of celibacy. As the sixth from the sixth is the eleventh house, the bādhak sthāna is very important to view as well. If the Bādhakeśa is in the sixth house, or the sixth lord is in bādhak sthāna, the native suffers from black magic due to enmity.

- Planets in the third house will invite conflicts, as Mars is the Kāraka for the same.
- Malefics in the sixth house will give terrible enemies, whilst benefics will give little or no enmity. Sun in the sixth house will give problems from government if associated with Saturn or Rāhu; otherwise, the native shall see auspicious results in the form of good health/physique and success in battles.
- There is a possibility of defeat in battles if the Kāraka Mars is in the seventh house, unless Jupiter is in Lagna or Mars is debilitated.
- The way the native deals with enemies is seen from the third and sixth houses from Ārūḍha Lagna, whilst the enemy's actions are seen from the third and sixth from the Ārūḍha of the sixth house.
- The native's ability as a fighter is seen from the third and sixth houses from Mars as this shows the native's reflexes and immediate reaction.

9.2.3 Case Studies

9.2.3.1 Injury and Ailments

Chart 123: Diabetes and Overweight

The native has Libra Lagna, and Venus is Ātmakāraka. Generally, those born with Venus as Ātmakāraka tend to suffer from diabetes. The second house is unoccupied while its lord is joined Venus and Jupiter, which indicates among other things, problems in retaining heat (Jupiter/fat) and problems in the production of serum from the endocrines. These planets also have Rāśi dṛṣṭi on the second from Ārūḍha Lagna confirming the problem. The second from pāka Lagna has the Sun and Mercury indicating overweight and diabetes because of problems in the endocrines. The presence of sixth lord has made this a source of immense pain and suffering for the native. The latter indicates that these diseases arise due to ignorance and bad habits, which the native is required to correct through meditation and guidance.

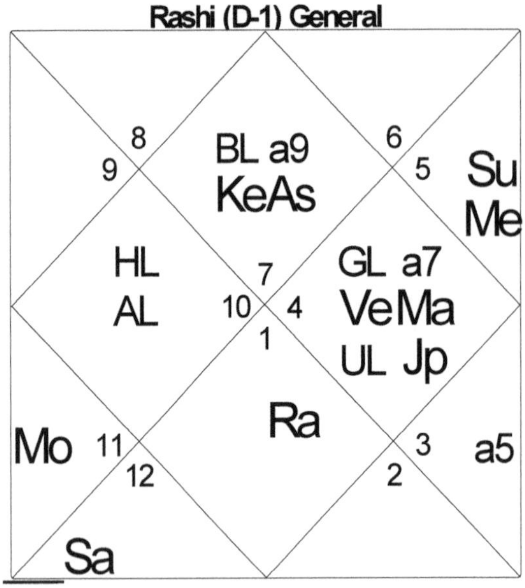

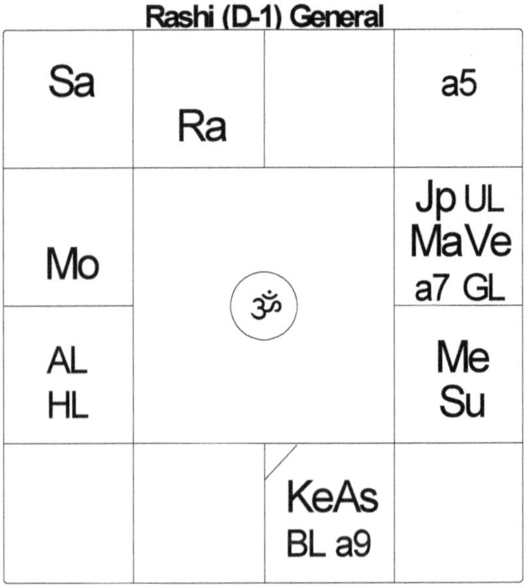

Chart 124: Diabetes

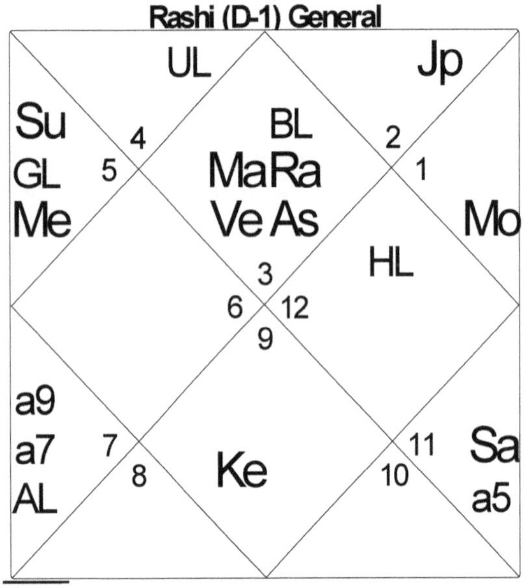

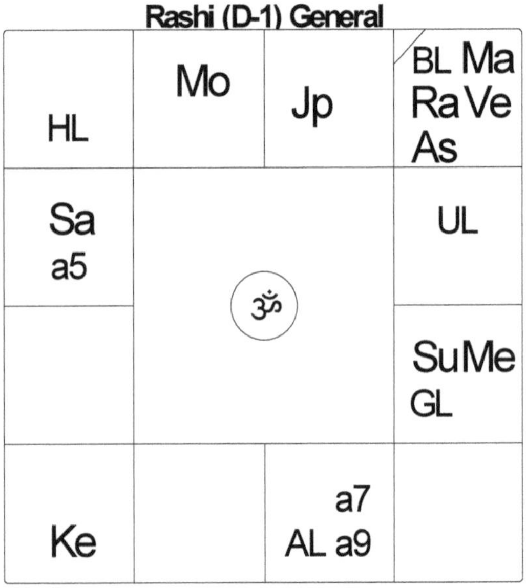

In the given chart, the native has Venus as Ātmakāraka, diagnosed with diabetes, which needs to be verified through analysis. The second from neither Lagna, nor Ārūḍha Lagna has the association of Mercury and Sun. The Lagna lord is Mercury and is in Leo. The second lord there from is Mercury itself who is joined the Sun, hence the yoga for diabetes is confirmed. The problem is quite severe due to the yoga being in second from Lagna lord and is sure to be chronic.

Chart 125: Hamilton Jordan

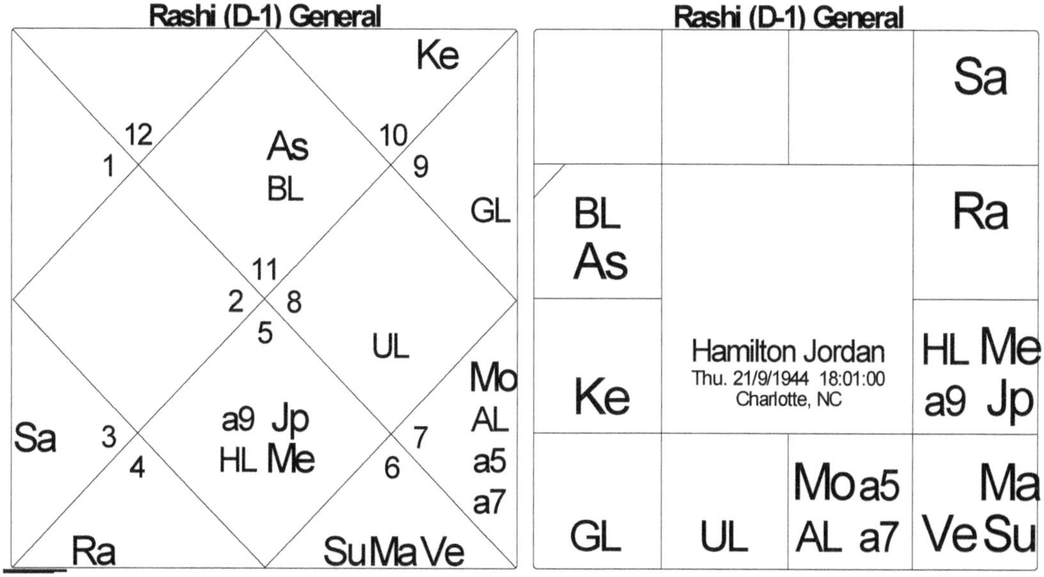

Hamilton Jordan, born 21st September 1944, 6:01 PM, Charlotte, NC, USA.

Weekday lord Jupiter is placed in a fiery sign showing strength and great energy for work. As the Nakṣatra is also lorded by Jupiter, he is more than capable of taking up hard and difficult work. However, with eighth lord Jupiter joining as Saturn and Rāhu both aspect the same, difficult diseases will also arise. Being in the seventh house these will arise towards the last part of his life. As the eighth lord is placed in Māraṇa Kāraka Sthāna, this will bring about near death incidents.

Venus is the Ātmakāraka, but the second from his Lagna lord Saturn has no connection to Sun and Mercury thus diabetes is not indicated in his chart.

With Horā lord being Venus, he would be drawn towards world affairs as Venus lords the ninth house. Being joined the seventh lord Sun he would be drawn to politics, and with Mars he will feel the need to joined the armed services as well. Vimśottari Daśā started from his Ātmakāraka Venus is applicable. Venus, Sun and Mars aspect the second house and in his second Daśā of Rāhu he met Jimmy Carter, who was then running for governor. The Antaradaśā was of Mars who is joined the combination and would have a lasting impact on Hamilton. He since then worked for Jimmy Carter however when Jupiter Daśā began he volunteered in the war in South Vietnam.

He had just finished his Bachelor of Arts in Political Science, and with Jupiter in the seventh house this is sure to bring about war issues. Jupiter lords the third and sixth from the Moon to bring him into the war. Being disqualified for military service due to his legs he worked as civilian aide assisting refugees. Saturn Antaradaśā the year after brought him home as Saturn lords the fourth house from the Moon and brings peace, but with disease. He returned home, discharged as he was ill with black water fever. Sun who is the seventh lord joined Mars in the eighth house of disease shows the fever during his military service. He suspects during this time that his exposure to the chemical *Agent Orange,* which was used as *herbicide warfare* in Vietnam, would later cause a great deal of health issues to him.

Jupiter Mahādaśā lords the fourth and tenth houses from the Sun promoting comforts and travel. By being placed in twelfth from Sun it causes Śubha Yoga for good associations and wealth. It further lords the Ghaṭika Lagna, joins the Horā Lagna and aspects the Lagna by Graha Dṛṣṭi to show power, wealth and great zeal in its Mahādaśā. This would be the most important political legacy of his life.

After recovering from his ails in Vietnam, he rejoined Carter for the 1970 gubernatorial race as his campaign manager. Carter became governor during this time. Saturn Antaradaśā was running and is lording over the fifth house from Moon giving power and position.

Carter being limited by one term as governor met with his aides in 1972. It was here that Hamilton presented a master plan that would lead to Carter entering the White House. Rāhu is the Amatyakāraka in the chart showing Hamilton's aptitude for politics, and Rāhu's lordship of the Lagna suggests an extremely shrewd and calculating mind making him the perfect spin doctor. Rāhu being joined the tenth lord Mars in the Navāṁśa chart proves that he will associate with the topmost in his field and its Vargottama position shows that he is a king maker! Hamilton presented an eighty-page memo on how Carter was to become president with every step of the road lined with how he should attain his goal.

Two years later in December 1974, Carter announced his run for the presidency. Hamilton is running Venus Antaradaśā during this time, being the dispositor of the Moon will give the attainment of one's desires. Jupiter Daśā, Venus Antaradaśā is rarely auspicious, but in this case Jupiter is placed in the seventh house with a Māraṇa Kāraka Sthāna Mercury. Venus being the Kāraka of the seventh will be responsible for their well being and being joined the Sun shows the blessings of overcoming the hurdles of Mercury. Venus further lords over the Ārūḍha Lagna, Darapada and Śrī Lagna bringing huge blessings during its Antaradaśā. Its lordship over the Moon's sign in Navāṁśa will bring new beginnings and the blessings of the Śankha of Kṛṣṇa to welcome a new era of politics.

In November 1976, in the Daśā of Jupiter, Antaradaśā of Venus and Pratyantaradaśā of Mercury Jimmy Carter became president, proving Hamilton's plan to be a success. Mercury is the fifth lord from Lagna giving power during its period. Jordan joined Carter to become chief of staff.

Rāhu placed in the tenth house from Moon will hurt reputation in ones work, and being in the sign of Cancer unaspected by any Graha, the Moon will act on behalf of Rāhu and Rāhu on behalf of the Moon. Jupiter Daśā, Moon Antaradaśā brought accusations upon Jordan of sniffing Cocaine and participating in anonymous sex in the infamous Studio 54 disco in New York. This occurred at a sensitive time leading to the divorce from his first wife. Lord of Upapada, Mars, is debilitated in Cancer in Navāṁśa thus ruining the first marriage.

After many months of being questioned, in May 1980 during Rāhu Antaradaśā the court decided not to indict him, but serious damage to the reputation of the administration had been done. Moon lords the eighth from the Ghaṭika Lagna indicating loss of power. Carter lost the re-election in 1980 and Hamilton began a new life. Rāhu is in trines to the Upapada, and in 1981 he re-married.

Saturn Mahādaśā began in 1982 and its aspect on the eighth lord as well as third from Ārūḍha Lagna would prove very dangerous. Mercury being the eighth lord should give the disease in the area indicated by its sign placement, i.e. Leo indicating the stomach area. The affliction by Saturn and Rāhu jointly suggests cancer as the disease. However, due to exchanging signs with the Sun, the entire disease will manifest in the sign of Virgo. Being in Virgo shows skin problems, i.e. skin cancer, whilst its junction with Venus ruins the lymphatic nodes. With Mars it attacks the nervous system as well.

Lagna is placed in the first ten degrees and the eighth lord Mercury is placed between ten to twenty degrees suggesting that the disease will affect the torso area. In the seventh house this is the *basti* or abdomen area.

Being that Saturn lords the sixth house from the Sun, its Mahādaśā can bring disease. Jupiter is the sixth lord from Moon and is joined Mercury, so also in Saturn-Mercury Daśā he suffered from lymphatic cancer. Neither Saturn nor Mercury are joined or placed in Māraka houses from Sun or Moon, hence Hamilton managed to recover from this. Venus is the eighth lord from Moon and in Saturn-Venus Daśā he was diagnosed with Melanoma cancer in 1991. He again persevered through this during Venus and Sun's Antaradaśā.

Mars is also joined Venus and in Saturn-Mars Daśā he was diagnosed with prostate cancer. Mars is a Māraka from the Moon and suggests surgery due to Mars placed in twelfth (hospitals/doctors) from Moon. The prostrate was removed and he was in remission.

Despite his ails, Hamilton continued a career within the media and also attempted to run for the senate, though unsuccessfully. He further worked tirelessly for causes of overcoming cancer.

Mercury Mahādaśā began in 2001. Mercury is joined Jupiter, who is the seventh lord from the Sun, thus becoming a Māraka. Venus, Mars and Sun are associated with the second and seventh houses from Moon and in Sun Antaradaśā he passed away due to cancer.

9.2.3.2 Enmity and War

Chart 126: Śrī Rāma

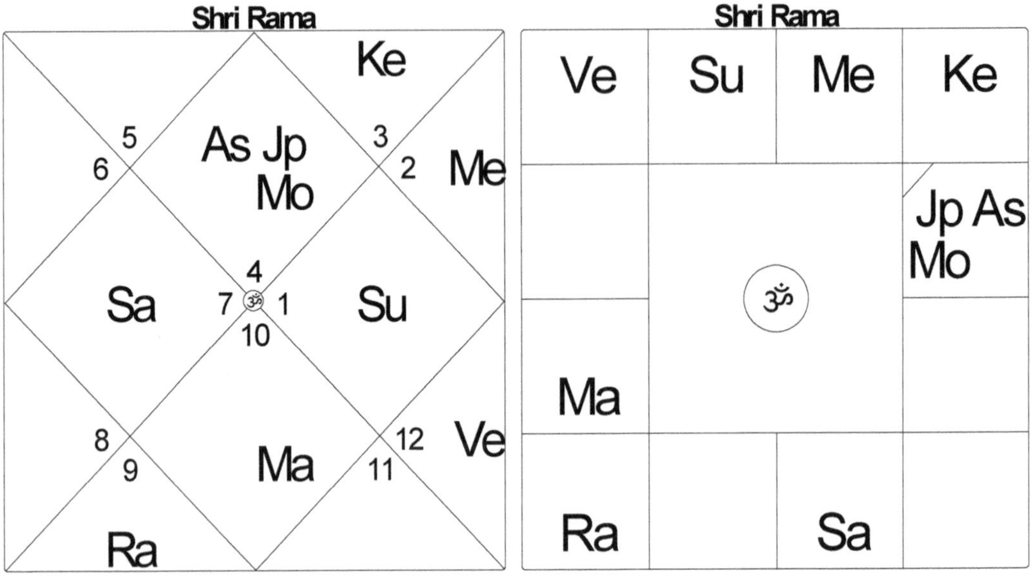

In the chart of Śrī Rāma, Rāhu, indicating strong and powerful enemies who will trouble the native, occupies the sixth house. It has graha dṛṣṭi on the 7th, 10th, 12th and 2nd houses; hence, the enemy will have his eyes on the native's spouse, throne, will plot against him secretly and will have an eye on his money. Rāhu is however debilitated indicating that Śrī Rāma will defeat this enemy.

The A6 is in Aquarius indicating that the enemy's Lagna would be an airy sign or the seventh there from, and Rāhu lords Aquarius, he could be a foreigner. The third house from A6 has an exalted Sun indicating a powerful warrior, who will be hard to defeat in battle. The sixth from A6 however has Jupiter and Moon, which are both strong and promising victory over the enemy. Jupiter and Moon are in Lagna hence the native's birth was meant to defeat the enemy. The Rāmāyaṇa tells us that this enemy is Rāvaṇa, the king of Lanka.

Mars in the seventh house threatens to defeat to Śrī Rāma, but the presence of Jupiter in the Lagna will bring the benefit to him and after a long struggle defeat his enemies and give him Rāja yoga. The conflict arose from Rāvaṇa's jealousy of Śrī Rāma and his lust for his wife Sitā, who is said to be an incarnation of Lakṣmī.

Chart 127: Adolph Hitler

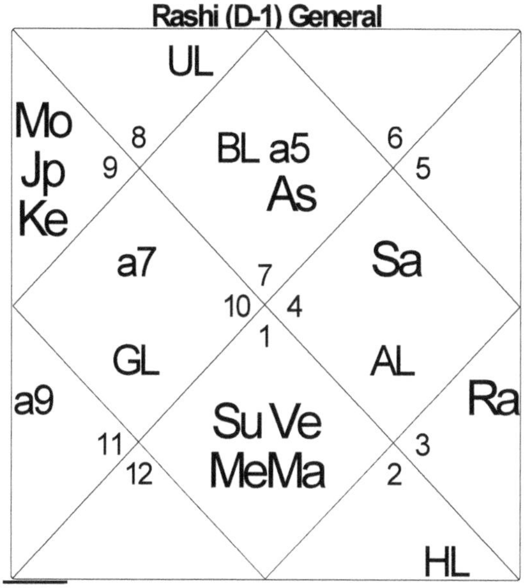

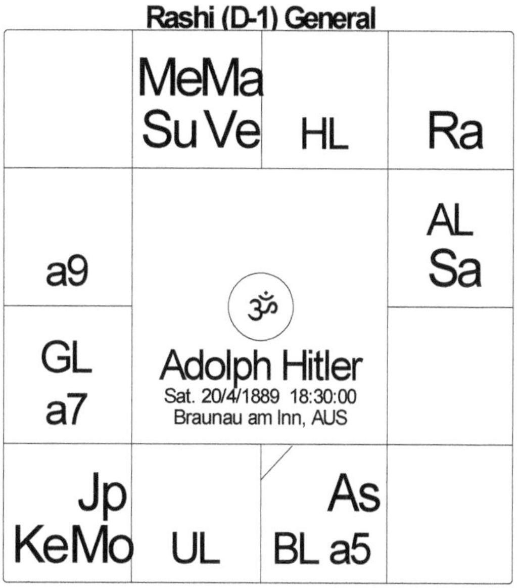

The story of Hitler is well known. Gajakeśarī Yoga in the third house indicates war for Germany, just as it did in the case of George Bush. Unfortunately, the sixth house is Pisces and its lord Jupiter indicates peaceful and spiritual people, who will be the target of the war-machine. Rāhu in the ninth house aspecting Jupiter and Moon causing the destruction of life through the infamous Śakti yoga confirm this[6]. As Jupiter and Moon are in the sixth from Ārūḍha Lagna and strong, it indicates that, this yoga will be a source of defeat Hitler. Mars is forming a strong Ruchaka Mahāpuruṣa yoga and leaders with such yogas usually do not hesitate to go to war. This same Mars is in the seventh house, hence defeat is imminent.

The nature of the enemy, who will defeat Hitler, is seen from the A6, which is in Gemini with Rāhu, indicating a very powerful enemy capable at battle. The Lagna of the enemy will be in trines to Gemini; Roosevelt who fought Hitler, had Libra rising.

Readers may appreciate to see the chart of Hitler's predecessor, Otto Von Bismarck.

6 The association of Rāhu and Moon with the ninth house forms Śakti Yoga. The planets joining it will suffer through their significations. In case of benefics, this is highly inauspicious which can ruin innocent beings, whilst malefics can cause the destruction of sin or evil.

Chart 128: Otto Von Bismarck

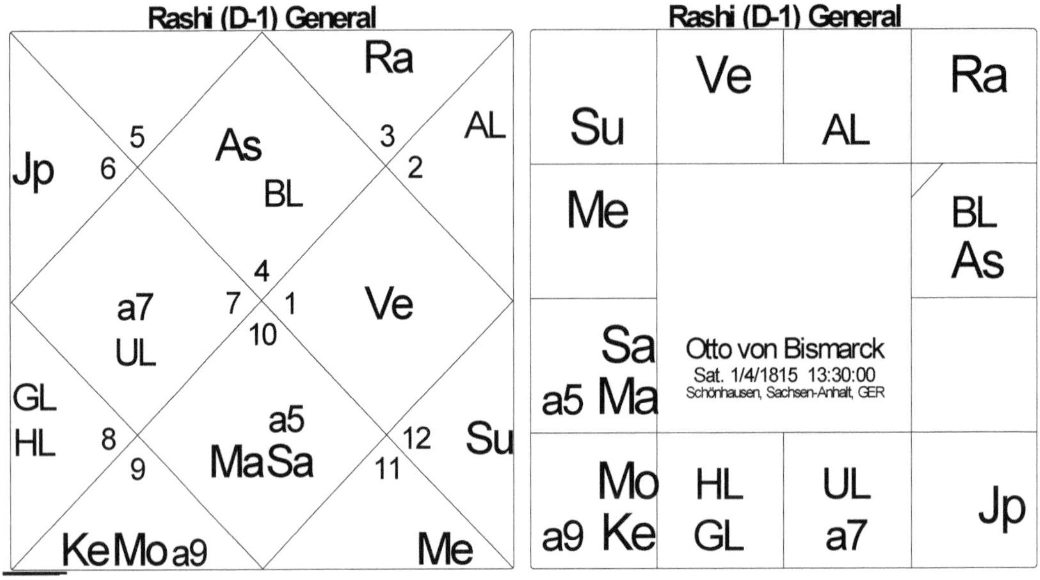

9.3 The Tenth House

The tenth house deals with accomplishments in life be this through hobbies, spiritual penance, or from work. It deals with various aspects of work, such as how the work sustains the nature of the work itself etc.

9.3.1 Occupation

Most ancient texts describe the use of the tenth house from Lagna and Moon to decide the aspects of the native's career. The Parampara teaches the use of Lagna, Moon, Sun, Ārūḍha Lagna and Amatyakāraka to get an idea about job and career. Each of these has different connotations.

- The tenth from Lagna indicates the work the native is interested in doing, i.e. what work supports his ideals.
- The tenth from Moon indicates that work which sustains the native in life. Here the issue is wealth/income.
- The tenth from the Sun indicates that work which brings status and position to the native, i.e. power and authority.
- The tenth from the Ārūḍha Lagna deals with the benefits of a job, i.e. the small benefits arising out of one's work.
- The lords of the above Bhāvas should also be seen
- The Amatyakāraka itself deals with the experience of the work place and the impact of one's employer on one's life.

Most people undergoing a troubled phase do so due to the graha dṛṣṭi or conjunction of transit Saturn on the tenth from Lagna, Moon or Ārūḍha Lagna. This is known as Kaṇṭaka Śani and causes trouble in getting a job/performing one's job, financial tension, and lack of fruits/profit from one's work. The best remedy for this is to recite the third anuvāka of the Rudra Chamakam.

While the above deals with the type of work the native does, the professions or status/positions the native takes on is seen from the Lagna and Ārūḍha Lagna. It is pertinent to understand that one's profession and occupation are two separate issues. business psychologists deal with the behaviour of clients towards products, whilst personal psychologists deal with helping people out of their mental abnormalities. In both cases the profession is that of a psychologist, hence the differentiation.

- Planets joining, lording and/or having Rāśi dṛṣṭi on the Lagna or Ārūḍha Lagna will indicate which traits the native identifies himself with and hence which professions they will enter.
- If the identified grahas are also in trines in the Navāṁśa, those professions will be long lasting.

9.3.2 Case Studies

Chart 129: Lata Mangeskar – Singer

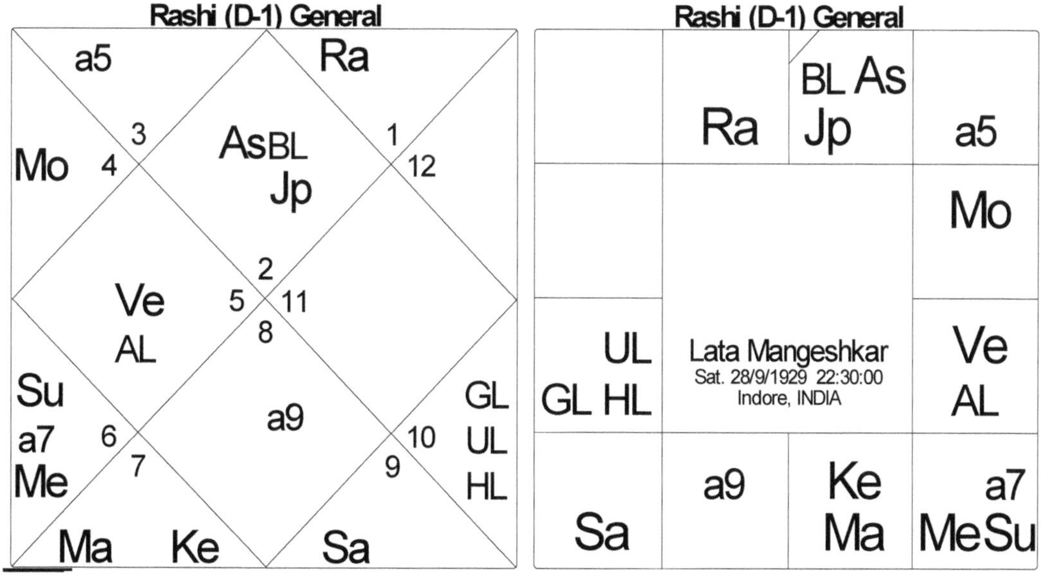

Given here, is the chart of Lata Mangeskar, a well-known Indian singer. Let us identify the profession of this native. The Varṇadā Lagna is in Aquarius, and the eleventh from it is unoccupied. The lord Jupiter indicates the main profession as a Brahmin. This could be a teacher, priest, singer, actor, writer, etc. Now let us list out the planets, which associate with the Lagna and Ārūḍha Lagna. Jupiter, Moon, Mars, the nodes and Venus associate with the Lagna and Ārūḍha Lagna. Among these, Jupiter, Ketu and the Moon are placed in the trines to Navāṁśa Lagna. Jupiter can indicate a profession as a teacher and Ketu as a mathematician. However, Ketu in the sixth will not prove auspicious, while the Moon indicates a profession as a singer or vocalist. Among these the Moon is strongest due to its position in own sign, and will dominate due to the native's comfort (svakṣetra) in that profession.

Chart 130: Sanjay Rath – Astrologer

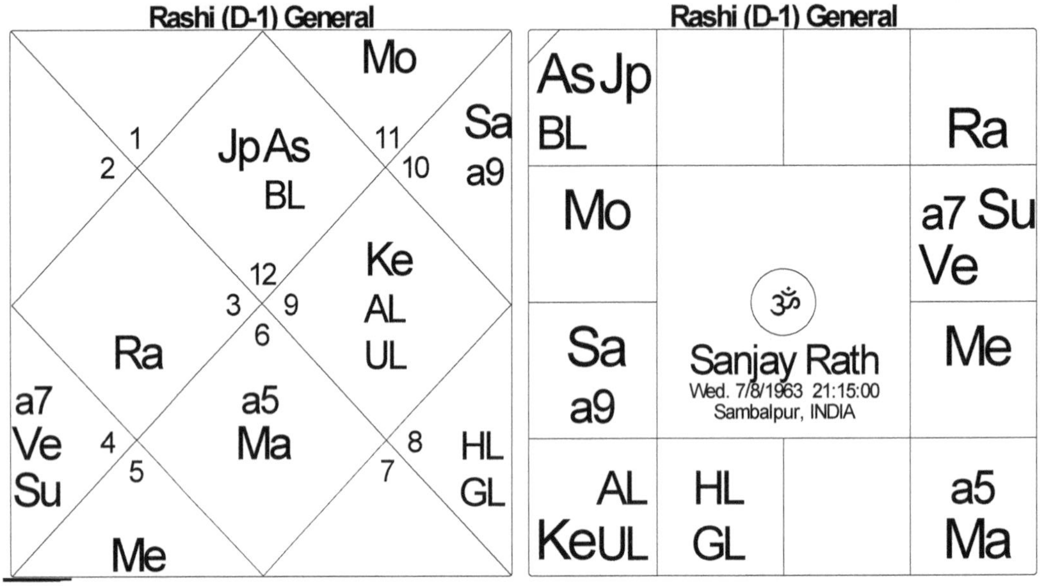

The Varṇadā Lagna is in Libra, and the eleventh there from is Leo. Mercury occupies Leo whilst Sun joins Venus. The native has worked for the government (Sun), is as an Astrologer (Venus), is involved with the publishing business and is a writer (Mercury). From the Lagna and Ārūḍha Lagna, the planets involved are Jupiter, Ketu, Rāhu and Mars. Of these, Ketu is the only one in trines to Navāṁśa Lagna, and indicates a profession as an astronomer, astrologer or some such similar line. Mars' placement in the seventh house in Navāṁśa did however get the native involved in defence during the beginning of the native's marriage.

Chart 131: Job Problems

In the given chart, the native has Gemini Lagna. Notably the tenth lord Jupiter is well placed in the tenth and is the tenth lord from the Sun, promising good working conditions and status and position in the job, especially after Jupiter Daśā. The tenth lord from Ārūḍha Lagna is Moon and placed in the twelfth house with Ketu in an inauspicious Grahaṇa (eclipse) yoga, which does not speak well of the native's job-benefits, and will cause mental instability due to strain. Analyzing the tenth from the Moon, we find Iṣṭa Devatā Mercury placed there, but its lords Saturn and Rāhu are very badly placed. Saturn is Amatyakāraka in Māraṇa Kāraka Sthāna causing instability on the account of the employer (Amatyakāraka), whilst Rāhu is in the sixth house indicating enemies and fierce battles. As the reference is the tenth lord from Moon, this will be in the scene of finances, bonuses, pay check, etc. During Rāhu Mahādaśā and Saturn Antaradaśā, the native had his pay check delayed for unknown reasons. The culprit is Saturn the Amatyakāraka indicating the employer.

Rashi (D-1) General

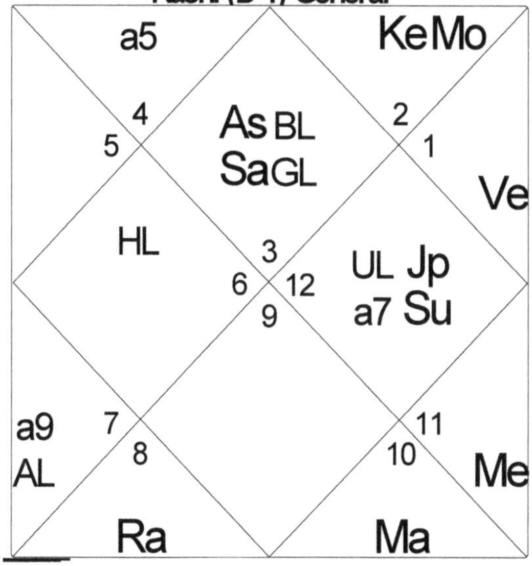

Rashi (D-1) General

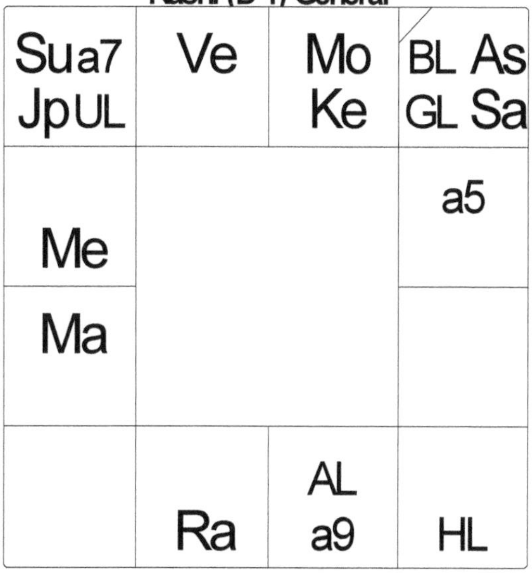

Analyzing the Varṇadā Lagna we find that the eleventh lord from Varṇadā Lagna is Venus whose Argalā on Taurus is blocked by Saturn, hence specifically the payment for regular work (pay check) was obstructed by the employer. The native mentioned that his mother has been encouraging him to change jobs. The Matṛkāraka is the Iṣṭa Devatā planet indicating that the mother will lead the native to his Iṣṭa Devatā, and the same planet is in the tenth from the Moon ensuring good finances as well as authority due to Mercury being in the sixth from Ārūḍha Lagna. The native was advised to follow the mother's advice and pray to the Iṣṭa Devatā.

यन्मण्डलं सर्वगतस्य विष्णोरात्मा परं धाम विशुद्धतत्त्वम्।
सूक्ष्मान्तरैर्योगपथानुगम्यं पुनातु मां तत्सवितुर्वरेण्यम्॥ १०॥

10

Third, Seventh & Eleventh
The Kāma trikoṇa

10.1 The Third House

The third house deals with matters related to copulation, weapons/fighting and siblings. The two former matters is dealt with in other chapters of this book, hence in this chapter, the identification of siblings from the natal chart will be examined. Ārūḍhas are used to identify siblings in a chart. This concept is based on the fact that siblings are related to us through parents, and indicates one's status in the family, i.e. whether one is the oldest, youngest etc. The Ārūḍha of the third and eleventh houses do not show our own siblings but those who can become brothers and sisters to us through close association. Instead our own siblings are seen from the third and eleventh from the Ārūḍha Lagna itself. Jaimini has given a range of dictums to help us understand this concept.

10.1.1 Houses of Co-born

All sages agree that the younger siblings are seen from third house, whilst the elder from the eleventh house. The Parampara teaches that when deducing results for siblings or children, the relevant houses involved are reckoned in direct or reverse motion, depending on the Lagna being an odd or even sign respectively. For example, the younger siblings are seen from the third house. Should the Lagna be an even sign, then this is seen from the eleventh house instead. This can change depending on the grahas in the Lagna. For siblings this applies to the Ārūḍha Lagna and the Drekkāṇa Lagna.

Should the person be female then this reckoning of siblings from the Ārūḍha is reckoned in reverse.

In analysis of the Ārūḍha Lagna examining the stronger between the Ārūḍha and the seventh house from it will determine where to examine the siblings and the person's life from.

10.1.2 Planets Denying Co-born

- Saturn is the presiding graha of the Vāyu Tattva, which is the cause of death and disease. Its association with Agni Tattva destroys the life-force/Agni of any being, and hence its association with the houses of siblings will cause death. Saturn's placement in the houses of siblings causes the demise of the siblings, after some time.
- If Saturn and Rāhu are in either of the houses of siblings then there is destruction of co-born. Rāhu is the destroyer of the ākāśa Tattva. His association with Saturn will deny siblings altogether, provided that Jupiter is not associated. However, even then the siblings may suffer premature death.
- Venus will cause loss through the destruction of the womb. Venus is Jala Tattva and is opposed to the Kāraka for siblings, Mars (Agni Tattva); as a result Venus becomes the prime Māraka for siblings. Venus will do so by destroying the pregnancy when placed in the houses of siblings. As this causes a Tattva doṣa, the binding Tattva, ākāśa needs to be strong to keep the pregnancy alive, hence Jupiter's association with the houses of siblings will ensure the survival of the sibling, even if Venus is placed in or aspects the bhāva of siblings. Further, Venus placed in the first or eighth houses from Ārūḍha Lagna can also inhibit elder siblings from being born.

10.1.3 Planets Friendly Towards Co-born

Mars, Jupiter, Moon and Mercury will give many co-born. Each graha mentioned has a role to play in giving co-born as given below.

- Moon, although a Jala Tattva graha has a higher energy-force than that of Venus. Moon has the purpose of feeding and sustaining the entire creation, which Venus cannot do, hence unlike Venus, Moon has the power to give siblings due to the mothers sustaining power. The Moon however, does not counter the aspect of Venus and increases the Jala Tattva to cause the destruction of co-born.
- Mercury being a Pṛthvī Tattva graha has the ability to debilitate Venus, and eliminates the evil indications of the Jala Tattva. Both Jupiter and Mercury can remove the evil of Venus, which causes the destruction of siblings in the womb.
- Jupiter is the ākāśa Tattva, removes any Tattva doṣa pertaining to the co-born, and brings the co-born into the world. The destroyers of ākāśa Tattva are the two nodes and hence they will end the count of siblings, as will their signs (Aquarius/ Scorpio). The nodes will not be able to do so if Jupiter associates with the houses of siblings, nor will Saturn be able to enforce his evil on these Bhāva. Should Jupiter be placed in or lording over the twelfth house from Ārūḍha Lagna then one may have suffered loss of elder siblings which makes on the eldest. So also Ārūḍha Lagna in Aries or Capricorn tends to make one the eldest sibling in the family.

- Mars is the Kāraka of third house and co-born, and has a strong predominance of Agni Tattva. It is due to this strong Agni, that siblings usually fight with each other, or have some sort of rivalry amongst each other. Mars is thus encouraging of siblings, especially younger ones. Just as is the case with Jupiter, should Mars be placed in or lord over the twelfth from the Ārūḍha Lagna then one may not have younger siblings.

Besides the examination of the Ārūḍha Lagna, analysing the Drekkaṇa (D-3) chart will give a more thorough view of each sibling. Herein the lord of the sign indicating the sibling will indicate the gender of the sibling. It is pertinent to note in this regard that the nodes for the purpose of examining śṛṣṭi or creation also take up the lordship of the Mūlatrikoṇa signs, i.e. Rāhu will lord both Aquarius and Virgo as Ketu lords over both Scorpio and Pisces.

10.1.4 Case Studies

Chart 132: Eldest Sibling – Prince Charles

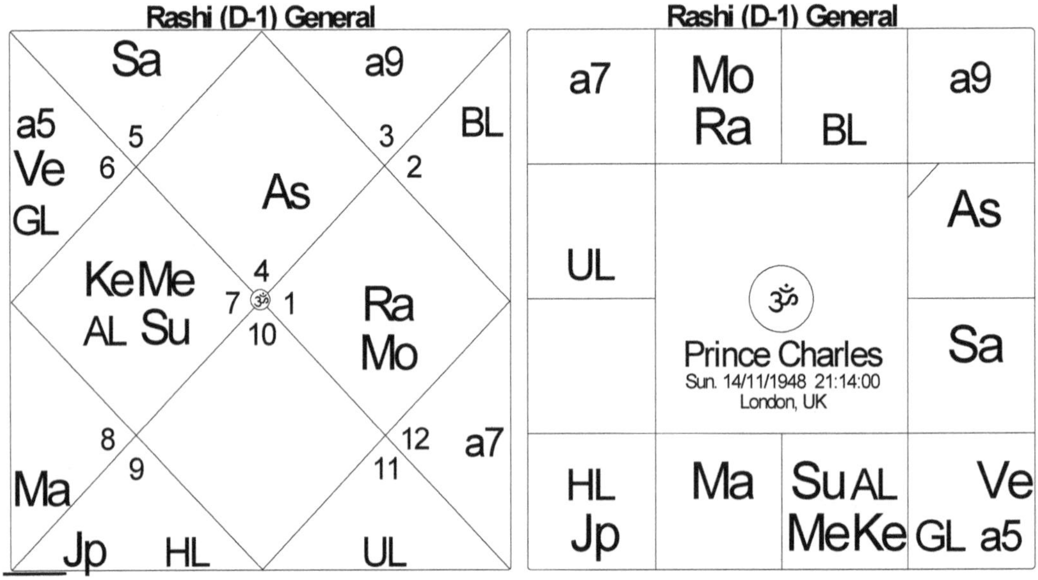

Charles, Prince of Wales, born Charles Philip Arthur George Mountbatten-Windsor, 14th November 1948, London, United Kingdom.

The Lagna is Cancer and the lord is in Aries, hence the Ārūḍha Lagna is in Libra. Among Libra and Aries, Libra is occupied by more planets and is stronger. Libra is an odd sign, and the eleventh from it will show the elder siblings whilst the third from it will show the younger siblings. These two signs are Leo and Sagittarius respectively. Leo is occupied by Saturn and receives the Rāśi dṛṣṭi of Rāhu. The native is the eldest. The Sun is the Ātmakāraka joined the Ārūḍha Lagna showing his image as the heir to the throne of England.

Prince Charles has three younger siblings. Jupiter is placed in the third from Ārūḍha Lagna and is also the lord placed in own sign showing two younger brothers. It further receives the Rāśi Dṛṣṭi of debilitated Venus giving one younger sister as well.

Chart 133: Male

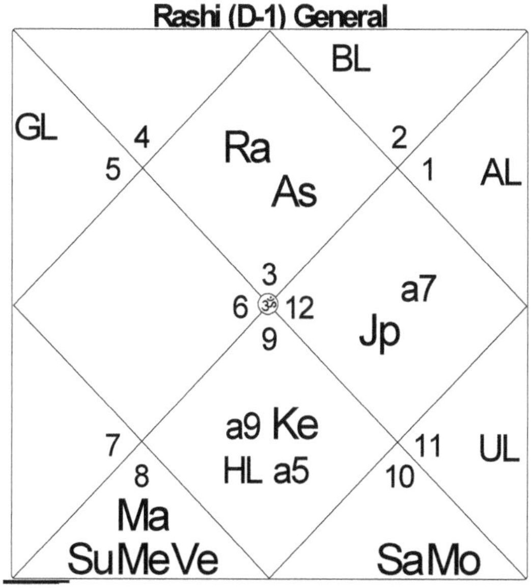

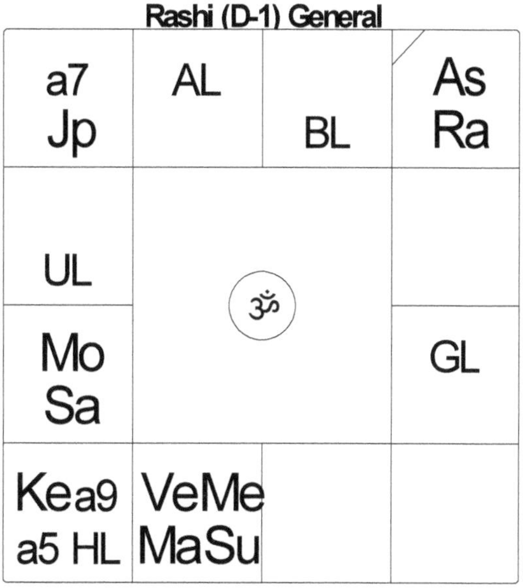

Chart of Male native, born 23rd November 1963, New Delhi, India.

Lagna is placed in Gemini as the Ārūḍha Lagna is placed in Aries. Among Aries and Libra, both are equally occupied. Due to the aspect of Mercury and Mars on Aries it may be assumed that Aries is stronger, however as Jupiter is in and lords the twelfth from Aries he should be the eldest sibling, which is not the case. Therefore Libra as the Ārūḍha is more appropriate.

Chart 134: Male - Drekkāṇa (D-3)

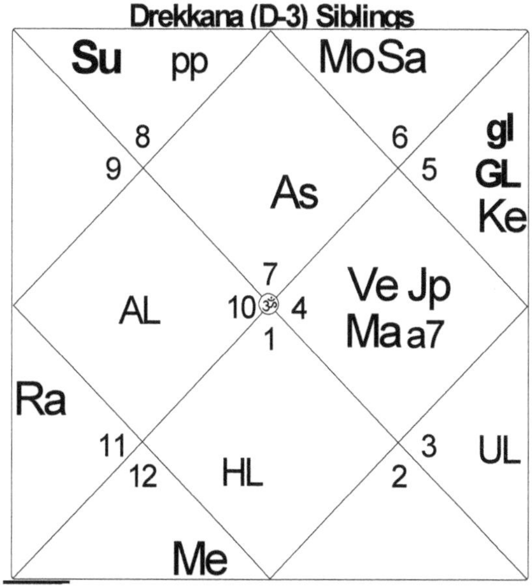

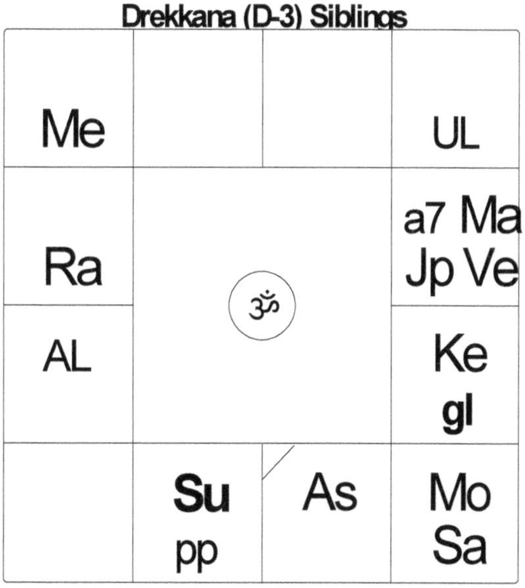

Libra is an odd sign and the younger siblings are examined from the third house from it i.e. Sagittarius. The position of exalted Ketu herein is good for younger sisters, but the Yāma yoga caused by Mars and Saturn's Papakartari on Sagittarius does not encourage younger siblings. The eleventh house from Libra will show the elder siblings and is Leo. Saturn and Moon aspect Leo by Rāśi Dṛṣṭi showing that some health issues may arise to elder siblings and may not live long. Lord Sun is joined three grahas of which one Venus is in Māraṇa Kāraka Sthāna. The native has two elder siblings.

The Drekkaṇa chart has Libra Lagna asking us to count the siblings in regular order. The eleventh house is lorded by Sun whose placement in Scorpio should have given an elder sister, yet the exchange of signs between Ketu and Sun reversed this to become an elder brother instead. The Papakartari of Mars and Saturn on Leo is detrimental and this brother did not live beyond the first year of his birth. The eleventh therefrom is Gemini whose lord Mercury is debilitated. The eldest child was a brother which the native has become enstranged from as Mercury is in the sixth house from Lagna.

This third house is lorded by Jupiter who is joined debilitated Mars and Venus indicating a younger sister. However treating the third house as the Lagna of the sister, the Lagna lord is placed in the 8th therefore and retrograde in its exaltation sign which is terrible for health, and on account of own accord. This younger sister did not live long out of own choice.

Chart 135: Eldest Sibling

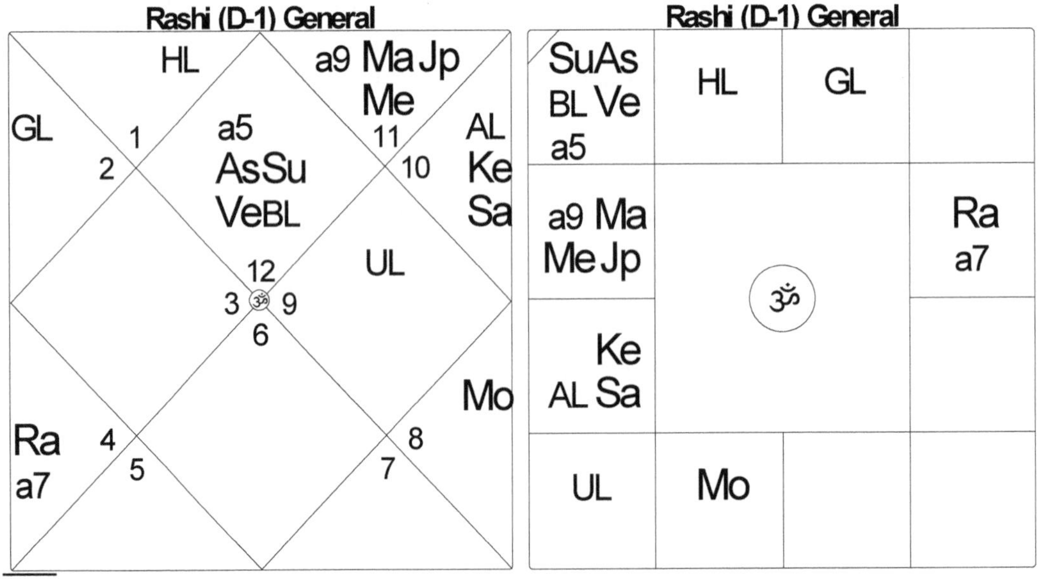

Male native born 28th March 1962, 6:29 AM, Kiri Buru, India.

In the chart, Ārūḍha Lagna falls in Capricorn an even sign. Normally we would count the siblings in reverse, however wherever Saturn is placed, it will make the counting go in forward/regular order. The younger siblings are indicated from Pisces whilst the elder one's are seen from Scorpio. Saturn is in Capricorn whilst Rāhu is in Cancer. They both have Rāśi dṛṣṭi on Scorpio, which is the sign of the elder siblings. The native is the eldest among his siblings. This is further justified being that the twelfth from Ārūḍha Lagna is lorded by Jupiter.

Chart 136: Eldest sibling - Drekkāṇa (D-3)

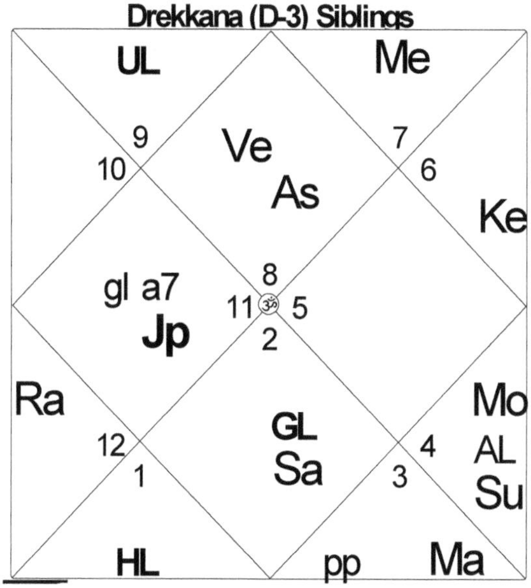

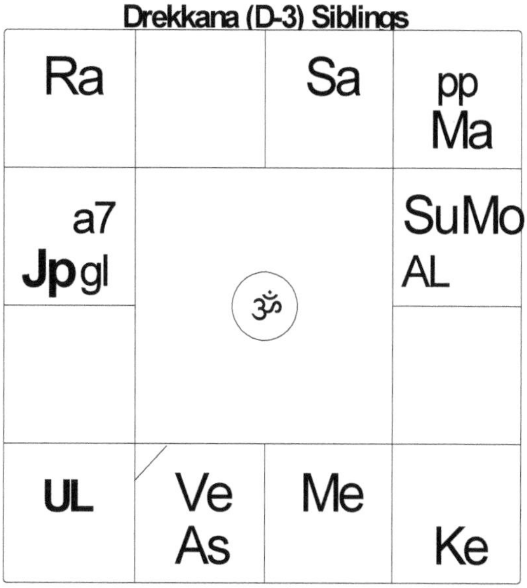

The younger siblings are examined from Pisces where the lord Jupiter is joined Mars and Mercury giving him two younger siblings.

The Drekkaṇa Lagna is Scorpio with Venus in it showing that he is the eldest sibling in his family. As the Lagna is an even sign the eleventh house will show the younger siblings. Virgo is the eleventh house and its lord Mercury is in Libra, a male sign, showing a younger brother. The eleventh therefrom is lorded over by the Moon and is joined the Sun suggesting the next sibling to be a brother as well.

Chart 137: Youngest Sibling

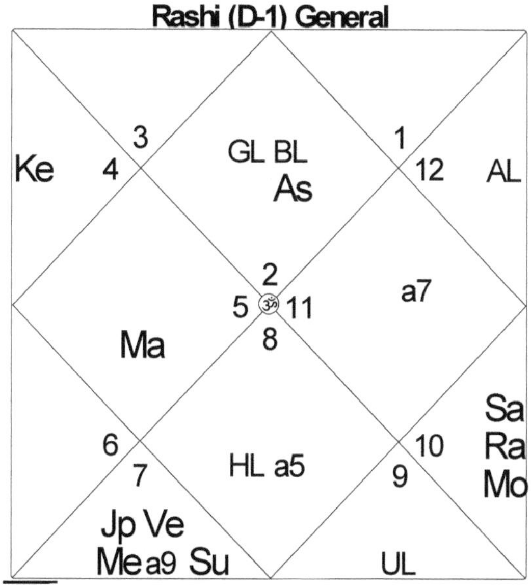

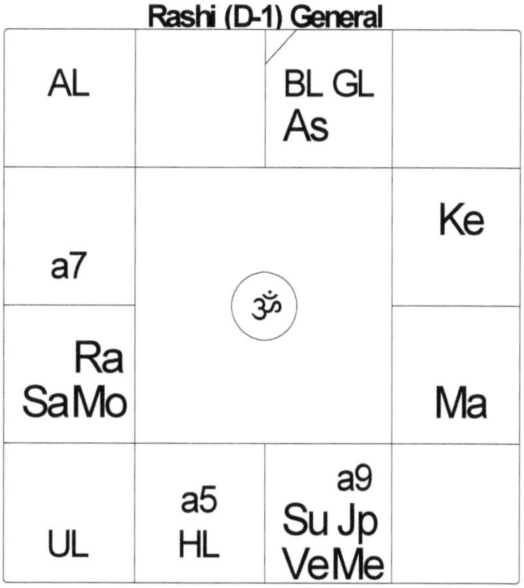

Male native born 12th November 1934, 6:19 PM, Cuttack, Orissa, India.

The Ārūḍha Lagna is in Pisces, so the elder siblings are seen from Taurus, whilst the younger will be seen from Capricorn. Saturn and Rāhu are in Capricorn with the Moon making the native is the youngest sibling. Saturn and Rāhu have Rāśi dṛṣṭi on Taurus, the house of elder siblings, but it did not deny the elder siblings, as Jupiter also has Rāśi dṛṣṭi on Taurus, ensuring the birth of elder siblings. The native has six elder siblings, of which two died prematurely. Hence, Saturn and Rāhu had their way in destroying the co-born.

Having understood the possible combination for co-born, Jaimini gives us an additional combination for the destruction of the co-born: *When Saturn and Mars both aspect these houses (3rd/11th/1st/8th), the siblings will be destroyed.* In Chart 137 in addition to the influence of Saturn and Rāhu, there is the influence of Mars causing the destruction of co-born.

Chart 138: Female - Eldest Sibling

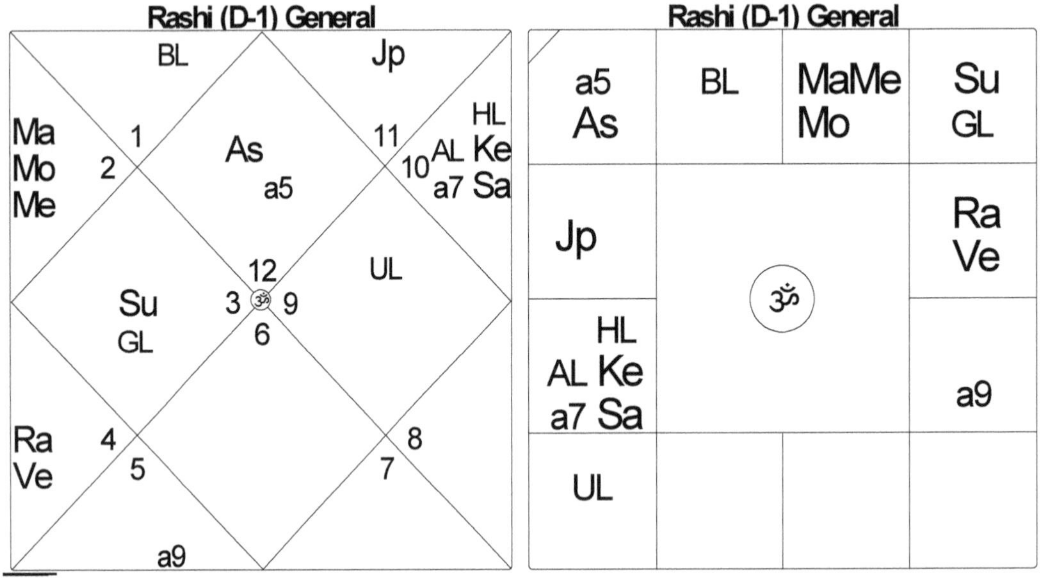

Chart of a lady born 30th June 1962, 0:13 AM, Calcutta, India.

Ārūḍha Lagna falls in Capricorn but the native is not the eldest sibling. Therefore treat Cancer as the Ārūḍha Lagna. Cancer has Venus and again should have made her the eldest however the parivartana between Moon and Venus brings elder siblings. The eleventh house from the Ārūḍha Lagna will show the elder siblings as the Ārūḍha is in an even sign and the chart is of a lady. Similarly the third from AL will show the younger siblings.

Taurus will show the elder siblings and the aspect of Rāhu, Mars and Saturn on the sign does not bode well for the health of elder siblings, whereas Moon and Mercury are protecting the same. The lord of Taurus reveals the count of siblings and Venus is joined Rāhu and aspected by Mars, Moon, Mercury and Jupiter. Being in the twelfth house from Lagna Jupiter is ignored in this case and she has four elder brothers. Mars in Rāśi Sandhi indicated one elder brother who passed away from a type of brain fever, whereas the other siblings are healthy and greatly successful.

The third from Ārūḍha Lagna is Virgo and should have brought younger siblings. However, Mars in the third from Lagna is not auspicious and she is the youngest in the family.

If Venus aspects/joins the 1st or eighth houses it will also destroy the pregnancy in the mother's womb (making one the eldest). This will occur in case of the eleventh house. If Venus is in the third house it will make one the youngest instead. This will not occur if Venus lords the houses of siblings, as it then takes on the objective of protecting the siblings.

10.2 The Seventh House

One of the most popular subjects in astrology (and the world) is marriage and relationships. The steps to analyze these are delicate and require careful approach. A house, which needs to be focused on, is the sixth house, which tends to obstruct relations from happening and cause separations. This and other relevant houses, such as the all-important Upapada, have been covered in this section.

10.2.1 Houses of Celibacy

The house responsible for celibacy is the sixth house, and the end of celibacy is the beginning of relationships, hence the seventh house is the māraka or "end" of the sixth house. It is the strength of the sixth house or its lord, which denies/delays marriage and causes separation. The sixth lord's position in a Kendra from Lagna will cause circumstances of separation between the native and their partner, whilst the trines indicate an unconscious prayer/desire for celibacy or prayers to celibate deities. The specific house will indicate the area of the problem.

Similarly, the placement of the seventh lord will enforce partnerships, or indicate the wish for the same. The placement of the seventh lord in the tenth house will give many relationship opportunities as this causes Jarā Yoga, giving excessive relationships. This will continue after marriage, and can cause problems. This also applies to the conjunction of the seventh and tenth lord. If on the contrary the seventh lord is in the sixth house it can cause separation for the couple as the spouse becomes inimical towards the native. The spouse may have a child with another, if the fifth lord is also involved here.

10.2.2 Bringing the Spouse/Marriage

The seventh house, its lord and its Kāraka must be analyzed to determine the native's ease in getting into relationships. See the relationship between the seventh lord and Venus. Mutual Kendra/trikoṇa placement is auspicious. Mutual 3rd/11th placement indicates some hardships or trials, whilst 2nd /12th and 6th /eighth mutual placement are inauspicious and causing a complete mismatch in circumstances between the native and his partner. If the seventh lord is Venus itself, then the relationship between seventh house and Venus should be reckoned using the same rules as above.

Delay in marriage or lack of partnerships will often arise as the result of a wrong attitude towards marriage, i.e. some shock or sorrow arising out of past relationships. This is caused by malefics influencing the seventh house by their graha or Rāśi dṛṣṭi. If malefics instead affect Venus, then the partners will have a wrong attitude/ phobia, which causes fear of rejection, anger, etc. If instead neither of the above is present and instead the Bādhakeśa is in the seventh or the seventh lord is in the Bādhaka sthāna, the native will face intolerable obstacles in attempting to marry, and marriage will be delayed. The native should hold dances/parties/festivals to appease this problem.

To see where one will meet the spouse and in which direction, the seventh lord from Venus should be examined. If the planet is in a movable sign the native must travel far to meet the spouse. Similarly reckon dual and fixed signs. The planets joining the lord will indicate the direction one needs to travel in order to meet the spouse. These should be seen in Rāśi or Navāṁśa depending on whichever is stronger. The seventh lord from Upapada must be reckoned in order to identify that which attracts the spouse. This does not change for subsequent relationships/marriages, and is a general indicator of what attracts/repels the spouse. Treating this planet as Lagna, if malefics are in the second house it will cause repulsion on account of ugliness. Saturn will indicate an ugly face whilst Rāhu can indicate repulsive teeth, especially if associated with Jupiter. Benefics will cause the opposite and attract. Worshipping this lord can enhance one's attractiveness.

Similarly, the trait one is attracted to in the spouse is seen from the seventh house.

- Sun in the seventh house, will give interest in a proud spouse, interested in reading, and hence learned.
- Moon in the seventh will give interest in a fair and emotional spouse. The native will have a wandering mind and will be constantly attracted to sex.
- Mars in the seventh house will give aggressive desires, and can cause interest in a short-tempered and maybe even short-lived spouse. Saturn and Jupiter may remove the evil of such a placement and calm down the fire caused by Mars, otherwise it could result in three marriages. There is sorrow related to marriage, due to the argalā of Mars on the fourth house.
- Mercury in the seventh house gives interest in a young intelligent, talkative and artistic spouse, but who may be promiscuous and make the native associate with other partners, unless Jupiter aspects the seventh house. If Moon is in trines or aspects Mercury, then low morals are indicated, while Saturn and Venus associated with Mercury can give a barren spouse.
- Jupiter in the seventh house is very auspicious and the native becomes lucky in choosing the right partners. The spouse is learned, intelligent and easily removes enmity and strife. There is fortune after marriage.
- Venus in the seventh house can give strange sexual appetites, and even association with prostitutes due to the rise of sensual desire, if Mercury and Ketu are involved. The spouse is sensual, artistic and very beautiful and has

very good manners.

- Saturn in the seventh can give interest in an industrious spouse, however older than normally expected and detached.
- Rāhu in the seventh house will give enmity towards the spouse, who will be short tempered and have a liking for war and fights, and behave like an evil spirit (piśāca). Such a placement could cause liaisons with prostitutes as well, provided the seventh is not a benefic sign nor aspected by Jupiter.
- Ketu in the seventh could cause disinterest in marriage, and even deny it. Marriage takes place with some difficulty and feels like a curse to the native, just as Gaṇeśa did not desire to marry.

Planets aspecting the seventh house will give the same results.

10.2.3 The Spouse

The state of the spouse is seen from the seventh lord and Venus. If both are afflicted then the spouse will incur some physical suffering. Should the affliction of these two arise in the Navāṁśa then physical suffering will arise after marriage. The involvement of other lordships/houses with the seventh lord indicates when the suffering will come, i.e. fifth lord may indicate childbirth while the sixth lord can indicate enmity or fights.

The Ārūḍha of the twelfth house, which is called the Upapada, will determine the Lagna of the spouse one wishes to marry. One has to determine the stronger between the Upapada, its trines as well as its lord. In cases where the seventh from Upapada is stronger than the Upapada, the trines to the seventh from Upapada should be reckoned instead. For example, if Libra is the Upapada, then the stronger between Aries and Libra must be reckoned. If Aries is stronger, then the Lagna of the spouse can be either of the fiery signs or a sign-placement of Mars. This can be applied to the other Ārūḍha padas, i.e. the Ārūḍha of the seventh house (A7) will indicate the Lagna of one's girl/boy friend, or partners in short-term relationships. If A7 strongly associates with the Upapada then the relationship matures into marriage. The amount of planets lording/joining or aspecting the Upapada indicates the number of people competing to become the spouse. In a modern, monogamous society, more spouses imply broken marriages; the second spouse is seen from the eighth sign from the Upapada, whilst the third spouse is seen from the eighth sign there from, i.e. third sign from Upapada. Similarly, subsequent spouses are seen in this manner.

Having found the Lagna of the spouse, the traits of the spouse can be ascertained from the predominant influences upon these. The second from Upapada will indicate the ailments suffered by the spouse and should be determined in a similar manner as the second from Lagna/pāka Lagna/Ārūḍha Lagna.

10.2.4 Marriage

Having found the spouse, marriage is the next step. It should however be kept in mind that finding a spouse does not imply marriage. To see whether the relationship will result in marriage, the Upapada and its lord must be seen.

- If the Upapada is afflicted by malefics, in a malefic sign, without any benefic involvement the native may not marry at all. A single benefic's involvement may alter this.
- If the Lord of the Upapada is defeated in planetary war or severely afflicted, or placed in the twelfth house, the native will not marry that person, and one should analyze the eighth from Upapada to ascertain the prospects of the next marriage.

Some additional clues are given:

- If the lord of Upapada is involved in a curse, the relationship will be a traumatic experience and will not result in marriage.
- If the curse mentioned before involves the Lagna lord and Ātmakāraka, the native will not enter a new relationship as a result of the trauma.

In-laws who openly oppose the marriage are seen from the seventh from Upapada, the planets placed there will indicate the people, i.e. Moon indicates mother in-law, whilst Sun indicates father in-law, Venus indicates sister in-law, etc. Similarly, the Bādhaka sthāna and its lord from the Upapada should be seen. The children arising from the relationship should be seen from the ninth from Upapada.

10.2.5 Sustenance of Marriage

The end of marriage is inevitable and the question is how it ends. The eighth house from the Lagna and the second from Upapada should be seen for the sustenance of marriage. If the second from Upapada has strong benefic influences, the marriage will last. Malefic influences will do otherwise unless they are strong, i.e. exalted or own sign. Similarly, debilitated or inimical benefics will cause problems. Strong benefics in the second from Upapada, will support the marriage, but can cause separation in the marriage if they are inimical towards the planets in/lording the Upapada, i.e. Rāhu in Upapada and Jupiter in the second. Ārūḍha padas in or aspecting the second from Upapada will indicate those people who may disturb the marriage. If A7 is involved these may be other partners/relationships, while A6 can indicate one's enemies.

The second lord from Upapada will indicate what is required to sustain the marriage. Its weakness can break the marriage, as the requirement becomes too high, whilst its strength indicates that little effort is needed to please it. Worship of this planet as Vishnu/Lakṣmī will ensure the sustenance of the marriage. If the future of the marriage seems to be dark, it is the eighth house from Lagna that should be analyzed to examine how the marriage breaks. Malefics placed here or if unoccupied or being lorded by malefics, can cause the end of the marriage through fights, sadness, shock, etc. benefics will cause a smooth and easy break. If the ninth house is associated with the eighth house, then the end of marriage could happen through the death of the spouse, as the ninth house shows the fighting strength of the spouse (third from seventh) and its association with the eighth house will end the life of the spouse prematurely.

10.2.6 Case Studies

Chart 139: Unmarried

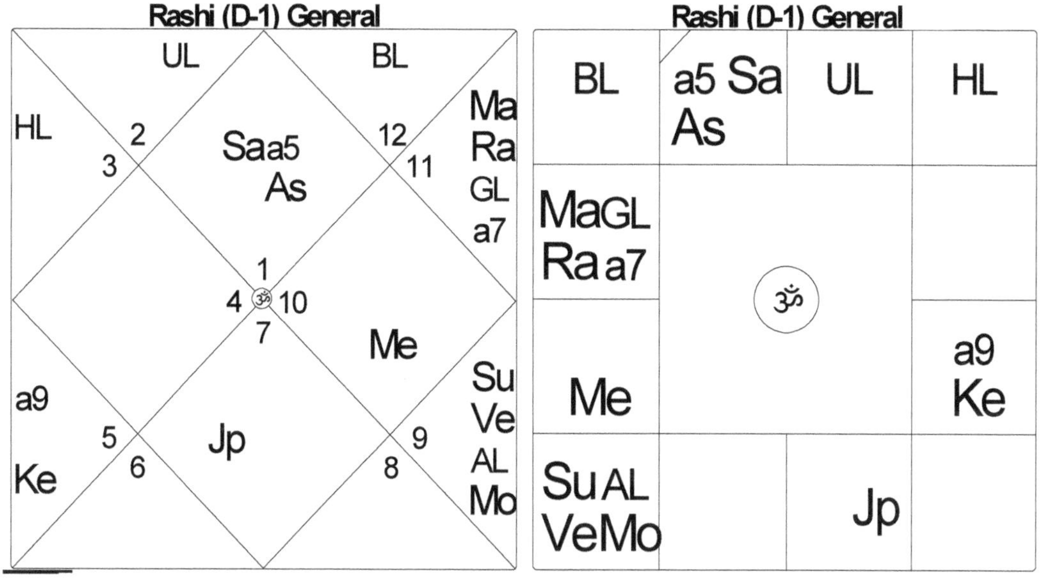

Female native born 6th January 1970, 12:52 PM, Nagpur, India.

The native has seventh lord in the ninth house, indicating a person who will go to the extent of doing sādhanā to get married as ninth house is the house of sādhanā and tapasyā. The sixth lord has gone to the tenth house, and as a result, she is yet to marry, but had broken relationships behind her. The native is employed at present. The seventh lord from Venus is Mercury and is retrograde, which will cause a delay in bringing the spouse. When the twelfth house from the Moon is the second or eighth house a risk of delay until forty-four exists and remedies are required to bring the marriage earlier. Because of the placement of the sixth lord, the native was advised to take more time away from work.

Chart 140: Unmarried

Male native born 22nd August 1962, 1:25 AM, Darbañga, India.

The native has seventh lord in the ninth house and attempted remedies to get married. The sixth lord is in Lagna, and whilst the native is a charming person the relationships break early due to reasons he cannot explain. The sixth lord in the Lagna implies that the appearance or behaviour can cause repulsion at times, due to circumstances beyond the native's control. This will especially be so during the transit of malefic planets over the native's Lagna. The seventh lord from Venus is Jupiter who is retrograde, which will delay the arrival of the future spouse. This Jupiter is also the twelfth lord from Moon again posing the delay.

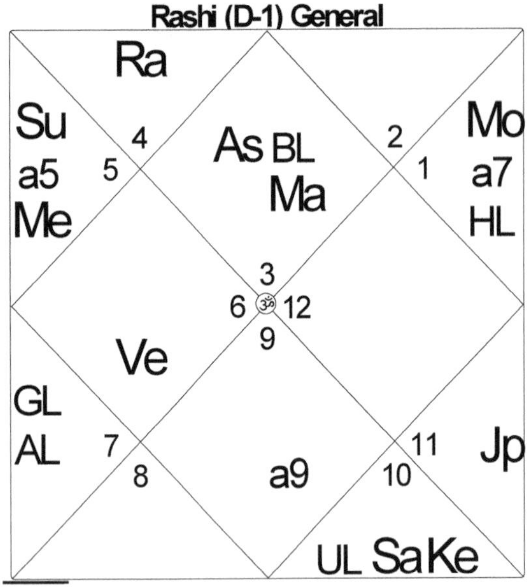

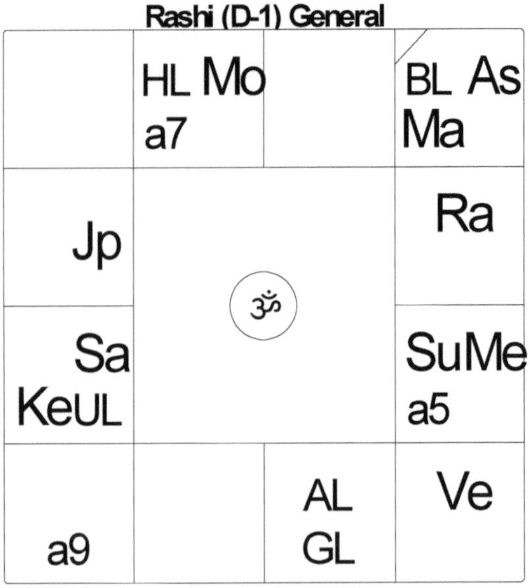

Chart 141: Long term marriage

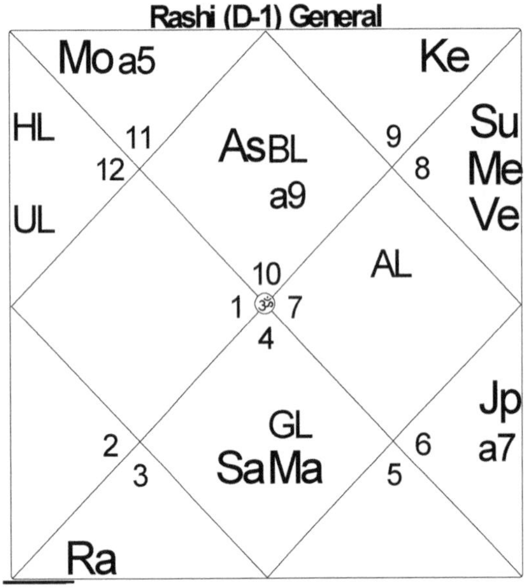

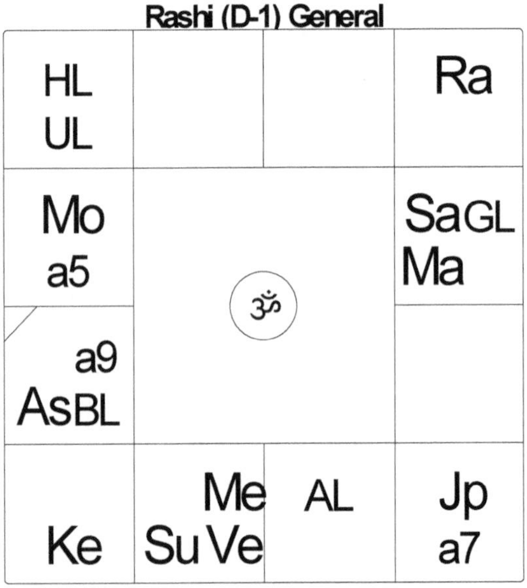

Male native born 12th December 1945, 12 PM, Sindal, Denmark.

The seventh house is occupied by Saturn and Mars, where Mars is trying to delay marriage as Saturn is removing the delay of Mars. Venus is well placed from both Moon and the seventh house showing a positive attitude and promise of happy marriage.

The sixth lord Mercury is placed in the eleventh house which is of no detriment towards marriage; however friends can give wrong advice to the native in matters of relationships.

The Upapada is placed in Pisces as its lord is well placed in the ninth house of fortune suggesting fortune after marriage and the birth of children (Jupiter in ninth house). As Jupiter also lords over the twelfth house the spouse may come from a foreign country. With the Virgo being stronger than Pisces the spouse may have her Lagna in an earthy sign or Cancer (Saturn in Cancer); her Lagna is Capricorn with Jupiter in it. Jupiter is further well placed from the Navāṁśa Lagna promoting the marriage to take place.

With Mars in the seventh house marriage is advised only after the 29th year, whereas Mars itself presides over the 27th and 28th years of age. Twelfth lord from Moon is Saturn and joined Mars making his meeting with his future spouse in his 27th year. The seventh lord Venus is Venus itself, and is also lord of the tenth house causing the workplace to be the cause of their meeting. Venus is placed in the eleventh house making the event a social function of the companies they worked for at the time.

Two years later in the 29th year in September 1974 the couple married, true to Mars' placement in the seventh house.

The second lord from Upapada is Mars who is debilitated in the seventh house. Initially the marriage met with resistance from the wife's family. Mercury is the seventh lord and is joined Sun showing that the father-in-law was spearheading the resistance. With fifth and sixth lords placed in the Badhaka Sthāna, prayers could have been made to break up the relationship. However, the Bādhaka Sthāna has mainly auspicious planets and the native and his spouse were able to persevere beyond any scrutiny of the inlaws.

Mars is further retrograde in its debilitation sign and thus acts as if exalted! Thus beyond any expectations the marriage is long lasting. The Yāma Yoga suggests longevity of the marriage until demise. The couple celebrated 30 years of marriage in September 2004.

Chart 142: Problematic Relationships
Male born 9th October 1976, 10:06 PM, Vineland, NJ, USA.

The seventh house in the native's chart is empty, and is aspected by Mercury and Sun. These are very auspicious planets as far as relationships are concerned, and indicate a good attitude towards these things. The seventh lord Jupiter is in the twelfth house, and this is no more inauspicious than the bad relationships between the seventh lord and Venus. Venus is in the sixth from seventh lord, indicating a lack of compatibility between the native and his partners.

The native is a very spiritual person who practices a lot of penance. He tends to practice penance at times when his partners seek his company, and when he seeks their company, they are not seeking his, or he misunderstands their intentions. A lack of compatibility is indicated. As Venus lords both the sign in which Jupiter and Venus itself are posited, the remedy lies in pleasing Venus. Moreover, Mars and Rāhu afflict Venus, indicating that the partners will have problems in their attitude towards relationships, or even have problems upon entering the relationship. As

Rashi (D-1) General

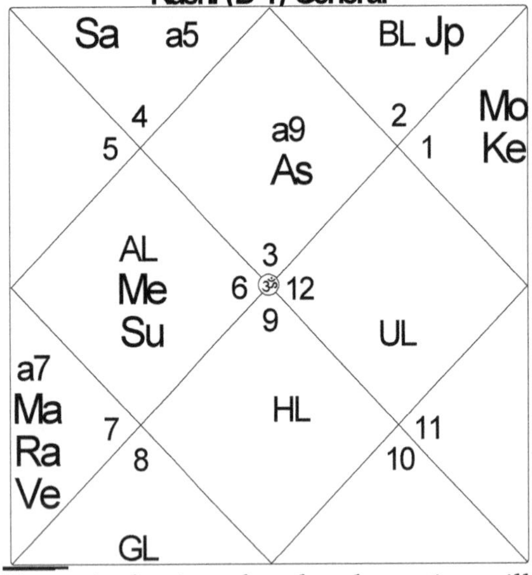

Rashi (D-1) General

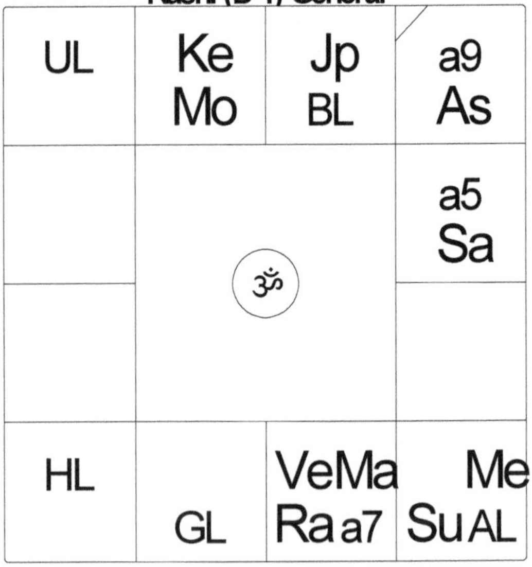

Venus is the Atmakāraka, the native will definitely face such scenarios in their life, and must worship the Iṣṭa Devatā to avoid such unpleasant situations.

The native has had relationships with women who have become mentally unbalanced during the relationship, or have expressed immense pain or sorrow. Venus, Mars and Rāhu are in Libra with A7, indicating that these relationships will be short lasting. Upapada in Pisces indicates marriage at a very mature age, and that too to a very spiritual person. The lord of Upapada is in twelfth house, which can indicate marriage to one from a poor background or first marriage does not happen. The person had a long term relationship earlier which did not result in marriage. Their second relationship is seen from the eighth from Pisces, i.e. Libra where Venus is in own sign, and being the Chara Ātmakāraka promises marriage. However a curse exists on Venus due to the conjunction of Mars and Rāhu making the marriage difficult to sustain, yet will bring a child as this is the fifth house from Lagna. The couple married and obtained a daughter.

Mars and Ketu lord over the second house from the Upapada and will indicate the length of marriage and its problems. Mars dominates being equipped with a body, and is involved in the curse suggesting problems in maintaining the marriage. Mars indicates quarrels and significant differences in opinion. Mars being in Libra with Venus suggests that the disagreement is regarding intimacy and love. As the eighth lord in Navāṁśa is Venus and is placed in the eighth house itself, the breakage of marriage occurs due to problems with love and intimacy.

Mars is further in third house in Navāṁśa which will cause considerable trials in making the marriage work and the couple will end up having turf wars with each other. Mars is in Libra Rāśi and Sagittarius Navāṁśa suggesting that after three years of marriage the couple would begin to become independent of each other. Following three years of marriage the couple decided not to continue the marriage, despite attempts of both parties to reconcile their differences. Considerable differences further exist in deciding the custody of their child.

Chart 129: Loss of Partner

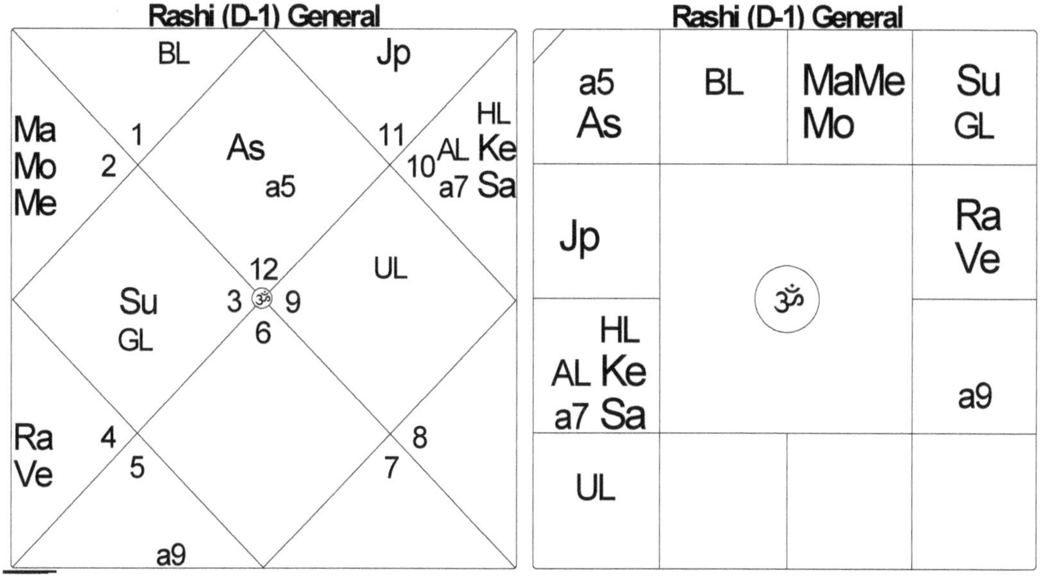

The native has the sixth lord placed in the fourth house. Ever since childhood, the native's mother has been advising the native not to marry, and to turn towards spiritual life. The native has had a few broken relationships as well. When the eighth and ninth lords associate, it can cause the premature demise of the spouse. The natives ninth lord Mars and eighth lord Venus are aspecting each other's houses by Rāśi dṛṣṭi. The native lost a potential spouse to a cerebral hemorrhage.

Chart 143: Broken Relationship

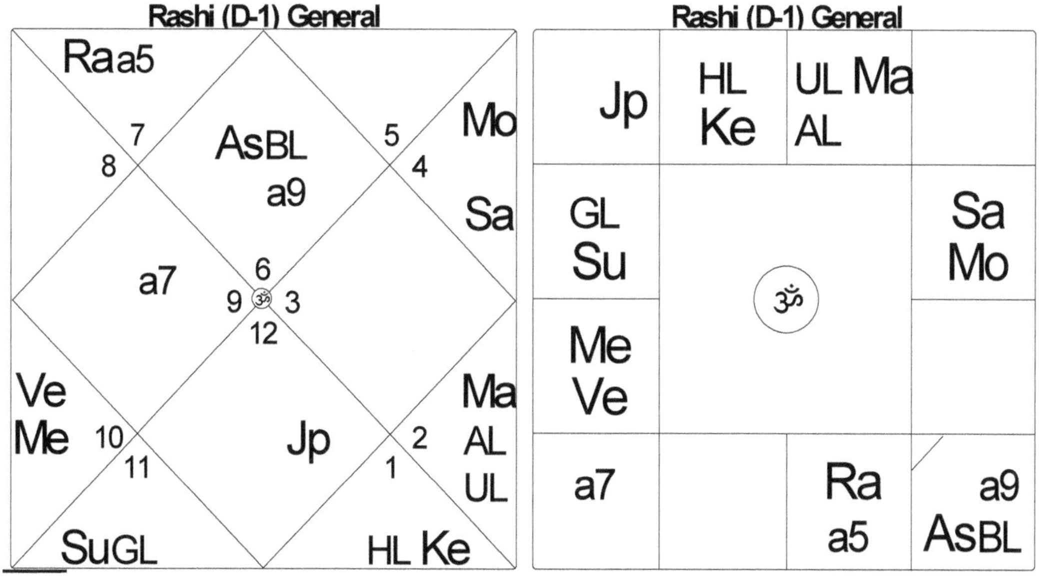

Male born 14th February 1976, 9:29 PM, Elmer, NJ, USA.

In the given chart, the Lagna lord is in the fifth house promising misfortune in begetting children. The second lord is involved as well. Jupiter is well placed both from Lagna and from the fifth lord, indicating no significant problems regarding children. The Upapada is in the ninth house whilst its lord is joined Mercury indicating a relationship during education. As the lord of Upapada is in Rāśi Sandhi, the relationship will not manifest in marriage. The ninth from the Upapada has Mercury and Venus while Saturn is the lord of the same, indicating denial of children from this relationship. However Moon is joined Saturn and will try to give a child, but this same child will not survive as Saturn causes the destruction of the Moon. The native's girlfriend had an abortion due to Saturn, Mercury and Venus denying children. As Mercury is also the second lord from Upapada, it caused the end of the relationship as well. Mercury's ability to cause the end of the relationship had a negative impact on the native's health, as Mercury is Lagna lord, making him suffer from tuberculosis following the termination of the relationship.

Chart 144: Denial of Marriage

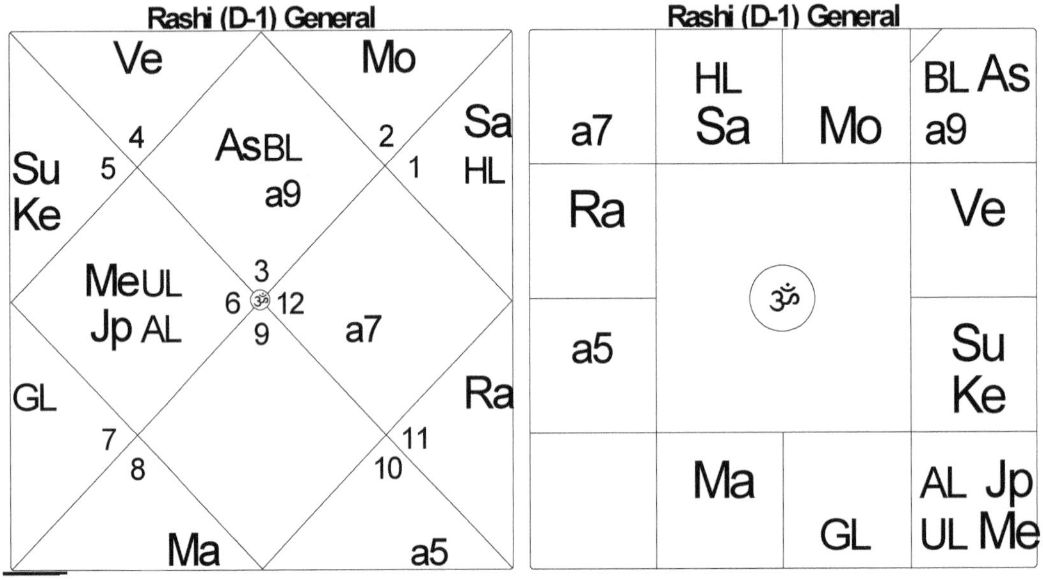

Male born 4th September 1969, 1:50 AM, New Delhi, India

The seventh house is unoccupied whilst its lord is joined Mercury, indicating an attraction towards young, artistic, learned women. The relationship between seventh lord and Venus is 3/11, indicating that some effort is needed to get involved in relationships, but no severe obstruction is there. The seventh house does not receive the dṛṣṭi of any malefics and the native has a good attitude towards marriage and relationships. Venus is suffering the affliction of Mars and Rāhu (Rāśi dṛṣṭi) indicating some anger and deception/shock directed towards the native by the partner(s), and being in a watery sign puts him in Tṛṣita avasthā, giving the native a strong desire or longing for relationships. This is tempered by the auspicious glance of the Moon in exaltation (Rāśi dṛṣṭi) which will give him comfort and remove the Tṛṣita avasthā. The seventh lord from Venus is Saturn who is in a movable sign in Rāśi but a fixed sign in Navāṁśa. The Navāṁśa is stronger due to Saturn's debility in Rāśi, indicating that the spouse maybe found in the same town/province in the western direction (Saturn).

The Upapada is in the fourth house indicating a spouse in one's home or family. As Jupiter and Mercury are joined in the Upapada this can indicate the same school or Gurukul, as the student (Mercury) and teacher (Jupiter) are together. Jupiter and Mercury have Rāśi dṛṣṭi on the fourth from Ārūḍha Lagna indicating that the native belongs to a large organization/family of the spiritual order, Jupiter. The native is a devotee of the Rāmakṛṣṇa Mission, where he met his partner. Next step is to analyze the Upapada and its lord to determine whether the marriage will happen or not. The lord of Upapada is Mercury and is joined the Upapada with Jupiter. This may seem auspicious; however Jupiter and Mercury are joined within one degree, indicating a planetary war. Jupiter having more degrees causes Mercury to be the defeated one, and so the marriage did not happen, though the native tried his best it left him in a state of sorrow/rejection.

The eighth from Upapada is the second marriage, which is Aries. Aries is joined Saturn (older lady), and whilst it is aspected only by malefics, Rāhu, Mars, Sun and Ketu, Sun will protect the marriage, as will Ātmakāraka Mars. Mars is in the sixth house and will require that there be celibacy in the marriage. The second from Upapada has an exalted Moon indicating that the marriage will be hard to break, as its lord Venus is in parivartana with the Moon ensuring the longevity of the marriage. The native married another devotee of the organization because of the sorrow encountered from the previous relationship. The spouse would marry only on the condition of celibacy in the marriage, and although the native agreed, he discovered later on that this was not in agreement with his ideals. The native tried to break the marriage but unsuccessfully. Venus is the second lord from Upapada showing intimacy as the requirement to sustain and also the cause of breakage of the relationship. Being in eighth house in Navāṁśa shows the desire to break the relationship.

Chart 145: John Forbes Kerry – Divorce

John Forbes Kerry, born 11st December 1943, 8:07 AM, Aurora, CO, USA.

The US Democratic Presidential candidate for the 2005 elections is in his second marriage. The seventh lord is Venus and the relationship between the seventh house and Venus should be reckoned. Venus is in the sixth from the seventh indicating that the spouse will usually meet him with desires for battle/change/rebellion. There would also be a significant incompatibility between him and his spouse. Venus receives the dṛṣṭi of Saturn, indicating that some sorrow will be experience by him in relationships. The seventh house is afflicted by Mars, Rāhu and Ketu, but exalted Moon is there protecting the native from too much conflict in that area.

The Upapada is in the ninth house with Rāhu. Moon has Rāśi dṛṣṭi on Rāhu indicating Śakti yoga, or the yoga for destruction. Rāhu has Rāśi dṛṣṭi on Mars and Sun, indicating that the destruction of wars/anger and the removal of the government heads was on the agenda when the marriage happened. The native married just after attempting to join congress on an anti-war platform in 1970. Although he fought

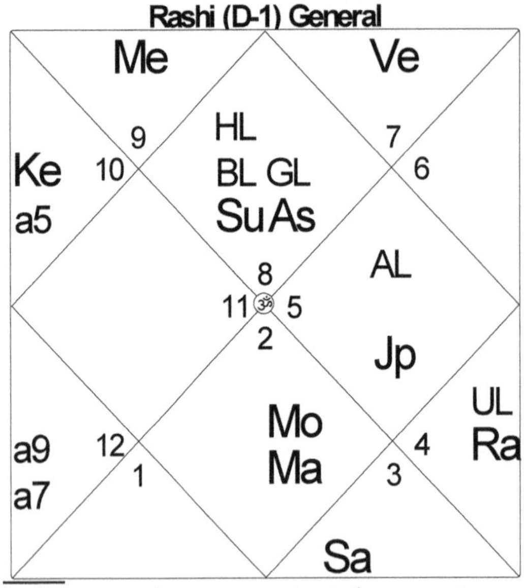

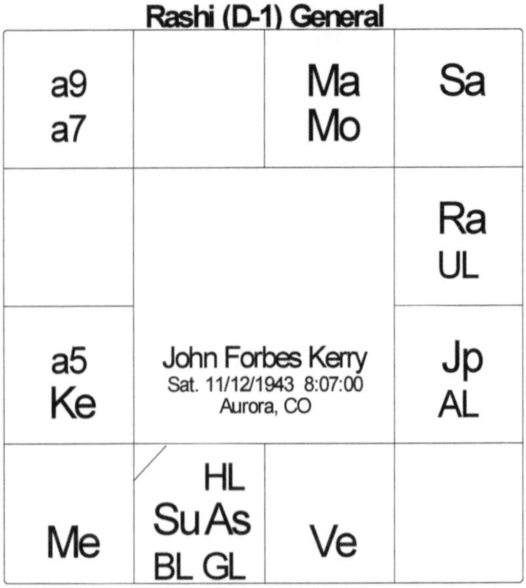

in Vietnam, he was against the ongoing war. In 1971, he became a leader in the organization of "Vietnam Veterans against the War." Jupiter is in the second from Upapada and joined in the Ārūḍha Lagna, hence there would be a very big difference in the ideals of the native and that of his spouse. This would cause separation in marriage, but Jupiter is strong in Leo, which makes a marriage last for at least sixteen years. After eighteen years of marriage (1988), the native was formally divorced. The eighth house from Upapada is Aquarius and it has Lord Saturn in Rāśi Sandhi and retrograde; it may be inferred that another relationship occurred after marriage, which did not last long and failed to culminate in marriage. The eighth there-from is Virgo whose lord Mercury is in Dhana yoga in the second house, indicating a very wealthy wife. The spouse had inherited a large fortune from her former husband. The ninth from Virgo is Taurus housing Mars while Venus is in Saturn's Navāṁśa, indicating adopted children from this marriage. Venus is strong in own sign in the second house from Virgo, Libra, indicating a long lasting marriage.

Chart 146: Hurtful Relationships
Male born 14th January 1981, 7:52 PM, New Delhi, India.

The native came to this author with a query regarding a relationship and its future. The native also mentioned the pain he had suffered because of the partner and had a suspicion that the partner was deceiving him. The Ārūḍha Lagna is in Libra, and the seventh lord from Libra is Mars whilst the Chara Dārakāraka is the Sun. Both are in the fourth from Ārūḍha Lagna, among which Mars is more inauspicious for the native's happiness, though the exaltation of Mars promises prosperity. It becomes pertinent to analyze Mars in the Navāṁśa to determine which spouse Mars indicates.

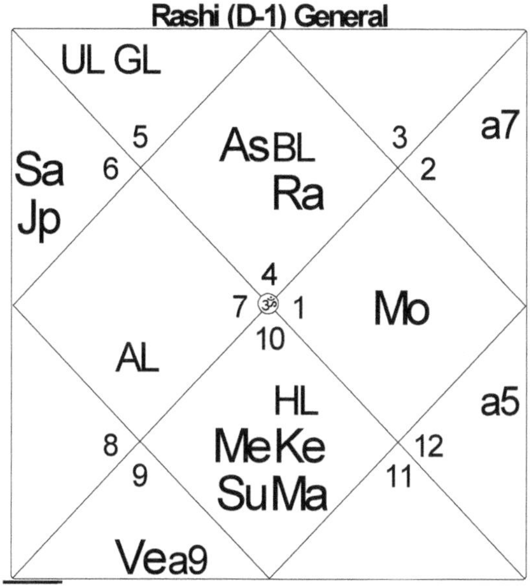

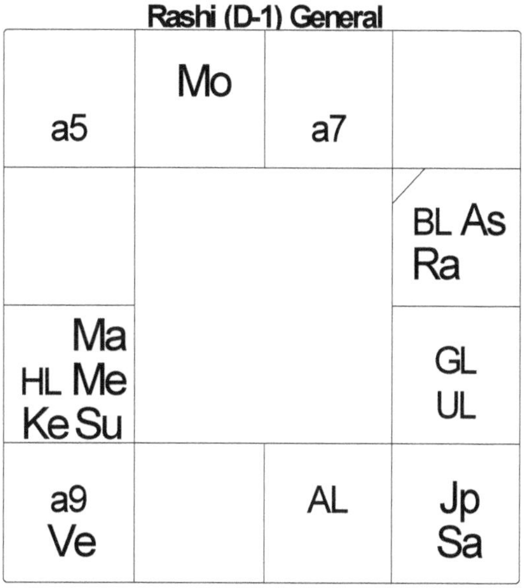

Chart 147: Hurtful relationships - Navāṁśa (D-9)

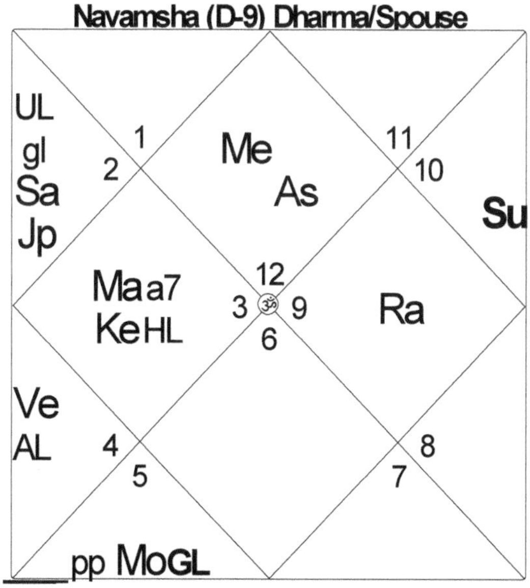

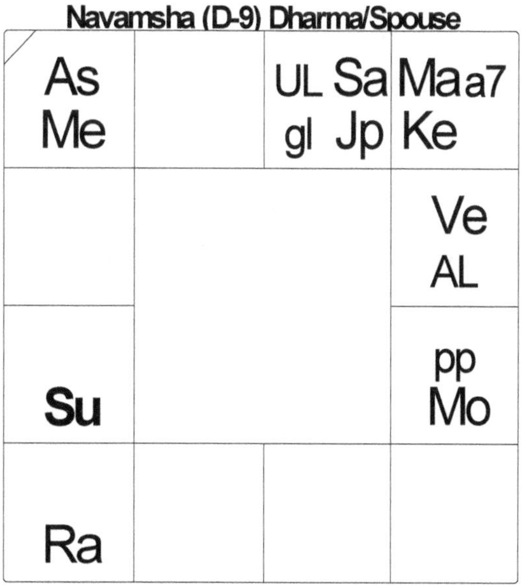

The seventh house in Navāṁśa is Virgo, and Mars is not in trines, nor does he own them. The second house is the next spouse and it is Aries, lorded by Mars, hence the native is talking about his second major relationship. The native indicated that he had not married before but had a serious relationship earlier. This is seen from the Upapada in Rāśi being lorded by the Sun, placed in Rāśi Sandhi. Sankrānti doṣa will arise in the first relationship and not result in marriage. In the Navāṁśa, the position of Mars must be analyzed. Mars is placed in the fourth house in Navāṁśa with Ketu causing the native to be deceived/cheated due to Kapaṭa yoga (refer: **4.2 Tatkālika (temporary) Sambandha**). The native was not wrong in his suspicions regarding the partner. We can hence confirm that the native is talking about their second relationship and we must analyze the eighth from Upapada in the Rāśi to understand the future of this relationship.

In the Rāśi, the eighth from Upapada is Pisces. Pisces is unoccupied and it was confirmed that the partner has Scorpio Lagna, which is in trines to Pisces. The lord of Pisces, Jupiter, who is joined Saturn in the third house, will determine the result of this relationship. Jupiter and Saturn are within one-degree range, and are in a planetary war. Although Jupiter is winning the battle as it has higher degrees, it is also in the Māraṇa Kāraka Sthāna, and indicates that whilst there will often be intense fights, between the native and his partner, he will be proven right. The marriage will not happen because of Jupiter's placement in the Māraṇa Kāraka Sthāna, creating a difficult situation. Usually deception begins in Daśā related to Rāhu, and the native was running Moon-Rāhu- Rāhu when the deceptions started. When Jupiter's Pratyantaradaśā came in Moon-Rāhu-Jupiter, the native's suspicion started and he sought the authors help in order to understand the situation. An important observation is the placement of Ātmakāraka Mars in the seventh house. The native was advised to begin worship to appease the malignant influences that this may have on his relationships.

10.3 The Eleventh House

The eleventh house is an often-misunderstood house. It is associated with gain, i.e. gain of objectives and articles. At the same time it is associated with punishment, as it is the sixth from the sixth i.e. the manifestation of punishment. These two extremes require explanation.

Table 72: Eleven Miseries

	Form	Meaning
1	Deva	The presiding deity
2	Dharmadeva	The deity enforcing justice
3	Phaṇi (Sarpa)	Serpents and nature
4	Pitṛ	Parents and ancestors
5	Guru	Ones preceptor
6	Brahmaṇa	Priests, astrologers and seers of God
7	Preta	The recently demised
8	Bhūta	Ghosts
9	Dṛṣṭi	Evil eye
10	Śāpa	Curses from past lives
11	Abhicāra	Black magic or enemy action

The deity who sits in the eleventh house is Śrī Hara, an aspect of Śiva as the one who ends the material creation. The objective of Hara is to give life force to the person, causing them to live in this world. When the native uses up this life-force or prāṇa, then their presence in this world is over, and Śri Hara leaves them. The yoga scriptures propagate eating less to live longer. At the time of leaving the native, Śri Hara is called Śri Rudra, as he causes people to cry and weep upon his leaving. This is why the eleventh divisional chart (D-11) is also called the Rudrāṁśa. Understanding the evil of the eleventh house, the eleven forms of misery have been listed out by the author Harihara in his monumental work Praśna Mārga.

The seventh house shows one's desires, and the eleventh is the fifth there from indicating the future of such desires, namely the fulfilment or denial of the desires. Such a fulfilment is considered as a gain to the native, and the reason the eleventh house is called the *lābha bhāva*. The people/grahas in the eleventh house indicate those whom you attempt to fulfil your desires with and those who will support one's dreams about the future, thus becoming one's friends

Some hopes/desires are inauspicious and could cause harm to others whilst attempting to reap the fruits of one's desires. To account for our misdeeds the eleventh house also acts as the natural house of obstruction or Bādhaka. The natural sign of Bādhaka is Aquarius being the natural eleventh sign in the zodiac, and its lords (1) Saturn, tempts us, and punishes us after death and (2) Rāhu causes our rebirth to suffer the results of the Bādhaka.

As Rāhu is the cause of Bādhaka, the Sattvic Grahas, Sun, Moon and Jupiter as well as the benefics, Mercury and Venus, when in association with the Bādhakasthāna are able to overcome the Bādhaka through remedies.

10.3.1 Bādhaka: the source of obstacles

For the three types of signs the Bādhaka changes due to the motion and steps of Rāhu.

Table 73: Sign and Bādhaka

Sign	Bādhaka
Movable	Eleventh
Fixed	Ninth
Dual	Seventh

These Bādhaka signs and their lords cause obstacles in our life, which are seemingly impossible to rectify for the native. This is especially so if the planets are badly placed. If the planets are well placed and associated with the Bādhaka sign or lord, then the planets will instead work towards the removal of obstacles, and all the doors of opportunities will be opened to the native, although their will be some obstacles at first, though. As the Bādhaka acts like Rāhu the good results could be reaped through travel, foreigners or foreign destinations. The following table describes the various types of Bādhaka.

Table 74: Types of Bādhaka

Bādhaka	Cause
Deva Bādhaka	The deity has been disrespected or done ill towards
Sarpa Bādhaka	One has acted maliciously towards serpents and nature
Pitṛ Bādhaka	Mistreatment of parents earns this Bādhaka
Preta Bādhaka	One has not resolved one's issues with a demised individual
Dṛṣṭi Bādhaka	One ignites jealousy and begets evil eye of spirits seeking some sort of offering or sacrifice from one
Abhicāra	One is the target of black magic

Whilst a multitude of combinations indicate the type of Bādhaka, some pointers are given below to ascertain the Bādhaka. Readers are further recommended to study Praśna Mārga, by Harihara and Vedic Remedies in Astrology, by Pt. Sanjay Rath, where the entire knowledge of this section has been derived from.

1) **Deva Bādhaka** – Bādhakeśa must be ill placed, and malefics must afflict the twelfth there from.

2) **Sarpa Bādhaka** – Rāhu influencing Bādhaka or Bādhakeśa causes sarpa Bādhaka. If the Sun is associated, then the serpents are intent on long term good. They are intent on evil if associated with the Moon. If Jupiter is the Bādhakeśa and placed in a Kendra from Rāhu and in a duḥsthāna then the curse is from divine serpents. These are inferior serpents if Gulika is in a Kendra.

3) **Pitṛ Bādhaka** – Sun or Moon must be in the Bādhaka house or joined the Bādhakeśa, and placed in a sign or Navāṁśa of Mars or Saturn. The displeasure of the parents can further be analyzed by the placement of the sixth lord in fourth/ninth houses, or fourth/ninth lord in the twelfth house. Position of Sun or Moon in the sixth house, is also conducive towards displeasure of parents.

4) **Preta** Bādhaka – Gulika or Ketu joined the Bādhaka house or joined its lord, causes the Bādhaka. The malefic signs or planets associated with Gulika or Ketu indicate how the spirit died. If Gulika or Ketu are placed in the fourth house, the spirit is a relative, otherwise not.

5) **Dṛṣṭi Bādhaka** – There are three types of Dṛṣṭi Bādhaka based on the desire of the evil spirit: Ranthu (causing worries and ill health), Hanthu (intent on killing) and Bali (wanting a sacrifice).

   a. **Ranthu Kamas** – Bādhaka and Lagna should be associated.

   b. **Hanthu Kamas** – Bādhakeśa and Lagna associated with sixth or eighth house.

   c. **Bali Kamas** – Rāhu or Gulika placed in fourth, fifth, seventh or eighth houses causes this. If instead placed in the sixth house, then enemies are to blame.

6) **Abhicāra** – Bādhakeśa associated with the sixth lord causes this. If associated with the Lagna, then Hanthu Kamas is indicated (see above). Additionally the placement of the sixth lord in the first, seventh or twelfth houses causes this problem as well when Mars joins or has graha dṛṣṭi on the Lagna. Similarly Ketu in first, fourth or tenth houses cause danger of possession if Mars joins or has graha dṛṣṭi on the Lagna. Special observance of the positions of nodes and Saturn or nodes and Mars should be done as these ignite the malign desire of spirits.

Regardless of the type of Bādhaka, the reason for the problem comes from the placement of the Bādhakeśa. For example, in the case of Deva Bādhaka, should the Bādhakeśa be placed in the second or eleventh houses, the problems arise from the misappropriation of the deity's wealth. If instead the Bādhakeśa is placed in the Lagna, then the idol of the Bādhakeśa has been disfigured or otherwise misappropriated depending on the malefics placed in the twelfth from Bādhakeśa.

It is possible that two types of Bādhaka may be present. For example, for Pitṛ Bādhaka, the placement of Bādhakeśa in the sixth house can bring the anger of parents and also black magic. If the Lagneśa is also involved, the health of the native will suffer. In case of confusion, the main source of Bādhaka will depend on the worst placed among the planets in the Bādhaka house or the Bādhakeśa. These principles should be intelligently applied based on the type of Bādhaka.

10.3.2 Bādhaka remedies

The details and remedies for the Bādhaka are here by given:

10.3.2.1 Deva Bādhaka: wrath of deity

Based on the graha involved, one can estimate which deity is displeased with the native and is causing the Bādhaka.

Table 75: Deva Bādhaka

Graha	Condition	Deva
Jupiter	All signs	Nārāyaṇa and all deities
Sun	All signs	Śiva
	1st drekkāṇa of dual signs	Kartikeya
	2nd drekkāṇa of dual signs	Gaṇapati
Moon	Strong Moon	Durga
	Weak Moon	Bhadrakālī
	Weak and Martian sign	Camuṇḍī
Mars	Odd sign	Male deities like Kartikeya & Bhairava
	Even sign	Camuṇḍī, Bhadrakālī
Mercury	Movable & Dual sign	Śri Viṣṇu avatar

Graha	Condition	Deva
	1st and 2nd drekkāṇa of fixed signs	Śri Kṛṣṇa
Venus	Sattvic sign	Annapūrṇeśvarī
	Rajasic sign	Lakṣmī
	Tamasic sign	Yakṣī
Saturn	All signs	Sastha & Kiratha

Rāhu and Ketu are excluded from the list, as they indicate Sarpa and Preta Bādhaka respectively.

The deity's displeasure comes from the placement of the Bādhakeśa.

- Placement in the fourth house indicates that the temple or home of the deity has been disturbed.
- Placement in the Lagna indicates that the idol or image of the deity has been ruined. Malefics aspecting the Lagna, indicate how this has happened.
- Placement in the second or eleventh houses indicates that the wealth of the deity has been abused or misused. The nature of this wealth will be indicated by Lagna being a metal, plant or living being, based on the sign or planets therein.
- Placement in the eighth house shows disruption of the Tattva.

Similarly the other houses can be judged. If placed in the twelfth house, then there is no Bādhaka, and instead all obstacles will be removed.

Remedies should be performed for the specific deity based on the house and planets involved. The planet dispositing the Bādhakeśa will indicate that which must be offered to the deity in regular worship.

Table 76: Offering to deity[1]

	Dispositor	Element	Remedy
1	Sun/Mars	Agni (Fire)	Lamp, Candle
2	Venus/Moon	Jala (Water)	Milk, Ghee, Sweetmeats etc.
3	Mercury	Pṛthvī (Earth)	Sandalwood paste, perfumed oils etc.
4	Jupiter	Ākāśa (Ether)	Flowers, garland
5	Saturn	Vāyu (Air)	Incense, Dress, Ornaments etc.

Furthermore the karma one should do to alleviate this suffering, is indicated by the house of the Bādhakeśa. The various karmas are indicated below.

1 Praśna Mārga śloka 12, chapter 5. The above translation is by Sanjay Rath from his book, Vedic Remedies in Astrology.

Table 77: Karma to do[2]

House	Remedy		
	Posture	Transliteration	Translation
1	Standing	Pratibimbadāna	Gift of idol or picture
2	Riding	Japa	Mantra Japa
3	Sitting[1]	Pūjā	Worship
4	Sleeping	Dhāma	Renovation of temple.
5	Standing	Santarpana	Presentation of oil/gifts, clothes etc.
6	Walking	Pratikāra Bali	Remedial offerings & dedication
7	Dancing	Nṛtya	Dances to be performed for deity
8	Sleeping	Bhūta Bali or Pūjā	Worship of the Tattva or element
9	Standing	Devopāsanā	Worship of Dharma Devata
10	Crawling	Danti-Skanda Bali or Pūjā	Bali Karma or Pooja for Ganesha (or Subra-manya/ Kartikeya)
11	Sitting[2]	Tarpana	Ritual offerings & Dedication
12	Sleeping	Gītam-Vādya	No affliction. (But music & song may be offered).

Example: If Bādhakeśa Jupiter is placed in the fifth house in Scorpio, then a lamp must be offered and the presentation of oil/gifts to Nārāyaṇa is required.

10.3.2.2 Sarpa Bādhaka: wrath of serpents

The particular sign of Rāhu indicates the source of the curse.

Table 78: Source of Sapa Bādhaka

Sign	Effects	Remedy
Moveable	Destruction of serpent eggs	Donation of copper/gold eggs
Dual	The killing of baby serpents	Offering copper/gold baby snake idols
Fixed	Destruction of trees and homes of ser-pents	Planting of trees

The number of eggs, idols or trees to donate/offer is indicated by the Lagna. If Lag-na is a movable sign then eleven. Nine should be offered incase of fixed Lagnas, and seven should be donated incase of dual sign Lagnas. This needs to be done at least once. Incase of house placement of Rāhu, the particular remedy must be performed:

2 Praśna Mārga śloka 14, chapter 5. The above translation is by Sanjay Rath from his book, Vedic Remedies in Astrology.

Table 79: Sarpa Remedy

House	Remedy
All houses	Sarpa Bali
Fourth	Installation of the image of sarpa devata or dedicating a Citra Kuṭa stone
Twelfth	Music and Singing must be arranged
First	Offering milk and water to the deity
Seventh	Singing of devotional music

10.3.2.3 Pitṛ Bādhaka: anger of forefathers

The remedy to appease the ancestors or parents is to serve them well whilst alive. In case of their demise, the proper and regular performance of their last rites must be performed to remove the negative Bādhaka associated.

10.3.2.4 *Preta* Bādhaka: anger of spirits/dead

It is said that when the last rites of a person have not been performed properly, and their inability to become liberated from this abode, they become ghosts. Incase of Preta Bādhaka, the malefic graha/Rāśi or Navāṁśa occupied by Gulika or Ketu will indicate how the demised spirit had their demise.

Table 80: Cause of death

Graha	Cause of death
Mars	Unnatural death, such as fire, spear, bleeding, etc.
Saturn	Due to sorrow, depression and misery
Rāhu	Serpent bite or poison

Similarly the placement in a watery sign can cause drowning, whilst in Sagittarius can indicate a fall from height. The astrologer can make a judgment based on the indications of the signs and planets involved. The sex of the spirit is based on its placement in an odd/even sign. Its age can be determined by the amount of degrees it occupies in its sign. Here the maximum age is 108. The remedy is based on the type of death and sex of the spirit.

Table 81: Preta Bādhaka Remedy[3]

Graha	Female	Male
Mars	Cāmuṇḍī	Kārtavīryārjuna, Ugra Hanumān, Ugra Narasimha
Saturn	Kāli	Ṣaṣṭa, Ucchiṣṭa Gaṇapati
Rāhu	Durga	Ugra Varāha, Sarpa Devatā

Praśna Mārga additionally advises Pārvaṇa Shraddhā[4] and Tila Homa[5].

10.3.2.5 Dṛṣṭi Bādhaka: evil eye

Position of Gulikā will indicate the person who is having the evil-eye towards you.

3 Remedies as advised in the tradition/paramparā.
4 Sacrificial rites during the new moon and full moon.
5 Offering of sesame.

The alleviation comes from the benefics associated. Incase of Bali Kāmas, the benefics in Kendra to Rāhu/Gulika will give the remedy. In case of Hanthu or Ranthu Kamas, the benefics aspecting the Bādhakeśa indicates the remedy. The gemstone's of the benefics should be worn, and the deities indicated by the benefics should be worshipped to remedy the problem.

10.3.2.6 Abhicāra: black magic

The sixth house and śatrupada (A6) indicates the strength and nature of the enemy, whilst the Bādhaka indicates the person who performed the black magic. Gulika indicates how the black magic was performed and which articles were used. Various remedies are known to be readily available in all religions, and almost among all deities of Vedic origin. Praśna Mārga advises Mṛtyunjaya recitation among the best remedies for this. This remedy not only removes all black magic but also ensures a disease-free life.

tryambakkam yajāmahe sugandhim puṣṭivardhanam।

urvārukamiva bandhanān mṛtyormūkṣīya māmṛtāt॥

10.3.3 Case Studies

10.3.3.1 Bādhaka

Chart 148: *Removal of Bādhaka*

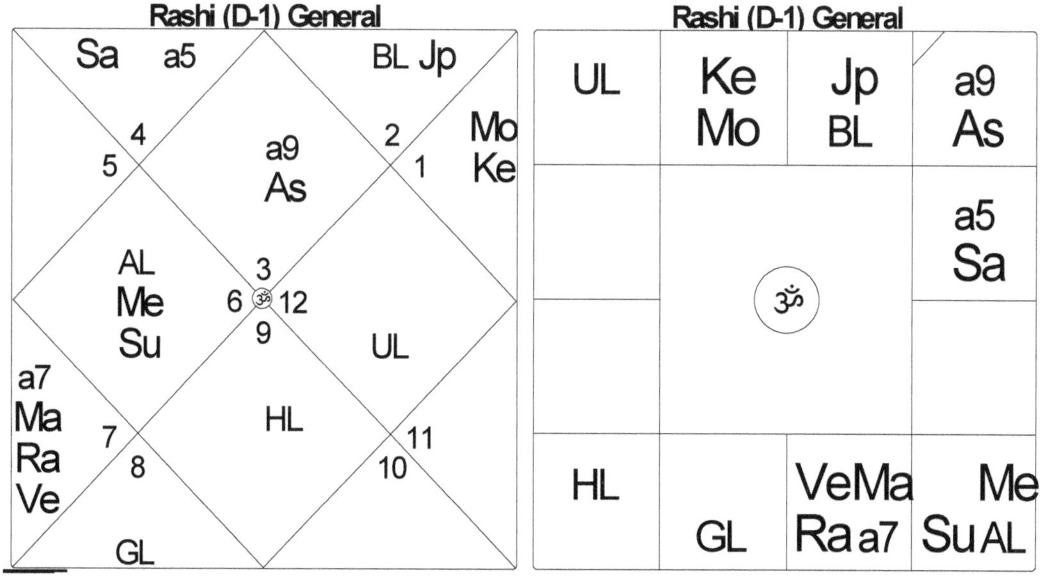

tIn the given chart, the Lagna rising is Gemini and being a dual sign causes the seventh house to be the Bādhaka house. No planets are placed in the seventh, whilst the lord is placed alone in the twelfth house. This is a very auspicious placement for the Bādhakeśa indicating that Jupiter causes the removal of all obstacles for the native through the Guru or a form of the Guru. During the Antaradaśā of Jupiter, the native was fortunate enough to find a very qualified teacher whom he learnt Sanskrit from at a very advanced level.

The ninth lord indicates the teacher, and the choice is between Rāhu and Saturn in this case. Saturn indicates the physical presence of the teacher, being a planet, and is placed in Cancer. Cancer is a movable sign and hence the eleventh from Cancer, namely Taurus, becomes the Bādhaka house. Taurus is occupied by the auspicious Jupiter, hence removing the bādhā from meeting the guru; however the lord of Taurus is Venus and is afflicted by Mars and Rāhu in Libra promising obstacles in this regard, especially from the opposite sex as Venus is Bādhakeśa.

The native has often been obstructed in his efforts to approach a qualified teacher. In some cases the teacher had their demise only days prior to him meeting them. Usually the obstacles in the native's life have been due to relationships. The wearing of a yellow sapphire or worship of the Guru will help the native remove these obstacles easily.

Chart 149: Removal of Bādhaka

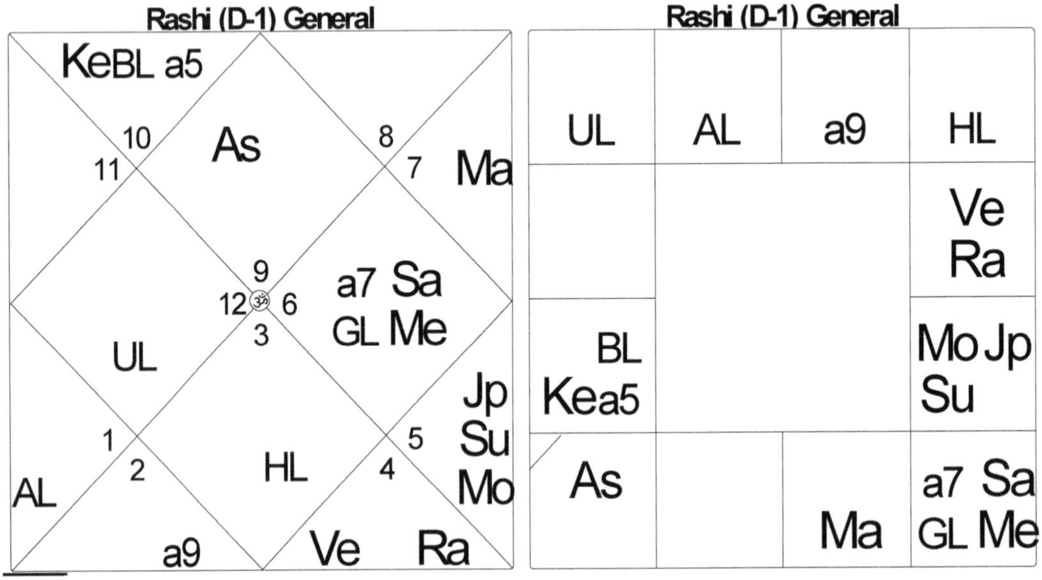

Female born 8th September 1980, 3:21 PM, Gracac, Croatia.

The Lagna is Sagittarius and seventh sign becomes the Bādhaka. Gemini is the Bādhaka house, and its lord Mercury is placed in the tenth house in exaltation. This is again an excellent position for the Bādhaka, causing Bhadra Mahāpuruṣa yoga, promising high ideals, expertise in yoga, and due to the conjunction with Upapada and Dārapada, the promise of love marriage/relationships due to the blessing of the Bādhaka. In this case the well placed Bādhaka removed obstacles for the native, and brought the native abroad in the Antaradaśā of Mercury, and gave strong and long lasting relationships.

The conjunction of second lord Saturn and seventh lord Mercury is also a Śrīmantah Yoga promising wealth and happiness to her due to their Rāśi dṛṣṭi on the Lagna. This will especially be prominent after marriage.

Chart 150: Queen Victoria of England

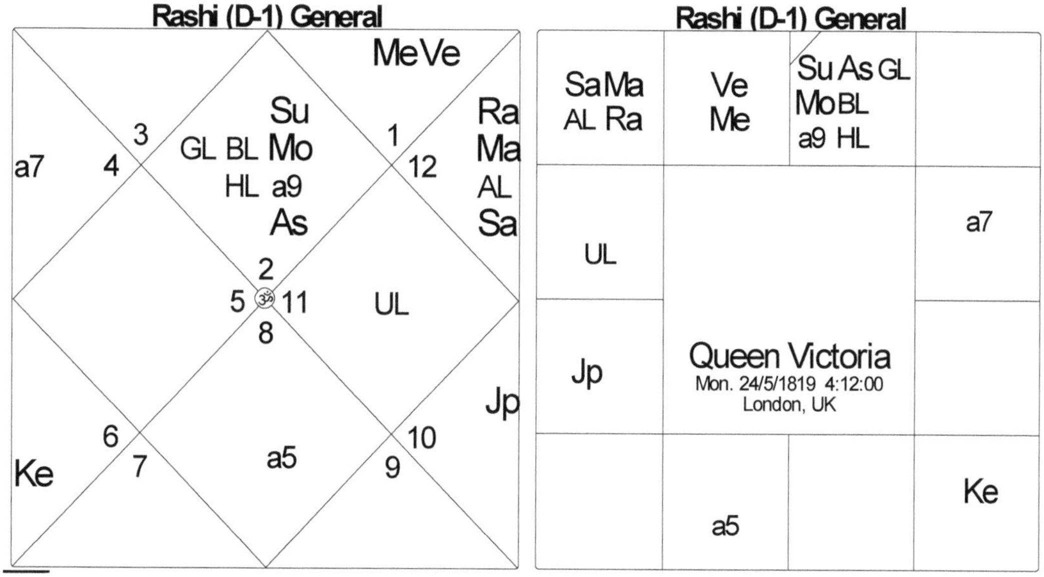

The chart of Queen Victoria rises with Taurus Lagna, making Capricorn the Bādhaka house. Jupiter is placed in Capricorn giving notions of Devabādhaka. However, the Devabādhaka is not present due to the lack of malefic influence on the twelfth house from the Bādhakeśa. Instead the Bādhakeśa being joined the Ārūḍha Lagna obstructs her achievement of status and position. Saturn is placed in the eleventh house with the seventh lord Mars forming powerful Dhāna yoga for great wealth. This is further confirmed by the conjunction of Ātmakāraka and Dārakāraka. Furthermore the conjunction of Chara Putrakāraka and Chara Ātmakāraka forms Maharaja Yoga for enormous power and sovereign. All this involving the Bādhakeśa and conjoined the Ārūḍha Lagna confirms the prediction of obstacles in ascension to the throne.

Victoria's father was the fourth in the line of succession to the United Kingdom, and it was highly unlikely that she would ascend the throne. However the maharaja yoga is involving Saturn and Rāhu in visible signs, promising the demise of the paternal side and ascension to the throne. An unusual phenomenon occurred in Queen Victoria's ascension. King George III was ruling, and his heir was his first son, the soon to be King George IV. To everyone's shock the only child and daughter of King George IV died during her child labor. The remaining sons had not married leaving the throne without an heir after King George IV. The only heir produced was Victoria born two years after the demise of the recent heir.

Moon Daśā and Rāhu Antaradaśā was running at Victoria's birth and is igniting the deadly yoga of Saturn and Rāhu in the chart. Eight months after birth, Victoria's father and grandfather the then King George III had their demise during the Antaradaśā of Rāhu. The pitṛ doṣa worked as Victoria was too young to perform the last rites of her father. The yoga is expected to strike again during the daśās of Saturn and Rāhu. On 26th June 1830, during Mars Daśā and Saturn Antaradaśā, King

George IV had his demise. King William IV took his place and as the new heir was also childless, Victoria became the new heir to the throne. The next Mahādaśā of Rāhu was to come in 1834, during which it was expected that Victoria would ascend the throne as queen. On 20th June 1837, during Rāhu Daśā and Jupiter Antaradaśā, King William IV dies heirless in Victoria's eighteenth year, making her eligible for the throne. She is crowned in the same year as Queen of the United Kingdom.

It's apparent how the Bādhaka removed the obstacles for the Queen to cause the Maharaja Yoga, and how the pitṛdoṣa of Saturn and Rāhu, worked towards her ascension to the throne. This same yoga brought her reign during the industrial revolution (Saturn), where England enjoyed great power and benefits. This was especially abroad in the foreign colonies due to the involvement of the Bādhakeśa.

Chart 151: Emperor Aurangazeb

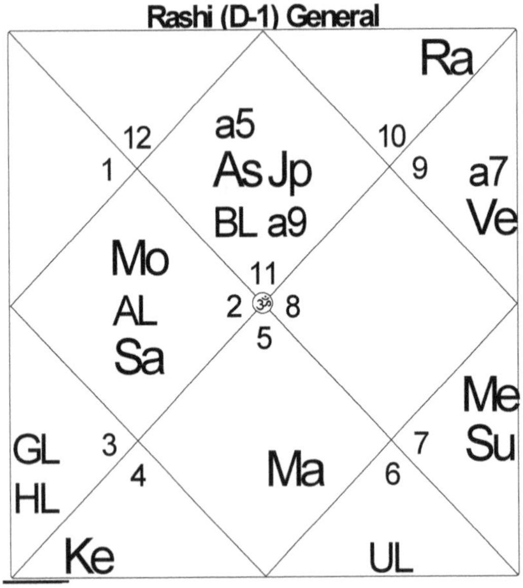

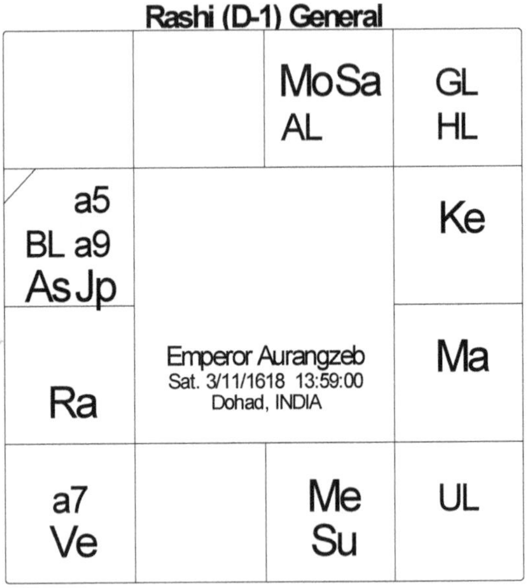

Abul Muzaffar Muhy-ud-Din Muhammad Aurangzeb, born 3rd November 1618, 1:59 PM, Dohad, India.

In the given chart, Lagna is Aquarius making Libra the Bādhaka house. The Bādhaka house is occupied by seventh lord Sun, and fifth lord Mercury forming raja yoga due to the conjunction of a Kendra and Trikoṇa lord in a Trikoṇa. Other strong raja yogas are formed by the placement of the Ātmakāraka Mercury. However the placement in the Bādhaka house and the debility of the Sun obstructs the raja yoga from functioning. Aurangazeb was the second son of the then Mughal Emperor. His elder brother (Bādhakeśa in the eleventh) stood to inherit the throne, and hence the promise of ascension was denied to Aurangazeb. Upon careful examination, we see that Sun is not only placed in a Martian Navāṁśa indicating that the wrath of father will rise, but Sun is also receiving nīca bhaṅga raja yoga due to its exaltation in Navāṁśa. This yoga causes a peculiar situation where the ascension to the throne earns him the father's anger.

Jupiter has graha dṛṣṭi on the planets in the ninth house and with the advent of

Jupiter Daśā, Aurangazeb father fell ill. Seeing an opportunity to seize the thrown, Aurangazeb imprisoned his father and challenged his brother for the thrown. He killed and beheaded his own brother and sent his head to his ailing father who then was imprisoned in Agra fort. This is a case of how an evil yoga helped the greed of one man to attain raja yoga.

Chart 152: Sarpa Bādhaka

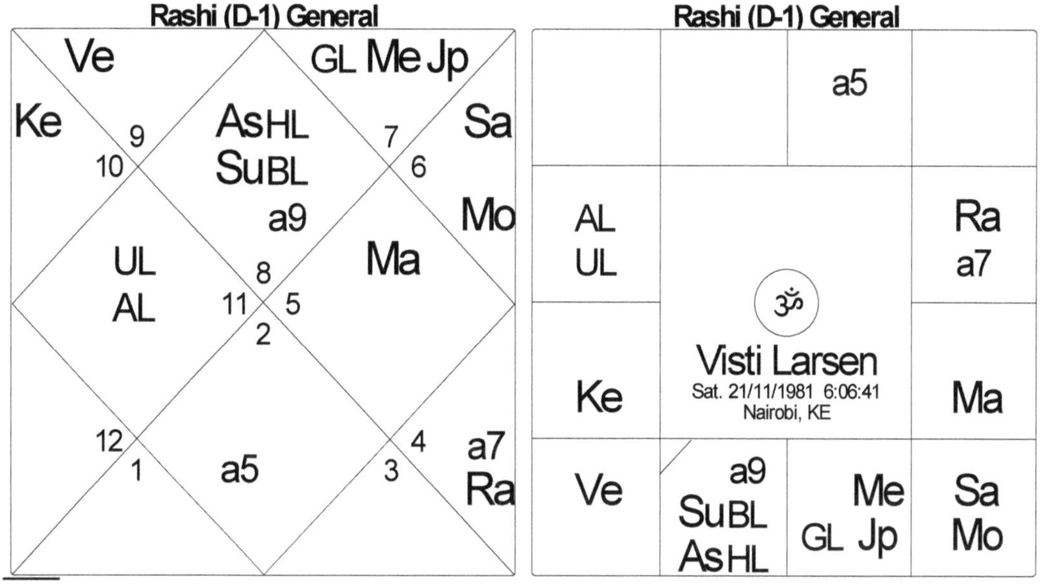

The native is born with Scorpio Lagna making Cancer the Bādhaka house. Cancer is occupied by Rāhu and indicates Sarpabādhaka. The sign is that of the Moon showing that these are evil minded serpents, intent on harm. Fortunately, Rāhu is also in mutual Rāśi dṛṣṭi with the Sun promising some good effects in the form of knowledge, name, fame and reputation as the Sun is posited in the Lagna.

The Bādhakeśa is placed in the eleventh house indicating that the wealth of the serpents was afflicted. The twelfth from the Bādhakeśa will reveal the harm the native did in the past life. Mars is posited there indicating some violent acts, which are only further promoted by the Rāśi dṛṣṭi of Ketu on Mars. The nature of the planet in the Lagna (or lord) being dhātu, mūla or jīva will indicate whether a form of metal, plant or life has been destroyed. Sun is in the Lagna and indicates that some plants, earth, trees or such objects have been destroyed.

The sign of Rāhu will reveal the root reason for the Bādhaka. Rāhu is in a movable sign indicating the destruction of the eggs of the serpents, due to which the native has received the curse. Since Rāhu is the Ātmakāraka, the native will surely see the curse as it is the root cause of birth. Its placement in Māraṇa karaka Sthāna can show near-death incidents occurring to the native. This is confirmed by the Moon's position in the eighth from Ārūḍha Lagna, which can cause accidents/death in water. In Moon Mahādaśā (Bādhakeśa) the native almost died on three occasions in water. On two occasions the native suffered injuries to the head whilst swimming, requiring hospitalization, whilst on a third occasion the native almost drowned. Moon is in the Navāṁśa of Aquarius, and the incidents all happened in swimming pools.

The Bādhaka will also arise in Rāhu Mahādaśā. Since Rāhu is joined the Dārapada this could happen through relationships, or being cheated in relationships or business deals. As Rāhu is in the ninth house, some adharma in relationships is expected from the native, but because Rāhu is the Ātmakāraka, the native will not cheat others, and instead himself be cheated. The native was advised to donate 9 golden or copper eggs to Nāgarāja or a Śiva Liñga, the sprinkling of milk on the Liñga on his birth Tithi, and the regular worship of Balabhadra. Additionally the performance of Sarpa Bali is advised.

Chart 153: *Deva Bādhaka*

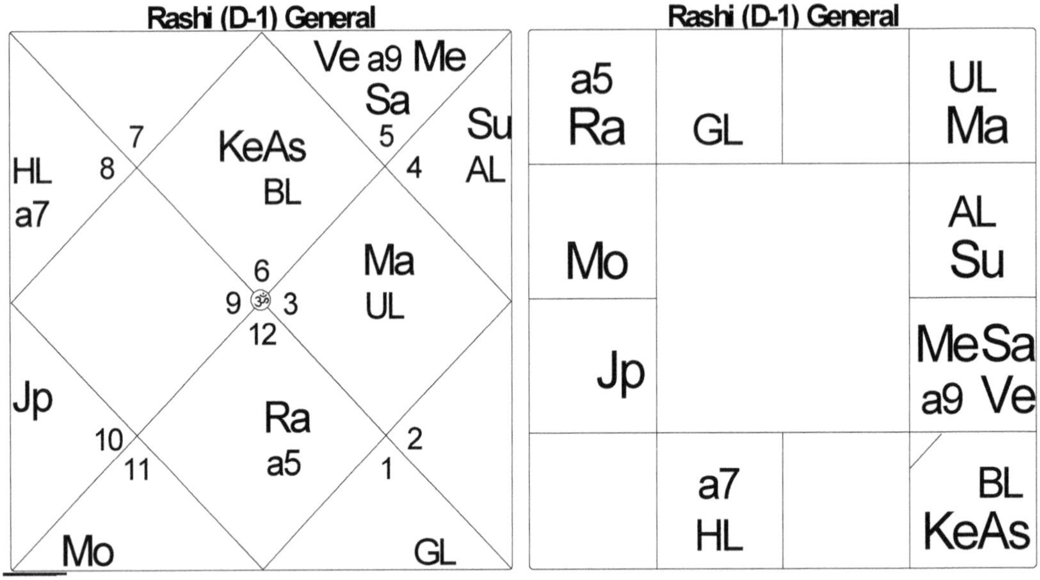

Male born 10th August 1949, 9:01 AM, Cuttack, India.

Virgo Lagna rises and Pisces becomes the Bādhaka house. Rāhu is in Pisces; however the lord Jupiter is debilitated indicating Devabādhaka. Jupiter is alone and indicates the supreme Brahmaṇ or Nārāyaṇa as the deity causing the Bādhaka. It is placed in the fifth house showing the forgetting or neglecting the worship of the deity in the past life. The twelfth house from Jupiter is afflicted by Mars, Rāhu and Ketu indicating the history of having shown great violence in the worship and abruptly ending the worship or abusing it. The Lagna indicates the abuse of life has happened, as it is a jīva sign occupied by a jīva graha (Ketu indicates insects or fish). Since Jupiter is Vargottama, this can affect his name, reputation or health, as Vargottama planets affect the first house. The position in the fifth house can indicate the loss of sanity which can cause the event. The native tampered with the worship of snakes and the dark arts as indicated by the fifth lord joined Venus in a duḥsthāna, though warned against this. This started during Jupiter Daśā and Venus Antaradaśā. Sun is the Khāreśa in both Drekkāṇa and Navāṁśa, and is placed in the seventh from Jupiter (Māraka) promising a very inauspicious incident. In Jupiter Daśā and Sun Antaradaśā, the native became schizophrenic after a sudden fire which occurred. Ketu occupies the Lagna, and is aspected by Mars, indicating black magic as well. All sorts of remedies have been tried to bring the native out of his condition, however because of the retrogression (denial) of the Bādhakeśa, none have been fruitful.

Chart 154: *Dṛṣṭi Bādhaka*

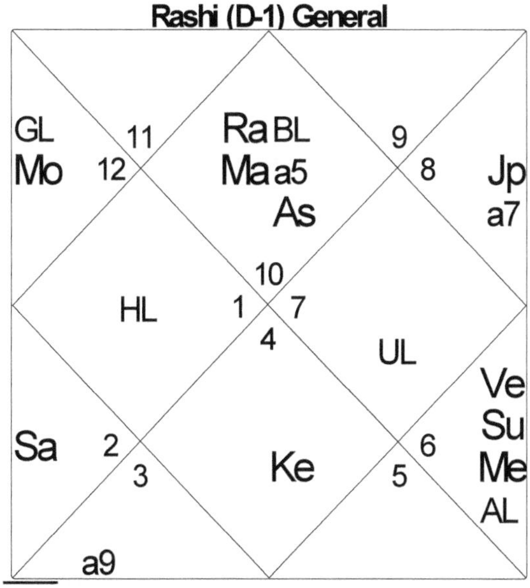

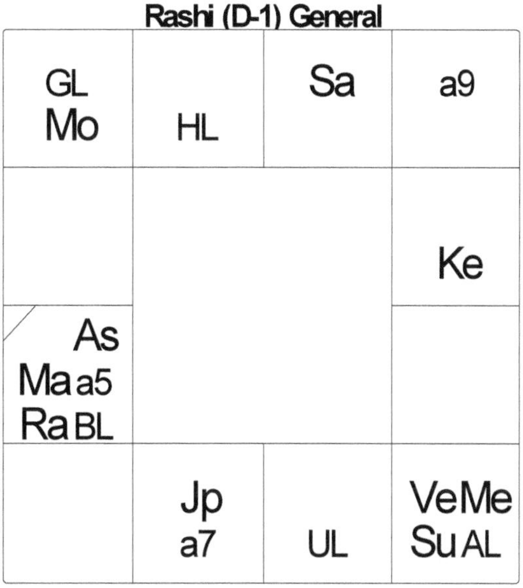

Lady born 4th October 1971, 10 AM, -10 EAST of GMT (146e48, 19s16)

The female native with Capricorn Lagna has Jupiter in Scorpio in the Bādhaka sthāna. Jupiter is well placed but Mars the lord is joined the Lagna indicating dṛṣṭi Bādhaka. Mars is exalted but its conjunction with Rāhu has spoilt his position. Since the eighth or sixth lords are not involved, the intention is not to kill the native but to trouble and distress the native as malefics are involved. The native complained of seeing ghosts recently after breaking a relationship, and during another relationship had ongoing dreams about snakes, indicating that the problem arises due to the relationships she chooses.

Gulikā is in a female sign indicating that a woman is causing the Bādhaka. The motive is seen from the Navāṁśa placement of Gulikā, which is that of Scorpio the natural eighth house, indicating the break of relationships. The native was advised the worship of Dattātreya, which removed the bad dreams and evils completely, however out of the native's dissatisfaction with the situation she ended her relationship.

Chart 155: Abhicāra

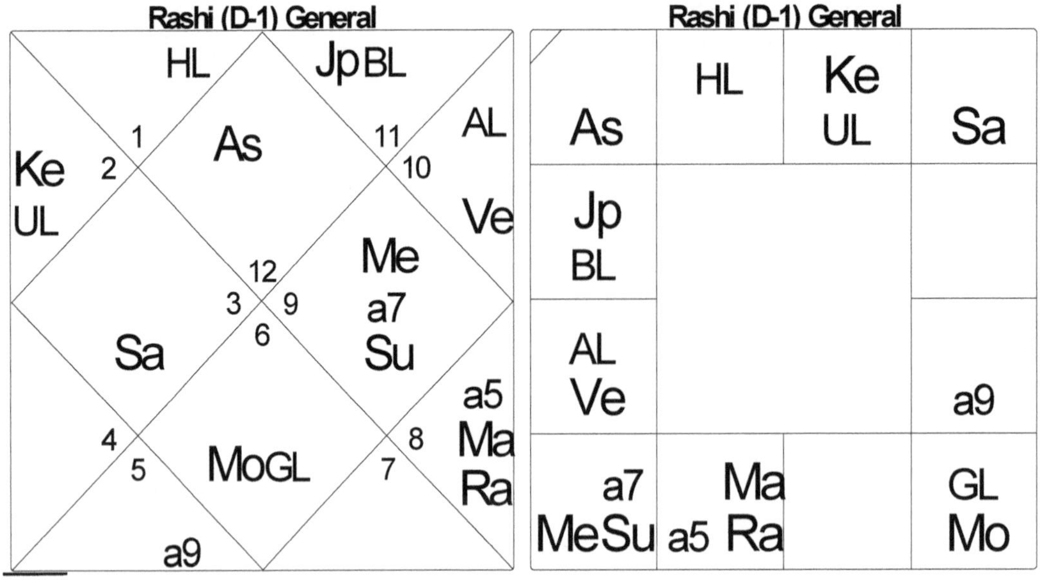

Lady born 3rd January 1975, 11:43 AM, London, United Kingdom.

The native has Pisces Lagna, and the seventh house becomes the Bādhaka house. The Bādhakeśa is joined the sixth lord Sun indicating troubles from enemies and black magic. The Ātmakāraka is Mercury, and the black magic is hard to avoid. Gulikā is joined the Lagneśa Jupiter, which can prove detrimental towards the health of the native. Furthermore Bādhakeśa is Vargottama and will definitely affect the health, name and reputation. Moon is in the Bādhaka house and is fifth lord which can give problems due to worship. Moon is in Capricorn Navāṁśa indicating that psychic disorders can result from this. With two malefic, Mars and Rāhu in the twelfth from the Bādhakeśa it suggests that this black magic is arising out of the anger of the Deva.

Gulikā will indicate when the native is cursed or poisoned by the black magic. Gulikā is in Capricorn and joined Venus; hence some food item in the form of liquids or drinks may be presented. The sixth lord is the Sun indicating devotees of Śiva or such enemies who would initiate the curse. The śatrupada (A6) is in Aries which is aspected by Rāhu, whilst its lord is joined Rāhu, indicating foreigners. In Rāhu Daśā and Mars Antaradaśā, during her stay in India, the native was presented some food item to eat; following which she lost her mental balance. Ever since then the native has been troubled by psychic disorders.

यन्मण्डलं ब्रह्मविदो विदन्ति गायन्ति तच्चारणसिद्ध सङ्घाः।
यन्मण्डलं वेदविदो स्मरन्ति पुनातु मां तत्सवितुर्वरेण्यम्॥ ११॥

11

Fourth, Eighth & Twelfth
The Mokṣa trikoṇa

11.1 The Fourth House

The fourth house is a vital house in the chart. Firstly it is a Kendra to the Lagna, and hence an important pillar of the native's life and secondly because it shows the native's happiness. Happiness is a state of mind and education first moulded by the mother; hence, the mother is seen from this bhāva. The bhāva tells us about the native's childhood, which is the time of initial learning or primary education. Having become independent, the native seeks happiness through his own home/property as well as luxuries; hence, home and luxuries/conveyances are seen from the fourth house. The many significations of the fourth house imply many grahas signifying each of them.

11.1.1 Mother

Unlike the father, the mother is always present at the time of birth; otherwise, the birth could not occur. However, it is the mother's presence after the birth that is important. To determine the presence of the relevant person in one's life, the house from the relevant Kāraka is used, i.e. fourth lord from the Moon will reveal the mothers presence in the native's life, and similarly the ninth lord from the Sun is seen for the father.

- Should the fourth lord from the Moon and ninth lord from the Sun both be badly placed/afflicted, the native's association with their parents maybe short lived and lacking.
- The most benefic planet(s) joining/aspecting the fourth from Moon will indicate the person who takes over the role of the mother after separation.
- Judge the ninth house from the Sun in a similar manner.

Generally observe that separation from the parents may occur when

- When the Sun is in exaltation or debilitation, in the first or seventh houses from either Lagna or Ārūḍha Lagna, the parents will abandon the native. This can also occur if the Kārakāṁśa is Scorpio.

- Father could be lacking from birth if the Dvādaśāṁśa (D-12) Lagna is Leo or Pisces[1], otherwise it will happen later. If the Dvādaśāṁśa Lagna is Cancer or Scorpio then mother's influence could be lacking in life. Planets signifying the mother or father placed in these signs in Dvādaśāṁśa are also relevant.

The fourth house and lord themselves will indicate the mother's health and the quality of her presence in one's life. The fourth lord when afflicted or badly placed, as well as its dispositor and the fourth lord from Moon can cause the early demise of the mother. The placement of malefic in the sixth or twelfth houses affects mother's health, as the fourth and tenth houses affect fathers health.

If the negative event doesn't happen in infancy, then for grahas in or lording the fourth or ninth house, their age based on the Viṁśottari Daśā will bring the negatives. I.e. for Moon lording the fourth house the age of ten would be relevant. For grahas joined the lords of these houses their natural age would indicate the event, i.e. Moon's natural age is 23 and the event could manifest at this time.

Before predicting the nature of the event, the Dvādaśāṁśa chart should be examined, and the timing should be confirmed from it using Daśā.

11.1.2 Property and Vāstu Faults

At the onset of an inauspicious Daśā, the most common change occurs in the home. In the home, a change of scenario may occur causing a Vāstu fault. This fault then starts showing up in the life of the inhabitants in the form of professional problems, financial problems, relationship problems, etc. If the problem can be corrected with the help of Vāstu, then the problem area must have some association with the fourth house. Hereunder are some combinations for Vāstu problems.

- Fourth house/lord joined a Māraṇa Kāraka Sthāna planet.

- Fourth house/lord joined Bādhaka Sthāna or Bādhakeśa.

- Fourth house suffering from low Rekha in the Sarvāṣṭakavarga scheme.

- Malefics in the eleventh or ninth houses will cause problems if property is bought during their natural ages – i.e. if a property is bought during the 36th year, and Saturn is in the ninth or eleventh houses, then sorrow, depression, lack of income, etc will hit the native. Mars in these houses will bring litigation and fights, if the property is bought during the 28th year. Similarly judge the nodes.

11.1.3 Ones community

It is common that people belong to large spiritual communities or are part of large organizations. These organizations can go to the extent of defining the native's life-

[1] The latter dictum is culled out of the scriptures. Pisces is the second from Aquarius, the natural 11th house where Śiva sits as Hara, whilst Leo is the 7th from Aquarius, another māraka house from Aquarius, hence possibly the origin of this dictum. A similar view is that these are both symbolic of Lord Śiva's anger, which will be inflicted upon one, if the D12 lagna is Leo or Pisces.

style and even limit the native's life. The organization which one belongs to is seen from the fourth from the Ārūḍha Lagna. The attachment one has to this organization is seen from the lord of the same. Strong benefics associated with the fourth from AL can make one part of a strong organization.

11.1.4 Education

Education or Vidyā is seen from the fourth house, where the native is educated in the necessary knowledge needed to survive in the world. This Vidyā is called Aparā Vidyā and is transformed into Jñāna i.e. knowledge which sits in the fifth house deciding the intelligence of the native. The native's own thoughts and working intelligence is hence seen from the fifth house. It is the fifth house which will show the Parā or spiritual Vidyā of the native, which arises through mantras and one's personal spiritual practices.

When the native works hard and earns a position in higher education (ninth is sixth from fourth house), they get to apply their own knowledge (ninth is fifth from fifth house) in seeking knowledge. Depending on their knowledge, (fifth) the higher education may become Parā Vidyā, or divine knowledge. This depends on the guru who comes into the native's life, signified by the ninth house. This is the clue to understanding the Siddhāṁśa (D-24), which is beyond the scope of this chapter. The Rāśi is important for identifying how one's quest for knowledge influences one's life in a holistic sense. Some important tools are given hereunder.

Learned in many branches

A person born with the fourth lord in the seventh house acquires knowledge of many branches. The seventh house is the 'Dvāra' or door through which we enter into the world and also represents the highest stage of academic knowledge. As per the Ṛg Veda (Gaṇeśa Gāyatrī), Gaṇeśa sits in the doorway to the gods, and a prayer to him ensures that any mistakes in our recitation of mantras are forgiven and the recitation is accepted. Similarly, any planet in the seventh house shows the blessings of Gaṇeśa in opening the doors to whatever activity the native may aspire to accomplish.

The fourth lord shows the fruits of one's education and when in the seventh house or joined the seventh lord, the native has the blessings of learning in many branches. Similarly, a broad faith and acceptance of all faith is caused by the fifth lord in the seventh house or joined with the seventh lord. This also applies to the ninth lord and fifth lord in the seventh house; however, it should be kept in mind that the education indicated by the same planets becomes useless, as the native does not apply the acquired knowledge.

Intelligent, yet devoid of learning

A person born with the third lord in Lagna will be intelligent yet uninstructed and/or unlearned. The third house is the desire of the guru, being the seventh from the ninth house, and for reasons already mentioned, its association with the Lagna or its lord causes Dhīmanta Yoga. Therefore the person is highly intelligent with third lord in Lagna and knows when and how to serve the Guru or mentor. However, because the third house is a negative house for both parents, the native may not have much social or cultural knowledge and does not know how to run a house hold or family, unless Moon is associated. Mercuries association ensures high academic qualifications.

In the same vain Parāśara has stated: should the third lord occupy the eleventh house, the native will be devoid of learning, yet be wise and intelligent. Here Parāśara states that the third lord in the eleventh house will make the person intelligent, yet devoid of proper teaching and guidance. The reason being similar to that of the placement in Lagna i.e. third lord in the eleventh will be opposite the fifth house of knowledge, making the person intelligent. Again this knowledge may not be from ones parents and one does lack the knowledge to run a household, unless Moon associates.

In both the cases of third lord placed in the Lagna and eleventh houses, it is seen that the Vidyā or education is reduced in the native. How it works is understood by counting from the house to its lord, and vice versa. In case of third lord in the eleventh house, the third lord is in the ninth from the third house. This causes the significations of the ninth house to suffer, and the guru or higher education is not present due to this. However, from the third lord, the third house is in the fifth sign hence, knowledge increases significantly – this is known as being street-smart.

In case of the third lord in the Lagna, the third lord is in the eleventh from the third house. This causes the eleventh house significations to suffer, however what is more important is that the third house significations are enhancing due to the third house being in the third from the third lord – hence the native will become more independent and the Kāraka Mars will become more prominent, causing the person to ignore the guru. Third lord in the fourth house will not damage the education, and will make the native very learned, as per Parāśara[2].

Abandonment of Knowledge

As per Parāśara one born with the twelfth lord in Lagna, will abandon their education due to lack of wealth. The lack of wealth is caused by the twelfth lord being in the second from the twelfth house, ensuring a suffering to the second house activities. The fourth house receives lābhārgalā from the second house, and controls the gains of the fourth house. This position further obstructs the fifth house, being the tenth from it. As a result, the native ends their learning and reaps no more fortune from education.

Similarly, the twelfth lord in the fifth house is the sixth from the twelfth house. The sixth is the second from the fifth ruling the sustenance of the knowledge/intelligence, and becomes weak in this case. The learning of the native hence becomes obstructed, unless modified by Jupiter's influence. This conforms with Parāśara[3].

The twelfth lord in the seventh house makes the native abandon their education in childhood. Here the principle can be satisfied through two methods:

---

2 sukhasthe sahajādhīśe sukhī ca dhanasaṁyutaḥ | matimān jāyate bālo duṣṭabhāryāpatiśca saḥ || 28|| - BPHS, Chapter on Bhava Lords, sloka 28.

3 vyayeśe sutabhāvasthe sutavidyāvivarjitaḥ | - BPHS, Chapter on Bhavat lords, sloka 137.

ι) Seventh house is the seat of Gaṇeśa, who is said to give the blessings of good education. The twelfth lord acting like Saturn would hence cause obstructions to the same. Further acting like Saturn, the tenth Dṛṣṭi on the twelfth lord is on the fourth house of education which suffers.

ιι) The twelfth lord is in the eighth from the twelfth house causing problems for eighth house matter. The eighth house is the fourth from the fifth and fifth from the fourth, being a very important house for the happiness derived from intellectual pursuits (fourth from fifth) and the application of one's Vidyā (fifth from fourth).

11.1.5 Case Studies

11.1.5.1 Separation from parents

Chart 156: Śrī Rāma's Vanavās

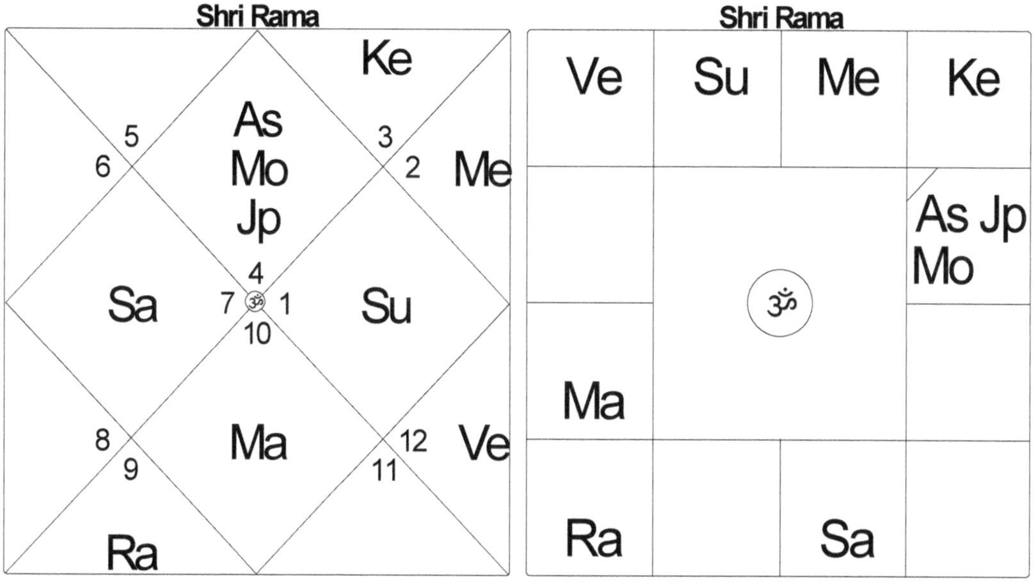

Śrī Rāma had to face exile because of his father's promise to his stepmother. This occurred due to the position of an exalted Sun in Ārūḍha Lagna. This did not occur at birth hence we may infer from the chart, that the Dvādaśāṁśa Lagna of Śrī Rāma was neither Leo nor Pisces[4]. The story says that this separation occurred due to a curse. This topic has been dealt with under chapter five.

Chart 157: Adoption

Female born 5th February 1995, 7:28 AM, (-8 hrs East), (102e43, 25n2).

In the given chart, the ninth lord from Sun and the fourth lord from Moon is the same planet, Mercury. Mercury is well placed in the Lagna however combust by the Sun. The combustion is within two degrees and very strong – as a result the native did not know her biological parents. Venus is the strongest benefic aspecting both ninth from Sun and fourth from Moon, showing a replacement-parent taking over

4 This eliminates the degrees 2:30-5:00 and 20:00-22:30 as his Lagna degree.

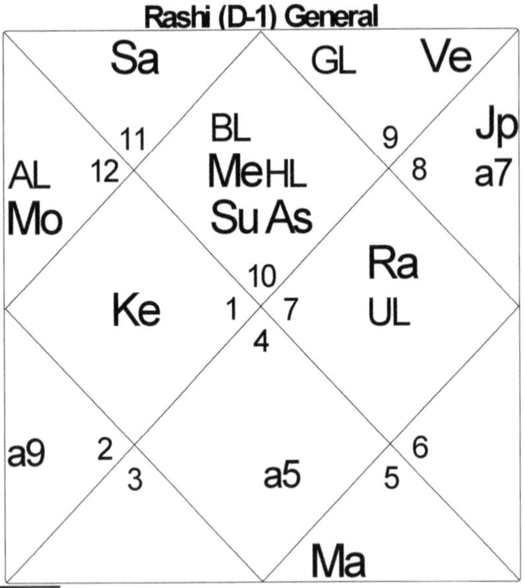

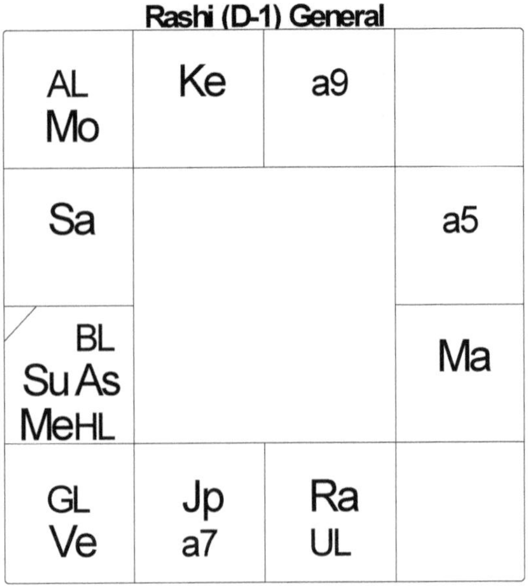

the job of the biological parents. The native was adopted in her early childhood and now lives a very pleasant life in her new home.

11.1.5.2 Education

Chart 158: Lack of Guidance

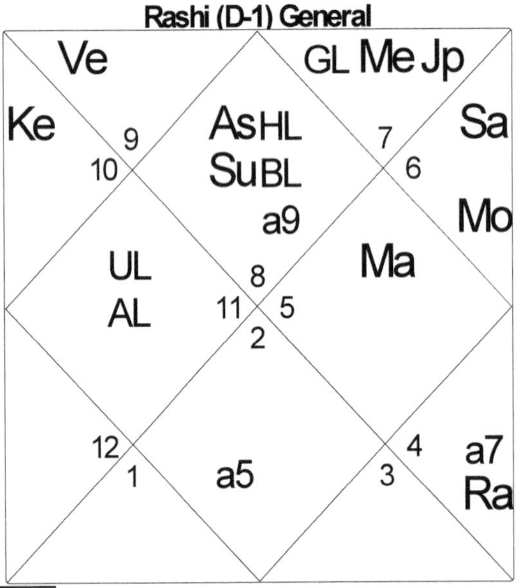

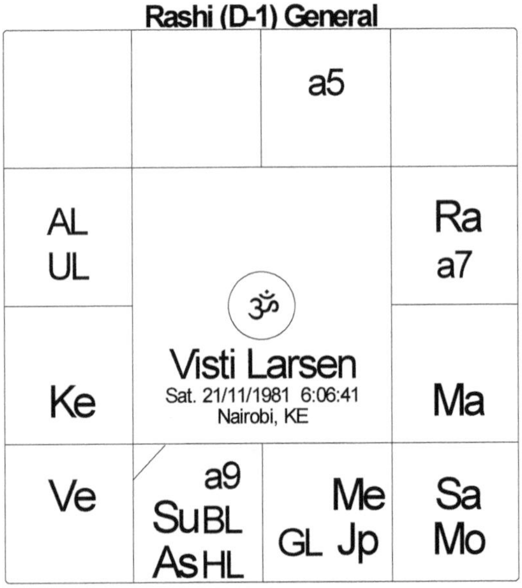

In the given chart, the native has third lord in the eleventh house. This also happens to be joined the dispositor of Ātmakāraka, leading the native towards knowledge of Jyotiṣa śāstra. Whilst the native was initiated into a Parampara of Jyotiṣa, he was initially without the guidance of his guru due to the third house lordship of Saturn and its placement in the eleventh house. This occurred during Mars Daśā – Moon Antaradaśā. Since Moon is joined Saturn in the eleventh house, it gave the effects of Saturn in this case. The native then took up the sincere worship of Guru Maharṣi Vyāsa (Mercury - Virgo) for one year, after which his association with his guru became stronger.

Moon being joined the third lord gives the person social education and understanding of social norms, which otherwise would be lacking, and also academic qualifications due to being in the sign of Mercury.

Chart 159: Change of education

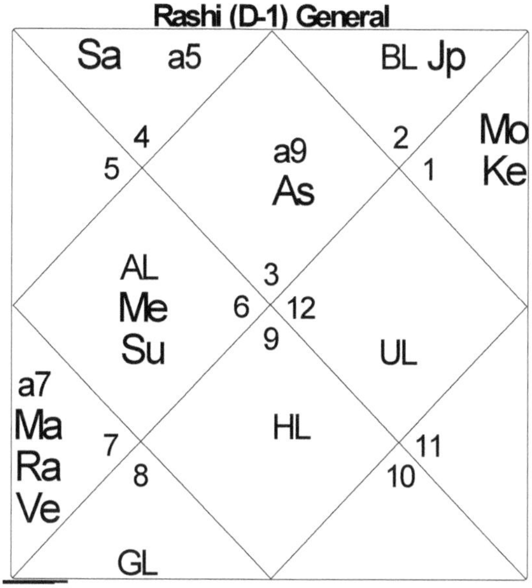

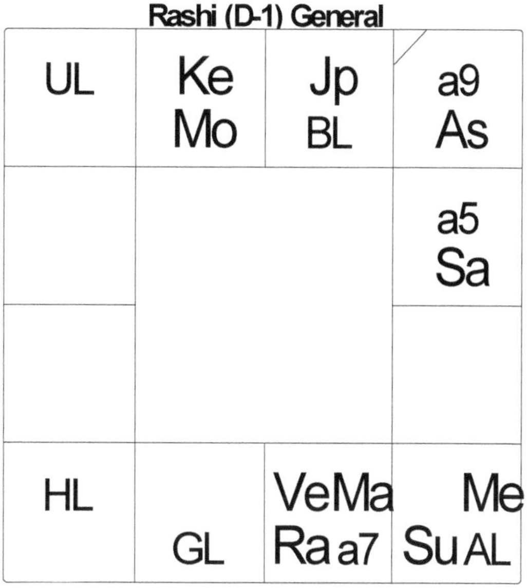

The native has twelfth lord Venus in the fifth house. During the end of Venus Daśā, the native decided to terminate his current education. As Venus is in its own sign, it would try to protect the education. The native chose a different line of study during the end of Venus Daśā, because of this yoga.

Chart 160: Abandoned by father and end of education
Male born 4th November 1979, 10:50 PM, Copenhagen, Denmark

The native has Cancer Lagna like in the case of Śrī Rāma, with Sun in debility in Ārūḍha Lagna. Moon is in quadrants to the Lagna, hence the mother will not abandon the native. It was enquired from the native, whether he had suffered some separation/abandonment with his father in life. The ninth from Sun has no influence of any benefic planets. Only Saturn has Rāśi dṛṣṭi and true enough, no father figure replaced the biological father. The native clarified that he had never known his father, and was brought up by his mother alone. The Dvādaśāṁśa Lagna was given as Aries, which the author rectified by five minutes to reach Pisces Dvādaśāṁśa Lagna.

The twelfth lord Mercury is in the fifth house with fourth lord Venus. Although the native is very intelligent due to the placement of fifth lord in Lagna, with the advent of Mars Daśā – Saturn Antaradaśā, the native terminated his high school education prematurely. Throughout Mercury Antaradaśā, the native did not have the inclina-

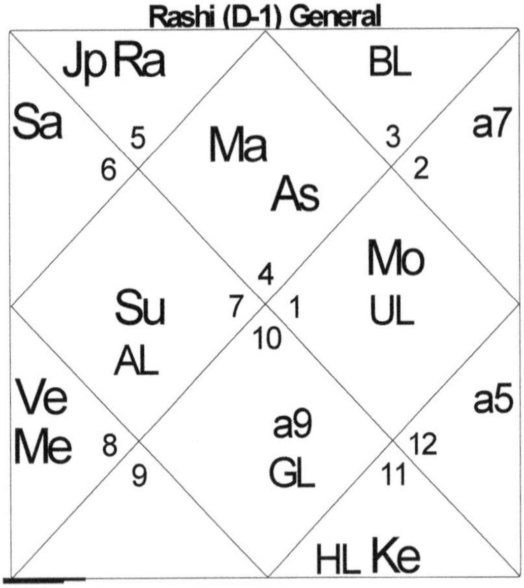

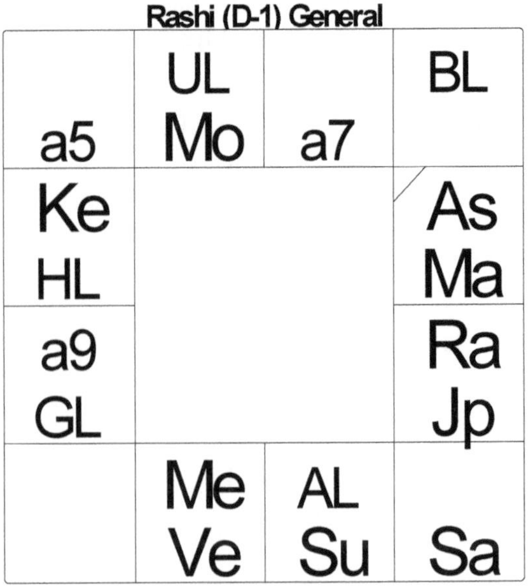

tion to study, however the upcoming Daśā of Ketu had to make the native study, due to Ketu's lordship over the fifth house. During Mars Daśā – Ketu Antaradaśā, the native enlisted for military service (Mars in Lagna and Kendra to AL, and Ketu – fifth lord) in the medical division (Venus and Mercury in fifth house), through which he learned extensively about the practice of medicine, first aid and such healing.

11.1.5.2 Property and one's Community

Chart 161: Vāstu Problems

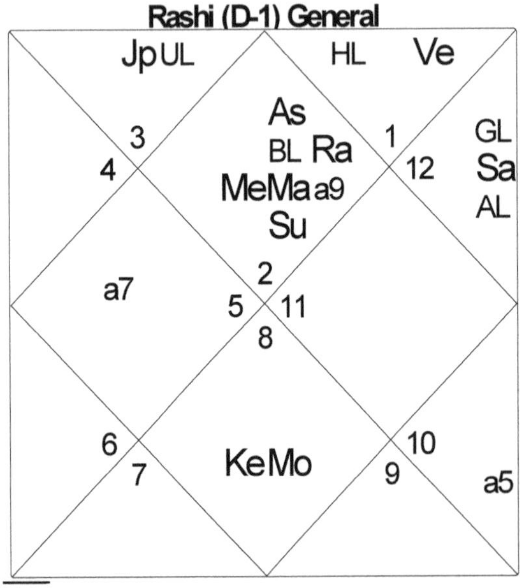

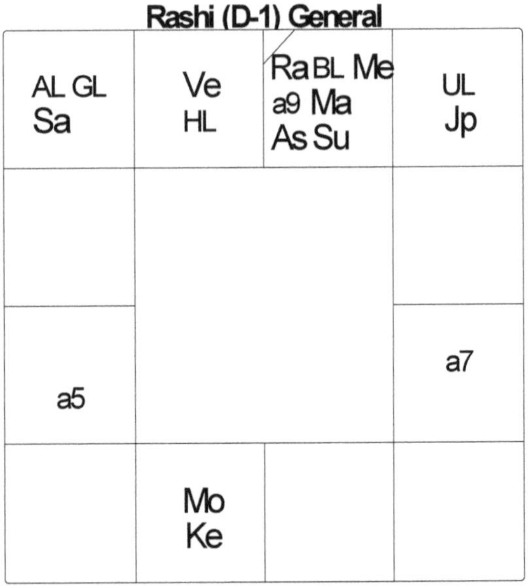

Male born 3rd June 1966, 4:45 AM, Muttukuru, India.

In the given chart, the ninth house is unoccupied, whilst Saturn occupies the eleventh house. The native had a very successful phase, having eight years of work-experience and is very competent. When the native bought a new property in his 36th year, he was suddenly jobless for two years. Jupiter aspects Saturn indicating that some guidance from astrologers, gurus or other advisors will prevail over the native. The native sold the property and moved house. He is currently working, with a good salary and a very nice job.

Chart 162: Property Problems

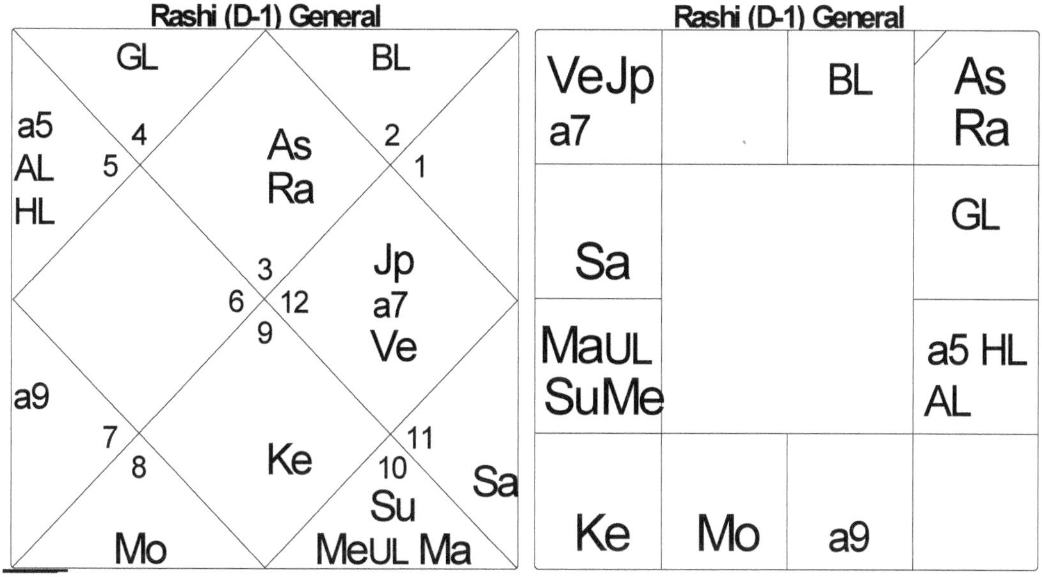

Male born 7th February 1964, 1:56 PM, Kanpur, India.

The native of the given chart decided to buy some landed property in his 36th year. Saturn is in the ninth house and does not bode well for such an acquisition. The fourth lord is Mercury placed in the eighth house in Capricorn; this can indicate land coming through an inheritance, an ancestral place, or place of the dead/spirits. The native bought a property, which officials later claimed, was an old Hindu cremation ground where the dead are burnt to ashes, and hence could not be used to build on. Mercury is with Mars and whilst this is good for landed property, it also shows litigation and 'mud-slinging' that will follow as Mercury and Mars are inimical towards each other. This is confirmed through Saturn's graha dṛṣṭi on the Ārūḍha Lagna. The native was advised to release any ownership of the property.

Chart 163: Vāstu Problem
Male born 12th November 1934, 6:19 PM, Cuttack, India.

In the given chart, the fourth lord Sun is debilitated and joined Venus who is placed in maraṇa Kāraka sthāna. This would imply a visible Vāstu problem in the home. In the southeastern direction (ruled by Venus), the family had a swimming pool, which had no water and was not being used and hence becoming a deep hole in the plot. As Venus is the Lagna lord and strong in the sixth house, it not only gives a

Rashi (D-1) General

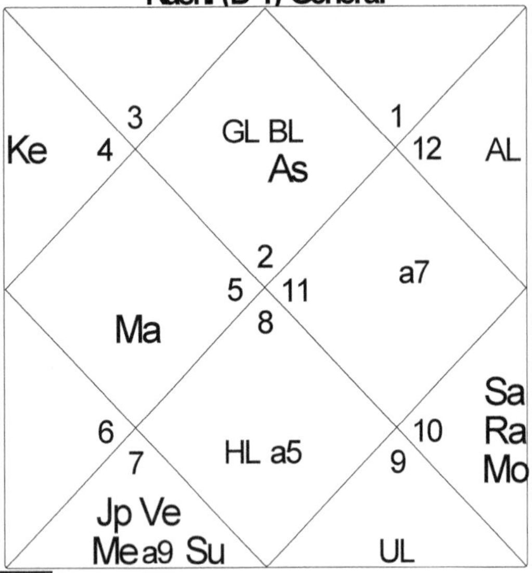

Rashi (D-1) General

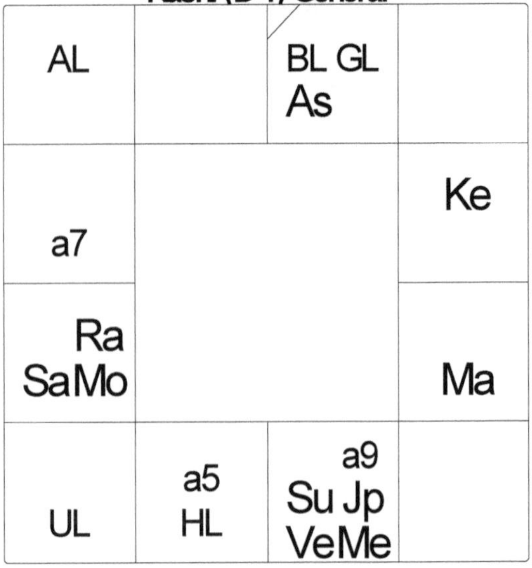

high level of intelligence in the native (dhīmanta yoga), but also a tendency to fight and pursue legal disputes. During the last 1/third of Leo Nārāyaṇa Daśā (fourth house), the native lost his property due to legal disputes. This coincided with the vimśottari Daśā of Saturn-Rāhu, which are both in the Bādhak sthāna causing the problem.

Chart 164: Female – Rāmakṛṣṇa Mission

Rashi (D-1) General

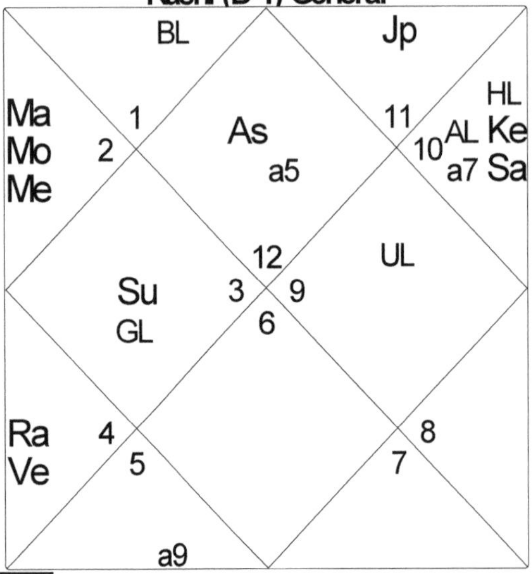

Rashi (D-1) General

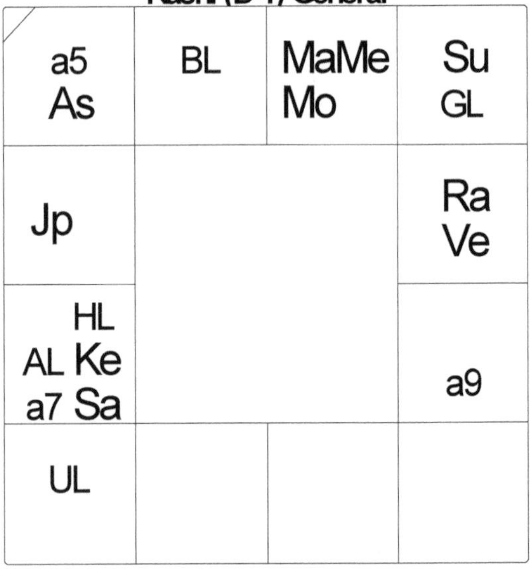

Female born 30th June 1962, 0:13 AM, Calcutta, India.

The native of the given chart has Ārūḍha Lagna in Capricorn. The fourth from Capricorn is Aries, aspected by a strong Jupiter in Aquarius. The native's family, especially the mother, has been a devout follower of the Rāmakṛṣṇa Mission, a spiritual organization established by Swami Vivekananda in the name of his guru, Śrī Rāmakṛṣṇa Paramahamsa. The connection to the organization has been since birth, however due to the lord Mars being weak in Sandhi (first or 30th degree of a sign) the native has slowly become more and more detached from the organization.

Due to the placement of Ketu on the Ārūḍha Lagna the fourth in reverse should be reckoned after the native becomes more spiritual. Venus lords the fourth house from Ārūḍha Lagna and joins Rāhu in a Śrī Yantra yoga for blessings from the divine mother. Jupiter and Mercury aspect Libra and promises a good link to the spiritual organisation. Venus suggests that this will be encouraged after marriage. After marriage the native and her husband took Dikṣa from the Śarada Math, an Ashram connected to the Rāmakṛṣṇa Mission.

Chart 165: H.H. Dalai Lama – Buddhism

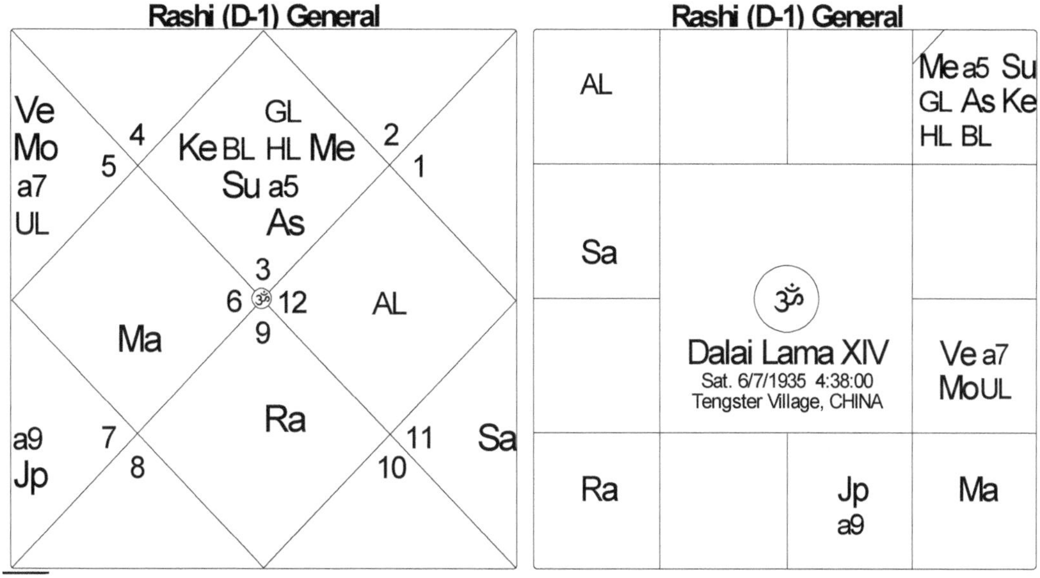

H.H. Dalai Lama, born Tenzin Gyatso, 6th July 1935, 4:38 AM, Tengster Village, Tibet.

The given chart is of H.H. Dalai Lama. The Ārūḍha Lagna is in Pisces. The fourth from Pisces is Gemini housing Ketu, Sun and Mercury. The strong Mercury in Gemini with the Sun is a very strong yoga for perfection in knowledge, whilst the involvement of Ketu supports spirituality and meditation in a big way. As this happens in the Lagna, the native's birth and name will be strongly associated with the organization. However, the lord Mercury though strong is receiving the Rāśi dṛṣṭi from Mars and Rāhu, both bitter enemies of Mercury. This can promise a disruption to the spiritual organization but will not end the same, as Mercury is strong in its own sign and the birth is during sunrise. During the AṣTottari Daśā of Mars the Dalai Lama caused much concern for his Buddhist followers and the people of Tibet due to the Chinese invasion. This happened after a breakdown of diplomacy between the two parties in Venus Antaradaśā (Venus is in sixth from Ārūḍha Lagna, causing defeat). Since then the Dalai Lama has lived a life of exile from Tibet, now China.

Chart 166: Śrī Śrīla Prabhupāda – founder of ISCKON

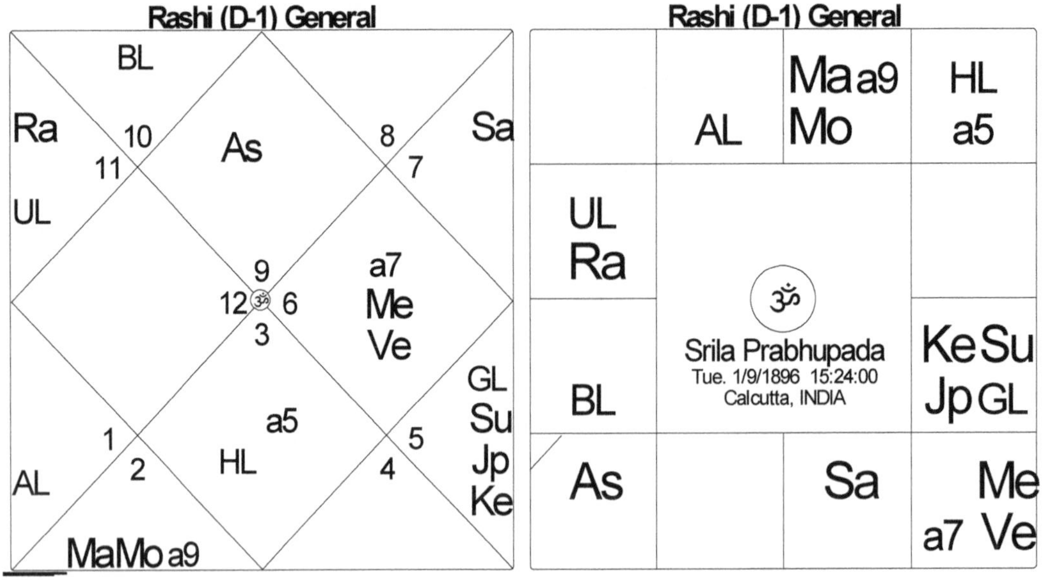

The Ārūḍha Lagna is in Aries. The fourth from Aries is Cancer and is unoccupied, whilst aspected by Moon, Mars and Rāhu. Neither indicate a very large organization, however the Moon is exalted and shows that an organization will grow. Moon and Mars are joined in the sixth house and Moon is Amatyakāraka, hence it will grow through work and service to society. Unfortunately the twelfth lord is joined the Moon showing a requirement to go abroad for the fructification of the same.

Śrī Śrīla Prabhupāda attempted the line of medicine, serving the common good by producing medicine for the public. Unfortunately, each time he attempted the same, he was robbed and/or cheated, and that too by his own workers at times. Moon is the Iṣṭa Devatā in the chart and joining the fifth lord Mars indicating that the service should be through the worshipped deity and as it is the Moon, Śrī Kṛṣṇa is indicated. At the age of 70 during the Caturaśītisāma Daśā of Mars, Prabhupāda went abroad to spread the word of Śrī Kṛṣṇa. He went to the United States of America and spent many years there, teaching about Śrī Kṛṣṇa and the Hindu ways, where he managed to establish 108 temples and build one of the biggest societies for spiritual consciousness in the world, namely ISCKON.

Chart 167: Śrī Caitanya Mahāprabhu – The Paramparā

The Ārūḍha Lagna is in Taurus, and the fourth there from is Leo, with a full Moon. Notably this is again a strong Moon just as in the case of H.H. Śrīla Prabhupāda. The Moon is joined Ketu and the Moon is itself twelfth lord showing a single-focus on attaining mokṣa and ending the cycle of rebirth. This becomes the karma yoga of his soul, as Moon and Ketu are in the tenth house from the Kāraka Lagna (Ātmakāraka). The lord of Leo is the Sun who himself is involved with the Full Moon, indicating the intensity of the organization and its never-ending presence in the world. The organization has becomes a symbol of truth due to the full Moon. Śrī Caitanya promoted the worship of Śrī Kṛṣṇa, and propagated the Mahāmantra[5],

5 Hare Rāma Hare Rāma Rāma Rāma Hare Hare| Hare Kṛṣṇa Hare Kṛṣṇa Kṛṣṇa Kṛṣṇa Hare Hare||

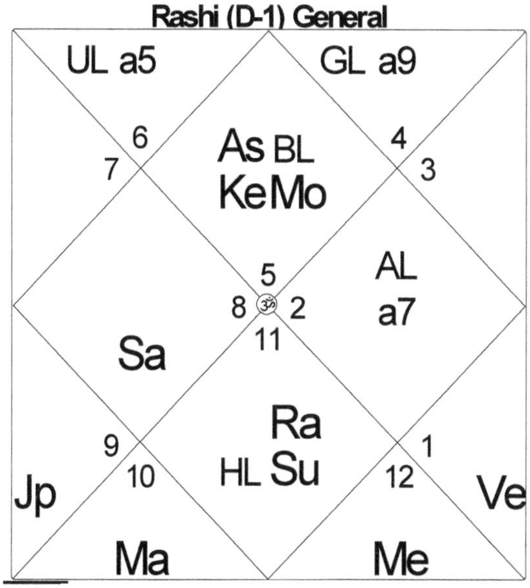

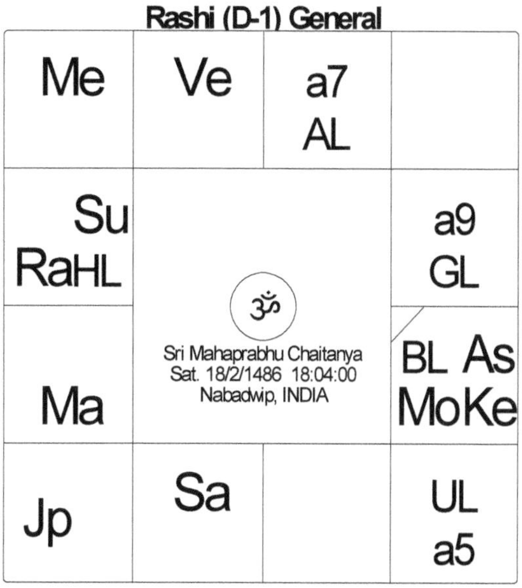

which was extolled by the saints of yore for the era of Kali (Kali Yuga). The Kali Yuga sign, Capricorn is occupied by ninth lord Mars, proving this to be the purpose of his birth. Notably Mars occupied the Ṣaṣṭyāmśa division of "Amṛta" meaning nectar, indicating that Śrī Caitanya's purpose of birth was to heal and help the souls of Kali Yuga.

11.2 The Eighth House

Most people consider the eighth house as the worst among houses. It is the house where death and suffering arises, and where we must endure the results of our past karmas. If wealth is coming following the demise of others, it can show inheritance. The eighth house shows the legacy the parents or relatives leave behind for you, and paired with the fourth house becomes important for one's property and home. It is the first definition of spirituality, as one becomes spiritual when trying to understand the cause of death and birth. For this reason, it is the house of occult practices or the practices done to raise the Kuṇḍalini Śakti.

11.2.1 Importance of Bālariṣṭa (infantile mortality) and Ages

आदौ जन्माम्गतो विप्र रिष्टारिष्टम् विचारयेत्।
ततस्तन्यादिभावानाम् जातकस्य फलम् वदेत्॥११॥
ādau janmāmgato vipra riṣṭā›riṣṭam vicārayet |
tatastanvādibhāvānām jātakasya phalam vadet || 1||

-*Bṛhat Parāśara Horā Śastra*, Chapter on evils, śloka 1.

"The wisemans first consideration at the birth of the child, is to judge the evils which may cause the death of the native, or the annulment of the same. Once having judged the evils or their cancellation, the fruits of the Lagna and the other houses in the birthchart, should be announced."

The above śloka by Parāśara clearly indicates the importance of analyzing the horoscope for bālariṣṭa effects, before judging the horoscope further. In fact, Parāśara does not allow the native to take **any step** in the chart analysis, before having analyzed the possibility of bālariṣṭa. Maharṣi Parāśara gives us an additional consideration to take into account before judging the chart:

चतुर्विम्शतिवर्षाणि यावद् गच्चन्ति जन्मतः।
जन्मारिष्टम् तु तावत् स्यादायुर्दायुम् न चिन्तयेत्॥२॥
caturvimśativarṣāṇi yāvad gacchanti janmataḥ |
janmāriṣṭam tu tāvat syādāyurdāyum na cintayet || 2||

- *Bṛhat Parāśara Horā Śastra*, Chapter on evils, śloka 2.

"Until the twenty-fourth year has passed from the time of birth, the possibility of premature death follows the native. The methods of ascertaining the longevity of the native are inapplicable to a person below this age."

This śloka has two implications, namely that one should not attempt to predict longevity for anyone below the age of 24. This is because one incurs the curse of Brahma upon doing so as one is incurring flaws upon his creation. Therefore astrologers do not speak of an infant's lifespan unless the parents inquire. The remedy to atone this flaw is through the Gayatrī mantra.

Parāśara later clarifies that among the 24 years, specifically the bālariṣṭa span is eight years and yogāriṣṭa is until 20 years (9-20 years of age). The rest is *alpa* (short) life. Hence, for a native of eight years of age or younger, the principles of bālariṣṭa apply fully, and the normal methods for calculating longevity such as piṇḍāyur, etc, do not apply.

Further to this Maharṣi states:

(mārakabhedādhyāyaḥ)

म्रियन्ते पितृदोषैश्च केचिन्मातृग्रहैरपि॥१३॥
केचित् स्वारिष्त्योगाच्च त्रिविध बालमृत्यवः।
mriyante pitṛdoṣaiśca kecinmātṛgrahairapi || 13||
kecit svāriṣṭyogācca trividhā bālamṛtyavaḥ |

- *Bṛhat Parāśara Horā Śastra*, Chapter on death, śloka 13

During these years (0-24 years) some die due to sins of father, evils inherited from the mother, or evil arising out of their own merrits.

The important learning arising from this śloka is that the father, mother and self are the prime causes of bālariṣṭa and yogāriṣṭa in the chart, and hence the Sun, Moon and Lagna, respectively, being the representatives of the Father, Mother and Self, become of utmost significance in deciding the initial lifespan of the person in the chart. The three points of reference viz. Sun, Moon and Lagna also form the basis of the "Sudarśana Cakra."

Table 82: Types of longevity

#	Term	Length
1	Bālāriṣṭa	0-8
2	Yogāriṣṭa	9-20
3	Alpāyur	21-32

#	Term	Length
4	Madhyāyur	33-64
5	Dīrghāyur	65-120
6	Divyāyur	121-1000
7	Amita	Limitless

Jaimini states that dīrgha āyu is for 108 years, and gives 36 and 72 respectively as the limits for Alpa and Madhya ayu. Parāśara states that the length of the ayuṣ khaṇḍa depends on the arrived longevity from the three pairs. Hence one khanda can be 32, 36 or 40 years long, making the maximum longevity 96, 108 or 120 years long.

Based on the type of longevity yoga existing in any being, we may determine the nature of the being born on this earth, i.e. if yogas exist in the chart for living till the end of a Yuga, then the native will have qualities akin to the nature of Viṣṇu. Yogas for limitless longevity indicate the birth of a sage!

11.2.2 The Sun: the Life Giver of the Universe

The graha, which gives light to the entire universe, is the Sun. The Sun through its light and warmth gives life to crops and ensures the beginning of creation. This Sun is hence associated with the father of the universe, and the two deities associated with the same are Brahma, as he is the creator of the universe, and Śiva, who is worshipped with the Mṛtyunjaya mantra to extend our lifespan in this abode. The Sun is also representative of the Dvādaś Ādityas, who are the cause of the entire material creation.

11.2.2.1 Sun's Placement

Since life is fully dependant on the light of the Sun, the signs, which do not receive the light or dṛṣṭi of the Sun, are destroyed. The places where no light resides are considered as the houses where shade or darkness exists in the form of Saturn. As Saturn's houses are the duḥsthāna houses, Suns placement in the duḥsthāna houses, especially the eighth house and twelfth house, become the worst placements of the Sun in the chart. Third and sixth houses are milder as Mars is Kāraka for them and is friendly towards the Sun.

Such a placement of the Sun can cause ill health due to low vitality, fatigue, weak immune system, and in worst cases death if other factors prevail, as the Sun will not be contributing to the strength of the Lagna. On the same note Parāśara states: "Sun is the Kāraka for Lagna"[t]. Hence, the Sun is the Kāraka of the first house itself and will have a direct bearing on the health of the native.

Parāśara has mentioned only one exception of Suns placement:

> व्ययस्थने यदा सूर्यस्तुलालग्ने तु जायते।
> जीवेत् स सतवर्षाणि दीर्घायुर्बालको भवत्॥६॥
> *vyayasthane yadā sūryastulālagne tu jāyate|*
> *jīvet sa satavarṣāṇi dīrghāyurbālako bhavet||6||*

- *Bṛhat Parāśara Horā Śastra*, Chapter on negation of evils, śloka 6.

"For Libra Lagna, if the Sun is placed in the twelfth house, the native has a long life of 100 years."

The cause behind this auspicious placement and seemingly contradictory statement is the fact that for Libra Lagnas, the Sun becomes Bādhakeśa due to its lordship of the eleventh house from a movable Lagna, and hence acts akin to Rāhu, the cause of the eclipse. It has been observed that the placement of the Sun in Libra Ascendant can be quite diabolical in disrupting the health and life of an individual. This one exception should be kept carefully in mind when deducing the results of the Suns placement.

11.2.2.2 The Lord of the Day

Since the Sun is the cause of sunrise, it is also the cause of the day. As a result, the entire day is defined by the period between sunrise and sunrise. This lord of the day has a vital say in determining the strength and overall health of the individual. This planet will indicate how the digestive fire/garbha-Agni in the body is burning... i.e. is it burning excessively or not at all. Preferably, it should be in the fifth house for best results.

- If the Sun is suffering from Sankrānti doṣa or such problematic placements, the Vāra lord becomes weak and can cause destruction to the houses it lords.
- Its placement in sixth or eighth houses from the Lagna causes troublesome ailments in the native and causes prolonged trouble from diseases and ailments. The body although healthy, could suffer severe troubles due to the ill placement of the Vāra lord.

11.2.3 The Moon: the Sustainer

The father, who holds the seed of life, creates the entire universe, just as the Sun pervades all darkness and ensures creation. In the same vain the mother is the sustainer of creation and is the initial protector of the child and sustainer in this world, in the form of the mother's milk... just as the Moon controlling the rains, ensures the sustenance of plants, crops, and feeds us with water. Hence, the Moon is of utmost importance in the chart. Among the three prime Godheads of Hinduism, the principle of sustenance is linked to Viṣṇu, as he is God in the form of the maintainer of the entire universe, hence it is said that the incarnations of Viṣṇu, also known as avatārs are born with a strong lunar influence on their Lagna.

Being governed heavily by the mind, the Moon is the Kāraka for human beings; hence, the strength of the Moon also shows the perfection in human beings. The blessing of the Moon is utterly important to sustain a person in this life. Among the most important factors in judging bālariṣṭa, the Moon is the key point of focus.

11.2.3.1 Inauspicious Placements of the Moon

Among all the grahas, Saturn despises the Moon the most. Saturn's ill relationship with the Moon is the cause of bālariṣṭa, and hence the Moon's placement in the houses of Saturn is susceptible towards bālariṣṭa. The houses of Saturn are the sixth, eighth and twelfth houses. Hence, the Moon in such a placement is conducive towards troublesome health at birth. Since the Moon becomes debilitated in Scorpio, a sign of Mars, the Moon also suffers heavily from the placement in the third house, whose Kāraka is Mars. Hence, Moon placed in the third, sixth, eighth or twelfth houses, can remove the sustaining forces of the individual.

पापन्वितः शशी धर्मे द्यूनलग्नगतो यदि।
शुभैरवेक्षितयुतस्तदा मृत्युप्रदः शिशोः॥१२॥
pāpānvitaḥ śaśī dharme dyūnalagnagato yadi |
śubhairavekṣitayutastadā mṛtyupradaḥ śiśoḥ || 12||
Bṛhat Parāśara Horā Śastra, Chapter on evils, śloka 12.

"Malefics accompanying the Moon, in the ninth, seventh or Lagna, and devoid of benefic aspect causes death"

Similarly, when the Moon is in gaṇḍānta, then bālariṣṭa is certain.

11.2.4 The Lagna: the Self

The father in the form of the Sun and the mother in the form of the Moon, come together to cause the conception and birth of the native. The birth itself and the native are seen from the Lagna, which is the union between the Sun's rays and Bhūdevī or mother earth. This union decides the rising sign.

11.2.4.1 Strength of the Lagna

The Lagna is like the Sun, and hence the placement Saturn or Rāhu in the Lagna can prove quite detrimental towards the health of the native, as both Rāhu and Saturn are inimical towards the life giver, the Sun. This is especially extolled by Vaidyanātha Dīkṣita:

"The third house for Jupiter, the seventh house for Mars, the first house for Saturn, the ninth house for Rāhu, the eighth house for the Moon, the twelfth house for Sun, the seventh house for Mercury and the sixth house for Venus are maraṇa (death) sthāna (houses/places). The involvement of malefics through conjunction or aspect on such grahas will cause a lot of pain." (Dikshita, 1992, p. 982)

Hence, it is clear that the position of Saturn in the Lagna is a death inflictor.

11.2.4.2 Lagna Lord: the Dhī

Jupiter rules the 'yoga' between Sun and Moon, being the binding element of the universe, and is the Dhī-Kāraka or the awareness of the native. This awareness is seen from the Lagna lord in the chart, whilst Jupiter will show the blessings of life force upon the native coming from Mahā Viṣṇu. Jupiter is jīva, which means life force. The weakness of Jupiter in the chart can prove detrimental towards the life force of the native, if neither the Sun nor the Moon is strong in the chart.

लग्ने भास्करपुत्रश्च निधने चन्द्रमा यदि।
तृतीयस्थो यदा जीवः स याति यममन्दिरम्॥९॥
lagne bhāskaraputraśca nidhane candramā yadi|
tṛtīyastho yadā jīvaḥ sa yāti yamamandiram||9||

Bṛhat Parāśara Horā Śastra, Chapter on evils, śloka 9.

"Saturn (Son of the Sun) in the first and Moon in the eighth whilst Jupiter in the third, will send the the person to the abode of Yama immediately."

Here Parāśara has shown how the ill placement/yoga of the Lagna, Moon and Jupiter will not hesitate to end the physical existence of the native. Since it has already been ascertained that the Sun is the Kāraka for the Lagna, and Jupiter is the Kāraka for the Lagna lord, we can finally conclude that the important facets of the horoscope:

1. Sun and Lagna
2. Moon
3. Jupiter and Lagna lord

If the above happen to be badly placed, weak or afflicted, then there is a serious possibility of bālariṣṭa in the chart.

11.2.4.3 The Three Lords

Having studied the Lagna lord, it becomes pertinent to study the eighth lord as well, as the eighth lord will decide the longevity of the native. To this Vyankaṭeśa Sharmā▫ states,

कर्मेश्वरेणापि विचन्यमायुदीर्घ सहत्सवोच्च युतेन तन।
केन्द्र स्थितै कर्म विलग्न रन्ध्र नाथैस्त्थै वायुरूदाहरन्ति॥
karmeśvareṇāpi vicanyamāyudīrgha sahatsavocca yutena tana।
kendra sthitai karma vilagna randhra nāthaistthai vāyurūdāharanti।।

"If the tenth lord is placed in friendly sign, own sign or exaltation sign, it confers long life. Similarly the location of the lords of tenth, first and eighth house lords in quadrants ensure long life."

–*Sarvartha Chintamani*, Chapter on eighth house, śloka 5..

Hence, it becomes pertinent to study the lords of the first, tenth and eighth houses when determining the longevity of the horoscope. Having understood the necessity of the first house and the longevity imparted to the native by the eighth house, it becomes necessary to explain the relevance of the tenth house.

The third from any house decides 'that which is necessary' for the house in question to perform its duties, i.e. the third house from the Lagna shows the skill and initiative of the native. Without this skill, the native cannot survive in this world. Similarly, the third from the seventh house is the ninth house, which shows how the morals and ethics of the native must be good for marriage to be fruitful. The third house from the eighth house will indicate that which ensures the longevity of the native, and this is the tenth house, one's karma.

The placement of these three lords in exaltation or own sign causes long life. Friendly sign gives medium life whilst inimical or debilitated sign give short life. Placement of these planets in duḥsthāna or Māraṇa Kāraka Sthāna will prove detrimental, whilst placement in Kendra or Trikoṇa will be auspicious.

11.2.5 Antidotes for Evils

Whilst evils may exist in a chart to extinguish life, the presence of specific yogas in the chart can remove the evil effects, and promote the life of a human being.

Parāśara states,

एकोऽपि ज्ञार्यशुक्राणां लग्नात् केन्द्रगतो यदि।
अरिष्टं निखिलं हन्ति तिमिरं भास्करो यथा॥ २॥
eko›pi jñāryaśukrāṇām lagnāt Kendragato yadi |
ariṣṭam nikhilam hanti timiram bhāskaro yathā || 2||

"If but one among; Jupiter, Venus or Mercury, be placed in the Kendras to the Lagna, all evils will be destroyed just as the Sun eliminates darkness."

- *Bṛhat Parāśara Horā Śastra*, Chapter on negation of evils, śloka 2.

Here Parāśara is clearly stating that the Kendras to the Lagna if occupied by benefics such as Jupiter, Venus or Mercury will protect the native. It should however be born in mind that Mercury if joined by malefics will not protect the child. Further to this Parāśara states:

एक एव बली जीवो लग्नस्थो रिष्टसंचयम्।
हन्ति पापक्षयं भक्त्या प्रणाम इव शूलिनः॥ ३॥
eka eva balī jīvo lagnastho riṣṭasañcayam |
hanti pāpakṣayam bhaktyā praṇāma iva śūlinaḥ || 3||

"Should one strong Jupiter be placed in Lagna, it will ward of all evils, just as a sincere bow to lord Śiva frees one from all sins."

- Bṛhat Parāśara Horā Śastra, Chapter on negation of evils, śloka 3.

The beneficence of Jupiter is eulogized here, and also the remedy to ward of indications of bālariṣṭa should Jupiter be placed in the Lagna. Similarly, the Lagna lord in quadrants to Lagna will also protect the native and remove evils that threaten premature death.

In those cases where survival seems impossible, it is found that if Venus is the strongest planet in the eighth house, or if unoccupied, Venus lords the eighth house, the native will be born prematurely. Venus in general indicates the Mṛtyunjaya Mantra, and its ability to save/rejuvenate lives.

एक एव विलग्नेशः केन्द्रसंस्थो बलान्वितः।
अरिष्टं निखिलं हन्ति पिनाकी त्रिपुरं यथा॥ ४॥
eka eva vilagneśaḥ kendrasamstho balānvitaḥ |
ariṣṭam nikhilam hanti pinākī tripuram yathā || 4||

"The Lagna lord placed in a Kendra can alone remove all evils, just as Pinaki (Shiva) destroyed the three cities."

- *Bṛhat Parāśara Horā Śastra*, Chapter on negation of evils, śloka 4.

11.2.6 Maheśvara: Lord Śiva

Maheśvara is the form of Śiva that detaches the ātmā (soul) from the mana (mind). Because of this concept, the Maheśvara in a chart is important from the spiritual perspective.

Calculations: Kāraka Lagna is the sign of the AK in the Rāśi.

1. The lord of the eighth house from Kāraka Lagna is Maheśvara

This follows the standard principle of ascertaining the Rudra in a chart.

2. If Rāhu or Ketu join the Kāraka Lagna or the eighth there from, then see the sixth from Kāraka Lagna.
3. If the sixth/eighth lord is exalted or in own sign, then the power to kill is delegated to the lord of the eighth/twelfth there from.

This rule implies that another graha takes on the power to kill from the original Maheśvara; this is an important principle.

4. If Rāhu or Ketu become Maheśvara then Mercury and Jupiter respectively become Maheśvara.

From the above one can observe that steps 3 and 4 are used solely to determine which graha will take on the power of Maheśvara to kill, but these planets do not actually become Maheśvara; hence, when we talk of Maheśvara from a spiritual perspective, only rules 1 and 2 apply. Reaching Maheśvara will help detach the ātmā from the *mana*. The position of Maheśvara in the chart will indicate how one can reach Maheśvara, or what events must transpire before that.

11.2.7 Kuṇḍalini

Scorpio is the natural eighth house and its colour is yellow. This yellow colour is akin to the colour associated with the Mūladhārā (root) Chakra, situated at the bottom of the spine. There are said to be seven chakras in the body, working as energy centers for various faculties of our being, i.e. the (Viśuddha) throat chakra when strengthened gives immunity towards diseases and diminishes lameness in the body. The energy is said to flow naturally in any animate being, however the intensity depends on how much energy is allowed to flow through these energy centres. The chakra hence works as a bottleneck. The goal of most occult practices is to widen this bottleneck to allow the flow of more energy through these centres. This is visualized as a lotus slowly opening its petals with the rising of the Sun in the morning. The increased energy allows for excess/mismanaged energy and this can in worst cases lead to mental or physical disorders. Once instigated the Kuṇḍalini rises from the seventh house and moves towards the Lagna where the Sahasrāra (crown) Chakra sits. Hence, the eighth house shows the instigation of the Kuṇḍalini, and planets associated with it will indicate how the native raises the Kuṇḍalini śakti.

- If Moon is associated with the eighth house, the native can through meditation and mantras raise the Kuṇḍalini.
- If Ketu is associated with the eighth house, the Kuṇḍalini rises spontaneously and the native is forced to deal with the energy. This can happen irrespective of whether they perform any spiritual practices, and can prove to be a very traumatic experience. This is a typical occurrence around the mid- 40's for any native.
- Venus in the eighth house will increase the Kuṇḍalini energy through the

practice of celibacy but this energy will be wasted unless Ketu's tempering effect is on Venus. This is also the blessing of the Mṛtyunjaya mantra.

- Generally, other planets in the eighth house will dissipate the energy unless tempered by Ketu.

The above combinations should be sought for in the charts of occult practitioners. For timing, the eighth house and the Ārūḍha of the eighth house (A8) should be analyzed.

- A Daśā related to the eighth house/lord can give the timing.
- The month will be indicated by the Sun's transit in the trines to the A8.

11.2.8 Case Studies

11.2.8.1 Bālariṣṭa: infantile mortality

Chart 168: Bālariṣṭa case

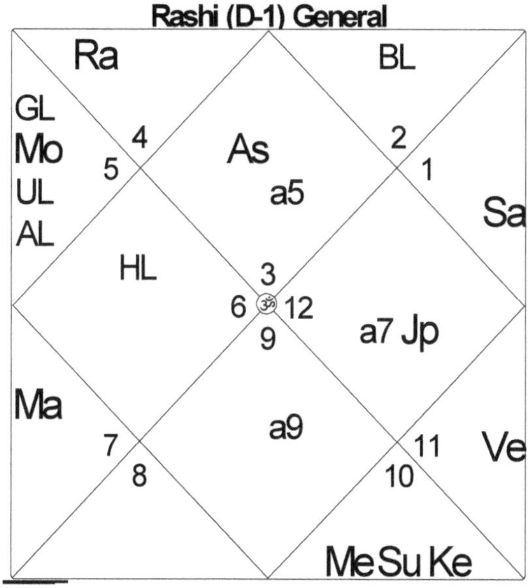

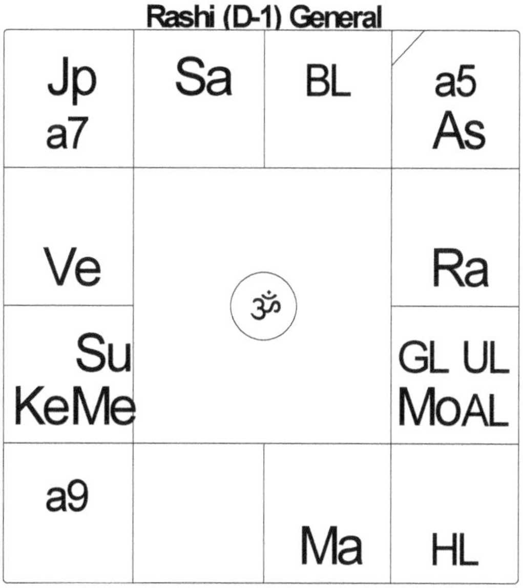

Male born 3rd February 1999, 3:25 PM, Bad Kreuznach, Germany.

1) In the given chart, the Sun is in the eighth house. This tells us that the native will have high susceptibility towards diseases.
2) The day is Wednesday, and hence the lord of the Day is Mercury. Mercury is also in the eighth house promising a very unstable life health wise.

The native has suffered severe health problems since birth, and has spent most of his infancy under medical care. Moon is in a duḥsthāna from the Lagna. The native has suffered fatal near death incidents in his childhood. Analyzing the three lords, we find the Lagna lord in a duḥsthāna, the tenth lord strong in the tenth house, whilst the eighth lord is in the eleventh house but debilitated. Jupiter is fortunately in a Kendra in this chart protecting and prolonging the native's life at every step.

Chart 169: Problematic health

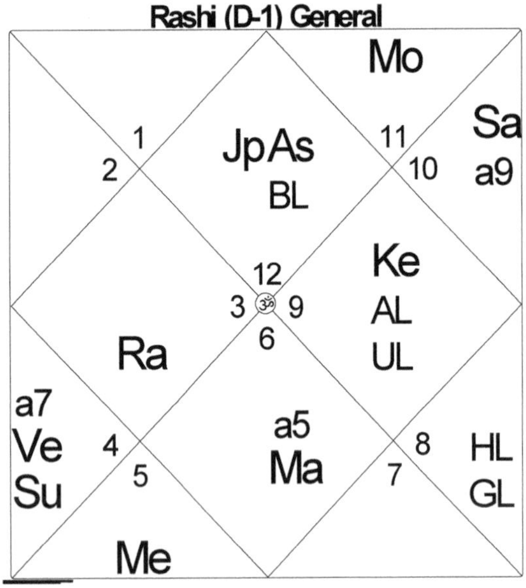

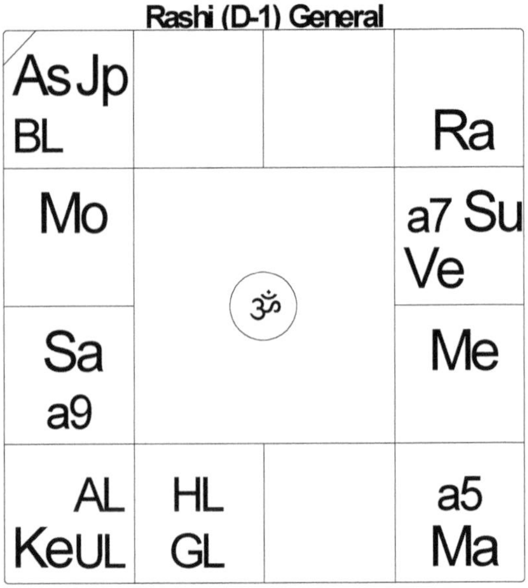

Male born 7th August 1963, 9:15 PM, Sambalpur, India.

1) The native's Sun is well placed in the trines to the Lagna, showing a strong vitality and low susceptibility towards diseases.

2) The lord of the weekday is Mercury, and is in the sixth house, showing that the native will often be troubled with health problems, as the body will be troubled by many ailments.

The native though having a strong immune system becomes heavily troubled by diseases at their onset. The native has problems with blood pressure and heart. Moon is in a duḥsthāna from the Lagna. Just as in the previous case, the native suffered fatal near death incidents in his childhood. Two such prominent cases were near-death due to drowning as an infant and dog bite during his early childhood. Jupiter is well placed in the Lagna, and proves to be a big blessing in the native's life, protecting him from any harm. Jupiter is in Lagna and in own sign, hence very strong. The native is an ardent worshipper of Śiva.

Vaidyanātha Dīkṣita (author of Jātaka Pārijāta) states that one born with Pisces Lagna occupied by Jupiter or Venus will prolong their life through the recitation of sacred hymns.

Chart 170: Baby Grossberg

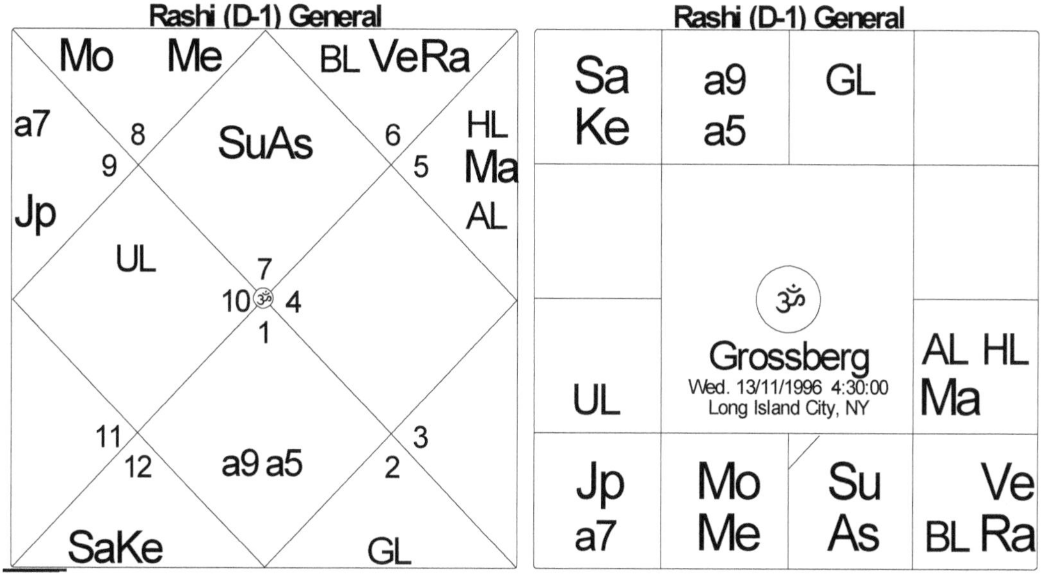

Baby Grossberg, born 13th November 1996, 4:30 AM, Long Island City, NY, USA.

The given chart is of baby Grossberg from the dramatic Grossberg-Peterson case. The Sun is in the Lagna, but since the Lagna is Libra, the Sun becomes the Bādhakeśa. The child died due to a blow suffered on the head (Sun) shortly after its birth. This proves that the Sun is not auspicious for Libra Lagna and its association with the Lagna can prove detrimental. This proves the statement of Parāśara.

The Moon is not in a duḥsthāna but is debilitated, hence causing a problem. The collective bad placement of Sun, Moon, Lagna and its lord is not helped by the placement of Jupiter in the third house. This is the maraṇa Kāraka sthāna, and proved to be extremely detrimental for the child. Note that neither of Jupiter, Venus, Mercury nor Lagna lord are placed in quadrants. The collective ill placement of important planets should compel us to judge the longevity using the three lords; the Lagna lord and eighth lord is not only debilitated but also in a duḥsthāna. The tenth lord is debilitated as well. The native lived less than a day.

Chart 171: Premature II

Male born 25th August 1974, 2:32 PM, Patratu, India.

In the given chart, the Lagna is Sagittarius and its lord is in maraṇa Kāraka sthāna. Moon is debilitated in a duḥsthāna whilst Jupiter, Venus nor Mercury are in Kendras. These factors confirm the probability of bālariṣṭa in the chart. Venus is in the eighth house and hence the birth will not end in demise but be premature, saving the native. Premature birth happens in or after the seventh month of pregnancy, and is an indication of great evil threatening the birth of the child. The presence of Venus in the eighth house averts the evil.

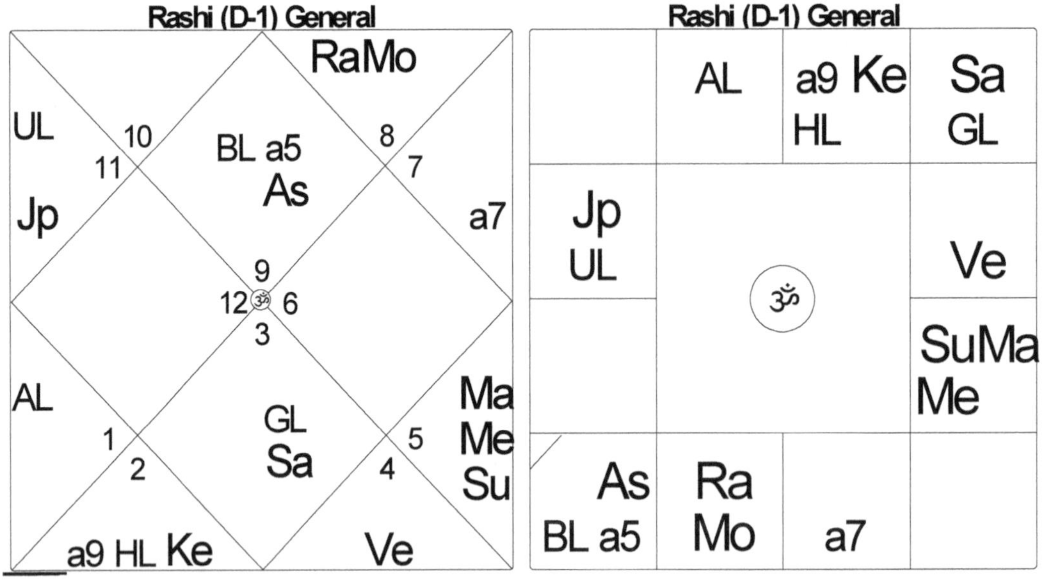

11.2.8.2 Kuṇḍalini Yoga

Chart 172: Jeddu Kṛṣṇamūrti

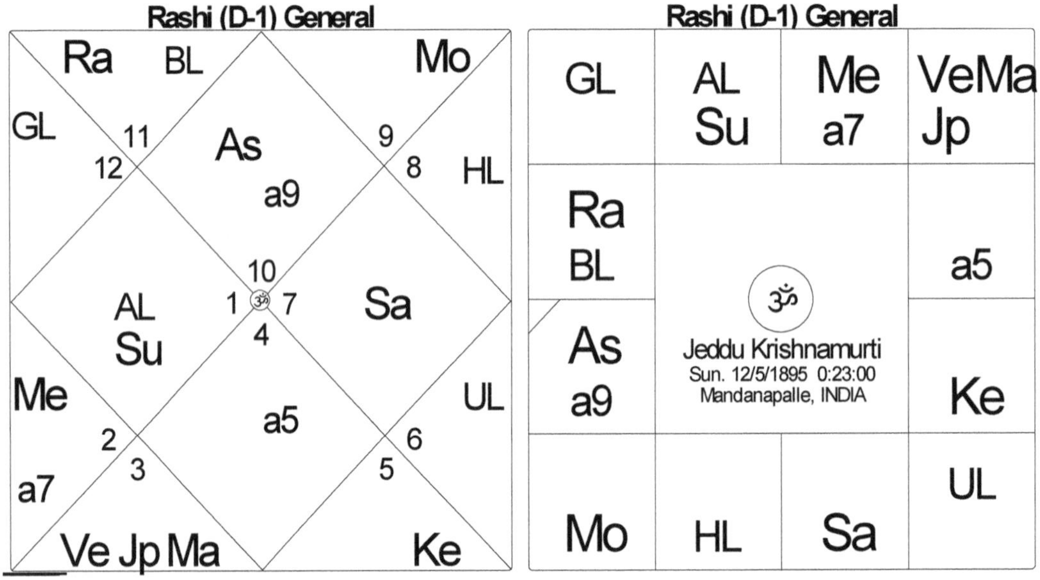

Jeddu Kṛṣṇamūrti born 12th May 1895, 0:23, Mandanapalle, India.

The given chart is of renowned teacher, spiritualist and philosopher Jiddu Kṛṣṇamūrti, who was closely involved in the theosophical society under the guidance of Annie Besant. The Ārūḍha Lagna is in Aries with Sun exalted in it, indicating a yoga for separation from parents. This began with the mother, whose demise came prematurely in 1905, only ten years after Kṛṣṇamūrti was born. The fourth lord from the Moon will reveal the details of the mother's presence in the native's life, and this Jupiter is in the sixth house, whilst debilitated in Navāṁśa. The eighth lord Sun is in the fourth house, showing possibility of a premature death of mother, whilst the fourth lord Mars is in a duḥsthāna threatening the health of the mother.

The person who will replace the mother is seen from the benefic influences on the fourth from Moon. The most benefic planet having Rāśi dṛṣṭi on the fourth house are Jupiter and Venus. One may note, that the ninth lord from the Sun is again Jupiter, however the ninth house and lord from Lagna do not suffer any severe blemish hence we may expect separation from the father, but not due to disease or demise. Jupiter and Venus are again the most natural benefic planets aspecting the ninth from Sun.

The guru is seen from the ninth lord, and its relationship with Jupiter and the Bhrātṛkāraka. The ninth lord is in a 2/12 relationship with Jupiter and the Bhrātṛkāraka, which will cause some disturbance in the association with the guru. Venus being the dispositor of Mercury is joined with Jupiter, and is causing the mutual association. This person will replace the mother, as mentioned previously, and later even the father. This guru is Anne Besant, who due to the fathers preoccupation and the mother's demise, took over the education of Kṛṣṇamūrti and his younger brother as a paternal guardian. It was during his twelfth year of age that Mrs. Besant began taking an interest in Kṛṣṇamūrti and his spiritual life.

Ketu is in the eighth house indicating the Kuṇḍalini Yoga, arising without conscious intention or meditation. The Lagna lord is in the tenth house, causing Siddha yoga giving Kṛṣṇamūrti the ability to perform serious penance and rites. The Lagna lord's retrogression would only make him try harder. These were the traits that Mrs. Besant was attracted to in the young boy, and the reason Kṛṣṇamūrti was specifically picked for a personal education. The guru's presence is seen from the ninth lord from Jupiter. Saturn lords the ninth from Jupiter and is exalted in the tenth house, hence the guru will always be close to the native and guiding the native. As Saturn is retrograde, and there will be a tendency to renounce or give up the association due to some sorrow or demise (Saturn).

Dṛg Daśā is the most appropriate for timing Kuṇḍalini awakenings and such incidents as it shows the path and experiences we take towards God. Kṛṣṇamūrti describes his early 20s to be spiritually profound, during which he was running the Dṛg Daśā of Sagittarius. Sagittarius is occupied by the Moon and A8 indicating the timing for experiencing important spiritual experiences. During Scorpio Antaradaśā, he was said to have experienced a Kuṇḍalini awakening whilst in Ojai, California. Scorpio is aspected by the eighth lord Sun and its lord, Ketu causing the awakening due to its placement in the eighth house. Whilst Kṛṣṇamūrti was a spiritual practitioner, he went to California looking for a better climate and possible cure for his ailing brother; hence, we may infer that Kṛṣṇamūrti did not seek Kuṇḍalini awakening at the time. In August 1922, the incident occurred. After August 15th, the Sun entered Leo which is in trines to the natal A8, indicating the precise time of the event.

When Kṛṣṇamūrti brother died in 1925, Kṛṣṇamūrti entered a period of grief and started to revolt against the restrictions imposed on him. In 1929, he broke free from the organization and became more independent; where after he wrote prolifically and was often labelled as a guru or Messiah of our times.

Chart 173: Śrī Lāhiri Mahāśaya

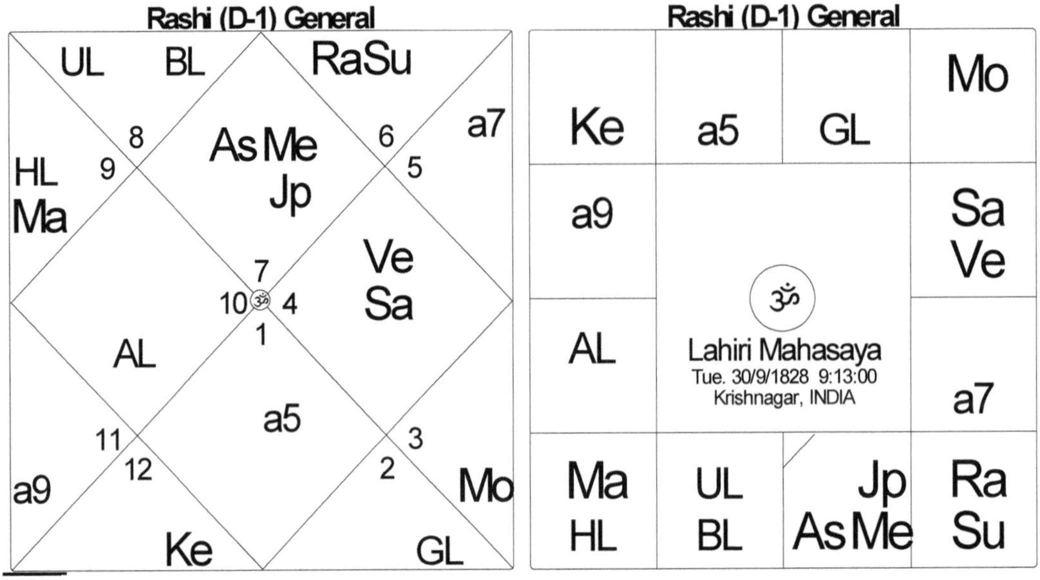

Śyama Charan Lahiri a.k.a. Lahiri Mahāśaya born 30th September 1828, 9:13 AM, Krishnagar, India.

In the given chart of renowned Krīyā yoga teacher, Lāhiri Mahāśaya, the Moon is in the eighth house with the Rāśi dṛṣṭi of Ketu, fulfilling all conditions for a Kuṇḍalini Yoga. Moon is the ninth lord in the chart and receives the graha dṛṣṭi of Jupiter, who not only is the natural Kāraka for the guru but also the chara Bhrātṛkāraka, which represents the guru. These factors show the strong influence of the guru in influencing the native's approach towards Kuṇḍalini yoga. The native learnt Krīyā yoga from the immortal Bābājī (also known as Gorakhnāth), and established a lineage for its teaching in India. Jupiter and Mercury are joined indicating the establishment of the Parampara.

Chart 174: OSHO Acārya Rajnīśa
Bhagawan Śrī Rajnīśa, born Chandra Mohan Jain, born 11th December 1931, 5:55 PM in Kuchwada, Madya Pradesh, India.

OSHO is well known for his books on philosophy of yoga, his greatest contribution to other practitioners being his personal experiences with the practice of yoga and his experiences of Kuṇḍalini rising. OSHO has eighth house unoccupied, whilst its lord Saturn is involved in a 5-planet yoga including the Moon. Four or more planets joined in a Kendra cause a person to renounce the world and live as a wandering monk. The eighth lord and the Moon are involved in such yoga. During his renunciation, OSHO would be compelled to attempt Kuṇḍalini yoga. For a person to take up such practices the ninth house/dharmapada (A9) must be involved, as such these practices should be taught by a guru. The lord of A9 is Venus and is in the

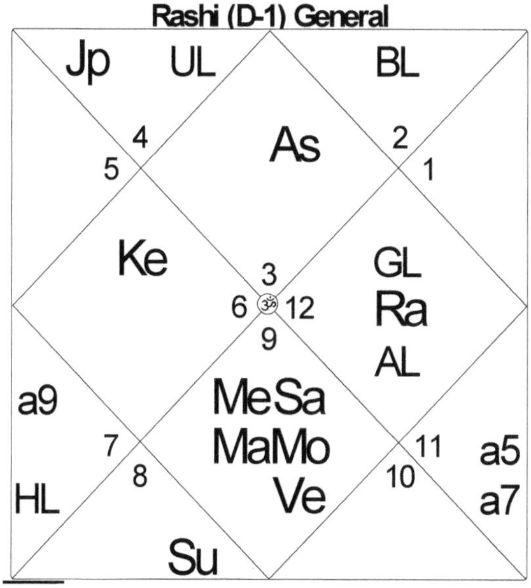

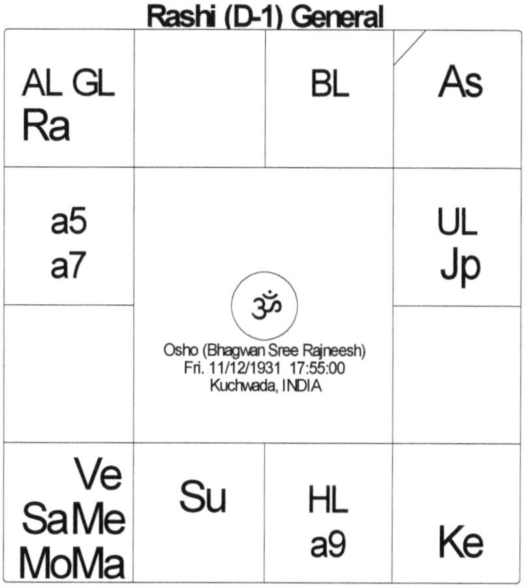

seventh house with the Moon and eighth lord.

OSHO was running Leo Dṛg Daśā aspected by the A9, indicating a time of spiritual practice and penance. The Antaradaśā was of Sagittarius wherein the planets causing the Kuṇḍalini yoga is occurring. Saturn being the eighth lord will indicate the timing of this awakening; since it is joined four other planets, and the most natural malefic planet will give its results through the most natural benefic planet. Venus is the most natural benefic planet and will indicate the timing. During Moon-Venus Vimśottari Daśā, the event occurred. The date was 21st March 1953, whilst the Sun was in Pisces, in trines to the natal A8 in Scorpio.

11.3 The Twelfth House

The twelfth house is an important house for marriage and relationships, as exemplified with the use of Upapada (Ārūḍha of the twelfth house). The twelfth house however does not deal solely with the concept of marriage. Marriage, as far as the twelfth house is concerned, is a concept derived from the act of giving or sharing. The twelfth house and its Ārūḍha deal with what we share with the world, and in cases where we do not share anything, our wealth maybe forced away from us. For this reason the Ārūḍha of the twelfth house also has another name, *Vyāyapada*, where *Vyāya* means that which is disappearing, decaying, passing away, is a source of expenditure or loss. This also means that the Upapada should not be ignored in the cases of people who do not marry.

11.3.1 Upa/Vyāya Pada

- ❖ When malefics are in the Upapada the native finds that, their giving/sharing is never appreciated. Instead, the native's wealth is forced away from him. This can go to the extent of making the person renounce marriage.
- ❖ The opposite will be the case in case of benefics in the Upapada.

To establish this further, Maharṣi Jaimini states that if Sun is associated with the Upapada, the native will have weak eyesight. How one sustains one's giving is seen from the second lord from the Upapada. Parāśara states that if this lord is in the second from Lagna, then the person will be a thief. This is because the native goes to any extent to sustain this giving, whatever maybe the cost. This will reveal the requirement for one's marriage to survive, and should be judged with similar rules as given in the seventh house chapter.

11.3.2 The concept of Giving

From this concept of giving, a very high level of spirituality arises, where the goal is to finally end the cycle of birth and death. The loss of self is at three levels of body (Lagna) mind (Moon) and soul (Ātmakāraka). The planet in the twelfth house from the Lagna shows that which you will always seek to protect. The native will always protect the Kārakatva of that planet, i.e. if Moon is in the twelfth house, the native will not like to leave their birth-place/country, whilst Mercury will make the native serious about their education. Malefics in the twelfth show inauspicious deeds, which the native devotes, time to and this troubles the native and manifests mostly through bad sleep patterns. This is also called Aśubha yoga. If the native does not devote time to these activities, the activities become a source of expense and the native suffers loss because of them. Where the native devotes his time is seen from the Lagna, hence if twelfth house and Lagna have a mutual association the native will be a spendthrift. Such people are very humble due to their ability to let go of wealth, and can be very giving in nature. This also ensures good sleep, as the blessings of Viṣṇu are upon the person, and sleep releases one from the bonds of this world.

11.3.3 Iṣṭa and Dharma Devatā

Having understood that the twelfth house from the Lagna shows that which releases one from the bonds of this world, the twelfth from Kārakāṁśa will show that form of God who will release the soul from the bondage of rebirth. The Kārakāṁśa is the Ātmakāraka in the Navāṁśa, and the twelfth from this position in the Navāṁśa reveals that deity, which will grant the soul Nirvana, or mokṣa. Identifying the planets placed there or if none, the lord of the sign will indicate the deity. That planet when worshipped gives solace to the native and carries a lot of peace with it.

Similarly, we should analyze the ninth from Kārakāṁśa to identify the deity, which will protect the soul's voyage through this birth. This deity should be worshipped for the attainment of one's objectives. The specific deity is seen from the planets in the sign. If unoccupied, the lord is to be taken. The deity is in truth a form of Viṣṇu, as Viṣṇu is the protector of dharma and the giver of mokṣa. However, the Iṣṭa Devatā can take any form for the native and one should chose that name or form which the person likes most. I.e. if Mercury suggests the Iṣṭa Devatā in a chart but the person prefers the divine mother, then the worship of Śrī Tripurasūndarī would conform the most for such a person.

Everyone should at least know their Iṣṭa Devatā.

Table 83: Iṣṭa and Dharma Devatā

House	Role
Ninth	Dharma Devatā – Protector of Dharma
Twelfth	Iṣṭa Devatā – Giver of Mokṣa/Nirvana

Table 84: Form of Viṣṇu/dharma devatā

Graha	Deity
Sun	Śrī Rāma
Moon	Śrī Kṛṣṇa
Mars	Śrī Nṛsiṁha
Mercury	Śrī Buddha
Jupiter	Śrī Vāmana
Venus	Śrī Paraśurāma
Saturn	Śrī Kūrma
Rāhu	Śrī Varāha
Ketu	Śrī Matsya

Worshipping the deity indicated by the specific graha is recommended to all persons, to ensure good passage through life and eventual emancipation to the soul. These planets can also be worshipped as other forms of God and not necessarily forms of Viṣṇu, however due to the advice of the Viṣṇu Purāṇa; we understand that the actual giver of liberation is a form of Viṣṇu. This is not to say that people who take a different name for God are not worshipping Viṣṇu. These planets should be judged in the Rāśi to understand the effects of this deity in moulding our life, or how God enters our lives.

11.3.4 Guru Devatā

The Chara Bhrātṛkāraka in Navāṁśa reveals the deity who will teach one about the universe, i.e. the inner and personal guru. We are taught that the guru of the universe is Jupiter and we worship him as Sadāśiva to remove our ignorance or at best as the Ātmaliṅga. However, guru can imply any living entity, which teaches us or removes our ignorance. The Guru Devatā is decided upon by seeing the Navāṁśa of the Chara Bhrātṛkāraka. If it is joined any grahas, the specific planet joining will indicate the deity. Otherwise, the Bhrātṛkāraka itself will indicate it. The eight Atmaliṅga of Śiva are preferred for this task.

Table 85: Guru Devatā

Graha	Atmaliṅga
Sun	Iśana
Moon	Mahadeva
Mars	Rudraliṅga
Mercury	Sarvaliṅga
Jupiter	Bhīmaliṅga
Venus	Bhavaliṅga
Saturn	Ugraliṅga
Rāhu/Ketu	Paśupati

The worship of the Guru Devatā is excellent for the native, and if the deity becomes pleased, it may bring one of its worshippers to the native as a guru. No matter the persons exposure, this worship changes life completely.

11.3.5 Case Studies

11.3.5.1 Eyesight Problems

Chart 175: Weak Eyesight

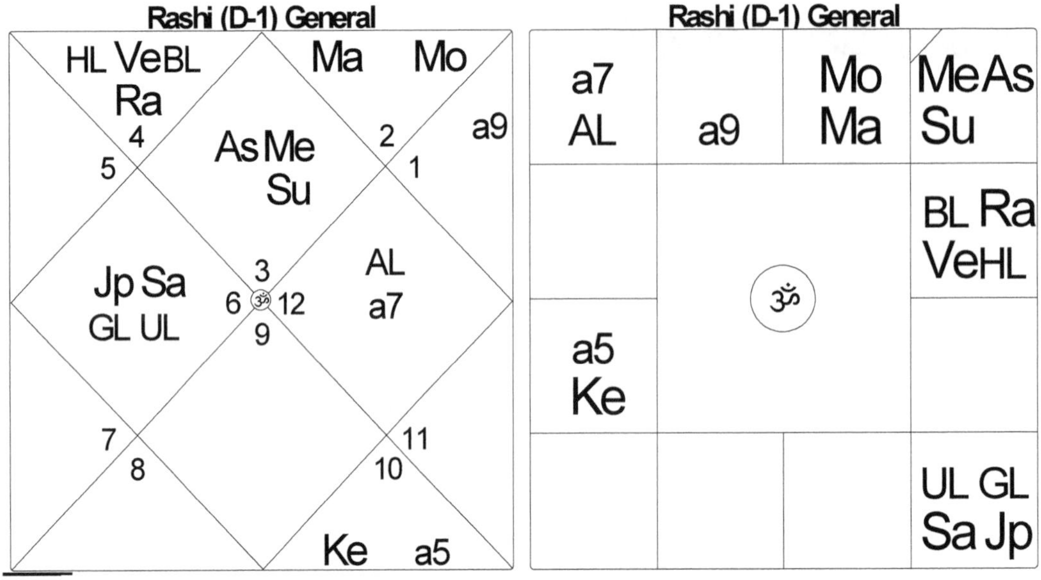

Lady born 29th June 1981, 4:42 AM, Tystrup, Denmark.

In the native's chart, Gemini Lagna rises, and the Ārūḍha of the twelfth house is in Virgo. Sun is in Gemini aspecting this Vyāyapada causing weak eyesight.

The tenth house rules eyesight and its lord Jupiter is joined Saturn in Virgo further diminishing the eyesight. The native has been wearing glasses since a young age and needs visual aid to be able to see properly. With Venus joined Rāhu it suggests that the eyes are weak and require care for her to maintain good eyesight.

Chart 176: Night Blindness and Weak Eyesight

Male born 20th March 1980, 6:05 AM, Copenhagen, Denmark.

The native of the given chart has had weak eyesight as long as he can remember. To further the same, the native is almost blind at night and is in constant need of visual aid. The Vyāyapada is aspected by the Sun by Rāśi dṛṣṭi, as Venus receives the Dṛṣṭi of Rāhu from Leo. This shows severe damage to the eye and a need for visual aid.

The tenth lord is Mars who is joined a curse of Brahmin in the seventh house showing that the reason for the eyesight problems is due to causing a wrong doing to a holy person in the past life.

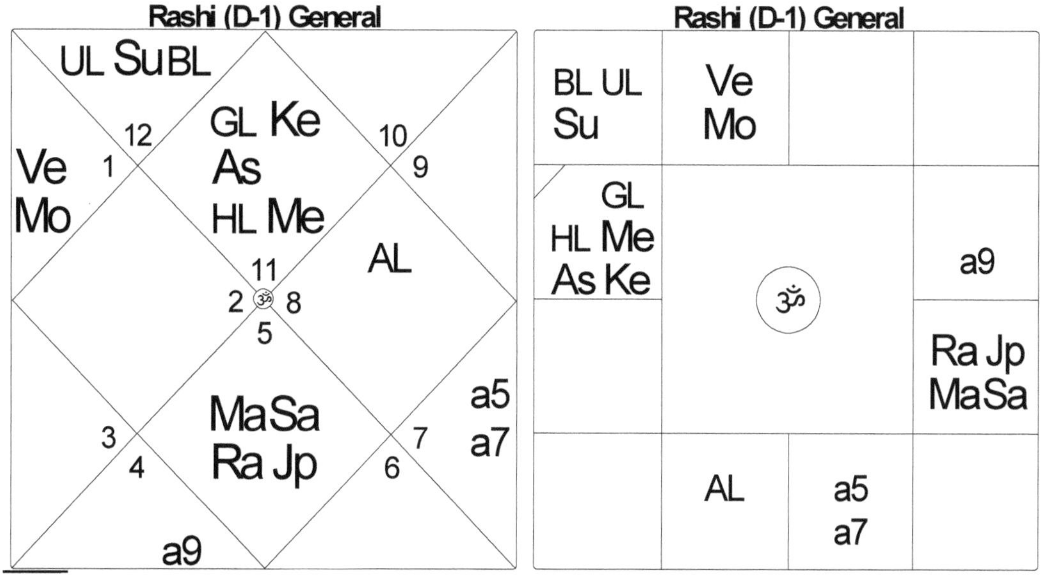

Chart 177: Author - Vyayapada analysis

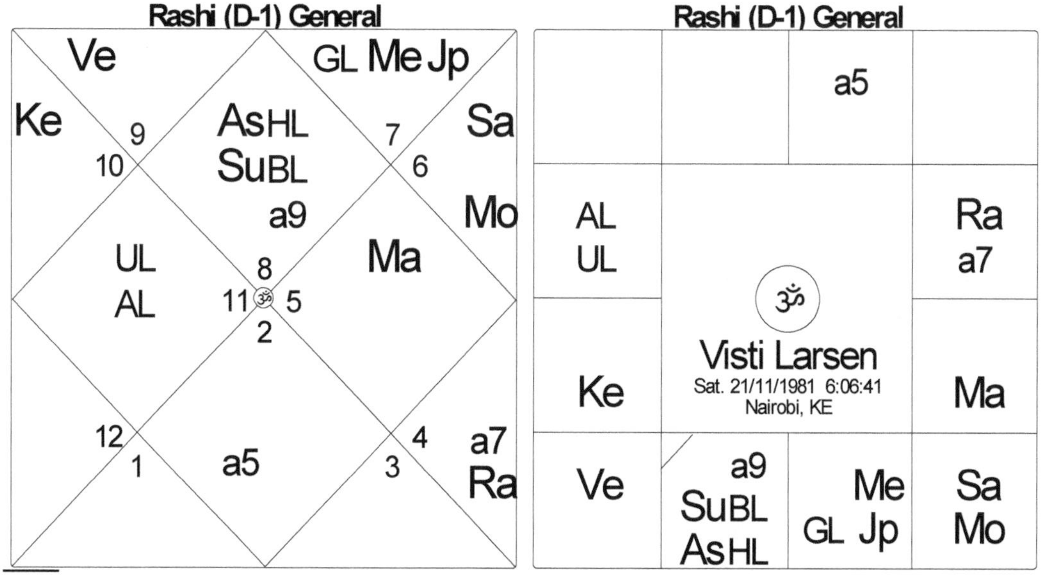

The native does not have eyesight problems, and the Sun is strong in the Lagna as tenth lord. The Vyāyapada is in Aquarius and is aspected by Jupiter and Mercury. Jupiter indicates the ability to hear or listen whilst Mercury indicates communicating, hence two important requirements for this native will be to listen and communicate with others. The native teaches many students on a frequent basis. Further the native suffers from chronic eczema in ears.

11.3.5.2 Iṣṭa Devatā: the liberator

Chart 178: Mahātmā Gandhi

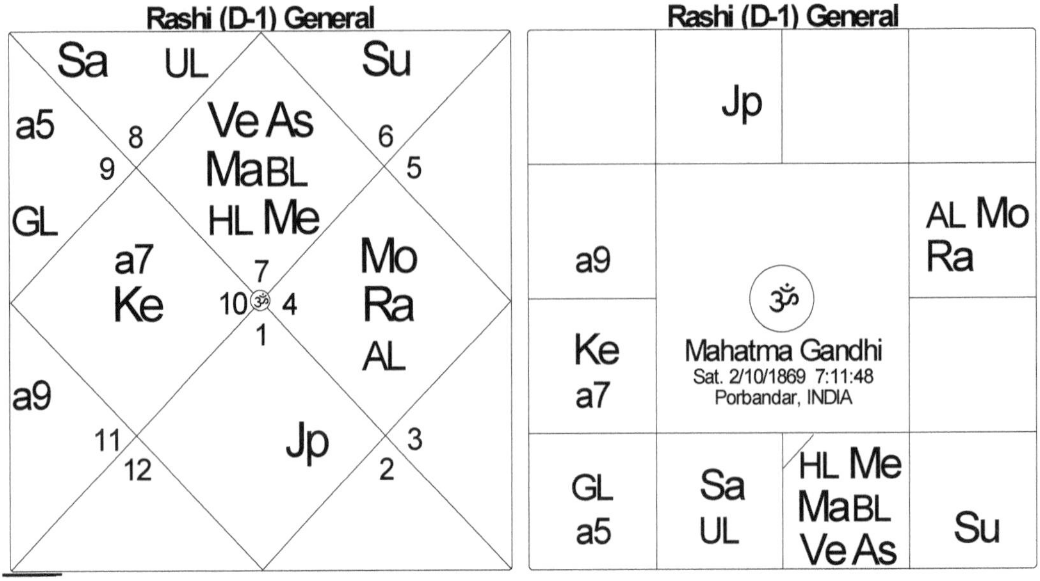

Mahātma Gandhi, born Mohandas Gandhi, 2nd October 1869, 7:11 AM, Porbandar, India.

Jupiter is the Ātmakāraka and is in Sagittarius Navāṁśa.

- The twelfth from Sagittarius is Scorpio, which is unoccupied. Scorpio is lorded by both Ketu and Mars. Mars is stronger as it is with more planets indicating Śrī Nṛasiṁha, Rudra/Hanuman or Bagalamukhī as the possible deities who will liberate the native.
- The ninth from Sagittarius is Leo, which is unoccupied. Leo is lorded by the Sun indicating Śrī Rāma as his protector.

The Sun and Mars should be examined in the Rāśi to see the results.

In the Rāśi, Iṣṭa Devatā Mars is in the Lagna whilst Dharma Devatā Sun is in the twelfth. Among these, Mars placed in Lagna joined two benefics in the sign of the scales (Libra) put Gandhi on a path of non-violence and justice. As this happens in the Lagna, this would have happened in his homeland. Gandhi returned to his homeland after having learnt and practiced law abroad for many years. Upon returning home, he turned a new leaf and entered the freedom struggle to liberate (Iṣṭa Devatā) India from the British Empire.

Sun the Dharma Devatā is in the twelfth house. In most cases this is a highly inauspicious placement, however the Sun is the lord of the eleventh for a movable Lagna, making its placement in twelfth very auspicious, as it takes away the inauspiciousness of the Bādhakeśa and the native may live free of many obstacles in life. Parāśara confirms this with the śloka:

"For birth with Libra Lagna, the Sun placed in the twelfth house will confer 100 years of long life on the native".

- *Bṛhat Parāśara Horā Śastra*, Chapter on negation of evils, śloka 6.

As it turned out, Mahātmā Gandhi was a sincere worshipper of Śrī Rāma, and as Sun is in the third from Ārūḍha Lagna, he even said the name 'Rāma' seconds prior to being assassinated in his garden (Virgo).

Chart 179: Jyotiṣa Guru

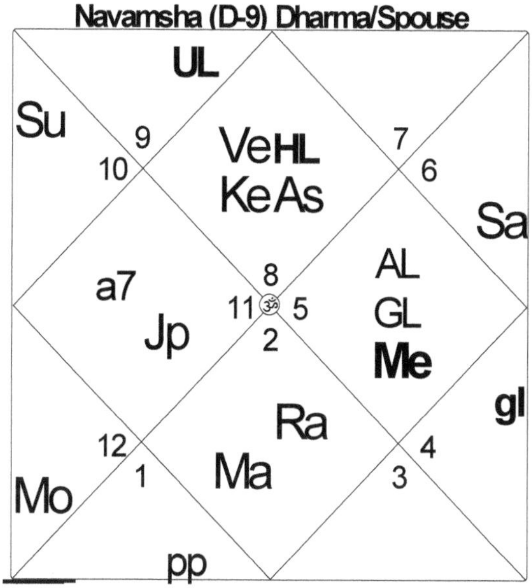

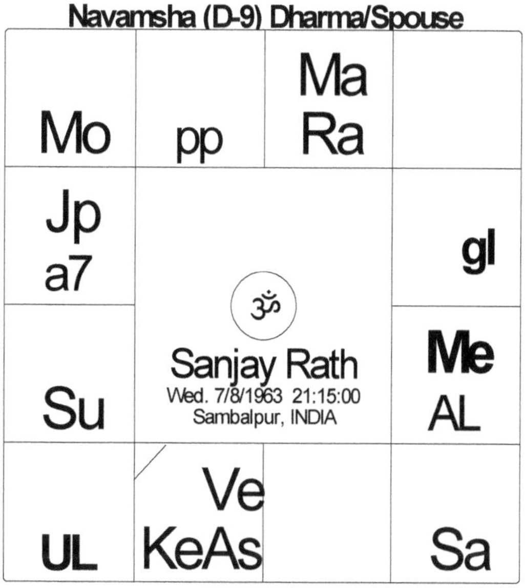

Pt. Sanjay Rāth born 7th August 1963, 9:15 AM, Sambalpur, India.

The native's Iṣṭa Devatā is Mercury, placed in the twelfth from Saturn in the Navāṁśa. Mercury is in the second drekkāṇa indicating Śrī Kṛṣṇa[6]. In the Rāśi, Mercury is opposite the Moon forming Śāradā yoga for divine knowledge and expertise. As Mercury is the fourth lord it will require a school to do so, and as Moon is the fifth lord, it will bring the students. At the advent of Mercury Daśā, the native felt compelled to start an organization for the sake of teaching astrology in the name of Śrī Jagannātha Śrī Kṛṣṇa.

Chart 180: Jyotiṣa Śiṣya

Visti Larsen born 21st November 1981, 6:06:41 AM, Nairobi, Kenya.

The native's Bhrātṛkāraka is Mercury unconjoined any planet in the Navāṁśa; hence Mercury will indicate the Guru Devatā. As Mercury is in the third Drekkāṇa of its sign, it indicates Śrī Viṣṇu. Whilst we should chose a form of Śiva as the Guru Devatā, the native worships Viṣṇu as the Guru (Śiva) in the form Vedavyāsa.

Mercury also happens to be the Iṣṭa Devatā indicating that the guru will also bring the native on the path of liberation. Mercury is in the twelfth house in Rāśi, indi-

6 Harihara (author of Praśna Mārga) is of the opinion that mercury in the first Drekkāṇa indicates Sri Rāma, whilst in the second and third drekkāṇas indicates Sri Krishna.

Navamsha (D-9) Dharma/Spouse

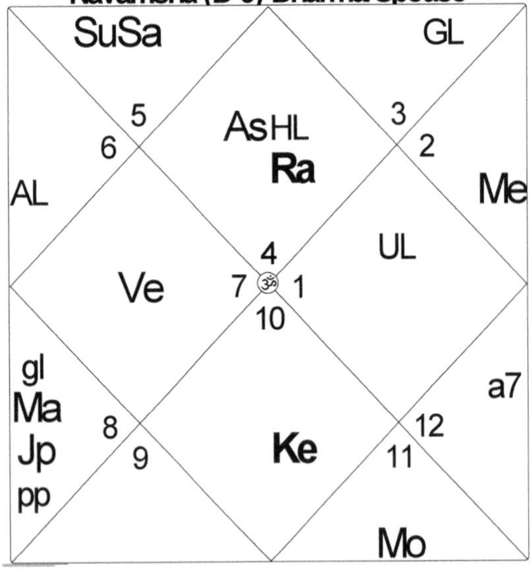

Navamsha (D-9) Dharma/Spouse

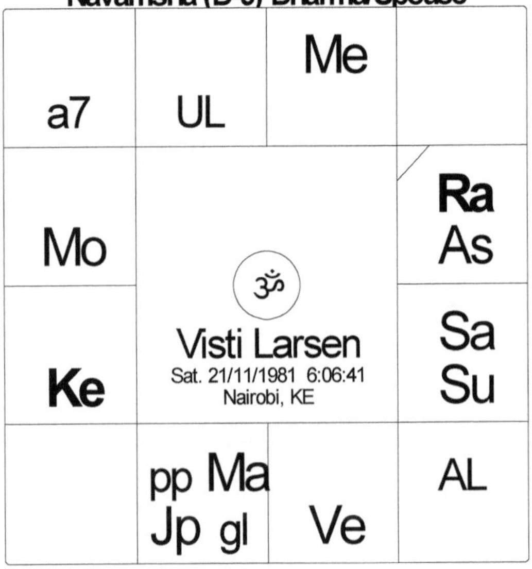

cating that the physical meeting between the guru and the native will happen in a country foreign from the place of birth. As this happens in a movable sign, it will be a long distance. Mercury is the eleventh lord showing that the guru will teach the native Jyotiṣa or occult Vidyā. As Mercury is joined Jupiter the guru has a strong Jupiter in his chart. The native's guru is a worshipper of Jagannātha, and resides in a foreign country.

The guru has Jupiter in Pisces Lagna, hence indicating the strong Jupiter. They met for the first time in London, UK (Libra). When there is such a combined involvement of Iṣṭa and Guru Devatā in a person's life, we may infer that the native incurred a blessing from the specific deity in prior births.

Chart 181: Swāmī Vivekānanda

Rashi (D-1) General

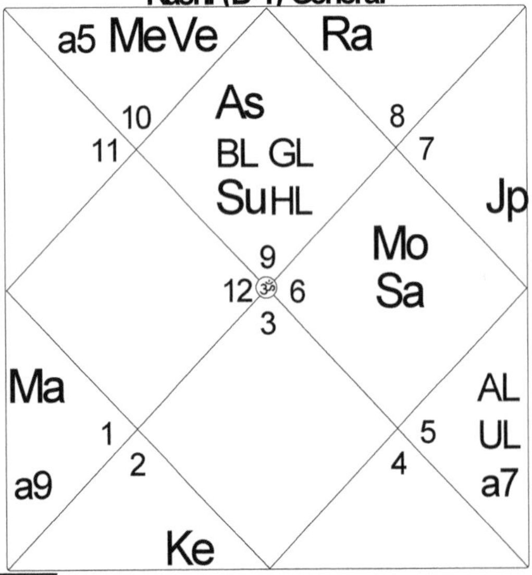

Rashi (D-1) General

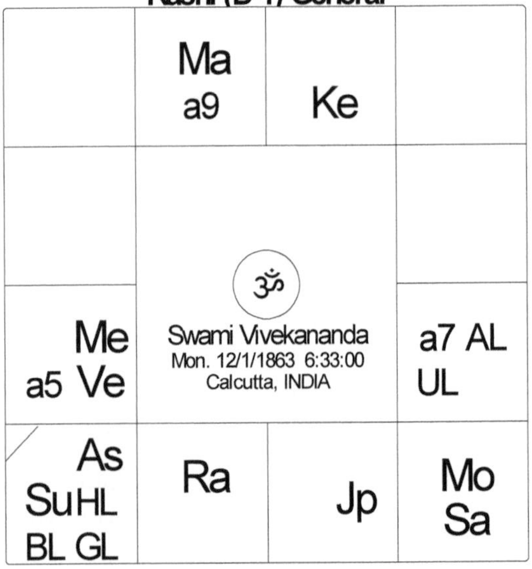

Swami Vivekananda, born Narendranātha Dutt, 12th January 1863, 6:33 AM, Calcutta, India.

The given chart has Saturn as Bhrātṛkāraka placed in the tenth house with the Moon. The native's guru was an avid worshipper of the divine mother, specifically as Kālī (Saturn specifically indicates Kāḷi). The native's guru was Śrī Rāmakṛṣṇa Paramahamśa. As the yoga occurs in the tenth house, the association with the guru requires some task or work to be performed. The result of this work will be widespread fame as Moon is in the tenth house.

Chart 182: Śrī Rāmakṛṣṇa Paramahamśa

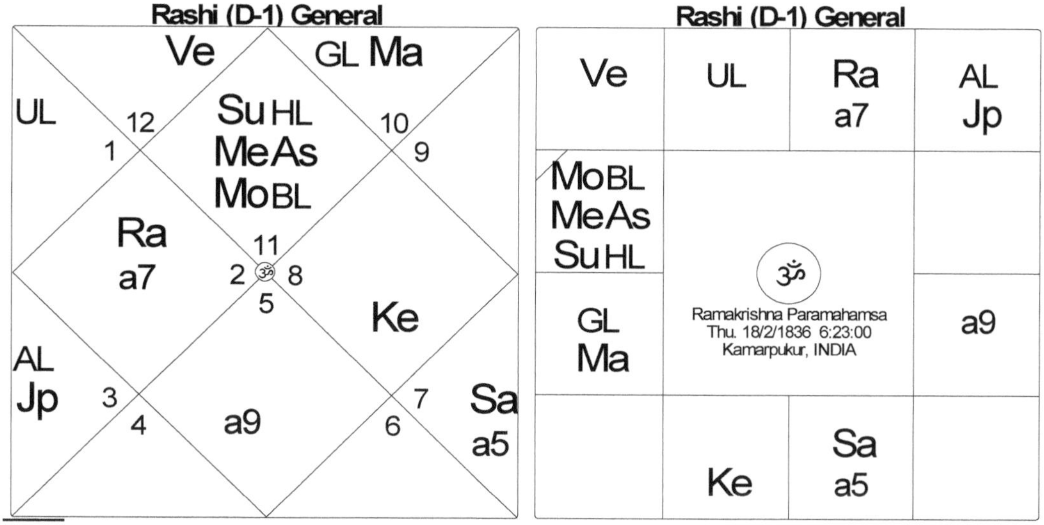

Śrī Rāmakṛṣṇa Paramahamśa, born Gadadhar Chattopadhyay, 18th February 1836, 6:23 AM, Kamarpukur, India.

Moon is the Bhrātṛkāraka and indicates devotion to the divine mother. The native worshipped the divine mother in all her forms and was well known for his saying; "only my mother knows who my father is." The native went to the extent of developing female features (Moon is in Lagna indicating the appearance) due to his intense penance towards the mother.

यन्मण्डलं वेदविदोपगीतं यद्योगीनां योग पथानुगम्यम्।
तत्सर्व वेद प्रणमामि सूर्यं पुनातु मां तत्सवितुर्वरेण्यम्॥ १२॥

12

Nārāyaṇa Daśā
Padakrama Daśā of Jaimini

In the available writings from Maharṣi Jaimini, a particular Daśā emerges which takes into account the peculiarity of the three types of signs, namely, the movable, fixed and dual signs. Some call this Daśā Padakrama Daśā, which literally means, series of steps or walking. Pada is equated with the ¼th portion; hence, it can refer to a series of quarters. In the tradition of Śrī Acyuta Dāsa, this Daśā is called Nārāyaṇa Daśā. The Daśā gets its name, as it encompasses the three types of śakti[1], which are said to reside in Nārāyaṇa. For this reason, the Daśā gets its name. The three types of signs, movable, fixed and dual, symbolize these three śakti.

This chapter will not deal with the calculation of the Nārāyaṇa Daśā in particular, but with its understanding and interpretation. Those interested in the calculations and other details may refer to the book *Nārāyaṇa Daśā*, by Sanjay Rath.

Understanding the Daśā

The Nārāyaṇa Daśā is a Rāśi Daśā, i.e. it gives the results of a sign and hence the Daśā focuses on places and circumstances. This is contrary to the graha daśās, which revolve around the entry of other souls into our lives, who may or may not support our own desires again symbolized by a graha. The Nārāyaṇa Daśā is the movement of Nārāyaṇa through our lives. Wherever Nārāyaṇa goes, the world follows, and hence this Daśā is excellent in seeing the progression of a person through life.

However it does not undermine the utility of Vimśottarī and other Udu daśās; in fact, the best way to use Nārāyaṇa Daśā is with Vimśottarī Daśā. Vimśottarī Daśā will show the mind of the individual and the manner in which it interacts with society. The mind however is subservient to the circumstances laid before it, and here is where Nārāyaṇa Daśā comes into play. Even if you want a job, you will not get one unless jobs are available. The desire is caused by the mind, but Nārāyaṇa provides the availability. The method in which we should apply the Nārāyaṇa Daśā is

1 Śrī Śakti, Bhū Śakti and Nīla Śakti; also known as Mahā Lakṣmī, Mahā Sarasvatī and Mahā Kālī.

from a circumstantial point of view, without taking into account the implications of people's longings and desires, unless we are using the Udu daśās.

Overall Results

The overall result of a Daśā is understood by treating the Daśā Rāśi as Lagna, and judging from it the placement of planets.

- Benefics in 1st, 2nd, 4th, 5th, 7th, 8th, 10th and 12th are auspicious; malefics are not.
- Malefics in 3rd and 6th are auspicious; benefics are not.
- Any planet in 9th or 11th is auspicious.

The individual results are given below.

- Benefic planets in the Daśā Rāśi will give direction, ideals, name, fame and happiness. Malefics in the Daśā Rāśi are highly inauspicious; causing disorders of the intellect, situations not conducive towards mental growth, unless they are well placed as far as the sign is concerned.
- Malefics should not be in both the fifth and ninth houses from Lagna, as this can cause bondage or a feeling of bondage, especially if equal amount of malefics are in these houses. If only the ninth house has planets, the result is not bad.
- Malefics in the second or eighth houses will give monetary strain and bad loans respectively. Benefics are auspicious here.
- Malefics in the third or sixth houses will give an aggressive posture leading to success in battles unless the malefics are debilitated in Rāśi or Navāṁśa. Benefics will give defeat and a path towards spirituality unless debilitated in Rāśi or Navāṁśa, where they will give material prosperity.
- Any planets in the ninth and eleventh houses will protect the native and give wealth to the native provided these houses are not the Bādhaka Sthāna, where the planets posited can give very evil results unless natural benefics. Planets in the ninth house will also indicate the nature of one's study during the Daśā. If auspicious planets are in these houses yet are afflicted by two or more malefics know that the native will be offered great opportunities will later end up becoming a curse for them.
- Malefics in the fourth will cause change of home, or moving away from home during the Daśā; benefics will do otherwise, yet can change home for a much better one.
- Benefics in the fifth will give supporters and blessings from children/followers; malefics will do otherwise and can hurt one's supporters/children/followers.
- The seventh house from Daśā Rāśi shows the desires of the native and this desire will indicate what direction the native moves in life i.e. a person with Saturn in seventh from Daśā Rāśi will have few desires, will be lazy and will sleep late.
- Malefics in the tenth house from Daśā Rāśi are not conducive towards good career growth; instead, they will cause bad name and destroy one's work. Rāhu

in the tenth can however specifically take one on pilgrimages. Benefics are preferred here for material success.

- Benefics are preferred in the twelfth house, instead of malefics, as they will form śubha yoga on the Daśā Rāśi and give good sleep and expenses on good deeds. Malefics, especially the nodes will cause one to lose the fruits of one's labour.
- The malefic/benefic nature of the planet is very important in deciding the fruits of the Daśā. Herein curses and such yoga must be taken into account for a final gleaning of the results of a graha.

These effects of treating the Daśā sign as Lagna become prominent especially in the portion of the Daśā trend associated with the sign.

Daśā Trend

With all Daśā systems, it is common practice to divide the Daśā into parts to decide the overall trend of the Daśā. Normally the division is into three parts. Such practice is useful in quickly judging the overall trend of the Daśā. In case of Nārāyaṇa Daśā, 1/3rd portion of the period equals four Antaradaśās, of which the qualified jyotiṣī can easily pick the relevant antara in which the event manifests.

The Rāśi daśās give their results as follows:

- Effects of the sign itself
- Effects of the sign lord
- Effects of the occupants and aspects on the sign
  - If the Daśā Rāśi is a Śīrṣodaya (rises with its head) sign, the results of the sign will give its results in the beginning of the Daśā.
  - Incase of Pisces as the Daśā Rāśi the results of the sign will come in the middle portion of the Daśā.
  - If the Daśā Rāśi is a Pṛṣṭhodaya (rises with its back) sign, the results of the sign will give its results in the end of the Daśā.

Table 86: The Three Parts of a Daśā

Daśā Part →	1st	2nd	3rd
Śīrṣodaya Rāśi	Sign	-	-
Ubhayodaya Rāśi	-	Sign	-
Pṛṣṭhodaya Rāśi	-	-	Sign

Having ascertained when the sign will give its results, the next step is allotting the results of the lord and the occupants/aspects on the sign. The effects of the lords will also depend on their beneficence in the chart. Malefic lords are more inclined to give results towards the end of the Daśā. The opposite principle applies for benefics. In the case of Leo, which gives its results in the beginning of the Daśā, the lord is a malefic, the Sun, hence the results of the lord will come in the end of the Daśā.

Finally, the occupants/aspects will give its results in the middle of the Daśā.

#	Result
1st	Sign Leo
2nd	Occupants/aspects
3rd	Lord Sun

Incase of Pisces which gives its results of the sign in the middle of the Daśā, the lord – Jupiter, will give its results in the beginning of the Daśā.

#	Result
1st	Occupants/aspects
2nd	Lord(s) Saturn/Rāhu
3rd	Sign Aquarius

#	Result
1st	Lord Jupiter
2nd	Sign Pisces
3rd	Occupants/aspects

Similarly, in the Daśā of Aquarius Rāśi, the results of the sign will be in the end as previously discussed and the lords Saturn and Rāhu will give their results in the middle. The results of the first portion will be given by the occupants who are more beneficial than the lord and the sign.

Effects of Daśā Trend

Daśā Sign

During the effects of the Daśā sign, the results are of two kinds. The placement of the Daśā Rāśi from the Lagna, Kāraka Lagna and Ārūḍha Lagna to derive what the native is receiving during the Daśā.

- Daśās of the second house from Lagna or Ārūḍha Lagna can cause ill health, accidents and even death. The same applies for the seventh house from Lagna. Similarly judge the other houses as given in classics.
- Daśās housing Ārūḍhas will give rise to those people indicated by the Ārūḍha.

Lordship

The lord of the Daśā Rāśi is the Pāka Rāśi. The Pāka Rāśi will indicate where the efforts of the Daśā are focused, and hence where the native himself will focus their energy.

The effects of the Pāka Rāśi can be measured in two ways.

- The placement of the lord from the natal Lagna(s), to see what the native is receiving from the world.

- The placement of the lord from the Daśā Rāśi to see what the native is required to do.

Occupants/Aspects

The effects of the occupants/aspects are similarly analyzed as above.

- The planets aspecting or joining the Daśā Rāśi, will give effects pertaining to their placement from the natal Lagna(s).
- In cases where the lord of Daśā Rāśi aspects the Daśā Rāśi, the effects will be carried to the 1/3rd portion where the lord is concerned.

The Daśā trend should be reckoned from Daśā Rāśi or its seventh, depending on whether the daśās were initiated from the Lagna or the seventh house respectively.[2]

Case studies

Chart 183: Bush, George W.

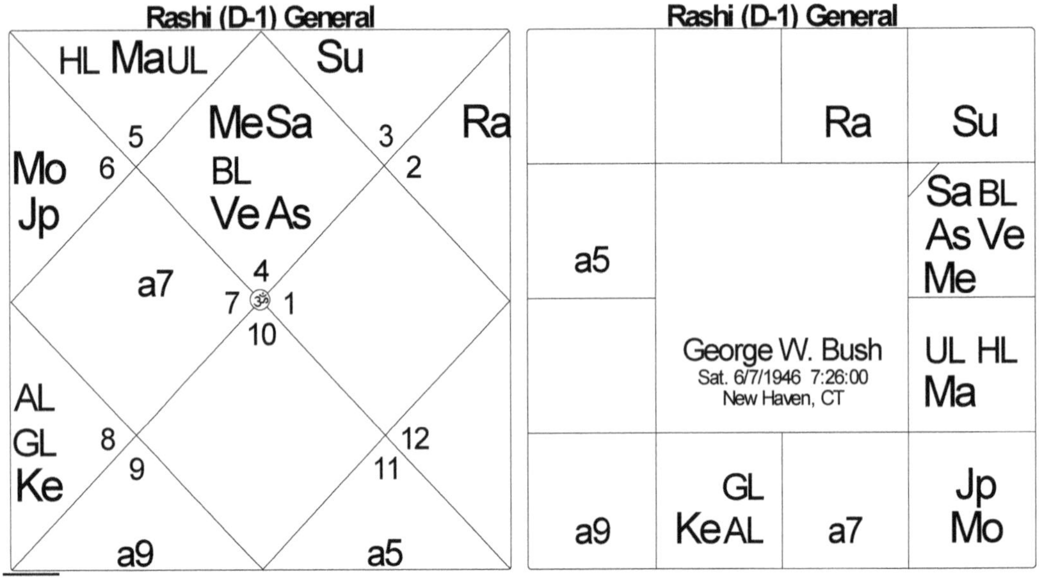

George W. Bush, born 6th July 1946, 7:22 AM, New Haven, CT, USA.

In the given chart of George W. Bush, Pisces Mahādaśā runs from 2000 to 2006. This period of six years is divided into three equal portions of two years each. Since Pisces is an Ubhayodaya sign it will give the effects of its lord in the beginning portion, its sign in the middle portion and the occupants/aspects in the last portion.

The first portion was from July/2000 to July/2002. Jupiter will indicate the overall results of this period and is in Māraṇa Kāraka Sthāna, forming Gajakesarī Yoga with the Moon. The results are contradictory and both indications will happen. It was during this time that Bush became president with the help of Jupiter (judges) and during the same period suffered the tragic 9/11 incident which sent the country

2 For more information, readers can refer to Bṛhat Parāśara Horā Śastra, Carādidaśāphalādhyāya (Chapter on the effects of chara and similar daśās).

into perpetual war against terrorists.

The second portion is from July/2002-July/2004. Here the result of Pisces' placement from the various Lagna is under scrutiny. Pisces is the ninth house and indicates a broadening of one's world-view, i.e. one travels and learns more about the surrounding environment. Pisces is occupied by the Ārūḍha of the sixth house, which will bring more criticism to the native and rise to more enemies. This will lessen one's popularity. The third and sixth from Pisces, has two malefic planets, Rāhu and Mars; this will require Bush to take a very aggressive posture and cause him to deploy his weapons/army. Sun is in the fourth from the Daśā Rāśi requiring Bush to leave his home, but the same Sun aspects Pisces, and will defer its results to the third portion. It was during this time that Bush attacked Iraq and gained a lot of unpopularity both at home and abroad.

The third portion is from July/2004-July/2006. Here the results of the planets occupying and aspecting Pisces will rise. The Moon is aspecting the ninth house Pisces which is very auspicious and promises fortune (ninth) and fame (first lord). The Sun aspecting Pisces is auspicious for health, but this same Sun is also in the eighth from the Ghāṭikā Lagna, which is relevant for power, and position. As a result, the Sun may not be promoting the continuation of power for Bush and could give him significant competition. It so happens that his main opponent during the elections of November 2004 has Sun in Lagna. Jupiter's effect came in the first portion, and hence is excluded from the reading.

Chart 184: Kerry, John Forbes

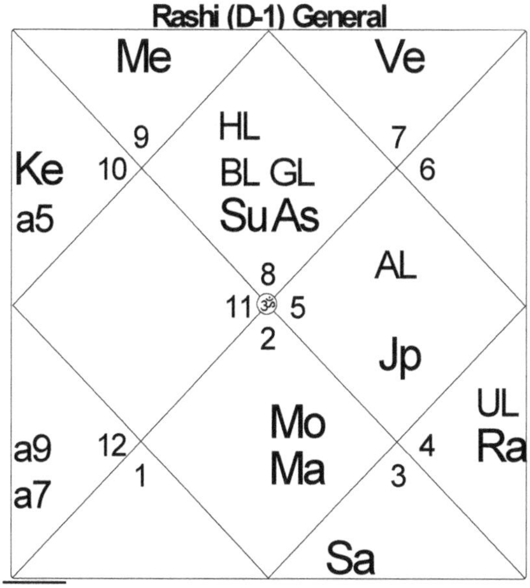

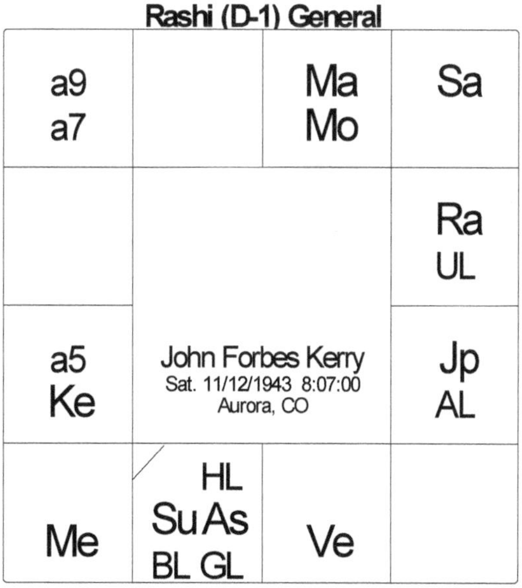

In the given chart of Kerry, the Sun is in the ghāṭikā Lagna in the Lagna. This is akin to the Sun in the eighth from GL in Bush's chart. Similarly, the eighth from GL in Kerry's chart houses Saturn, which happens to be in the Lagna in Bush's chart. Daśās start from the seventh house, and normally one should reckon the results from the seventh from Daśā Rāśi, however as Kerry's Lagna lord is in the seventh house, the results can be seen from the seventh house itself.

Kerry is running Leo Nārāyaṇa Daśā from 1996–2005. Leo rises with its head and gives the results of the sign in the first portion; the results of occupants/aspects will manifest in the second portion whilst the lordship will give results in the third portion. From 1996-1999 the effects of Leo itself would be given, housing Jupiter, showing good name and reputation. Mercury in the fifth house is giving a strong support, especially from those interested in communications and technology.

1999-2002 will give the results of the occupants/aspects. Jupiter is conjoined other planets and is the fifth and second lord in the tenth house from the Lagna giving a lot of good work and favorable circumstances. This Jupiter is joined Ārūḍha Lagna increasing the persons name and fame in the world. Jupiter is in the tenth from the ghāṭikā and Horā Lagnas, which indicates an increase in the authority and wealth for Kerry. Venus is aspecting, who is in the twelfth from the Lagna causing an auspicious śubha yoga, protecting Kerry from any harmful events. Venus in the third from Ārūḍha Lagna shows an act of renunciation or stepping down; whilst Kerry was popular among the democratic candidates, election time had come and Vice President Al Gore was running for presidency among the Democrats, hence Kerry had no reason to join the election-race.

Ketu gives Rāśi dṛṣṭi to Leo from Capricorn, and is the Lagna lord in the third house. This shows a need to fight i.e. a need to contest, which makes one courageous like a lion and makes one take bold steps. It was during this time that the 9-11 incident took place and Kerry and his fellow senators had to prepare the country for wars against terrorism.

2002-2005 will give the results of the lord Sun. Sun is in the Lagna joined Ghāṭikā Lagna and Horā Lagna indicating that the time for rising to power has come. Sun is the tenth lord showing that many accomplishments will be made during this time. From the Daśā Rāśi, the lord has gone to the fourth house showing a need to be cautious and change residence.

Chart 185: Job Problems

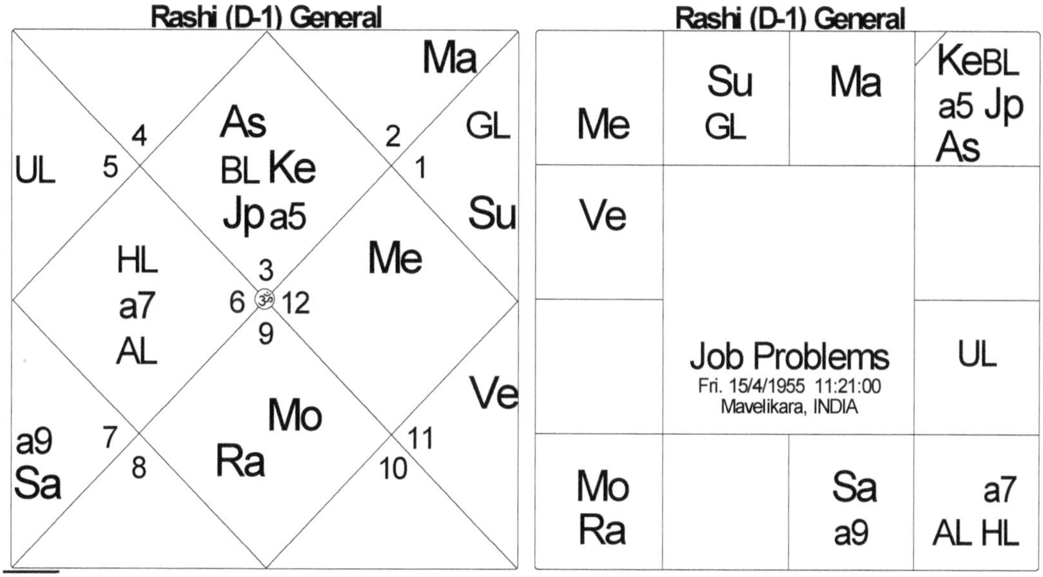

Male born 15th April 1955, 11:21 Mavelikara, India.

In the given chart, the tenth lord from Moon is Mercury who is debilitated in the tenth house. As a result, one may expect some disturbance to the native's career when this Mercury is activated. Usually when the tenth lord from Mercury is weak the native may not even enter the job-scene, however due to nīcabhañga caused by Mercury and Jupiter the native will enjoy some fruits from his work and profession. Virgo Daśā started in 2002 and ends in 2007. The results of Mercury's lordship will rise in the middle of Virgo Daśā, and correctly, in 2004 the native experienced the effects of this debilitated Mercury. Simultaneously there was concern of having to relocate, as Mercury is the fourth lord.

Results of the Daśā

The Daśā trend is useful in determining the general auspicious/inauspicious nature of a Daśā. However within a trend some auspicious and some inauspicious events will occur, only diminishing or enhancing the traits of the Daśā-trend. The method to ascertain these events is given below.

There are various points of reference given by the sages to judge the results of the entire Daśā from different perspectives. These points will give their results throughout the Daśā, but more prominently during the specific Antaradaśā activating them. Following are the specific points mentioned by Jaimini:

- Dvāra Rāśi
- Bāhya Rāśi
- Bhoga Rāśi

Dvāra and Bāhya

The Daśā Rāśi is the Dvāra. Dvāra means door or doorway. The Dvāra Rāśi will show the events, which directly influence the native. It is the place where Nārāyaṇa sits. These events can affect one's physical health directly.

Dvāra shows Deha

As the Daśā Rāśi shows the place where Nārāyaṇa sits, it indicates the body of Nārāyaṇa. This Rāśi will show the events and circumstances, which immediately affect the native. This directly influences the body of the native and is therefore known as the deha Rāśi. If the deha Rāśi is a malefic sign, the native will suffer ill health during the Daśā, especially if it is lorded by Saturn, or placed in Saturn's houses (duḥsthāna). As the Kāraka for the health is Sun, the position of the Sun from the deha Rāśi is all-important. Similarly take the kārakas of other people and decide their health.

Kāraka

The Kāraka of various events can through their aspect or placement from the Daśā Rāśi, cause their events to fructify.

- Venus and Ketu joining or aspecting the Daśā Rāśi can bring marriage.
- Sun in Kendra from Daśā Rāśi can bring a new beginning, new job or new start of life.
- Moon in Kendra will boost one's place in life and bring success and good name in whatever one sets out to accomplish.
- Rāhu in 6th, 8th or 12th from Daśā Rāśi shows wrong desires, which lead one to suffer during the Daśā.
- Rāhu in Bādhaka sthāna from the Daśā Rāśi is especially detrimental to one's success in life, and will cause problems with the government, enemies, trouble during travels and risk of imprisonment.

Ārūḍha

The Ārūḍha occupying the Daśā Rāśi will rise or fall depending on the sign being benefic or malefic respectively. This goes to show that the Ārūḍha will rise or fall depending on whether the circumstances Nārāyaṇa sets forth are auspicious or inauspicious i.e. if the circumstances are evil enough to cause bad health, the Ārūḍhas in the sign will fall with the health. Exceptions come to Ārūḍha of the sixth and eighth houses, which actually rise because of inauspicious planets. Malefic signs are well placed in third, sixth, ninth or eleventh from AL – otherwise results are inauspicious. Benefic signs do not auger well in third or sixth from AL, whilst in other houses they promote the Ārūḍha.

With reference to Ārūḍha Lagna, the Daśā can be of three types generally.

- That which causes gains to the Ārūḍha (join/aspect eleventh or second from AL).

- That which causes loss to the Ārūḍha (join/aspect 12th from AL).
- That which causes rise to the Ārūḍha (join/aspect the AL itself).

In this manner, the overall results of the Ārūḍha can be determined from the Dvāra Rāśi.

Bāhya

Count the distance between Lagna and Daśā Rāśi. Count the same distance from Daśā Rāśi. The result will be the bāhya Rāśi. Bāhya means 'exterior' and shows the events, which unfold around the native in their life. It shows what the native is "experiencing." The same count can be done between Daśā Rāśi and Antaradaśā Rāśi. This will show what specific experience the native is getting during the Daśā/ Antaradaśā. The bāhya shows the exterior results, arising from the influence of Nārāyaṇa in our life, i.e. Nārāyaṇa sits in the Daśā Rāśi deciding the circumstances or means through which the native's life will unfold, and the bāhya shows what events unfold around this. See the planets in/aspecting the bāhya Rāśi, especially the Bādhaka sthāna from bāhya Rāśi, as these will reveal any obstacles the native faces in their life.

Pāka and Bhoga

Pāka shows the native's focus

The lord of the Daśā Rāśi is the pāka Rāśi. The pāka Rāśi will indicate where the efforts of the Daśā are focused, and hence also where the native themselves will focus his energy. If the pāka is well placed in a Kendra/trikoṇa from Lagna, without being in maraṇa Kāraka sthāna, auspicious results will obtain. Similarly see the strength of the lord of Daśā Rāśi to determine whether the efforts will lead to auspiciousness or inauspiciousness of the Daśā. The yoga of the pāka Rāśi will manifest due to the pāka Rāśi i.e. pāka Rāśi joined 2nd/7th house or lord could lead to Śrīmantah Yoga results during the Daśā.

Bhoga shows the fruits

The Ārūḍha of the Daśā Rāśi is called the bhoga Rāśi. The bhoga Rāśi shows the fruits the native receives during the Daśā. The results of the bhoga Rāśi should be reckoned with regard to the Ārūḍha Lagna. The bhoga Rāśi should be placed in a Kendra or trikoṇa from the Ārūḍha Lagna, to give auspicious fruits during the Daśā. The grahas joining/aspecting the bhoga Rāśi will indicate the type of fruits received during the Daśā.

Case Studies

Chart 186: Marriage
Female born 24th January 1970, 12:46 AM, Chennai, India.

The signs aspected or joined Venus/Ketu are the most likely to give marriage. In the given chart, no significant delays to marriage exist, and hence we need merely identify the Mahādaśā aspected by Venus/Ketu. Libra and Scorpio Daśā are eligible

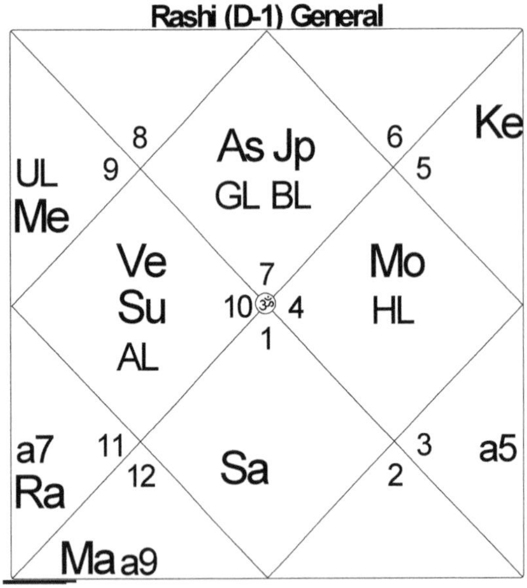

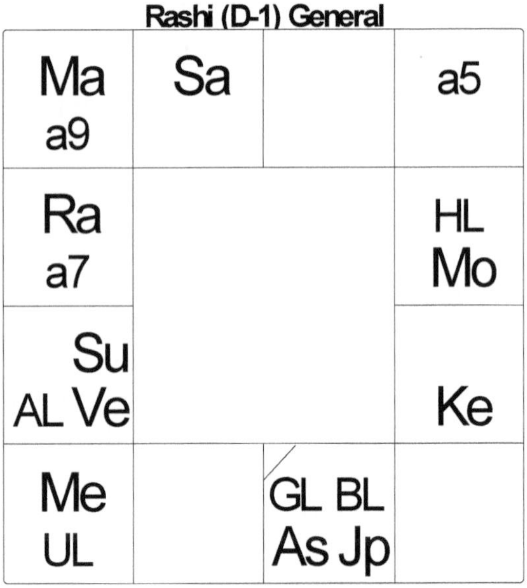

between 1970-1982 but the native is too young during this time. Sagittarius is out of the question, while Capricorn from 1992-2000 is perfect. Capricorn houses Venus and is aspected by Ketu from Leo. Counting from Lagna to Capricorn, and the same distance from Capricorn we get the seventh house as the Bāhya Rāśi. This indicates that the experience the native is having is related to marriage.

Chart 187: Bāhya and Marriage

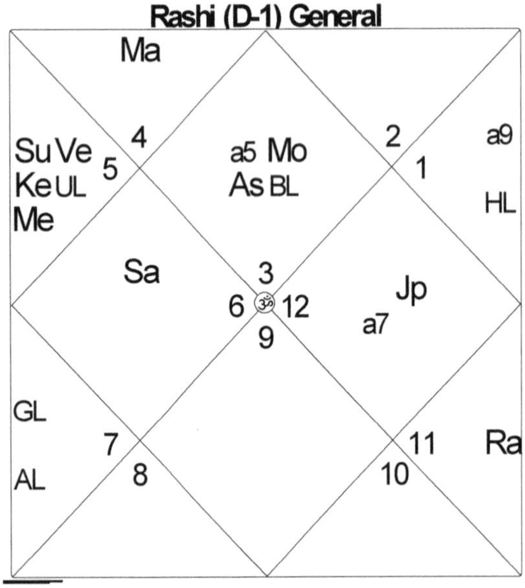

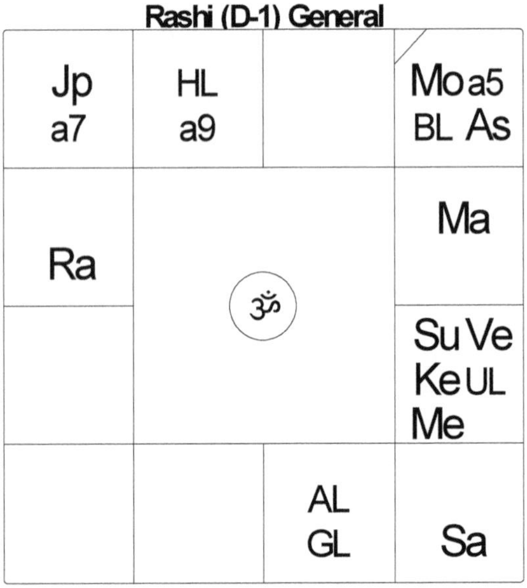

Female born 27th August 1951, 1:59 AM, Sidcup, United Kingdom.

The native of the given chart has been married twice. Looking at the Nārāyaṇa Daśā Libra, being aspected by both Venus and Ketu comes between 7-17 years of age, which is an unlikely age to marry. Capricorn Daśā is the next eligible Daśā, aspected by Venus and Ketu, running between 21-25 years of age. We may infer that the possibility of marriage exists in this Daśā. Counting from the Lagna to Capricorn, we get eight signs. The eighth sign from Capricorn is the Bāhya Rāśi, namely Leo, housing among others, Venus, Ketu and the Upapada. This confirms that the main experience, which will colour the native's life during this Daśā, is marriage.

To analyze the length of marriage the Upapada and its second house must be analyzed carefully. The Upapada is in Leo with the Sun in it, indicating the marriage and the spouse, but Saturn the dire enemy of the Sun is in the second there from in Virgo. This can cause separation in the marriage. The lord Mercury, if strong, will make the marriage last at least 17 years (Vimśottari Daśā length of Mercury), otherwise this could happen prematurely. Mercury is in the third house, Leo, with third lord Sun, sixth lord Ketu and twelfth lord Venus, forming a Viparīta Rāja Yoga. This implies the end of marriage as the yoga causes the fall of Mercury who is responsible for sustaining the marriage.

Analyzing the Daśā, the native got married at the end of Capricorn Daśā (Aug 1976), and the next Daśā of Sagittarius did not break the marriage, as aspecting Saturn, the Daśā is in the seventh house, protecting the marriage. The next Daśā of Leo activated the Viparīta Rāja Yoga, and ended the marriage. This occurred in the middle of Leo Daśā (January 1984). The next Daśā of Aries, aspecting the combination in Leo, gave marriage as soon as the Daśā started (September 1991). Unfortunately when analyzing from the subsequent Upapada Pisces, Aries is the second house there from and its lord is debilitated which can end the marriage through the ill health of the spouse. Before the end of Aries Daśā, the spouse's unfortunate demise came in January 1991.

Those who analyze carefully will notice that the *curse of a brāhmiṇ* resides in the chart, as Rāhu and Saturn both have graha dṛṣṭi on Jupiter and that too a retrograde and unwavering Jupiter. The lordship of Saturn and Rāhu over the eighth and ninth houses for Gemini Lagna is very inauspicious for marriage, and as a result end the marriage, possibly with the demise of the spouse. The individual Upapada is analyzed to see the exact nature of the results.

Chart 188: Martha Stewart - Wealth and Imprisonment
Martha Stewart, born Martha Kostyra, 3rd August 1941, 1:30 PM, Jersey City, NJ, USA.

The Ātmakāraka is Mars, who lords the second house, and is in the sixth house. This shows a person who can be aggressive and will not hesitate to use such means to sustain himself in the world. This amounts to an increase in enemies. The Horā Lagna is in the sixth house indicating a person who will attempt to earn through the service industry. Stewart's first business was in catering. Whenever the Ātmakāraka is joined or placed in trines to the nodes, Mars or Saturn, then the native will experience bondage in the form of imprisonment or the likes. Often such people are held back in customs. Mars is AK and is joined Ketu, hence indicating the possibility of bondage. The physical bondage of a person should also be analyzed from the Lagna. An equal amount of planets in 2/12, 3/11, 5/9 or 6/8 can cause imprisonment. In Stewart's chart it occurs along the 3/11 and 6/8 axis.

Rashi (D-1) General

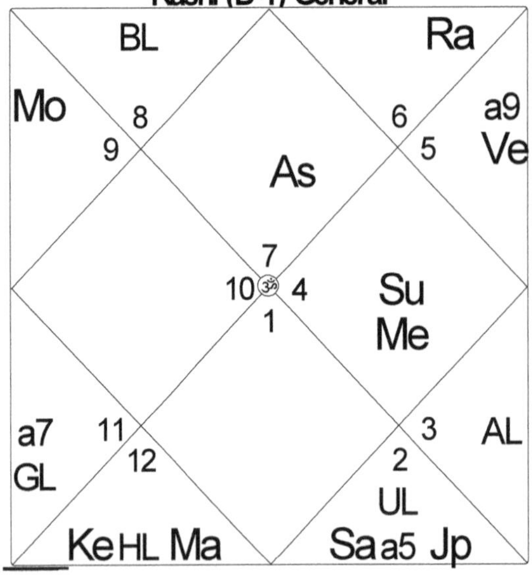

Rashi (D-1) General

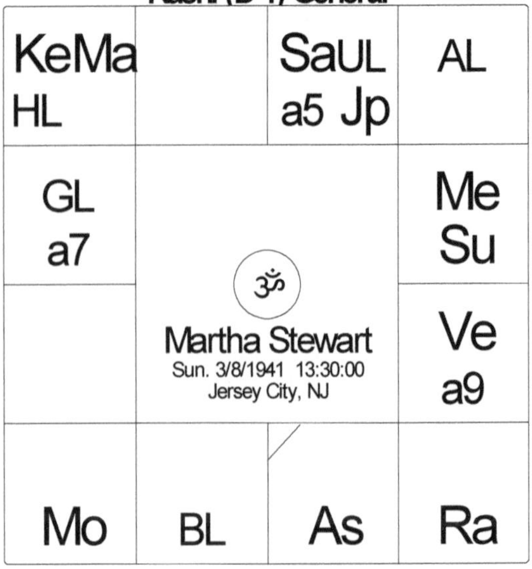

Stewart has been under the scrutiny of authorities and always with respect to matters related to money (AK joined Horā Lagna). Mars lords the eleventh house from Ārūḍha Lagna and it was notably during the Daśā or Aries that Stewart made her greatest wealth, notably at the end of Aries Daśā in 1997 when she made a profit of $25 million. Venus aspects Aries indicating the limelight, show business or the likes; Stewart produces magazines, books, videos specializing in the home-department. When the Daśā of the Bādhakeśa has to come, it is inevitable that any past wrongdoings, mistakes or the likes will come to haunt the native. For Libra Lagna the Sun is the Bādhakeśa and is in Cancer; it is during this period that the possibility of imprisonment can exist.

Allegations of insider trading were upon her, regarding a sale of 4,000 shares in 2001 only the day before the stock fell drastically due to an announcement that affected the stock-price negatively. Stewart stated that she had a deal with her stockbroker to sell the stock if it fell below $60. In 2002 June, the scandal broke and escalated. Gemini Daśā is running, housing the Ārūḍha Lagna, receiving aspects from Rāhu, Ketu and Mars, all of whom are giving the bad name. In 2004 during Cancer Daśā, she was convicted of obstructing justice and of conspiracy, as well as lying about the nature of her stock-transactions. The Antaradaśā at the time of imprisonment should be linked to Rāhu. She was convicted during Cancer Daśā and Pisces Antaradaśā, which receives the aspect of Rāhu from Virgo.

Chart 189: Swāmī Vivekānanda

In the given chart of Swāmī Vivekānanda, the first ten years were of Sagittarius Daśā, followed by Leo Daśā. Leo Daśā has the Ārūḍha Lagna, with benefics occupying the third and sixth there from. This was the time when Swāmīji (then known as Narendra) took on the spiritual path more seriously and joined the Brāhma Samāj. However, Swāmīji was not satisfied and his search continued for the knowledge of true spirituality.

Rashi (D-1) General

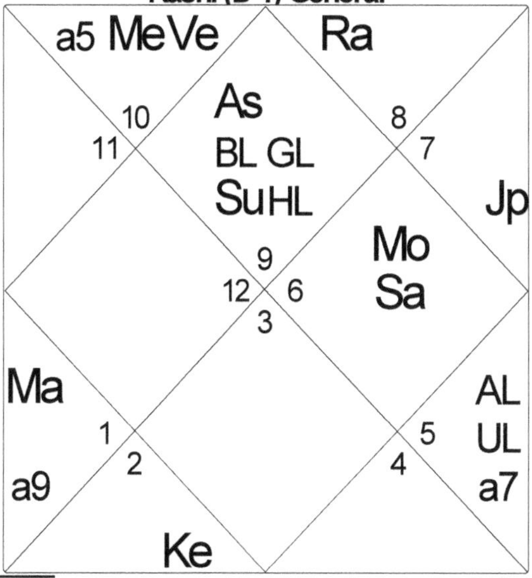

Rashi (D-1) General

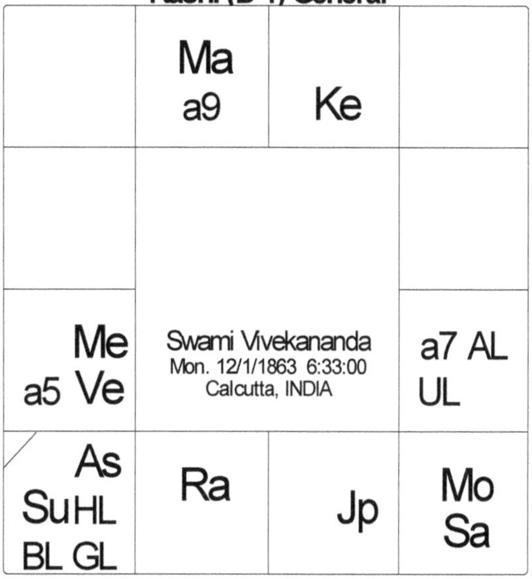

Aries Daśā followed that of Leo, and is in the fifth house causing Dhīmanta Yoga with the Lagna lord Jupiter. During this time Swāmīji's real learning about God started. The A9 is in Aries highlighting the coming of the Guru; however, Rāhu's aspect on the A9, whilst placed in the eighth from the Daśā Rāśi does not bode well for the health of the father and the guru. Swāmīji's guru was quite old when they met, and demised during the same Daśā. Father's demise also occurred during this Daśā, as Pitṛkāraka is in the eighth from Daśā Rāśi.

Following the demise of his father, the family of Swāmīji was subject to complete poverty, even denying them food; this is indicated by the placement of the nodes along the 2/8 axis. To help their situation, Swāmīji began a teaching profession, which was the only one he could get though he was overqualified for it. The Amatyakāraka Moon is in the sixth from Daśā Rāśi hence the denial of good profession. Bhrātṛkāraka, which is the Kāraka for guru, is in the sixth from Daśā Rāśi and next person to suffer is the guru. Śrī Rāmakṛṣṇa fell ill and began teaching Swāmīji vigorously. Mars in the Daśā Rāśi will give intense knowledge of Mantra and Tantra. In 1886, the guru left his body, only two years after the father's demise.

Swāmīji renounced and attained the name Vivekānanda. He started a Math and began teaching the devotees philosophy and Sanskrit, in which he was proficient. Towards the end of Aries Daśā Swāmīji's urging desire for renunciation culminated in his leaving the Math for pilgrimage. In 1890, Swāmīji returned from his pilgrimage. Pisces Daśā started in 1893, a Kendra sign and showing a change in the life's direction. Pisces is the sign of the maharṣi, and is aspected by the ninth lord Sun (temples and ashrams) whilst Sun is joined ghāṭikā Lagna and Horā Lagna, giving a magnanimous Rāja Yoga. In the same year, Swāmīji attended the World Parliament of Religions in Chicago, USA. This trip left a strong impact on the attendants, and Swāmīji's words resounded through the entire world. Swāmīji spent his time traveling in the West and in India, and in 1897, he established the Rāmakṛṣṇa Mission, in the memory of his guru's teachings. Mars is in the second from the Daśā Rāśi, receiving the dṛṣṭi of Jupiter, indicating lavish resources and wealth. It was during this time that Swāmīji showed his ability as a leader.

Scorpio Daśā followed that of Pisces, which is the twelfth house, occupied by Rāhu. After exhausting journeys throughout the world, Swāmīji retired to his Ashram. Rāhu in Daśā Rāśi gives strain on the mind. The A8 is occupying the same and indicates the time of death or demise. Swāmīji left his body in 1902, leaving behind a legacy, which will last him many more lifetimes.

Chart 190: Author

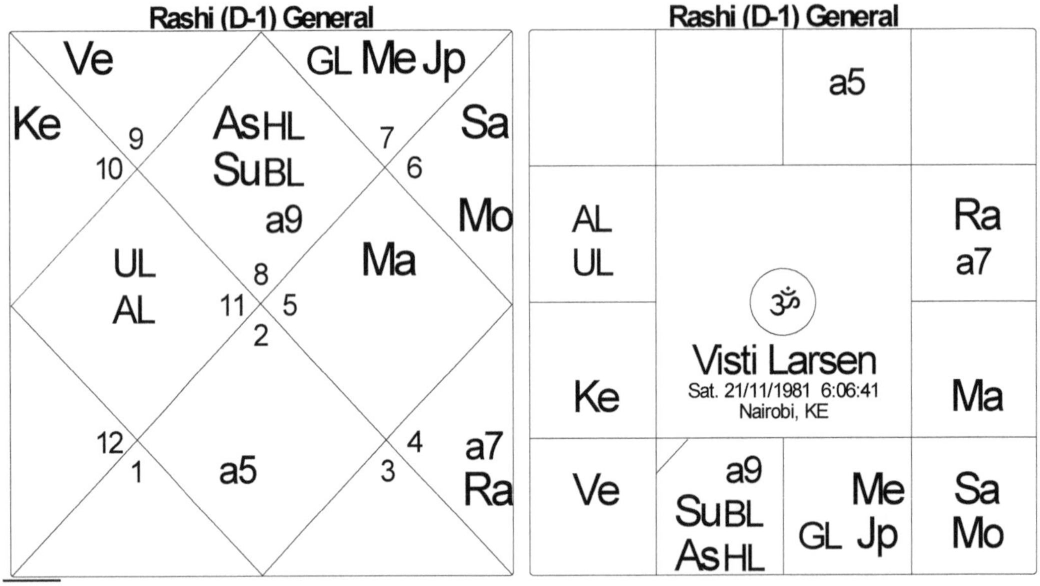

The native was born in Scorpio Daśā, of the Lagna lasting from 1981-1990. During this time the fourth house from Daśā Rāśi is Aquarius, which is a malefic sign and will indicate a move, however one without much importance as no grahas are in it. The native's family moved from the nation's capitol to a coastal area. Sun is in the Daśā Rāśi indicating strong health and body, and a very active nine years of childhood. Venus in the second house shows good food and habits, whilst the twelfth house is well occupied by two benefics indicating good and sound sleep. During the latter part of the Daśā, the effects of Saturn in the eleventh from Daśā Rāśi came to light where some friends at school bullied the native.

Gemini Daśā (1990-1994) followed that of Scorpio and the fourth from Gemini has Saturn indicating a significant change in home/residence. The native's family moved to Denmark from Kenya only 1-2 months before the Daśā started and finally settled in Denmark towards the beginning of Gemini Daśā. The native changed school and his friendship circle. Gemini is the eighth house and some unhappiness must manifest during the Daśā with the native coping with the new culture and friendship circle was often bullied by his peers and due to third and sixth houses from Gemini being occupied by two strong malefics, Mars and Sun, the native retaliated very aggressively leading to many fights. Venus in the seventh from the

Daśā Rāśi can show the beginning of an interest in the opposite sex during this period and may have been a reason for the tumultuous events with the native's peers.

Gemini indicates games, and the native began playing soccer seriously during this time. The fifth from the Daśā Rāśi has two benefics, Mercury and Jupiter, and it was during this time that the native's study skills improved significantly, and the native showed a knack for excellent memory and good ability for languages. Rāhu is in the second from Daśā Rāśi indicating the intake of new food, and the native became less particular about his eating habits. Gemini is the tenth house from the Moon, which indicates the time when the native will begin working; the native started delivering newspapers for some extra pocket change.

Capricorn Daśā (1994-1998) followed that of Gemini and is the third house, which is an inauspicious house. Ketu is occupying it indicating sudden accidents. The native was in a bike crash, which injured his knee (Capricorn). The native also lost interest in studies due to Ketu's presence in the Daśā Rāśi, as Ketu is inimical towards Mercury the Kāraka for Vidyā. The native began an interest in the paranormal during this time, and was very interested in unexplained and mysterious phenomena such as UFOs etc. Mars is in the eighth house indicating a time of mismanagement of finances and paying of debts; this especially became so after the native changed from primary school to high school in the summer of 1997, where the native spent lavishly on his social activities, due to Venus in the twelfth from Daśā Rāśi. Sun is in the eleventh house, which was a significant improvement for the native's friendship circle since primary school. The native got a new job with much better pay and less work/strain as two benefics are in the tenth from the Daśā Rāśi.

Leo Daśā (1998-2007) follows that of Capricorn, and is a Kendra sign, indicating a change in character and direction in life. Mars in the Daśā Rāśi is in parivartana with the Sun in the Lagna, showing the change of character from the aggressive Mars, to the knowledgeable Sun. This change will occur with the coming of a new community or family, as Sun is Chara Jñātikāraka. The third from the Daśā Rāśi has benefics ending the past aggressive tendencies and moving the native more towards spirituality. The disinterest in school continued due to Mars in Daśā Rāśi but the interest in higher knowledge such as spirituality and religion rose significantly during this time. The native took up the study of astrology seriously (based on the Ruchaka mahā pūruṣa yoga, Mars makes one interested in astrology, mantras and tantra). Mars will always ignore the planets in the twelfth from it, where the A7 is, indicating that some of the native's habits will include practice of celibacy or separation from the opposite sex. Venus in the fifth from Daśā Rāśi does promise some relationships during Leo Daśā. In fact, the native began dating with the advent of Leo Daśā, but towards the end of Leo ended the same.

Saturn and Moon in the second from Daśā Rāśi promised high rises and lows in the native's finances, and the native had really spent a lot of money during Leo Daśā. As Saturn and Moon are in the eleventh from Lagna, this shows spending money on occult knowledge. Mercury being in third from the Daśā is aspecting the Daśā Rāśi indicating the time for writing. It is during this Daśā that the native wrote this book for the benefit of other astrologers. As Jupiter is joined Mercury, the writing comes from a lineage of interaction between teacher and student, a paramparā.

Appendix 1: FAQ

Frequently Asked Questions

Question 1: Why do both exalted and debilitated planets give great wealth?

Answer: Mahāṛṣi Jaimini states; "taśmin ucche neeche va śrīmantaḥ", namely that both exalted and debilitated planets make one wealthy. The state of the planet will indicate the mind-state of the people who will give one wealth. When a planet is exalted the person is very happy and extremely joyful, and will give lots of money to experience more joy. One could be satisfying others with enjoyment in the form of entertainment, selling holidays, movies, etc. Instead a debilitated planet indicates a person in great fear and in need. To remove their fear they will gladly give away their money to ensure their security, i.e. as a repairman or involved in security. Inimical planets due to their disgust, will not give any money at all, and if any it will be very little, whilst neutral, and friendly planets will give more money, followed by own sign, Mūlatrikoṇa and exaltation/debilitation which give most.

Question 2: When malefics are strong do they become more malefic or less malefic?

Answer: Thankfully Praśna Mārga gives us the answer to this. Chapter 4, śloka 35: "Benefics if strong contribute good fully. Malefics if weak give evil in full." Here it may be inferred that the weaker a planet, the less auspicious it becomes.

To add to this we need to examine the houses that the grahas are in to undersand more. Auspicious houses such as Kendra or Koṇa are responsible for giving us blessings. Strong benefics here make the blessings received nicely and one benefits. Strong malefic here block these doors and the blessings are spent on fighting. Therefore malefics are preferred weak in the Kendra and Koṇa. Similarly the Duḥsthāna are where our energy is spent and leaves us. If strong malefics sit in the Duḥsthāna then our energy doesn't leave us whereas strong benefics here makes the energy leave more rapidly. Hence benefics are preferred weak in Duḥsthāna for material prosperity.

Question 3: If a planet is a benefic but lord of a duḥsthāna, will it still give beneficial results?

Answer: To clarify, Harihara the author of Praśna Mārga has answered, in chapter 4, śloka 37: "A planet capable of giving rise to both bad and good, confers only good results if he is strong and only evil results if he is weak." This answer also clarifies the case of natural vs. functional benefics or malefics.

Question 4: Saturn is Kāraka for dukha or sorrow. Does the sorrow become worse when Saturn is strong?

Answer: Praśna Mārga answers this as well. Chapter 4 śloka 32: "When the planets from Sun onwards are strong, their karaka is predominant in life. If weak they will exist only in name. However, if Saturn is strong his inauspicious karaka will be felt less." This is in line with the answer to Question 2, regarding the strength of malefics.

Question 5: What are the results of the various types of bala/strength?

Answer: The Parampara teaches that the various bala have different effects. Many of them are based on the planets position in the sign or house, and will confirm the astrologer's prior estimation of the chart. Many astrology software's do not take into account the position of planets from points other than the Lagna, and the astrologer should not let their prediction rely solely on the strength calculations of a planet.

Vimśopak bala: A planet strong in vimśopak bala gets great support from the world. Here the ten and sixteen varga-scheme is used for human beings, whilst the six and seven varga scheme is used for Praśna and Muhurta respectively. This can be useful in predicting the results of electoral support.

Śadbala**:** Literally 'six strengths' based on the planets position, time, direction, motion, sight and nature. Each of these strengths can be used independantly, but the result in its entirety can be used to determine the strength of the planets Kāraka.

Iṣta and Kasta phala: This method of strength is used to decide the amount of auspicious/inauspiciousness that one may face in a Daśā. This can be moderated by the Antaradaśā. Adding the points of the mahā and Antaradaśā and dividing by two can be used to decide the results of the Antaradaśā. If the number is below thirty, then the results are inauspicious. Incase of the nodes, they will give the results of the planets they are joined, or the planet lording their sign if unconjoined.

Āṣṭakavarga **bala:** A small introduction into the finer principles of Āṣṭakavarga have been given in this book, however some clarification is given. The strength of a planet in its own Bhinna Āṣṭakavarga will indicate the more help that it has been given from other Kāraka. Example: In a mundane chart for a nation, the strength of the Sun in its Bhinna Āṣṭakavarga will show how much support the king or leader is getting to do his work. The planets which contribute will show who is supporting the king. If in a natal chart Saturn in is own Bhinna Āṣṭakavarga has many points it is inauspicious, as it shows how many sources of sorrow or sin are prevalent in the natives life, hence making its strength inauspicious. This cannot be used to determine the strength of yogas, only the amount of resources drawn by the planet.

Vaiśeṣikāmsa bala: This source of strength is used to determine the extent or height that one's raja yoga or dhāna yoga can take one to. This is the correct method to determine the strength of raja yogas.

Question 6: In case of Parivartana (exchange) yoga between planets, will the Daśā effects also exchange results?

Answer: Some changes occur when in a parivartana, and the type of change will depend on the type of parivartana being in: Rāśi, Nakṣatra or Navāṁśa. But in all cases the nature of the planet, its placement and lordship will not change.

Rāśi parivartana: When a parivartana occurs in the Rāśi, the two planets are working together to cause a change. This change is from the nature of one planet to the nature of the other, i.e. from one Guṇa to another. Example: A parivartana between Sun and Mars is a change in Guṇa from Sattva to Tamas, or from Tamas to Sattva as these are the Guṇa of Sun and Mars. The change also involves the houses, Kāraka and Tattva of the planets, to give the exact details about this change. Which of the two comes first in this exchange, depends on who the change is affecting the most. If one planet is in the Lagna, Ārūḍha Lagna or joined Lagneśa, then the transformations result will be of that planet. If one of the planets in the exchange is badly placed or afflicted, then the result of the exchange leaves the person indicated in bitterness.

Nakṣatra parivartana: A parivartana in the Nakṣatra causes a change in the minds of the people in society, and can heavily modify the Daśā for people who live in the limelight of society. The results of the parivartana should be judged from the planets placement from the Moon.

Navāṁśa parivartana: the Navāṁśa indicates the relationships one has with people. If a parivartana occurs, then it can change the nature of the people one associates with during an entire Daśā.

Question 7: What is Kuja doṣa?

Answer: Kuja doṣa, Manglik doṣa is commonly understood as the affliction of Mars. This is one of the most commonly talked about afflictions in marriage cases. It happens when Mars has graha dṛṣṭi on the seventh house in a chart. Here particularly its fourth and eighth house dṛṣṭi is considered most evil. For this reason Mars in twelfth, fourth and seventh is considered kuja doṣa. Mars in fifth house is not considered inauspicous as it sits in the house of worship. Additionally Mars' placement in the eighth house is considered evil for the sustenance of marriage. The placement in the twelfth, fourth and seventh house is said to delay marriage until after the twenty-eighth year of age, unless Saturn associates. Jupiter's association does not remove the delay but promises marriage when the native has matured. Marriage before twenty-eight is usually not advised, as it can cause violence and severe fights in the marriage – regardless of Saturn's association. Jupiter's association will however calm this down, but will not remove the delay.

Mars in the eighth house gives fear of early break of marriage or the premature demise of the spouse, which should be further analyzed from the second from upapada. In any case the yogas with the seventh house should always be confirmed by analyzing the upapada.

Question 8: Which is the best remedy to solve marital problems?

Answer: Fasting on the day of the Upapada is the best method to solve marital problems, proven time and time again. The fasting should be performed from sunrise to sunset. The more sincere the fast, the better the results. Water is allowed, if necessary. If absolutely necessary the native may have uncooked foods such as fruits. This fast is not recommended if the lord of the Upapada is also the lord of the second house. In such cases Tithi fasting is advised based on the house of the lord of Upapada, i.e. if the lord is placed in the third house then fasting on the 15th day of the bright fortnight is advised. This Tithi is lorded by Saturn and if the second lord is Saturn then again fasting is not recommended.

Question 9: Why is the Ārūḍha of the twelfth house considered for marriage, and not the Ārūḍha of the seventh house?

Answer: Both are used, however the Ārūḍha of the seventh house or dārapada is used to see our mate in matters of sexuality, just like animals have a mate. However human beings go a step further and have the option of spending their entire life with one mate, and this cannot be considered as a mere sexual partner, as is the case with the dārapada. Upon being born we have earned a debt to our ancestor's up to seven generations back. To repay this debt we have only 2 choices; 1) marry and have children to continue the lineage (Kāraka Jupiter). 2) Renounce perfectly (Kāraka Saturn). If we do not perform either of these, our ancestors will not be at peace. In fact some say the consequences are much more extreme, and we will carry this debt to our next lives. Now this debt is not some duṣṭa karma which is seen in the eighth house, but a debt to our creator. The creation is caused by Sūrya when he transits the twelve Rāśi, and hence the name Sūrya or Āditya also means twelve. It is from this basis that the sūryāmśa or dvadaśāmśa is created which shows our parents and grandparents according to Pārāśara. It is a debt for having being created, which is seen in the twelfth house.

Now we've established that the twelfth house shows how we repay our debt to our ancestors (and also the deva). This debt is repaid either through marriage or perfect renunciation, and how we are repaying this debt is seen from the Upapada, as this is how our debt is manifesting in the world, i.e. through the Ārūḍha. That is why Pārāśara and Jaimini state that malefics in the upapada can cause renunciation.

So the Upapada shows either our marriage or the lack of the same. It also shows who we will choose to marry (if the choice is ours), and hence can indicate the Lagna of the spouse. It shows how long the marriage will last in society as a marital contract, and can also show whether such a contract was written or not for the relationship.

Question 10: What is the main difference between grahas and upagrahas?

Answer: The word 'graha' comes from the word 'grahaṇa' or 'to eclipse/seize'. This refers to the ability of the planets to take control of our minds and make us think and act like them. The prefix; 'upa' refers to those planets which are secondary in significance, i.e. they are lower in significance. An Upagraha cannot take control of our mind, but of particular body functions, causing spasms, blockages or freak episodes. Hence an Upagraha cannot control our way of acting, as the grahas do, but they can control specific limbs and organs, and cause accidents or problems.

Question 11: The duḥsthāna are supposed to be inauspicious, but which is more evil; the duḥsthāna from Lagna or the duḥsthāna from the particular bhāva?

Answer: Again Praśna Mārga comes to our help. Chapter 4, śloka 42: "If the lord of a bhāva occupies a favorable house from itself, then the effects of that bhāva will be full. If the lord occupies a favorable house from the Lagna, the effects of the bhāva will be well experienced". In other words; if the lord of a bhāva is in a duḥsthāna from Lagna, then the native will experience sorrow and misery on account of that bhāva. But if the lord of the bhāva is placed in a duḥsthāna from the bhāva, then the bhāva itself will suffer, but one'self may not experience this sorrow or misery.

Question 12: What are the results of kendrādhipati doṣa?

Answer: Kendrādhipati doṣa means; the 'the affliction ascribed to the lords of quadrants'. It refers to the ability of malefics lording a Kendra to shed its malefic results, whilst the benefic lording a Kendra to shed its benefic results. The benefic lording a Kendra will not shed its benefic results if it is well placed, in a Kendra or a trikoṇa. Instead the benefic will become more benefic as a result.

For malefics, their malefic influence is not completely shed unless placed in a duḥsthāna, whereas its placement in a Kendra or trikoṇa will not allow it to shed its malefic results. If the malefic is also lord of a trikoṇa or joined a trikoṇa lord, then it produces vipareet raja yoga.

Question 13: If the Rāśi chart and the divisional charts are showing contradictory results, which will dominate?

Answer: The Rāśi chart covers the entire life, but unfortunately is only indicative of what the future may bring. The divisional charts are complementary to the prediction and can help get the exact details about the particular events which may occur in a person's life. Example: from the Rāśi chart we can ascertain the amount of children that the native may have, but the details about each pregnancy their sex and the fortunes experiences by each child is seen from the saptāmśa. In this way the divisional charts are complimentary to a detailed prediction.

Question 14: Can one consider the exaltation/debilitation states of a planet in the divisional charts?

Answer: Yes, as long as we are considering the placement of planets in certain signs and drawing a new chart, we a required to also consider the state of that planet in that sign, as well as its relation to other signs. Graha dṛṣṭi and Rāśi dṛṣṭi are also considered in divisional charts.

Question 15: If the Rāśi chart and bhāva chalit chakra are showing contradictory results, which one will dominate?

Answer: The difference between the bhāva chalit chakra and the Rāśi chakra will be greater when the Lagna degree is in the beginning or end of a sign. When the Lagna degree is placed such, the intellect of the native becomes distorted to some extent. This distortion causes a different perception of the events revolving around the native, and this new perception is seen from the bhāva chalit chakra. It is important to point out that one's perception creates a reality for us. Example: perception can lead us to think that we can establish a successful business, and we may even go ahead and try to establish it. However the business may not last if the perception is not true. Hence the Rāśi chart always dominates as it is the truth, but we need to analyze the perception from the bhāva chalit chakra.

Question 16: I did my marriage matching for my wife and I, and the Kuta-matching is really low. But instead our relationship is very good with each other, why is this?

Answer: There are various points to address here. Firstly, most people only perform the matching based on the moons of the couple. However the matching of moons (especially moons-Nakṣatra) has a stronger relevance in the matching of the two couple's families or the society that the two belong to. Instead if matching is done between the Lagnas of the two, the intellectual and mental matching will be more clear and consistent in giving results.

Secondly, some matching techniques are more or less important to apply in the couple, which disproves the use of the point system. Gotra matching is more important in couples who work together, or where their principles shouldn't clash. Similarly Varṇa kuta is also important for couples who work together.

Stri-dīrgha kuta is always worth analyzing to determine the support that the wife is getting in society from the husbands family and social circle. If the Strī-dīrgha is bad, then the support will be stronger from the wife's side, and not be present from the husband's side.

Vaiśya matching is usually only temporary, and only necessary if it is required to attract the two partners.

Rajiu matching from Moon and Gana matching from Lagna should always be considered and are very accurate.

Question 17: There are many Daśā systems used in Vedic astrology. Which one should I choose for successful results?

Answer: An astrologer, who is predicting the events for other people's lives, should choose the Daśā based on (1) their own ability or preference, (2) applicability in the clients chart.

(1) To identify which Daśā suits the astrologer best, the three Graha; Sun, Moon and Jupiter should be seen in the natives chart. Their place-

ment in Kendra/Koṇas is auspicious for the native, whilst duḥsthāna is inauspicious. If the Sun is best placed, the native should develop their ability with Naisargika Daśā, Kendrādi Daśā (Mūla, Ātmakāraka Kendrādi, etc) and Rāśi based Daśā. Notably, Naisargika Daśā should be applied in all charts. If instead the Moon is strong, the Nakṣatra Daśā are the most preferable, including Mūla Daśā. If Jupiter is the strongest, then Nārāyaṇa Daśā, Buddhi-gati Daśā and other Lagna based daśās are the most preferable.

(2) In a native's chart, the Daśā which best explains the native's theme of life should be preferred. Spiritual people require the use of Dṛg Daśā, whilst business men need to know their su-Daśā. The conditional Udu Daśā take into account these differences in ideals and paths in the criteria for the Daśā.

Finally the astrologer should aspire to master at least two Daśā for general predictive-purposes and two Daśā system for longevity based predictions. In the tradition, for general purposes Naisargika Daśā is compulsory whilst for longevity Śūla Daśā is compulsory.

Question 18: I've seen astrologers calculate Vimśottari from Lagna, but most people say that vimśottari from Moon should be used, which is accurate?

Answer: In śloka 33 of the 18th chapter of Jātaka Parijata, Vaidyanath Diksita states that Vimśottari Daśā should be calculated from four positions; (1) Lagna Nakṣatra (2) moons Nakṣatra (3) name Nakṣatra (4) moons Nakṣatra during praśna. Further in śloka 34 and 35, the use of vimśottari from the fourth, fifth and eighth Nakṣatra from the Moon is used for longevity. This gives a total of seven options to start vimśottari from!

Among these for natal charts, most people use Vimśottari from Lagna or Moon, depending on which is stronger. Both are applicable, but in cases where the Lagna is stronger (more planets in Kendra), the events will be clearer from Lagna-vimśottari. The Vimśottari from the fourth, fifth and eighth Nakṣatra from the Moon, is used in natal charts to time failings in health and the demise of an individual.

Question 19: How does astrology account for the birth of twins, where the birth times are so close?

Answer: Since Vedic astrologers rectify birth times with a precision down to one vighati (twenty-four seconds), a better question would be how astrology accounts for people born on the same birthplace at the same birth time. Finding such cases is usually reserved to logicians and not astrologers. Invariably the past-life karmas of the two individuals cannot be the same; hence the sixtieth divisional chart (ṣaṣṭyamśa) will be the different in the case of twins.

Specifically for twins, the tradition holds some keys to differentiate between the events in the lives of twins, triplets or other multiple births. I.e. the last born among the twins is said to be the first conceived and if the twins share the same Lagna then this child is said to be the Lagna and the other (first born) is the third house. The interpretation of the chart is then done from those houses as Lagna for the respective twin. Should the Lagna be an even sign then instead of the third house the eleventh house is examined. For triplets the Lagna will be the last born, the third will be the second born as the fifth house will be the first born. In this way the twins, triplets, etc. can be deduced from the chart.

Question 20: I was told that I have kāla sarpa yoga in my chart. How to reckon this in my chart?

Answer: Many people are born with kāla sarpa yoga or its sister; kāla amṛta yoga. This yoga is like a cage of sorts, involving all the planets. Draw a line from Rāhu to Ketu, splitting the zodiac in half. If all the grahas occupy one half, then it is kāla sarpa/amrita yoga. If they occupy both halves, then there is no such yoga. Next put your finger on Rāhu, and move zodiacally through the zodiac until you reach Ketu. If you have passed all the grahas when doing so, then the yoga is kāla amrita yoga. If you pass none, then it is kāla sarpa yoga.

Planets conjoined the nodes, or placed in the first or seventh houses from Lagna, help break the yoga in their natural ages. The person does not see real success in life before 42 or 45 depending on whether its kāla sarpa or kāla amrita yoga respectively.

Kāla Sarpa Yoga means the native is trapped in a community of serpents and is being asked to continue the spread poison in the society. This can cause damage to the environment, to the social structure and people. Depending on the Lagna the person may not accomodate this and instead of enslaving people will decide to free them. Kāla Amṛta Yoga is the opposite, namely one who is asked by the community to seek freedom for the world, its occupants and to give nectar to the world. These are people exposed to highly spiritual philosophies and if the lagna supports such as person will break all social norms in seeking freedom. An example is given of the author:

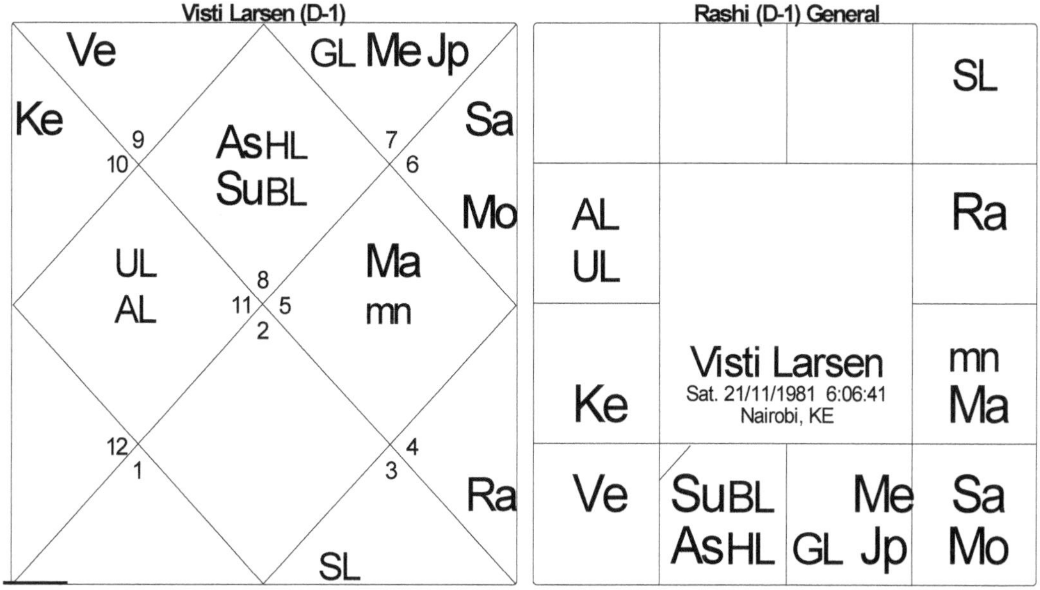

Visti Larsen, born 21st November 1981, 6:06 AM, Nairobi, Kenya. All planets are hemmed between Rāhu and Ketu, where when counting zodiacally from Rāhu to Ketu we find all planets within. Thus Kāla Amṛta Yoga is born and a true freedom seeker is born. The Lagna is Scorpio and is surrounded by benefics and a sattvic graha - Sun on the Lagna, thus this person will wanto support and agenda of doing good for the world and giving happiness and freedom to people. Further Ketu, being the king of the Kāla Amṛta Yoga, is also lord of the Scorpio Lagna indicating a person who will go out of his way to pursue spirituality. Lagneśa in the third house is also Dhimantaḥ Yoga indicating the pursuit of knowledge being the key focus. With dispositor Saturn in the 11th house this is clearly the pursuit of Jyotiṣa knowledge under a Guru's tutelage. Thus an average kid born to parents of a western society, went out of his way to pursue a path of spiritual knowledge.

Question 21: People tell me that I'm running sade sathi and that this is very inauspicious, yet I've been doing fine in life, why is this?

Answer: Sade Sathi is the 7½ year transit of Saturn over the twelfth, first and second houses from the natal Moon sign. However whilst most astrologers apply this in the Rāśi chart, the tradition teaches to apply this in divisional charts as well. This is based on the understanding that the transit of Saturn in the Rāśi chart, only affects the body/health; whilst in the divisional charts it can affect particular areas of life like marriage (Navāṁśa) or career (dasāmśa). Example: if Moon is in the Navāṁśa of Leo, and Saturn enters Cancer in the Rāśi chart, then the intimacy in marriage/relationships will suffer. Some people call this method of using transits; "Bhṛgu transits".

Also each 2½ year transit has a special significance; the transit over the twelfth from Moon causes personal life and relations to suffer. The transit over the Moon sign itself causes one to make wrong decisions, mistakes and delays one in attaining one's desires. Finally the transit over the second from Moon gives bad or little food, little resources and wealth and many worries.

Further, the effects of each year can also be analyzed based on the Nakṣatra transited by Saturn, whilst the Navāṁśa of Saturn's transit tells us about the span of a three month period, and how it affects us. Such principles can be learnt from Chandra Kāla Nāḍi (Deva Keralam).

Question 22: I have a planet in retrogression yet in debilitation; does this make the planet behave like exalted?

Answer: Yes it does, however it should be kept in mind that retrograde planets have two primary states; (1) having just entered retrogression and moving towards the peak of retrogression. (2) Having attained the peak of retrogression and slowly ending its retrograde state and moving into stationary motion. Incase of (1) the desire of the graha is very strong and very determined. Such an individual will strive very hard to attain the desires indicated by the planet. Incase of (2) the native is slowly ceasing his/her desires and moving towards equilibrium.

Question 23: Does retrogression apply to divisional charts?

Answer: Retrogression is a pure astronomical phenomenon, and a planet in a state of retrogression is retrograde in all divisional charts as well. The same applies to combustion. However, in interpretation this is ignored in the divisional charts.

Bibliography

Acharya, D. S. (2003). *Daivagya Śrirāmāchārya Virachitah Muhūrta Chintāmani.* (G. C. Sharma, Trans.) New Delhi: Sagar Publications.

Aditya, S. V. (1997). *The Surya Siddhanta: a tekst-book of Hindu astronomy.* (P. Gangooly, Ed., & R. E. Burges, Trans.) Delhi: Motilal Banarsidass Publishers Private Limited.

Dikshita, V. (1992). *Jataka Parijata.* (V. S. Sastri, Trans.) Delhi, India: Ranjan Publications.

Jaimini, M. (1997). *Jaimini Maharishi's Upadesa Sutras.* (S. Rath, Trans.) New Delhi: Sagar Publications.

Narada, D. Darsha Jananashanti. In *Shaanti-kusumaakara-paddhatinah.*

Parashara, M. (1999). *Brhat Parasara Hora Shastra.* (G. C. Sharma, Trans.) New Delhi: Sagar Publications.

Rath, S. (2007). *A Course on Jaimini Maharishi's Upadesa Sutra.* New Delhi: Sagittarius Publications.

Rath, S. (2008). *Brhat Nakshatra.* New Delhi: Sagittarius Publications.

Rath, S. (2002). Charakaraka and Spirituality.

Rath, S. (1998). *Crux of Vedic Astrology - Timing of events.* New Delhi: Sagar Publications.

Rath, S. (2006). Focus on Nepal. *The Jyotish Digest Vol 2 Issue 4* , 14-21.

Rath, S. (2010). Vedic Reading Process. *BAVA Workshop.* London: BAVA.

Sharma, V. (1986). *Sarvartha Chintamani.* (J. Bhasin, Trans.) New Delhi: Sagar Publications.

Sibly, E. (1784). *The New and Complete Illustration of the Celestial Science of Astrology.* London.

Varahamihira. (1997). *Brhat Samhita.* (M. R. Bhatt, Trans.) Delhi: Motilal Banarsidass Publishers Private Limited.

Index

J

K

L

V

W

Y

Milton Keynes UK
Ingram Content Group UK Ltd.
UKHW051035301023
431590UK00006B/37

9 788799 506309